PRIVATE FINANCE, PUBLIC POWER

Private Finance, Public Power

A HISTORY OF BANK SUPERVISION
IN AMERICA

PETER CONTI-BROWN AND
SEAN H. VANATTA

PRINCETON UNIVERSITY PRESS

PRINCETON & OXFORD

Published by Princeton University Press
41 William Street, Princeton, New Jersey 08540
99 Banbury Road, Oxford OX2 6JX

press.princeton.edu

GPSR Authorized Representative: Easy Access System Europe - Mustamäe tee 50, 10621 Tallinn, Estonia, gpsr.requests@easproject.com

All Rights Reserved

Library of Congress Cataloging-in-Publication Data

Names: Conti-Brown, Peter, 1981– author. | Vanatta, Sean H., author.
Title: Private finance, public power : a history of bank supervision in
    America / Peter Conti-Brown, Sean H. Vanatta.
Description: Princeton : Princeton University Press, [2025] | Includes
    bibliographical references and index.
Identifiers: LCCN 2024042299 (print) | LCCN 2024042300 (ebook) | ISBN
    9780691232829 (hardback) | ISBN 9780691233468 (ebook)
Subjects: LCSH: Banks and banking—State supervision—United
    States—History. | Banking law—United States—History. | BISAC:
    BUSINESS & ECONOMICS / Banks & Banking | BUSINESS
    & ECONOMICS / Business Law
Classification: LCC HG1778.U5 C66 2025 (print) | LCC HG1778.U5 (ebook) |
    DDC 332.10973—dc23/eng/20250108
LC record available at https://lccn.loc.gov/2024042299
LC ebook record available at https://lccn.loc.gov/2024042300

British Library Cataloging-in-Publication Data is available

Editorial: Joe Jackson, Emma Wagh
Production Editorial: Elizabeth Byrd
Jacket: Karl Spurzem
Production: Danielle Amatucci
Publicity: James Schneider, Kathryn Stevens

Jacket image: Courtesy of Historic American Buildings Survey (HABS),
Historic American Engineering Record (HAER), and Historic American
Landscapes Survey (HALS).

Printed in the United States of America

10 9 8 7 6 5 4 3 2 1

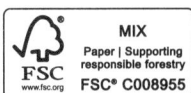

To our children, with love

Remnants of the past that don't make sense in present terms—the useless, the odd, the peculiar, the incongruous—are the signs of history. They supply proof that the world was not made in its present form. When history perfects, it covers its own tracks.

—STEPHEN JAY GOULD, *THE PANDA'S THUMB* (1980)

CONTENTS

Introduction

IN THE spring of 2023, Silicon Valley Bank (SVB), a major player in the tech and venture capital world (but little known outside it), announced that it needed to raise more equity capital from investors. Such announcements from banks are usually not very good news for bank stakeholders. It suggests at best that current shareholders will be "diluted," that is, see the relative value of their investments diminished by the inclusion of more investors for the same firm; at worst, it suggests that some terminal financial illness is consuming the bank from within. In the case of SVB, it was the latter, and it arose from a seemingly innocuous bet. At the height of the COVID-19 pandemic in 2020, the bank, awash in liquidity from a flush venture capital industry, thought that interest rates, near 0 percent, would stay that low for a long time. SVB invested most of its portfolio in very safe, liquid securities like U.S. Treasuries that paid more than what the bank paid its depositors but not much more. The bank needed time to digest what had been a period of explosive growth—from about $70 billion in deposits in 2019 to $212 billion in 2022—and these safe securities seemed like the prudent strategy.[1]

SVB bet big, and it lost. In March 2022, the Federal Reserve began raising interest rates more quickly than it had in forty years, seeking to combat rising inflation that few had anticipated. SVB was stuck. Rising rates slashed the market value of its low-yielding investments while requiring SVB to pay more to its depositors. At the same time, trouble in the start-up ecosystem meant that SVB depositors were running down their balances, portending a reckoning when the bank would have to realize losses on its bond portfolio. What had once been safe, boring sources of positive income turned into stranded assets that were underwater on essentially every dimension.

Hence the need to raise more equity. SVB's capital call was not met by disaffected investors wondering about the consequences of shareholder dilution.

It was met by all hell breaking loose. After the 2008 global financial crisis, the federal government promised not to bail out another bank. SVB's depositors, whose holdings were well above the federal deposit insurance line, began hasty withdrawals. Within days, $42 billion left the bank. Depositors who couldn't get their money out before government officials closed SVB clamored to be made whole, despite no plausible legal claim in their favor. On March 12, 2023, Treasury Secretary Janet Yellen vowed that there would be no federal rescue: "The reforms that have been put in place [after 2008] mean that we're not going to do that again." Hours later, the federal government sidestepped those reforms and provided precisely that bailout, especially to SVB's depositors who in some cases held billions of dollars more than the deposit insurance limit. The Federal Reserve even invoked its "unusual and exigent" emergency authority. The country had a proper banking crisis, just fifteen years after the last one that was, in Barack Obama's famous words, supposed "to put a stop to taxpayer bailouts once and for all."[2]

In the months thereafter, given the profound repudiation of the government's anti-bailout commitments, commentators pointed fingers in many directions for the bank's spectacular failure. Almost everyone agreed that the failure was one of risk management, with plenty of condemnation for the bankers at SVB's helm who had mismanaged these risks. But another group that became the focus of SVB's failure were those who never owned a share of the bank's stock, never cashed a bank's check, almost certainly did not hold an account, and if they ever attended a bank board meeting, did so as a not-very-welcome guest. These were the bank supervisors that worked for various federal agencies, not for the bank itself, but who knew more about the risks the bank had taken than many of the banks' own employees.

The Federal Reserve's own postmortem took it for granted that this private bank's failure was in fact an indictment of public governance, concluding that "supervisors did not fully appreciate the extent of the vulnerabilities as Silicon Valley Bank grew in size and complexity."[3]

Of course, blaming politicians for corporate failures is not new to the United States in 2023. But in an avowedly capitalist society, it may seem odd to affix blame for day-to-day risk management failures not on careless bankers but on mostly unknown civil servants. The regional banking crisis that SVB helped initiate did not lead to a national cataclysm and did not suggest any deeper, systemic public policy failures. Why, then, did such a broad consensus develop that SVB's risk-taking was the responsibility not of this private bank but of public officials whose job it was to prevent such risk-taking in the first place?

It is a good question, and we can start with the answer. These public officials are responsible because that responsibility is a cornerstone of modern finance. The truth is that the system of banking in the United States is composed of private finance, backed inescapably by public power. Even though banks are private institutions with private shareholders, boards of directors, profit motives, customers, and competitors, they aren't managed that way. Banking is private finance, to be sure; yet, it is public power that we ultimately expect to manage those risks, even when public officials would like to shift responsibility to the private sector. Public institutions, plural and often in conflict, play foundational roles in deciding what risks banks take, how and when they take them, and to what end.

The expression of and responsibility for the public power that manages the risks of private finance has a name. It is called bank supervision. It is unusual in American society, and it is unusually American, at least in origin. This book is a history of what this striking and curious institution of financial risk management is and how it came to be.

Supervision, Not Regulation

The first question a book on bank supervision must address is the definitional one: What does bank supervision even mean? Scholars, policymakers, and other stakeholders have not reached a consensus on this question. One reason is that supervision is often conflated as a synonym with a much more common term, "regulation," the rules that govern banking. To those closer to the action, the two terms often travel as close companions in a single phrase—"supervision and regulation," or "soup and reg" for short. The Greeks called this kind of pairing a hendiadys, a double noun joined by a conjunction that provides extra emphasis for a single idea. In this case, the idea is that public officials create rules for risk management (and other purposes), with supervision and regulation as the mechanism to ensure compliance with those rules. At some level of abstraction and in some contexts, the two terms function in precisely this way, especially in contrast to other ways that the government manages systemic risk (for example, through national defense, monetary policy, food safety, or other mechanisms).

However, if the intent is to understand how, precisely, these practices function—and where they come from—then the conflation and companionship of regulation and supervision are errors that obscure what makes public supervision distinct within our system of nominally private finance. What supervisors do in fact is manage situations that require active policy tradeoffs pursued through official discretion, and in such cases supervision and regulation might have very little to do with each other. Those who want to understand the intersection of public power and private finance need to know better not only what the rules say but also what the curious institution of supervision is, how it has evolved, and for what purposes.

This book isolates American bank supervision as a unit of study and accounts for its historical evolution. As developed here, supervision is bilateral institutionalized discretion that the government uses to identify, monitor, manage, and resolve the residual risks that private actors generate through the financial system. It is not simply the synonym of writing the rules that implement congressional actions, the pith of "regulation." Nor is it the basic verification that those rules are being followed by individual banks, though some supervision operates as compliance. It is much broader than this. Sometimes bank supervisors look like cops on the beat, issuing fines, enforcing laws, and even assisting the real police in hauling crooked bankers off to jail. Sometimes bank supervisors look more like fire wardens, alerting banks when their risks are a threat to themselves and their customers and calling for the public fire engine to bring relief when those downside risks ignite. Sometimes they act like accountants and auditors, sometimes as the tormentors of bankers hoping to innovate and experiment, and sometimes as those bankers' loyal collaborators. Sometimes they are public officials, duly endowed with public power. And in others, supervisors are private actors, exercising discretionary oversight in service of bankers' individual or collective self-interest.

Above all else, bank supervision is the space between public and private, where government actors work with private bankers to manage the risks thrown into the economy and society through the basic, foundational, and vital enterprise of banking. This definition is a broad but important one. It reflects no specific pinpoint in history, no ability to say what the relationship between the government and private banks was always about. It describes instead a middle ground, a negotiated space where the private and public sometimes contest power, sometimes collaborate in it, but always manage that power together in a way that is more extensive and more pervasive than in other parts of American society. Bank supervision is, in short, institutionalized discretion used to manage residual financial risk as it occurs in individual private banks and across the private banking system.[4]

In our account, bank supervision is therefore a dynamic space. Some supervisory tools, such as chartering, gained and lost discretionary power at different points in time. Others, such as bank examination, became more consistently dynamic in the risks that examiners evaluated and in the methods that they used, even as the examiners and the content of examinations changed. In defining bank supervision as institutionalized discretion to manage bank risk, we seek to understand who used discretion, for what kinds of risks, using what tools, for what purposes, and how the complex of institutionalized decision-making evolved. *Private Finance, Public Power* therefore offers a positive theory of how bank supervision works now and explains how, through experimentation, error, and the slow building of sometimes redundant, often warring institutions, that same machinery that sprang to the rescue of Silicon Valley Bank came to be.[5]

The Layered and Evolving Institutions of Bank Supervision

That process of building redundant, warring, but ultimately effective institutions to co-manage private risk is a remarkable but mostly ignored instance of what political scientists call "institutional layering," or the process by which "new elements are attached to existing institutions and so gradually change their status and structure." After Congress created a system of federally chartered banks during the Civil War, federal officials sought to provide robust public support to the new national banking system. The Comptroller of the Currency, the first federal bank supervisor, offered the new national banks under its supervision everything from practical banking advice to fraud detection. Yet supervisors lacked the institutional capacity to realize their ambitions. After the 1870s, individual and systemic bank failures, along with official corruption and scandalous fraud, led federal officials to shift risk management away from the public and onto private shareholders and bank directors. This occurred at the level of individual banks, through corporate governance and shareholder liability, and through private clearinghouses that could provide liquidity in moments of strain. Supervisors gathered and mobilized information, continuing to steer banks toward safety with the latent threat of closure if they detected insolvency or fraud, but private liability management anchored the system.[6]

Across the late nineteenth century, the rise of bank deposits as a major component of the national money supply, combined with decennial banking panics that endangered those deposits, gave rise to deposit insurance and central banking as alternative risk management strategies to the Comptroller's information model. The last of these Gilded Age panics, that of 1907, led to the embodiment of those strategies as institutions—the Federal Reserve System and state deposit insurance schemes—but not at the exclusion of the Comptroller, state bank examiners, or private clearinghouses. Contemporaries largely understood these as competing frameworks—deposit insurance *or* central banking; public examination through the Comptroller *or* private examination through the clearinghouses. And in this competitive mode, supervision—public and private—unambiguously failed during the 1920s agricultural depression, the 1930s banking crises, and the Great Depression that followed from these catastrophes. The first half of *Private Finance, Public Power* tells the story of these origins, evolutions, and failures, each of which contributed to the mostly durable system of bank supervision that emerged from the critical period in the 1930s.

The second half tells the story that evolved from there. During the New Deal, complementarity eclipsed competition, so that, notwithstanding their Depression-era failures, the public supervisory institutions not only evolved but expanded. Modern bank supervision emerged in the wake of these central, pivotal moments of intense experimentation. Franklin Roosevelt's administration forged information provision, central banking, deposit insurance, and public ownership into a reinforced supervisory structure that would, once and for all, stabilize the unstable financial economy. In the face of new public institutions, each layered on top of the others, the New Dealers curtailed but did not eliminate the institutions of private risk management. They sought to maintain private control of the banking system even as the public provided more support with a more expansive set of tools. After World War II, in an era of financial calm that seemed to validate the New Deal approach, various stakeholders wrestled with two core and competing questions: (1) how and whether to extend the scope for private risk-taking; and (2) how and whether to use institutionalized discretion to advance new policy goals, including antitrust and antidiscrimination. By the time financial instability forcefully reemerged in the 1970s, the shape of the supervisory system had solidified, even as these debates grew more intense.[7]

The institutional layering that built up over the postwar period provides an essential window through which we view the supervisory successes and failures that followed. We track three in particular. First, the chartering prerogatives of the Comptroller of the Currency and the state banking authorities, each jealous of the other in an unsteady equilibrium known as the "dual banking system," created a dynamic space of charter competition that defies usual conceptions of federalism in the provision of law. This was neither a race to the top nor a race to the bottom, although there was indeed some kind of competitive race afoot. Second, the Federal Deposit Insurance Corporation (FDIC), the institution created during the height of the Depression in Franklin D. Roosevelt's first hundred days in office, initiated a new, encompassing focus on insurance underwriting and the preservation of the Deposit Insurance Fund. Although the FDIC relied on the Office of the Comptroller of the Currency and the Federal Reserve for supervisory insights in its first frantic years, it eventually became a juggernaut of its own, spanning the federal and state divide, and employing the largest corps of supervisors. And third, the Federal Reserve System, the nation's central bank evolved through the twentieth century to focus on supervision as subordinate to and in the service of broader conceptions of macroeconomic stability. These institutional prerogatives over risk management were almost constantly in conflict from the 1930s onward. Those conflicts—over chartering, insurance provision, and macroeconomic stability—defined risk, its management, and the political economy of bank supervision from the New Deal through the 1970s.

Institutional Evolution in *Private Finance, Public Power*

In telling the story of institutional layering in bank supervision, *Private Finance, Public Power* is an institutional history as much as it is a financial and political history. By institutional history, we mean the focus on the dynamic ways that institutions form and evolve. Here, we build on the work of new institutional economists like Douglass North and historical institutionalists from political science and sociology. These scholars focus more on the processes that proceed from the founding of institutions and more on the ways that later institutions build upon these earlier moments. Institutional layering is, of course, part of this institutional analysis, but so too is the recognition that institutions adapt to fit their contingent historical moments. Sometimes, those moments (as in those studied by the new institutional economists) are on the order of revolutions and constitutions. Other times, they are responsive to changes in political administrations or the structure of the economy. And in other instances, these moments of change occur because one person was appointed Comptroller of the Currency and another person wasn't. In *Private Finance, Public Power*, we look at critical junctures of all such moments (and many others).[8]

We can think, then, of bank supervision as the evolutionary outgrowth of a series of unrelated decisions made by politicians, bankers, legislators, policymakers, citizens, and many other stakeholders, eventually creating a system that creaks and groans as mismatched parts, crafted at different times for different purposes, grind against one another, all while still serving useful and well-adapted purposes.

Evolutionary biologist Steven Jay Gould referred to such evolutionary adaptations in his 1980 book, *The Panda's Thumb*, to explain why the giant panda's elongated wrist bone survived despite its ungainly appearance and imperfect functionality. His insight is that complex systems like the panda's thumb—or, in our application, the financial risk management across the public-private divide—leave behind hints of a past that is much more complicated than our present uses of those systems seem to support. As we quote in the book's epigraph, "remnants of the past that don't make sense in present terms—the useless, the odd, the peculiar, the incongruous—are the signs of history. They supply proof that the world was not made in its present form. When history perfects, it covers its own tracks." Bank supervision in its institutional forms is full of "the useless, the odd, the peculiar, the incongruous," proof that the abiding challenges of risk management have been met again and again—and must continue to be met—in specific historical circumstances, meetings which have left ample evidence of history's failure to "cover its own tracks." (For a long time, we called this book *The Banker's Thumb*, but many of our early readers had no idea what we were talking about or referring to, hence the title change at the strong encouragement of our editors!)[9]

This evolutionary basis of supervision's historical trajectory means that bank supervision is not some sleek, efficient machine ordained by farsighted legislators. Rather, many of the most important innovations to bank supervision resulted from supervisory officials' creative repurposing of statutory constructs. In the 1860s, Congress authorized ad hoc bank examination in the National Banking Acts, which supervisors made into routine, periodic, and surprise inspections. Congress set strict eligibility rules for Federal Reserve discounting in 1913, onto which the Reserve Board layered discretionary acceptability criteria. What makes supervision as it evolved so functional is that it provides a negotiated and negotiable space through which risk can be managed across the public-private divide. Through this space, occupied by partisans and technicians alike, both sides discover profoundly important information not otherwise available through other mechanisms of risk management. This negotiated, liminal space means that the financial system of the United States cannot and need not ever be completely "future-proofed" through legislative design. Bankers and bank supervisors, on the ground and behind closed doors, can manage risks on an open vector, assessing changes as they come with better speed and better protection of competing interests than the legislative process could ever possibly deliver.

To make an implicit point explicit: Just because supervision can work this way does not mean it has or will. Often, over supervision's long history, officials managed risks poorly or failed to confront risks they could neither see nor understand. Officials in different agencies and at different levels of government pursued conflicting and counterproductive risk management strategies, while bankers, caught amid opposing forces, played for advantage. Legislative reforms, incremental and wholesale, could change the field quite dramatically but did not on their own determine the subsequent movement of the players.

In this sense, recognizing that the development of banking supervision is not simply a teleological march toward greater and greater perfection informs how we approach history in another important respect. Just as bank supervision took a somewhat circuitous path toward reaching functionality, its history can't be told in a crisp series of genesis moments when certain institutions were called into being by an enlightened Congress. This is the province of the heavily leaned-on genre of constitutional history, which tends to replay the moves of the "founding generation" and defines, through their thoughts and intentions, institutions from free speech to affirmative action, gay marriage to gun control. In the case of banking history, scholars might focus on the legislative acts that created new supervisors, such as the National Banking Acts or the Federal Reserve Act, as if those acts cast the institutions in stone—supervision as it was and always should be.[10]

We don't neglect those key moments in *Private Finance, Public Power*. All the legislative stars of banking are here. The history of bank supervision, though, is not merely legislative history. We want to tell the history of the organizations and practices of bank supervision not just as they were designed but also as they evolved. What the Lincoln administration thought they were doing in creating the national banking system, or the ways that the creation of the Federal Reserve System altered supervisory institutions, or the curious advent of federal deposit insurance supervision in 1933—all of them elucidate much of what bank supervision would become. Not completely, however, so our history is not focused exclusively here either.

The Faces of Institutionalized Discretion

Since our theoretical conceit is that history is contingent and unpredictable, the history of *Private Finance, Public Power* focuses both on structural changes—war and peace, economic growth, and changes demanded by citizens through political processes—and on the individual words and actions of bankers, politicians, supervisors, and other historical players as they engaged in the tug-of-war that defines bank supervision. In these historical spaces, we start to see the many contests to define how residual risk should be managed and where in the space between public and private that management should occur. Our historical actors agree on very little. These disagreements themselves generate the content that defines what bank supervision evolves to become over the course of our account.

The disagreements also define the core logic of bank supervision and what separates it from rival epistemologies of government action: Supervision is about the public's institutionalized discretion in the management of and, subsequently, ultimate responsibility for the risks taken by private actors. Discretion is, by its nature, inexact and hard to predict, as supervisors have long recognized. In 1884, the Comptroller of the Currency acknowledged the uncertainty: "The exact line at which the Government shall interfere and the point at which Government discipline shall commence is a matter of some delicacy to determine." In 2020, Randal Quarles, the former Vice Chair for Supervision at the Federal Reserve, put the same sentiment somewhat more colorfully: Identifying the line between regulation (which generally follows the crisp rules and procedures spelled out in law) and supervision (which is harder to track) only becomes clear after "fasting and much prayer."[11]

The discretion in supervision has become, in the 2020s, something of a controversial flashpoint in legal circles, with some arguing that "the confidential and tailored nature of supervision sits uncomfortably with the responsibilities of government in a democracy," while others defend bank supervision's basic compatibility with those responsibilities. This book does not assess the legal arguments that these disputants make, but we do trace in this history the irreducible centrality that such discretion has had in federal financial oversight. The use of discretion in assessing the risks taken by private actors is one of the few throughlines that we discuss in *Private Finance, Public Power*. The way that the institutions of bank supervision evolved to place such discretion, exercised to manage a large and growing number of various kinds of risks, is in an important sense the entire argument of the book.[12]

We are, of course, not the first to emphasize the discretion inherent in bureaucratic authority. Most prominently in administrative law, Jerry Mashaw argued that the discretion exercised in the Social Security Administration threatened the very stability of our bureaucratic system. Similarly, in political science, a thriving literature on "street-level bureaucracy," that arose roughly at the same time as Mashaw's critique, focuses on the "challenges" of discretion to the rule of law, costs that other mechanisms must correct.[13]

These and other efforts to taxonomize and diagnose the strengths and weaknesses of discretion come down to the same basic arguments: It is ubiquitous in our system of government, and it can be used for good and ill. We do not dispute these basic premises. There is no question that bank supervisory discretion is both valuable and potentially ripe for mismanagement and abuse. But the institutionalization of supervisory discretion is about much more than the implementation of law enforcement in individual cases. Defining the boundaries and potential of supervisory discretion is a major part of our narrative, primarily because it was a major project through the two centuries of history that we narrate.[14]

Supervision as Residual Risk Management

The foregoing theoretical context of *Private Finance, Public Power* leads to four basic insights. Supervision is (1) about the relationship between individual actors in government and individual financial institutions, where public power meets private finance. It is further defined by (2) evolutionary processes and is resistant to efforts to impose a single defining ethos, instead leaving supervisors— and Congress—to use (3) supervisory discretion to choose among competing conceptions of what that individual relationship should be.

The most important payoff of this account is the fourth insight—that this system has (4) proven so functional, even if often inefficient, because institutionalized supervisory discretion works as a risk absorber for the entire financial system. Bank supervision is the promise that the government will participate with the private sector to manage and take responsibility for the residual risks that design choices about the American financial system will always produce. Contrary to other categories of risk—national security after September 11, 2001, for example—financial scandals, panics, crises, and other events have come to be viewed as more or less the cost of the American system. Supervision, then, isn't just about punishing wrongdoers or responding to panics; it is about managing a large and ever-growing system of risk that we, as a society, have decided we want to take, using a variety of tools and strategies that sometimes converge, sometimes conflict.

Supervision is, in that way, about managing the moral hazard that the financial system creates in so much abundance, and with so much controversy. The concept of "moral hazard" comes from nineteenth-century insurance, denoting concern that people or firms that take out insurance to protect themselves against specific kinds of risks will be less dutiful about avoiding those risks.

Eliminating moral hazard is often cited as the defining problem of institutional design in the financial system. The fact that banks and bankers are perceived to privatize the benefits of finance while they socialize the costs is a recurrent scandal in its own right. One of the reasons that the regional banking crisis of 2023 caused such alarm was not the risks to the overall health of the financial system but the seeming betrayal of the promise to end government bailouts of private actors in banking (especially large uninsured depositors who should be competent to manage their own risks).[15]

We argue, however, that moral hazard is irretrievably baked into the American financial system: Banking, by its very nature, will always involve risks that are prosocial in nature with no effective mechanism of rendering the costs and benefits of that system symmetrically socialized or privatized. Perhaps the political promises coming out of 2008 implicated an end to government bailouts, but the architecture of public-private risk management would never permit such a policy commitment. That fact means that bank supervision will always entail a contest and collaboration between public and private actors on how to manage that risk, including the provision of public insights and responsibilities for private action and inaction. Once understood in that light, moral hazard isn't a policy problem to solve for bank supervisors. Managing moral hazard is the job description.[16]

Audiences

Although we have aimed to capture the attention of readers with no prior knowledge of the sometimes arcane and technical details discussed in *Private Finance, Public Power*, we have no illusions about our target audience. This is a book primarily written for scholars of financial regulation in law, economics, political science, and history; as well as for bank supervision's stakeholders and participants across the public-private divide. We hope too that the book will be of interest to a variety of scholars from fields as diverse as administrative law, finance, sociology, and various subdisciplines of history beyond financial history (especially political and legal history). We recognize, of course, that some of this material will be substantively and methodologically different from those normally encountered by supervisory participants and practitioners in these other disciplines. We hope that it will generate debate as to the application of bank supervision in these contexts, even if by contrary comparison.

Our intervention in debates about the historical foundations of bank supervision comes at a propitious time for the field of financial regulation, the field to which we hope the book will be most relevant. As recently as the early 2000s, this field was relatively small and focused. The financial crisis of 2008 changed this. As the field has grown, conversations have become more specialized and more fragmented, a natural outcome of any expanding field. Financial regulation scholars have made contributions to monetary theory,[17] market structure,[18] sustainable finance,[19] systemic risk regulation,[20] the political economy of crisis,[21] congressional reactions to financial crisis,[22] financial innovation,[23] digital finance,[24] financial inclusion,[25] payment systems,[26] financial regulation and bankruptcy,[27] bank antitrust,[28] and law and macroeconomics[29] (a nonrandom but still partial list). If anything, the COVID-19 pandemic— and the financial crisis that it sparked in the early spring of 2020—has solidified the intellectual energy around financial regulation as an important subfield of business law.[30]

The problem, as with so many areas of scholarly specialization, is that these subfields have become evermore siloed such that those who focus on, for example, central bank governance are rarely engaged with those who are interested in market microstructure. This is lamentable, because there are genuine insights to be gained by keeping the subfields of financial regulation in conversation together, even on such disparate topics.

Private Finance, Public Power shows that bank supervision can be the connective tissue that brings these conversations together, thereby filling an essential role in unifying the field of financial regulation. In the chapters ahead, we address each of these literatures and many others as supervisors grapple with early changes to bank capital accounting, changes to institutional governance and market structure, antitrust overhaul, financial innovations, panics and crises, crime and scandal, and so much else. Bank supervision can provide the table around which these subfields can gather on a common set of insights and conversations.[31]

Indeed, our argument is bolder than that: Reliance on theory, legislation, and regulation alone—the primary tools of financial regulation scholars—is insufficient to understand any of these issues. Bank supervision is where these important ideas become tangible. To ignore bank supervision is to risk failure to grasp what really matters about each of these fields. Bank supervision is where the practice of government actually occurs in finance. Studying the development of legal rules and even institutions writ large cannot get close enough to offer much by way of description or interpretation of how public power is exercised in the financial system. The study of bank supervision thus facilitates that exploration much more authentically.[32]

Supervision and History: State Capacity
and Administration

Our other primary audience, beyond scholars focused on contemporary financial governance, are historians interested in the American administrative state. Our story about the development of bank supervision uncovers an important throughline in the nation's political and financial history, and especially contributes to debates about the evolution of state capacity and administration in the nineteenth century through the New Deal and on the process and consequences of the rapid growth of finance in the postwar period.

Private Finance, Public Power adds its voice to the chorus correcting the still-stubborn myth that American state capacity only came online during the Progressive Era. Others have expanded our view much more broadly, extending periods of experimentation deep into the nineteenth century. We join the revisionists but with a correction of our own: These scholars ignore bank supervision, one of the most creative and entrenched spheres of government action in the era. Federal bank supervision predated the Interstate Commerce Commission—the conventional starting point for bureaucratic development in the United States—by more than two decades at the federal level. It existed in the states for three more decades before that. In understanding the origins and rise of the bank supervision in the nineteenth century through the beginning of the New Deal, we learn about key aspects of state capacity that confirm some accounts and challenge others. These aspects include the array of institutional choices that confronted legislators and policymakers, judicial resolution of conflict versus bureaucratization, and, of course, the exercise of discretion in ordering private markets.[33]

We also contribute importantly to the vast and still growing literature on the New Deal and the postwar period, focusing again on questions of state capacity. Here, the argument is not *whether* the government engaged forcefully in private markets—no one disputes these central facts of the New Deal and beyond. The question is more about the throughlines of such engagement, how much of a policy departure these moves represented, and what endured into the post–World War II era. The principal debates regard the intellectual content of the New Deal, including whether it was chaotically experimental or part of longstanding commitments, and the efficacy of the policy choices themselves. We engage in this literature directly to describe the key predecessors to New Deal bank supervision but also the extraordinary, seismic, and enduring moment that New Deal supervision represented, not least

that it was through supervision—in the form of the Bank Holiday of 1933—
that Roosevelt created space without which the New Deal could not have
materialized. The creation of deposit insurance and the reformulation of the
Federal Reserve in the 1930s established conclusively the federal ownership of
financial risk. Finally, we engage in debates about antitrust and financial concentration in the postwar era, as well as the role of state capacity used against
said concentration and in favor of consumers and racial minorities as bank
supervision arrived as a set of tools for managing residual risk beyond the
safety and soundness of the banking system.[34]

Overview of the Book

The book proceeds as follows.

In chapters 1 to 3, we discuss the longest historical period in the book, covering 1789 through 1907, including the period during which the institutions of
supervision were most contingent and least resolved. In this part, we describe
the state-based approach to bank supervision that existed in the nineteenth
century, an ad hoc system that looked much more like "street-level bureaucracy" and much less like the system of institutionalized discretion that bank
supervision would ultimately become. The origins are important, though, for
the choices they reflect. In the nineteenth century, federal and state officials
developed a variety of supervisory tools, including chartering, examination,
publicity, private liability, liability insurance, forbearance, and receivership, all
with the aim of limiting bank failure and failure's consequences for bank counterparties. The balance of public and private power ebbed and flowed during
this period, but repeated public failures—whether early liability insurance
schemes before the Civil War or efforts at robust bank examination after it—
led officials to fall back on private risk management within individual banks
and collectively through private clearinghouses.[35]

Chapter 4 then outlines the origins of the first competitive pressure among
supervisory entities at the federal level with the advent of the Federal Reserve
System in 1913, which sat uncomfortably alongside the Comptroller of the
Currency (created in 1863) as a federal bank supervisor. Within the Federal
Reserve System, the individual Federal Reserve Banks lacked the "chartering"
authority of the Comptroller and the state banking authorities that usually
brought supervision into existence. Instead, the Reserve Banks, built on the
clearinghouse model, extended supervision through the practice of bank liquidity management by deciding which assets to discount or whether to

discount at all. Finally, chapter 4 outlines the continued limitations of "for-bearance" as a method of supervision—that is, supervisory decisions to with-hold action on non-performing loans in the face of crisis. This practice would become a familiar one, highlighting supervisory absorption of risk at the be-hest of politicians for purposes other than bank profitability.

Chapter 5 covers one of the biggest tests in the history of supervision: the Bank Holiday of 1933. We recast this landmark event as a triumph not of grand rhetoric and presidential charisma but as a successful invocation of bank su-pervision to legitimize uncertain political experiments that had already been attempted and had failed during the Hoover administration. This chapter also outlines the important relationship between supervision, legitimacy, and poli-tics, a theme developed later on. Chapter 5 is the fulcrum of the book, placed between the origins of supervisory institutions and the solidification of risk management and discretion (backed by an unwavering public commitment) as the raison d'être of those institutions.

In chapter 6, we discuss the alternatives to the two models already tried and found wanting in the banking crises of the Great Depression—namely, the informational approach of the Comptroller and the states, and the liquidity approach of the Federal Reserve. Added to that mix are the Reconstruction Finance Corporation, one of the most important institutions of the New Deal, and the much more enduring Federal Deposit Insurance Corporation. The FDIC is, after Social Security, arguably the most important and successful innovation of the New Deal era. It also permanently and radically altered the orientation of bank supervision away from private conversations between bankers and the government for the purpose of protecting bank stakeholders writ large and toward a consumerist ethos that protected depositors (and, by extension, the deposit insurance fund). The other models did not disappear but remained as forceful sources of conflict between and among rival worldviews.

Chapter 7 narrates the problem of financial concentration and financial complexity by taking up the major postwar focus of bank supervision: mergers and acquisitions. Banking had been a special category within antitrust since the 1914 passage of the Clayton Act. In the 1950s, following a wave of bank consolidations, merger review became the explicit focus of bank supervisors as well. This change occurred alongside increasing challenges of supervising complexity. The model of the nineteenth-century unit bank that could be ex-amined in a couple of hours by an aggressive and underpaid supervisor fell away. Financial department stores became increasingly the norm.

In chapter 8, the first cracks in the New Deal order are revealed as personnel changes in the Kennedy administration led to a fundamental reevaluation of the intellectual purposes of supervision as the residual risk manager of the financial system. Chapter 8 functions as a kind of public biography of James J. Saxon, the Comptroller of the Currency and sparring partner of virtually all of official Washington. Saxon was a pugilist; he was also an institutional innovator who sought to alter the risk tolerance in finance through supervision, efforts that did not succeed in his day but that planted the seeds of a radical alteration of those risks in the future.

Finally, chapter 9 concludes with a discussion of how civil rights and consumer protection became key parts of the supervisory apparatus through 1980. Chapter 9 illustrates Congress's enthusiasm for multiplying the paradigms of supervisory discretion into areas far beyond micro- and macroprudential risk. Bank supervision absorbed, increasingly, political risks as well. In doing so, supervisors took a cue from Congress and gave consumer protection more weight than antidiscrimination—because Congress included stronger penalties that could endanger bank safety in its consumer legislation. Following a pattern of institutional layering found throughout the book, federal supervisors' failures to adequately manage civil rights in finance led Congress to give these supervisors yet more tools—through the Community Reinvestment Act—with which to do so.

In this book, we track major transformations in banking and government over two centuries, and yet our conceit is that supervision is in a sense profoundly interpersonal and discretionary, worked out in conversations and correspondence between specific people, in specific institutional and historical contexts. At the best of times, many of the conversations that animate the nature of bank supervision are protected by high walls of secrecy. We have encountered many varied barriers as historians trying to document the nature of bank supervision. In the sweep of two centuries and in the face of such restrictions, some of the most important details can sift out. To answer these problems—and perhaps to indulge our own interests in the people we study—we have included interludes between the chapters, which we hope will reveal some of the substance of private and public interaction.

Bank Supervision After 1980

This book is not a comprehensive history of supervision to the present. We stop in 1980 for important reasons. Around 1979, the world changed. Chaotic experiments with monetary policy shifted the economic landscape increasingly toward the Federal Reserve through its monetary policy powers. What later became known as the neoliberal consensus exploded onto the scene on a transatlantic basis with the presidential campaign of Ronald Reagan and the installation of Margaret Thatcher in the United Kingdom. The financialization of the U.S. economy left the nation's agricultural and industrial sectors behind.[36]

Bank supervision underwent important changes during this critical period too. The basic apparatus of bilateral, institutionalized discretion that functioned as a manager and absorber of risk stayed the same, but its uses evolved substantially. Part of these changes came through the rise of the Federal Reserve as the preeminent financial supervisor, with a preference for stability through monetary policy. Part of this change came through the advent of greater financial concentration. Part came through the dramatic expansion of other non-prudential categories of bank supervision, principally consumer privacy protection and, even more so, anti-money laundering. And part also came through the crystallization of capital regulation as the primary mechanism for prudential regulation. *Private Finance, Public Power* uncovers the origins of these changes but leaves for another book the exploration of just how the state capacity of supervision was deployed during this neoliberal era.

Even so, this book provides many important insights for the 2020s (the decade of its publication). In key respects, the supervisory conflicts and opportunities that the United States faces in the twenty-first century—from massive financial crises such as in 2008, questions about climate change, combating terrorist financing, federalist conflicts around marijuana banking, and what to do about cryptocurrency and cyber security—all flow through the same institutional apparatus that was forged in the fires of the nineteenth century, the New Deal, and the postwar era. While these debates in their particulars would be foreign to the bankers, supervisors, and politicians whose stories we tell in this book, in general there would be much that was familiar.

———

We began our collaboration on this project in 2014. At the time, we planned only to write an article on the history of the Examination Report, a document whose form—we then thought—stayed remarkably stable from the 1860s to the 1950s. We imagined the Examination Report as a cultural artifact and example of the state attempting to render financial markets more "legible" for state control. As we pulled that thread, though, we began to see bank supervision as something much larger than bank examination and its associated paperwork. It is the story not only of bank examiners and politicians, but of con artists and lobbyists, racism and federalism, financial crises and monetary theory, and those who view bank mergers as the protection against financial collapse versus those who saw such mergers as the cause of that collapse. In the pages ahead, we tell their stories—along with many others—through the lens of a unique set of institutions that, in important ways, defined the development of the American state far beyond the Examination Report.[37]

1

Origins

THE EARLY REPUBLIC AND
THE FREE BANKING ERA

MICHIGAN, RESOURCE-RICH and capital-starved, had the ill fortune of joining the federal political union just as the federal banking union, anchored by the Second Bank of the United States, had ended, leaving Michiganders to their own financing devices. It was not great timing. In 1837, its first year of statehood, Michigan's lawmakers enacted the nation's first "free banking" law, creating an administrative process for investors to charter banks, unencumbered by legislative oversight. Soon, Michigan's woods and hollows teemed with financial life, some of it virtuous, much of it predatory. Would-be bankers flooded the state with a flurry of private banknotes before retreating into the wild, hoping to thwart those interested in turning paper promises into the gold and silver they nominally represented. It was in this financial frontier that such banks earned the fitting nickname "wildcats."[1]

State legislators had anticipated the incentives to bank from the shadows. The "free banking" law that allowed these banks to flourish also called for state officers to examine them, making sure that the paper notes they issued were backed by more than vapor. In the first winter of the free banks' existence, state examiners trekked from bank to bank, each more remote than the last. As they did so, they noticed something odd. On every leg of their journey, a fresh set of heavy sled tracks was always ahead of them. This was no mere passenger rig but something carrying sizable cargo.[2]

To their dismay, they learned that their shared paths were not coincidental: The sled hauled a cache of silver, successively filling the vaults of the banks they were coming to inspect. The bankers, with knowledge of the examiners' likely path—there weren't many options in early nineteenth-century

Michigan—had created a mobile specie reserve. When inspected, each bank looked sound, even though none were. "Gold and silver flew about the country with the celerity of magic," the state banking commissioners reported, "its sound was heard in the depths of the forest; yet, like the wind, one knew not whence it came or whither it was going." Michigan's experiment with free banking was, not coincidentally, a short-lived disaster.[3]

Bank supervisors were often chasing silver sleds, literal and figurative, then as now. Before Congress created the national banking system in the 1860s, and with it the beginnings of the modern federal supervisory structure, some of the most important institutional tools that Congress would adopt had been tried by state oversight officials—and at times found wanting. Some, like special chartering, which granted banking privileges to favored investors at state legislatures' discretion, clashed with insurgent political ideologies of antimonopoly and laissez-faire. In the age of emerging mass democracy, special chartering—castigated as favoritist, corrupt, and reeking of aristocratic privilege—carried too many political risks. Other approaches, like on-site examination, struggled to overcome problems of distance and time. Government officials could not observe banks often enough. When they did try, their power to change behavior was often limited and ill-defined.

Still, antebellum politicians, state and federal, recognized that banking was too important to leave entirely in the hands of private capitalists. What they struggled to define was what role the public would play in understanding, shaping, punishing, or promoting those private interests. Nevertheless, across seventy years of economic growth, imperial expansion, and episodic panic, they experimented with managing the public's interest in private finance. Some of their efforts endured, most turned to failure, but regardless, the period of antebellum bank supervisory experimentation set the stage for the important debates and departures that followed thereafter.

Money and Banking in the Young Nation

The rise of supervision as a mechanism for discretionary risk management begins, as with so much else in finance, with Alexander Hamilton. The global order that the revolutionary generation inherited, dominated by the United Kingdom, defined silver and gold as the foundation of monetary value—either as money itself or as the necessary backing of any circulating currency. The American colonies, however, proved chronically short of specie, lacking suitable mineral deposits of their own. One solution to these constraints was government-issued paper currency, supported by the public taxing power, which the Continental Congress liberally employed during the Revolution. Another was the banking alternative, where private or public institutions made loans by issuing paper notes redeemable in specie. These private notes circulated as money, creating few problems so long as the promise of redemption remained credible.[4]

At the national level, antebellum banking politics were a constant tug between Hamilton's vision of a centralized financial system and Thomas Jefferson and his successors' antagonism toward concentrated financial power (a canonical political dispute that has never been fully resolved). The Articles of Confederation gave the Continental Congress "the sole and exclusive right and power of regulating the alloy and value of coin struck by their own authority, or by that of the respective States." The Congress also had the authority to "emit bills on the credit of the United States." But in the 1780s, the confederated government didn't exercise these prerogatives. Instead, ten of the thirteen former colonies issued forms of paper money, to greatly mixed effect and significant national, commercial confusion.[5]

To rein in the chaos, the framers of the 1787 U.S. Constitution specifically barred the states from issuing paper currency and implicitly discouraged the federal government from doing the same. As one delegate to the convention stated plainly, the Constitution was meant in part "to shut and bar the door against paper money." They had had enough of the paper experiments of the revolutionary era and were ready for something new.[6]

Hamilton was the author of that "something new." What the federal government might not do directly, Hamilton encouraged it to do indirectly. In his *Second Report on the Public Credit*, Hamilton proposed a "National Bank" as an "institution of primary importance to the prosperous administration" of the new country's finances. The First Bank of the United States, modeled on the Bank of England, would serve as the fiscal agent of the Treasury; pay out interest on the public debt; receive subscriptions for new issues of government securities; pay government salaries; facilitate foreign exchange; moderate the outflow of specie; provide foreign specie to the mint; and lend to individuals and businesses by issuing banknotes that would circulate as money. In other words, it would dominate nearly every aspect of the new nation's financial life.[7]

Like the Bank of England, Hamilton's proposed Bank of the United States would be a private institution imbued with public purpose, with the federal government a mere minority shareholder. "Public utility is more truly the object of public Banks, than private profit," Hamilton wrote. "Such a Bank is not a mere matter of private property, but a political machine of the greatest importance to the State." To provide these public benefits, though, the bank needed independence from public control. The Bank of the United States "shall be under a *private* not a *public* Direction, under the guidance of *individual interest, not of public policy.*" Congress accepted the proposal almost exactly as Hamilton made it, passing legislation to grant the bank's charter in 1791, over the vehement protests of Jeffersonians and others who opposed the bank both on the merits and as a violation of constitutional principles of federalism.[8]

Jefferson's hostility toward Hamiltonian finance grew to such a feverish peak that he viewed the bank's creation as "an act of treason" by the U.S. Congress against the states, such that anyone who participated in commerce with the bank should be "adjudged guilty of high treason and suffer death accordingly."[9]

As president, though, Jefferson waffled, both on constitutional principle and to a lesser extent on the merits of the bank itself. That is, he never lost his disdain for the institution, even as his letters no longer called for the execution of the bank's counterparties. He still regarded the Bank of the United States as "one of the most deadly hostility existing against the principles and form of our Constitution," but he did little to antagonize the institution during his presidency. Neither he nor his party members pursued the constitutional question with any vigor. His successor and ally, James Madison, had mostly, if weakly, acquiesced in favor of the bank.[10]

Even so, when the bank's recharter came due in 1811, Congress, in the hands of Jefferson's Democratic-Republicans, declined without conviction to renew it. With the War of 1812 on the horizon, Congress's timing could not have been worse. During the war, state-chartered banks, the notes of which now supplied the nation's paper currency, largely suspended specie payment. Noteholders could no longer convert their paper promises into cash and were left holding only promises. Without a specie anchor, the value of these notes floated, then sank.[11]

Lacking a functional currency, the government struggled to finance the war effort. In its wake, Congress, led by John C. Calhoun, chartered the Second Bank of the United States in 1816, a more robust version of the original.[12]

Threat of Redemption: U.S. Banks and the Currency Model

The bitterly contested and short lives of the First and Second Banks of the United States are well-traveled terrain in the history of early American banking. What is less understood is the evolving supervisory relationship between these federal banks and the smaller, state-chartered financial institutions. Though the

Constitution had attempted to bar the states from printing their own currency, it said nothing about state-chartered corporations doing the same, a loophole that worked even when the state directly owned the bank.

Seeking to lubricate the wheels of commerce and drive local economic development, states chartered banks at a rapid clip, a move anticipated (and even desired) by Hamilton's design. In 1791, there were only five banks in operation in the United States; by 1820, there were more than 300. Many of these early banks were partly or wholly owned by state governments, indicating the extent to which some state legislatures saw currency creation and finance-led development as essential public functions. The consequence was not only the decentralization of banking services, even as the First and Second Banks exerted strong gravitational force, but also the proliferation of different banknotes functioning as a medium of exchange. With so many banks issuing so many notes, the currencies of the United States were confetti—there was hardly any standardization at all.[13]

Though the federal government could not prevent the expansion of state-chartered banks, the quasi-public Banks of the United States exercised supervisory control through counterparty exposure, a mode of market-based oversight we call the "currency model" of supervision. This system was relatively straightforward. When the Banks of the United States received the paper currency issued by state-chartered banks, they would present these notes to the issuing bank and demand specie in return. If the issuing bank could not provide it, the federal banks could cut offenders off from business and make known their redemption failure (direct action, like suits for redemption, were politically risky and unlikely to succeed in local courts). The exercise preserved the quality of the circulating currency through the practice—and manifest threat—of note redemption. Note redemption ensured private institutions could deliver on the promises their notes made.[14]

The Banks of the United States were not strictly necessary for this market-based process: Banknotes were tested every time a customer came to the counter and traded notes for coin. What made the Banks of the United States' actions significant was their size, geographic reach, and discretionary application. The First Bank, capitalized at $10 million, had eight branches in the young republic's major trading centers; the Second, capitalized at $35 million, had twenty-five branches, many reaching deep into the booming frontier. Scale and scope were manifest power. "The general scheme of administering the Bank," the Second Bank's President Nicholas Biddle explained in 1825, "is to preserve a mild and gentle but efficient control over the monied institutions of the United States so as rather to warn than to force them into a scale of business commensurate with their real means." With these warnings, the Banks of the United States restrained credit growth, state banknote circulation, and monetary inflation.[15]

Importantly, the currency model of supervision, even when undertaken by the federal banks, operated between private entities each acting on market information. At this point, no federal inspector could go behind the counter and inspect their counterparties' books. Proof came when notes were redeemed in coin—or when they weren't.

Visiting the Banks of the United States

Congress relied on the currency mode of supervision not for its virtues but for the lack of alternatives: It had no other means of monitoring state-chartered banks. Overwhelming deference to federalism created a bright line between state and federal powers. "The [federal] Government have no means of ascertaining the system or principles upon which these different banks conduct their business," Vermont Congressman James Fisk lamented in 1811. "The treasury cannot inspect their books, nor ascertain their funds." State-chartered banks came into existence as extensions of sovereign state authority. Monitoring and oversight—for banks and other corporations—were the prerogative of the sovereign, exercised through the common law "visitorial power." Rooted in English ecclesiastical and charity law, visitorial authority enabled founders—and in later civil corporations, the sovereign—to ensure that charter provisions were being followed and to take corrective action if they were not.[16]

The federal government had no such power over state corporations, but under the same logic, it exercised monitoring and visitation over the Banks of the United States. For the First Bank, Congress only required that it furnish balance sheet information to the Treasury, which the institution appears to have done. The bank's stockholders asserted that such information ensured "the confidence of the Government," based on "a constant knowledge of the interior management and condition of the bank."[17]

A "constant" knowledge likely overstates the nature of federal supervisory authority, and in practice the limited scope of public oversight reflected Hamilton's vision of a predominantly private federal bank. When Congress chartered the Second Bank in 1816, however, it granted itself more affirmative investigatory powers. In November 1818, the House used this authority, sending five Representatives to inspect the main bank in Philadelphia, along with

branches in Baltimore, Richmond, and Washington, DC. They made good use
of their visitorial powers, going behind the counter and determining whether
the corporation was abiding by the terms set by the sovereign chartering authority. The investigators found four significant violations of the Bank's charter
and called for them to be corrected. Resolutions to remove federal funds from
the Bank and to revoke its charter were also advanced but rejected. Discretion
carried the day: better to call for correction than destroy the institution so
recently won.[18]

Although the Second Bank of the United States competently managed the
nation's highly decentralized financial system in the 1820s and early 1830s, the
power it wielded won it abundant enemies. Many Americans distrusted banks
in general, and they elected politicians who promised to abolish them. Banks,
by issuing credit that circulated as currency, increased economic activity and
economic instability. For agrarians, from Jefferson forward, instability—
economic and social—was the thing to be avoided. As financial writer and
Andrew Jackson confidant William Gouge wrote in 1833, banks were the
"*principal* cause of social evil in the United States." Others saw the problem
differently, resenting at once the "restraint upon individual cupidity, and the
exercise of state power." The nation did not have too many banks but too few.
They wanted to lift the monetary barriers that checked entrepreneurial and
speculative energy.[19]

These opposing movements, anti-bank and laissez-faire, united behind
Democrat Andrew Jackson. Marching under a Jeffersonian banner, Jackson's
Democracy decried the influence of centralized financial power in the hands of
the Second Bank and its president, Nicholas Biddle. Biddle did little to help his
cause. He recognized that the Bank commanded a popular majority among the
people and the Congress. He tried his luck, making the Bank's charter renewal
a political cause. So provoked, and despite the majority support for the Bank's
renewal in both houses of Congress, Andrew Jackson vetoed its recharter in
1832; the Bank's advocates could not summon the votes to override it.[20]

The demise of the Second Bank, true to the hopes of the nation's expansionists and enterprisers, unleashed a wave of speculative energy, especially along
the cotton frontier of the new Southwest. The chaotic spread of banking without effective supervision, in turn, fueled the panics of 1837 and 1839, which
decimated the banking industry and delegitimized finance even further. The
federal bank still remained popular with the developmentalist and rival Whig
Party. Yet their accidental president, John Tyler, a strict constitutionalist who
assumed office following the death of William Henry Harrison, vetoed an

attempt at a Third Bank of the United States in 1841. Almost his entire cabinet resigned in protest. Despite the common view that there should be public participation in banking, this series of contingent events meant that the first American experiment with central banking was over once and for all.[21]

The Jacksonian attack on concentrated financial power and its catastrophic financial consequences empowered anti-bank forces and convinced many state governments to prohibit banking altogether. None of these bans proved permanent, and in the long run, the 1830s panics encouraged states to shift financial risk more fully onto private stakeholders. State governments got out of the business of running their own banks. "The role of governments," in the words of banking historian Bray Hammond, became "supervisory rather than proprietary."[22]

Hammond was right. What was less clear was what the "supervisory" role would mean in practice.

Antebellum State Supervision: The Currency Model and Its Tenuous Alternatives

The state banking explosion following the demise of the Second Bank of the United States did not extend the British model of central banking and currency supervision. An alternative, fluid system of legislative, administrative, and judicial oversight arose instead. Consistent in these supervisory efforts was the often-unstated assumption that the government would play an important oversight role to ensure simultaneously that economic and developmental energies would flow forcefully, while also maintaining system liquidity, noteholder protection, and bank soundness. In the process, states began to experiment with practices that became enduring parts of a supervisory toolkit, including a searching process for bank chartering, onsite visitorial powers, and the active government management of bank failure. The evolution of this toolkit did not mean that the government would fully displace private parties in risk management. With limited state capacity, public officials sought to harness private self-interest to promote financial risk management.

Chartering as Supervision

The antebellum period is defined by two distinct forms of state-controlled bank chartering that tracked corporate chartering more generally. The first model, which had existed since the beginning of the Republic and lasted in many states until the eve of the Civil War, required a special legislative charter to operate a bank. State lawmakers voted on specific bills to charter each new bank, and in doing so, they implicitly guaranteed that bank organizers would serve the public interest. As one legislator observed in 1831, "it is the duty of the Legislature to ascertain by competent testimony, whether the amount of business and capital in the place where the bank is to be established, are such, as to require the accommodation; and above all, whether those who ask the privilege, are men of unsuspected character."[23]

The second model, "free banking," included Michigan's attempt described in the chapter's introduction. Free banking referred to the mechanism by which banks obtained a charter and on what terms. Under a free banking system, entrepreneurs could secure a charter on the basis of clear (and easy-to-satisfy) rules, most often linked to minimum capital standards and requirements to back note issues with bonds deposited with the state.[24]

Agitation for free banking began in New York in the 1820s, a state where special chartering was criticized as a vehicle for political favoritism and factional control of vital financial infrastructure. Though the established system of legislative chartering did entail a form of public supervision—in large measure because risk-averse politicians did not want to be held responsible when specially-chartered banks failed—the state also suffered from endemic chartering corruption. Well-connected capitalists could grease the palms of their legislative sponsors, while those without such connections could not.[25]

From New York, free banking gradually spread to other states, opening banking privileges to entrepreneurs with the desire and necessary capital to operate a bank, without the need of special political connections. The expansion of free banking was part of a larger Jacksonian project to replace political discretion over finance and commerce with a more democratic—and perhaps ironically, more administrative—system. In the 1840s and 1850s, just as free banking began to spread, legislatures also began to permit corporations to arise generally, without specific legislative authorization. At the onset of the Civil War, more than half of the thirty-three states had free banking statutes.[26]

Free banking did not mean banking free from government oversight. Instead, state free banking laws made chartering regulatory rather than supervisory; that is, states issued bank charters if organizers met fixed standards rather than satisfying the discretionary evaluations of legislators. In most cases, legislatures vested this chartering authority in new administrative agencies—state banking commissioners—who verified that bank organizers had satisfied chartering requirements. Further, the same free banking statutes that threw the door open to bank ownership generally either created or expanded the purview of administrative agencies once banks were open for business. Bank commissioners often collected and published periodic bank balance sheet information, facilitating continuous public and private monitoring, and undertook visitorial examinations, ensuring charter compliance. The era of the delegation of bank oversight from the legislature to the administrative state began in the free banking era.[27]

This delegation of authority meant that the legislature did not engage in a supervisory assessment at the moment of chartering. Anyone who met the clear (and simple) standards could start a bank, whether or not they met the administrative standards to continue one. Some contemporaries criticized this free chartering process, removed as it was from evaluating the quality of the bankers under consideration. In 1888, Hugh McCulloch, formerly an Indiana banker during the free banking era and the first Comptroller of the Currency, recalled: "Anybody who could command two or three thousand dollars of money could buy on a margin the bonds necessary to establish a bank, to be paid for in its notes after its organization." Without initial oversight, these banks did not fare well. "Their life was pleasant, but short; their demise ruinous and shameful." McCulloch was likely overstating his case, in part to justify the supervisory discretion he imposed as Comptroller on the national banking system, itself modeled on the free banking regime. Experiments like Michigan's, moreover, did not heap glory on free banking. Yet states also learned from their peers' mistakes and sought to improve free banking regulation and supervision over time.[28]

Note Redemption

As chartering evolved into a regulatory process rather than a discretionary supervisory one, states adopted other forms of supervisory oversight that they could exercise once the banks were in business. The currency model of supervision thrived in this era of market-based note redemption. Without a central bank to manage the process, however, the logistics of currency supervision became more complex and its effects more difficult to coordinate and manage. Many states ceded note redemption to market participants, relying on private means for these public ends. The federal version of note redemption under the Banks of the United States worked well because the Banks were themselves counterparties to those state banks that issued notes. After their fall, the state chartering authorities lacked the same mechanisms.

The private efforts flowed from a profit motive rather than a public franchise. In financial hubs, such as New York and Philadelphia, private note brokers made a business of buying, selling, and occasionally redeeming the notes of far-off banks. Because they took the risk that banknotes might change in value, note brokers had a keen interest in monitoring banks and publicizing information about their condition. Brokers like Robert T. Bicknell (Boston) and T. B. Peterson & Bros (Philadelphia) published price lists that often doubled as guides for detecting counterfeits. In this sense, note brokers created a market for competing forms of money, substituting decentralized discipline for the concentrated force of the Banks of the United States.[29]

Motivated bankers also organized their own note redemption institutions. In New England, Boston's Suffolk Bank fashioned itself, without official sanction, into a quasi-central bank. To create currency uniformity in New England, the Suffolk Bank consolidated the notes of country banks received by Boston bankers and sent them out for redemption in specie. The so-called Suffolk System required rural banks to back their notes with adequate coin or restrain their currency emissions, which ultimately allowed the limited stock of New England banknotes to circulate at par, or face value. Coordinated redemption also encouraged country banks to develop correspondent relationships with city banks, which enabled the streamlining of redemption through offsetting deposits. State officials did not manage this system, but many praised it. "This system of par redemption seems to be a most perfect regulator upon all the New England banks," Connecticut's bank commissioners wrote in 1848.[30]

Other state supervisors were less enthusiastic. When a group of Cincinnati banks undertook a plan similar to the Suffolk System in 1839, Ohio's bank commissioners condemned it. "Among the causes which have increased the drain of specie from the banks of the state, and driven them to a rapid curtailment of their circulation, is the hostile attitude they have assumed toward each other." Instead of stability, zealous redemption produced a continuous bank run, preserving the value of the currency by limiting the very banking activity—lending—that generated currency in the first place.[31]

Despite its promise in some corners, private supervision-as-redemption was ultimately not a good fit for the fragmented financial system of the antebellum United States. Lawsuits to force redemption—the ultimate recourse that gave currency supervision its bite—were difficult to win and, because of the costs involved, usually not worth the effort. State officials—legislators, executives, and judges—often undermined this process, relieving banks of the responsibility to redeem their notes in times of stress, believing it was better to have an uncertain currency than no currency at all. In effect, because state officials couldn't employ discretion to force redemption in the market, they managed redemption risk by employing discretion through legislative or judicial forbearance.[32]

Note redemption thus fell between two stools. The private system worked well in times when there was no reason to doubt it. The public efforts seemed most effective only in times of chaos, and even then through cumbersome legal processes. The system also faced geographic impediments and significant information asymmetries. Even as note brokers created an integrated national market in banknotes, the inefficiencies in the system continued to invite wild-catting entrepreneurs to make money by printing banknotes in one state and lending them in another.[33]

To overcome the shortcomings of note redemption, many states began requiring bankers to pledge bonds equal to their note issue with the supervisory authorities—provisions that also created a market for state bonds. By ensuring that notes could eventually be redeemed through the sale of the underlying assets if the issuing bank failed, bond-backing created trust in ultimate redemption and tempered pressure to check solvency by redeeming notes over the counter in specie. Notes stayed in the market; specie stayed in the vault.[34]

The Examiner

Ultimately, note redemption as a mechanism of supervision forced bankers to make fewer loans, issue fewer notes, and hold more specie reserves than they otherwise would in the absence of the redemption threat. Those who craved stability in the system defended this model; those who wanted growth condemned it. Increasingly, toward the end of the antebellum period, states were searching for something that permitted growth while managing stability, something less rigidly wedded to fixed rules and more permissive of a balanced approach.

Enter the bank examiner, the first public instance of the institutionalized discretionary approach to bank supervision, and with it regular public inspection within banks as an alternative to private note redemption in the market. How and when examination attained prominence vis-à-vis note redemption as the supervisory preference is difficult to pinpoint with precision. Before the 1820s, bank examinations sometimes occurred but were ad hoc affairs, usually taking place when chartering officials, believing a bank to be insolvent, used their common-law visitorial authority to investigate the bank. As noted above,

Congress had attached similar authority to the Second Bank of the United States, which it had likewise used in extraordinary circumstances (and in the later days of the Bank, for partisan dirt-digging).[35]

A critical juncture occurred in 1829, when Martin Van Buren, days away from becoming vice president of the United States, took the only notable act of his three-month governorship of New York by instituting what the legislature called the Safety Fund, a rudimentary liability insurance scheme designed to protect the state's banking system by insuring individual bank liabilities in the case of bank failure. The safety fund guaranteed both banknotes, which circulated among the public as money, and bank deposits, which performed a similar function through bank drafts and the emerging techniques of check clearing.[36]

The Safety Fund Act also expanded bank supervision into a more discretionary, responsive, and government-oriented risk management system. The Act created a novel class of examiner, three state commissioners with the duty and power to inspect each participating bank once every four months—a process of regular, proactive examination designed to actively monitor and influence bank behavior. The Safety Fund created three levels of risk management. First, private note redemption continued to operate as a check on banknote issuance, backed by stricter rules about the ratio of notes to bank capital. Second, liability insurance protected noteholders and depositors by creating indirect claims on all participating banks. Third, bank examination protected bankers and bank liability holders by ensuring state regulations were followed. Bank examination meant that bank commissioners and, through commissioners' reports, state lawmakers received not only information available in the market but more intimate details of an insured bank's business.[37]

Several states followed New York's effort to insure bank liabilities, and with it to institute regular bank examination. These states pursued two different models. Michigan and Vermont followed New York in creating liability insurance funds. Participant banks paid into a central pool that would repay creditors of failed banks (mostly depositors and noteholders), indirectly binding insured banks, through the state fund, to the health of their peers. In these states, politically appointed bank commissioners exercised limited supervisory authority. They could close insolvent banks, but they could not force banks to improve management or curb excessive risk-taking. Indiana, Ohio, and Iowa, by contrast, created mutual insurance systems. Participating banks were collectively responsible for their colleagues' liabilities, and thus had a more direct interest in the solvency of their counterparties. In these systems, the bankers themselves appointed supervisory officials who could and did address risk-taking and mismanagement by using their authority to change banking practices.[38]

By the end of the antebellum era, bank examination had emerged in tandem with liability insurance but was soon taken up as a standalone risk management strategy. In the 1850s, Massachusetts commissioners visited the state's banks annually to evaluate their "condition and conduct." This power often carried with it the authority to sanction conduct the examiners deemed imprudent. The same year that Connecticut's bank commissioners declared the Suffolk system a "most perfect regulator" of New England's banks, they forbade the Quinebaug Bank from paying dividends "until they could furnish undoubted evidence of their ability to do so." Through direct, preemptive oversight, state officials worked to improve individual bank performance in the present and inform policymakers on how to improve system performance in the future.[39]

Bank examination was not universally regarded as a successful risk management strategy. In New York, the early innovator in examination, the experiment lasted only fourteen years. Following a crisis that led to the failure of the Safety Fund, the New York legislature, "despairing that [bank examiners] could curb improper banking practices, but without effort to improve their capacity to do so," abolished the Board of Bank Commissioners in 1843 (see the interlude following this chapter for an account of the long running official dissatisfaction with this weakened authority). The state returned to a system of examination only on suspicion of insolvency. In this sense, the rise of state bank examination did not guarantee its continuation. Public management of private financial risk was a process of experimentation, one that could retreat as well as advance.[40]

Managing Failure

As would be the case throughout the nineteenth century and beyond, bank failure loomed over nearly every aspect of banking practice and policy in the antebellum era. Bank failure was ever present and politically ominous, not merely because a failed bank wreaked havoc on bank stakeholders and the economies they supported but because privately owned banks supplied the nation with the media of exchange. Bank failure meant monetary failure. And bank and monetary failure was widespread and frequent: More than 15 percent of antebellum banks closed without redeeming their notes at full value.[41]

The frequency and familiarity of a failed bank did not make bank failure easier for state policymakers to manage. Before the Civil War, chartered banks wound down their operations largely through judicial receivership, a process structured by state law and managed by local courts and judges. The legal death of a bank could begin in many ways—a contemporary treatise listed eleven—but generally fell into three categories: Bank stockholders could voluntarily close their bank; bank creditors could sue to close a bank that did not meet its obligations; or public officials could sue to close a bank found violating its charter. In all these cases, the party initiating the closure tended to have the first opportunity to nominate a receiver, which, if not objected to, the court would appoint as its officer to represent all stakeholders in the liquidation and distribution of the bank's assets. Receivers were meant to be disinterested, "a man of business and integrity," but contemporaries saw the benefits of nominating a friend rather than being subject to an opponent's nominee.[42]

As contemporaries recognized, court-appointed bank receivers faced an enduring tradeoff between speed and recovery. If the receiver liquidated a failed bank's assets quickly, likely at a significant discount to their par value, it would get some cash into the hands of creditors but not make them whole. On the other hand, a receiver that patiently managed the wind-down, while returning more to the bank's claimants, would tie up those claimants for a much longer period of time. Courts were meant to handle the discretionary elements on these questions, but that mostly meant resolution in favor of the latter equilibrium. Bank supervision by judicial oversight was present in the antebellum period as an alternative to administrative processes but carried with it significant costs.[43]

In some cases, states decided, after hard experience, that these thorny questions were better answered by expanding the discretionary authority of banking officials. New York's 1829 Safety Fund law, for example, originally required a failed bank's assets be liquidated before the Fund could be tapped. When three Buffalo banks failed in the Panic of 1837, legislators realized the delay required by law would negatively impact noteholders, who would see the value of their notes fall as the liquidation process dragged on. The legislature amended the law, expanding the role of the State Comptroller to "take any such measures as he may deem necessary . . . to prevent any loss to the holders" from "depreciation." This provision and others like it demonstrated lawmakers' recognition that the judicial process of bank supervision traded accuracy for delay; delegating through administrative processes and administrative officials the discretion to move quickly would, they hoped, remove the dilemma by promoting both accuracy and timeliness.[44]

In this period of expansive experimentation, states pursued financial risk management beyond the insurance funds, bond-backed note redemption, and bank examination already discussed. States also looked to the banks' capital structures and experimented with different shareholder liability regimes in an early version of capital regulation. When an incorporated bank failed (as opposed to those organized by partnership), generally only corporate assets, held by the corporation or by state officials on its behalf, were accessible to meet creditor claims. Such is the nature of the limited liability corporation that dominated early American banking (differently, it should be noted, from the banking industry in the United Kingdom). In this model, if bank managers ran their bank into the ground while increasing their private fortunes, there was little forlorn creditors could do. The financial turmoil that was commonplace for much of the nineteenth century convinced some state officials that limited liability shifted too much risk from bank shareholders to the public. As Ohio's banking commissioners wrote in 1842: "The great and fundamental error in the banking system, may be traced to the want of individual liability of the directors and stockholders, to pay the debts they contract, and redeem the paper they put into circulation." What would later be called "skin in the game" was a focus for some state banking officials who sought to force the question of risk management more squarely into the hands of bank shareholders by assigning them liability above and beyond the value of their investments.[45]

Increased shareholder liability offered an alternative model for protecting bank creditors from the possibility of failures: private risk management by bank owners. By putting the fortunes of bank shareholders at stake, increasing shareholder liability was designed to encourage more concentrated bank shareholding and more attentive oversight by those shareholders. Enhanced liability rules worked best when bank shareholders had adequate personal resources to meet creditor claims. When this fact was known to bank creditors who might depend on these resources in the case of bank failure, it was thought, their incentive to put liquidity pressure on the banks went down. Still, in cases of bank failure, recovery worked through slow, uncertain judicial processes. "Individual liability affords no certain security to the holders of bank notes," Michigan's governor argued in 1849, "it at best but enables them to recover and collect their amount, by the tardy process of law."[46]

The "tardy process of law" is a good label for the alternative to discretionary, administrative bank supervision. Initially, policymakers conceptualized these different approaches to managing bank risk as distinct. Michigan's governor decried enhanced liability in favor of asset-backed note issuance, coupled with state supervision. When adopting the Safety Fund, New York moved from enhanced to limited liability but expanded examination and liability insurance.[47]

In the 1850s, though, states began bundling these mechanisms, combining asset-backed note issuance and enhanced shareholder liability within free banking statutes, with the former securing noteholders and the latter securing bank depositors, often overseen by bank examiners. The problem of financial crisis, whether in an individual case or more systemically, was a problem that any single risk management approach did not seem to solve. In the variety of antebellum systems that the states created, they recognized this need to layer risk management systems. So it was that, in fits and starts, the state-dominated systems were taking shape.[48]

Then, the Civil War changed everything.

The Civil War and the New National Banking System

On the eve of the Civil War, federal participation in bank supervision existed as historical memory. Despite state efforts to build more robust banking structures, by 1860, the archipelago of state-chartered banks and the dizzying variety of state-sponsored systems meant to manage the risks that these banks generated was not equipped to endure four years of sustained armed conflict. Indeed, the banking system barely survived six months.

When Abraham Lincoln assumed the presidency in March 1861, South Carolina troops were already laying siege to Fort Sumter, while the federal Treasury lay virtually empty. Meanwhile, the federal government, still cowering under Andrew Jackson's long shadow, could only deal in hard currency, not bank credit. To finance the coming conflict, Treasury Secretary Salmon P. Chase developed a plan: The federal government would sell bonds for gold. The plan was simple and poorly conceived. The nation's bullion largely sat in vaults of its state-chartered banks, providing the solid foundation undergirding the national money supply that relied on specie redemption as its institutional anchor. Chase—who stubbornly demanded that the gold be transferred to the Treasury rather than held on deposit in the banks, as recent emergency legislation allowed—removed this foundation. In short order, New York's banks suspended specie payments and gold fled to private hordes and overseas. Chase also proposed significant tax increases to at least draw some gold back into federal coffers, but Congress ignored them. By December, the federal finances were in worse shape than when the war began.[49]

As Secretary Chase struggled to fund the war effort, he undertook an even more ambitious side-errand: reclaiming the federal government's constitutional power over the currency from the states and their banks. Chase, it should be said, was no financier. A lawyer and politician, he saw questions of banking and money through the lens of law and politics. Building on ideas submitted to him by others, Chase proposed a new national banknote currency, issued by private, federally-chartered banks and secured by federal bonds, essentially a federal version of common state approaches. Chase imagined this system would generate ready money for the government: Bankers would buy the government's bonds in specie, while bankers' own notes would be backed by government promises, not gold reserves.[50]

In the crisis of December 1861, with the nation floundering to pay its soldiers, sailors, and suppliers, Congress had as much interest in Chase's banking proposals as it had in his tax proposals. Instead, Congress authorized Chase to directly issue national legal tender notes, circumventing the banks entirely. This policy built on an earlier issuance of demand notes, which had been redeemable in gold at the Treasury until December 1861, when the Treasury likewise suspended gold payment. The new legal tender notes were *fiat* currency—the notorious greenback—the first experiment with federally issued currency since the Revolution. With specie scarce and private banknotes uncertain, the public took an initially favorable attitude to the new invention. Greenbacks offered a bold public challenge to private money creation; they demonstrated conclusively that the federal government could nationalize the money supply, and in doing so wrest power from private financiers.[51]

This experimentation at the federal level, prompted by military crisis and overseen by politicians and lawyers, soon revealed its flaws. Despite the initial enthusiasm from the public, the greenbacks suffered significant depreciation, and by 1863, with tax receipts and bond sales more buoyant, Chase decided to halt the purely public monetary experiment and instead more evenly balance public and private financial interests. The national banking system Chase envisioned, which Congress enacted in the National Bank Act of 1863, guaranteed private control of the financial system by adopting a decentralized system of private banks that enabled the federal leviathan to avoid the politically fraught concentrated power of a third Bank of the United States.[52]

The first National Banking Act was also shaped by decades of state experimentation. The Act was a free banking measure, providing a streamlined administrative process for chartering national banks. A new administrative official, the Comptroller of the Currency, would have additional discretion to investigate banks while leading the Currency Bureau, a new agency within the Treasury Department. The law also relied on bond-backing to secure the currency, where banks would receive circulating notes equal to 90 percent of the market value of U.S. bonds deposited with the Treasury. Fractional reserves likewise safeguarded bank deposits.[53]

Chase did not grasp, however, that with the rise of deposits as an alternative form of money—held on the books of a bank rather than in the hands of the public—banks with existing state or new federal charters could profitably perform banking functions without issuing notes at all. Many of the system's subsequent flaws were tied to Chase and Congress's relentless focus on creating national banknotes that would act as currency and ignoring deposits which served as money.[54]

In legislative design, Congress was not especially creative: The nation's new bank supervisory regime borrowed extensively from state experience in its reliance on chartering and note redemption to manage market entry and its use of enhanced liability and market surveillance to ensure compliance. However, Congress also wrote the statute with sufficient ambiguity such that its administrative implementers could define their own role as they understood it.

Hugh McCulloch, the first Comptroller and later Secretary of the Treasury, found enough statutory authority to do something more than the "currency model" of supervision. McCulloch was the policy catalyst who took this skeletal structure and gave it form. From the uncertain legislative foundations anchored primarily on the antebellum model of note issuance, McCulloch would decisively shape the early practices of federal bank supervision by making the Currency Bureau an effective, autonomous institution and by essentially creating the system of regular federal bank examination. If the failure of the rechartering of the Second Bank of the United States and the subsequent state experimentation in supervision constituted the first major rupture in designing the supervisory system, McCulloch's leadership—more even than the passage of the National Banking Acts themselves—constituted the second.[55]

———

By the time Ulysses S. Grant accepted Robert E. Lee's surrender at Appomattox on April 9, 1865, a new dawn had come not only for a nation scarred by war but for a national banking system that was forged in those same fires. But the national banking system that arose from the state model would not replace what had come before. The new institutions of the national banks and the national bank supervisors would be layered on top of the state banking apparatus that had preceded it. The national banking experiments would not end those of the states. Some of the most important innovations—deposit insurance, for example—would come from state banking authorities and their legislative sponsors.

What arises from this critical antebellum era is the recognition that banks pursuing profits create costs and benefits that the bankers, their shareholders, and even their customers do not enjoy exclusively. Economists call these externalities. Banks illustrate both the positive and negative sides of the externalities that they impose on the economy and society. On the plus side, a well-managed antebellum bank provided more than just financial services for its clients and customers. It contributed to the economic well-being of the entire community. On the negative side, a single poorly managed bank could throw that same community—and, through the contagion that spread quickly, many other neighboring communities—into depression and despair.

The national banking system, created during the Civil War, institutionalized and nationalized key parts of that evolutionary process of residual risk management. The war's aftermath would be its testing ground.

Interlude: Supervision
on Suspicion

TO THE extent that Millard Fillmore, the thirteenth president of the United States, is remembered, it is not as a banking reformer. He's hardly remembered at all, one of a string of nineteenth-century presidents unable to halt the nation's march toward civil war. In his brief stint as New York's chief bank supervisor in 1848, however, Fillmore discerned the key failings of the state's free-banking era oversight regime. Being Fillmore, he did little about it.

Born in a log cabin in upstate New York, Fillmore made his name as a Buffalo attorney and politician, first as an anti-Mason opposed to the candidacy of Andrew Jackson, and later as a Whig. He was a prominent member of the House of Representatives in the late 1830s, briefly retired to private life in the early 1840s, before being elected New York State Comptroller in 1847 on the way to the Vice Presidency in the election of 1848.[1]

As Comptroller—the state's chief fiscal officer—Fillmore inherited a vestigial bank supervisory authority, one which he deemed wholly insufficient. In 1843, the New York legislature abolished the state's Board of Bank Commissioners, the office which had undertaken quarterly examinations of the state's Safety Fund banks. In doing so, the legislature did not abolish bank examination as an administrative function, or at least not entirely. Instead, it granted the Comptroller authority to examine banks when credible information suggested that they had made false reports or were in unsound condition. How the Comptroller would acquire such information, without regular examination authority, was left unstated.[2]

New York lawmakers added one further feature: Whenever the Comptroller used this exceptional examination authority, the law required that he publish the results in the newspapers for the benefit of the public. Examination would thus be an adjunct to the reporting and market surveillance regime, providing information to private bank counterparties, without any scope for negotiation with bankers or discretion by state officials (this was a century-plus before Congress would begin the process of rendering any such disclosure completely illegal).

Writing in January 1849, on the eve of assuming the Vice Presidency, Fillmore castigated the state's system of examination on suspicion of wrongdoing or insolvency as a wholly inadequate compromise between public and private risk management. "Whatever might have been the object, there can be no doubt that the effect of this law is to prevent examinations that might be useful," Fillmore complained.[3]

Fillmore's ire had been raised by the failure of the Canal Bank of Albany in 1848 and the near failure of other banks connected with it. There was a political element to this dispute. Democrat Edwin Croswell, newspaper editor and Fillmore's political rival, controlled the Albany bank. Early in July, Fillmore had "heard some intimations unfavorable to the [bank's] solvency," and under the provisions of the law, he dispatched two examiners. Upon arrival, they immediately took possession of and closed the bank. The partisan press leapt on the story, gleefully skewering Croswell and his partners. "Among the many disgraceful bankruptcies in this State, there has probably never occurred one worse than this," the *Albany Atlas*, a rival paper, chortled.[4]

The media reaction may not have been hyperbole. Fillmore's examiners found utter chaos inside the bank. The bookkeeper had "grossly neglected his business" leaving the books of the bank in "mystified and confused condition." After five days of work, state officials could only offer a partial report. They identified more than $300,000 in liabilities, including $189,000 in circulating notes and $63,000 in state deposits, against $1,102 in coin and "good current bank bills not exceeding *ten or fifteen dollars.*" When they presented their full findings a month later, the examiners reported a nearly $200,000 hole in the bank, caused by the officers' habit of lending freely to "particular favorites" and to themselves.[5]

Examination on suspicion of insolvency, the model under which Fillmore operated, had replaced regular examinations by public officials under the Safety Fund legislation. It was a method that provided no check on the "illegal and improper practices" that had "for some years been perpetrated by bank officers."[6]

That is not to say that examination on suspicion was useless: It could quell unfounded rumors against sound banks. Immediately after the Canal Bank's failure, *Thomson's Bank Note Reporter* listed the Pratt Bank of Buffalo as holding a large redemption account with the Albany bank. This was an error Pratt's officers sought to correct, yet the Canal Bank's examiners initially found supporting evidence in a $91,000 debt owed by the Pratt Bank on the Albany bank's books. In light of this apparent debt, "calculated to arouse at once . . . a strong suspicion of your stability," Fillmore ordered an examination of the Pratt Bank. Soon after, Fillmore published a brief report, which found the bank "in sound condition and prudently managed." With this supervisory reassurance, pressure on the Pratt Bank subsided. Indeed, the Canal Bank's examiners later discovered that the Pratt loans were dummy entries that allowed the Albany bank's officers to lend still more money to themselves.[7]

The public exoneration of the Pratt Bank suggests the one benefit of New York's examination system: The state could vouch for the soundness of suspect banks. Given the state's deep partisanship and the earlier failures of the Safety Fund's examination regime, it is not obvious that market participants would always credit such state pronouncements. The real weakness of supervision on suspicion, as Fillmore understood, was that undertaking public oversight in any but the direst circumstances posed an extreme danger. "Because it is known that an examination can only be made where there is ground of suspicion, the very fact of making it brings discredit upon the bank," Fillmore observed.[8]

Fillmore had a solution: He called for annual examinations, undertaken by surprise, and "left to [the Comptroller's] discretion whether the report of such examination should be published." Such a system "would tend greatly to restrain any abuse and to prevent fraudulent practices," an observation keenly informed by the Canal Bank's years of illegality and mismanagement. Surprise examinations, undertaken by public officials and published at the supervisor's discretion was a risk management system that had not been tried before. It was also one with an obvious conceptual flaw: Would the Comptroller publish only the bad reports or only the good reports?[9]

Fillmore, though, was on his way up and out; the legislature declined to adopt his proposals. In 1854, lawmakers transferred the latent examination authority to the State Banking Superintendent, the official charged with overseeing New York's free banking system. Throughout the 1850s, state banking officials remained dissatisfied with the scope of their authority, while bankers found new ways to avoid the limited powers officials did have.

By December 1858, Superintendent James M. Cook had had enough. Cook, a Whig turned Republican, served as a state senator, Comptroller, and nearly secured the Republican nomination for governor. He picked up Fillmore's critiques and carried them forward. The power to examine on suspicion of wrongdoing or insolvency, he argued, created the false impression that the Superintendent had the capacity to determine when reports were fraudulent, or to somehow detect bank insolvency through the reports bankers filed themselves. "Figures and affidavits are never made by bank officers to expose insolvency or defalcations. They, the figures, are most useful adjuncts to conceal the real condition of affairs."[10]

Worse, Cook found that bankers, subject to the damning scrutiny of examination, further avoided even weak public oversight by throwing themselves upon the mercy of friendly courts. In his one attempt to exercise his examination authority, Cook complained, "by the time his agent had obtained a slight insight into the real condition of the affairs of the bank, he was politely met by its receiver, appointed by the court at the solicitation of the officers themselves, and told that his duties were ended, and that the property and effects of the bank were beyond his control and power, even for examination." Once in the hands of a court-appointed receiver, the bank was no longer subject to administrative oversight.[11]

The law, Cook complained, gave a public imprimatur to private lies that the superintendent was powerless to root out, so that the implicit promise that the Superintendent could investigate created "an ostensible responsibility" for verifying the truth of bankers' statements "which it is utterly impossible . . . to fulfil." Instead of following Fillmore's call for permanent public examination authority, Cook pursued what he called a "radical" path, seeking to push oversight fully onto the private sector. Examination on suspicion, Cook argued, was "a delusion and . . . purely a cheat of the people." Better to strip away the fantasy that public power could protect private interests, and let the people look after themselves.[12]

"When banking capital in this State . . . finds itself in danger of loss, (and the loss under the law falling alone upon depositors and stockholders,) it, through its managers, entrenches itself in a position . . . which looks to ultimate solvency instead of large profits," Cook opined. "The great and controlling law of self-interest, once learned through the rough road of experience, is a far more effectual rule of human action than any statutory provision, however strictly enforced." The private interest would always trump the public power.[13]

Cook's program, like Fillmore's, went nowhere. Both men imagined supervision could be something much different and much better. The debate about whether that something should be public or private would rage for another seventy-five years.

2

The Rise and Retreat
of Supervisory Discretion

IMPLEMENTING THE NATIONAL
BANKING ACTS IN THE 1860S

THE LINCOLN administration chose Hugh McCulloch (1863–1865), an Indiana banker, as the inaugural Comptroller of the Currency. It was a surprise pick. McCulloch came to Washington, DC, in 1862 to lobby against Treasury Secretary Salmon P. Chase's proposed national banking system. He feared that Chase intended a new Bank of the United States, "a mammoth corporation with power . . . to control the business and politics of the country." Chase converted him to the view that the new national banking plan would be no such centralized, financial mammoth but would instead balance public needs for a reliable currency against the private interests of local unit bankers. Convinced, McCulloch agreed to lend his support, support Chase ultimately asked for in the form of helming the new office.[1]

As the first Comptroller of the Currency, McCulloch would define much of what that office would be. He asserted his greatest influence by giving content to bank examination, a task Congress identified but on which it provided very little guidance. Congress had provided for examination regimes before. In 1838, it created a system for inspecting steamboats—which, like banks, could sometimes explode. Initially, local courts managed steamboat inspection, but in 1852, Congress revised the legislation to create a permanent Board of Supervising Inspectors within the Treasury Department. This experience likely influenced the design of federal banking examination (since much of the National Banking Acts were written by the Treasury), though Congress took a step backward, returning to the more ad hoc system prevalent under the

original 1838 Steam Act. Under the National Banking Act of 1863, the Comptroller could appoint bank examiners on a temporary basis, "as often as necessary and proper." Federal bank examiners received identical compensation as
the original steamboat inspectors—$5 for each workday, plus $2 per twenty-
five miles traveled—charged to the bank being examined. In the same way that
steamboat captains paid the government to certify their seaworthiness, bankers would pay the government to certify their creditworthiness.[2]

Despite identifying bank examination as a supervisory authority in the 1863
Act and its 1864 revision, the structure of these laws does not suggest that
Congress intended bank examiners to be a vital administrative force. Rather,
Congress emphasized a system of publicity and market surveillance, through
which bankers would publish their balance sheets at set intervals and bank
counterparties would continue to verify bank promises through activities like
note redemption. Private oversight also operated through bank shareholders,
who faced double liability in the case of bank failure. The public role appeared
small by comparison. The section authorizing the Comptroller to appoint
examiners sat between provisions holding directors liable for violations of
the law and provisions describing penalties for embezzlement. Federal examiners would act as visitors, in the sense of common law, serving as deputized
charter enforcers and fraud detectors; they would seek out and punish illegal
behavior that market participants and bank shareholders could not see. In
the 1860s, the modality of risk management for private finance remained
largely in private hands.[3]

From these meager legislative beginnings and with a broad grant of statutory discretion given to him, McCulloch (and his successors) built something
bigger than private power in financial risk management. Beginning as Union
armies slowly ground down the Confederate war machine and continuing
during the forestalled political and social transformation of the postbellum
South, the role of the bank examiner became central to the exercise of federal
power over private local action. For a time, it appeared that bank examiners
would become increasingly powerful representatives of a newly powerful federal government.

What they would actually do with that power remained an open question.
McCulloch knew they were trying something new. A banker in the national
system, McCulloch wrote, "is engaged in an experiment, which, if successful,
will reflect the highest honor upon all who are connected with it." McCulloch
also promised bankers they would not be alone in this endeavor: "The sincere
efforts of the Comptroller will not be wanting to make the system a benefit to

the country." Neither McCulloch nor anyone else knew how effective—or even what exactly—those sincere efforts would be. In this context, Mc-Cullough and his successors grasped a set of discretionary governance tools—the chartering, examination, receivership, and forbearance initially developed at the state level—and turned them to federal use. Federal supervisors interpreted their congressional mandate broadly, developing practices to match what McCulloch called "the spirit and intention of the law," and not the hard text of the law itself. In part, these innovations were borne by necessity: Congress hadn't provided much hard text to work from. But in part, this was borne by institutional experimentation. The risks that McCulloch sought to manage were not so easy to categorize. To meet them, McCulloch and his successors placed official discretion in interpreting and managing those risks at the heart of the way he would supervise banks, individually and as a system.[4]

Despite McCulloch's ambitious goals, federal officials and bankers quickly learned that supervision faced important limits. Examiners' poor compensation and long travel times between banks restricted the attention they could give each institution. Political, financial, and practical impediments meant that bank supervisors could not reliably prevent all bank fraud or bank failure. More fundamentally, this first institutionalized foray into bank supervision did not yet answer the most basic of questions that supervisors must answer: What, exactly, were these new officials supposed to do in their examinations? Perform an audit? Look for fraud? Tell bankers how their competitors did it better? As Comptrollers sought to resolve these ambiguities, a series of crises and scandals in the 1870s undermined any reputation the office had for procedural and performative competence, leading to a retreat and reframing of what public supervision could and would accomplish.[5]

Supervision Through Chartering, 1863–1866

Under the National Banking Acts, Congress sought to create a national currency system through the instrumentality of federally chartered banks. Mc-Culloch, in turn, needed to quickly charter the national banks, which would circulate the new national currency. Congress provided clear criteria for financial entrepreneurs "to commence the business of banking," including requirements governing paid-in capital, corporate bylaws, and directors' oaths. Consistent with the National Banking Acts' status as essentially free-banking statutes modeled on state law antecedents, Congress identified the Comptroller's chartering duty as straightforward and limited: to "examine into the condition of such association" and, if the Comptroller was satisfied that the organizers had complied with the law, then "the comptroller shall give to such association a certificate" authorizing them to commence business. In other words, Congress provided rules for securing national bank charters, with little room for supervisory judgment about risk management. The chartering examination was pure compliance, the verification of facts as opposed to a searching supervisory risk assessment.[6]

McCulloch saw this statutory role as insufficient for the job at hand. He understood that the new laws created a national *banking system*, and with it significant new financial risks for the federal government. With that in mind, McCulloch had no intention of handing out charters as indiscriminately as the Acts described. So it was that McCulloch rendered chartering as equal parts regulatory (enforcing widely applicable chartering rules) and supervisory (evaluating the necessity for and viability of prospective national banks). In so doing, McCulloch infused significant discretion into chartering where Congress had all but instructed his office to be mechanical in its approach.

McCulloch used this discretion with two primary objectives in mind. First, McCulloch sought to strengthen the infant national system by incorporating existing state banking capital and managerial talent. The transfer from state to federal authority was core to what federal policymakers hoped to accomplish through the National Banking Acts. As part of the 1863 law, Congress imposed a 2 percent tax on state chartered banks' notes, an explicit effort to draw such notes from circulation and pull state bankers into the national system. The tax proved too low to be effective. With conversions slow and state banks still abundant, Congress raised the tax to a more prohibitive 10 percent in 1865. "The national banks were intended to supersede the state banks," Senator John Sherman explained. "Both cannot exist together." Still, McCulloch recognized that not all state banks would bring credit to the new national system. He instructed bank organizers to submit references "from gentlemen of well-known character and reputation" and directed examiners to determine the "banking experience and business qualifications" of bank officers. In this way, McCulloch used chartering discretion to prevent "men without capital, and adventurous speculators" from operating under a national bank charter.[7]

McCulloch's second use of discretion was to accomplish almost the opposite goal of extending national bank charters. He recognized that each new bank would be a source of new, inflationary money, and he restrained charter extensions in service of monetary policy. His "duty" obliged him to "discourage, in many instances, the organization of new banks, and in more instances

to refuse my sanction to the increase of the capital of those already organized."
McCulloch acknowledged that employing chartering discretion was controversial. "I may seem to have exercised a power not warranted by the act," he
wrote, "but if not sustained by its letter, I have been by its spirit, and I am willing to let the future decide as to the correctness or incorrectness of my course."
In the first instance of supervision as the exercise of institutionalized discretion, it was the supervisors—not Congress—asserting the prerogative.[8]

Currency Bureau, Open for Business

Just as establishing a national banking system required experienced, reputable
bankers, chartering these banks required government officials with the right
combination of expertise, influence, and skill. Here again, Congress provided
little guidance. The National Banking Acts gave only a vague outline of how
the Currency Bureau should be organized and how many staff it could employ.
The law allowed the Comptroller to "employ, *from time to time*, the necessary
clerks to discharge such duties as he shall direct." It required him, "*as often as
deemed necessary and proper*," to "appoint a suitable person or persons to make
an examination of the affairs of every banking association." The rest was left to
the Comptroller to decide.[9]

Once again, McCulloch pushed the bounds of his authority to build a
new, functional administrative agency. He did so first by making his corps of
examiners permanent and concentrated rather than ad hoc and dispersed. By
1867, the Currency Bureau employed fifteen examiners, based primarily in the
commercial centers of New York, Pennsylvania, and Massachusetts, reaching
up into New England and out into the midwestern states. Two years later,
eighteen examiners spread further, and their territories changed shape. Two
focused on single cities—Boston and New York—a few others covered individual states, and several were responsible for multistate territories. Pliny T.
Sexton, an upstate New York attorney and bank cashier, ranged across the
"Southern States." None yet covered the West Coast.[10]

Given his ambitions for the national banking system, McCulloch recruited
examiners with significant political connections, meaningful banking experience, or, ideally, both. Andrew Mygatt, for example, apprenticed in his father's
bank in New Milford, Connecticut, while developing his political career, eventually serving as president pro tempore of the state senate in 1861. From 1862 to
1865, Mygatt was also one of Connecticut's three bank commissioners. Among
the first cohort of examiners, Elihu Baker (Iowa), Asa R. Camp (Vermont), and

E. C. Sherman (Massachusetts) had also served as state banking officials. Other examiners came from significant political and administrative careers, or, like R. W. Derrickson (Pennsylvania) and Butler Ward (New York), drew their experience from banking (though they likely had political connections as well). These men provided McCulloch with legitimacy, prestige, and specific knowledge of local banking markets that would enable him to exclude speculators and weak state banks.[11]

A staff of clerks in Washington provided the bureau with a swelling—and likewise permanent—reservoir of administrative capacity. The clerks, housed in the Treasury Building, managed the Comptroller's informational machinery, processing charter applications, receiving and reading examination reports, and instructing bankers on how to comply with the spirit and intention of the law. The files they compiled documented the life course of each national bank. Clerks also served as a pool of future examiners, while top staff provided leadership continuity. McCulloch's principal successors, Hiland R. Hulburd (1867–1872) and John Jay Knox Jr. (1872–1884) each served as Deputy Comptroller before ascending to the top job. After Knox, Comptrollers tended to be outsiders. By then, the Comptroller's bureaucracy had momentum. Although the Currency Bureau, like other agencies in wartime Washington, was a hotbed of ambition—some of it legitimate, some of it not—it fast became the central node in a sophisticated information and surveillance network, through which the Comptroller exercised authority "as often as deemed necessary and proper."

The Timing and Practice of Bank Examination, 1866– 1872

By 1866, just two years after the passage of the 1864 Act, the pace of chartering slowed and the Comptroller's emphasis shifted from certifying new banks to supervising existing ones. Here again, McCulloch and his successors reached further than Congress intended, touching the question of supervision's fundamental purpose: Was the Comptroller's office meant to guard the currency through enforcement of rules or to guide banker activity through exercise of judgment? From the Comptroller's perspective, it could only do both.[12]

As Comptroller Hulburd observed in 1869, "it is a common saying among bankers, when speaking of governmental supervision, 'Take care of the currency; make that as secure as possible, but do not interfere with the business of the banks.'" The bankers might have preferred that categorical separation, but the idea of noninterference was a canard, as Hulburd well knew. "The business of issuing circulating notes is so involved with the lending of money," Hulburd wrote, that "it is impossible to apply safeguards to the currency, without applying prudence and reasonable restrictions to the business of lending." Congress legislated a banknote currency; such money came into existence through bank lending, either as currency handed across the counter or as deposits that could be converted into cash at the depositor's convenience. The currency was only as secure, therefore, as the lending practices of banks. It was the Comptroller's duty to influence those practices.[13]

This dance—taking care of the currency, which bankers supported; interfering with the business of banking, which bankers hated—provided the mechanism for supervisory expansion far beyond monetary management. McCulloch and his successors transformed the visitorial authority provided by Congress in the National Banking Acts—meant in common law to be a power in reserve—into continuous oversight. By the late 1860s, national bank examiners had become permanent envoys of the spirit and intention of the law.

Having determined that bank examination would be continuous, early Comptrollers next had to answer the threshold questions of which banks should be examined, and when. Because Congress had not answered these questions, McCulloch claimed them for himself. "The theory," one examiner explained, "is that examinations are to be made once per year." In practice, McCulloch took the discretion afforded him and turned it over to the examiners themselves: He sent each examiner a list of banks and authorized them to "proceed to examine at your pleasure."[14]

With no other structure to their schedule, examiners also kept their ears to the ground, listening for sounds of trouble. "Sitting in the reading room of [his] hotel," one examiner was drawn to "some gentlemen [who] were conversing in so loud a voice that [he] could not avoid hearing them." The substance of their conversation was a "thoroughly rotten" Memphis bank. The examiner conveyed the conversation to the Comptroller and within a week was on his way to Tennessee.[15]

Such emergencies were unusual, though. In the ordinary course of their work, federal bank examiners developed supervisory routines aimed at verifying compliance with charter provisions (making the currency as secure as possible) and guiding bankers toward an idealized set of business practices (applying prudence and reasonable restrictions to the business of lending).

As with any bureaucracy, paperwork played a central role in this institutionalization. By the late 1860s, standardized examination forms encouraged a set routine, creating a thick surveillance infrastructure that reinforced publicly visible call reports—the periodic balance sheets that national banks were legally required to publish in their local newspapers. The examination form's first page mirrored call reports, foregrounding the examiner's auditing role. When an examiner arrived at a bank, he usually instructed the officers to inventory the bank's assets. "When such a statement is furnished," examiner John Bull explained, "I commence to examine the assets to verify the statement." First, Bull would check the bankers' math. "If the statement shows that the bank has $200,000 in greenbacks," Bull continued, "I go to work and count the greenbacks. . . . If it appears the bank has 7-30's"—30-year bonds paying 7-percent interest—"I count the 7-30's."[16]

Simple counting confirmed that bankers were honest and minimally competent, but examiners needed to look deeper, assessing the quality of the bank's internal operations rather than the mere quantity of assets on the balance sheet. "The bank might have a very large deficiency in reserve, and large amounts of over-drafts, or a great amount in suspended paper," a clerk at the Currency Bureau explained. "These things would not be shown by the report; they would appear only by an examination of the books of the bank." Examiners also inquired about the status and security of loans, a process that required knowledge of current market conditions, securities prices, and the reputations of local businessmen. Here, as in chartering, the Comptroller's decision to employ examiners with local knowledge and public reputation secured and— perhaps more importantly, projected—competence. Expert examiners not only enforced rules but also exercised judgment about sound bank lending. When examining the North National Bank of Boston in December 1868, examiner Chandler Ransom uncovered a large loan held collectively by the bank's president, cashier, and directors. Criticizing the loan, Ransom observed, "instead of its being considered as an element of strength, as would appear upon its face"—and to any external readers of the bank's call reports— "it is in fact the opposite . . . a drag on the interests of the Bank." After a stern chat with the directors, Ransom assured the Comptroller's office that the bank would collect and close out the loan: "There is no doubt they will act in accordance with our suggestion."[17]

Examination forms also directed examiners to look up from the ledger books and evaluate the bank's physical condition, which expressed the competence of the bank's officers in material form. McCulloch was especially concerned that bank organizers obtain a "suitable and safe banking-house or room," with "a good vault or safe, (which ought to be both burglar and fire proof)." Robbery and fire remained potent financial risks. After describing the "iron lined" vault and safe at the First National Bank of Evansville, Indiana, examiner Butler Ward noted an additional precaution: "A man sleeps in the office."[18]

Information about a bank's condition did not stay as a dialogue between examiners and bankers. Examiners provided bank management with immediate and candid assessments, but they filed their final reports with their superiors in Washington. The bankers had to wait on the Comptroller for the official word on how they weathered the exam. Clerks read and evaluated examiners' reports; they then wrote to bank officers, under the Comptroller' signature, detailing any violations of the letter or the spirit of the banking laws and demanding prompt correction. The bank's officers were required to respond, explaining how they would comply. "We can only promise to do better in the future!" one banker—himself formerly a national bank examiner—wrote back after being scolded for a persistently deficient reserve. The paper machinery also went into motion when the banks' periodic call reports showed deficiencies, thus allowing the Comptroller to repair minor problems before they became major ones. Ultimately, the early examination regime, consistent with McCulloch's invocation of a grand experiment in which private bankers could expect sincere public efforts, was geared to redirecting bankers toward sound banking practices rather than punishing them for past mistakes.[19]

Instructions and Suggestions for Bankers (and Examiners)

McCulloch self-consciously developed these norms and institutions. In an 1863 pamphlet, revised and extended in 1864, he provided bank organizers with instructions, advising them not only of the chartering rules but also suggesting how to pursue what McCulloch understood as legitimate banking. Specifically, he encouraged bankers to make small loans in relation to their capital, to distribute them widely in their communities, and to record them assiduously. By following these practices, bank officers would remain free from the influence of dominant clients and would underwrite the political legitimacy of the new system by making credit widely available.[20]

McCulloch wrote his pamphlet for bankers, not examiners, yet absent other guidance, his Instructions and Suggestions became an early version of a bank examiner's manual. Officials like R. W. Derrickson, who examined banks in Pennsylvania in the late 1860s, used McCulloch's framework to describe bank behavior and guide bankers toward practices that McCulloch and his team viewed as appropriate and legitimate. Some banks, like the First National Bank of Indiana, Pennsylvania, a farming community fifty miles east of Pittsburgh, perfectly encapsulated McCulloch's vision. The bank was "doing a safe + very profitable business," Derrickson reported, with "money loaned in very small [amounts] throughout this county." Safety and profitability kept a bank in business and promoted public confidence. Wide loan distribution ensured safety and underwrote local political legitimacy. The bank fulfilled the public obligation that came with the privileges conveyed in its corporate charter.[21]

Not all banks fared so well. Working through the banks in Erie, Pennsylvania, in November 1868, Derrickson found that the Keystone National Bank was "doing a safe and profitable business," but the First National Bank of Erie "does a small business" and "is of no public benefit." The First National had $150,000 in capital but only lent $64,399, almost half of which went to the bank's officers. By contrast, the Keystone, with $250,000 in capital, had $315,622 in loans outstanding, only 20 percent of which were in the hands of officers.[22]

Derrickson elaborated his dissatisfaction in a lengthy critique of the First National Bank of Girard, which he examined later that month. "This bank," Derrickson wrote, "does but very little if any business outside of the six stockholders who own the bank. The president informed me that they would not take the risk of loaning out their circulation when they could purchase U.S. Bonds with it." Although the national banks existed to monetize the national debt, supervisors expected them to also serve the public, even if they were not always clear on the mechanism of enforcement of that public interest. "I would deem it very advisable if legislation could be had to take the priveledge [sic] granted away from these gentlemen, and give it where it could be used as was intended," Derrickson urged. National banking's explicitly public purpose meant that both hoarding banknotes for monetization and redeploying those notes exclusively to insider lending were disfavored, subject to criticism at the examiner's discretion, and perfectly legal under existing statutes.[23]

In the end, the practical consequences of discretionary supervisory remonstrations appear uneven. From 1867 to 1876, the two banks Derrickson praised maintained loan-to-capital ratios of around 1.5, lending more into their communities than the shareholders contributed to organize the banks. On this measure, the First National Bank of Erie improved its performance, coming into line with its peers by 1876. The directors of First National Bank of Girard, however, remained stubbornly committed to returning safe profits to themselves without lending in the wider community. Despite a change in management in 1872, their bank never lent more than 65 percent of its capital in this period. Public power could guide but not force private actors to halt disfavored practices.[24]

Creating Legal Discretion:
Supervision Through Resolution

As the contours of bank supervision took shape in the 1860s and 1870s, an apparatus beyond market discipline and discretionary federal examination loomed over the relationship between the Comptroller and the national banks: the ultimate threat of receivership and liquidation. As with bank examination, early Comptrollers sought to expand the scope of this power beyond what Congress initially authorized.

Under the National Banking Acts, the Comptroller's power to appoint a receiver was constructed around closing and liquidating banks that violated clear rules, which, by implication, strictly limited the Comptroller's discretion to shut banks for insolvency. The law charged the Comptroller with dissolving banks that failed to maintain a reserve, failed to maintain a surplus, failed to select a place to redeem its notes, failed to maintain its capital stock, or improperly certified a check. Violation of those rules constituted valid reasons to close and wind up a bank. They also signaled poor business performance but did not, in themselves, indicate insolvency. Rather, the Banking Acts defined insolvency in relation to national banks' monetary powers. The 1864 Act authorized the Comptroller to appoint a receiver if "any association has refused to pay its circulating notes." Congress had created the national banking system to provide a uniform banknote currency, and failures of redemption— failures of sound money—constituted a near automatic basis for liquidation. Yet such a conception of solvency appeared to limit the scope of supervisory action. When a bank examiner suspected a bank might be insolvent, after discovering large credit losses for example, his only option was to present the bank's notes at its counter and see what happened next.[25]

As written, then, the National Banking Acts enabled the Comptroller to close potentially solvent banks that violated charter rules, while curtailing officials' capacity to close insolvent banks unless bankers refused to redeem their notes. Federal banking officials viewed such limited, rule-bound liquidation as insufficient. They needed the authority to act decisively on the strength of their own judgment, first to close insolvent banks, and then to liquidate them in the interests of bank creditors. In the 1860s and 1870s, Comptrollers pushed

their authority in federal courts, while also lobbying Congress to institutionalize this broad discretion.

The courts acted first, gradually granting the Comptroller and his receivers
discretion over how, and then whether, to proceed to liquidate a bank. In an
1869 case about when a receiver could pursue shareholders' liability, the
Supreme Court observed that the National Banking Acts "referred to [the
Comptroller's] judgment and discretion, and his determination is conclusive,"
and that said judgment and discretion "was not to be questioned in the litigation that may ensue." In an 1873 case, a federal district court extended this logic,
finding that the Comptroller had sole authority to determine when to close and
wind up a bank. In the midst of the Panic of 1873, depositors sought to force a
suspended Chicago bank into court-administered bankruptcy under the 1867
federal bankruptcy law rather than waiting for the Comptroller to appoint a
receiver. "The currency act . . . does furnish, through the functions of an important public official—the comptroller of the currency—a very complete and
detailed . . . plan for administering the affairs of an insolvent national bank," the
court ruled. Creditors could apply to the Comptroller, not the courts, to determine whether a bank was subject to receivership and liquidation.[26]

Meanwhile, Congress incrementally expanded the Comptroller's power to
place an insolvent bank in the hands of a receiver beyond mere failures of note
redemption. By 1876, Congress's language was blunt and direct: "Whenever the
Comptroller shall become satisfied of the insolvency of a national banking association, he may . . . appoint a receiver." Congress thus made the Comptroller
the sole arbiter of bank solvency. While courts had suggested as much before
this amendment, the Supreme Court left no doubt after: The Comptroller's
"conclusions as to the facts [of insolvency] are final, and not reviewable by the
courts." The discretionary mode of bank supervision had, within a single
decade, become the sole basis for insolvency review.[27]

How did this awesome power work in practice? When contemporaries described the Comptroller putting a bank into the hands of a receiver, they
meant it literally. The receiver took physical possession of the assets and records of the bank, usually locking them in the bank's own safe. Examiners often
assumed the role temporarily, either because they discovered the insolvency
or because they were nearby and could close the bank quickly. Examiners also
had the skills and knowledge to determine whether the bank could be saved.
They could bring order to the chaos of its unexpected closing and, if a bank
had indeed failed, pass it on to a dedicated receiver to see the long-term
process of liquidation through.[28]

Once the examiner-qua-receiver took over a failing bank, he then had to try to salvage the assets, which often contained past-due loans, worthless bonds, and unwieldy collateral. Managing the wind-down, receivers engaged in a fundamental tradeoff experienced by their state forebears and reverberating down to the present: Liquidators could move quickly, or they could maximize recovery, but usually not both.

Theodore M. Davis, the receiver for the Ocean National Bank, a prominent failure in 1871, faced this dilemma. The New York City bank had lent more than $500,000 to the organizers of a Michigan canal company, secured by the canal company's bonds. Without additional funding, the canal would never get built and the bonds would be worthless. Davis took extraordinary measures, organizing a syndicate to finance the completion of the canal, on the promise that once completed and operational, the reorganized canal company would repay the debts to the bank. There was no obvious legal authority to take such actions as receiver, but he did it anyway. After a thorough investigation, the House Banking Committee initially supported this use of extralegal discretion. The story didn't end there. Six years later, the same committee reversed course, condemning Davis's action. "He exercised a discretion which, even if well intentioned, was unwise and in violation of the law," wrote two committee members who offered the most favorable rendering of Davis's activities. Their colleagues, meanwhile, accused him of outright corruption. To be fair, by that point Davis was the well-compensated president of the canal company, and the promised returns to the bank had not materialized.[29]

Institutional Frailty: Informational and Financial Disadvantage

During the early years of the national banking system, McCulloch and his successors worked to infuse chartering, examination, and receivership with discretionary authority not obviously present in the National Banking Acts. They did so with an expansive view of federal power, one that grew from their conviction that the national banking experiment was necessarily an unequal partnership between private bankers and public officials, with public officials in the lead. Officials believed that the new banks could not succeed without guidance and supervision; they expected bankers to conform to their vision of sound and prudent banking. "If they carry out this policy a little more thoroughly," Comptroller Hulburd wrote in 1869, "they will be less at the mercy of the borrowers, will be better able to protect the legitimate interests of their customers, and better entitled to the fostering care of the government." Yet federal supervisors faced a set of informational and institutional impediments, which became increasingly apparent by the 1870s, thus throwing that "fostering care" into a new light and undermining the reputation of bank supervision among bankers and the public.[30]

The first problem was statutory. Under the initial regime of public reporting and private surveillance created by Congress, bankers self-reported their condition to the Comptroller and the public, allowing market participants to evaluate their vitality. Initially, Congress fixed the dates for bankers' quarterly reports on the first Mondays of January, April, July, and October. Bankers knew when their reports were due and could clean up their balance sheets in advance. "It is certainly a point to be gained to know that the banks can make a good showing at least once every quarter," Hulburd quipped. Fixed dates also created opportunities for speculators. Bullion prices rose in advance of each reporting day. In 1869, Congress amended the law, requiring the Comptroller to request "not less than five reports during each and every year," leaving the timing to his discretion. The new system enabled Comptrollers to perform a rudimentary form of what would become stress-testing, picking moments, like spring planting or fall harvest, when banks typically faced seasonal strains. Randomization made call reports "far more valuable and gratifying," resolving the "previous preparation on the part of the banks and the opportunity afforded to speculators to manipulate the money market."[31]

One informational challenge was fixed, but another persisted: Generating examiner reports required good examiners, and good examiners needed appropriate compensation. When Congress enacted the National Banking Acts, it followed an established system of paying government employees, in one scholar's words, "immediately and objectively, on the delivery of services and the achievement of outputs." As noted above, examiners were paid through a system of per diems, $5 for each workday, plus $2 per 25 miles traveled, charged directly to the bank examined. This pay reflected the temporariness of the work; Congress never intended federal bank examiner to be a full-time job. Almost immediately, McCulloch recognized that such rates were insufficient to recruit and retain the caliber of examiner he thought necessary to secure the reputation of public oversight. "I found I was getting so short," John Bull explained of his own decision to leave the examination force, that "I did not care to be a bank examiner."[32]

For the examiners who stayed on, earning a decent living meant following the incentives to their logical conclusion: Examiners needed to cover a lot of banks, quickly. R. W. Derrickson, the examiner who complained bitterly about banks that failed to lend to their communities, is a case in point. According to his examination journal, he inspected the First National Banks of Indiana and Johnstown, both small towns in West Central Pennsylvania, in a single day in December 1868. The towns are an hour drive apart in 2025; Derrickson likely could not have made the trip so expeditiously. The examinations must have been done in haste. Derrickson hardly ever slowed down. After spending Christmas in Hollidaysburg, where he examined the town's bank on December 28, Derrickson moved on to Clearfield fifty-five miles away, where he cleared the town's two banks on successive days. By the 31st, he was in Curwensville, about ten miles southwest, examining the bank there. One day off on New Year's Day, then on to Bellefonte fifty-one miles away, then fifty miles to Huntingdon, then thirty-six miles to Lewistown, and then fifty-seven miles to Harrisburg, one per day, day after day. Hulburd may well have had Derrickson in mind when he advised Congress that "the labors of examiners are very severe, involving work by day and travel by night; while the rigid and careful scrutiny required to investigate fully the condition and accounts of the banks is wearying and exhausting" (see the interlude after chapter 3 for the fictional rendition and the implications of this frenzied examination schedule).[33]

Economic necessity drove examiners to speed, which compromised the element of supervisory surprise. When Derrickson arrived in Erie, Pennsylvania, in November 1868 and inspected the first of the town's four national banks, the others had ample warning that he would soon come calling. So did the bankers in neighboring Girard and North Coast. Once Derrickson left, these bankers knew he wouldn't be back for some time. In cities with more than a handful of banks, examiners might inspect only a few at a time, as Derrickson did when he visited Pittsburgh in late November 1868, leaving the remainder for when they passed back through or for other examiners working the same territory. Ultimately, compensation and geography undermined supervisory stealth.[34]

The speed that low pay encouraged had some benefits. Haste meant that each examiner would visit many, many banks. They could recognize quickly when a bank was, as Derrickson wrote, "in the very best of order." They also knew, in many cases, when circumstances looked amiss. Unfortunately, such haste was not particularly conducive to a more exhaustive evaluation of managerial competence or solvency.[35]

McCulloch tried to address poor compensation creatively, charging larger banks more to account for the time and effort necessary to thoroughly vet them. But McCulloch's new plan was not authorized by the statute, a fact that bankers noticed and protested. Reacting to what seemed to him like a cursory examination followed shortly by a $25 assessment, an irate Massachusetts banker balked, asserting that the Comptroller "has *no* authority to charge to such an extent." Then serving as Deputy Comptroller, Hulburd agreed with the banker on the hard language of the statute, even as he sought to justify the higher charge. "The amount is not assessed according to a technical construction of the law," Hulburd wrote, but it "is intended to pay such a salary as will enable the Department to employ a competent man to make these examinations." As Hulburd, later as Comptroller, wrote to Congress hoping to make the dubious expedient legal, "the compensation allowed by law is totally insufficient to pay the right kind of men to undertake this duty." Congress amended the law in 1875, expanding the pay scale for larger banks, while allowing the Comptroller to fix the salaries for key examiners in reserve cities. Yet in exchange for raising examiner pay, Congress eliminated mileage, further encouraging examiners to take the most direct (and predictable) routes.[36]

The fee system, which required bankers to pay for their own examinations, complicated and confused bankers' relationships with their supervisors. It was not clear whether bankers were paying for services rendered or being taxed to fund an adversarial process. The difference was not semantic: It would define what the information generated through examination would mean and who would lead whom in this shared process of risk management.

Many bankers believed that one way or the other, examination existed to serve their interests. "There are two sides to these examinations," the aforementioned irate Massachusetts banker observed, "not only is the Government to protect stockholders by a rigid examination of banks and bank-officers, as if they might all be rogues; but . . . bank-officers themselves will demand . . . that the examinations shall result in positive proof to their employers that they are worthy of their trust, and that the banks are sound and well managed." In this framing, examiners and their certifications were a product that bankers purchased to provide assurance, if not quite insurance, to bank stakeholders: Federal examination certified that bank managers were operating according to the government's high standards. For shareholders facing the potential of double liability, this was a welcome assurance indeed. More fundamentally, bank examination was meant to provide every party with the confidence that the promises banks made—to noteholders, depositors, and borrowers—were indeed credible.[37]

At bottom, this also meant that examination certified that bankers were not committing fraud. The idea that bank examiners were fraud detectors was not just preferred by bankers but also supported by the statute and promoted by Hulburd. "The examinations made . . . have been instrumental in developing irregular and dishonest practices in time to prevent loss to the bank in quite a number of cases," Hulburd wrote approvingly in his annual report in 1871.[38]

Unfortunately, this enthusiasm to monitor on behalf of other stakeholders would soon prove an impossible dream. "It is not to be supposed that the short time usually spent in the examination of a national bank will be sufficient in all cases, to detect bad management or defalcations," Comptroller Knox, Hulburd's successor, acknowledged in 1873. It was a sheepish admission born of hard experience. Examiners would never know as much as the bankers they supervised; they could never examine banks as frequently or thoroughly as they might like. Whatever bank examination was, it was not—and could not be—a certification of competence or honesty of bankers or, unfortunately, even of the examiners themselves.[39]

The Corruption of Bank Examination

Underlying the conflicts over the fee system were foundational problems of public corruption. This generalized problem in the 1870s had a specific manifestation for bank examination. If examiners were not paid, they could be bought or might extract favors for favorable treatment, including, especially, certifications of solvency of undeserving institutions.

These were not idle concerns. The massive expansion of the federal government during the Civil War united patriotism and profiteering, contracts and corruption. In this environment, the Comptroller did not escape the stench of impropriety. After all, the Comptroller could grant—or withhold—valuable corporate charters. Clerks handled vital and valuable commercial information. Examiners could be searching or cursory, their reports accurate or adulterated. McCulloch had used supervisory discretion—in his own estimation—to keep the rogues out of the national banking system. His successors, wittingly or not, accepted rogues within their ranks.[40]

For example, in August 1866, George R. Rutter came to Washington to discuss certain "irregularities" in his Tennessee National Bank, discovered and reported by examiner John Bull after listening in on tavern chatter. Rutter had some notion of how to fix the problem. He either offered Comptroller Hulburd a $500 bribe or $500 to help him select a competent cashier to run his ailing bank. Witnesses disagreed. What is not in disagreement is that Rutter bought Hulburd a fine carriage and harness, whether at Hulburd's insistence or intimation we do not know. "I mean to say that the Comptroller gave me to understand that unless I gave him something," Rutter later explained to a congressional committee, "I would have trouble." Though he admitted accepting the carriage, Hulburd denied the corruption charges. He had also, against the advice of his clerks, given Rutter more time to get his troubled bank in order. Time, however, could not save the "thoroughly rotten" Tennessee National Bank. In 1867, it failed, taking the funds of Tennessee's state school system with it.[41]

Rutter may have been, as receiver Theodore Davis called him, "the veriest rascal that walked," but he seems merely to have played the prevailing game without the requisite skill or subtlety. He certainly was not playing alone. The inquiry into his bank's failure revealed a Comptroller's office filled with strivers and the self-described hangers-on of financiers like Anthony Drexel and Jay Cooke. The Comptroller's clerks thought little of taking oyster lunches with Rutter or hobnobbing at Cooke's Philadelphia residence. Rumors swirled that national bank charters could best be obtained through the influence of Hulburd's brother. That, at least, was what was "generally understood." Even as officials framed discretionary oversight as a vector for the spirit and intent of the law, it carried—by implication, rumor, and accusation—the corrupt spirit of the age.[42]

It was corruption from the highest to the lowest level. Looming over the 1872 inquest into Rutter's failed bank were the misdeeds of examiner Charles Callender. A native of New York, Callender had worked as a bank teller in Boston, before serving as a captain in the Union Army. By 1865, Callender was serving as a clerk in the Comptroller's office, quickly advancing to examiner. That's where the trouble started. Beginning his examiner career in Philadelphia, when he found banks in weak condition, he apparently used his authority to solicit loans in return for favorable examination reports. Eventually he borrowed more than $400,000 from fifteen banks, first in Philadelphia and then in New York City (Callender had been transferred to the latter city to replace its previous examiner, John Bull, whom Callender had implicated in petty bribery).[43]

In October 1871, Callender examined the Ocean National Bank, whose troubles included a close association with New York's notorious William "Boss" Tweed—who was briefly a director—and a major robbery in 1870. Following his by-now usual pattern, after discovering the bank's precarious position, Callender secured a $76,000 loan from it. In consideration, he declined to file an examination report with the Comptroller. He did praise the directors on the bank's "most gratifying and prosperous condition."[44]

The New York Clearinghouse Association, which had managed interbank transfers in New York City since 1853, didn't share Callender's rosy assessment. Because the Clearinghouse extended temporary credit as part of its interbank payments business, it closely supervised its members, sometimes in consultation with the Comptroller, more often on its own initiative. The Clearinghouse was skeptical of the Ocean Bank because the bank was a consistent debtor at the Clearinghouse. This should almost never occur, since payments should ultimately net out through settlement, leaving the Clearinghouse exposed only in circumstances suggesting insolvency or fraud or both. Consistent debtor status would mean that Ocean Bank was failing to make good on its transactions.

In mid-December, the Clearinghouse, not trusting the Comptroller's process managed by Callender, sent its own examination committee, made up of officers of other Clearinghouse banks. They found the Ocean Bank in "very critical condition." They also found Callender's loans, which had been dutifully recorded. In light of these discoveries, the Clearinghouse suspended the bank from membership on December 11. They called for Hulburd, who arrived the following morning with Callender in tow. Callender remained the examiner for New York; he and Hulburd took possession of the bank and placed it in the hands of a receiver. A week later, once the full story became public, Callender was arrested and charged with fraud.[45]

Callender's actions inspired hot outrage. "A graver charge was never laid at a man's door," the *Chicago Tribune* declared. "Not alone because he was bleeding weak banks by blackmail, not alone because he was using his official position to illegally increase his income, but because he was aiming a direct blow at the commerce of the country by bolstering rotten banks." The corrupt examiner became, in effect, a byword for federal corruption, reinforced by the fact that Callender twice escaped conviction because of hung—and possibly bribed—juries. There was, at least, a measure of earthly justice: He was ejected from his church, by a resounding vote of 175 to 5.[46]

Callender's misdeeds fundamentally undermined the legitimacy of the public power which sought to steer private finance within the nascent national banking system. When news of the Ocean Bank's failure broke (but when the public still did not know of Callender's role in it), the *Commercial and Financial Chronicle*, one of the nation's leading business periodicals, brimmed with confidence in the examination regime. "For among the severest checks on bad banking and the most dreaded barriers against some of the dangers in which unskillful or unfaithful bank officers involve themselves," the paper observed, "is the frequent visit of an accomplished, faithful, incorruptible bank examiner."[47]

As Callender's full story came to light, editorial views of the incorruptibility of the bank examiner started to change. In January 1872, the New York magazine *Financier*, which dubbed itself "a trustworthy and capable exponent of American monetary interests," objected to the entire enterprise of bank examination. Public officials' predictable visits to private businesses, the editors argued, created a streamlined machine for extortion and fraud. Congress authorized examination only when necessary, the magazine vented, urging strict adherence to common law visitorial authority as a mere reserve power. "There is no authority in law," for continuous oversight, the editors insisted. "No such office as bank examiner was ever created." Examination was not only illegitimate but, in its pretensions to permanence, illegal.[48]

To the *Financier's* chagrin, perhaps, the Callender affair did not end federal supervision. It did, however, subvert the balance between public and private that McCulloch had tried to install. By 1872, that balance was shifting to the private, and in particular to the New York Clearinghouse—on terms set by the New York bankers (incidentally, *Financier's* primary audience). During the Civil War, the Clearinghouse and its members had resisted the new national banking system. Only revisions of the law in 1864, which made New York a central reserve city and preserved the preeminence of the New York money market, convinced prominent city banks to adopt national charters. Even still, the Clearinghouse maintained a tense relationship with the new national authority. "The best thing to do with [Callender's] position," the *Financier* editors wrote, "is to leave it unfilled altogether and let Mr. Callender's odium remain as its memorial."[49]

In a sense, the Comptroller almost did precisely that. Rather than a pure abolition of the post, the Comptroller invited the Clearinghouse to nominate Callender's replacement, an informal tradition that continued into the twentieth century. That is, the Comptroller would no longer exercise its appointment power over examiners in the nation's financial center—the private-sector Clearinghouse would control that prerogative (the Boston Clearinghouse gained a similar privilege during this period). In this way, the Callender episode solidified the Clearinghouse's role as a complementary supervisory institution within the new national banking system, one distinct from the Comptroller but nevertheless closely tied to it. The Panic of 1873, which began in the New York money market and ended through decisive action by the Clearinghouse, cemented and further shifted risk management from public authority to private actors.[50]

Crisis and Forbearance: The Panic of 1873

Informational asymmetries and corruption prevented McCulloch's vision of supervisory discretion in "the spirit and intention of the law." Comptroller Knox and his successors fully embraced a more formalistic project, retreating from McCulloch's visible and activist oversight.[51]

John Jay Knox was an appropriate figure to lead the transformation. Before his appointment by President Ulysses S. Grant in 1872, Knox had been a banker and was something of a banking scholar, publishing a nearly 1,000-page history of banking in the United States. Over his long tenure, Knox downplayed the power and authority of federal supervisors, emphasizing instead the responsibilities of bank directors to supervise their own banks on the private side of the public divide. Knox elevated corporate governance as the preeminent modality of risk management. His posture recognized the limits of federal supervisory power but also in an important way gave federal supervisors more leeway to work behind the scenes in a more consultative role with bank managers and directors.[52]

Indeed, Knox did not abandon discretion per se, although he did reduce its use in imposing discipline on banks. Instead, he crafted an alternative tool, what we now call forbearance—the intentioned choice not to exercise authority available to a bank supervisor for some other purpose of risk management (note that the concept of forbearance would not apply to the Rutter or Callender corruption, where money flowed to prevent supervisory actions for criminal purposes). Forbearance, in its initial and subsequent uses, was a tool made for crisis. The National Banking Acts did not provide the Comptroller with effective powers to manage market disruptions or financial panics: that was not Congress's purpose. The very idea of public-private management of financial crises was still under development at the time of the National Banking Acts' passage. That same decade, however, in Great Britain and to a lesser extent the United States, ideas were cohering around the concept of lender of last resort, through which a *private* bank endowed with a public purpose would lend into the crisis, providing necessary liquidity to convert illiquid bank assets into ready money and thus enabling banks to meet panicked creditors' demands for cash.[53]

Although the point of the lender-of-last-resort function was to restore credibility to financial markets, the mechanism rested almost exclusively on a functioning balance sheet. The Comptrollers in their first decade hoped very much to establish that credibility but lacked anything like a balance sheet. In the absence of that balance sheet but in the quest for that credibility, forbearance became the Comptroller's most potent tool. Choosing not to act was, in itself, a powerful discretionary action.

Forbearance was a consistent feature of early federal bank supervision. In their reports, bank examiners frequently noted behavior that *could* be grounds for initiating receivership but in practice seldom was. In the early 1870s, the question of forbearance coalesced on bank reserves, the money national banks had to keep close at hand to pay out deposits or redeem their notes. The National Banking Acts required banks in large "reserve cities" to keep a 25 percent reserve against their notes *and* deposits, while banks in the rest of the country (so-called "country banks") needed to maintain a 15 percent reserve, 60 percent of which could be held on deposit with a reserve city bank. Reserve city banks, in places like Chicago and St. Louis, could also hold their deposits in the central reserve city, New York.[54]

This institutional architecture created a financial pyramid whereby country banks counted on reserve banks and reserve banks counted on New York City. Money from around the country flowed into New York banks for safekeeping—often at attractive rates of interest. Seeking profitable outlets for the nation's reserves, New York banks lent this money where there were profits to be had, including to Wall Street speculators. Seasonal demands for currency in the interior periodically strained the New York money market, while the unrealized schemes of financiers could unleash panic and financial ruin on unsuspecting country banks.[55]

The National Banking Acts empowered the Comptroller to curtail, and ultimately exterminate, a bank's business if it failed to maintain its reserve. The law forbade deficient banks from making new loans or declaring dividends, and authorized the Comptroller, with the approval of the Treasury Secretary, to close under-reserved banks. Closing a deficient, albeit otherwise solvent, institution was necessarily a drastic action that implicated difficult political realities. In practice, examiners noted violations and strongly urged correction, to varying effect. These negotiations remained private; bankers had the good sense to keep reserve deficiencies out of their public reports. The Comptroller and his examiners would, in these private conversations, forbear any more drastic actions.[56]

In moments of financial strain, whether seasonal or because of flighty speculative capital, the challenge of maintaining reserves intensified, especially for large reserve banks that were likely to experience heavy outflows as country banks called back their reserves. By creating a system concentrated in New York City, the National Banking Acts did not explicitly make the exercise of supervisory authority different for systemically important banks. Yet in times of stress, the implication of the Banking Acts' model of reserve pyramiding was precisely toward more patient forbearance for these large institutions in the interests of stability in the wider money market. "The failure of one of these New York City banks in a time of monetary stringency," Comptroller Knox observed, "would embarrass, if not ruin, many banks in the redemption cities, and, in turn, the country correspondents of these banks."[57]

The Great Chicago Fire of 1871 posed the first significant test for the reserve system, forcing officials to decide whether and how to act when New York City banks experienced large reserve deficiencies. In October 1871, much of Chicago, including the central business district, burned to the ground. As the fire raged, the city's bankers worked feverishly to rescue their cash and account books from the blaze. Just a few days after the ashes cooled, most banks had opened temporary offices and were prepared to pay out depositors. In the months that followed, money flooded out of New York to replenish Chicago's banks and rebuild the city.[58]

For several months in early 1872, a few prominent New York City banks failed to maintain reserves, an anomaly broadcast by their mandated public reports and amplified by the financial press. The banks also continued to make loans in violation of the law but in clear accordance with necessity and with the full knowledge of the Comptroller. This was public, not private, forbearance. The financial media cheered the system on. "Who can doubt that the intent of the law was, to leave to [the Comptroller's] discretion merely the power *not* to do this, in the case of some extraordinary emergency, such as the great fire, for instance?" *The Financier* argued. The "this" referred to the power to forebear on the law's demands that the reserve banks in New York City curtail lending or close shop. In exercising leniency in the face of illegality, the Chicago Fire and the Comptroller together opened the question of when the law would be enforced and for which banks—some of which were simply too big to fail.[59]

The Chicago Fire highlighted the extent to which reserve pyramiding in New York City created the appearance of systemic stability—the reserve banks could pool correspondent reserves and channel funds to meet isolated local challenges—while in fact undermining those very principles. Systemic collapse loomed if reserve banks could not meet all demands or if they got into trouble through their own activities. The Comptroller knew that these correlated risks were a problem and was powerless to address it. In November 1872, Knox explained to Congress that the equivalent of one-fifth of all the banking capital in the nation was deposited with New York City banks. The failure of one of these banks, Knox explained, would be "wide-spread disaster." Closing one for failure to maintain its reserve would bring the same consequences. The only choice was forbearance, allowing the banks to continue lending and shifting risk management responsibility from public enforcement to private judgment.[60]

The financial press, in turn, used the disjuncture between the law and its enforcement to attack the law. "The wise policy for banks, especially for bankers' banks, in panic times, is to lend freely, to *use* the reserve which they have accumulated in good times; but the American law says the banks are not to lend," the British writer and editor Walter Bagehot observed in *The Economist* that December. "The existence of such a regulation will certainly be very apt to increase the general apprehensiveness when anything goes wrong." Knox may have forbore in 1872, but there was no guarantee that future Comptrollers would do the same.[61]

The full test of the forbearance approach came the following year. In September 1873, the merchant banker Jay Cooke overextended himself. When his bank failed, one of the largest financial panics of the nineteenth century ensued (see the interlude after chapter 2 for an account of part of this failure and its many spillovers). Country banks called in their reserves and cash drained from New York. There was nothing the Comptroller could do: Banks and their counterparties demanded money, but the Comptroller had no way to provide it.

If the Comptroller was powerless, the New York Clearinghouse Association was not. The Clearinghouse had something that the Comptroller did not: a balance sheet. In response to the crisis, the Clearinghouse pooled member bank reserves, so that any bank could draw on the central fund to meet demands. At the height of the panic, New York banks, many with national charters, were on average far below their legally required reserve. But since the Clearinghouse centralized reserves, every bank could draw on a fund far in excess of 25 percent of its individual liabilities. "The bold and fearless fashion in which the Clearinghouse committee exercised the power which was placed in its hands," economic historian Oliver M. W. Sprague wrote a generation later, enabled the New York banks to survive this great panic. And with the New York banks, so too did the American financial system.[62]

For the New York bankers, the Panic of 1873 emphasized two principles. First, it underscored the practical irrationality of reserve requirements and the indignity, in the bankers' view, that falling below them could constitute a legal basis for liquidation. In their postmortem crisis report, the Clearinghouse Committee, confident in their ability to manage their own risks, vigorously attacked the Banking Act's reserve provisions.[63] "There seems an intrinsic absurdity in a law requiring that a 'reserve' must be always kept, which was created on purpose to be used, or that a bank officer who draws upon his reserve, under circumstances for which it was intended, is false to the oath which he takes to obey the law." Knox had little patience for this position. "The object of the reserve is to enable the bank at all times to pay its Debts," he wrote after the Panic. "In times of panic the depositors of a bank, and not its officers and directors, are its masters." It was more important, in Knox's view, to preserve the depositors than to preserve the bank. Reserve pyramiding, which placed bankers' deposits in New York City, was the problem, not reserve requirements. Even still, Knox had demonstrated in practice what he could not say: In the throes of a crisis, the Comptroller would not close a major bank for failing to maintain its reserve.[64]

The bankers took a second lesson from the Panic of 1873: Supervision, as constructed in the National Banks Acts and developed through the Comptroller's office with great, hopeful enthusiasm, was not equipped to confront financial crisis. As with the Chicago Fire, the Comptroller's tools—chartering, examination, liquidation, and now forbearance—provided no basis for confronting and halting financial panic. In times of crisis, supervisors needed money, and plenty of it, to convince frightened country bankers that they could all draw on their reserves at once. Money, ironically, was the one thing the Comptroller of the Currency did not have.

Writing the same year as the crisis, Bagehot famously observed that panics are "a species of neuralgia, and according to the rules of science you must not starve it. The holders of the cash reserve must be ready not only to keep it for their own liabilities but to advance it most freely for the liabilities of others." Bagehot was describing the lender-of-last-resort function that he had popularized in previous years. The Comptroller could not fulfill this role because there was no financial mechanism to accomplish it. Neither could the reserve city banks, acting individually, since doing so would violate the law. In 1873, the New York Clearinghouse Association brokered a compromise, but one which depended on the willingness and capacity of private actors to cooperate. The Comptroller remained responsible for the banking system's health, even as private bankers, working together, made it so. For a time, this cooperative, corporatist supervisory framework kept the era's episodic panics from breaking into full-blown crises. When cooperation strained and split at the turn of the century, reformers would seek to imbue the public with more assertive crisis-fighting authority.[65]

Reimagining Examination

While the Panic of 1873 exposed federal supervisors' inability to stem financial crisis, the information asymmetries at the heart of public bank oversight gradually undermined examiners' collective reputation for competence. Specifically, although the National Banking Acts had implied a public role in detecting and punishing bank fraud, the persistence of financial malfeasance showed that examiners were not likely to be an effective police force rooting out unfaithful bankers. In one notorious case, two successive examiners found cashier Oscar L. Baldwin a "good officer" and "a competent and efficient officer" before it was revealed that Baldwin had competently ransacked $2.5 million from his bank. Examiners' failings were well enough known to be the subject of poetic ridicule in the brand-new *Life* magazine:

> The Bank Examiner! Didn't he come?
> Well—he wasn't exactly deaf and dumb;
> Nor was he one of the fungus kind
> With a wooden head and eyes so blind.
> He seemed to be sharp and bright and quick,
> But he wasn't up to my little trick.
> With all his sharpness he couldn't see
> How the bank was mismanaged by me—
> For I kept things looking neat and fair
> The business seemed to be done on the square.
> He looked at the books and counted the cash,
> And said, in a way that now seems rash,
> That the Bank's condition was healthy and sound
> As any Bank he ever had found
> And with such directors and such a cashier
> There would never be anything to fear.

From the perspective of less poetic bankers, if examiners could not root out embezzlers, why should they submit to the labor and annoyance, much less the expense, of an examination? What, meanwhile, could stockholders gain from such federal oversight?[66]

A good set of questions that McCulloch's answers, only a generation old, could not adequately resolve. Under intense public and congressional scrutiny, Knox sought to temper expectations about what bank examination could accomplish. "The examiner can have but a limited knowledge of the habits and character of those employed in the bank," Knox explained to Congress in 1881. "If the teller is making false entries, and daily abstracting the funds of the bank . . . it is not possible for an examiner, in a day or two, to unravel this evil work." Knox's successor, Henry W. Cannon (1884–1886), built on this theme: "A rogue or dishonest man who acquires the confidence of his associates to such an extent that he can appropriate the funds of the bank to his own uses can have but little trouble in deceiving an examiner and of hiding his peculations from him." Even with the element of surprise, the examiner would always be an interloper in a fraudster's machine.[67]

Knox and his successors were staging a strategic retreat and seeking to place more emphasis on private corporate governance as the central locus of supervisory activity. Bank directors, representing private shareholders, needed to take responsibility for the internal workings and internal risks of national banks. "The men employed by them in the banks are under their supervision," Knox argued. "The directory must continuously look after its own servants. The examiner looks after the acts of the directors."[68]

As Knox revised the scope of public risk management in the private banking system, he instructed federal examiners to conceptualize their roles, not as police but as management consultants with the power to place their "clients" under oath. "All violations of law developed in the course of examinations should be pointed out in a courteous manner to the managing officers," Knox instructed. With courtesy, too, Knox encouraged examiners to coach up bank managers. "Any improvements in books and the method of keeping accounts which would add to the safety and efficiency of the conduct of the business," Knox continued, "should be suggested in such a way as will best secure their adoption." In doing so, federal supervisors still aimed, as McCulloch set forth, to promote upright and legitimate banking. Only now, that promotion was meant to be gentle, consultative, and constructive but without the claim that supervision would bear any of the responsibility should events turn sideways. Bank supervision had some ability to spot issues but not much more. The residual risks that the financial system would generate could not fall to the Comptroller and his supervisors to manage.[69]

In the final analysis, examiners would highlight the "restrictions . . . intended to protect these institutions, by imposing upon them general rules, which experience has shown may be properly done by the government *without its thereby becoming the guardian of the bank, or of the moneys of its depositors or stockholders, or being in any way responsible for the management of its funds.*" The italics are original, but we would have likely added them if they weren't.

The fostering care of government was gone. Private actors had to hazard their own risks.[70]

Conclusion

The early years of federal supervision were defined by contingency. From a thin statutory outline, Hugh McCulloch sought to craft robust institutions of public risk management, ordered around discretionary chartering, examination, and receivership. Yet the inherent weaknesses of the supervisory project—caused by information asymmetries, corruption, and the inability to combat crises—coupled with the deep national preference for private over public power, undermined the activist supervisory posture. Beginning with Knox, Comptrollers shifted risk-and-discretion supervision to the background, downplaying its capacity to force proactive change. The enthusiasms of a public-private partnership in the Lincoln administration gave way to the realities of a private responsibility that would sometimes, in idiosyncratic ways, receive a bit of help and a bit of scolding from the public sector.

In giving up on the public-private nature of bank supervision, however, federal officials opened the door to alternative ideas about national financial management. In the vacuum, proponents of state chartering, self-regulation, central banking, and deposit insurance all challenged the Comptroller's position at the peak of the financial hierarchy. The slow-building momentum for reform would break free in the early twentieth century but only after a period of extended supervisory muddling. The institutions of supervision would eventually grow far beyond the organization of the Comptroller of the Currency.

Interlude: The Freedman's Bank

IN FEBRUARY 1873, Charles A. Meigs, the national bank examiner responsible for New York City, concluded an examination report with a touch of Jeffersonian flair: "The destinies of any nation are safe in the hands of a people who are the owners of the soil." The people Meigs referred to were not the White yeoman farmers Jefferson would have had in mind but the more than 70,000 formerly enslaved men and women who had entrusted their savings to the Freedman's Savings and Trust Company. The Freedman's Bank, as it was widely known, received a federal charter on March 3, 1865, the same day Congress created the Freedmen's Bureau, the central institution for post–Civil War Reconstruction. Over the previous two years, Congress had enacted the National Banking Acts as war measures aimed at financing an undecided conflict. The Freedman's Bank, by contrast, was the project of a country on the cusp of victory and eager to make plans for rebuilding the broken nation.[1]

Like the White Northern elites who conceived the Freedman's Bank and lobbied Congress to create it, Meigs saw the institution as a means of inculcating thrift, a value which White paternalists thought was inaccessible under slavery. Unlike those elites, who sought to transform formerly enslaved people into free laborers fully invested in market capitalism, Meigs grasped that freedmen and women sought landed independence outside the market rather than wagework within it (an ambition Meigs understood narrowly through the male-headed household). "In hundreds of cases the freedmen, through the influence of [the Freedman's Bank], have been taught habits of thrift, which have resulted in their becoming the owners of small patches of land, and it is needless to describe the elevation of the man which this simple fact at once produces," Meigs wrote.[2]

Meigs's praise, appearing at the end of a carefully worded examination report published by Congress in March 1873, came at a decisive and dangerous moment for the new institution. Although Congress had created a system of bank supervision to safeguard the national banking system—one which Hugh McCulloch had shaped into proactive oversight—the legislature retained for itself supervisory authority over the Freedman's Bank. The last clause of the charter read, "The books of the corporation shall . . . be open for inspection and examination to such persons as Congress shall designate or appoint," language similar to that governing the First and Second Banks of the United States. Until Meigs visited in 1873, no such designee darkened the bank's door, an oversight failure that enabled the downfall of the bank, and with it the very practice of legislative supervision.[3]

Congress had not been entirely negligent in its design of the Freedman's Bank. Understanding the bank as fundamentally a philanthropic institution, lawmakers entrusted oversight to a board of trustees, headed by the Reverend John W. Alvord and composed largely of New York businessmen. This was a different form of supervision through corporate governance: Trustees were meant to be disinterested rather than self-interested; they had no capital in the bank and no liability for any of its failures.

Congress also took precautions by limiting the risks the bank could take. Consistent with the bank's purpose as a savings institution, the charter restricted trustees to investments in safe U.S. government securities. But there was some leeway. Up to one third of deposits could "be left on deposit at interest or . . . in such available form as the trustees may direct." Without meaningful public oversight, this loophole became an invitation to private enrichment and insider fraud.[4]

For the first two years of its corporate existence, the Freedman's Bank was a nonentity, as formerly enslaved people and their Northern allies fought against efforts by Southern landholders to reconstitute a slavocratic system by another name. In 1867, the bank moved its headquarters from New York to Washington, DC, and over time it established thirty-three branches in Northern and Southern cities. The trustees also recruited Henry D. Cooke to help turn the bank into a vital institution. To the naïve trustees, Cooke, who headed the Washington, DC, branch of his brother's firm, Jay Cooke & Co., was an enlightened choice. Under Cooke's management, the Freedman's Bank grew dramatically.[5]

Henry Cooke was not a man to be trusted with a bank. "Never can there have been a bank executive who was much less of a banker than Henry Cooke!" wrote Jay Cooke's biographer. Rather, Henry was "an assiduous lobbyist," as well as "a spendthrift, a 'good fellow,' easily influenced, lacking in business judgment, with an exaggerated opinion of his own importance, and inclined to tie up the business of the firm in speculative enterprises and loans to politicians."[6]

In 1870, Henry used his congressional connections to liberalize the bank's investment authority, and he soon made the Freedman's Bank an adjunct to his brother's financial empire. The bank siphoned the freedmen's savings to Washington, DC, where it fueled just the kind of "splendid financiering" Mc-Culloch sought to bar from the national banking system. Jay Cooke, who had led the Union's bond selling campaign during the Civil War, turned to railroad speculation as the federal bond market dried up, using the bank's resources to further his schemes. Henry Cooke, meanwhile, loaned money for fanciful real estate deals across the capital. "Many of the loans are of a character that should not appear upon the records of a savings bank, and will finally result in some loss to the institution," Meigs observed, "but the probable amount of such ultimate loss it is very difficult to determine at this time."[7]

In liberalizing the bank's investment powers at Cooke's insistence, Congress made a critical mistake. It allowed the Freedman's Bank to take on more risk without, at the same time, creating any new scope for risk management. Only after significant runs in October and November of 1872 did Congress instruct the Comptroller to examine the bank, reversing its earlier error of relying on legislative (non-)supervision instead of the administrative supervision that was, by then, standardized and refined administrative practice.

Meigs, convinced of the Freedman's Bank's positive influence and invested in its continued existence, walked a careful line in his examination report. He was vague about the losses that Cooke's reckless strategy had imposed on the bank, encouraged by improvements in accounting practices and investment standards, and praising of its officers. He also urged Congress to reinscribe investment limits, "having reference more to *safety* than *profit*." "With proper legislation and necessary restrictions," Meigs explained, "the bank would be able to correct the mistakes already made, to retrieve its present and prospective losses, and be enabled to continue a business of great usefulness to the class of depositors for whose benefit the institution was organized."[8]

These hopes were misplaced. True to the logic of supervision on suspicion of insolvency—the pre–Civil War practice that Millard Fillmore, as New York Comptroller, had so reviled—by revealing the bank's troubled state, Congress's investigation hastened its collapse. Over the next year, the bank suffered a series of significant runs. Its deposits fell by 20 percent, forcing it to liquidate it best assets. The Panic of 1873, caused by the failure of Jay Cooke &

Co., further undermined the value of the bank's holdings, which were still too intertwined with Jay Cooke's railroad speculations and Henry Cooke's shady local dealings. A second examination in early 1874 revealed that the bank was insolvent, its branch offices in disarray.[9]

To salvage the confidence of Black depositors, the trustees elected the prominent abolitionist Frederick Douglass president of the bank in March 1874. By then, the bank was foundering. Douglass, as he recalled, was "married to a corpse"—"The LIFE, which was the money, was gone." Congress sought to reorganize the bank but in doing so ignored Meigs's pessimistic valuation of the bank's assets. Nine days after Congress authorized changes to the National Banking Act to permit the reorganization, in June 1874, the bank closed forever. The era of legislative supervision was over.[10]

Congress created a commission to wind up the bank, a duty which, in 1881, passed into the Comptroller's hands. Of the $2.9 million in deposits held by the bank at the time of its failure, only $1.8 million in dividends were declared, with strict time limits on when they could be claimed. Comptroller John Jay Knox Jr. (1872–1884), who had overseen Meigs's examination of the bank, prepared the final two dividends. For the rest of the century, successive Comptrollers, acting formally as Commissioner of the Freedman's Savings and Trust Company, urged Congress that, in Knox's words, "it would be little more than just for Congress to make an appropriation for the payment in full of all the creditors . . . instead of allowing them to lose 40 per cent of the scanty means which they had deposited." Congress had plainly failed to supervise the Freedman's Bank, and the federal government, a line of Comptrollers argued, should stand behind the deposits.[11]

With the end of Reconstruction and the rise of Jim Crow, these arguments went nowhere. Rather, by the end of the nineteenth century, fully administrative supervision became yet another institution bent on curtailing economic opportunities for freed people, by excluding them—as proprietors and participants—from the banking system.[12]

3

Competition and Crisis
in the Gilded Age

IN DECEMBER 1872, England's *The Economist* magazine, under the editorial
pen of Walter Bagehot, observed that while "our own [banking] act of 1844
deals only with currency, the American legislators [in 1864] were more ambitious. They seem to have reasoned that an important object was to have sound
banking as well as good currency." Discretionary federal oversight was the key
to this second ambition, yet stubborn geographic impediments, poor pay,
official corruption, and undetectable fraud by turns constrained and delegitimized the supervisory project. By the 1870s, renewed hostility to activist government under the framework of legal formalism cast definite limits on official
discretion, limits which federal officials often imposed on themselves. Supervision's survival required restraint and redirection. After John Jay Knox
Jr. (1872–1884), Comptrollers promoted a corporatist oversight regime where
public officials would collect information and exercise real power only in cases
of absolute necessity—essentially, total bank failure. The responsibility for risk
management prior to failure would shift much more emphatically to bank directors, managers, and shareholders, with coordinated oversight from institutions like the New York Clearinghouse.[1]

Federal officials retreated from discretion as the American banking and currency systems underwent a fundamental change. Already by the 1860s, when
the experiment in federal bank supervision launched, bank deposits held within
banks, rather than notes held outside banks, were increasingly the dominant
source of bank liabilities, bank profits, and public money. In the interests of
good currency, federal supervision was meant to police banks' note issuance.
The growth of deposit banking raised new questions about both the purpose
of public supervision and the capabilities of private risk management to protect

not only the interests of noteholders but also the interests of depositors. The problem was not only that depositor protection looked different from note-holder protection. The bigger issue was that while only national banks could issue banknotes, national and state banks could create deposit liabilities. Federal bank supervisors had almost zero insight into the workings of these state-chartered institutions: In an important sense, state banks were shadow banks to the national authorities (and vice versa).

No insight, but still major responsibility. Through reserve and correspondent balances, bankers (state and national) held deposits of other banks (state and national), integrating bank balance sheets into a nationally interconnected system with disjointed supervisory oversight. In good times, deposits and monetary integration promoted liquidity, inter-regional payments, and economic growth. In bad times, they provided deadly vectors of financial contagion.

The period from the end of the Civil War through the beginning of the Wilson administration is often styled "the Gilded Age," in Mark Twain's turn of phrase. What was not gilded was the incessant financial panics that spread through this brittle and uneven system. The rise of deposits and the episodic financial panics that rocked the Gilded Age financial system encouraged the emergence of new risk management frameworks that at times complemented, and at other times competed with, the Comptroller's chartering and corporate governance model. State governments reemerged as significant players in bank chartering and bank oversight. Populist reformers took up deposit insurance, a risk management regime with antebellum roots, and initiated a sustained debate about the relationship between deposit security and bank runs. Building on the English experience of central banking, meanwhile, the New York Clearinghouse Association and its peer clearinghouses in other cities developed modes of decentralized central banking, coordinating private action to provide liquidity in times of panic. Central banking had an even more private orientation than the Comptroller's corporate governance, yet in its American instantiation, it suffered from coordination problems among self-interested and self-preservationist banks. Through these changes, the Comptroller did not remain static but experimented with information gathering and forbearance as tools that would enable federal supervisors to improve bank performance in good times and preserve sound institutions in bad.

This fragmented supervision—not only between public and private actors but across national and state lines—failed the nation during these critical decades. Risks crossed boundaries where risk managers could not. As the drumbeat of financial panic thumped louder with each successive crisis and each successive decade, federal officials and financial reformers alike recognized that the federal government remained politically responsible for the fate and function of the financial system. Where Knox had hoped to push the management of that residual risk back to the private sector, the public and their politicians—and very often the bankers too—refused to ratify that change. After the Panic of 1907, the public would seek to reassert control.

The Millionaires' Panic of 1884

Among the many Gilded Age banking panics, the one in 1884 was a modest affair, "a panic of the millionaires and the stock gamblers," a contemporary observed. The fact that it was modest was owed to decisive supervisory action, led in the first instance by national bank examiner Augustus M. Scriba (appointed the year before at the request of "every New York banking institution"), whose public power was backstopped by the private balance sheet of the New York Clearinghouse.[2]

The trouble began with the failure of the Marine National Bank on Tuesday, May 6, and with it the associated brokerage, Grant & Ward. The bank's president, James D. Fish, was a partner in the brokerage. Ferdinand Ward, a self-styled "young Napoleon of finance," led the brokerage and was a director of the bank. Ward speculated fervently and recklessly. By early May, he had overdrawn his accounts, and the bank had illegally certified his checks as secure (former President Ulysses S. Grant, who lent his name to the firm, disavowed involvement, though the failure humiliated and impoverished him). When the New York Clearinghouse demanded that the Marine Bank settle its $555,000 balance on the morning of May 6, Fish ordered the bank to close. Forlorn depositors watched as the porter rolled down the heavy iron shutters. Within two hours of the Marine Bank closing, Scriba was on the scene, running briskly up the steps and lodging himself in the bank. Although depositors hoped for some recovery, Scriba declared the bank "hopelessly insolvent" on Sunday, May 11. Two days later, the Comptroller appointed a receiver.[3]

The quick fall of the Marine Bank and the collapse of Grant & Ward set off tremors throughout New York's financial sector. Stock prices fell over the next few days, exposing many brokers who had speculated on borrowed funds, thus exposing their bankers too. Attention turned to the Second National Bank and John C. Eno, its young president. Eno, "the principal customer of half a dozen houses in the Street," was a major player in railroad stocks. Rumors circulated that Eno had taken and lost more than $2 million of the Second National's funds. On Wednesday, May 14, press accounts confirmed these speculations. The stock exchange was overrun. Seven brokerage firms suspended; with these suspensions came new pressure on the banks. "One of the ugly features of the day was the ruthless manner with which the names of banks were bandied about," the *New York Times* reported on May 15. "Scarcely a bank within a radius of half a mile of the Stock Exchange escaped suspicion."[4]

As depositors lined up outside the Second National and brokers panicked on the stock exchange floor, Wall Street's collective suspicion fell heaviest on the Metropolitan National Bank. Not only was the bank's president, George I. Seney, a well-known speculator, his sons were partners in one of the failed brokerages. Facing a $576,000 clearinghouse balance he could not meet, Seney closed the Metropolitan on his own initiative. "Then," the *Commercial and Financial Chronicle* reported, "the wildest kind of panic raged."[5]

What is remarkable about the Panic of 1884 is that it flared hot and cooled nearly as quickly once the clanky, public-private supervisory system lurched into motion. Scriba's work on the frenzied day of Wednesday, May 14, began at the Second National. The bank's problem was simple: Corporate governance failures had enabled John Eno, a dandy and a crook, to loot the bank. With the sure knowledge that Scriba would close the Second National if it could not meet the urgent demands of its creditors, the board of directors—and primarily John Eno's father, Amos R. Eno—shouldered not only their legal obligations but "their entire moral responsibility." When Second National opened to lines of fearful depositors, Amos Eno "stood up like an old Roman," and declared, "a million today and a million a day for a fortnight, if it is necessary."[6]

Scriba, on site for Eno's grandiose commitments, placed federal authority behind the private promise to recapitalize the bank. With private funding assured, Scriba pasted a note to the bank's front doors: "After an investigation of this bank I am satisfied that it is in a perfectly sound and solvent condition." To the crowds gathered outside, however, bank supervisory assurances alone carried little weight. "The lines of panic-stricken depositors never wavered," the *Times* reported. Only cash in hand—funds Scriba relied on Amos Eno to provide, since he had nothing of the kind to offer—could subdue the run. Fortunately for Scriba (and Second National's depositors), Eno the Elder delivered. As depositors looked on, two express wagons unloaded $1,700,000 in coin and currency. By the next day the run was over.[7]

Having dealt with the Marine and Second National banks, Scriba turned to the larger and more important Metropolitan. The failure of the Marine and the near failure of the Second National made the panic a New York City affair. These were local banks engaged in local business. The Metropolitan National Bank, by contrast, was a major correspondent bank and held the deposits of bank customers throughout the country. Metropolitan was a systemically important financial institution. As a key node in the national banking system that anchored the nation's payment infrastructure in the New York money market, the Metropolitan's suspension threatened to spread financial contagion across the country.

Again, Scriba was on the scene, taking possession of the Metropolitan Bank early the same afternoon. The following day, May 15, he declared the bank solvent. And with that, the panic was over.[8]

Scriba moved fast. He used his discretionary authority—authority to close banks if necessary—to encourage equally prompt private action. And it was this private action, shaped but not directed by public authority, which ended the Panic of 1884. The same day that Scriba took possession of the Metropolitan Bank, the New York Clearinghouse met and agreed to issue loan certificates against the sound assets of its members, enabling them to convert sound, illiquid assets into a money equivalent. The Clearinghouse's action gave broad assurance that all major New York banks would be liquid and able to pay out any deposit claim. The Clearinghouse also focused specific attention on the Metropolitan. Around 3:00 P.M., a team of Clearinghouse examiners arrived at the bank and confirmed what Scriba had already discovered: The Metropolitan was embarrassed but not insolvent. After midnight, the committee publicly declared that the Clearinghouse would fully back the bank.[9]

The next morning, it was Scriba who informed customers that the bank would open at noon. "I'll take full responsibility," he said. "The bank is all right now." It was, however, the Clearinghouse's support, not Scriba's, that made the difference. "The Clearing House settled the business," Scriba explained to reporters after the bank had reopened. "The bank resumes business now backed by the New York Clearing House Association." Again, private liquidity, not public assurances, ended the panic.[10]

Bank Supervision in the Age of Deposits

Brief and sharp, the Panic of 1884 was at once a victory for corporatist supervision and a portend of greater trouble to come. Scriba used his public authority to threaten, coax, and legitimize, thus giving a public face to decisive private action. This was by design. Corporate governance and private networks remained the ruling risk management framework of the Gilded Age, with public officials working offstage, if they were relevant at all. After the panic, Comptroller Henry W. Cannon (1884–1886) emphasized that federal officials had not been surprised by the banks' troubles: "Many of the transactions of the national banks which failed . . . were looked upon with disfavor, and that these associations . . . had been frequently reprimanded for irregularities." Absent clear insolvency, however, the Comptroller could—and would—do little more than reprimand. Bank directors held ultimate responsibility for monitoring their firms, a point Cannon underscored. "Bank failures are not so much due to the inadequacy of the law as to the failure on the part of the directors to maintain a proper supervision of the affairs of their associations and of the conduct of their officers."[11]

What saved the banking system, though, was not only private risk management through corporate governance but especially that same risk management through the Clearinghouse. "The New York Banks . . . are the last resort of this whole nation," George S. Coe, president of the American Exchange Bank, reflected after the crisis. Without Clearinghouse support, "a general financial and commercial derangement" would have prevailed "throughout the country." Coe knew of what he wrote. As the de facto leader of the Clearinghouse from around 1860 to 1890, Coe guided the New York banking community toward a shared understanding of mutual responsibility, especially in times of crisis. In this framework, the Clearinghouse provided America's answer to the Bank of England, offering central banking on decentralized principles.[12]

This combination of individual and mutual private responsibility, coupled with the public information-gathering and legal power of the Comptroller, formed the basis of the corporatism of bank supervision in the Gilded Age. The Comptroller did not provide the "fostering care of the government," as one of Cannon's predecessors described the new federal supervisory regime; the Comptroller was a partner, often a junior one, in a maturing public-private system.[13]

The Panic of 1884, however, hinted at troubles to come, linked to two interrelated problems which would magnify in succeeding decades. First, the national banking system's reserve city pyramid was exceedingly delicate. In good times, reserves and payments could flow quickly through an interconnected financial system. In bad times, as Coe recognized, the failure of any New York reserve bank, like the Metropolitan, could cripple its interior correspondents, causing "calamity of widespread dimensions." Such a failure—or its threat—caused cascading responses. The risk of losing access to their reserves encouraged interior banks to run on all the reserve banks at once. Only decisive action from the Clearinghouse could keep payments flowing and halt such contagion.[14]

Retail deposits posed a second, distinct but related problem, revealed by the Second National Bank run. Under the National Banking Acts, U.S. bonds held by the Comptroller provided security for national bank noteholders. Depositors enjoyed no such protection. They had to rely on assets inside of banks, and once these were exhausted, on shareholder liability. As deposits became a larger proportion of bank liabilities, these backstops—impossible for depositors to evaluate and always incomplete—became woefully insufficient. Depositors had to trust bank officers and that trust could vanish quickly. Amos Eno and his directors agreed to shoulder "their entire moral responsibility," but it was a legal and financial one too—only cash on hand, whether from bank assets or shareholder liability, could keep the Second National open.[15]

The growth of deposits—as interbank balances and as household and business savings—fundamentally altered nineteenth-century banking and the structure of the U.S. money supply. In the broadest sense, rising deposits reflected growing national wealth, which Americans chose to save within banks rather than as cash or other assets outside of them. More importantly for federal supervisors, by the early 1880s, it was no longer profitable for national banks to issue banknotes. National banks had to back their notes with U.S. bonds held by the Comptroller. With the gradual resumption of the gold standard in the 1870s, the United States experienced significant and continuous deflation. Bond prices rose, so that bonds eventually cost more to purchase than they could generate in lendable currency.[16]

Instead of handing notes across the counter, banks made loans by crediting borrowers' checking accounts. Borrowers could then write checks against deposit money *within* the bank rather than spending cash that circulated outside of it. As a result, deposits increased steadily, both absolutely and in relation to bank capital. In 1867, there were roughly $1.70 in deposits for every dollar of circulating currency (specie, greenbacks, and banknotes). By 1890, the figure reached $5 to $1. By 1914, there were more than $10 in deposits of every dollar in currency. Even as debates about the substance and value of American currency raged—first between greenbacks and gold, and then between gold and silver—deposits quietly became the primary form of American money.[17]

Deposits inside of banks were convertible into physical currency, but the two types of money were not equivalent. Physical currency was finite, limited to coin and paper notes. Deposits, however, could and did grow much larger than the stock of physical money. Banks created deposits through lending, generating an asset (the loan) and a liability (the deposit) simultaneously. Interconnectedness created greater systemic risks, as deposits of one bank were the assets of another, and then the liabilities of still others. The expansion of interconnected credit money through lending (good lending, bad lending, ugly lending—it made no difference) could fuel economic growth, while the rise of deposits encouraged greater financial integration and interconnection among bank balance sheets. Money traversed the country, not as physical notes backed by U.S. bonds but as balance sheet notations inside the banks themselves.[18]

The immateriality of deposits created another key vector of bank runs, since depositors could—and, when spooked, did—demand their money in hard cash. During periods of high activity, like crop-moving season, the need to convert deposits to cash at scale strained the banking system. During panics, all bets were off. When depositors rushed to convert plentiful, immaterial deposits into scarce, material currency, the system could come crashing down.[19]

The rise of deposits coincided with important changes in the banking system and larger economy. During the late nineteenth century, the United States gradually evolved from a commercial economy, which thrived on trade and grew by expanding the reach and scope of markets, to an industrial economy, which grew through intensification and expanding use of capital. Congress had designed the national banking system to facilitate commerce. In line with the prevailing banking theory, known now as the "real bills doctrine," banks existed to provide short-term credit to finance real transactions, bridging production and sale, or transit and sale. Industrial firms, by contrast, required long-term financing and working capital over an indefinite horizon. The agricultural economy, moreover, continued to expand; the National Banking Acts, which prohibited loans secured by real estate, had never been a good match for the needs of farmers. Thus, the ideas of what constituted sound banking and appropriate bank assets—embodied in law and encouraged by supervisors—gradually diverged from the needs of the U.S. economy and the actual practices of the nation's banks.[20]

Writing in 1884, in the aftermath of panic and amid these tumultuous economic changes, Cannon grappled with the transformation of American banking by reflecting on the relationship between bank lending, bank failure, and supervisory oversight. Within the note-issue paradigm that ruled when the National Banking Acts became law, earlier Comptrollers like Hugh McCulloch

(1863–1865) had conceptualized bank failure as a species of bank fraud, which threatened public confidence in the nation's sovereign currency—the notes issued by national banks. Banks that adhered to the real bills doctrine by making only self-liquidating loans tied to real commercial transactions should not have been able to fail. Fraud or improper lending needed to be afoot. By 1884, this association of fraud and failure was clearly incomplete. Cannon stated what was then obvious: It wasn't the fraudsters that should cause supervisors the most concern; the honest and incompetent or unlucky could bring down a bank just as quickly. Banks failed because of "injudicious banking, bad management, or adventurous speculation." If bank failure was not de facto fraud, and if individual bank failure threatened, through the reserve system, to ignite general panic, what could and should federal supervisors do? Cannon was perplexed. "The exact line at which the Government shall interfere and the point at which Government discipline shall commence is a matter of some delicacy to determine," Cannon lamented.[21]

Cannon had clear ideas for how to address the "delicacy," but the available solutions did not align with the Comptroller's understanding of the public role in financial risk management. If injudicious bank lending caused bank failure, he reasoned, then national bank examiners might do more to monitor national bank lending. Cannon, who favored private risk management over public control, raised the idea only to dismiss it. With "more than $1,240,000,000" in aggregate loans and discounts in the national banking system, there were simply too many assets for public supervisors to monitor. "It is of course not the province of the bank examiners to supervise the making of these loans," Cannon explained. This admission was an obvious extension of the corporate governance framework: Bankers had to manage their own risks, not turn to the government to do so.[22]

Cannon was motivated by more than a desire to keep risk, finance, and control all in the same private hands. Even if federal officials could monitor bank lending, he emphasized, it was against their interests to do so. "It is well known," Cannon wrote, "that banking can be carried on under the laws of most of the States of the Union with but very little interference and scarcely any espionage on the part of the officials of the State government." If bankers were unhappy with invasive federal oversight, they could seek a state charter instead, continuing to generate risks for the nation's banking system even as they sat outside the corporatist risk management framework and the Comptroller's field of view.[23]

Alternative Risk Management Paradigms

In choosing to restrain the role of federal risk management rather than expand it, officials in the Comptroller's office opened the door to new risk management alternatives, both competitive and complementary to their oversight. First, because banks could generate profits without issuing notes, state chartering emerged as a viable competitor to national banking (despite the expressed hopes that the National Banking Acts would extinguish state banks). As a result, state-level supervision reemerged as a competing risk management ecosystem. Second, because deposits, rather than bond-backed notes, made up a larger proportion of bank liabilities (and thus the money supply), populists and other activists sought federal protection of depositors comparable to federal protection of noteholders. Third, as the linchpin of the reserve system, the New York Clearinghouse had asserted its dominance in the immediate postbellum period as a key institution in the management of systemic risk. Over succeeding decades, other cities created their own clearinghouses, which facilitated payments, enhanced system liquidity, supervised their state and federal members, and served as lenders of last resort. They did so for the primary benefit of their paying members, not for the overall banking system.[24]

That is not to say that federal supervision in the 1880s and 1890s stood still. Most powerfully in that institutional evolution, and despite Cannon's insistence that federal examiners could not supervise bank lending, supervisory loan evaluation emerged as a potent instrument in the toolbox of national bank examiners. The Comptroller's emphasis on loan criticism, in turn, cemented federal supervision's role as an information regime of socializing insights about loan quality rather than an enforcement regime meant to shutter misbehaving banks. In this era, the supervisory charge was to guide and forbear, not discipline and punish.

State Chartering

As Secretary of the Treasury during the Civil War, Salmon P. Chase set out to destroy the state banking system and return sovereignty over the nation's money supply to the federal government by taxing state banknotes. This worked to a point: By 1870, there were more national banks than there had been state banks at the start of the Civil War. Meanwhile, less than 20 percent of antebellum state banks remained in operation under their state charters. State banks, however, were poised to make a sweeping return. The transition

from note-issue to deposit banking, combined with lower capital requirements, wider investment privileges, and sometimes less rigorous supervision,
all made state charters appealing for financial entrepreneurs. Where the national banking system grew through mere addition in the late nineteenth
century, state banks multiplied, doubling from 1870 to 1880, and then almost
tripling in each successive decade from 1880 to 1910. In 1880, there were 620
state-chartered banks. In 1910, there were more than 12,000.[25]

The reemergence of state chartering undermined rigorous charter vetting
as a viable supervisory tool. To protect the new national banking system
against speculation and fraud, McCulloch and the early Comptrollers evaluated charter applications against formal legal rules and pursued extralegal inquiry into the reputations and prospects of would-be bankers. Facing renewed
state competition, later Comptrollers disclaimed chartering discretion almost
entirely. "The Comptroller has no discretionary power," Knox explained in
1881, "but must necessarily sanction . . . such associations as shall have con-
formed in all respects to the legal requirements."[26]

Knox's repudiation of supervisory discretion, consistent with his larger
effort to shift responsibility onto private entrepreneurs, demonstrated the
evolutionary backpedal of "desupervision," abandoning discretion for the
predictable, self-implementation of fixed rules. Comptrollers maintained
the rhetorical commitment to free federal chartering until the next century
and, in the face of state competition, urged Congress to reduce the national
bank chartering requirements. In 1900, Congress obliged with the Gold
Standard Act, which, among other provisions, substantially reduced the
capital needed to organize a national bank, especially in rural areas. The
number of national banks doubled in the decade after enactment, but state
banks expanded faster still.[27]

Nevertheless, even as state competition restrained supervision through
chartering and led to a liberalization in national chartering standards, it did
not simply create a race to the bottom or, as a later Comptroller would term
it, a "competition in laxity." In a world of deposit banking, state officials recognized that depositors and bank counterparties needed confidence in bank
safety and soundness. That confidence rested on credible oversight. States,
therefore, experimented with new strategies and supervisory tools. They developed professional supervisory institutions, paid examiners fixed salaries
rather than intermittent fees, and examined banks frequently. States also gave
their supervisory officials more power to force intermediate corrections, enabling them to order "discontinuance of unsafe and unsound practices" rather

than bluntly closing banks. In short, bank failure held political risks for state officials too, and they reached for public power to prevent it.[28]

In places, these powers exceeded those granted to the Comptroller, but this wasn't quite a race to the top either. It was a race for charters. In some cases, bankers would seek credible supervision. In others, bankers would seek different benefits, including relative freedom to pursue their interests as they saw fit. Financial, organizational, and legal innovation ensured that the variety of banking organizations that proliferated within the United States at the turn of the twentieth century was dizzying in its complexity. In all of this, state banks remained outside the bounds of federal supervision, a shadow system of financial risks that the Comptroller could neither see nor shape.[29]

Deposit Guarantee

The opacity the defined the Comptroller's (non)relationship to state banks was also a central and destabilizing feature of depositors' relationships to the banking system overall. Banknotes, secured by U.S. bonds, enjoyed transparent protection, while depositors had to rely on the value of bank assets and the wealth of bank shareholders to secure their claims. Yet depositors had, at best, limited means of evaluating these safety measures. The supervisory system was structured as a dialogue between examiners and bank managers and was not geared toward instilling depositor confidence beyond an occasional certification of solvency (communicated privately to bank managers, not depositors).

Following the Panic of 1884, populist politicians began to argue that the lack of security of bank deposits vis-à-vis banknotes created financial instability by encouraging bank runs. At any hint of danger, depositors would rush to convert insecure deposits into secure cash—potentially destroying the bank and the value of their deposits in the process. The solution, populists insisted, was to provide an equally robust federal deposit guarantee and, in doing so, fulfil the National Banking Acts' original promise of securing the national money supply. One proposal, introduced in Congress in 1886, called for a fund that, in the case of bank failure, would convert deposits nearly instantaneously into notes, thus forestalling runs by ensuring depositor savings would not be lost or tied up in long liquidations. With this security, former Iowa Governor Samuel Merrill predicted, "panics would pass into history, and become subjects for novel-writers as things in 'times of old.'"[30]

Deposit guarantee proposals, which sought to collectivize financial risk, stood in stark opposition to the prevailing corporatist framework, which privileged individualism and risk-taking as the heart of the nineteenth-century economy. A federal deposit guarantee, the *Chicago Tribune* opined, would "deaden the sense of responsibility" among bank management and "lead to a relaxing of the vigilance of directors and officers." Individuals needed to safeguard themselves. "Depositors in National banks are of a class who ought to be able to watch their interests."[31]

Underlying these arguments was the hotly disputed question of where run risk came from. Bankers and their allies, unable to protect depositors, blamed them for feeding the flames of panic, often pitting the self-possessed, responsible depositor against his feminized, hysterical counterpart who would line up at the first sign of trouble. When depositors ran on the Second National Bank, the *New York Times* reported, "the women outnumbered the men two to one." They "pushed past the big policemen with gentle but resistless force."[32]

Comptrollers initially embraced this view, but their thinking evolved as deposits became the dominant form of bank liabilities. Following bank runs during the Panic of 1893, Comptroller James H. Eckles (1893–1897) blamed the national depression on the "panic-stricken depositors." In reform debates that followed the panic, however, Comptroller Charles G. Dawes (1898–1901) came to different conclusions. Depositors should expect the same security as noteholders, Dawes reasoned, though he did not call for a federal deposit guarantee. Instead, Dawes insisted that public supervision should orient more fully toward depositor protection. "The detection of untrustworthiness in banks is, as a matter of fact, not one of the duties with which the depositor . . . charges himself," Dawes argued. Rather, "he has come to leave that to the officials of the National and State Governments." In taking up the cause of depositors, Dawes participated in the gradual reconceptualization of supervision as depositor protection, both in the interests of depositors and in the interests of the banking system to which they posed an acute systemic risk. Without new tools to make that commitment more than rhetorical, however, depositor protection would continue to rest on the foundation of corporatist risk management.[33]

Clearinghouses

Agitation for deposit insurance reflected the growing importance of deposit liabilities for national and competing state banks, growth facilitated by the nationwide expansion of the fully private city clearinghouses. Clearinghouses existed primarily to settle interbank claims, such as drafts and checks, without recourse to cash. As bank customers sent and received payments to other bank customers using these media, bankers aggregated and then netted out claims against each other in the clearinghouse, settling any outstanding balances by a fixed time each business day. Claims tended to offset, with no permanent net creditor or debtor when the system functioned well. In this way, clearing-houses also reduced the risk of loss from theft. As a Washington, DC, banker explained on the founding of that city's clearinghouse in May 1887, "each bank saves itself the risk of loss or robbery resulting from the sending of its messengers from bank to bank," laden with cash and coin.[34]

Over the nineteenth century, clearinghouses multiplied, largely following the trends of urbanization and industrialization which were reshaping the United States. In 1870, there were only twelve clearinghouses, mostly clustered in the Northeast and Midwest. By 1905, there were 103, representing most major cities, as well as far-flung communities like Helena, Montana, and Beaumont, Texas. Clearinghouses vastly simplified and expedited interbank payments, encouraging depositors to use checks in lieu of cash for local transactions. Comptrollers supported and promoted these institutions. "Over ninety per cent of all business transactions in the United States, accomplished through banks, are represented by credits," Comptroller A. Barton Hepburn (1892–1893) observed approvingly in 1893. "The Clearing-House affords the most remarkable instance of the extent to which a simple device of bookkeeping can minimize the use of money."[35]

Centralized clearing made payments more efficient and reduced the risk of theft, but it introduced the potential for deeper systemic instabilities. By making transactions easier, clearinghouses encouraged more transactions. When markets were stable, such improvements in the payment system created more liquidity and encouraged greater economic activity. Greater local liquidity also encouraged the geographic integration of capital markets across the United States, so that banks in clearinghouse cities participated in deeper correspondent networks, holding reserves, collecting claims, and brokering transactions with banks in other parts of the country.[36]

This is how clearinghouses worked in good times; in bad times, the clearing-house system became very bad indeed. Clearinghouses increased liquidity while also increasing liquidity risk, especially within the context of a banking system that hitched the cyclical financing needs of the agricultural economy to the speculative financial activity of Wall Street through the pyramiding of bank reserves in New York City. When trouble emerged—on Wall Street or on Main Street—clearinghouses increased the speed and scale of bank runs. The Panic of 1884 demonstrated the risk. The Marine and the Metropolitan shut their doors in the face of large clearinghouse deficits. When banks couldn't meet their obligations, the clearinghouse, either as individual creditors or the institution as a whole, was on the hook.[37]

To mitigate these risks, clearinghouses performed two primary supervisory functions over the national and state banks that comprised their membership. First, through their daily operations, clearinghouses centralized the private, counterparty supervision that remained an essential element of individual bank risk management. Daily transactions gave banks a clear sense of their peers' positions. When a bank failed to consistently meet its obligations or called on the clearinghouse for support, as the Metropolitan did in 1884, clearinghouses employed a second tool: examination. In the nineteenth century, this function remained ad hoc, performed by clearinghouse bankers when a member bank appeared to be in trouble. After the Panic of 1907, many clearinghouses institutionalized examination by hiring salaried examiners. Systemically important clearinghouses also shaped government oversight— recall that the Comptroller allowed New York and Boston clearinghouses to select the national bank examiner assigned to their respective cities.[38]

Clearinghouses could also, as epitomized by New York, act as lenders of last resort by pooling member resources and using the clearinghouse's balance sheet to convert illiquid assets into liquid funds during times of financial stress. This was not a permanent solution, however, because clearinghouses performed this role inconsistently and selectively. Clearinghouses established high barriers to entry, which excluded some national and many state banks from membership. In turn, they only provided direct protection for banks in their circle, protection often further contingent on the position of the bank. Systemically important banks, like the Metropolitan, got help. Lesser firms, like the Marine and Second National, faced their fates alone. Banks that were not members, while still subject to liquidity risk when the system strained, could make no claim for clearinghouse assistance. Ultimately, clearinghouses, as private and decentralized risk management networks, operated in the interests of their members and at arm's length from public authority. Like state supervision, the clearinghouses generated and managed risks that enriched and endangered the national banking system, even as the Comptroller remained on the outside, not even looking in.[39]

Supervisory Evolution and Experimentation
Under Resource Constraint

With the reemergence of state chartering and the expansion of clearinghouses, together with the accelerating transition from banknotes to deposits, federal supervisors struggled to identify tools that would enable them to proactively manage the nation's growing financial risks. Comptrollers continued to insist on a highly rigid, regularized system of supervision that lacked much governmental discretion. Bank supervisors were, Comptroller Edward S. Lacy (1889–1892) remarked, "mainly charged with the responsibility of indicating to bank managers what they shall not do." Supervisors could mark out the boundaries of the law but had few corrective options if bankers stepped over the line. They could, in limited circumstances, bar a bank from paying dividends. Otherwise, the only punishment for violating the National Banking Acts was the revocation of a bank's charter. Or, as Comptroller William B. Ridgely (1901–1908) put it, "there is no punishment but death, even for misdemeanors."[40]

At the same time, bank examiners continued to be paid on a fixed fee-per-examination basis, limiting their capacity to work cooperatively with bankers to improve bank performance. Examiners, in short, could not afford to spend sufficient time in banks. In 1892, there were 42 national bank examiners and 3,759 national banks, 89.5 banks per examiner. As Comptroller Dawes complained to Congress in 1900, "the amount allowed an examiner for the examination of smaller banks is not sufficient to compensate him for the time necessary." The numbers only got worse. In 1903, Ridgely reported, the bureau's 75 examiners performed 10,914 examinations, or 145 per examiner. In 1905, 78 examiners performed 11,716 examinations; 150 each. The outcome was obvious to all involved. "The present system," Dawes continued, "encourages to too great an extent superficiality in examinations, and interferes greatly with the proper and wise apportionment of time of examiners among the different banks."[41]

It is difficult to discern a century later which of these factors—limited examiner time, limited legal remedies, and a strict formalist vision of supervision—most drove Comptrollers' retreat from supervisory discretion. It is not clear that they knew. Whatever the reason or combination of reasons, by the end of the nineteenth century, Comptrollers continued to lean more heavily on corporate governance and stockholder liability to manage bank risk and much less on a discretionary model of bank supervision.

This model of supervision-by-regulation did not mean that the Comptroller would give up discretionary oversight entirely. Instead, the federal officials continued to develop an evolving informational regime of supervision through examinations, call reports, and correspondence with banks. Supervision generated insights into individual bank practices, maintained continuous records of those practices, and conveyed relevant information about those practices to bank boards. The Comptroller thus cultivated an information model of risk management, not an action model.

The evolution of loan evaluation demonstrates this information model in practice. In their work as charter enforcers, national bank examiners valued bank assets to determine whether a bank's capital was impaired, barring it from paying dividends, or whether it was insolvent, necessitating closure. Yet such valuations proved difficult, as they involved significant judgment about the underlying quality of borrowers, bankers, and local economic (and even political) conditions. "As a rule," Lacy explained in 1891, "examiners find the greatest difficulty in . . . ascertain[ing] whether or not impairment or insolvency exists." To guide examiners, Lacy amended the examination forms in the early 1890s to include a final "recapitulation" section, which called on examiners to consolidate a list of problematic assets and provide an estimate of the "probable loss" arising from banking activities.[42]

The small change altered both the kinds of information examiners collected and how the Comptroller's office used that information to engage with bank boards. Recapitulation formalized the appraisal and categorization of assets, encouraging examiners to consider the *quality* of bank assets, not just their *legality*. Before this change, examiners focused their criticisms on loans that violated provisions of the National Banking Acts, particularly those that exceeded 10 percent of bank capital. Recapitulation, in a sense, arose from that same compliance function: As a blunt enforcement device, recapitulation enabled examiners to add up losses, subtract them from capital and reserves, and thus determine solvency. Yet for most examiners, in most interactions with banks, the point of the exercise was improvement, not enforcement. Comptrollers and bankers recognized that, as one expert put it, "many bank failures are due to the gradual acquirement of undesirable assets." Recapitulation became a way of identifying those undesirable assets clearly and in one place, and then encouraging dialogue between supervisors and bankers as assets moved on and off the list with each examination. Thus, although Comptroller Cannon argued in 1884 that it would be inappropriate and, as a practical matter, impossible for examiners to enforce good bank-lending decisions, by the turn of the century, examiners used loan categorization and recapitulation to do just that.[43]

The Persistence of Panic

Had these emergent risk management frameworks—state bank examiners, loan criticism and evaluation, robust clearinghouses—spelled the end of the bank failures and financial panics that motivated them, the financial and political history of the United States would have unfolded very differently. The deposit revolution and the changes it abetted, however, introduced systemic risks into the banking system that at once crossed over the fragmented risk management institutions and grew asymmetrically in relation to the power of those institutions—acting either (more often) individually or (less often) collectively—to manage. By the early twentieth century, federal bank examiners' reliance on bank shareholder liability and the balance sheets of clearinghouses was no longer sustainable. More deposits meant that individual banks were riskier in relation to their shareholder's liability. Clearinghouses encouraged deposit growth, which increased system liquidity in good times but could offer only inadequate protection for their own members when times were decidedly not good (never mind what they offered nonmembers). As the scale and scope of panics increased, Comptrollers tried to harness their powers, especially new information about bank asset quality, to forestall banking panics. Ultimately, the inability to make deposits secure or—barring that—to convert unsecured deposits into secure cash only encouraged depositors to run faster. In rapid succession, three crises—1890, 1893, and 1907—revealed the risk management inadequacies of the national banking system, the federalist dual banking system, and the clearinghouses' private supervision. Corporatist supervision was broken. After 1907, although there was a cacophony of views on what should succeed it, there was unison on that central point.

1890

The Panic of 1890 followed a similar pattern to that of 1884. Monetary stringency tied to foreign gold exports and autumn crop-moving strained financial markets from August through mid-September. The Treasury intervened by buying bonds until mid-October, which eased the monetary pressure by injecting cash into the New York money market. After that, foreign sales of U.S. stocks and the contraction of the call loan market drove the prices of U.S. securities down below the 1884 trough. On Tuesday, November 11, brokerage Decker, Howell, and Co. failed. "Away went the stock market tumbling," the *New York Times* reported.[44]

The market crash immediately cast doubt on several Clearinghouse member banks. Recognizing the danger, the Clearinghouse, led by George Coe and Chase National Bank president—and former Comptroller—Henry Cannon, authorized loan certificates the same day. "The radical action . . . brought new calm into Wall Street," the *Times* observed. The calm held until Saturday, November 15, when the English firm Baring Brothers & Co. collapsed. Panic selling resumed, but the Clearinghouse held firm, and so did the banks. The Bank of England swept in to rescue Barings, while the Boston and Philadelphia clearinghouses also issued loan certificates to aid specific firms. By the end of the week, the panic was largely over, reflecting the epitome of private success. The Comptroller was barely involved, just the way he liked it.[45]

1893

The system put in place through the Panics of 1873, 1884, and 1890 forestalled a test of the resilience of the American banking system, including whether and when the public would own the residual risks of that system in panic. That test came in 1893, and the system failed it.

Unlike previous Gilded Age panics, the epicenters of which tended to be Wall Street and the New York money market, the Panic of 1893 began in the interior. Overexpansion of railroads, crop and mercantile failures, and the declining price of silver all spelled trouble for "country" banks, especially in the South and West. Bank failures began in May (Chicago), and spread in June (Milwaukee, Los Angeles, and Detroit) and into July (Portland, Kansas City, Denver, and Louisville). Interior banks pulled reserves out of regional and New York City correspondents. The domino effect followed from there.[46]

At first, reserve banks, assisted by clearinghouses, met these demands, though the time it could take to ship currency from New York City to Denver might still spell doom for a bank besieged by depositors. In early August, however, New York banks suspended payment—they would not pay out deposits in cash—sending shock waves nationwide. "For weeks there was no rest, night or day," recalled Thomas P. Kane, deputy to Comptroller James Eckles who Grover Cleveland appointed on the eve of the crisis. "Every hour of the day and late into the night telegram after telegram was received announcing additional suspensions of banks or new complications which had to be promptly met." In all, 158 national banks closed, unable to meet their obligations. The Comptroller did not have enough staff to handle all the failures. Banks outside the national system fared worse; 415 state and private banks failed as well.[47]

As the crisis unfolded, city clearinghouses provided some assistance, but they were soon overwhelmed. As the panic escalated in June, East Coast clearinghouses, led by New York, authorized loan certificates to enable members to keep lending to solvent customers. The panic put those commitments to test, and the currency demands from the interior meant that New York reserve banks with large bankers' balances needed what the clearinghouses could not provide. The demand was for real currency—the so-called clearinghouse "scrip" would not do. Unlike in 1873, however, the New York Clearinghouse banks did not pool their reserves, and by August, many suspended cash payment (George Coe, near retirement and ill with pleurisy, could no longer command cooperation).[48]

Suspension, in turn, encouraged hoarding, further undermining system liquidity. In Chicago and Kansas City, national bank examiners asked the leading banks in the cities' clearinghouses to aid troubled members. The banks refused, citing their own poverty and distress. Worse, they stated publicly that they would not allow correspondent withdrawals, generating further momentum for hoarding. With no central institution strong enough and united enough to drive a collective strategy, individual banks pursued risk management as self-preservation to the distinct detriment of the nation's banking system.[49]

With the clearinghouse member banks attempting to fortify their individual balance sheets at the expense of systemic liquidity, the Comptroller faced the panic without the backstop of his private partners. Eckles resolved to use the tools available, relying on the Comptroller's accumulated information and newly rediscovered discretionary authority to push forbearance further than it had gone before. Eckles, Kane observed, "proposed to exercise to the fullest extent the discretion vested in him by law."[50]

In 1872, Comptroller Knox had extended some forbearance when the reserves of many New York banks fell below the legal mandates. In 1893, Eckles pushed further, choosing not to initiate receivership in cases where banks refused to pay depositors—that is, banks "suspended" redemption of deposit claims, normally an "act of insolvency" that would have required liquidation. Eckles recognized that many of these banks suspended not because they were insolvent, but because they were illiquid: They could not get cash to pay local depositors because their reserves were, in turn, locked in the vaults or accounted as ledger entries in other banks. Of the 158 national banks that closed their doors during the panic, ninety-three resumed business without official sanctions of any kind. This was forbearance on a grand, national scale.[51]

Despite the dubious legality, it was essentially the only discretionary policy lever Eckles could pull. As Eckles explained: "With a full knowledge of the general solvency of these institutions and the cause which brought about their suspension, the policy was inaugurated of giving all banks, which, under ordinary circumstances would not have closed, and whose management had been honest, an opportunity to resume business." This "full knowledge" came from the examination regime, and from the shelves of examiner reports and correspondence documenting the business of these banks. Sound before the panic, Eckles could have some confidence they would be sound afterward, so long as the economy didn't collapse entirely.[52]

In this way, forbearance built on the Comptroller's information regime in an attempt to forestall contagion, creating breathing room from frantic bank runs and avoiding messy and expensive receiverships that might put additional firms in jeopardy. The very fact that loan criticism and solvency determinations were so dependent on market prices and market dynamics meant that harsh conclusions became self-fulfilling, referenda not only on bad banks but a death sentence to the entire system. Eckles, through forbearance, was trying to forestall that outcome.

By reopening some banks while keeping others closed, the Comptroller appeared to exercise judgment. Yet forbearance could encourage banks to close preemptively, since liquidation was not automatic, which would likewise encourage depositors to run faster still to get their money out or forswear trusting money to banks in the first place. Most troubling of all, Comptrollers might forebear by keeping banks open, creating no discernable difference between the living and the walking dead.[53]

As in the 1870s, forbearance was a tool born of necessity and crisis, in this case the clearinghouses' failure to provide needed liquidity to the larger banking system. Unlike 1873, 1884, and 1890, the New York Clearinghouse faced internal fracture between local institutions and nationally focused reserve banks. As such, it could not pool member reserves internally, nor lead other clearinghouses to accept mutual responsibility. Self-preservation prevailed. Eckles, lacking tools to provide liquidity or provide any guarantee to depositors, used the information and power at his disposal to not make the crisis worse.

1907

The Panic of 1893 and the other financial cataclysms that followed turned what might have been a mild recession into a major depression. Indeed, before the extended recession of the 1930s co-opted the name, the Great Depression in American history referred to this critical decade of economic contraction, which lasted from 1893 to 1897. One practical legacy of this tumult was the election of 1896, a close-run affair that pitted ideological juggernauts against each other: the Great Commoner William Jennings Bryan who railed against the financial powers of eastern elites versus the quiet, amiable, mostly boring Ohio Governor William McKinley, who represented those elites exactly as they preferred. McKinley won, and it wasn't particularly close. As a result, the Panic of 1893 did not create momentum for any major changes to the laws and practices of American bank supervision.

Once economic growth resumed, the financial system grew apace, with much of that expansion coming outside the national banking system. In addition to the continued multiplication of small, state-chartered banks, a new type of urban institution emerged as an adjunct to securities markets: the trust company. Like commercial banks, trust companies were largely funded by deposits. Under permissive state laws, they enjoyed wide investment powers. These firms provided liquidity to the stock market but held meager reserves. By 1906, New York trust company lending was roughly equal to that of New York national banks. Trust companies represented a new source of systemic risk, by design outside the view of the Comptroller, and by choice beyond the reach of the New York Clearinghouse. In 1907, they ushered in yet another major panic.[54]

The Panic of 1907 began on the West Coast. The 1906 San Francisco earthquake triggered a major payout in insurance, causing the City of London (and the Bank of England) to react by pulling up interest rates in accordance with the demands of the global gold standard. Higher rates and economic headwinds created a drag on the U.S. economy throughout 1907, but the financial system, though nervy, remained resilient. Beginning on October 16, however, it all came crashing down. On that day, a long building effort to corner shares of United Copper Company by Charles W. Morse and F. Augustus Heinze collapsed. Morse and Heinze had built their stake on funds borrowed from banks and trust companies that Heinze controlled. When the corner collapsed, suspicion turned to these institutions.[55]

The New York Clearinghouse, somewhat chastened by its failures the decade before, stepped in immediately. It examined the troubled banks and certified many of them solvent and ready for business. Instead of circulating clearinghouse scrip, syndicates of clearinghouse members made loans directly to the banks affected by the collapse of copper stock on the condition that Heinze and his associates step down as directors. Here was powerful private supervision, which enabled the Clearinghouse to remake the banks while saving them. Over the following weeks, the New York Clearinghouse used the power of judgment backed by its balance sheet to make solvent banks liquid, ensuring that the banks would regain the market's confidence. Indeed, the Mercantile National Bank, formerly headed by Heinze, did so by offering its presidency to the Comptroller, William Ridgley (he declined).[56]

Whatever the state of the Clearinghouse's own self-supervision, the trust companies were outside of that perimeter. Overextended financiers, not merely those connected with the copper corner, were facing the same interest rate pressures that all global finance faced in the aftermath of the Bank of England's rate hikes. By October 21, depositor panic, which had focused on the Heinze-associated banks, turned now toward those trust companies that could not operate successfully in this new interest rate environment.[57]

At first, these trusts turned to the Clearinghouse for help. Having preserved its members, however, the New York Clearinghouse threw up a wall. The Knickerbocker Trust, the primary target of depositor runs, requested a loan. "It was decided that the advance of money for the protection of depositors is limited to its own members," the Clearinghouse determined. The next day, October 22, the Knickerbocker suspended, later failing outright. "The financial community," the *Chicago Tribune* reported, "is tonight standing on the precipice of doubt." Soon they tumbled over the edge. Trust companies with connections to the copper speculators lost 53 percent of their deposits in three months, while non-affiliated companies lost 23 percent. Faced with a vacuum of leadership, financier J. P. Morgan, with support from the U.S. Treasury, made emergency loans to the beleaguered trusts, shoring up the New York market.[58]

Nevertheless, banks in the interior, fearful that a panic in New York might cut off their access to their reserves, rapidly pulled their funds from New York banks, hastening the fulfillment of their dire prophecy. When the crisis shifted from specific institutions to general panic, the Clearinghouse again reverted to self-protection. Faced with heavy demands, the New York Clearinghouse issued loan certificates and suspended cash payment on October 26. Suspension and derangement rippled throughout the country. National banks and city clearinghouses followed New York's lead. Cash traded at a premium to deposit money and hoarding became widespread. Eventually clearinghouses and private firms issued substitute currencies. As the historian F. Cyril James remarked, "the banking system ceased to operate as an organized mechanism, and every city and township supplied its own circulating medium and its own financial facilities."[59]

In the face of the money panic, Comptroller Ridgely used what tools he had to make money available and to reassure depositors that the national banks were sound. In concert with the Treasury, Ridgley encouraged banks to free up and convert U.S. bonds into banknotes. Heeding Ridgely's call, banks deposited more bonds with the Comptroller, and by early November, Ridgely was issuing $1.5 million in national banknotes a day. Ridgely also marshalled his office's publicity machinery. On the advice of Chicago bankers, Ridgely delayed a scheduled call report in late October, which bankers feared would reveal their weakened reserve position. Ridgely then highlighted the report when it was published in December, hoping to draw attention to the improved position of the banks. He also simply stopped announcing national bank failures. Lacking the full machinery to stop bank panics using a public balance sheet, bank supervisors controlled the only tool they had—information, or its absence.[60]

Nevertheless, even these small actions overemphasize the Comptroller's constructive role. The Comptroller simply had too small a view of the financial system and too few tools to absorb its cascading risks. He also lacked legitimacy. The nephew of an Illinois senator, Ridgely was looking for an offramp. As the crisis raged, the media's interest in Ridgely focused not on his tools for calming the crisis but on which of the private sector bank presidencies he would accept when he retired. In the end, Ridgley could urge banks to resume, but it took months for the system to come back right, while credit remained scarce for months after that.[61]

Forward to Reform

The U.S. banking system tottered along in the Gilded Age like a drunk man confident in his ability to make it home while bystanders look away in embarrassment. The Panic of 1907 was, in a sense, the last time the bystanders would look without acting. The panic revealed the profound inadequacies of a supervisory system that was only equipped to observe, advise, advertise or fail to advertise information about banks rather than actually discipline them in good times or help them in bad.

The critical mismatch between the national banking system as a currency system, designed to provide a stable, bond-backed banknote currency, and as a banking system, which created flexible, insecure deposit money, had matured into a major problem of public policy and institutional design. Panic came when depositors—banks and trusts, big companies and small enterprises, wealthy individuals and ordinary citizens—could not convert those new (and growing) deposits into the old (and certain) currency. "Our bond-secured bank notes offer no help to a bank in any sudden call for deposits," Ridgely argued. "From their very nature they are fixed currency, issued on the secured-currency principle, as distinguished from the credit or banking principle."[62]

Comptrollers had been wrestling with this distinction, between the currency principle and the banking principle, since the founding of the national banking system. "It is impossible to apply safeguards to the currency," Comptroller Hiland R. Hulburd (1867–1872) wrote in 1869, "without applying prudence and reasonable restrictions to the business of lending." Deposits and notes, Ridgely argued, were and must be, in practice, the same thing. They should be "daily and hourly, if necessary, convertible from one to the other."[63]

But they weren't. Not even close. Private clearinghouses, Ridgley recognized, could not perform this task; doing so required a true central bank with the full power to create a circulating credit currency. Only then would central bankers have the capacity to halt panic, using oversight, in concert with lender-of-last-resort powers, to convert deposits to notes—daily and hourly. Only then could a bank, Ridgley proposed, "be sure that at any time, as long as it was solvent, it could go to the central bank and get any amount of cash needed on the notes of its customers, or other good security."[64]

The critical factor, as Ridgley emphasized, was that the borrowing bank be solvent. But who would make that determination? More importantly still, who could provide the needed liquidity to ensure that such categories made sense to the panicked depositors? The financial panics of the Gilded Age proved that supervision as merely an exercise of information hoarding or information publicity was ill equipped to handle the liquidity demands of the sprawling U.S. economy. As Ridgely knew, direct oversight was necessary to determine which banks were solvent and which were not, but it was not sufficient. Solvency remained a supervisory fact, one that emerged from supervisory knowledge and supervisory judgment; convincing others of that fact required real money. Announcing solvency was not enough. Supervision needed something more.

Interlude: O. Henry and
J.F.C. Nettlewick

SET IN a dusty Texas town, O. Henry's "Friends in San Rosario" remains arguably the most vivid portrait of a bank examiner in American literature and film. The competition is fiercer than that sentence suggests, with *It's A Wonderful Life* and the W. C. Fields film, *The Bank Dick,* also vying for this title.[1]

That depiction, published in 1908, is meant to convey three truths about bank examination in the pre-Federal Reserve era: Bank examiners were cold, they were foreign, and they were easy to fool.

J.F.C. Nettlewick, the examiner, "dressed in the prevailing Eastern style," arrived on the 8:20 A.M. train with plans to examine San Rosario's two national banks. The last train out would depart in three and a half hours. He would get $25 for each bank he examined but would spend the weekend in "this uninteresting Western town" if he were late. He did not want to be late.

To the national bankers in Nettlewick's Texas territory, Nettlewick's ways were not their own: "There was something so icy and swift, so impersonal and uncompromising about this man that his very presence seemed an accusation. He looked to be a man who would never make nor overlook an error." Behind the counter, Nettlewick supervised as an auditor, maybe as a compliance officer, but not as a friend—"the coins whined and sang as they skimmed across the marble slab from the tips of his nimble digits." This fact made him out of his depth. Nettlewick was all system and rules. Banking was much more than this. Banking, to O. Henry's country bankers, was about relationships and trust.

Nettlewick was impatient with trust. He was no match for San Rosario's bankers, who knew how to manipulate bank examination to their favor. By the end of his first examination, Nettlewick "felt that he had been made the victim of something that was not exactly a hoax but that left him in the shoes of one who had been played upon, used, and then discarded, without even an inkling of the game." He also missed his train.

O. Henry, née William Sydney Porter, wrote from good authority. In the 1890s, the decade the story was set, Porter was a banker in Austin, Texas. He was also a crook. In 1895, federal bank examiner F. B. Gray discovered Porter's defalcation of $850 from the First National Bank of Austin, Texas, where Porter was both teller and clerk. Porter planned to face the charges honorably, but he lost his nerve and fled to Honduras. With his wife near death in Austin, Porter returned and stood trial. He was convicted and served three years in prison. There he discovered his flair for writing, eventually becoming a short-story writer of such acclaim in New York City that his stories commanded a market comparable to Rudyard Kipling.[2]

"Friends in San Rosario" is not O. Henry's most famous story (that would probably be The Gift of the Magi, about the poor husband who sold his watch to buy his wife a comb only to discover that she had sold her hair to buy him a watch chain). But it does show a singular glimpse into how O. Henry and his readers viewed the practice and institutions of bank examination as it had evolved in response to the scandals and crises of the Gilded Age. The story pits the exacting formalities of eastern banking officials against the wholesome if somewhat rakish efforts of country bankers to keep their communities in business. Major Tom, the president of the First National Bank, waylays Nettlewick to buy time to favor his crosstown competitor. Bob, president of the town's other bank, the Stockmen's National, had to make good a depleted cash reserve—an error very similar to the one that put Will Porter in the penitentiary. As O. Henry teases out the yarn, a story whose denouement we have already spoiled, Nettlewick underestimates his banker interlocutors and is oblivious to their machinations. The waylaid examiner stays with Major Tom long enough for Bob to get the cash delivery he required, both banks passed their examinations, Nettlewick missed his train and had to stay the weekend against his wishes.

Friends in San Rosario illustrates a financial industry and a relationship between banks and government in transition. By the 1890s, the frontier had closed, White settlers had staked or stolen their claims, and the fierce identity of America required reinvention. As the land filled in, small towns and small banks multiplied and would continue to do so. The dominance of small banks in the United States continued for decades to come. But the rise of the industrial economy, the refinement of "modern" management techniques, and the spread of "scientific" banking theory all pressed against the prevailing ethic of community banking. Despite J. P. Morgan's famous declaration that "the first thing [in credit] is character," made only a few years after O. Henry wrote with similar fondness for relationship banking, the supervisory ethos had shifted. Character alone could not secure a debt. The proper forms would need to be in order, the paper correct and self-liquidating. The story highlights the enduring competition among American banking ideals: San Rosario, where banks were built on trust, local knowledge, and flexible risk-taking; for Nettlewick and the modern corporatist, industrial republic he represented, banking required formality, uniformity, and strict compliance with the rules.[3]

In this contest, O. Henry is clearly taking sides. Indeed, Nettlewick is memorable because he is a caricature. All eastern style, Nettlewick "was a finished product of the world of straight lines, conventional methods, and formal affairs." He arrives in San Rosario because the Comptroller of the Currency has rotated his examiners, a new practice instituted, presumably, to protect against too friendly relations between the supervisor and the supervised, a change O. Henry's bankers detested. Nettlewick is an envoy from the world of paper and typescript. He introduces himself not with a handshake but with a calling card. He checks every claim against their records. However, his was only a pretense to power, not the power itself. His entrance into the story promises as much: "His air denoted a quiet but conscious reserve force, if not actual authority." He has a rulebook but no discretion—no freedom to decide and act.

Such devotion to formality, O. Henry indicates, is a patently poor fit. Nettlewick gives rote advice to San Rosario's bankers, doubtless pulled from the latest textbook. "I would recommend the calling in of your large loans," he tells Tom, "and the making of only sixty and ninety day or call loans until general business revives." In urging liquidity, Nettlewick urges the liquidation of the community (O. Henry clues us into the consequences of calling such loans in another story, where the borrower tries to hold up a train).[4]

In his straight-lined formality, Nettlewick doesn't make the bank better; he reveals that rote compliance fails to capture the spirit of banking, economy, and society in San Rosario. The First National's cashier was a "gentleman of deliberation, discretion, and method." Nettlewick does his initial work quickly, because "the running order of the bank was smooth and clean." Nevertheless, San Rosario's bankers are obliged to take risks and to have faith. Bob lent the last of his cash to finance a sure cattle trade, on notes secured only by honor. "Pink Ross and Jim Fisher are two of the finest white men God ever made," Bob reassured Tom, asking for time. "They'll do the square thing."

Besides reflecting on the White masculine tropes of the day—we assume but are not told that "Major" Tom earned his military commission fighting to overthrow the U.S. government on behalf of slavery and the Confederacy—O. Henry wants us to think about banking as an allegory of community under siege. It's a useful story in a critical period of transition for a nation on the verge of entering the American century. It was also a period of transition in bank examination. In the nineteenth century, federal supervisors varied in their approaches, from supervision on suspicion of insolvency to supervision as a consultancy to, eventually, a strict compliance ethic. By the end of the nineteenth century, bank supervision looked increasingly like rules without real authority, legitimacy, or liquidity behind them. They were thus easily manipulated, even if not quite so flamboyantly as in San Rosario. At the same time, a stiff breeze was liable to blow over Stockmen's National and all its depositors with it. Bob may have put his faith in Pink Ross and Jim Fisher, but the government needed something more. Rules, by themselves, did not appear to be the answer.

4

Central Banking and Bank Supervision

COMPLEMENTS AND ALTERNATIVES IN THE FOUNDING OF THE FEDERAL RESERVE

IN THE aftermath of the 1907 Panic—generally considered the last of the panics of the Gilded Age—observers of all stripes recognized that the American financial system had to change. Banks were too small and too unstable. Money flowed, or failed to flow, unpredictably. Regulation and supervision—public and private—had not solved these problems. Although bankers and policymakers had debated remedies since the turn of the century—and indeed throughout the Gilded Age—the panic thrust banking reform to the center of political debate. The status quo of constant instability and impending collapse could not continue. But what should that reform be? There were as many diagnoses and cures as there were reformers, and it seemed that everyone in 1908 had something to say about the state of the banking system.[1]

Through the cacophony, some fundamental questions emerged. Which risk management strategies would finally succeed in making the nation's banking and currency systems stable? And which actors would be ultimately responsible for that stability? Would the government—federal or state—formally take on the residual risk of the banking system, not just in word but in deed? Or would private actors—responsible and self-interested—build on mixed successes of the nineteenth century to provide that stability themselves? Or would America continue on some middle path between these poles?

In the years that followed the 1907 Panic, Congress took sides on these issues. Deposit insurance, popular in the South and West and championed by presidential candidate William Jennings Bryan, lost at the ballot box with

Bryan in 1908, and was rejected by Congress thereafter. State governments took up the policy, ultimately with poor results. Another alternative, expanding private-sector risk management through the clearinghouses, inspired policy choices but did not dictate them. Instead, Congress, for the first time since 1836, embraced central banking, focusing on liquidity provision and currency management based on gold and sound commercial bills, following examples set in London and other European capitals. This central banking system would, however, have American characteristics. Congress devised a quasi-federalist structure, with power shared nationally through subnational districts. Within each district, a private bank—a Federal Reserve Bank—was charged with undertaking bank supervision in ways that Congress left ill-defined. In Washington, DC, a public Federal Reserve Board, the "capstone" of the Progressive experimentalist Woodrow Wilson, would ostensibly govern the whole system.[2]

Policymakers developed America's unique central bank through contentious negotiations that spanned three presidential administrations and four congresses. The system that emerged reflected important realities about the way that public power would manage private finance. The new Federal Reserve System, bold and imaginative and confusing as it was, did not wipe the slate of bank supervision clean. Congress imposed the Fed on top of the existing structure of bank oversight, including dual chartering, examination, liquidation, and corporatist risk management. The Federal Reserve Act was aimed, Congress wrote, "to Establish a More Effective Supervision of Banking," but Congress left the practical details of this ambition to the interested stakeholders to work through once the system was established. The legislation only declared authority to push forward into supervisory experimentation, authority now shared horizontally across federal actors—the Comptroller and the Federal Reserve, primarily—and vertically through the dual banking system that the Federal Reserve reified in important respects. The deposit revolution of the late nineteenth century had revitalized state banking as an alternative to the Comptroller's public financial oversight. The Federal Reserve System maintained these parallel supervisory lanes, even as its authority overlaid them.[3]

This institutional layering is vital to understanding the way that bank supervision moved forward through the new Federal Reserve System and beyond. Between the Panic of 1907 and the passage of the Federal Reserve Act in 1913, the Comptroller had pursued a mission of professionalization, information gathering, and cooperation with state officials and private clearinghouses. Although some critics, such as Roosevelt's Treasury Secretary Lyman

J. Gage, thought that the Comptroller's mode of chartering supervision was unnecessary for and perhaps even detrimental to the new central banking experiment, the Comptroller gained status and authority under the new System. The Comptroller's informational approach to bank supervision thrived in this ecosystem, even as its alternative—a liquidity-based risk management system governed through private central banks—did so as well. What remained unresolved was whether these risk management practices would operate as complements or competitors. Bankers, meanwhile, sought their own alternatives, pursuing branch banking, and with it bank size and diversification, as yet another private risk management alternative, one which opposed both the national banking system's unit banking model and the efforts to restrain branching by the Federal Reserve Board. Congress tried to bring harmony to the competing risk management models in the 1927 McFadden Act. With depression on the horizon, its makeshift solutions would not hold.[4]

The 1907 Reaction: Deposit Insurance, Private Risk Management, or Central Banking?

As the dust settled on the Panic of 1907, reform fires burned hot. William Jennings Bryan, the Nebraska populist who had run on free silver in 1896 and anti-imperialism in 1900, again led the Democratic ticket in the presidential election of 1908. Bryan had championed deposit guarantees since 1893 and made bank reform and depositor protection the heart of his campaign. Recognizing the gravity of the banking problem, Republicans in Congress needed their own theory of reform. Some legislative leaders, like Rhode Island Senator Nelson W. Aldrich, sought to approach the question of banking reform outside the glare of presidential electoral politics. Aldrich recognized that the nation's banks posed continuous danger to the economy. With a large and growing ratio of insecure deposits to secure circulating notes, any slip in confidence initiated a rush to convert the first into the second. There were simply not enough cash reserves to satisfy all the claims of these well-motivated, rationally insecure depositors, either at the individual bank level or in the entire system. To resolve this, Aldrich proposed enabling national banks to issue emergency currency, backed by local government and railroad bonds, a plan that did not require any larger reordering of American banking. The national banks would become their own central banks on their own authority.[5]

Where Aldrich framed reform narrowly, House Banking Committee Chairman Charles N. Fowler sought to transform the balance of public and private

authority in banking. A Republican banker from New Jersey and close ally of
influential Chicago banker James B. Forgan, Fowler represented the interests
of bankers outside New York City. As Bryan championed federal insurance as
the proper backstop of bank deposits, Fowler called for private bankers to
form guarantee associations and remove the federal supervisory role entirely.
Bankers, mutually responsible for each other's liabilities under Fowler's model,
would undertake more vigorous supervision, making "every banker . . . a
guardian of the banking interests." Fowler's bill passed the House in early 1908,
but Aldrich blocked it in the Senate. To clear the impasse, Republicans cobbled bits of competing proposals into the Aldrich-Vreeland Act, mostly to
push the problem of permanent reform into the future.[6]

The delay was not simply political procrastination: Aldrich wanted time to
consider larger changes, a cooling period so to speak. For that reason, perhaps
the most important part of the legislation was the creation of the National
Monetary Commission, a congressional commission with the charge to "report to Congress . . . what changes are necessary or desirable in the monetary
system of the United States." Aldrich took the chairmanship of the commission for himself, a maneuver which, following Bryan's defeat, barred the door
on a federal deposit guarantee and pushed reform toward something the
banker-allied Aldrich would prefer.[7]

The states sensed an opening in the delays provided by Aldrich. Since state
governments could not legislate a more flexible currency nor charter a central
bank themselves, their responses instead focused on deposits—more oversight over their creation in the state banking systems and schemes to guarantee
them through deposit insurance funds. With a greater proportion of the public
holding bank deposits as opposed to hard currency, state policymakers saw
vividly that the costs of bank failure were political affairs as much as financial
ones. Yet while formal supervision was common in the Northeast and Midwest before 1907, most states in the South and West relied instead on double
shareholder liability and the responsibilities of bank boards to address financial risk. The panic and the non-response from Congress spurred states to initiate and expand their supervisory activities. Between 1907 and 1914, seventeen
states created banking departments to provide government-led oversight of
existing banks. Some, like New York and California, also returned discretion
to chartering via new rules aimed at limiting charters to those that were "necessary" and "convenient" for the local economic conditions.[8]

Several states went further. The Oklahoma legislature, inspired by Bryan's
proposals, was the first to enact deposit insurance in 1907, its first year of

statehood. Over the next decade, seven states would follow, nearly all unit banking states dominated by small, rural banks. Oklahoma lawmakers made the deposit guarantee inclusive, permitting nationally chartered banks to participate. Comptroller William B. Ridgely (1901–1908) refused to permit it, however, a decision later affirmed by the U.S. Attorney General. Wishing to avail themselves of the guarantee law, many small national banks switched to state charters. The state government, in turn, hastily hired a host of examiners to inspect the state's banks before the plan got underway.[9]

Under state deposit guarantee plans, state officials often gained new authority to supervise the banks that might impose losses on the insurance fund, but like their federal counterparts, state examiners were stretched thin. In South Dakota, which adopted state deposit insurance in 1915, each examiner made, on average, 125 examinations a year. Other states suffered from poor timing. Mississippi and Washington, which adopted plans in 1917, did so during local economic downturns. Deposit insurance might protect individual banks against irrational runs—depositors confident in eventual repayment may not act hastily on rumors of insolvency—but deposit insurance provided no answer for actual, widespread insolvency caused by protracted market collapse.[10]

The deposit guarantee states faced another disadvantage in their attempt to use insurance as the risk management mechanism. Oklahoma's deposit guarantee came online in the very weeks after the Panic of 1907, which initially proved propitious. Depositors moved money to Oklahoma for safekeeping and deposits increased from $18 million to $50 million. The scheme failed when Oklahoma's bankers started using these new deposits to speculate in oil and real estate. As banks went under, the guarantee fund did as well. The supervisors associated with the fund were taken entirely by surprise by the bank failures and the fund's failure as well.[11]

Deposit insurance was not the only risk management alternative to the federal reform plans Aldrich was developing through the National Monetary Commission. Another came from clearinghouses, the decentralized central banks whose coordination failures during the Panics of 1893 and 1907 made them increasingly unreliable at their core function of liquidity provision. Despite these failures—or perhaps because of them—clearinghouses decided to undertake more proactive supervision of their members. Because clearinghouse membership included state and national banks, clearinghouse bankers recognized that the parallel systems of public oversight each provided only a partial picture of the risks concentrated in the clearinghouse. Following the near catastrophic failure of one of its members in 1905, the Chicago Clearing-house was the first to hire a permanent examiner in 1907 (one Chicago banker, believing that his defalcations would be discovered once the clearinghouse examinations went into effect, absconded to Tangier).[12]

After the 1907 Panic, other clearinghouses moved quickly to hire their own examiners, often framing private clearinghouse supervision as an alternative to government oversight. In Republican California, the Los Angeles and San Francisco clearinghouses recruited examiners beginning in 1908, a foundation on which the state bankers association constructed a plan for statewide private examinations to "make California banks failure proof." Surveying the prolifera-tion of clearinghouse examiners in 1909, a writer in *Bankers Magazine* pre-dicted that "national and state examinations will be abolished." This was not idle boasting. The organizing principles of the banking system—whether the system would be ultimately public or private—were on the table. With Re-publican plans for bank-issued emergency currency and the gradual cohesion of central banking reforms centered on private reserve associations, bankers saw private clearinghouse examination as essential institution-building for a future where private interests gained full control of the banking system. Even Comptroller Ridgely, while not advocating the abolition of public authority, identified distinct advantages of private oversight. "The examinations by a national-bank examiner . . . are necessarily . . . limited to the discovery of specific violations of the national-bank act, and criticisms and recommenda-tions . . . cannot always be made sufficiently mandatory. The information ac-quired by clearinghouse committees, through their own examinations, has in many cases resulted in their being able to enforce better methods and more conservative policies."[13]

Even so, clearinghouses understood their power as more limited than what Ridgely imagined, and despite pockets of enthusiasm, many came to view their own examination forces as an insufficient standalone risk management strat-egy. "On the whole we have done a great deal of good, but we cannot manage the banks by examining them," James Forgan, Chairman of the Chicago Clearinghouse Association, observed in 1908. "Conditions have to be very bad indeed before we take drastic action." This fact dispirited some, but the need for some kind of risk management, public or private, remained strong. The *New York Times*, reflecting on the rise of clearinghouse examination, offered a balanced view. Public and private risk management need not be competitors: "One looks to the safety of the public, the other to the safety of the banking community, but, in reality, both coincide in result."[14]

The Comptroller Asserts His Hold

Despite the urging of Treasury Secretary Lyman Gage to abolish the office, the Comptroller of the Currency not only survived the immediate aftermath of the 1907 Panic, but it thrived. The reason was Lawrence O. Murray (1908–1913), whom Theodore Roosevelt appointed Comptroller in February 1908. Murray, a frequent tennis companion of the president, had enjoyed a varied career in government, including stints at the Comptroller's office and the Commerce Department (in the latter role, he reorganized the U.S. Steamboat Inspection Service following a major disaster in 1904). A business progressive in Roosevelt's image, Murray shared the view that bank supervision was a public-private affair whose vitality would become stronger only if reform focused on both sides of this apparent divide.[15]

As reform coursed along divergent paths through Congress, the states, and the private clearinghouses, Murray drove institutional change from within the Comptroller's office. Murray simultaneously pursued more public information gathering and more aggressive oversight, asserting more public power to foster private coordination and control. Doing so meant expanding the discretionary power of government, which Murray did self-consciously. "When I became comptroller it seemed to me that we needed three things," Murray explained to the National Monetary Commission in 1908. "A more efficient law for the comptroller to work under, whereby he would be taken out of the category of a common scold and given the power to do something; better examinations of the banks by bank examiners; and more cooperation or direction by the directors." As he waited on the law to give more concrete and specific tools, Murray worked toward his remaining goals with vigor (subordinates dubbed Murray's tenure "the period of the reformation").[16]

Murray accomplished his tasks without Congress, first by bureaucratizing and then by professionalizing the examination corps. Prior to Murray, federal bank examiners worked independently, a status reinforced by the fee system. Examiners managed their time, planned their routes, and learned their trade through experience. Murray imposed bureaucratic hierarchy and more information exchange among federal examiners. He divided the nation into geographic districts and created chief examiners for each district. He instructed examiners to meet yearly, where they would discuss strategies for improving supervisory methods. Through professionalization, Murray expected the quality of oversight to improve. By 1911, he required examiners to take personal responsibility for the soundness of the banks they examined, ordering examiners "to certify that the bank is absolutely solvent, in his judgment, that the bylaws are satisfactory, and are being followed, that the management is safe and that the books show the bank's real condition, being so kept that the examiner's scrutiny of the bank may be thorough." This was no easy task, as Murray acknowledged, but he would accept no alternative. If "you are unable to discover the true condition of a bank," he admonished, "do not send excuses; send in your resignation."[17]

Despite placing this existential authority in the hands of examiners, Murray wanted examination to strengthen risk management practices for bank boards, not displace them. To accomplish this task, Murray changed the way the Comptroller communicated with bankers. Before Murray, examiners might discuss their findings with bank management, but it was clerks in Washington, DC, who digested examination reports and wrote to bank directors demanding action. Murray insisted that examiners engage directors immediately, convening the board following examination and demanding correction that minute. Even where the bank proved sound, Murray insisted on the meeting—the point was to initiate a conversation about the health of the bank and their duties as directors. "Now the directors know at first hand exactly what the examiner finds," Murray boasted.[18]

As he increased direct interaction, Murray also scaled back communication from Washington on the theory that supervision should prioritize only important problems, those matters that required the most attention. "I think it is a great mistake to fritter away what real power for good we have by writing letters to good banks on trivial things," Murray told a meeting of the National Association of Supervisors of State Banks, a new organization founded in 1902 to coordinate state bank supervision. "Let us get at the vital things and correct them." As he waited for reform, Murray campaigned to make the existing institutions of public oversight and private risk management more effective.[19]

The change wrought by Murray appears clearly in the experiences of the First National Bank of Canton, Pennsylvania. After an examination in June 1908, the Comptrollers' office wrote a spare three paragraphs, noting a reserve deficiency and demanding correction. In December, after Murray took over, the board got three full pages. The examiner had sniffed out a "dummy note" used to conceal illegal stock ownership as well as a bundle of small loans that hid the full liability of the borrower, the cashier Louis T. McFadden. Scolding from Washington did little to change the Canton bank's behavior. Under the examination and correspondence method of supervision Murray inherited, the forces of law and personal liability existed in some future courtroom, after the bank had failed. As they read the Comptroller's letters, some boards might have seriously contemplated that future and their corporate governance responsibilities. Bank boards also tended to be confident in the management they had chosen. A chiding letter did little to change that. Where the scolding letter approach failed, Murray turned to the scolding examiner. With the force of law standing in the room, the board of the Canton bank looked at every loan on their books.[20]

Murray could not invest his examiners with new disciplinary authority: The most—and least—he could do was close a bank. Yet Murray did control the timing, frequency, and extent of examinations. Bankers who did not cooperate could expect to engage with more searching federal oversight more often.

Murray's bureaucratization campaign also focused on expanding the Comptroller's capacity to gather and mobilize information. Within the examination districts, Murray's staff began compiling credit files on firms borrowing from national banks, which enabled examiners to spot problem borrowers across institutions. Consolidating such information diminished the importance of any single examiner's knowledge and influence, allowing Murray to rotate his examiners among different districts. Murray expected information gathering to be cooperative, and he opened lines of communication with both state bank supervisors and clearinghouse examiners. "You and I are interested in having strong banks," Murray told the state bank supervisors in September 1910, a commitment he enacted through coordinated examinations, when state and national banks were held under common ownership. Murray also promoted private risk management at the clearinghouses. Because the clearinghouses stood behind their members—making loud public commitments to do so following the Panic—Murray proposed sharing supervisory information about troubled banks, enabling private supervisors to act quickly. He hoped that clearinghouses would return the courtesy, and many agreed to do so. For Murray, private and public supervision should reinforce—rather than replace—each other.[21]

In the vacuum between the Aldrich-Vreeland Act and the National Monetary Commission's pending proposals, Murray made a forceful case for cooperative and coordinated risk management that included federal officials, state officials, private clearinghouses, and bank directors. He did so through the mobilization of information, wrenching the Comptroller's office into the corporate age. Murray was, according to the *New York Times*, a "controller who controls."[22]

Murray's reformation, though, was not universally welcomed. Some career officials in the Comptroller's office viewed Murray's efforts to push supervisory reform without congressional approval as illegitimate. Other critics, following William Howard Taft's election in 1908, concluded that Murray's program of reining in the department's excessive letters was aimed at appeasing bankers. Murray, for his part, wanted to give his version of more intensive, collaborative bank supervision a chance. He knew that "there is not a bit of power in the comptroller to force [bankers] to do a single thing that he asks them to do." With the path of reform uncertain, Murray made his best case for the continuation of the Comptroller within a robust, multipolar, and information-driven supervisory order.[23]

Supervision and the Federal Reserve System

At the end of 1913, debates about bank supervision reflected those about the future of American banking in general. Republican politicians and influential, big city bankers sought to privatize financial risk management—through size and diversification, on the one hand, and counterparty oversight through clearinghouses, on the other. They favored private finance, private power, and private control. Many Democrats, drawing on populist traditions, insisted on greater public authority through enhanced government oversight and even full deposit guarantees. Murray, a Democrat in a Republican administration, straddled this divide, making the case that public and private risk management needed strengthening and coordination from overarching public power. The private and public were in this view reinforcing forces, not opposing ones.

It was into this mix that Congress inaugurated the Federal Reserve System as yet another risk management alternative. In some ways, of all the reform options under consideration, central banking appeared the least likely following the panics of the Gilded Age. The National Monetary Commission, through the careful orchestration of Nelson Aldrich, changed this. Eager to reshape American finance in the image of its European competitors, central banking advocates among the coastal bankers and their Republican allies sought a private central bank modeled on the Bank of England and the German Reichsbank. They hung their hopes on Aldrich's eponymous Senate bill, drafted at a now-famous November 1910 meeting of Aldrich and a coterie of bankers at the Jekyll Island Club, a members-only resort off the coast of Georgia. The bill, introduced in January 1912, stalled. In the chaotic 1912 election, Republicans lost control of Congress, the White House, and as a result, the entire program of banking reform.[24]

The Aldrich Plan, as it was known, became anathema among Democrats. Ironically, it also became the model for their own reform efforts. The basic idea from Aldrich was to effectively create a nationwide clearinghouse with power centered in New York, backed by the full faith and credit of the federal government but under the private control of New York bankers. After the turnover in political power in 1912, a purely private basis for the new national clearinghouse faded, but much of the rest of the Aldrich Plan survived (Aldrich, by then retired from the Senate, hated the legislation that emerged with a personal intensity; most of his compatriots from Jekyll Island recognized their handiwork and backed it).

The bankers might have been especially willing to compromise because, in the heat of the 1912 campaign, their political standing came under direct and sustained attack. Beginning in March 1912, Louisiana Democrat Arsène Pujo, himself a member of the National Monetary Commission, initiated a set of hearings focused on the "Money Trust," which sought to demonstrate that Wall Street bankers controlled the flow of credit throughout the country. The hearings were a sensation, dominating the headlines and capturing national attention. Leading bankers, including the august J. P. Morgan, were compelled to submit to congressional grilling. When Morgan died a few weeks after his testimony at the age of 75, his friends and family blamed the hearings and the rough press treatment that the hearings inspired. Although few parties (including most of the politicians) cared particularly about the technical details of banking reform, there was broad agreement that the time for private control of private finance was over. The Aldrich Plan did not appear poised for implementation in any form.[25]

Woodrow Wilson, the newly elected president, was one of the many who had only a passing familiarity with the technical business of banking. Nevertheless, he decided to make currency reform one of the keystone efforts of his administration. Wilson, formerly a Princeton University professor and governor of New Jersey, was an uncommon politician, not because he had substantial political skills, but because he was a theorist who took questions of governance seriously. In Congress, Virginia Democrat Carter Glass, a conservative who assumed control of reform in the House, initially retained the Aldrich proposal's private emphasis, even as he rejected placing control in the hands of New York bankers. Wilson sought a different compromise. Pressured to assert full government control by populist allies—including William Jennings Bryan, whom Wilson had appointed Secretary of State—Wilson worked to cement a public-private alliance but with the public firmly in command. Wilson sought to institutionalize the public supervision of private finance by placing a governmental body at the core (in Washington, DC) and private "reserve banks" spread throughout the country. The core government power came in the form of a new Federal Reserve Board, a "capstone," composed of political appointees, modeled in part on the Interstate Commerce Commission.[26]

It was clear that the new central banking system, then, would sustain private finance (in the form of the Federal Reserve Banks) and public power (through the Federal Reserve Board). Yet within this framework, the ways supervision would operate among the Board, the Reserve Banks, and the rest of the banking system were framed in outline but not in detail—an invitation to struggle among the various parties already deeply interested in bank oversight at the national and state levels.[27]

In some cases, the statute was quite clear in the changes to supervision it intended. For example, the Act institutionalized Murray's professionalization project for national bank examiners. The law finally provided an affirmative mandate for continuous federal oversight, replacing the Civil War–era directive to examine national banks "as often as shall be deemed necessary and proper" with definite instructions to examine them twice a year, and more often if necessary. The law also abolished the fee system, authorizing salaries for national bank examiners set by the Federal Reserve Board. These changes, which motivated that Act's subtitle, "to establish a more effective supervision of banking," were late additions. The National Monetary Commission had devoted substantial attention to bank oversight by surveying bankers, clearinghouses, and bank examiners about supervisory practices and examiner compensation. However, no meaningful reforms made it into Aldrich's proposals (lobbying by Murray and state bank supervisors seems to have convinced Aldrich not to abolish government oversight altogether, something he contemplated). It was only with Wilson's determination to place public officials at the head of financial reform that Murray's efforts to make examination continuous and examiners salaried made it into the legislation.[28]

What was a little less certain was the supervisory relationship that the statute created between the Federal Reserve Banks and the Federal Reserve Board. The Act created the unambiguously private Federal Reserve Banks—or more accurately, identified the delegated, administrative process for their creation—on a similar basis as national banks, with a 20-year federal charter, a private board of directors, and private banks as shareholders. Yet, where the Comptroller was given a specific statutory right to examine the national banks at the outset, the Federal Reserve Board's authority to supervise the Federal

Reserve Banks was more penumbral. The chairman of the board for each Reserve Bank would also serve as the "Federal Reserve agent" and would be required to "make regular reports to the Federal Reserve Board" regarding the bank's performance; branch offices of the Reserve Banks could only be created subject to regulations imposed by the Reserve Board; the Board would approve all bank applications to become members of the Federal Reserve System; and the Reserve Banks' facility of loans and discounts to member banks was "subject to the provisions of law and the orders of the Federal Reserve Board," among many other provisions. In other words, the public Reserve Board was deeply involved in not only in setting the broad rules for the private Reserve Banks but also in making sure that each bank would abide by them. The relationship between them was essentially supervisory.[29]

The supervisory relationship between the Federal Reserve System—that is, the Reserve Board and the Reserve Banks—and the private banks, state and national alike, that would join the system was even less well-identified. On the one hand, the Reserve Banks, as lenders to their member banks, would employ counterparty supervision similar to that used by the Banks of the United States a century before. Yet because the Board supervised the ways Federal Reserve Banks would loan money—on what terms, and according to which theories of lending and liquidity—the balance of power over counterparty supervision, between the Board and the Reserve Banks, remained ambiguous. So did the Federal Reserve System's examination authority. The statute preserved for the Reserve Board the prerogative of *authorizing* "examination by the State authorities to be accepted in the case of State banks" and "special examination of member banks" whatever the status of their charter. The statute did not specify *who* would conduct these examinations, only that the Federal Reserve Banks and the Federal Reserve Board would share the responsibility.[30]

Contemporary observers were left to wonder what, precisely, the new supervisory regime would be, something that Congress failed to answer with clarity. The Fed's statutory charges to "furnish a more elastic currency" and "establish a more effective supervision of banking in the United States" were closely related. Monetary policy, such that it was in 1914, primarily operated through the individual Reserve Banks discounting "real bills," short-term commercial loans made by member banks to support definite commercial transactions (such as the purchase of raw materials, transit of goods, and stocking of inventory), not speculative investments. Discounting was the practice of purchasing such loans at a discount to their face value, which enabled member banks to convert assets into cash or reserves held at the Reserve Banks (also, Reserve Banks could lend to member banks with real bills as collateral, which amounted to the same thing). The discount rate, the price the Reserve Banks charged to perform this form of credit intermediation for the member banks, dictated the volume of discounts for such bills. This, in turn, influenced the money supply. The advent of "open-market operations," or the practice of buying and selling securities in the open market to influence their value, only arose later.[31]

In this model of finance, there was very little public power exercised at all. The currency itself was in the hands of the essentially private Reserve Banks, which they created by buying or lending against private bank assets generated through private commercial transactions. For proponents of central banking as the answer to the instabilities of the early twentieth century, this was precisely the point. Public power should be, at most, peripheral to the main business of banking. Central banking under this model was a rules-based, self-executing approach to managing liquidity, reserves, and emergency loans that itself operated with a profit motive (since the Reserve Banks guaranteed dividends to stockholding member banks). If private bankers could practice disciplined lending on the basis of real commercial transactions, then the quantity of money in the system would adjust almost naturally. At most, bank supervisors in this model provided nudges to this natural equilibrium.

This classical model of central bank supervision appears to have been the congressional intent of the Federal Reserve System. If that is true, it would not last.

The Supervisory Ethos of the Federal Reserve

As the ink dried on the newly signed Federal Reserve Act, the Federal Reserve System opened for business. The law compelled national banks to join, but state banks could choose. Few jumped to participate. In the unstable compromise that emerged, the Comptroller and the state supervisors continued their "condition" examinations of national and state-member banks. The Federal Reserve Board confined its examination activities to the Federal Reserve Banks, while the Reserve Banks provided supplementary examinations, primarily but not exclusively of the state-members. Within the Reserve Banks, the Federal Reserve agent, responsible for discounting paper in accordance with the guidelines of the Federal Reserve Act—that is, purchasing loans originally made by member banks to their customers—performed the examination function relative to the member banks. This institutional placement demonstrated that Reserve Bank supervision of member banks would be different than the condition examinations of the Comptroller and the state examiners, instead focusing on vetting the credit quality of eligible bills rather than determining whether member banks were safe, sound, and abiding by the terms of their charters.

As they organized and opened for business, the Federal Reserve Banks unpeeled layer upon layer of ambiguity about their supervisory roles. The first key question centered on the real bills doctrine, the banking theory that underlay the Federal Reserve System. By allowing the Reserve Banks to discount *only* real commercial bills, the system's architects anticipated a near-automatic improvement in the safety and stability of American banks. Commercial bills, short in duration and tied to definite business activity or goods in transit, offered a "secondary reserve" of liquid assets that could be borrowed against or sold in order to increase reserves or meet deposit withdrawals. The existence of a central bank, standing ready to convert quick assets into cash, should have encouraged bankers to reshape their balance sheets into the ideal image of sound banking. To realize these ambitions, Congress had to define what real commercial bills were. The Federal Reserve Act thus created regulations for *eligibility*, authorizing Federal Reserve Banks to discount "notes, drafts, and bills of exchange issued or drawn for agricultural, industrial, or commercial purposes," at ninety-day maturity for industrial and commercial notes and up to six months for agricultural paper. The framers of the Act had a very good idea what these categories meant, but in cases of uncertainty, the Federal Reserve Board would "determine and define the character of the paper thus eligible for discount."[32]

Much easier written than accomplished, as it turned out. Eligibility requirements entailed significant changes in commercial banking practice. Before the Federal Reserve Act, U.S. bankers practiced relationship banking. They looked to the borrower, not the fine details of the loan. Bankers compared a borrower's quick assets to their liabilities, and if the former exceeded the latter, the bank was inclined to lend without too deep inquiry into the loan's intended purpose. For security, bankers took the borrower's promissory note.[33]

Eligibility, however, required knowing what the money would be used for, which required information. As Reserve Banks quickly realized, bankers and borrowers often did not have the information at hand. In its initial circulars describing eligibility, the Federal Reserve Bank of New York acknowledged that "especially in the smaller banks, many of the notes are discounted by persons, firms or corporations not accustomed to making statements." To overcome these deficiencies, the central banking project became one of modernizing bank information systems, including teaching bankers and their customers how to make proper statements.[34]

Even with full information, reserve bankers struggled to apply simple rules to complex businesses. At first, the Board advocated a heuristic that accorded with prior experience: If a borrower had more quick assets than liabilities, Reserve Banks could assume loans were for commercial, rather than speculative, purposes and thus eligible for discount. The deeper reserve bankers looked into borrowers' balance sheets, the murkier the rules became. By 1921, Board counsel George L. Harrison was fed up: "the purely theoretical questions whether they borrow for a commercial purpose or whether they borrow to avoid the necessity of selling their investments to procure funds for a commercial purpose is one which depends upon a state of mind that is impossible to determine, even were it wise to attempt to do so." Although theoretical, Harrison's questions were hardly idle, sparking major disputes among the Reserve Bank governors.[35]

The Federal Reserve System's founders and early managers expected bankers to concentrate on real bills: This was fundamental to the risk management logic of central banking. The Federal Reserve Board, as the final arbiter of what a real bill properly was, struggled to establish functional rules for Reserve Banks to apply.

With the intellectual framework of central bank risk management, the formal category of eligibility was intended to draw bright lines around assets that were safe, liquid, and discountable at the Reserve Banks. Eligibility rules failed to satisfy these goals. Complicating matters, the Reserve Banks layered a second, informal category, *acceptability*, onto their discount decisions.[36]

In short, if eligibility measured liquidity, then acceptability measured credit quality. Complicating matters still further, eligibility determinations were regulatory, made by the Federal Reserve Board for the entire Federal Reserve System; acceptability determinations were supervisory, made bilaterally between Reserve Banks and their members, with the encouragement of the Board as the supervisor of the Reserve Banks (layers and layers and layers).[37]

Because they took on the credit risk of discounted paper, the Reserve Banks wanted to be sure that discounted notes would be paid at maturity. Mere eligibility was not enough. Determining credit quality required yet more information about member banks and their borrowers. To obtain it, the Board instructed Reserve Banks to use their examination authority. The Board, conscious of the duplication of effort and expense, created a division of responsibility between Reserve Bank examiners and the other public and private supervisors already engaged in bank examination, albeit with different goals in mind. "The primary object of Federal Reserve examinations will be to obtain more detailed information as to credits," the Board wrote the Reserve Banks in 1918. "It would be well to consider the work more in the nature of a special credit investigation."[38]

The Reserve Banks would evaluate the individual, discountable assets of member banks, as well as overall member bank lending policies. They would do so to apply eligibility and acceptability criteria, with the aim of protecting the Reserve Banks' own balance sheets.

The discretion, which inhered in acceptability standards, provoked deep controversy within the Federal Reserve System. This stemmed in part from the system's design. Reserve Banks discounted paper endorsed by member banks, meaning that the member banks would repay the debt if the original borrower defaulted. The health of these banks was thus a primary concern for Reserve Bank examiners. Yet in the European banking systems that the Fed's architects sought to recreate, banks tended to be few, well-known, and strong. In the United States, unit banking ensured that banks were many, obscure, and often weak. Reserve Banks confronted these institutions not as chartering authorities with the power to shut them down but as a lending institution designed to prop them up.

To prop them up or, in the failure to lend, to freeze them out. The negative power implied by the discretionary acceptability determination threatened some of the political legitimacy of the new central bank. Recall that the Federal Reserve was promoted as a risk management alternative to deposit guarantees that were, in the 1910s, still growing in prominence in various states. The point of deposit insurance was to guarantee *all* paid-in banks' deposits, which usually meant all of a state's banks. This expectation of comprehensiveness put the Federal Reserve Banks in a bind. As private institutions, they had no interest in lending to weak members—there was no profit in lending to banks that would go belly up. In moments of crisis, however, they faced difficult choices. "Declining credit I have always maintained was the worst type of discipline," New York Federal Reserve Bank Governor Benjamin Strong (1914–1928) wrote to Federal Reserve Board member Adolph Miller (1914–1936) in July 1922. If Federal Reserve Banks refused to lend on eligible paper and a bank failed, "a storm of protest" would result, leading either to a Reserve Bank defying popular demand and inviting challenges to its legitimacy, or acquiescence to such demand, thus encouraging forbearance.[39]

For ambitious Federal Reserve officials, the combination of credit examinations and a discretionary discounting policy opened the door to more robust forms of bank supervision than had been practiced in the United States. It also opened the door to bank supervision that would evolve into macroeconomic management. For example, a week after the armistice of the Great War in 1918, the Board worried that member banks were engaged in heavy discounting to generate reserves which would support speculative lending. "The directors of the Federal reserve banks should exercise reasonable prudence . . . and should be satisfied, by proper inquiry and investigation, that the accommodation sought is for legitimate local requirements," the Board admonished. Put differently, the Reserve Banks should use their acceptability evaluations to tame overenthusiastic economic expansion.[40]

Such policies, often dubbed "moral suasion," constituted a negative power, but some officials wanted to do more. Credit "examination is a necessary and appropriate instrument of credit administration under the Federal Reserve System," Board member Adolph Miller wrote to Strong in July 1922. Such "credit administration" extended beyond liquidity, implying the power to favor member-bank lending to some industries over others and thus direct the course of local economies. This was more than conservative bankers like Strong could countenance, but it presaged ideas about economic management that would resonate into the future.[41]

In the long run, the assiduous efforts by Federal Reserve Banks to collect data about their members, their members' businesses, and the broader economic conditions within their districts provided a storehouse of information. Federal Reserve Banks pursued this data collection for different purposes than the Comptroller, but in doing so they nevertheless generated records on each member bank that, as a historian of the Federal Reserve Bank of Cleveland explained, enabled a "comprehensive appraisal of its condition over time," so that "the trend of affairs in any institution may readily be seen." What the Reserve Banks could or would do with this information, though, remained open—and highly contested.[42]

The Comptroller Grinds On

As the Federal Reserve Banks and Board stood up to craft their new supervisory ethos, made so formidable by the new combination of a balance sheet and an informational regime, Comptroller Lawrence Murray stepped down. In 1914, Woodrow Wilson appointed John Skelton Williams (1914–1921).

Williams, a wealthy Virginian, had been a banker and railroad president before joining the Treasury Department as Assistant Secretary following Wilson's election. Williams was, according to one contemporary, "a man of strong impulses and prejudices . . . devoid of subtlety, and relentless." These prejudices included a commitment to white supremacy, and Williams had been instrumental in segregating the Treasury Department before assuming the comptrollership. He proved a domineering presence. A Federal Reserve Bank governor recalled that Williams was "the only man I ever knew who could strut while sitting down." Where Murray sought cooperation and strength through coordination, Williams pursued the Comptroller's interests first.[43]

In some ways, Williams continued the incremental experimentation of his predecessors, seeking to make national bank supervision more effective through the collection and mobilization of information. In the first instance, he refined examiners' loan assessment work by aligning loan categorization with the real bills doctrine. In the 1890s, Comptroller Edward S. Lacy (1889–1892) had introduced loan categorization to help examiners determine bank solvency, eventually creating "doubtful" and "loss" categories, which indicated loans where some or a total loss was expected. Examiners used loan categories to identify threats to solvency, but only retrospectively. With time, examiners added another category, "slow," identifying loans that were being serviced but were not of short duration. Slow loans suggested not insolvency but rather illiquidity. Williams formalized the organic slow category, nudging examiners to evaluate liquidity in addition to solvency.[44]

The Comptroller's loan categories thus mirrored those used by the Federal Reserve. The Comptroller mandated solvency, as embodied in the doubtful and loss columns, and preferred liquidity. The Fed mandated liquidity, through eligibility criteria, while the Federal Reserve Banks exercised their strong preference for solvency (i.e., credit quality) through acceptability criteria. In this way, the Comptroller's information regime, while lacking its own balance sheet to make solvent banks liquid, guided bankers toward practices that would ensure their loans were at once quick-paying and eligible for discount at a Federal Reserve Bank.

To bring these diagnoses to bankers, Williams maintained the emphasis on the supervisory dialogue with bank boards that Murray began, ratcheting the engagement with bank examiners, managers, and directors. In 1916, Williams began giving bank directors facsimiles of the formal examination reports, something that not even Murray had done (the latter sent summaries only). Williams also began requiring field examiners to impress upon directors their duties and responsibilities in risk management. As his changes took root, Williams congratulated himself that the plan "has resulted, in thousands of cases, in giving to the directors of banks, as well as officers, a clearer insight as to the bank's condition, and a better comprehension of its management and operations than they ever had before." As importantly, because national bank examination was now a twice-yearly affair, Williams needed to offer small bankers clear value for money. Giving them examination reports enabled "them to dispense with costly examinations, which some of them have heretofore been receiving periodically from special accountants." By 1918, Williams claimed that strict examination, in collaboration with more active directors, had given national banks "immunity from serious losses or failure."[45]

Williams also revitalized the call report, an old and mostly ineffective tool of supervision, into something much more powerful. Throughout the nineteenth century, the call reports fronted a system of disclosure and private risk management. The Comptroller compelled bankers to publish their balance sheets and market participants used the information to make decisions about the security of bank liabilities and the value of bank stocks. Because the Comptroller determined when reports were called, he could effectively test the resiliency of the system in moments of seasonal credit stringency.

Williams pushed further. On the one hand, he gathered more and more information, increasing the number of questions from fifty-four in 1914 to 134 in 1921. He also used the reports to compel compliance with law. Williams insisted that the stability of individual banks and the banking system rested on bankers "observing strictly the provisions of the national bank act and of conforming closely to the rules and regulations prescribed" by his office. In his hands, call reports became a weapon for this compliance. In one typical episode, Williams admonished bankers for charging higher interest rates than legally permitted in their home state. He then required them to list all loans on which they charged more than 6 percent in the call report. In his last act as Comptroller, Williams called on banks to publish officer salaries.[46]

Williams's campaigns infuriated bankers who viewed his efforts as a usurpation of their private prerogatives. Their irritation was a problem for the Comptroller's office. With the establishment of the Federal Reserve and the strengthening of the state systems, the Comptroller had significant competition. Without a balance sheet to provide liquidity, the Comptroller could only use information to cajole or to scold, to defend banks against other government actors, or to accuse them (there was active debate about whether the

Federal Reserve Act had further limited the Comptroller's enforcement powers by nullifying the power to prohibit dividends). The scolding Comptroller could alienate the national banks who might opt for a state charter while still enjoying the benefits of Fed membership. Given that dynamic, so long as banks remained solvent, the Comptroller's options were few.[47]

McFadden vs. the Comptroller

The Comptroller's weakness in the face of banker intransigence is evident in the case of the First National Bank of Canton, mentioned above. Even after Murray put the examiner in front of the board in 1909, the bank continued to face stern criticism, often for excessive loans to insiders. Chief among these insiders was Louis McFadden, the cashier and, after 1916, bank president. McFadden also happened to be a Republican member of Congress. In February 1917, after an examiner again found excessive loans, the Comptroller's office warned the bank: "If the next report of examination shows a violation of law with respect to the limit of loans it will be necessary to place your bank on the special list for frequent examinations and such other action taken as may be deemed necessary." In July, the excessive loans remained. The Canton bank was on the list.[48]

The Comptroller's office had always been able to single banks out for additional scrutiny, but the codification of twice-yearly exams made more frequent examination a potent marker. The bank's directors knew this and plead for forbearance. The excessive loans had been paid, they said. Subjection to a special examination "would reflect seriously locally on the general standing of this bank, and would place a powerful instrument in the hands of our competing bank." The Comptroller instructed the bank to await the results of the next examination. When that examination occurred, it revealed new and excessive insider lending. A number of loans and other financial services had arisen "of which the President of the Bank appears to be interested." As the violations continued, so too would the examinations.[49]

By May 1918, Deputy Comptroller Thomas Kane expressed the dire condition of the bank in the clearest possible language. "The bank continues to violate the law," he wrote, something he attributed to a "lack of proper management." He went further: "The bank will not observe the law or regulations of this office as long as President McFadden is the managing director, because the other directors seem to take no personal and active interest in the bank, and permit President McFadden to use the bank for his personal interest without due regard to safe and sound banking." Kane gave the directors an ultimatum: "This condition will not be permitted longer to continue," he wrote, adding that "if President McFadden is not inclined to observe the instructions of this office and the law, he should be required to resign and the board should elect someone else as president who will." As Kane would later explain, his intention was to activate the corporate governance machinery, in part by driving home to directors their liability for employing a president who deliberately and persistently violated the law.[50]

If the Comptroller's staff did not lack for boldness, neither did McFadden. In February 1919, he brought his fight into Congress, seeking an investigation of Williams and hearings on a bill he introduced to abolish the Comptroller's office. Williams responded quickly. In a letter to McFadden that leaked to the press, Williams asserted that the Canton bank "had been under rebuke and criticism of the Treasury Department for more than twenty years, through five comptrollerships and by fifteen bank examiners." Only the constant correction by government officials had saved McFadden's bank from ruin.[51]

McFadden, pursuing his claims in the Treasury and Congress already, decided to add the judiciary. In May, his bank sued Williams, seeking an injunction to prevent any further special examinations. The suit accused Williams personally of attempting to destroy the bank (although it was his staff that instigated the special examinations). The Comptroller's office played the publicity game too, releasing the correspondence with the Canton bank going back to 1904, along with affidavits from examiners and supervisory staff showing how poorly the bank had fared over so many years. The squabble gained additional gravity in 1920, when Republicans swept into Congress and McFadden became Chairman of the Banking and Currency Committee. His campaign to abolish the Comptroller's office moved from petty to plausible as the new Congress was gaveled into order.[52]

Hostility and Division: The Institutional Fracturing of Bank Supervision

McFadden's crusade was the sharp edge of long-building conflicts among the nation's divided supervisory institutions. Some of the hostility reduced to personal animosity—between McFadden and Williams, and between Williams and nearly everyone else. Yet the divisions in supervisory responsibilities and the consequences of institutional layering were much more structural than personal. The Federal Reserve Act created a central bank that balanced public and private control but which exercised power by providing liquidity through the private Reserve Banks. The Comptroller, meanwhile, remained a fully public official charged with enforcing the provisions of the National Banking Act, using that authority to guide or compel bankers toward solvency. The states and the clearinghouses were still in the picture—the former as yet another public competitor experimenting with alternative risk management strategies, and the latter increasingly supplanted by the Federal Reserve Banks. Wilson's compromise thus did not solve the issue of public versus private control. It merely shifted the fight onto the supervisory institutions.[53]

This conflict erupted early as the public Reserve Board and the private Reserve Banks battled over the information about member banks' businesses collected by the Comptroller's examiners. From the inauguration of the system, the Comptroller and national bank examiners strongly objected to opening exam reports to perusal by Reserve Bank directors, most of whom were bankers or their close associates (two-thirds of the Reserve Banks' board seats were elected by private banks directly and two of the three remaining directors had to have "tested banking experience"). Williams and members of the Federal Reserve Board immediately recognized such information-sharing could put sensitive business details in the hands of competitors. "Under no circumstances should any information contained in the Bank Examiner's reports be open for the inspection of the directors of any Federal Reserve Bank," an early member of the Federal Reserve Board wrote to reassure Williams in December 1914.[54]

Still, the Board was not completely on the side of the government. It wanted Fed examiners and Federal Reserve agents to have access to the Comptroller's examination reports—access that Williams, on the advice of his examiners, refused to grant. The Federal Reserve Act allowed but did not require the Comptroller to share reports with the Board. Williams determined to share only as much information as the Reserve Banks needed to determine that a borrowing bank was solvent.[55]

Information sharing implicated the larger issue of examination authority. The Comptroller's examiners argued that the law authorized Reserve Bank examinations only for exceptional circumstances, not the routine oversight that defined the Comptroller's place in the financial ecosystem. The Reserve Banks were, after all, banks. They needed no more information than their private counterparts to make lending decisions. Neither the Second Bank of the United States, nor any contemporary central bank, enjoyed searching examination power like that practiced by the Comptroller.[56]

Eventually, in 1916, Williams relented. As he had begun sharing facsimiles of examination reports with bankers and bank directors, he assented to sharing the same reports with Federal Reserve agents (though he also withheld confidential material from both). By 1918, meanwhile, the Fed had decided to focus much more exclusively on credit examination, emphasizing types of information—like the balance sheets of borrowing businesses—that the Comptroller's examiners did not collect. This division also mapped onto the state-chartered member banks. State supervisory officials had neither the time nor the inclination to perform the Reserve Banks' credit checks. Although the Board sought to convince state examiners to adopt the Fed's credit forms, its staff recognized that it would be "difficult to accomplish," leaving the Reserve Banks to expand their examination forces and credit supervision regime.[57]

The peace suggested by divided responsibilities did not last. Fed officials, like many others in Washington, had grown weary of Comptroller Williams. The friction, in part, focused on control. The Federal Reserve Board determined whether to admit state-chartered banks and exercised authority over changes in capital or mergers for all member banks. The Comptroller maintained chartering authority, and with it a passkey into the Federal Reserve System, since all national banks were admitted to the Federal Reserve System automatically. The Comptroller, competing with states, issued charters that the Fed would rather decline. At the same time, the Fed struggled to convince state banks to join its system. Small banks did not receive enough benefits to justify the costs of abiding by the system's reserve requirements and conforming with eligibility and acceptability. There were too many gatekeepers making redundant determinations about who could be a bank, such that the entire ecosystem ran on institutional friction.[58]

These frictions were also, at their heart, a conflict about whether the American banking system would be one of private control or public control. Reflecting on an intervention by the Federal Reserve Bank of New York to rescue an upstate bank, Federal Reserve Governor William P. G. Harding (1916–1922) was uncompromising in his appraisal that the private power of private liquidity provision was now the dominant supervisory framework, having displaced public power completely. "No matter how vigilant the Comptroller of the Currency might be, he could not have [rescued the bank] by himself, because he did not have the power. The Federal Reserve Board could not do it. It was only the Federal Reserve Bank which had both this power of examination . . . and then the power to apply the remedy." Harding, testifying before McFadden's committee, supported McFadden's efforts to abolish the Office of the Comptroller of the Currency, utterly dismissing its supervisory ethos. "The great defect in the comptroller's powers is that he can give advice, instructions, caution, and all that sort of thing, but the only remedy he had was the drastic one of revoking the charter." In effect—as McFadden well knew—that was no power at all.[59]

Harding's remarks were intended as fighting words and were taken as such. But behind the grandstanding, the Comptroller and the Fed faced a real and irreconcilable conflict. The Comptroller's mode of risk management centered on identifying threats to bank solvency and then using the lever of shareholder liability to compel corporate managers to keep their house in order or to exit while their personal losses remained manageable. Federal Reserve liquidity provision worked at cross-purposes. Instead of facing up to insolvency and bowing out when losses to shareholders—and depositors—might remain small, bank directors could gamble for redemption, mortgaging a bank's good assets to the local Federal Reserve Bank on the chance they could make up losses. Fed liquidity provision was not a lifeline but an anchor, one made heavier by the still resonant political claims of depositors. It was more expedient for the Comptroller and the Fed to feign strength by keeping banks open rather than showing strength by closing them. In this, the supervisors were on common ground, taking orders from private power rather than exercising public control.[60]

Bigness: A. P. Giannini vs. Louis McFadden

The friction between the Fed and the Comptroller could be chalked up to institutional growing pains if it did not overlay a smoldering financial crisis. After World War I, the still-teething central bank instigated a sharp deflation, seeking to bring prices back in line with the prewar gold standard. Commodity producers, especially farmers, who had borrowed to invest when prices were high, underwent a wrenching shock, as did their banks. Hundreds of rural banks failed each year, the majority of which were state-chartered institutions too small for Federal Reserve membership. State governments were not equipped to cope with the slow immolation, and bankers, depositors, and politicians all sought alternative strategies to rescue small banks from the agricultural depression. Deposit guarantees continued to capture the popular imagination, even as many state systems floundered and failed. Congress did better, repurposing the War Finance Corporation—which had lent to industry during World War I—into an agricultural lending agency. Yet neither of these public strategies could overcome the fact that too many small, rural banks were entirely invested in local monocrop economies at the mercy of global commodity price swings.[61]

Faced with too many small, weak, and poorly managed banks, many bankers and bank reformers argued that bank size, generated through branch banking, offered the ultimate private risk management technique, combining geographic diversification with internal liquidity. Bigness, however, posed political and supervisory difficulties. The Comptroller, the Fed, and state banking officials held conflicting views about the merits of branch banking, while the nation's long tradition of unit banking—predominant since the fall of the Second Bank of the United States in the 1830s and inscribed in the national banking system since the 1860s—created a resolute constituency of unit bankers who adamantly opposed the extension of branching privileges.[62]

California, where branching extended furthest and fastest, offered both a proving ground for large-scale branch networks and a stage for supervisory conflict. Drawing on the same reform impulses unleashed by the 1907 Panic, California adopted a statewide branching law in 1909. State banks expanded slowly through the war years, and then rapidly thereafter, often absorbing national banks and converting them into branches. By 1924, eighty-eight state-chartered California banks operated more than 450 branches. Some, like the Mercantile Trust Company of San Francisco and the Security Trust and Savings Bank of Los Angeles, focused on discrete urban markets. The Bank of Italy, by contrast, pursued true statewide branching, both in its own name and through affiliated banking groups controlled by founder Amadeo P. "A. P." Giannini. "The word 'revolutionary' can be overworked in connection with the Bank of Italy," the banks' biographers wrote. Following the Panic of 1907, Giannini took to branch banking like a divine calling.[63]

California banking officials saw themselves at the forefront of a branch banking revolution. "In the distribution of credit with a knowledge of the needs of every part of the territory involved, far better results may be accomplished than through the agency of many smaller institutions," the state's banking superintendent wrote in 1921. But as branch banking heated up after World War I, state officials pumped the brakes. Independent bankers had political influence, and they lobbied against the rapid expansion of branch networks, especially Giannini's Bank of Italy. State supervisors enjoyed discretion on whether "the public convenience and advantage will be promoted" by a new branch. Arguing that too rapid expansion could cause instability, superintendent Johnathan S. Dodge (1921–1923) used this authority to prohibit state

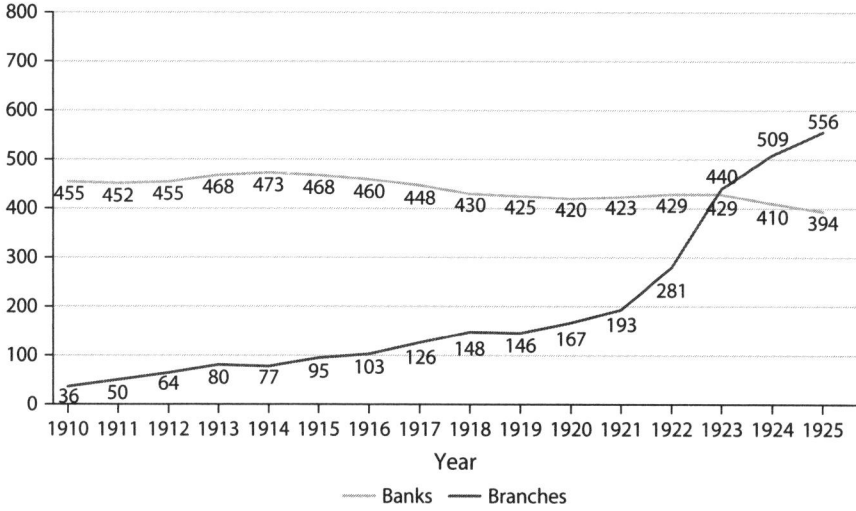

FIGURE 4.1. Banks and bank branches in the California, 1910–1925
Source: Annual Reports of the Superintendent of Banks of California, 1909–1925;
Shirley Donald Southworth, *Branch Banking in the United States* (McGraw-Hill,
1928), 54.

banks from opening de novo branches outside the city where their main office
was located.[64]

For Giannini, this was a bitter pill, but one he swallowed by creating nominally independent banking chains that he controlled through a ramified web of
holding companies. This corporate structure was always an unwelcome expedient: Giannini wanted a unified bank. In 1926, he asked permission to consolidate
his empire, principally composed of four banks, 155 branches, and $464,000,000 in
deposits. The State Superintendent of Banking said no, emphatically, arguing
that Giannini's empire was too big to supervise and beyond any public power to
control. "We ask you . . . to inform us how it is possible for the State Banking
Department of California to know what the condition of this chain is?" wrote
Superintendent J. Franklin Johnson. "Kindly state, also, at what point, if any,
short of the elimination of the independent banker, you propose to stop."[65]

California embodied the fears of federal officials who saw state branch
banking as an existential threat to the national banking system, to the Federal
Reserve, and to public control of banking. By the early 1920s, state branch
banks dominated major urban markets in cities like Cleveland, Detroit, and
New Orleans, and momentum seemed to be growing. Unit bankers, especially

through the influential American Bankers Association, waged increasingly apocalyptic lobbying campaigns against further branch expansion. Holding firm to still-resonant Jacksonian ideals, unit bankers sought to maintain the power, prestige, and preferential credit access that came with local financial control. Federal supervisors, echoing California officials, voiced concerns about effective oversight. Branch systems were difficult to supervise, they complained. Public examiners struggled to comprehend the often complex relationships between large banks' central offices and their branches, making public oversight even more dependent on privately controlled and managed information.[66]

More ominously, national banks were leaving for more permissive state charters, where federal officials could not monitor them at all. State branching "is having a positively alarming tendency to keep banking capital and organizations out of the national" system, Comptroller Daniel R. Crissinger (1921–1923) observed. "National banks cannot compete." When they left the national banking system, bankers left the Federal Reserve System as well. In their greatest fears, large chains on the scale of the Bank of Italy would operate alongside the Federal Reserve, exercising private monopolistic control over national flows of credit. Comptroller Henry M. Dawes (1923–1924) expressed this fear with all the emphasis he could muster: "*The issue is a clean-cut one as to whether the country prefers a system of privately owned branch banks or a reserve system under Federal control.*"[67]

Federal officials recognized some advantages to branching, especially in citywide bank networks, but they were indecisive, using their discretionary authority to toggle between permissiveness and opposition. Crissinger, formerly an Ohio banker, read the National Banking Act to permit national banks to open subsidiary offices—not branches—within the city where the bank was located, authorizing the first for a Los Angeles bank in June 1922. Dawes reversed course, working with McFadden to snuff out branch banking within the national banking system. The Fed likewise waffled. In 1917, the Board admitted the Bank of Italy into the system with an explicit assurance that it would not impede Giannini's branching ambitions. In the early 1920s, after determining that "the Bank of Italy already had more branches than the Federal Reserve Bank [of San Francisco] had machinery to properly supervise and examine," the Board changed course, adopting a version of California's de novo rule, prohibiting member banks from branching outside their home cities.[68]

Discretionary federal supervision had little power to forge a decisive resolution on branching as long as the state and national systems operated under substantially different rules. To resolve the question, Congress needed to act. In 1923, Dawes surveyed bankers and national bank examiners and, in 1924, he sent a reform bill to Congress, which McFadden, as House Banking Chairman, took up with vigor. The draft legislation made some concession to size, permitting citywide branches for national banks in states that allowed branching. Unit bankers, however, would brook no compromise. The congressional fight raged for two years, as unit bankers sought to halt the spread of branching entirely. The tide turned in 1926 when the American Bankers Association, meeting in Los Angeles, dropped its opposition.[69]

The McFadden Act, forged in the waning fires of anti-branching politics, has long been overshadowed by the Federal Reserve Act on one side, and by the New Deal banking reforms on the other. But it is important for supervision in several respects. It reflected the tentative acceptance of size and diversification as legitimate private risk management strategies. Congress also partially affirmed the private risk management of the nation's fragmented central bank, granting the Federal Reserve Banks perpetual charters.[70]

At the same time, Congress—and perhaps the bankers and bank examiners who provided fodder for the law—recognized the inadequacy of the experiment. Central bank risk management, as conceptualized by the Federal Reserve's architects such Paul M. Warburg and others, required limiting commercial banks to commercial bills—which provided good assets on their own, as well as the prospect of central bank discounting when money got tight. Instead of holding bankers to this narrow path, McFadden pushed toward diversification, authorizing banks to engage in risk management through securities markets. By enabling banks to buy bonds, the Act enabled them to build up a secondary reserve of liquid assets—indeed, after 1927, the very term "secondary reserve" came to mean bonds, not eligible real bills. Instead of looking to the central bank, bankers could look to bond markets for liquidity. As it turned out, 1927 was hardly an ideal moment to venture into the bond market.[71]

Conclusion

The last of the immiserating panics of the Gilded Age in 1907 made plain to all that the creaky mechanisms for managing residual risk had fallen apart—if they had ever even held together at all. Congress and states considered all kinds of alternatives before settling on what Wright Patman, a later critic of the Federal Reserve, would call institutionally and constitutionally "a pretty queer duck." Despite the basic endorsement of important features of both the private clearinghouses and the European central banks on which the Fed was modeled, Congress made more of an impact on the structure of bank supervision in the Fed's creation for what it didn't resolve: It refused to clarify which of its creatures would use which parts of a complex ecosystem of supervisory authority. The advent of the phenomenon of multiple and overlapping federal and state authority over bank supervision would continue to be a dominant theme of bank supervision in the twentieth century, compounding in the years ahead with the creation of still more institutional actors. There was method to this madness, even if that method revealed itself not from legislative laboratories but from the lived experience of supervision throughout the system. As the Fed took its place as a supervisor of reserves and currency, it necessarily looked at questions of residual risk differently than the approach taken by the Comptroller—the latter viewing its mission to support, defend, cajole, and sometimes punish the banks that were part of the national banking system, mostly based on the careful gathering of information gained from inside the banks themselves.[72]

The national banking system presented federal prerogatives in a way that the hybrid Federal Reserve System—both public and private, national and local—did not. "The Comptroller of the Currency should," Comptroller Henry Dawes intoned solemnly in 1923, "be the representative and the partisan of the national banks." The Federal Reserve looked at similar questions differently. The Fed *was* a mostly private system. It was not a partisan for bankers on their behalf because the Fed was essentially the banker itself. That common identification with private sector prerogatives was the end of their overlap, however. The Comptroller used information as its primary tool and resource in managing the risks that individual banks and the national banking system imposed. The Fed used both liquidity and information, in that order. This meant a very different set of questions for what kinds of support would be required in the event that residual risk would be realized on the doorsteps (figuratively) and balance sheets (literally) of bank supervisors. Whether federal bank supervisors wanted this or not, they were about to experience their first major test.[73]

Interlude: Sioux Falls Falls

IN SIOUX FALLS, South Dakota, the Banking Crisis of the Great Depression did not begin in 1933, or even 1930—it started in 1924. On January 11 that year, a national bank examiner closed the Sioux Falls National Bank, the third largest bank in the city, "because conditions had warranted it." Those conditions included a balance sheet clogged with "doubtful" agricultural paper and even more doubtful loans to the bank's directors.[1]

Under the watchful eye of receiver Charles H. Wilcox, a committee of "responsible men of this community" worked to reorganize the failed bank but not in time to stem a growing panic that gripped first the city and then the region. Sioux Falls boasted a modest clearinghouse, and many of the small state-chartered banks in South Dakota, North Dakota, and Minnesota kept their merger reserves there. A crisis in Sioux Falls promised regional repercussions. That's exactly what happened. After the larger state-chartered Sioux Falls Trust and Savings Bank shut its doors on January 14, these country banks quickly folded too. The severity of the crisis was immediately clear to authorities. On January 18, President Calvin Coolidge announced plans to aid banks, promising loans from the Federal Reserve Bank of Minneapolis and the still-humming War Finance Corporation (a lending agency from the World War I era that Congress repurposed in 1921 to aid the distressed agricultural sector). Within days, the WFC's managing director, Eugene I. Meyer Jr. (1919–1920, 1921–1927), and the Comptroller of the Currency, Henry M. Dawes (1923–1924), were both in Sioux Falls to provide a human presence to the federal promises.[2]

That presence and those promises, too, did not halt the runs. The International State Bank of Sioux Falls failed on January 22. The Commercial and Savings Bank followed on January 25. By that point, closed banks held $10,000,000 in frozen deposits, twice the deposits held by those banks still struggling to stay open. Dakota Trust and Savings failed on May 12. "The general public is in an ugly and suspicious state of mind toward all banks," Wilcox reported to the Comptroller the next day.[3]

These failures were not simply the irrational panic of uninformed depositors. The farm economy that the Sioux Falls banks served had been teetering for some time. During World War I, American farmers, encouraged by European demand and federal lending programs, took out loans and planted wheat from fence to fence. With the return to normalcy, farmers faced the acute problem of oversupply. Wheat prices fell; farm loans stayed in place. Depressed markets and crop failures pushed an already precarious situation to the edge of ruin. When farm loans went bad *en masse*, the banks that had made them without diversification closed. And when the banks closed, given the fragility of the South Dakota deposit insurance program initiated only a decade before, depositors lost some or all of their savings. In the face of such losses, depositors did not panic irrationally; they panicked rationally, pulling their money at the first sign of trouble, speeding the very collapse they feared.[4]

The examiner's decision to close the Sioux Falls National Bank pushed the first banking domino, and the resulting cascade intensified the Comptroller's supervisory duties. The widespread failure made Wilcox's work of reorganizing and, when that failed, liquidating the bank that much more difficult.

Reorganization demanded cooperation with depositors. None was forthcoming. The reorganization committee planned to split the bank's assets in half, placing the "rejected assets" in a liquidating trust and the sound assets in a recapitalized bank. Depositors with more than $50 would take an immediate 50 percent haircut but over time would receive some payout from the proceeds of the trust. "The alternative to the plan is a Receivership," by which they meant liquidation, "which is destructive and expensive," the committee warned. The committee needed all depositors to approve their plan, but several would not go along. Eight state banks with substantial deposits were "very hostile" and "stubborn." The committee also had "some difficulty" with the State Banking Department. It held claims on the deposits of several closed state banks and there was "considerable antagonism between the State Banking Department and the National Banks," Wilcox reported.[5]

Soon this technical problem became a political one. William H. McMaster, South Dakota's Republican governor, stoked that considerable antagonism, barnstorming the state in early 1924. McMaster did not blame the agricultural economy or its overdependence on wartime wheat production. He did not blame the bankers that failed to diversify or the depositors whose simultaneous (if rational) withdrawals caused the collapse that they feared. The governor put the responsibility entirely at the feet of the Federal Reserve and the Comptroller of the Currency.[6]

He might have put more blame at the feet of the depositors. In Sioux Falls, the holdouts scuttled the first reorganization plan. Wilcox's next option was an assessment on the shareholders to recapitalize the bank. If the bank went into receivership, the stockholders were liable for $150,000, equal to their interest in the bank and consistent with the prevailing double liability regime. The threat of a full assessment, Wilcox hoped, would convince them to pay in some lesser amount that, with additional outside cash, could bring the bank back from the brink. But the stockholders had little incentive to sign on. The necessary buy-in to rescue the bank would be so close to their full liability as to make no difference. With the economy collapsing, there was no outside cash to be had.[7]

The stockholders, like the depositors, followed the rational (if destructive) course. In that environment, the recapitalized bank looked likely to fail all over again, wiping out the stockholders again (and potentially imposing a second wave of double liability). Stockholders were better off trying their luck in court. In the meantime, deteriorating economic conditions drove down asset prices. "Further delay is inimical to the interests of the depositors and creditors of the bank," the Comptroller urged. Wilcox agreed. In May, he wrote, "I believe I should now proceed with the liquidation and push every matter just as hard as local conditions will permit."[8]

Wilcox knew the liquidation would be long and messy. He estimated it would take between three to five years to complete. "I am likely to be on one side or another in several hundred different suits before I succeed in getting everything cleaned up," he reported. To manage the receivership, Wilcox recruited two assistants. One, D. L. McKinney, had been a member of the reorganization committee and formerly an officer of the bank. The conflict was obvious, but Wilcox needed manpower and McKinney knew the business. The second, T. M. Bailey, was a corporate lawyer, independent of local interests. Both, Wilcox was careful to note, were Republicans like the governor and South Dakota's congressional delegation. For the next year and half, Wilcox did his best to cajole, negotiate, threaten, and economize. He typed all his own letters on the bank's stationery to save money. But with six of Sioux Fall's eight banks belly-up, liquidation was "rather difficult." Local markets were flooded with assets no one had money to buy. By the end of 1926, depositors had received only 32 cents on the dollar.[9]

The immediate failure of Sioux Falls' banks obliterated local purchasing power and flattened the regional payment system, with clearinghouse exchanges falling 61 percent from 1923 to 1925. Depositors in the state banks that collapsed had the nominal promise of South Dakota's deposit guarantee fund, but it too folded under the weight of the failures. By the end of 1926, the state owed depositors $43,000,000, but the legislature would not guarantee the obligation. The state supreme court soon declared the fund insolvent.[10]

The Sioux Falls National Bank receivership concluded on August 10, 1934, half a decade behind schedule. By that time, the receivership had paid 50 percent of the claims. It had paid Wilcox and his staff $217,510 in salaries and legal expenses. Sioux Falls National was the 746th national bank to fail since 1863. By the time its receivership concluded, 2,133 more national banks had failed. The Depression that claimed them all started, in an important sense, in Sioux Falls.[11]

5

The 1933 Bank Holiday and the Legitimacy of Supervision

ON SUNDAY, March 12, 1933, newly elected President Franklin D. Roosevelt began addressing the nation's unprecedented economic crisis with the line: "I want to talk for a few minutes with the people of the United States about banking."[1]

Broadcast over radio to a nervous but hopeful public, the first of Roosevelt's "fireside chats" was designed to reassure the nation that his administration was solving the banking and economic crisis. In avuncular tones, the new president explained how vital banking was to "keep the wheels of industry and of agriculture turning." Roosevelt detailed why he had declared a national bank holiday—which had closed all the nation's banks the previous week—as "the first step in the Government's reconstruction of our financial and economic fabric." Finally, he reassured his listeners that these bold efforts would ensure that "no sound bank is a dollar worse off than it was when it closed its doors last Monday."[2]

The stakes could not have been higher. Between 1929 and 1933, real GDP had fallen by 23 percent. The unemployment rate topped out in 1933, with nearly one in four Americans jobless. Between January 1930 and March 1933, 5,722 distressed U.S. banks had merged or permanently closed. In the two months preceding Roosevelt's inauguration, more than forty states shuttered their banks to prevent further failures. Compared to the economic wreckage of the Great Depression, the Panic of 1907 looked like a garden party.[3]

Just as alarmingly, the failure of the banking system had occurred despite the significant institutional redesign of U.S. banking supervision over the previous generation. The credibility of the Comptroller of the Currency's informational approach collapsed as bank customers recognized that supervisory reassurances were hollow. The Federal Reserve's liquidity approach to bank supervision, if anything, made matters worse as Reserve Banks gave bankers enough liquidity to gamble for redemption, while leaving depositors with devalued assets when banks failed.[4]

Roosevelt also understood that if the banking and economic crises remained unchecked, political upheaval could quickly follow. Around the world, extreme economic hardship translated into increased support for both communist and fascist political solutions. The same month as Roosevelt's speech, the newly empowered Nazi Party began sending political rivals to Dachau. Liberal democracy itself was on the line. If the bank holiday failed, there was no assurance that the nation could succeed.[5]

The day after Roosevelt's chat, depositors stood in line at their banks not to extend the panics but to return their hoarded cash. The holiday succeeded, and with it the financial recovery, the New Deal, and arguably, American democracy itself. Although further reforms—most importantly the devaluation of the dollar through the abandonment of the gold standard—would be necessary to revive the economy, the holiday was the vital precondition for all further action. Indeed, Roosevelt's banking policy and currency policy were inextricably linked. To devalue the dollar, his administration first had to save the banks. Only then would he have the credibility to transform the currency. Only then could the financial system function in a world without gold.[6]

Contrary to the popular narratives that arose almost immediately after the holiday, its extraordinary success wasn't simply the result of Roosevelt's winning charisma. As the new president soothed the American public with his words, bank supervisors invited American depositors back into the system with their expertise. This expertise had not come cheaply. Limits on the scope of supervisory action and institutional conflict among competing agencies had prevented supervisors from halting the rolling destruction of the U.S. banking system. But these failures obscured what supervisors contributed to the resolution of that collapse. Over two generations, from the advent of the national banking system to the crisis itself, federal officials and the Federal Reserve Banks had built up an information-gathering regime that equipped them to make decisive judgments about the condition of the nation's banks. They had not lacked information but the political authority to turn knowledge into action. Roosevelt gave them precisely this authority.[7]

The holiday may have been a cooling-off period for panicked bank customers, but it was also a moment of unprecedented mobilization for supervisors. During that frenzied week, supervisors used their files to restore life or pronounce death on thousands of individual firms. Although their work was frantic, bleary-eyed, and subject to important political constraints, it was essential to placing the financial system on a sound footing. Roosevelt, for his part, needed the bank supervisors too. Supervisors provided the technocratic foundation to Roosevelt's lofty rhetoric, grounding his promises in the expertise of long-serving federal bureaucrats. Supervisors who had strained their credibility keeping troubled banks open during the slow boil of the crisis could now confidently close them. It was only by closing insolvent banks that the public was assured that the banks which did reopen were sound.[8]

Before the holiday, supervisors had engaged in a constant contest over the boundaries of public and private risk management responsibility. With the holiday, the public—and specifically the federal government—took firm control. It was and remains the watershed moment in the history of bank supervision, an enduring resolution of the key question: Who, at bottom, controls financial risk?

The Landscape of Supervisory Authority and the Coming Crisis

On the eve of the banking crises, the U.S. banking system retained its uniquely byzantine institutional and supervisory complexity. Instead of locating power in one centralized institution, individual state banking departments and the federal Comptroller of the Currency both maintained authority to charter and oversee banks using a mix of public and private risk management. After 1914, the new Federal Reserve System overlaid this structure. The Fed incorporated both state and federal institutions, and it pursued a distinct supervisory approach—risk management through liquidity provision. Leading up to the crises that set off the Great Depression, these supervisory institutions, never in harmony, sharply diverged, laying bare shortcomings that would compound in the face of systemic crisis.

The banking system's most important weakness was that state and federal chartering competition enabled the formation of too many weak banks. By 1920, the nation was blanketed by nearly 30,000 individual banking firms, most of them small, under-capitalized, geographically confined, rural, and ripe for collapse during the long agricultural depression that followed the end of World War I. Between 1921 and 1929, more than 600 banks failed each year, nearly ten times the average for the previous decade. At the same time, banks in urban centers were expanding through new branch networks and holding

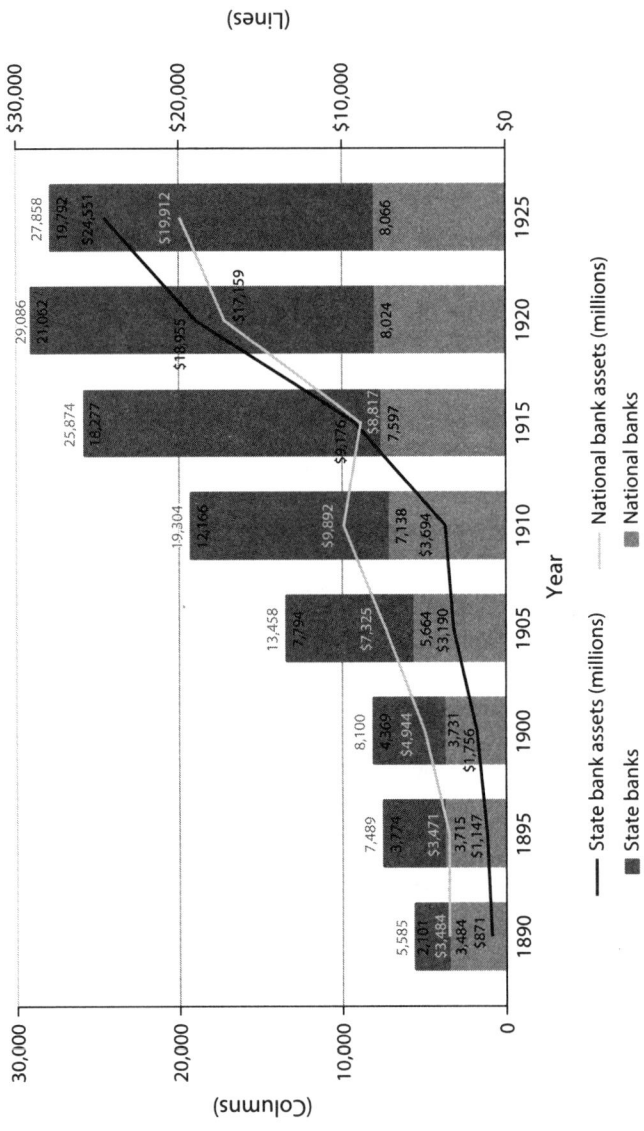

(Lines)

$30,000

$20,000

$10,000

$0

	1890	1895	1900	1905	1910	1915	1920	1925
	5,585	7,489	8,100	13,458	19,304	25,874	29,086	27,858
	2,101	3,774	4,369	7,794	12,166	18,227	21,062	19,792
	$3,484	$3,471	$4,944	$7,325	$9,892	$9,176	$18,955	$24,551
	$871	3,715	3,731	5,664	7,138	$8,817	$17,159	$19,912
		$1,147	$1,756	$3,190	$3,694	7,597	8,024	8,066

Year

— State bank assets (millions)   — National bank assets (millions)

■ State banks   ■ National banks

30,000

20,000

10,000

0

(Columns)

FIGURE 5.1. Banks by charter and assets, 1890–1925

Source: Eugene Nelson White, *The Regulation and Reform of the American Banking System, 1920–1929* (Princeton University Press, 1983), 12–13, 132 (after 1914, deposits substituted for assets).

companies. Depending on the bank, their growth in scale and scope offered stability or speculative opportunity. In all cases, their large size made government oversight more difficult.[9]

Federal supervisors at the Comptroller and the Federal Reserve Banks incrementally developed new methods with which they sought to guide bankers toward sound banking. The Comptroller used the loan quality system—loan criticism—refined in the 1910s as the primary tool for diagnosing and improving distressed banks. During their inspections, examiners characterized problematic loans as "slow," "doubtful," and "loss"—which represented a scale of illiquidity (slow) and poor credit quality (loss). A bank with too many slow loans was "frozen"—incapable of new lending and in danger if its deposit base dried up. A bank with too many losses was insolvent and promptly closed.[10]

Supervision through loan criticism was one of the most important developments of the early twentieth century. Although it appeared to be technical and objective, loan criticism entailed significant supervisory discretion. Loans did not announce themselves as "slow" or "doubtful"—they required not only supervisory judgment but supervisory negotiation between bankers and examiners about category decisions. The Comptroller "would not make a hard and fast rule as to what assets would be considered slow or doubtful," Fed researchers explained in 1933 in a retrospective assessment of loan criticism and supervision.[11]

Despite the implicit enforcement judgment in these characterizations, for most banks, loan criticism brought not enforcement but information. Public evaluations of asset quality relied on the cooperation of bank directors and bank managers to make good on the intelligence they provided. This was private finance, private control, and public warning but not more. The Comptroller could send sternly worded letters, but in the 1920s, the only genuine enforcement power the office retained was the messy process of liquidation. As one Comptroller phrased it, "there is no punishment but death."[12]

Loan criticism created real information that, federal officials argued, might have prevented more bank failures if backed by more forceful public authority. The 1933 Fed retrospective focused on 225 bank failures between 1925 and 1930, finding that examiners had criticized assets for years before the banks finally failed. "You left us in the situation of officiating at the birth of a bank, and at its death, but as a doctor in between with no power to make the patient take medicine," former Acting Comptroller Francis G. Awalt (1932–1933) complained to Congress in 1934. Under the balance of public and private power that prevailed before the banking holiday, the Comptroller could only examine, evaluate, and warn.[13]

The Federal Reserve Banks operated within a similar window of rules and discretion, even as they exercised a distinct form of power. As with the clearinghouses on which they were based, Reserve Banks undertook their most important supervisory work through counterparty lending. The Fed provided liquidity by lending against bank assets at a discount, offering a reliable source of cash in periods of market pressure. By law, the Reserve Banks could only rediscount what came to be known as "real bills," or liquid, commercial loans. The law was silent about the credit quality of those loans. Because Reserve Banks assumed the credit risk of the underlying collateral, the Reserve Banks developed "acceptability" requirements, using rediscount policy to influence member bank lending behavior. Like loan criticism, acceptability standards were fundamentally discretionary and varied among the Reserve Banks; unlike loan criticism, a denial at the discount window could have real consequences that some Reserve Banks were willing to impose and others eager to forbear.[14]

In the throes of the nineteenth-century banking panics that led to the creation of the Federal Reserve System, public supervisors knew intimately the difference between solvency issues (on which they could act) and liquidity problems (about which they were virtually powerless). The 1920s provided the Federal Reserve Banks ample opportunity to demonstrate that the liquidity problem had been solved. None proved more adept at this job than the Federal Reserve Bank of Atlanta, especially in its efforts to rescue failing banks in sunny Florida.[15]

In spring of July 1929, a fruit fly epidemic devastated Florida's citrus groves. Depositors, fearing that farmers would not repay their loans, ran on their local banks. Citizens Bank in Tampa, which sat at the center of a large correspondent network, suspended operations on July 17, 1929, threatening to take down the entire network. Two large national banks in the area, hubs of similar networks, faced sustained runs and prepared for the same outcome. It looked to be the Florida version of the fall of Sioux Falls (see the interlude preceding this chapter). The ending turned out much better. On the same day of Citizens Bank's failure, but before the failure of the others could occur, the deputy governor of the Federal Reserve Bank of Atlanta flew to Tampa in an airplane loaded with $1 million in Federal Reserve Notes—i.e., cash—and a directive to do all he could to aid the banks with that cash, fruit flies be damned. An additional $5 million arrived the next morning. The gambit worked. "The sight of the money in huge stacks in the cages of the bank tellers had a reassuring effect," the *Financial Chronicle* reported.[16]

In such moments, Reserve Banks could take on the role once filled by private clearinghouses: converting deposits into cash—and proper currency too, not mere clearinghouse certificates. In the short run, this looked like the implementation of the celebrated advice from central bank theorist Walter Bagehot in 1873—central banks like the Atlanta Fed (or, in Bagehot's case, the Bank of England) needed to "lend to merchants, to minor bankers, to 'this man and that man,' whenever the security is good," Bagehot wrote. "In wild periods of alarm, one failure makes many, and the best way to prevent the derivative failures is to arrest the primary failure which causes them."[17]

The downside of the Bagehotian strategy occurs when the panic is slow-boiling, the roots of the problems are deeper, and the illiquidity of the collateral is in fact evidence of insolvent institutions (Bagehot's "whenever the security is good" caveat does a lot of work in his prescription). As the 1920s ground on, some Reserve Banks habitually propped up weak member banks, keeping troubled banks open and undermining the Reserve Banks' ability to respond in a crisis. Hundreds of Fed members carried increasingly large debts to their Reserve Banks. Perpetually indebted banks were "made subject to special inquiry," but they were not cut off. To do so would have been, as New York Fed Governor Benjamin Strong opined, "the worst type of discipline." By opting for forbearance, the Reserve Banks hoped that the booming economy would enable troubled banks to right themselves, even where sectors of the economy (like agriculture) teetered on the brink of collapse. Many member banks stayed in debt, committing their eligible collateral and limiting the ability—and in some cases the willingness—of Reserve Banks to inject liquidity when full panic struck. By the time the banking crisis arrived in force, bank supervisors' power to know outstripped their power to act.[18]

The Coming Crisis

The 1930 failure of Nashville-based Caldwell & Company, which precipitated the first of the Depression's banking crises, demonstrated the foundational weaknesses of overlapping federal oversight. During the 1920s boom years, Rogers C. Caldwell built his company into the largest financial conglomerate in the South, a highly leveraged empire of brokerages, insurance companies, industrial firms, and affiliate banks. Like many financial empire builders, Caldwell drew firms together through a complex ownership structure with little underlying capital, shuffling cash and paper promises throughout the group to give the appearance of strength. By the end of the 1920s, Caldwell and his associates controlled sixty-three banks in Arkansas and Tennessee, which they used to finance ever more speculative ventures. The empire, constructed on borrowed funds at the height of the bubble, floated well on calm waters.

After the 1929 stock market crash shattered market confidence, Caldwell scrambled for cash.[19]

As Caldwell headed toward insolvency, the National Bank of Kentucky, headed by speculator James B. Brown, agreed to step in. Brown and Caldwell were a well-matched pair. For a decade, Brown had managed the National Bank of Kentucky in "utter disregard for the law and the regulations of the Comptroller's office." Beginning in 1925, the banking practices in Brown's institution got bad enough that national bank examiners were sent in to comb through the Kentucky bank's books, demanding charge-offs and corrections amounting to millions of dollars of slow, doubtful, and worthless paper. None of this slowed Brown. Rather, irritated by the Comptroller's incessant criticism, Brown sought to denationalize and continue banking under a state charter. He could not do so, however, until he repaid $8 million in loans to the Federal Reserve Bank of St. Louis. Brown sought to raise the cash by wrapping his banks into a Delaware holding company and selling stock to investors, affiliating with Caldwell to pull the venture off. The deal collapsed, however, when a national bank examiner let slip that the National Bank of Kentucky had long been insolvent.[20]

Although the story of the examiner's indiscretion is possibly apocryphal, it reflected the Comptroller's assessment of the Kentucky bank. It also demonstrated the Comptroller's fundamental challenge: Unless examiners could unambiguously demonstrate insolvency, they could only criticize. By the end of the 1920s, national bank examiners had enough information to predict that Caldwell and Brown's banks were extremely sensitive to panic. Without a viable enforcement mechanism, their supervisory criticism could do little to change the recalcitrant bankers' behavior. By November 1930, it was too late.

On November 7, the Tennessee Banking Superintendent closed one of Caldwell's banks. Contagion burned through Caldwell's affiliates. Meanwhile, corporate depositors and correspondents pulled their deposits from Brown's Kentucky bank. Twenty-five percent of its deposits vanished in ten days. The Federal Reserve Bank of St. Louis offered no help. The Kentucky bank had rediscounted all its eligible paper, and from the Reserve Bank's perspective, there was no other good security on which to base any further loans. Panic gripped the Mid-South and Midwest. In two weeks, hundreds of banks shut their doors.[21]

Once the panic struck, the Reserve Banks offered the best hope for rescue from the depositor stampede. The Atlanta Federal Reserve—whose jurisdiction covered the eastern halves of Tennessee and Kentucky, with the St. Louis Fed responsible for the western halves—determined that some, although not all, of Caldwell's banks could be saved. Over the next several days, the Atlanta Fed repeated its rescue of the Tampa banks, flooding Tennessee with currency and walling off the runs.[22]

However, the crises extended to banks across the South and into the Midwest, some of which were under the St. Louis Fed's authority. While the Atlanta Fed exercised its discretionary power in favor of ample liquidity, St. Louis continued a longstanding policy of restraint even as runs on banks and closures continued aggressively. The Reserve Bank had imposed rigid acceptability standards and made no move to relax them as the crisis accelerated. When the panic spread to Mississippi, another state evenly split between the St. Louis (north) and Atlanta (south) districts, the Atlanta bank lent aggressively, while the St. Louis bank did not. Panic burned hot on the St. Louis side.[23]

The Caldwell failure and subsequent contagion revealed both the impotence of the Comptroller's supervision, as well as the dangers and inconsistencies of the Fed's quasi-private, geographically fragmented, discretionary liquidity. The chartering authorities' regime of information provision and corporate governance could not persuade Caldwell or Brown to walk safer paths in the months and years before their implosion. Meanwhile, Fed liquidity gave reckless bankers facing insolvency more money to plow into risky ventures, while sound member banks facing illiquidity were left at the mercy of discretionary Reserve Bank policy—a function during the Caldwell crisis of whether they operated within the St. Louis Fed's district or without.

No More Bank Failures

The bank failures at the end of 1930 deepened the nation's growing financial crisis, setting federal supervisors on a path of somewhat counterintuitive decisions. The well-publicized bank failures made depositors nervous, prompting them to withdraw cash and hoard their savings. To meet their depositors' enormous demands, bankers sought liquidity in the market by selling bonds. As bankers sold, prices on the bonds dropped, which in turn eroded the balance sheets of banks that continued to hold listed securities (see the interlude following this chapter for an account of the origins of these problems and Comptroller's effort to solve them through institutionally creative means). This spiraling dynamic steadily increased the number of banks nationwide teetering on the edge of liquidation as banks' equity capital—the difference between their assets and liabilities—continued to drop.[24]

The Fed and the Comptroller recognized the severity of the crisis. However, their legitimacy, shaped by continuous public pressure for depositor safety, came not through closing banks but by keeping them open. Officials hoped that with time and gradual supervisory influence, conditions would improve, bankers would clean up their balance sheets, and unsound institutions would muddle their way to soundness. When time ran out on these insolvent banks, supervisors felt they had no other option: Whether through failures to liquidate (at the Comptroller) or failures to cut off lending (through the Fed), supervisors pushed forbearance further. Strikingly, what supervisors did not lack was information. Through their sophisticated examination and reporting regime, they saw the severity of the crisis. But they also knew that their tools could not restore solvency as the market prices of bank assets fell. To prevent any more bank failures, federal officials extended their discretion on foreclosure further and further.

Of course, the entire categorization framework of "slow," "doubtful," and "loss" was an exercise in forbearance to some degree. The problem now was that a bank's assets consisted not only of bespoke loans whose values were determined by supervisory negotiation and discretion but also of bonds with deep secondary markets whose values bank examiners could determine by consulting a newspaper. In a time of crisis, with bonds depreciating by the day, this "more accurate" information was a threat to the solvency of scores of banks.[25]

To keep the banks open, examiners began to look at bank balance sheets very differently. In January 1931, Comptroller John W. Pole (1928–1932) instructed examiners to give consideration "to the present and what is believed to be a temporary condition of the bond market" and urged them to limit write-downs on bonds "which are believed to be intrinsically sound." Examiners, not bond markets, would make that judgment. Pole, the only Comptroller to begin his career as a national bank examiner and work his way through the ranks, understood the power inherent to such discretion. He was also responding to political pressure. President Herbert Hoover instructed the Comptroller "not to do anything to rock the boat, and not to have any more bank failures."[26]

As the banking system deteriorated—790 banks failed in the first half of 1931—federal officials united behind extraordinary forbearance. In August 1931, the Federal Reserve Board and the Reserve Bank governors unanimously agreed to urge the Comptroller—the only one with the power to do so—to extend discretion to declare banks solvent. By December 1931, Pole was ordering examiners to actively "disregard market depreciation upon bonds not in default." When this memo came, New York Fed officials estimated that an astonishing 60 percent of New York banks, based on the market value of their securities portfolios, were impaired or insolvent. These banks remained open and notionally solvent only because examiners declared them so.[27]

Hoover's insistence on extreme forbearance was in line with his overall approach to the country's larger financial crisis: public optimism, light-touch supervision, and faith that private banks would ultimately sort themselves out. In other words, he insisted on private finance with some limited consultation from public officials. A self-made man, administrative guru, and symbol of sober business modernism, Hoover remained committed throughout the crises to a vision of guiding, rather than interventionist, government. He demanded forbearance from the Comptroller to give bankers time and space to get their businesses in order.[28]

In September 1931, however, Great Britain abandoned the gold standard, sparking the next major banking crisis of the Great Depression. By October, Hoover accepted that supervisory forbearance could no longer, on its own, maintain depositor confidence. Even after he decided that intervention was necessary, however, the president remained unwilling to throw the full weight of the federal government behind the banking system. Instead, he sought to convince bankers to self-organize their rescue efforts. At an October 4 meeting in the Washington apartment of Treasury Secretary Andrew Mellon, Hoover strong-armed the nation's leading bankers into forming a private corporation, the National Credit Corporation (NCC), which would pool cash and purchase bank assets not eligible for discount by the Federal Reserve. The plan was initially greeted with public acclaim. *Literary Digest* called it "Hoover's Golden Torch to Thaw Frozen Assets."[29]

The fully private National Credit Corporation failed to live up to Hoover's hopes, in part because it replicated one of the existing problems of the quasi-private Reserve Banks. The corporation required banks to open up their books so the corporation—managed by seconded bank executives, sometimes competitors to the banks examined—could evaluate the collateral assets. Weak banks hesitated to undergo such scrutiny. The corporation, seeking to protect its balance sheet, also hesitated to lend. By December 1931, just two months after its formation, the NCC had clearly failed.[30]

As banks continued to tumble, Hoover was finally forced to inject more public control into the field of private finance. He approved—begrudgingly at first—a proposal for the Reconstruction Finance Corporation (RFC), a public corporation modeled on the World War I-era War Finance Corporation, which would attempt to do what the private NCC would not. Established by

Congress in February 1932, the RFC lent to troubled banks against high-quality collateral as a preferred creditor. Money flowed, but with the consequence that claims of troubled banks' other creditors—especially depositors—became subordinated, secured only by a weaker pool of assets. Declining market confidence and depositor runs often accompanied RFC assistance. Troubled banks needed more capital, not more debt.[31]

For the Hoover administration—the bank supervisors very much included—the chief function of supervision remained keeping banks open, not forcing them to close. Yet the policy of keeping unsound banks open undermined supervision's legitimacy, as bank directors, clients, and depositors became wise to this increasingly desperate charade. Through 1931, scores of "solvent" banks continued to close because of bank runs. "We closed very few banks," Comptroller Pole explained defensively in March 1932, "their depositors closed them." By then, however, examination had ceased to be an engine of public confidence. Pole nonetheless urged examiners to hold the line on forbearance. In July 1932, Pole wrote to his national bank examiners in frustration: "Reports of examinations received by this office recently clearly indicate that some examiners have not fully grasped the meaning of previous instructions." He again urged examiners to "exercise extraordinary discretion."[32]

In 1932, on the eve of the collapse of the U.S. financial system, government officials had pushed forbearance to and beyond its limit. Hoover's campaign for a second term rested on bold statements of optimism, but what was needed were bold commitments of positive government action. Such a public commitment, however, was antithetical to the prevailing theory of supervision, which emphasized guiding, rather than directing, private activity. As the overall economy continued to decline into 1932, extreme forbearance's fiction of solvency became harder to maintain. Supervisors could no longer secure the public's confidence. The bluff of paper solvency worked for a time, but when the collapse came, it exposed supervision as essentially powerless.[33]

Winter War, Spring Holiday

On November 8, 1932, Franklin Delano Roosevelt defeated Herbert Hoover in a landslide. Four days later, Francis Awalt, Acting-Comptroller in place of John Pole (who had resigned in September due to ill health caused by the "severe strain" of the banking crises), painted Hoover's Treasury Secretary Ogden Mills a bleak picture of the nation's banking system. Local banking conditions were, district by district, "menacing and unstable," "unsatisfactory," "deplorable," and, when Awalt apparently ran out of adjectives, just plain "bad." Major banks, vital to their local markets, were "frozen and dangerously extended," "either insolvent or . . . seriously impaired," and simply "embarrassed." The Comptroller's policy of not doing anything "to rock the boat" had kept these embarrassed banks nominally open for business, but supervisory officials recognized a reckoning was imminent. Over the next few months, the banking system unraveled completely.[34]

The end began in Detroit, where four-fifths of all deposits were held by two banking groups, the General Motors-backed Detroit Bankers Company and the Ford-affiliated Guardian Group. Both firms were in abysmal shape, and their examiners knew it. The Detroit Bankers Company's lead bank, the First National Bank of Detroit, "was not rotten," Chief Examiner Alfred Leyburn confided, "it was putrid" going "back a considerable time." The Guardian Group, which Leyburn called "a promotion scheme," was not much better. Much like Caldwell, each group bought up banks at the height of the bubble and then shuffled paper to avoid collapse. Examiners duly and actively criticized them, but Detroit's bankers had no intention of following supervisory guidance.[35]

To manage these banks' all-but-certain collapse, Hoover administration officials urged Michigan's governor, William A. Comstock, to declare a state banking holiday. After midnight on February 14, 1933, Comstock closed the state's banks. "I was at that time against a banking holiday in Michigan," Awalt recalled. "I felt sure it could not be localized and that it would spread to other states." He was right. By the end of February, Indiana, Maryland, Arkansas, and Ohio had all declared holidays. Early March brought an avalanche. In the first three days of the month, twenty-four states—then, fully half of the country—shut their banks.[36]

Many early states blamed Michigan, but by March 1933, the nation's banking system was overwhelmed by at least three converging forces. First, eroding public confidence intensified the ongoing solvency crisis, which supervisors had been battling from behind the curtain since 1930. As the depositors withdrew their funds from troubled banks, bankers, out of options, had to convert assets into cash at market prices—rather than the balance sheet values inflated by forbearance—when there was a market at all. Later that month, confidence was further eroded by the vivid testimony attorney Fernand Pecora elicited before Congress of corrupt financial practices. Congress also made public the recipients of the Reconstruction Finance Corporation, exposing these troubled banks to additional public scrutiny that turned quickly into depositor calamity. Second, fears about bank solvency had blended with corporate concerns that state holidays would freeze business assets, instigating a run by corporations on banks and then, in turn, by banks on other banks. Local banks withdrew their deposits from New York correspondents to meet withdrawals by large corporate clients. The corporations, in turn, redeposited their cash directly with the New York banks, leaving their former local bank partners without one of the few sources of reliable liquidity they had left. Finally, international financial turmoil and mounting uncertainty about Roosevelt's commitment to the gold standard led to heavy foreign withdrawals, depleting the reserves of the Federal Reserve Banks. There was, in short, a massive erosion of public confidence in the already fragile financial system.[37]

Despite the obvious and abundant need for action, Hoover refused to act after his electoral defeat. Hoover administration officials did consider instituting a nationwide holiday, but they decided the legal basis for such an action was dubious and risky. Although some officials, including Fed Governor Eugene Meyer (1930–1933), felt that the legal basis—built on the World War I-era Trading with the Enemy Act—was amply justified, those who were more conservative squelched any such enthusiasm. Ogden Mills felt that such an authorization "was not free from doubt" and that Hoover should not move forward "without the consent and approval" of the incoming Roosevelt administration. William D. Mitchell, Hoover's Attorney General, agreed, calling the legal authority "a shoestring."[38]

The legal concerns may well have been a sideshow. Ultimately, Hoover wanted joint action with the incoming administration to handle a crisis that he attributed to public panic at Roosevelt's election (despite the fact that the public had just overwhelmingly approved Roosevelt's program at the polls), not to any underlying instability in the U.S. banking system. Hoover was not indifferent to the swirling crisis per se; he simply wanted to pre-commit the president-elect to policy concessions that Hoover deemed in the country's best interests. Roosevelt, however, refused to lend a cent of his electoral mandate to Hoover. Divided by egos, ideology, political sensibilities, and even a sense of the unfolding crisis, the two men refused to talk. Instead, discussions filtered from Hoover to Mills in Washington, from Mills to incoming Treasury Secretary William Woodin in New York, from Woodin to Roosevelt in Washington, and back again. The standoff had real costs: "The procedure, incidentally, is not only ridiculous but criminal," Fed official Emanuel Goldenweiser noted at the time. "With the country on the verge of financial collapse, the inability of the incoming and outgoing administrations to talk to each other direct[ly] is utterly and totally unpardonable."[39]

The day after Goldenweiser recorded these thoughts, Roosevelt was inaugurated the thirty-second president of the United States. In his inaugural address, justifiably remembered for its towering rhetoric, Roosevelt confronted the crisis. "The money changers have fled from their high seats in the temple of our civilization," Roosevelt declared. "We may now restore that temple to the ancient truths." Behind these grand statements, Roosevelt offered little vision of the process, except that it would be a supervisory one. "There must be," the new president insisted, vaguely, "a strict supervision of all banking and credits and investments."[40]

The following day, with substantial help from Hoover administration holdovers, the economic team presented Roosevelt with a plan to close the banks. What emerged was essentially the same plan Hoover had rejected, the central component of which was a presidential declaration of a nationwide bank holiday using the Trading with the Enemy Act. This time, the president—Roosevelt, not Hoover—was ready to accept the advice and act.

He wasted no time. "Say this Roosevelt is a fast worker," comedian Will Rogers joked on the front page of the Los Angeles Times on March 6, the day the banking holiday took effect. "Even on Sunday, when all a President is supposed to do is put on a silk hat and have his picture taken coming out of church, why this President closed all the banks, and called Congress in extra session." As Rogers's jest implied, the new administration recognized that any durable solution to the crisis needed to rest on the full, undivided political authority of the federal government. In addition to closing banks, Roosevelt summoned Congress to special session on Thursday, March 9 to address the crisis. The shoestring theory, even backed by a firm electoral mandate, was not enough to legitimize the holiday. The administration needed not simply legal authority and political rhetoric to change the minds of American depositors; it needed something more.[41]

The Work of the Holiday

Together, Hoover's beleaguered staff and Roosevelt's now-engaged team recognized that the holiday afforded them one—and only one—opportunity to rescue the banking system. The easy part came first: At 1:00 A.M. on Monday March 6, Roosevelt issued Proclamation 2039 prohibiting "all banking transactions" and requiring "no such banking institution or branch [to] pay out, export, earmark, or permit the withdrawal or transfer in any manner . . . of any gold or silver coin or bullion or currency." The holiday thus simultaneously permitted some breathing room on the question of dollar devaluation, while giving supervisors the space to address the solvency crisis first.[42]

Two days before the holiday was announced, Mills had explained to Woodin, his successor, that success "would depend on the frankest disclosure to the public of existing conditions and an unyielding determination to resist all pressure to deal with individual banks on any other basis than reality." This was easy advice to give on the way out the door and precisely the opposite of what Hoover administration officials had been privately instructing bank examiners. Still, Mills's injunction wisely urged the mobilization of supervisory knowledge that, despite the years of forbearance, supervisors had assiduously collected through the entire series of crises. The government's capacity to apprehend "reality" relied on the supervisory system's unique stores of information, albeit in ways that required reimagination. Some banks, Mills explained, were "hopelessly insolvent and incapable under any circumstances of reopening." As powerful as Roosevelt's inaugural rhetoric had been, his administration could only save the banking system by determining which banks fell into this category and keeping them closed.[43]

It was Hoover's staff—primed by years of struggle—that put forward a plan for this moment. Roosevelt's team was clearly in charge, but it was the previous administration's plan (and their intimacy with the critical supervisory information) that went into motion. "Two main questions confronted us" on Inauguration Day, Awalt recalled: "(1) what banks could be opened quickly in order that the country might function; (2) how to keep them open."[44]

While Treasury officials couldn't evaluate state banks, their biannual examinations of national banks led them to estimate that perhaps 2,200 out of 5,938 national banks "could be reopened at once and meet all demands on them." To facilitate the reopening, Hoover's staff developed a simple classification system, labeling these liquid banks "Class A." The banks that were "doomed to failure" were designated Class C. The essential work of the holiday, they thought, would be drawing the lines between these categories and then working out a means of opening as many Class B banks as quickly as possible. By Tuesday, March 7, Woodin had fully committed to the Hoover team's plan. In a stroke, he wed the legitimacy of the three-day-old Roosevelt administration to the Hoover administration's supervisory apparatus.[45]

First, the administration needed to convince Congress that there were enough Class A banks to serve the basic needs of the country. But it also needed Congress to provide new tools so the supervisors could reorganize and reopen class B banks. On Wednesday, March 8, Woodin asked the Comptroller of the Currency and each Federal Reserve Bank (which could at least assess those state banks that were members of the Federal Reserve System) to send a list of the member banks they regarded to be solvent "on fair appraisals not on liquidating basis." The clear implication was that the commitment to "reality" did not mean that current market conditions would carry the day. Even after committing to closing some banks, supervisors would use discretionary judgment to shape the broad grey edges of liquidity and solvency. Throughout that day, the twelve Chief National Bank Examiners sent telegrams naming which banks could be reopened. Awalt's staff marked the banks with pins on a map. "The president thought it great," Awalt recalled. Nevertheless, despite a fair geographic distribution of Class A banks, Awalt though, "it was obvious that the country would still be paralyzed unless we could open more banks."[46]

The Reserve Banks were more cautious, fearful of being held responsible for keeping troubled banks open. They had balance sheets to protect, and Board members worried that they would be called on to support reopened institutions unconditionally, exposing the Reserve Banks to "heavy losses." To reassure the Fed, Roosevelt promised to persuade Congress to cover their losses and urged them to liberally assess the balance sheets of distressed banks. "There is a very definite obligation on the Federal Government," Roosevelt assured the board, "to reimburse the 12 Regional Federal Reserve Banks for losses which they may make on loans under these emergency powers." In this pivotal moment, the president convinced Congress to protect the Fed from any losses stemming from the actions it hoped the Fed would take. Roosevelt thus added financial capital to his political capital by ensuring that the process of supervision was fully guaranteed by the federal government.[47]

Meanwhile, the Emergency Banking Act that would ratify the holiday on stronger legal footing rocketed through Congress. The law was drafted by Fed officials and Hoover administration staff and read by very few legislators. Beyond ratifying the holiday, it created "conservatorship," a new supervisory tool which enabled the Comptroller to take possession of a bank, with the aim of ultimately reopening it rather than winding it down. Insolvency would no longer be a death sentence; supervisors could act forcefully to repair troubled banks, while also bolstering confidence that the banks that remained open were sound.[48]

Carter Glass, who ushered the bill through the Senate, relied on Awalt's estimate that the Roosevelt administration could eventually open 5,300 national banks with the legislation and 2,600 without. As Glass assured his fellow senators, "only those banks which are literally rotten, and which ought to have been permitted to fail long ago, will not be allowed to open."[49]

Congress was, the senators recognized, about to provide bank supervisors with new authority to act decisively, not to keep banks open but to close them—some temporarily, others permanently. For Michigan Senator Arthur Vandenberg, this represented a shocking expansion of public power. "The Comptroller," Vandenberg objected, "is about to decide tonight what banks in America are solvent and what banks in America are not solvent." What Vandenberg likely knew but did not acknowledge was that the Comptroller always had that authority; it just lacked the political will to use it. That evening, Roosevelt signed the hastily passed law and extended the holiday indefinitely, giving supervisors time to deliver on the vision of a political and technocratic approach to the crisis's resolution.[50]

The following day, March 10, Roosevelt issued an order establishing the procedure for reopening the banks. National and state-chartered banks that were Fed members would submit applications to their local Federal Reserve Bank. The Reserve Banks, in consultation with the chief examiners from the Comptroller's office, would then evaluate each application. A national bank essentially needed three independent approvals, from the examiners in the field, from its district Federal Reserve Bank, and from the Comptroller's office in Washington. The Secretary of the Treasury, upon whose authority they would open, "would not be able to take up each case individually," as Awalt explained. For state banks outside the Fed system, reopening decisions lay with the state banking authorities, a calculated gamble which relied on state supervisors' incentives to maintain the legitimacy of state-level governance vis-à-vis their federal counterparts. Banks in Federal Reserve cities, Roosevelt told the press, would open on Monday, March 13. Banks in cities with clearinghouses on March 14, and all other banks on March 15.[51]

This schedule left the supervisors just one weekend to determine, as best they could, which banks should open immediately and which should not. Writing in 1939, historian Frederick Lewis Allen suggested that the success of the reopening was only possible because people didn't realize "that it was impossible, in a few days, to separate the sound banks from the unsound." Barry Eichengreen, writing decades later, likewise viewed the sheer speed of the behind-the-scenes supervisory work as implausible: It was "hardly possible to conduct careful inspections of each and every financial institution." What these skeptics failed to grasp was that the sorting process did not begin with

Roosevelt's announcement on March 10; it was decades in the making. The holiday didn't rely on new information, nor did it rely on new officials. Rather, its genius was to mobilize and transform the supervisory information regime by giving supervisors the authority to act upon the knowledge and judgments they had been making all along.[52]

That is not to say this was an orderly affair. Each Reserve Bank devolved into chaos as examiners combed through old examination reports, searching for a plausible if generous basis to permit the banks to reopen. At the New York Fed, the board convened every day from 10:00 A.M. to 6:00 P.M. As examiners analyzed examination reports, they passed the files up to senior officers, who in turn made the case for each bank to the board. Meanwhile, distraught bankers milled around the lobby of the New York Fed on the theory that "money had fled from small towns to New York, therefore New York might have money," as longtime New York Fed employee J. Herbert Case recalled. In what Case called a "keep your shirt on" operation, the former president of the New York State Bankers Association was dispatched to spend the holiday reassuring these worried men. The Richmond Fed was similarly packed. "The auditorium is full," Richmond Fed Governor George J. Seay (1914–1936) reported. "The directors' room has been full, our discount room is full, and the lobby is pretty well occupied, and most of the desks have bankers conferring—we are trying our best to avoid physical breakdown of the officers."[53]

The stress was intense, the pace unrelenting. "Sleep was practically unknown to many of us," Awalt recalled. "My usual routine was to arrive home in the morning, around seven, get a hot toddy, prepared by Mrs. Awalt, sleep for at least an hour, have a shower and return to the Treasury." According to reporter Ernest K. Lindsey, "the main participants in the drama were too numerous and they emerged from long days and nights of tension with blurred and conflicting memories." The task was "so onerous and responsible, and performed under such a cruel limitation of time," that the head examiner at the Philadelphia Fed suffered a breakdown that "compelled him to rest for a year before his health was completely restored."[54]

Amid their hurried and fevered labors, officials confronted decisions that were at once politically and technically difficult. A major test arose with California's Bank of America, formerly the Bank of Italy, an empire of 410 branches and more than a million depositors built up by the domineering entrepreneur, A. P. Giannini. Like the Detroit banks, Bank of America was part of a sprawling financial conglomerate, Transamerica, which had grown rapidly in the 1920s boom and suffered significant losses in the Depression years. On Sunday, March 12, San Francisco Fed Governor John U. Calkins (1919–1936) refused to grant the bank permission to reopen. Calkins, citing recent examiners' reports, declared it hopelessly insolvent. Woodin intervened. Armed with updated financial information from Giannini, and the conviction that the bank's failure would destroy the economy—and the new president's political credibility—along the West Coast, Woodin confronted Calkins. If the Federal Reserve would not take responsibility for opening the bank, then at least Calkins would take personal responsibility for closing it. Calkins balked. "Well then," Woodin said, "the bank will open."[55]

Only Sound Banks

As supervisors exhausted themselves hurriedly deciding the fate of the nation's banks, the administration planned for Roosevelt to address the country by radio in a frank, candid, reassuring tone to explain the banking crisis and what would happen next. As New York governor, Roosevelt had already made a name for himself in broadcasting, "taking the issues to the people." But the stakes in the first "fireside chat" were much higher than they had ever been in Albany. Roosevelt believed that the only way to restore unerring confidence was to promise Americans that only "sound banks" would open. As the draft speech circulated among those working tirelessly on the examination process, that promise caused the banking staff intense apprehension. "In our hurry to complete the program," Awalt told the president, "there might be some exceptions." Roosevelt understood the gamble and understood that he had to restore unerring confidence. "He stated in no uncertain terms that that was what we were going to do, 'open only sound banks,'" Awalt recalled. "I had nothing more to say."[56]

The gamble illustrated just how much the political (Roosevelt) and the technical (bank supervisors) combined to create the legitimate. Roosevelt, even with his electoral mandate and his larger-than-life persona, could not simply will away the financial and economic crisis. He needed what only the bank examiners could offer: the assurance that the banks that opened were indeed "sound" on some defensible criteria. In their hurry, examiners would—and did—make mistakes, but the credibility of the enterprise required a public commitment to supervisory expertise that meant that banks that reopened could do so because some other banks had failed and been closed.[57]

The legitimacy of the moment depended on both forces—the political and the technical—to work in harmony. This is clear from the fireside chat itself, in which Roosevelt founded his government's commitment to preventing "another epidemic of bank failures" on the work of federal supervisors. "We start tomorrow," Roosevelt explained, "with the opening of banks in the twelve Federal Reserve Bank cities—those banks which on first examination by the Treasury have already been found to be all right." He followed up this explanation by laying out a roadmap for the restoration of the banking system. "On Wednesday and succeeding days banks in smaller places all through the country will resume business, subject, of course, to the Government's physical ability to complete its survey. It is necessary that the reopening of banks be extended over a period in order to permit the banks to make applications for necessary loans, to obtain currency needed to meet their requirements and to enable the Government to make common sense checkups." Roosevelt invited his listeners to imagine examination, physical surveys, and commonsense checkups, because the flurry of supervisory activity that enabled the banks to open was largely hidden from public view.[58]

When the banks that survived supervisory scrutiny opened in Federal Reserve cities on Monday, March 13, Americans expressed their confidence in the administration through a flood of cash and gold deposits. "The people," Woodin remarked, "have responded." In many communities, bank reopenings brought more than financial stability. When Philadelphia's only African American-owned bank was licensed to reopen on March 13, it was, according to the *Philadelphia Tribune*, "epoch making." Depositors were "electrified with racial pride." After the first three days, about half of all banks, representing 90 percent of deposits, had opened. "The reopening of the banks restored in the mind of the public confidence in the banking structure," the Federal Reserve Bank of Boston concluded.[59]

The bank holiday was not the only executive move to restore financial order. Just as the declaration of banking holidays—state and federal—involved the destructive convergence of banking and currency panics, so too did reopening involve the redemptive convergence of new banking and currency policies. Once again, under the authority of the Trading with the Enemy Act, Roosevelt stabilized the currency by criminalizing gold hoarding. Even before the holiday concluded, hoarders clamored to return bullion to the banks. Most deposited their stashes rather than exchanging them for paper currency, a trend which continued after formal reopening. A day after the holiday ended, one Chicago bank reported opening 2,500 to 3,000 new savings accounts, explaining: "In many cases these people frankly said they had been hoarding but that their confidence had been restored and they wanted to get their cash back into bank accounts." By the end of March, $1.25 billion in currency, 17 percent of that in circulation, had been placed in bank vaults—deposits that helped further stabilize the shakiest of Roosevelt's sound banks. For its first few weeks, the success of the New Deal was measured in such deposits.[60]

Capitalism had been saved, but many of the capitalists were not. When the holiday concluded on March 15, only 75 percent of national and Federal Reserve member banks had reopened, leaving 1,400 national banks and 221 Fed member banks in the hands of federal conservators or similar state-level officials. Some reopened later, others only after reorganization, some never again. Nearly 15 percent of national and Federal Reserve member banks closed permanently after the holiday. The picture was similar for state-chartered, nonmember banks. About 3,000, or 30 percent, remained unlicensed for reopening by mid-April 1933, 1,173 of which would suspend permanently.[61]

The administration sought to make clear that banks which did eventually open were just as sound as those which had opened immediately. In his fireside chat, Roosevelt said, "a bank that opens on one of the subsequent days is in exactly the same status as the bank that opens tomorrow." Behind the scenes, however, officials urged caution. "It seems to me fundamental," Awalt wrote, "that we should be very rigid, both in examination and requirements, from now on in order to keep these banks sound." Roosevelt had promised to only open sound banks; bank supervisors kept the promise by keeping unsound banks closed and committing themselves to making sound banks earn their status on an ongoing basis.[62]

In this way, the holiday transformed supervision into a decisive institution of federal power, which, in the years ahead, would enforce the government's guarantee that open banks were sound. In 1933 and 1934, supervisors used their new authority to manage the transition from Roosevelt's implicit guarantee to formal federal deposit insurance. Their most common technique was compelling bankers to accept recapitalizations from the Reconstruction Finance Corporation as a condition of membership in the new Federal Deposit Insurance Corporation. These recapitalizations, authorized as part of the Banking Act of 1933, brought public power to bear through direct public ownership. Emboldened examiners in this initial period were occasionally too stringent; even Roosevelt urged them to ease up. Nevertheless, the legitimate exercise of supervisory judgment remained central to federal financial governance in the New Deal and, as we shall see, well beyond.

Conclusion

Roosevelt's first fireside chat implied a government guarantee with various components. It was a reputational guarantee as he tied his political mandate to the results of the holiday. It was a financial commitment, which guaranteed the liabilities of the Reserve Banks. It was also a guarantee made possible by an army of federal bank supervisors relying on years of critical expertise that had laid fallow in the era of criticism and forbearance. This stood in stark contrast to Hoover's policy of refusing to close banks, which amounted to an endorsement of all the banks and, ultimately, an endorsement of none of them. As a result of Hoover's dogmatic efforts to keep the banks open, supervisory forbearance was pushed beyond its functional limits. Roosevelt and his team—including policy architects from Hoover's staff—had a different insight: recovery required legitimacy, legitimacy needed expertise, and expertise required banks to fail.

In this way, the holiday became the Bank Holiday of 1933, a reconstitution and expansion of the legitimacy of the supervisory apparatus. In the process, the purpose and modality of supervision changed. In 1923, well before the crisis, Comptroller Henry M. Dawes (1923–1924) had written that the chief function of supervisors was to keep "banks from failing." During the crisis, supervisors stuck with this ethos—they "did not close banks." Yet it was precisely failure—and the supervisors' capacity to declare failure—that was vital to creating legitimacy, even if the actual decision-making process was hurried and imperfect. Closing the banks, and keeping some banks closed, changed the rules of the game. It enabled supervision to begin a halting transition from associational governance—seeking to guide bank behavior—to a more decisive bureaucratic power. The bank holiday worked, in the last analysis, not by opening banks but by keeping them closed.[63]

Interlude: Banking on Bonds, for Better and Worse

IN JANUARY 1932, Comptroller John W. Pole (1928–1932) faced a dire and growing crisis. More than 400 national banks had closed their doors the previous year. Prospects looked little better for the year ahead. Banks' bond portfolios proved an acute source of stress, not only those of banks which managed to stay open—in part through Pole's aggressive forbearance campaign—but especially those of banks which had closed and now lay in the hands of receivers.[1]

Banks fail for various specific reasons but only for one general reason: They do not have adequate assets to meet the demands of their depositors and other creditors. Through the history of American banking, those assets were primarily loans that banks underwrote and held to maturity. By the crises of the Great Depression, this had radically changed, and most closed banks held at least some marketable securities on their books, purchased on the bank's account or taken as collateral for defaulted loans. National bank receivers, however, usually lacked experience dealing in bonds, and the failed banks they managed tended to be situated in communities far from active markets. This created a special problem: How could these inexperienced receivers find value in assets they did not understand?

Typically, receivers solved this failure of sophistication by bundling a failed bank's securities as a single lot and offering them for sale through an urban broker for whom such placements would be routine. Bids to that broker reflected the value of the best securities in the lot, with "the least desirable securities . . . given scant consideration." Offloading bonds this way yielded value that the receiver could not otherwise secure, but prices tended to be low and brokerage fees high. In 1932, given the number of failed banks, receivers competed to sell the same bonds, pushing down prices and with them both returns to depositors and portfolio values in going banks.[2]

Pole understood the problems his receivers faced: Unlike any of his predecessors, he had worked in the trenches of bank examination. Reviewing several proposals to deal with the bond valuation problem in early 1932, Pole rejected them all. He turned instead to an expert for help, telephoning Dr. Paul M. Atkins and asking Atkins to visit with him in Washington, DC.[3]

Atkins was, in a way, the obvious choice. An economist and engineer by training, Atkins had developed a career in the 1920s as a financial expert and consultant, including as an advisor to the Peruvian government with the famed money doctor Edwin Kemmerer and as an economist for Ames, Emerich, and Co., a bond house with offices in Chicago and New York.[4]

In the latter role, Atkins built a public profile as a banking expert, championing bank investments in marketable bonds. In public talks, trade press articles, and his book, *Bank Secondary Reserve & Investment Policies*, Atkins argued that bankers should maintain a "secondary reserve" of high-quality, liquid securities that would generate income when held by a bank and be quickly salable to meet depositor withdrawals or other demands. A secondary reserve of bonds, in this case, offered a complement (or alternative) to other ready sources of liquidity, especially loans from the Federal Reserve Banks.[5]

In the context of the slow-burning rural banking crisis of the 1920s, which began to flare after the stock market crash in 1929, Atkins's influence grew. He soon had the ear of state banking associations and federal supervisory officials. Writing to Atkins after they shared the podium at the Pennsylvania Bankers Association conference in 1929, George W. Norris (1920–1936), governor of the Federal Reserve Bank of Philadelphia, praised Atkins's work and asked for his help. For "banks outside of the centres, the importance of secondary reserves needs to be emphasized," Norris wrote to Atkins. If trouble struck, a bank's cash reserves could evaporate in hours, and a portfolio of eligible loans could not guarantee liquidity. "Under these circumstances, there is often no time for a correspondent bank or even a Reserve Bank to make such an examination of its note portfolio as would justify a large loan."

In other words, the Fed's primary representative in Philadelphia admitted, on the eve of the banking panics of the Great Depression, that the Reserve Banks could not perform their essential lender-of-last-resort function for lack of timely supervision (Norris knew this was a significant confession—he closed by writing, "I have expressed myself freely upon your assurance that what I write will be treated as confidential").[6]

Atkins gained the confidence of officials across the spectrum of bank supervisory institutions. "Given a little time," he wrote to his colleagues at Ames,
Emerich, and Co. in 1930, "I am certain that we shall have not only all national
bank examiners but practically all Federal Reserve Officials and many state
banking commissioners actively supporting our work."[7]

For Atkins and his firm, promoting bondholding as the foundation of bank
liquidity was entirely self-interested. "We are getting the best of publicity and
active official support," Atkins wrote in a follow-up letter. "If we do not profit
by this it will be because we do not take advantage of the opportunity. In other
words, we must sell more bonds to banks."[8]

The irony that Atkins's self-interested enthusiasm for a secondary reserve in
marketable bonds set banks up for fire sale liquidations was lost on apparently
everyone. Nevertheless, bankers' widespread embrace of bonds as secondary
reserves proved, in hindsight, profoundly ill-timed. Before November 1930,
national banks could and did sell marketable bonds to raise cash. With the
failure of Caldwell & Company that month and the deterioration in bond
markets that followed, banks tended to hold onto bonds rather than sell them
at depreciated prices. Instead of a source of liquidity, bond portfolios became
a threat to solvency. And because banks held onto their bonds, when they
failed, receivers were left with more bonds to manage.[9]

Atkins gave no sign of appreciating his role in spreading this specific vector
of financial contagion. Instead, meeting with Pole in January 1932, Atkins—by
his own recollection—offered a timely solution to Pole's predicament: consolidate the bonds held by receivers at a central office in New York and assign
an experienced bond trader to manage the sell-off. Pole agreed and asked Atkins to take the job.[10]

Pole quickly made the necessary arrangements with the Federal Reserve
Bank of New York and the Treasury. "The unloading of any substantial
amount of these bonds at one time will adversely affect the bond market,"
Pole explained to the Secretary of the Treasury, seeking permission to undertake the consolidation plan. With permission granted, Atkins got to work in
February as the Special Liquidator of Securities, a new office of the Comptroller based in the New York Fed. From that point on, whenever a national
bank receiver was granted court permission to sell an insolvent bank's securities, the receiver forwarded the bonds to the Federal Reserve Bank of New
York. There, the bank held the bonds in trust to the appropriate receivership,
while Atkins collected interest and worked to discern when bonds could be
sold "to advantage."[11]

Pole granted Atkins significant autonomy and discretion, ordering him to balance returns to individual receiverships against protecting the wider bond market. Pole, Atkins recalled, wanted bonds sold "as rapidly as possible," accepting a good price immediately even if values seemed likely to rise in the future. At the same time, the Comptroller "did not want the liquidation to proceed so rapidly as to damage the weak market for securities."[12]

"These two policies were mutually incompatible," Atkins recalled pointing out. "I know that," Pole replied, "your task is to steer your way between them."[13]

The steering was made more difficult by the quality of bonds Atkins received. Most "were of distinctly low quality: tax exempt bonds of unsatisfactory quality—Florida bonds, special assessment bonds, drainage district bonds, bonds of communities which had become notorious for their defaults; public utility bonds, especially those of the top holding companies which fell into such low repute, many of them eventually defaulting; foreign dollar bonds, particularly German, Hungarian and Latin American bonds, most of which also defaulted; real estate bonds, most of which were in difficulty." In sum, failed banks unsurprisingly had ugly bond portfolios, cobbled together during better times on the theory of secondary marketability that was significantly impaired during the crisis.[14]

The records of the Special Liquidator bear this out. To take one of Atkins's categories, the U.S. National Archives holds binders full of receipts that document bankers' ill-conceived investments in Latin America. The Noble County National Bank of Caldwell, Ohio, located in a small farming community in the southeastern part of the state, invested the equivalent of half its capital in Sterling-denominated Brazilian government bonds. The First National Bank of Waterloo, Iowa, invested a similar proportion across Brazil, Argentina, and Bolivia. Other flyspeck banks invested in Latin American provincial and municipal bonds, most of which defaulted by 1931. In the 1920s, Atkins and others promoted these as sound components of a secondary reserve; in the 1930s, Atkins sold them off at cents on the dollar.[15]

The Special Liquidator's work started slowly in 1932, as it took time for receivers to process the necessary paperwork to ship bonds to New York. Atkins, overconfident and initially underworked, reckoned that the Special Liquidator could become a full-service, publicly managed bond brokerage, with expertise "in all kinds of securities." He even proposed taking on the securities of going banks to help them advantageously liquidate low-grade bonds.[16]

Atkins's confidence quickly gave way to dread. By July 1932, the department—understaffed, overwhelmed, and "behind in our work"—faced five times the volume of liquidations Atkins had been led to expect. Atkins had anticipated disposing of roughly $50,000,000 of par value securities; by July he revised this estimate up to $250,000,000. At its peak, the Federal Reserve Bank of New York dedicated thirty-eight full-time staff to processing the Special Liquidator's paperwork.[17]

Over his five years of service, Atkins's abiding challenge was securing good prices, which required a continued cat-and-mouse game with the brokers he sought as counterparties. Bond buyers recognized that Atkins ultimately had to sell, and once they discovered that he held particular securities, they often lowered their bids. To maintain an informational advantage, Atkins did not advertise his holdings and accepted only unsolicited bids from interested brokers. If he had the securities they were looking for and if they offered a good price, Atkins would deal.[18]

Poor information control undermined Atkins's strategy. Sometimes receivers shared the contents of a broken bank's bond portfolio with interested local elites, information that quickly found its way to the street. "If it is possible to stop the leaks of information it will greatly facilitate the success of the work of this office," Atkins wrote in frustration. Atkins also coached his office staff not to volunteer anything. "When answering telephones," he instructed, "no information whatsoever [is to] be given to the caller. That is, they are not to be told whether we have the bonds they might mention for liquidation or that we expect to have them." Confidentiality saturated even this unusual outpost of the Comptroller's office.[19]

Although the transition from Hoover to Roosevelt presaged dramatic changes in other supervisory domains, initially Atkins continued to process the remains of dead banks without significant interruption. In November 1933, J. E. Fouts, the supervising receiver, explained that "we have been so absorbed in getting our banks open and getting receivers appointed in banks which cannot open, that we have not had a great time to devote to liquidation." With the deadline to qualify for federal deposit insurance pending at year's end 1933, Fouts anticipated soon turning to the liquidation work. "If I am not mistaken, I believe we can keep you busy next summer."[20]

Atkins stayed busy over the next few years, as the Roosevelt administration turned toward liquidation to get deposits out of failed banks and back into the economy. The administration frequently pushed Atkins to "clean-out" the last bonds held by receiverships, often the least marketable, most distressed securities. The political symbolism was paramount. In November 1936, one receiver was "quite satisfied to have the above-described securities liquidated as he believed that it would enable him to pay another dividend by Christmas."[21]

These were some of the last securities that Atkins sold. The par value of the Special Liquidator's bond sales increased year by year, from $35 million in 1932, to $51 million in 1933, $55 million in 1934, and $79 million in 1935. Sales fell off in 1936, with a par value of only $23 million. Atkins attributed this to changes in the Comptroller's staff and liquidation policy that he "believed to be undesirable." He resigned at the end of 1936 to resume private business. During Atkins's tenure, the Special Liquidator's office handled more than ten thousand different securities issues, representing $242,000,000 in par value, which Atkins and his colleagues sold for $143,000,000. "Perhaps the greatest measure of the success of the work of this office under the direction of Dr. Atkins," he recalled in the third person, "was the lack of publicity which attended it."[22]

Paul Atkins, the preacher of the secondary reserve as an alternative to bank supervision, proved an abject failure. Paul Atkins, the cleanup artist hired to rescue the banks that bought into his plan, succeeded much better.

6

Supervision's New Deal

THE COMPETITIVE INSTITUTIONALIZATION
OF THE 1930S

THE BANK Holiday of 1933 eliminated any doubt about who would manage the residual risk for the financial system. The nineteenth-century push-and-pull between the private sector banks and the public officials supervising them was fundamentally resolved in favor of the government. But what exactly did this commitment to own the residual risk mean? And who, exactly, was the government? Officials in the post-holiday New Deal quarreled over both questions without reaching firm resolution. In the aftermath of the Roosevelt administration's critical early days, four different entities vied for dominance, and with it for authority to determine the forms and functions of bank supervision in the new era of assertive public risk management.

Two of these agencies offered novel approaches to federal oversight of individual bank risk, which in different ways shifted supervision's emphasis from the retroactive evaluation of bank assets to proactive efforts to improve bank management. As part of the 1933 Emergency Banking Act, the Hoover-era Reconstruction Finance Corporation (RFC) gained power to buy preferred stock in national and state banks, a policy aimed at restoring solvency through government recapitalization. Under the chairmanship of the dynamic Texan Jesse H. Jones (1933–1939), the RFC took equity stakes in roughly 5,000 banks and used its position as a part owner to impose public corporate governance and strengthen bank management. Likewise, under the leadership of Wisconsin banker and politico Leo T. Crowley (1934–1945), the Federal Deposit Insurance Corporation (FDIC) gradually shifted from determining bank solvency—the defining qualification to participate in the fund and the impetus for many RFC recapitalizations—to evaluating managerial competence to limit public insurance losses by limiting the likelihood of private failure. Before the New Deal, the federal government, largely through the Comptroller of the Currency, had supervised banks through information provision, giving private managers and bank directors retrospective evaluations of bank performance and leaving any remedial action to private corporate governance backstopped by private shareholder liability. By contrast, supervision through public ownership and public insurance aligned around a future-oriented view of risk management, where the government would evaluate bank managers to improve performance and prevent failure.

For the RFC and the FDIC, supervision focused on protecting government stakes as owner and insurer in individual banks. Faced with the difficult recovery from the Great Depression and embracing the emerging conception that, as Franklin D. Roosevelt said in April 1938, "the prosperity of the United States is of necessity a primary concern of Government," the Federal Reserve pursued a distinct vision of supervision as a force for macroeconomic stability. Here, Federal Reserve Chairman Marriner S. Eccles (1934–1948), former Utah banker and Keynesian sympathizer, provided the guiding light. Through a reformed and more robustly public Federal Reserve System, Eccles wanted to use bank supervision in concert with monetary policy and credit management to smooth the fluctuations in the business cycle. For Eccles, the risks of any individual bank failure were less consequential than the risks that misguided government supervision, which sought safety when the economy needed risk-taking, posed to the macroeconomy.[1]

Finally, there was the Comptroller of the Currency, the original federal bank supervisor that had scrappily survived threats to its existence through corruption scandals of the Reconstruction Era, financial panics of the Gilded Age, redundancy during the Progressive Era, and failure during the Depression. The Comptroller's regime of information and corporate risk management had transformed in the crisis years into one of information and forbearance. With the holiday, national bank examiners repurposed their accumulated knowledge to decisively close hundreds of banks. Even so, the early years of the New Deal brought uncertainty. With government power ascendant through the RFC, the FDIC, and the Federal Reserve, and with private risk management through double liability in retreat, the Comptroller's role was unclear. What now could the Comptroller do that the other agencies, all with more skin in the game, could not do better?

Institutional layering in the public-private management of residual risk continued unabated in the 1930s. Three of these four models would survive and even thrive during this period of the New Deal's intense experimentation (the Reconstruction Finance Corporation would shift tack during the full mobilization of World War II before its eventual discontinuation in 1957). Institutional layering, however, did not mean institutional harmony. The Fed and the FDIC sought to consolidate supervisory authority around their distinct visions; the Comptroller fought merely to survive. The supervisory conflicts that arose in this critical period would define bank supervision throughout the remainder of the twentieth century. It was more than simply a series of turf wars and personality conflicts (though there was plenty of that). It was a fight about how the fact of governmental ownership of the financial system's residual risk would be administered. Different institutions approached that question in profoundly different ways. Those differences defined the era.

Layering on Deposit Insurance

After the hurried enactment of the Roosevelt administration's emergency legislative provisions, Congress geared up for more fundamental reform. Amid the competing proposals, federal deposit insurance sat poised for an unexpected return, one that would ultimately recast the intellectual foundations of federal bank supervision. Where national bank examiners focused on informational flows and Federal Reserve Bank examiners focused on their own balance sheet exposures, the New Deal politicians created something new: the bank supervisor as an insurance underwriter.

The path to federal deposit insurance highlights the contingent, layered, and evolutionary path of bank supervision. Deposit liability insurance had a long and unhappy career as a political cause and risk management strategy in the generation before the Great Depression. Advocates had hoped that, by providing depositors confidence that bank promises would be honored even if the bank failed, insurance would halt deposit runs before they began and "panics would pass into history." Yet state-run systems suffered from moral hazard and adverse selection, the threats that insured banks would act recklessly, while strong banks would exit the insurance system. In states with deposit insurance, participating banks tended to be small and weak, and many of the insuring states suffered most during the 1920s agricultural crisis. By the time of the bank holiday in March 1933, the state deposit insurance experiments were three years gone—the last going bankrupt by 1930.[2]

The failure of state insurance plans in the 1920s did not recommend deposit insurance as a central plank in the New Deal. Unsurprisingly, it was nowhere in

Roosevelt's 1932 campaign literature. Southern and western Democrats, led by Alabama populist Henry B. Steagall, strongly supported the proposal, a version of which the House had enacted in May 1932. Steagall was keen to shore up community-based, unit banking; as the newly elevated chairman of the House Banking Committee in 1931, he was in the position to do it. He also thought that the failed state systems were no impediment for federal reforms. The management and implementation of these state-level schemes failed, not the concept. "Because of bad banking, lax enforcement, and weak regulation," the state funds ran out of money. Rather than condemn federal deposit insurance, for Steagall the state experiments "pointed the way to a sound national insurance system," one which would overcome the moral hazard and adverse selection inherent in piecemeal state systems by providing national coverage.[3]

Steagall's plans met Carter Glass's fierce opposition in the Senate. Glass, the patrician patriarch of the Federal Reserve System, did not view the protection of unit banks as a priority. Instead, Glass saw large branch banks, with modern financial management and diversified portfolios, as the proper path to safe banking. He also recognized the political power of unit bankers, who would oppose legislative efforts to manage risk through bank size. Thus, Glass's reform proposals focused on throwing regulatory walls around the commercial banking business. In Senate legislation, Glass sought to recommit commercial banks to real commercial lending rather than investment banking and other sidelines, while also restraining price competition for bank deposits. Deposit insurance, Glass believed, would only protect bad bankers and perpetuate the system of unit banking that had so clearly failed over the previous decade.[4]

The collapse of the banking system and the interventions of the holiday opened the door to reforms focused on panic prevention. Roosevelt had assured the public that their deposits were safe in the banks that the government allowed to reopen, thus creating, in effect, a federal guarantee of the banking system. The question remained what long-term form this guarantee would take. With Steagall's insistence and the provision's overwhelming popularity for depositor-voters, deposit insurance went from possible, to plausible, to preordained. "It's coming," Glass told Roosevelt in June 1933, "so we'll do the best we can."[5]

Glass, who a generation earlier had molded the Federal Reserve System into a predominantly private central bank, sought a similar resolution for deposit insurance. In the legislation that emerged, Congress delivered insurance through a federally chartered corporation, funded in the first instance by bank insurance premiums. It also made the new Federal Deposit Insurance Corporation an institutional appendage of the Federal Reserve. "I have opposed guaranteeing deposits," Glass said in the Senate, "but this is not a Government guaranty of deposits." The quasi-private Fed was in charge. Where Steagall saw an opportunity to build new institutions, Glass wanted to strengthen existing ones. The Glass-Steagall Act allowed state banks to join the insurance fund and required them, after two years, to qualify for and join the Federal Reserve System, a requirement that would force them to grow, merge, or lose their insurance coverage.[6]

Perhaps this last requirement—to unite federal deposit insurance with the Federal Reserve System—explains why, at its birth, the FDIC had few supervisory powers of its own. Congress created it by amending the Federal Reserve Act and by requiring the Federal Reserve Banks to provide nearly half of the fund's initial capital ($139 million, with the Treasury obligated to contribute $150 million at call). Even its board was not its own. Congress conjoined the new corporation not only to the Fed, which would eventually have authority over all the fund's banks, but also to the Comptroller, who was an ex officio member of the corporation's three-member board. The final bill made the entire deposit insurance experiment temporary—it would last only two years unless Congress deemed otherwise. As a last-minute amendment, the law eliminated double liability on *new* national bank stock. Instead of allocating risk to bank shareholders, Congress now shifted risk to the FDIC—and behind it, the U.S. Treasury.[7]

Making the Banks Sound: Capital Infusions and Insurance Coverage

As Congress debated Glass and Steagall's provisions, it moved more quickly to reconfigure and revitalize the Reconstruction Finance Corporation. If, in the long run, deposit insurance stood as the New Deal's enduring legacy, the RFC was a spark of bright, expedient, and temporary power. Houston banker Jesse Jones, who joined the RFC as a Hoover appointee in 1932 and led it as chairman from 1933 until 1939, grasped this power with both hands.

In his memoirs on the Depression, Hoover listed the RFC first among his administration's depression-fighting accomplishments. But the version of the RFC that Jones and the Roosevelt administration used was not the RFC that Hoover had weakly supported (after his favored privately organized rescue efforts foundered). Hoover's RFC lent against bank assets, trading liquidity for collateral. While it was true that troubled banks needed cash to meet depositor outflows, what they really needed was equity capital to make good their losses and restore them to solvency.[8]

The RFC's staff under Hoover recognized the flaws in the tools at their disposal but had to wait for the new administration to implement something more transformative. The March 1933 Emergency Banking Act, besides ratifying the Roosevelt administration's actions during the bank holiday, provided a roadmap for how the government's ownership of residual risk should be operationalized through direct investments in the banks. The law enabled national banks to issue preferred stock, without the double liability that had previously attached to bank ownership. The legislation also authorized the RFC to purchase preferred national and state bank stock, enabling the government to infuse capital into, and thus become beneficial owner of, banks receiving such investments. After March 1933, the RFC moved beyond the business of lending to banks and into the business of owning them.[9]

Empowered with new authority to reorganize and reopen unlicensed banks, the RFC faced a daunting task. Of the 18,390 banks operating at the start of the holiday on March 3, 1933, 12,756 had reopened by March 15, with an additional 1,300 banks in need of minimal government aid reopening by mid-April. By then, there were 4,215 unlicensed institutions, including 1,108 national banks, 148 state member banks, and 2,959 nonmember banks. Many of these proved beyond saving; more than 1,100 were liquidated by the end of the year. With hundreds of millions of dollars of deposits frozen inside the 3,100 or so banks that remained, the Roosevelt administration faced tremendous pressure to open them up or close them out.[10]

The Comptroller's informational regime had been effective at determining which banks could safely reopen, but these problem banks required more assertive interventions. To accomplish this task, the RFC worked closely with the Treasury Department and the Comptroller to craft reorganization plans that would make suspect banks safe and sound. Jones developed partnerships between the government, bankers, and the communities where the banks operated. He insisted that any infusion of RFC capital be matched by at least an equal portion of locally owned common stock, compelling community elites to stand behind their banks. Community support did not mean unhampered local management. Jones expected control to follow from government ownership. Preferred stock meant voting rights, rights the RFC exercised to improve bank performance. "When we felt a bank was well run we did not raise our voice as to its management," Jones recalled, "even though our investments were sufficient to afford effective control." When a bank was not well run, the RFC used its power accordingly.[11]

Before the holiday, federal supervisors had used corporate governance and double liability to nudge bank directors to monitor bank managers; now, with preferred stock ownership, the federal government provided corporate governance directly. At particularly troubled banks, the RFC placed government officials directly on corporate boards "to keep an eye on the management."[12]

Despite the political urgency and ailing banks' desperate need for capital, the RFC made scant headway. "Our preferred stock program moved at a very slow pace," Jones recalled. Bankers resisted government ownership out of principle and feared that association with the RFC would signal weakness to their customers, competitors, and communities. RFC capital was expensive: The corporation required banks to pay 6 percent annual dividends, the maximum allowed by law. It also required banks to set aside a proportion of their profits to buy the stock back from the government. Government ownership of the nation's banks was always conceived as a temporary measure. Although Jones constantly used outright nationalization as a stick in his negotiations with bankers, his ambition, aligned with that of the Roosevelt administration, was for private actors to remain the leading force in finance. Still, bankers remained reluctant. RFC recapitalizations, after an early surge in March 1933, gradually lost momentum, fully stalling out by August. In October, 2,300 banks remained closed.[13]

The slow uptake of RFC recapitalizations had direct implications for the new deposit insurance corporation, which was slated to begin insuring banks on January 1, 1934. The Glass-Steagall Act mandated that only "solvent" institutions could qualify for insurance. For state banks outside the federal supervisory purview, the statute left the determination of solvency in the first instance to the state banking supervisors. It also required the FDIC to examine and approve that certification, reflecting perhaps some discomfort with the quality of state bank supervision.[14]

In late August 1933, with four months until the congressionally mandated insurance deadline and no members formally appointed to the FDIC's board, the job of federal solvency certification fell to Comptroller J.F.T. "Jefty" O'Connor (1933–1938) and Assistant Treasury Secretary Walter J. Cummings. Cummings, a Chicago industrialist and longtime associate of Treasury Secretary William Woodin, joined the administration in April 1933 to help reorganize and reopen troubled banks. O'Connor, who assumed his post in May, had organized Roosevelt's presidential campaign in California and enjoyed the backing of California Senator and former Treasury Secretary William G. McAdoo, O'Connor's former law partner. O'Connor's political connections compensated for his lack of banking experience, and the ambitious Comptroller aimed to use his high-profile administration post as a launching pad for higher office (although it had been—and would again become—a political backwater, the banking crisis briefly made the comptrollership a plum appointment).[15]

O'Connor and Cummings debated different approaches to evaluating and admitting state banks. O'Connor, following the Comptroller's informational model, favored a system where applicant banks would submit certified condition statements, attesting to their solvency as part of the state certification process that the federal government was meant to verify. Under O'Connor's light touch proposal, the insurance fund would supervise banks by checking paperwork in Washington rather than sending examiners out into the field. Cummings, however, advocated a "strict" plan of examination. Here, federal examiners in each state would oversee the process in cooperation with local officials but not in complete deference to them. With the integrity of the new insurance fund at stake and with limited time available, Cummings insisted that entry requirements ought to be more rigorous than bankers initially expected. Behind the scenes, O'Connor prepared to follow Cummings's proposal. He wrote state officials and U.S. senators, requesting names of experienced examiners who might check up on state banks in places where state examinations would not be sufficient.[16]

Conceptually, Cummings had the better of the argument, but the lack of time ultimately cut in favor of easier entry standards. In September, with less than four months to approve state banks for insurance, bankers and state examiners grew increasingly nervous. The American Bankers Association urged delay. State bank supervisors worried that the fund could not examine and accept all the state banks that wished to apply, even with RFC recapitalizations. Because Fed-member and national banks would be automatically admitted to the fund—their federal certification was what the holiday had been about, after all—any delay for state banks would place them at a disadvantage. Bank runs remained a live possibility. State bankers also saw the FDIC as an existential threat to the federalist experience of dual banking. The FDIC's own money was at stake, and state banks could not expect what they had experienced during the holiday: a federal guarantee without federal interference. Following the holiday, the federal government stood behind the banking system; through the FDIC it would ensure the entire banking system—state and federal—was worthy of its support.[17]

In early September 1933, amid this drama, Roosevelt appointed a full board to the new insurance corporation, formally selecting Cummings and Utah businessman E. G. Bennett to join O'Connor, the ex officio member. The board got to work, mailing out over 8,000 blank applications, fully fifty bags of mail. They requested office space in every state capital, so that national examiners could work directly with state banking authorities in what amounted to a new process of quasi-chartering. The Comptroller's staff handpicked forty-eight national bank examiners to assist in the effort, while the FDIC Board sought qualified examiners anywhere they could find them—the states, the Federal Reserve, even the banks themselves. The new corporation's minutes were crowded with examiner appointments as the staff swelled to 1,676 examiners and 900 office employees by December 1933. This was a massive effort. At the time, the Comptroller only employed around 150 clerks and 200 examiners. Meanwhile, the FDIC Board began a process of organizational proliferation, splitting off functions into subsidiary divisions as institutional exigency required. This insurance underwriter, in a few short months, had become a bona fide bank supervisor.[18]

The rush to get banks enrolled in the federal insurance system coincided with a significant change in the administration's posture toward the banking industry. Roosevelt was anxious to get closed banks open and open banks lending to aid the recovery. As the FDIC assembled its field force, Roosevelt announced "an intensive campaign to reopen the nation's closed banks," signaling his commitment to recovery over all competing concerns.[19]

At the FDIC, this policy manifested as a significant easing of enrollment standards. Though Cummings had proposed "strict" examination of state banks in August, a few weeks later he advertised "liberal" guidelines for entry to the insurance fund. To be admitted, a state bank needed only be solvent, Cummings explained to the *Wall Street Journal*, which he defined as having "sound assets to pay out all its depositors 100%." Since examiners would determine the soundness of bank assets in their evaluations of solvency, this description only underscored the "liberal" effort to get banks into a system of risk management that relied as heavily on the projection of safety and soundness as on its technical demonstration. In other words, from the very beginning of the deposit insurance system, the management of residual risk was largely located in the guarantee itself.[20]

This distinction, between federal assurance versus a technical demonstration of solvency, is highlighted by the fact that even as the banks that remained closed required significant government aid to reopen, thousands of open banks, even under generous supervisory valuations, could not meet Cummings's standards. To fulfill the administration's expectations for recovery, the banks required insurance *and* fresh capital. Congress and Roosevelt, as well as

Cummings and Jesse Jones, made clear that both would come from the government. Public power would stand behind private finance, whether the bankers liked it or not.

Roosevelt followed the issues closely. In September 1933, Roosevelt pleaded with the bankers. "Never before in its history has the nation had greater need of courageous bankers," he wrote in a statement delivered to the annual convention of the American Bankers Association, convened at the Stevens Hotel in Chicago. Jones was blunter. In a stinging address to the same convention, he commanded the assembled bankers "to be smart, for once" and "take the government into partnership with you." The alternative to public and private partnership, Jones lectured, would be nationalization. Bankers could decline the government's offer of aid, he said, but "if that is the program, and we want the government to do our banking, what is to become of our high-priced bank talent? The office boy can say no." He was met with silence. Afterward, Eugene R. Black (1933–1934), governor of the Federal Reserve Board, gave a follow-up address that Jones remembered as "devoted to apologizing for my speech."[21]

Asked to speak again after dinner, Jones responded that he had already spoken, and the bankers had not liked his remarks. He would only add that "half the banks represented at the gathering in front of me were insolvent, and no one knew it as well as the men in our banqueting room." Jones recalls this speech as the turning point in the RFC's recapitalization program.[22]

The looming FDIC deadline and the threat of nationalization seemed to do what previous efforts had not: capital infusions accelerated from October 1933. The program was also aided by a number of other factors, including the endorsement of the New York Clearinghouse, the symbolic acceptance of RFC equity by many of the nation's largest banks, and a commitment that the RFC would ease, significantly, the associated supervisory requirements. Although the RFC only purchased $3.3 million of preferred stock and capital notes in August and $3.75 million in September, it bought $89.6 million in November and $311 million in December. By then, the federal corporation had direct ownership stakes in more than 1,000 banks.[23]

Government capital infusions came at a critical moment for the banking system. The banks were still in terrible shape. More than half of the banks that the FDIC examined had impaired capital; approximately 1,000 were fully insolvent. As the insurance deadline approached, Jones, in consultation with O'Connor and newly appointed Treasury Secretary Henry Morgenthau Jr., agreed to recapitalize insolvent banks with a 90 percent ratio of liberally valued assets to deposit liabilities. Jones worked out a deal with Morgenthau, where "if Morgenthau would certify the borderline banks as solvent [Jones] would guarantee to make them solvent in six months" using bank equity investments and every other tool at the RFC's disposal. By the end of December 1933, the deposit fund offered temporary coverage to 500 state banks, pending their acceptance of RFC funds. If this program represented, as Jones insisted it did, a "partnership" between the public and private, it was clear that there was a senior partner (the government) and a junior partner (the banks).[24]

The administration's unflinching commitment to reopening through equity infusions, no matter the state of the bank's assets, scandalized some examiners. At the height of the December 1933 rush to clear applicant banks, a field examiner put his foot down over the Citizens Bank of Pekin, Indiana. In Pekin, a town of 500, economic conditions were "bad." The bank's "management has been unsatisfactory." Its "cash position" was "inadequate." As the examiner wrote, "this case raises the simple issue of whether under the present open bank program all banks are to be bailed out merely by the addition of new funds, or whether some attempt is to be made to secure new management or to wind up obviously unsound institutions." He urged the insurance application be declined. Despite these objections, the RFC stepped in to recapitalize the bank, leaving the FDIC's regional examiner to wonder whether they were now stuck with the present management, or if further changes could be orchestrated.[25]

Despite these objections, the breathless push to extend insurance coverage, backed by RFC recapitalizations, stabilized the banking system. It also substantially federalized it. In four months, the FDIC's hastily assembled force examined 7,785 banks. "No one thought it could be done," O'Connor congratulated himself in his diary. In their flurry to meet the law's examination mandate, FDIC officials collapsed the distinction between state and federal supervision completely. At the top, the corporation's bank examiners headed the examination team. They adopted the Comptroller's examination forms, applying the federal rubric to state banks. Some state officials, like New York Banking Commissioner Joseph A. Broderick (1929–1934), welcomed national unification. "With the system thus unified," Broderick argued, "it will be possible to standardize methods of examination, establish uniform measures for appraisals and determination of values, and erase the differences and distinctions which heretofore have existed between national and state institutions."[26]

Broderick's vision did not entail weakening state supervision but strengthening it, and with it the dual banking system. The FDIC brought the federal government into state banks but did not erase the federalist division in banking. State banks, in turn, were the FDIC's primary constituency, and with them the state bank supervisors who continued to enjoy authority from state legislatures. These legislatures were not idle. They often had to authorize state-chartered banks to sell preferred stock to the RFC and to participate in FDIC insurance. During those legislative sessions, lawmakers also expanded state supervisory powers. At the September 1933 meeting of the National Association of Supervisors of State Banks, for example, the assembled officials were especially envious of their colleague, Arkansas Banking Commissioner Marion Wasson (1933–1937). As Wasson explained: "Right after the banking holiday, our state passed the Dictator Bill which gives the Bank Commissioner authority to do anything outside of first degree murder."[27]

Recovery and Reconfiguration

By early 1934, the Roosevelt administration could take pride in their heroic efforts to stabilize the banking system. The previous year had begun in catastrophe, followed by a massive but fragile victory in the holiday and an even more substantial, and slightly less fragile, intervention through the FDIC certification campaign. True stability, however, remained elusive. "Banking is as yet one of the big unresolved problems," Jones confided to former administration official Raymond Moley in April 1934. Emergency capital infusions and qualification for deposit insurance helped, but neither offered magic cures for the nation's still-troubled banks. More work was required to get them on solid footing. Stability, moreover, was not recovery. As Roosevelt looked over the horizon to the New Deal's first electoral test in the 1934 midterms, the pressure to achieve visible economic progress built. Bank lending would be the core of any recovery program, Roosevelt believed. The question was how to achieve it.[28]

For answers, Roosevelt turned again to his supervisory staff, a group that transformed and solidified in the early months of 1934. Jones and O'Connor remained in place (the latter after declining repeated entreaties from Bank of America Chairman A. P. Giannini to run for governor of California). Henry Morgenthau Jr., gentleman farmer and Roosevelt's Hudson Valley neighbor, had formally replaced the ailing William Woodin as Treasury Secretary in 1933. Morgenthau, in turn, hired Utah banker Marriner Eccles as a special assistant. An advocate of government economic management in a Keynesian mold, Eccles quickly gained Roosevelt's confidence, eventually ascending to the governorship of the Federal Reserve Board. At the FDIC, Walter Cummings resigned to accept the chairmanship of Continental Illinois, an appointment secured by Jones to protect the RFC's considerable investment in the Chicago bank. Roosevelt appointed Wisconsin banker and politico Leo Crowley as Cummings's successor. For the remainder of the 1930s, these men—O'Connor, Eccles, and Crowley especially—would determine the course of federal bank oversight.[29]

In the early months of 1934, federal supervisors remained focused on recapitalization, with a new emphasis on shoring up banks' capital-to-deposit ratio as a counterweight to public deposit insurance, an early version of federal capital regulation. Under the still temporary deposit insurance plan, the fund guaranteed bank accounts up to $2,500, which fully protected 94 percent of depositors. Crowley and other officials wanted to build up bank capital—preferably private but public if necessary—as a first line of depositor protection. Supervisors settled on a 10 percent capital-to-deposit ratio, for which, a later commentator observed, "there appears to be no scientific basis for this . . . ; it is simply a good round decimal, easy to calculate at a glance." Supervisors gave this rule of thumb the force of law to protect the FDIC from moral hazard, to induce and maintain private investment, and to compel bank owners to exercise corporate governance. Where private funds were inadequate, the RFC continued to take temporary ownership stakes, amounting to $430 million in capital infusions in the first quarter of 1934, an amount nearly equal to the $431 million invested in the final quarter of 1933.[30]

Jones's recapitalization program succeeded in enabling insured banks to make stronger technical demonstrations of solvency, but the results for lending and economic recovery proved disappointing. Commercial bank loans outstanding peaked at $42.2 billion in October 1929. By December 1932, that figure cratered to $26 billion, and fell further through Roosevelt's first year to $22 billion by the end of 1933. With bankers apparently unwilling to lend, Jones turned up the pressure. Speaking at the meeting of the New York State Bankers Association in February 1934, Jones challenged those assembled: "Will our banking be continued in private hands or, of necessity, be supplanted by the government?" Jones was dead serious. The Texan intended to marshal all available forces to drive recovery. Two months later, still unsatisfied by bankers' progress, Jones began lobbying for authority for the RFC and the Federal Reserve Banks to make direct loans to businesses, bypassing private banks entirely. Congress enacted that reform in June 1934.[31]

Roosevelt was willing to use public funds where necessary, but his strong preference remained in favor of private action. Roosevelt had a keen understanding of the local power bankers wielded in the highly fragmented U.S. political system, and through 1934 he sought to keep bankers on the side of the New Deal. The president listened attentively to rumbling disquiet within the banking industry and demanded that his supervisors take banker concerns seriously.

Bankers had two interrelated complaints that Roosevelt heard and amplified. First, bankers argued that examination had become too strict, driving bankers away from any but the safest investments. Examiners leaned heavily on the familiar regime of loan categorization, using designations of slow, doubtful, and loss to pressure banks to pursue only short-term, self-liquidating loans and to collect and close out on working capital loans, even those to high-quality borrowers. Second, bankers complained about supervisory duplication, a concern that pre-existed Roosevelt's administration but one that intensified during the New Deal. Now, with the RFC and FDIC joining the other revitalized examiners, supervisory redundancy was especially acute. Completing reports for multiple agencies was expensive and time-consuming, especially for smaller banks. The two problems also reinforced each other. Redundant supervision increased examiner scrutiny, bankers argued, because examiners sought to prove their toughness to counterparts in other agencies. When Jones alerted Roosevelt to banker complaints about national bank examiners in May 1934, Roosevelt urged Jones to connect with O'Connor. "I *personally* know of so many cases in other banks, where the examiners have not used *common sense*, that we *must* do something!" the president commanded.[32]

The issue simmered through the summer of 1934, as the administration fought for a congressional extension of the still temporary deposit insurance fund. In August, Morgenthau decided to act, summoning the heads of the four banking agencies, "to try to get . . . a uniform policy as to examinations." After an initial meeting produced "a general discussion leading nowhere," Morgenthau instructed Jacob Viner, a University of Chicago economist working as Morgenthau's assistant, to organize a follow-up meeting and draft an initial report.[33]

The next day, the officials assembled in the Federal Reserve boardroom to consider both tough examinations and supervisory duplication. The officials agreed that, in their efforts to cultivate bank soundness, bank examiners may have exerted "undue deflationary pressure" on bank lending. No one could tell, though, whether the bank supervisors were the problem or whether it was a function of a lack of borrower demand or banker timidity. Resolving this question would take further study, which Viner undertook first through a short survey in the Fifth Federal Reserve District, headquartered in Richmond, and then in a much more comprehensive study in and around Chicago. With this information not yet available, the group agreed that "common sense" should prevail. Crowley insisted that once banks were insured and well capitalized, "the authorities should become lenient with regard to bank assets."[34]

The discussions also revealed an emerging reconceptualization of supervisory priorities in light of the federal government's ownership of financial risk and the new tools federal supervisors possessed. Loan categorization was an informational instrument crafted for an era when bank risk management fell primarily in the private domain, with government able to advise but not compel behavior. It also rested on the real bills doctrine, the banking theory which emphasized both liquidity and solvency as essential metrics for safe bank lending. With central banking, deposit insurance, and direct federal equity infusions all available, government pressure for bank liquidity was unnecessary and counterproductive, the assembled officials agreed. "Examining authorities should consider primarily the matter of the soundness of the assets and depend on rediscount privileges for liquidity," Viner instructed the group.[35]

Compared with determining the causes of restrained bank lending, supervisory duplication seemed an easier problem to solve. The officials acknowledged that they had likely been too aggressive in requiring reports from bankers in 1933, as they attempted to expand the information regime after its success during the holiday. By the time of their meeting in August 1934, they insisted that the lines of bank reporting and information sharing had been clearly demarcated, so that there was "no duplication, in actual practice, in the examination of banks by Federal agencies." The Comptroller oversaw national banks; the Fed oversaw state member banks, in partnership with state supervisors; the FDIC did the same with nonmember state banks; and the RFC accepted reports from the examining agencies.[36]

The question of duplication, though, implicitly raised the possibility of consolidation. As Morgenthau recalled: "A number of those present seemed quite frightened, particularly [First Deputy Comptroller F. G.] Awalt, who seemed to think that I had in mind . . . doing away with the Comptroller's office." Although this may not have been Morgenthau's initial intention, the momentum for consolidation grew over time, and with it a more fundamental contest about which supervisory approach would become the primary mode of federal financial risk management.[37]

Increasing Pressure

Morgenthau wanted to work out the details of a uniform examination policy in private, given the "many prima donnas involved." Yet in September 1934, the chief examiners of the various banking agencies convened in Washington, DC, for the first joint Federal Supervisory Conference, and their deliberations quickly became front-page news. With the 1934 midterms near at hand, and business opposition to the New Deal rising, the administration was eager to revive the flow of credit and pay deference to banker concerns.[38]

Roosevelt, despite his public reliance on a stricter conception of bank supervision during the holiday, now resolutely viewed the problem from the bankers' perspective. He told reporters covering the drama "that bank examiners were preventing bank credit expansion by throwing out good but 'slow' loans." Roosevelt echoed Francis M. Law, president of the American Bankers Association. Law told the examiners in Washington that "as long as examiners . . . constantly hammer on loans that are admittedly good, only because they are slow, it will have the effect not only of forcing banks to exert unnecessary pressure on such loans, but will prevent them from making new loans except those that are liquid and of short duration." Bankers, the *Wall Street Journal* reported, clipped stories describing how strict examinations were stalling the recovery and pinned them to their desks for the next examiner to see.[39]

In the meantime, Crowley took up the president's implicit charge to rethink loan categorization in the new risk environment and to discard liquidity as an essential supervisory metric. In a separate meeting with FDIC examiners during the September conferences, Crowley called the doubtful category "lazy and useless." He railed against the slow column as well. Slow loans were illiquid, but not all illiquid loans reflected poor risk management. Citing a recent Treasury report which found that national bank examiners had classified 20.83 percent of all loans and discounts as "slow," Crowley urged examiners to distinguish between loans that were slow and "safe," and loans that should be properly criticized because of poor credit quality. It was the latter, which might portend losses to the FDIC fund, that should concern examiners. Although examiners would maintain the slow designation, the category, Crowley insisted, would only be used to bring attention to loans likely to move into the doubtful and loss columns.[40]

As Crowley reconfigured loan categorization, he also oriented FDIC examiners' attention away from bank balance sheets, which told only a retrospective story of past decisions, to bank management, which enabled examiners to evaluate a bank's future prospects. The change reflected a difference in what it meant to supervise as an insurance underwriter versus supervision as a counterparty (the Fed), a chartering authority (the Comptroller), or an investor (the RFC). "We are now in the position where we insure and guarantee the mistakes of the other fellow," Crowley told the assembled FDIC examiners. "We should constructively help them retain or secure good management." Examiners and supervisory agencies had always been implicitly concerned with bank management, but with the insurance fund at stake, the FDIC was especially focused on managing moral hazard. Crowley's ambition was to make managerial competency more transparent and measurable. A bank with suspect loans but sound management could be trusted to work its problems out; a similar bank with weak management would be kept on a tighter leash. For Crowley and other high-ranking FDIC officials, asset and management quality could not be considered independently.[41]

The interagency meetings in September went further than repeating the constant calls for more informal supervisory coordination through standardized reports and forms. There was now a growing enthusiasm for a specialized supervisory corps housed in a single agency. In the week after the meetings, Morgenthau privately offered Crowley the governorship of the Federal Reserve, "with the idea that we would put the examination of banks" with the Fed. The Fed already had secondary examination authority over national banks, and all banks insured by the FDIC were slated to become Fed members by 1937. Crowley was game. "He said he would do everything that I wanted him to," Morgenthau recalled.[42]

O'Connor, aware of the maneuvering, fought back, using Crowley's past as a blunt bureaucratic weapon. It was easy to do; Crowley had lived a checkered life. The Wisconsin politico had risen to prominence as an industrialist, banker, and backer of Democratic governor Albert Schmedeman. Crowley, it was said, owned Schmedeman and with him Wisconsin's Democratic patronage machine. A stint as chairman of Wisconsin's Banking Review Board had elevated Crowley's national profile. In 1932, Crowley barnstormed the state, reorganizing more than eighty state banks. Impeccably dressed and physically imposing, Crowley commanded confidence, even as he convinced depositors to accept losses as the price for keeping local institutions open. During Crowley's Senate confirmation proceedings, however, it was alleged that Crowley was corrupt and had managed his business empire with peculiar indifference to banking law and good corporate governance. When the administration encouraged Crowley to produce an examiner report that would answer the allegations,

Crowley complied by commissioning the necessary report from a trusted confidant. So vindicated, Crowley received his confirmation; the vindicating examiner, meanwhile, soon became a high-ranking official at the FDIC.[43]

O'Connor, at the administration's behest, had shielded Crowley during his confirmation hearings, but he now engaged in institutional warfare as he sought new evidence of Crowley's misdeeds in Wisconsin. It wasn't hard to find. In the later words of Crowley's biographer, Crowley's was a "darker story of the businessman as speculator embezzler . . . deeply involved in conflicts of interest a later generation would find unacceptable and even incomprehensible." O'Connor passed along his evidence to Morgenthau, prompting the Treasury Secretary to call Crowley to account. Although his explanations satisfied Morgenthau, they also ended any further talk of the Fed governorship.[44]

Morgenthau moved on from Crowley at the Fed but not from Crowley at the helm of a consolidated bank supervisory apparatus. In a November memo to Roosevelt, Morgenthau proposed merging the Comptroller's office with the FDIC through administrative action. Because existing law allowed the FDIC to examine all banks, it could easily assume the Comptroller's duties. Key to this plan was getting O'Connor out of the way. The most promising post seemed to be a position at the Federal Reserve Bank of San Francisco, a job Roosevelt urged O'Connor to take.[45]

As O'Connor mulled the offer, Morgenthau turned to Eccles, recently confirmed as Federal Reserve governor after securing Roosevelt's commitment to comprehensively reform the Federal Reserve System. Morgenthau wanted Eccles to include supervisory consolidation in those reform plans. Eccles was nonplussed. "This amalgamating of your examinations and the question of charters," Eccles explained in early December, was "not material" to his ambitions, which were much more focused on wresting power from the private Reserve Banks and consolidating control of the Federal Reserve System within the public Federal Reserve Board. In other words, Eccles wanted consolidation but within the Fed, not beyond it. Eccles did heartily support Morgenthau's interest in sending O'Connor to California. Never one to mince words, Eccles put the matter simply: "We've got to get rid of him." It had to be a soft landing, though. O'Connor was politically important in California and California was politically important to Roosevelt. When O'Connor declined the offer of the governorship of the Federal Reserve Bank of San Francisco, there was no alternative but to stay the course with O'Connor—and his stubborn opposition to any attempt to reduce the Comptroller's influence.[46]

FDIC and Liquidation

The institutional disputes moved on one track; conceptual disputes about supervisory risk management traveled along on another. The growing consensus that liquidity was no longer a meaningful supervisory category derived in part from the federal government's implicit and explicit guarantees during the Bank Holiday of 1933 and its immediate aftermath. The federal government, in the most meaningful senses during the New Deal, *was* bank liquidity. The Federal Reserve, newly authorized to discount a variety of bank assets, would provide liquidity to sound banks through its discount window. The RFC would unleash a massive co-ownership program by buying bank stock and infusing government capital and cash. The FDIC would, in promise and in effect, liquify otherwise frozen deposits in the event of bank failure. Under this framework, examiners, that had once focused on banks' ready ability to convert their assets to meet depositor demands, needed to adjust their attention to other matters.

Each supervisory agency took different approaches reflecting their different missions in defining what supervision should be. For the FDIC, Crowley and his staff had to map the process for liquidating a failed bank in a way that would defend the value of the new deposit insurance fund. This was an especially important task given the problems of supervision and solvency that plagued deposit insurance in the states. The core policy they sought to implement was speed of process. Deposit insurance worked when depositors had quick access to their money, otherwise the incentive to run remained, whatever the government promised. More fundamentally, slow liquidation was a drag on the entire economy. With the overhang of thousands of bank receiverships after the 1930s crises, billions in deposits remained out of reach and out of circulation from a still-shriveled economy. To work, deposit insurance needed to work quickly.[47]

The congressional architects of the FDIC focused on solving these problems in ways that aligned with their other efforts to revive the banking system. The FDIC's 1933 temporary liquidation powers were the intellectual extension of the Emergency Bank Act's conservation authority—in the same way that conservators were tasked with managing banks toward reopening rather than wiping them off the map through receivership, so too would the FDIC liquidate failed banks by creating new banks. Under the Glass-Steagall Act, the FDIC was required to pay insured depositors through a newly chartered Deposit Insurance National Bank (DINB). When an insured bank closed, the

FDIC would open a new DINB to take its place, at least temporarily—until depositors were paid out or private investors took over. This strategy reflected New Dealers' ambition to preserve local banking facilities and Congress's understanding that, with billions in deposits tied up in receiverships, the old system of court-supervised liquidation was completely inadequate.[48]

Glass-Steagall transferred authority over national bank receiverships from the Comptroller to the FDIC, and state banking officials could appoint the FDIC receiver for insured state banks if they chose. Congress thus gave the FDIC a keen interest in orderly receiverships that generated the most return for a bank's creditors—it not only served as the liquidator of the failed banks, it also had to protect its own insurance fund through the process. In this the agency could be patient; it could afford to wait for local conditions to improve before liquidating assets, "having," as Congress mandated, "due regard to the condition of credit in the locality." Congress and bank supervisors understood from hard experience that fire sales devalued the assets of going firms, threatening a contagion of insolvency as market prices collapsed. Orderly liquidation was the only sound alternative.[49]

Despite the vision of the statute, the lines of authority in failed bank liquidations remained muddled, split among the federal agencies and between the FDIC and the states. The FDIC's interest in orderly liquidation was obviously strong but so, too, was every other relevant institutional interest. The first bank to fall into the FDIC's hands illustrates the challenge. That bank was the Fon du Lac State Bank in East Peoria, Illinois, which at the time of its failure had $237,892 in deposits, less than half insured. The Auditor of Public Accounts for the State of Illinois closed the bank on May 26, 1934, after a state examination. When the examiner determined that reorganization of the bank was impossible, the state auditor placed it in receivership on June 13, 1934.[50]

Illinois law allowed stockholders ten days to sue to halt the receivership, and during that time, FDIC examiners scoured the bank, collecting information necessary to identify assets with which to pay the insured depositors. The FDIC also sought a charter for the Deposit Insurance National Bank of East Peoria from the Comptroller of the Currency, as required by law, and requested a deposit account for the new national bank at the Federal Reserve Bank of Chicago. Given the novelty of this procedure, the Chicago Fed sought permission from the Board in Washington, which, ever cautious about experiments in banking, granted it "with the understanding that such action is to be considered only as an experimental step and not as a precedent to be followed in any future cases."[51]

Once the Comptroller issued the charter, the receivership transferred the Fon du Lac State Bank's insured deposit liabilities to the DINB, while the FDIC transferred cash into the DINB equal to those liabilities. As a result, the FDIC held a primary claim on the receivership for proceeds from the sale of assets. On July 3, 1934, the creaking institutional machinery finally issued Lydia Lobsiger, "a scrawny bespectacled widow" from East Peoria, check no. 1, for $1,264 (her entire life savings of $1,250, and $14 saved for her granddaughter).[52]

Lobsiger was the ideal recipient: Newspapers carried her picture, granddaughter in her arms, receiving her check with dignity from the bank teller window. The payment, the FDIC explained, "marks the first time in the history of the United States that deposits in a closed banking institution have been protected against loss through a national system of deposit insurance." Other writers hailed it as the embodied promise of the New Deal's new phase of "social security."[53]

Lydia Lobsiger's cover story warmed hearts; the backstory of how her check finally arrived was a Rube Goldberg liquidation process, one that continued to hammer and spring long after she claimed her funds. First, despite Congress's aim to preserve banking facilities, there was no successor bank to the Deposit National Bank of East Peoria, Illinois. Indeed, no one at the FDIC wanted there to be. In 1934, its first year of operation, the agency was more interested in consolidating weak "little banks." Officials did not wish to encourage new small banks to replace failed small banks. Although the FDIC existed to preserve unit banking, officials hoped to construct bigger, stronger units by merging failing banks before liquidation.[54]

In its first institutional iteration, the FDIC was seldom in control, epitomized when Illinois appointed its own receiver rather than the FDIC. That left the corporation to submit a claim, albeit a preferred one, just like other creditors. Like any failed bank, the Fon du Lac's affairs were messy. It had violated Illinois law by taking deposits far exceeding its capital, leading to cascading suits over the priorities of creditors' claims. With the most at stake, the FDIC participated in these suits, undertaking most of the legal work. Yet the Illinois receiver resisted paying the corporation's attorney fees directly, instead seeking to attach those claims to the receivership (where they would only be partially paid). In the meantime, the receiver vastly overpaid his own attorney—money which came out of the receivership to the detriment of the federal agencies. The receivership, initiated in 1934, was not resolved until 1941.[55]

So much for speedy resolution.

Supervision as Economic Management

To the great benefit of the country but to the detriment of the FDIC receivers who needed practice with this new institutional arrangement, there were only nine bank failures in the entire country in 1934, Fon du Lac among them. The broader questions of supervision during that year focused on deeper intellectual issues of how to organize this new, divergent, unwieldy supervisory system that showed itself impervious to organization and consolidation.[56]

Bank lending, or lack of it, remained the foundational puzzle for New Deal supervision. When supervisors met at Morgenthau's insistence in August 1934, and then *en masse* in September, they had only anecdotal evidence about why bank lending remained below expectations. Perhaps supervisors were being too strict. Perhaps bankers were being too cautious. Perhaps borrowers did not exist. No one was sure. Viner, the Chicago economist charged by Morgenthau to get to the bottom of these problems, went to work. Determining that the Seventh Federal Reserve District, which covered the midwestern states situated around Chicago, was suitably representative of national conditions, Viner and a team of researchers fanned out to survey banks and borrowers about credit conditions.[57]

In late December 1934, Viner circulated his preliminary findings. Surveying bank lending practices, Viner and his staff found that a post-crisis mania for safety had engendered a deep-seated conservatism in *both* examiners and bankers. While Chicago-area bankers claimed they were eager to lend, Viner found that these bankers were actively closing out long-term working-capital loans and providing only the short-term, self-liquidating credit prized by traditional banking theory. The lack of working capital seriously impeded industrial recovery. "This wave of 'righteousness' among the banks and the bank examiners accounts for a very large portion of the current discontent over the unavailability of bank credit," Viner reported.[58]

Even though bankers and examiners shared allegiance to the discredited economics of the real bills doctrine, that did not mean bankers voluntarily assumed responsibility for the lack of lending. Bankers complained bitterly about their examiners. Of the bankers surveyed, 72.4 percent criticized examiner practices, focusing especially on pressure for liquidity, examiner criticism of real estate and capital loans, and general strictness. "He won't let us do a banking business," one bank president complained to Viner's researchers.[59]

The Viner report revived again the fundamental question of what bank supervision was supposed to accomplish in this new world where the residual risk, which supervisors and bankers were meant to manage together, was not simply about the risks to a community served by a failed bank about the macroeconomic and political risks of a failed economy. Viner had a view. With the advent of the FDIC, he argued, liquidity, still relevant, should no longer be examiners' primary concern. Viner pressed forward an alternative supervisory epistemology: Supervision appeared to be procyclical, adding momentum to the swings of the business cycle. On the upswing, examiners followed bankers in their optimism. On the downswing, examiners tightened their standards, pressuring bankers to liquidate questionable loans. For a government committed to stability and recovery, these tendencies had to be checked. Strict loan classifications by examiners, the report argued, "are assuredly entirely out of place in the incipient stages of a recovery." Instead, they should be used only "in a period when a restrictive policy is desirable."[60]

This was something new. Supervision, the report stated at times and implied in others, was not only about individual bank safety but also credit policy and economic management. The way to accomplish this change, Viner thought, was through consolidated supervision. In this way, Viner's take appealed both to Morgenthau, always eager to consolidate supervision, and Marriner Eccles, who was coming to view supervision in a similar light.[61]

What examination was meant to become and what would become of examination were central questions that the administration grappled with as it prepared a legislative agenda for a new Congress in 1935. On the one hand, Crowley and the FDIC were eager for legislation that would place the insurance corporation on a permanent footing, maintaining the goodwill of bankers, while providing necessary supervisory powers to protect the fund. On the other, Eccles accepted the governorship of the Federal Reserve conditional on the legislative centralization of its monetary powers. Ignored in this consolidation of banking authority was O'Connor and the Comptroller of the Currency. With an expanded central bank to guide the economy and robust deposit insurance to protect depositors, it was not clear what role the Comptroller would play in the new, consolidated supervisory system.[62]

The Institutionalization of Supervisory Conflict

Spoiler, as it turned out. Throughout the fall of 1934, O'Connor continued to undermine Crowley, spreading rumors of Crowley's unseemly past to anyone who would listen. In early January 1935, Morgenthau summoned Crowley and O'Connor to his office to stage a confrontation. Crowley, Morgenthau's secretary observed, "broke down and cried. He became quite hysterical." Crowley's sincerity saved his position, but O'Connor won the day. The ambitious Comptroller, sights set on higher office in California, determined that his political interests were best served by holding onto his post in Washington. So it was that O'Connor blocked Morgenthau, Eccles, and others who sought to eliminate the office and bring institutional coherence to bank risk management in government. Instead, the administration sidelined supervisory consolidation in its legislative program; the institutional disarray, and with it supervision's conceptual disharmony, would persist.[63]

Roosevelt was not pleased. Consolidation, the president believed, would appease his banker critics and temper the industry's persistent opposition to his agenda. Determining, though, that there was no political path to consolidation given the inability to agree on legislative reforms, the administration adopted the argument that O'Connor had made all along: The boundaries between banking agencies were sufficiently clear, "there really is no duplication." Crowley, cowed but not yet defeated, offered to stay on until the banking legislation—Eccles's reform of the Federal Reserve, coupled with permanent authorization of the still-temporary FDIC—could be secured.[64]

As Eccles and Crowley lobbied for what would become the Banking Act of 1935, they focused on different supervisory problems. Eccles wanted to rid the Federal Reserve of its chaotic structure, the cause, he believed, of much of its policy errors in the past twenty years. Among other benefits of such consolidation, Eccles's plan meant that Fed supervision would rest squarely with the Federal Reserve Board and not the conservative, self-interested Federal Reserve bankers who had withheld so much liquidity in the name of protecting their own balance sheets. Crowley, for his part, wanted to reform the herkyjerky action of FDIC liquidation and sought new supervisory powers to ensure the safety of the deposit insurance fund, along with its permanence beyond the temporary authorization in 1933. In broadest strokes, Crowley offered Congress two options. The FDIC could "be a charitable institution which will pay for the mistakes, bad banking, and dishonesty of bankers," he suggested. "Or, by being placed on a sound basis, the Corporation may be used as an instrument to improve the standards of bank management and reduce the losses to depositors through bank failures."[65]

Put in these terms, there was only one option. The problem the FDIC confronted, Crowley continued, was that too many small, weak state-chartered banks had survived the previous crisis and too many new, small banks (2,000+) had formed since the crisis. When the topic of these tiny institutions was broached in Crowley's congressional testimony, Carter Glass interrupted the FDIC chairman to ask, "Do you call those banks?" If such institutions were solvent, Crowley continued, the FDIC had to insure them, even as shifting economic currents threatened to drown these banks by the thousands. Crowley, playing to his audience, argued for more authority so that the FDIC could eliminate "banks which cannot economically survive."[66]

Congress largely granted Crowley this authority, and in doing so, institutionalized and enshrined far more expansive supervisory power than the 1933 Act imagined for a government corporation initially charged with verifying insurance eligibility and providing orderly liquidation for banks that suddenly failed. The 1935 Act made the FDIC a permanent institution, still entwined with the Comptroller and the Fed but with its own examination authority and without the obligation that all participating state banks join the Federal Reserve System. Although the 1935 Act did not give the FDIC formal chartering power—that remained with the Comptroller for national banks and with the states for state banks—Congress did grant the FDIC power to deny insurance for nonmember state banks and to revoke insurance for any participating bank. This power was functionally the equivalent of the supervisory death sentence long possessed by chartering authorities. Congress also empowered the federal insurer to stop insured banks from branching, reducing capital, or merging with uninsured banks—historically, questions negotiated between state officials and state banks' private boards of directors. Finally, the FDIC could draw upon the deposit insurance fund to make loans or guarantees to facilitate mergers between weak and healthy banks that "will reduce the risk or avert a threatened loss to the Corporation." This was not liquidation authority that came in after the fact but preemptive managerial authority to exercise ahead of crisis.[67]

Crowley thus secured statutory independence for the FDIC. Eccles sought comparable treatment for his new vision of the Fed as a banking and economic stability supervisor. Eccles wanted to centralize power within the Fed in the hands of a new class of government bureaucrat: the public central banker. The most important of these changes was the consolidation of authority over open market purchases to stabilize the money supply and over supervisory control. Eccles also sought to excise the real bills doctrine from the bank's rediscount policy, substituting the old phrasing of "eligible paper"—ninety-day commercial bills or nine-month agricultural loans—for "any sound asset." While Glass was Crowley's ally in reforming the FDIC, he was Eccles's implacable foe. Glass still ascribed to the real bills doctrine—or, as he called it, "The

Commercial Loan Theory of Banking"—and he whittled away at Eccles's plan. The Federal Reserve Banks would retain much of their statutory power, even as a newly created entity, the Federal Open Market Committee, would be dominated by a new Board of Governors in Washington, DC. By the end, Glass gloated, "we did not leave enough of the Eccles bill to light a cigarette."[68]

Roosevelt played a careful game. He feigned sympathy with those who would have prioritized the FDIC reforms, severing and sinking the Fed changes. Meanwhile, he worked behind the scenes to ensure the enactment of the whole package. It helped the administration that the Senate was also taking up a raft of legislation that would come to be known as the Second New Deal. Among these was the creation of social security, the passage of the Wagner Act (which would define labor relations for the next ninety years), and the passage of the Public Utilities Regulation Act, among others. The Banking Act was not the top priority for many members beyond Glass, and part of Roosevelt's strategy was to give Glass the room to claim victory. In fact, both Title I (the reforms to the FDIC) and Title II (the changes to the Fed) mostly passed as Crowley and Eccles wanted.

The 1935 Banking Act was, in a way, an effort to reformulate the crisis legislation of 1933 in the light of the experience of 1934. Economic recovery—slow, halting, but steady—raised the political stakes. Americans, seeing progress that they attributed to New Deal reforms, wanted more. They turned to figures like populist Huey Long, radio preacher Father Coughlin, and journalist-turned-novelist-turned-California gubernatorial candidate Upton Sinclair to deliver more radical changes. To diffuse these leftwing pressures, Roosevelt worked to outflank them during the 1936 campaign. Gone was the reasoned accommodation with bankers and business of 1934. Instead, in a speech at Madison Square Garden in October 1936, Roosevelt thundered to an exuberant crowd that "government by organized money is just as dangerous as government by organized mobs . . . they are unanimous in their hate for me—and I welcome their hatred." It worked. In 1936, Roosevelt went on to win a sweeping victory.[69]

In Roosevelt's victory, Eccles saw his moment to place countercyclical economic management at the heart of the federal bank supervisory structure. In an avalanching November 1936 memo, Eccles urged Roosevelt to take revolutionary action with his overwhelming mandate. The time had come for a "fundamental reconstruction." The dual system of federal and state chartering left half the banking system outside of federal control, and enabled inexperienced, incapable bankers to open small, weak, and dangerous unit banks. These "mushroom miscalled banks" accounted for "the greatest holocaust of bank failures" causing "the greatest losses and misery among their depositors," Eccles insisted. Supervisory control over the banking system needed to be complete. He didn't just want consolidation within the Federal Reserve System, or even harmonization at the federal level. He wanted all supervisory authority, state and federal, in one place to manage for one purpose: countercyclical economic stability. The time for deference to state authority and unit banking was over.[70]

For Eccles, this meant consolidating financial oversight in the Federal Reserve, and in doing so, unifying bank supervision, monetary policy, and national credit management. Before the Depression, the commitment to the gold standard had worked as a moderating force on private money creation in the banking system. With the gold anchor more nominal than real after Roosevelt's 1933 ban of private gold holdings, the Federal Reserve, as the monetary authority, needed more power to control private credit creation. Such currency management, moreover, was intimately tied to Federal Reserve management of the business cycle. In this way, Eccles had firmly converted to Viner's proposition that supervision could best serve financial risk management by managing the economy as an adjunct to monetary policy. "Clearly," Eccles wrote in his memoirs, "if the [Federal Reserve] System is committed to a policy of monetary ease in times of depression, then bank-examination policies should follow a similar commitment."[71]

Writing to Roosevelt, Eccles revived his 1935 proposal to eliminate the Comptroller, an agency now worse than "obsolete." "The Comptroller's office," Eccles explained, "has repeatedly pursued a policy of restraint when it should relax and vice versa, directly contrary to correct central bank policy." Eccles assured Roosevelt that he had Crowley's support. Cooperation with O'Connor, however, was "out of the question." Roosevelt told Eccles to take it up with Morgenthau, who received the idea favorably, but coolly. When Eccles pressed, arguing that his chief concern was "taking O'Connor out of the picture," Morgenthau demurred. Before a meeting with Roosevelt in December, Eccles confided to Morgenthau, "I want you to join me alone and get rid of this man O'Connor," after which, "you and Crowley and I can sit down and decide what the future banking system for America should be." Morgenthau—surprisingly, given his early antipathy to O'Connor—seemed scandalized. "I would be no part or parcel of any such thing," he recalled soon after.[72]

Though bold with Roosevelt and Morgenthau, Eccles would not confront O'Connor directly. Perhaps he feared that O'Connor would take Crowley down with him. Whatever the reason, Eccles's inability to pursue his reform program left the administration stalemated on the big issue of consolidation. When the heads of the supervisory agencies convened in January 1937 to consider administration proposals to send to the new Congress following Roosevelt's victory, they had little of significance to offer. O'Connor wanted statutory clarification on whether the 1935 law's provision for "semiannual" dividends allowed for quarterly dividends. Eccles wanted a new bill to split the positions of Federal Reserve Bank agent and chairman. "That's words," Jesse Jones said, exasperated. "You're just talking about words." With no one willing to propose bold steps, the administration declined to put forward any banking program when the new Congress met in January. Instead, they agreed to meet again in March 1937 to reconsider the issue.[73]

They would not have the chance. After the election, Roosevelt overreached in his efforts to assert executive dominance not only over Congress (which he enjoyed thoroughly in his first term) but over a hostile judiciary too. In February 1937, he announced plans to "pack" the Supreme Court, adding a new member for each justice over 70 years old. Younger justices, appointed by the president, might view New Deal programs more favorably. Despite his overwhelming popularity and congressional majorities, the politics were disastrous, stymying the reform momentum promised by Roosevelt's 1936 victory. Any hope for sweeping bank reorganization was over. With reform ended and the economy recovering, Roosevelt returned to his inherent fiscal conservatism, preaching fiscal rectitude and balanced budgets in 1937, at a time when the weak economy could not abide it. The decision sparked the recession in 1937, notorious for extending the Great Depression even after Roosevelt—and the voters—had expected its end.

Consolidation and Compromise

With the economy in trouble, Roosevelt turned to familiar scapegoats—bank supervisors. In April 1938, Roosevelt forwarded a letter to Eccles from a New York state senator. The senator complained that "the small banks . . . are harassed by two sets of examiners visiting them at the same time and throwing these small loans out of the window." Roosevelt continued to see strict examination as a barrier to economic recovery. Eccles, in turn, reopened his bid for supervisory consolidation and countercyclical supervisory policy. Eccles urged Roosevelt to "put examination functions under the same tent and . . . see that examination policy takes account of changing economic conditions just as monetary policy does." Roosevelt, always supportive in principle, was moved enough to include the proposal in a larger program of federal spending and credit measures aimed at fighting the recession. In a message to Congress outlining these proposals later that month, Roosevelt expressed hope "that federal banking supervision can be better coordinated" toward macroeconomic ends. Although Roosevelt addressed the suggestion to Congress, he also instructed the supervisory heads, once again, to work it out themselves.[74]

Crowley, meanwhile, had clung to power at the FDIC and the 1937 recession catalyzed his plans to reformulate bank supervision in line with the New Deal's political economy of strictly regulated finance. Just as Eccles geared up his campaign, Crowley moved forward with changes in examination policy across the federal supervisory agencies that the FDIC chairman had long advocated. First, Crowley planned to cut the last cancerous cells of the real bills doctrine out of bank supervision by getting rid of the "slow" designation from examination forms. Second, Crowley sought to impose an intrinsic value standard on banks' bond holdings, not only to protect bank solvency during market downturns but also to shield bankers from the temptation of betting on the upswing. Banks would hold highly rated bonds at the purchase price, so that, Crowley declared, "banks will thus no longer be able to profit from securities speculations."[75]

Although these proposals might have provided macroeconomic benefits (for example, by divorcing bank balance sheets from fluctuations in bond markets), Crowley, in contrast to Eccles, remained focused on risk management at the level of the individual bank. After four years at the helm of the FDIC, Crowley saw supervision purely through an insurer's lens. "Bank examination is for the protection of depositors," he told Morgenthau in a June 1938 meeting. "Marriner is leaving the impression that [it] is supposed to be mixed up with some other things." Morgenthau, who opposed Eccles's plans to modulate supervision with the nation's economic fortunes, made the point more strongly: "Who the hell's money is it? It's the depositors' money. And [Marriner] sits up all night trying to find sloppy ways in order to loan this money."[76]

Crowley and Eccles were on a collision course. Crowley saw Eccles's bid for countercyclical supervision consolidated within the Federal Reserve as a power grab, plain and simple. "I don't think you will find any difference of opinion as to what spirit that you are trying to bring about in the way of uniform policies," Crowley explained to Morgenthau, who Roosevelt had again tasked with finding agreement. "I think you will find a lot of opposition if anyone is trying to take over something that belongs to somebody else." If consolidation should occur anywhere, Crowley said, it should be in the FDIC. Unlike the Fed, Crowley's agency worked hand-in-glove with forty-eight state banking commissioners. Eccles was just stirring up trouble. He was "trying to make the bank examiner the goat for this recession."[77]

In the meetings that followed, Morgenthau set himself as arbiter and, given his sympathies, channeled discussion toward the changes favored by Crowley. To get an agreement on uniform examination policy, Morgenthau brought together the feuding agency heads, their deputies, state bank supervisors, and a handful of trusted bankers. Agreement on how to evaluate banks' bond portfolios was easiest to reach. Before the New Deal reforms, bonds functioned as a "secondary reserve" that bankers could sell to meet liquidity squeezes in secondary markets that were typically well suited to the purpose. In that previous system—where private bankers were expected to manage liquidity risks with informational, not financial, assistance from the government—bond prices had to be evaluated in parallel with the creditor claims that the bonds might be sold to satisfy. During downturns, a collective rush for liquidity could spark mass insolvency, vividly demonstrated by the collapse of bond prices in the early 1930s, and a live concern as officials debated reforms with a recession churning in the background. With the federal government now ready to answer all calls for liquidity, the Fed and the FDIC agreed that highly rated bonds should be valued at their purchase price, thus locking in solvency by shielding bank portfolios from market fluctuations "on a basis of 'damn the ticker.'"[78]

The debates over the slow column were more contested because they opened up deep questions about how public examination worked as a means of influencing private bank behavior. At a first pass, all agreed that the slow designation, with its inherent emphasis on liquidity, was no longer fit for purpose. Supervisory definitions already reflected this change: Since 1934, slow loans were defined in relation to credit quality as "loans which in [the examiner's] opinion will become doubtful or worthless in whole or in part unless placed in proper bankable shape by the bankers." Yet the category continued to be called "slow," and examiners continued to criticize long-maturing assets, thus discouraging productive private lending, which the administration still understood as necessary for economic growth. The question was how to deal with this problem. Some officials favored simply renaming the column something more benign and continuing loan criticism under the prevailing definitions. Others, aligned with Eccles's view, sought to eliminate the first category of criticism entirely to encourage bankers to lend without fear of examiner rebuke.

Perhaps surprisingly, the assembled bankers sought to keep the initial category in place. "There is where you get your trend—in the slow column," one banker observed. Another made the point more bluntly: "I tell you, if you cut that out you might just as well quit examining your banks."[79]

These bankers' objections carried in them assumptions about how federal examination worked and what it was meant to accomplish, which had been deeply unsettled by the New Deal. Their arguments reflected the old information regime, where public officials provided guidance on which private bankers and bank directors—holding the risk for bank failure—would act or not act. Yet over the preceding five years, the federal government's relationship to the banking system had fundamentally changed. As the ultimate backstop against the risks of bank failure—managed through information provision, public central banking, deposit insurance, and public ownership—the public had asserted overwhelming power to make banking safe. Yet from Roosevelt down, the administration also remained committed to banking as a system of private entrepreneurial risk-taking, undertaken primarily by small, community institutions, and overseen through the unchanged process of periodic oversight by a rotating cast of government employees. The structure of the banking system and the mechanics of banking oversight looked the same, even as the balance of public and private authority had changed dramatically.

Put simply, before the New Deal, public officials could suggest, but not mandate, safety; after the New Deal, they found they could suggest but, not mandate, risk-taking.

The debates about how to structure federal examination forms thus revolved around this larger paradox, which Morgenthau and his colleagues considered through the frame of three interrelated problems. The first was the problem of private risk-taking. The assembled officials and bankers shared a collective belief in private action. They looked with apprehension at the proliferation of public lending programs, which Congress enacted to generate the loans that bankers appeared unwilling to make. The federal government, they feared, was becoming the risk-taker of last resort. With these concerns motivating them, officials spent hours debating the best way to present bank examiners' evaluations without discouraging bankers. Should there be a first column, or not? Should the column be totaled, or not? Should there be new columns for "good loans" to boost bankers' confidence?[80]

Even if they could perfect the forms, that would not resolve the second problem: consistency. Bank examination continued to operate through the judgment of individual examiners, judgments that now carried more significant consequences. Finely tuned examination forms would only work if examiners interpreted categories consistently, instead of, as one Fed governor feared, "throw[ing] notes promiscuously from one column to the other." Officials recognized that interpretations varied from examiner to examiner, as well as among differently oriented federal supervisors. The government never spoke with one voice.[81]

And here, Morgenthau's group confronted the last and perhaps most intractable problem: consolidation, or its persistent failure. The assembled agency heads understood that perfecting the examination forms would not solve their underlying philosophical differences—protecting depositors, for example, as against macroeconomic management. They agreed on the basic problems of supervisory incoherence and agreed even more that they must guard their own institutional turf. As long as officials argued over columns on the examination report, they were not getting closer to answering these foundational questions. It was, as Jones said, just words.

And so, they settled on words, known formally as the "Uniform Agreement on Bank Supervisory Procedures," which the agencies agreed to in June 1938. Although it could not touch the foundational paradox, the agreement nevertheless had consequences. It instituted a new regime of loan criticism, finally abandoning "slow," "doubtful," and "loss" in favor of escalating categories of loan quality. The agreement also embraced Crowley's plans to use fair value accounting for bank bond portfolios, eliminating profits on the upside, as well as losses on the downside. Finally, the agreement adopted a moderate version of countercyclical supervision, instructing supervisors to avoid "examination pressure to liquidate intrinsically sound assets in time[s] of deflation." This was a divided mandate, left to each agency to interpret. Eccles had wanted and fought publicly for more, launching a last-ditch effort to consolidate countercyclical supervision in the Fed. He failed to rally sufficient support. Instead, federal supervision remained divided along lines of chartering (Comptroller and states), liquidity (Federal Reserve), and insurance (FDIC), with ownership (RFC) fading away as the banking system regained solvency and the nation geared for war. Despite the agreements in principle, these divisions would sow seeds for broader and wider disagreements about what it meant to manage residual risk across the public-private divide for decades to come.[82]

Conclusion

A dominant metaphor in evolution is the gladiatorial-style "survival of the fittest." The fights over supervisory consolidation appeared, superficially, to be precisely this kind of contest. Combatants were politically connected and intellectually motivated institutional designers that squared off against each other in the last years of the Great Depression. They worked together at times, as when they rushed to set up the FDIC and used the best tools available to accomplish the enormous task of certifying—and indeed creating—the solvency of thousands of banks. Sometimes they turned on each other, claws out, to reach for dominance, even when they in fact agreed on the importance of shifting supervisory priorities away from retrospective critiques of illiquid loans and toward a system of workable solvency assessments that could be actionable well before a bank's demise.

The personalities in this chapter—Crowley, O'Connor, Eccles, Morgenthau, and of course, Franklin D. Roosevelt—were surely gladiators, but another metaphor helps us understand what the New Deal did to bank supervision and what it could not do whatever their best intentions. The supervisory system the New Dealers established—temporarily first, permanently thereafter—did not remove the preexisting institutions (such as the OCC or Federal Reserve Banks), despite many concerted efforts to do so. Instead of consolidation, there was a profound sense of multiplication, as the FDIC's role as an insurance provider morphed into a supervisory authority that was just different enough from others in the federal and state government to constitute a new force for managing banks' residual risk and the government commitment to provide liquidity to the system in times of crisis. The institutional layers that evolved from this process constituted an ungainly extra digit on the hand of the state, a "banker's thumb" that was not the product of thoughtful design but the outcome of contentious processes that yielded a mechanism for risk management that mostly worked, its obvious shortcomings notwithstanding.[83]

These deeper processes were far more important to the way public officials and private bankers would practice the negotiation of bank supervision in the years that followed than some of the contemporaneous debate suggested. For example, it is dubious to blame—as Eccles did and as the Uniform Agreement seemed to imply—bank examiners for causing 1937 recession, the double dip of the Great Depression. The scholarly literature on that recession does not mention examiners much at all, blaming instead industrial policy, fiscal policy, or tighter-than-needed monetary policy. But the late

1930s highlight an important element of a supervisory system in punctuated equilibrium. Even in the New Deal's frenzy of institutional creation, a central tendency of supervision was evolving. As the government took ever firmer control over liquidity for the system, bank supervision transformed to provide the superstructure of the risk management that would govern the deployment of that liquidity.[84]

Interlude: Supervising
Japanese Banking

ON A trip to Kobe in September 1948, Dr. Paul M. Atkins, formerly the Special Liquidator of Securities (1932–1937) and now special advisor to the Supreme Commander of the Allied Powers (SCAP) in occupied Japan, took a passing interest in East Asian architecture. Why, he wanted to know, did the corners of Japanese temple roofs curve upward? His hosts, including Chu Okazaki, President of the Bank of Kobe, had no ready answer. In subsequent weeks, Okazaki would thank Atkins for a "good many suggestions . . . of great significance" to the bank, but he could shine no further light on the architectural riddle. Apparently, a temple's deep eves protect the building's open windows from typhoon rains, while the upturned ends allow light to enter in sunny weather.[1]

Atkins was not in Japan to see the sights, although there was plenty to see in post–World War II Japan. He was instead a representative of the United States conferring with local and military authorities to make "a thorough inventory of banking statistics and related data as a first step toward appraising these statistics and recommending necessary improvements." Truman administration officials, still deeply rooted in New Deal banking sensibilities, worried that financial instability and a slow economic recovery would encourage the rise of extremist political groups, especially Japan's budding socialist and communist parties. Atkins was sent to find an effective supervisory information regime that would facilitate safe, responsible banking, in turn ensuring economic and political stability. Atkins was perfect for the job. He had earned (perhaps undeservedly) a reputation as a banking savant in his work, first, evangelizing—ill-advisedly—a secondary reserve in bonds in the 1920s and, second, liquidating—most successfully—those same bonds during the 1930s. Since then, he had reinvented himself as an international banking consultant for the U.S. government, working in Iran from 1942 to 1944 and as part of the American Mission for Aid to Greece from 1947 to 1948.[2]

The work of financial governance in Japan did not flow through the domestic banking agencies like the Federal Reserve, FDIC, or Comptroller of the Currency; as with everything else in the critical postwar period, that work was accomplished through the U.S. military. At the request of Major General William F. Marquat, head of the Economic and Scientific Section (ESS) of SCAP, Atkins set about evaluating the pending American plans to reform the Japanese banking system. He did so at a moment when military reformers prioritized "democratizing" Japanese institutions, including the nation's mammoth quasi-public banks. This transformation was easier said than done. Determining what democratization would mean in practice elicited strenuous debate among the occupying forces.[3]

By the time Atkins arrived in August 1948, the Japanese banking system had already faced dramatic upheaval. In the 1870s, the Japanese had first modeled their banking institutions on the U.S. national banks. Yet Japanese commercial banks proved ill-suited to the needs of a rapidly industrializing nation. Ultimately, Japan more closely followed the continental European model of large, universal banks, albeit with tighter public control unique to Japan's imperial system. After more than a decade of imperial, globe-spanning conflict, Japanese banks were fully invested in the war-making economy. In the first year of the U.S. occupation, following the end of the Pacific campaign in August 1945, the Japanese government (which, following the purge of its conservative leadership, continued to function) kept its economy afloat by continuing its payments to war contractors, first directly through indemnities and war insurance, and then indirectly through easy monetary policy and bank loans. This activity kept industrial firms and the banking system solvent but at the cost of rampant inflation.[4]

In this strained environment, the U.S. occupation forces worked with the Japanese Ministry of Finance to implement a complex plan to demilitarize and then stabilize the Japanese financial system. First, American officials arrested inflation by imposing a new currency, requiring that exchanges from old to new money occur through bank deposits, not—except for very small amounts—in cash. The new currency policy forced money into the banks, where accounts were essentially frozen. At same time, SCAP forced the Japanese government to end indemnities to the war industries, presaging mass bankruptcy among Japanese industrial firms. Because two-thirds of Japanese bank loans were for military production, the move also promised mass insolvency of Japanese banks.[5]

To forestall a complete breakdown of the Japanese banking system, officials undertook an intensive supervisory process, identifying "special" war-related markdowns of bank assets and then offsetting those losses against the rest of the banks' balance sheets, first eroding profits, then marketable reserves, then shareholder equity, and then by taking haircuts from large frozen deposit accounts of Japanese firms. The process was, in intent and effect, a conservatorship and reorganization of the entire Japanese banking system.[6]

The process took more than a year, but the reorganizations, like the 1933 Bank Holiday, instilled confidence in the Japanese banking system through the shock and awe of decisive action and the continued commitment by technical, informed bank supervisors. And as the Americans had done in the 1930s, the Japanese government also created a Reconstruction Finance Bank to channel credit toward pivotal industries, reviving financial flows by other means.[7]

With the system stabilized, American officials approached banking reform in Japan in the only way they knew: by inscribing the elemental features of American-style banking and with them, American-style economic democracy, including their conflicts, tensions, and cross-cutting incoherence. For example, antitrust had been a contested pillar of the New Deal, with Roosevelt sometimes relying on coordinated industries and sometimes warring against them. In Japan, this tension manifested in SCAP's approach to the incumbent banks. Edward C. Welsh, a veteran of the Office of Price Administration, headed the ESS Antitrust and Cartels Division. Welsh and his staff were determined to eliminate "excessive private concentrations of economic power" across the Japanese economy, with banking as a central area of policy emphasis.[8]

Welsh and his colleagues wanted to democratize by deconstructing. Their vision of economic pluralism centered on a unit banking ideal where financial firms were accountable to local economic interests. The idealized political economy of small finance that the antitrusters imagined ran headlong into the Japanese *zaibatsu*, large banking and industrial holding companies which had straddled the Japanese economy since the Meiji restoration, and into the more general trend of nationwide branch banking. Welsh sought to break it all up. "Banks should be organized so that primary direction of the bank management is to serve the local public," Welsh wrote. "It is not in the interest of banking management efficiency nor in the interest of deconcentration to have bank operations of any one bank extended generally throughout a large geographic area."[9]

In a plan put forward to the ESS in February 1948, Welsh proposed dividing Japan into geographic districts and barring branching across district borders (a reform model that had already been imposed on occupied Germany).[10]

As had occurred so many times in the United States, the localism of unit-style banking ran full steam into the national (and global) wishes of other parts of the economy and government. The plan advanced by Welsh and the antitrust division was met with adamant opposition from the ESS Finance Division, which until that time had jurisdiction over Japanese banking reconstruction and reform. The head of the division, former First National City banker Walter LeCount, predicted "complete financial collapse" if the antitrust plan was followed. "Finance Division feel strongly that the plans or ideas for the breaking up of the branch banks advanced by Antitrust are not practical or feasible," though they "will be highly effective if the objective is the disintegration of the banks."[11]

The finance division championed an alternative New Deal impulse: counter-organization. Where the antitrust division sought to impose democracy by making big banks small, the finance section sought to level the competitive playing field by making weak banks strong. The task was not to simply scale the banks to larger size, although the finance division was hardly opposed to such moves. The method involved a particularly activist approach to bank supervision. Officials imposed a standardized reporting regime on Japanese banks and formulated bank-by-bank reorganization plans, working to enable specialized savings and trust banks to compete with the slightly pared-down *zaibatsu* banking firms.[12]

Although the finance division's reform proposals did not favor size per se—note the focus on savings banks and trust companies, for example—they did focus much more on centralization and public supervision rather than the fragmentation and local discipline favored by the antitrust division. These tensions between antitrust and finance echoed the ongoing disputes in U.S. domestic bank supervision. If the antitrust division approximated the FDIC, with its focus on state-chartered, nonmember unit banks, the finance section was the Fed, keen to meet the needs of macroeconomic stability with larger banks managing risks against the cycle. In a way, this parallel was literally true, at least in the finance division—Caroline E. Cagle, who crafted finance's bank- ·ing law reforms, had long been an economist and adviser at the Federal Reserve Board.[13]

The antitrust and finance divisions fought to a stalemate in early 1948. Career military officers staffed the upper echelons of SCAP, and they sought guidance from policymakers in Washington. With Japanese recovery stalling and communism on the march in Asia, Washington officials shied away from the antitrust division's draconian reforms. Stability—both economic and political—became the most important method of understanding Japanese bank reform. There was no institutional layer in Japan built on unit banking. Imposing it on the near tabula rasa that the war produced was not the path, these officials decided, to accomplish the paramount task of stability in Japan.[14]

With the deconcentration agenda scuttled, the initiative shifted to Cagle and the finance division. In May 1948, Cagle submitted a memo outlining his plans, which sought to reshape the Japanese banking system as a mirror image of the Federal Reserve, not just as it was, but as Chairman Marriner S. Eccles (1934–1948) had long wanted it to be. Cagle proposed a central board "responsible for the formulation and enforcement of all monetary and audit policies of the Government," and which would "regulate and supervise all banks and all other credit granting institutions." Eccles had tried repeatedly—and failed repeatedly—to make the Federal Reserve the central institution for national monetary and financial management down through the supervision of individual banks. Now Cagle sought to impose on Japan what Eccles could not win for himself in America.[15]

The irony, that Atkins saw clearly but that most American officials could not or would not see, was that the Japanese banking system was already highly sophisticated and organized to Japan's particular practices of government-directed industrialization. In his primary investigation, for example, Atkins found that financial information gathering in Japan was as good or better than in the United States. While Cagle called for annual balance sheet reporting, the Bank of Japan was moving to establish a system of continuous reporting, requiring banks to submit information every ten days. "The banking statistics now being compiled in Japan [are] relatively good," while "some of the banks are doing really superior work in collation of statistics for their own use," Atkins reported.[16]

Atkins did see opportunities for improvement, advancing proposals that aligned with the centralization thrust of Cagle's reforms, focused especially on securing more effective bank supervision. "Inspections," Atkins observed, "lack the definiteness and completeness attained in the case of bank examinations in the United States." He called for a Bureau of Audits and Examinations to be established "with very little delay."[17]

But where Atkins implicitly sided with Cagle's call for centralization, he took a dim view of the remainder of the finance division's proposals. "The proposal for a new banking law appears to be an attempt to transplant, with some variations, the Federal Reserve Act . . . from the United States to Japan without adequate consideration of the many fundamental differences which exist between the two countries and with little regard to Japanese customs and psychology," Atkins wrote to his military superior at SCAP. In this sense, Atkins understood much better the nature of institutional evolution than either those in the antitrust or finance divisions. "No greater error can be made than to assume that, because certain laws have been proved to be desirable and effective in the United States, they are equally desirable and may be expected to be equally effective in other countries where economic, financial, social, cultural and psychological conditions are radically different from those existing in the United States."[18]

In essence, the United States' banking system—its legal and institutional framework—came about through a distinct process of national evolution. Japan's banking system had developed in the same way but under very different historical and institutional conditions. Thus, in places where the Japanese adopted American supervisory practices, like the enhanced bank examination Atkins advocated, the results were less than the sum of the parts. Following guidance from FDIC officials (including training with the FDIC manual designed for examining unit banks that were uncommon in Japan), Japanese bank examiners began to focus more on collecting fine-grained balance sheet data. By practicing what one scholar calls "manualization" and "mechanization," they sacrificed older practices of wholistic evaluation and high-level dialogue between examiners and bank managers.[19]

At the scale of the banking system, Japanese officials took the same view as Atkins and successfully whittled down Cagle's reform proposal, eventually leveraging the building Cold War conflict in Asia to reassert sovereign autonomy over finance. The supervisory system that emerged was more informationally sensitive and reflected more of a public-private partnership in risk management than what came before. Yet in sheer numbers and size of banks, the American reforms made almost no difference, and by 1952, the brief American efforts to impose versions of the New Deal banking reforms in Japan had ended.[20]

7

Supervising Concentration

HOLDING COMPANIES AND MERGER
REVIEW IN THE POSTWAR YEARS

THE QUEST for the soul of supervision amid the New Deal's institutional and personal conflicts gained some common purpose through World War II. Institutional complexity thrived but so did the singularity of the enterprise: Everyone was focused on total war against Nazi Germany and Imperial Japan. War may have brought consuming hardship, but it also greatly simplified residual risk management in the financial sector.

Banking, like every other industry, joined the war effort with enthusiasm. "A nation fighting for its life is not stopped by considerations of finance or credit; it is stopped only by military defeat or economic exhaustion," Chase National Bank's board of directors wrote in its annual report of 1942. "On that basis, the main objective of wartime finance is to provide a smoothly working mechanism for implementing the fiscal transactions involved in the all-out prosecution of the war." Chase was not alone; banks everywhere, with the support and sometimes the insistence of the supervisors, set themselves to patriotic work. Federal supervision, crafted especially in the aftermath of economic depression to be ever more engaged in public risk management, remained a potent tool for martialing the nation's financial resources for war.[1]

The end of hostilities in 1945 brought a profound release of pent-up energy in the United States in virtually every sector, with banks and financial services providing the lifeblood of economic growth. This was a market economy the likes of which banks had never encountered before. While much of the wartime apparatus of government faded away, the New Deal bank supervisory system—creaky in ways, comprehensive in others—stayed in place. The Roosevelt administration had created a thick regulatory structure to channel credit toward public priorities, including housing, small businesses, and public infrastructure. Economic security, above all, was the guiding principle of government. In banking, supervisory agencies aligned to ensure that security by minimizing financial risk to the greatest extent possible. Whatever private risk management preferences banks might have had prior to 1933 were no longer operable; the government now owned the residual financial risk of the banking sector, definitively.

What the New Deal had complicated rather than resolved was the question of what form banking would take as banks reduced their wartime obligations and turned toward wider local, national, and even global markets. Many bankers and policymakers hoped the country would develop large, efficient, far-reaching banking firms appropriate to America's new role in world affairs. Yet they ran into a uniquely American constraint: the phenomenon of unit banking. The nation's longstanding political preference for a system of financial localism, with each bank operating a single office under an individual charter, still thrived in the postwar era, thanks to the continued political influence of thousands of small bankers. Other countries did not go this way. At the end of 1929, before the banking panics of the Great Depression, there were 25,300 banks and thrifts in the United States. By 1945, that number was 14,725, with 4,186 branches. In Canada, by contrast, eleven chartered banks operated 3,923 domestic branches in 1953, by which time the U.S. figures had adjusted to 14,552 banks and 6,227 branches.[2]

While the question of how to manage the sprawl of unit banking had been a topic of debate since at least 1907, the failure of so many thousands of small banks during the Depression raised questions about the virtues of so hyper-localized a banking sector. Rather than resolving these questions, the New Deal created strong and competing constituencies on both sides of the issue. Marriner S. Eccles (1934–1948) and the Federal Reserve favored a goldilocks policy, seeking banks that were neither too big nor too small. The FDIC, created by Congress to prop up the unit banking system, was foundationally committed to unit banking and argued assertively that large banks endangered the deposit insurance fund. With its state banker and supervisory allies, the agency sought to preserve and extend unit banking against branch banking competition.[3]

Behind the first order question of bigness versus smallness lay more specific concerns about bank management and bank risk management for the postwar era: Were big banks or small banks more conducive to economic freedom and economic growth? Which were likelier to promote financial stability? Which intruded more on the functioning of democracy? If small was better, should antitrust laws from 1890 and 1914 be applied to banking as they applied in other industries? Or should antitrust laws be applied idiosyncratically to banking to encourage large banks that served public convenience? Should bank branching be forbidden by state laws, or superseded by national law? Should nonbank corporations face few, or many, constraints on owning banks? The answers, if anything, outnumbered the questions. The currents and crosscurrents of bank risk management, the deep-running politics of antimonopoly, and the growing preference among the bank supervisors for reducing the number, but also the complexity, of banks drove a contentious, sprawling debate that launched in earnest in the 1950s. These debates remain with us today. Some bankers saw size as a path toward efficiency, diversification, and profitability. Others condemned anything larger than the local community bank as evidence of monopoly.

This chapter tells the story of how bank supervision confronted a postwar era of unprecedented economic growth and defined the role for banks—and bank supervisors—to participate in it. It explores two major debates related to these questions of supervising banking with an eye toward power and concentration, but each focused on sufficiently distinct concerns. First, we explore the ways that supervisors, politicians, and bankers confronted questions of *bank holding companies*. Since the turn of the century, bank holding companies had provided a tool for circumventing restrictions on branch banking and regulatory divisions of banking and commerce. From the New Deal through the war and postwar years, policymakers struggled to contain one holding company in particular: A. P. Giannini's Transamerica, which the mercurial entrepreneur built into a colossal West Coast financial conglomerate. The bank holding company fight centered both on bigness—Transamerica's largest bank, Bank of America, held more insured deposits than any other—and on the capacity of bank supervisors to identify, manage, and control risks that existed in private corporations that were not technically banks.

Congress temporarily resolved the bank holding company problem with the Bank Holding Company Act of 1956, and then turned its collective attention to our second area of focus: *bank mergers*. The postwar merger debates continued a longstanding antimonopoly tradition going back to Louis Brandeis but also diverged significantly from Brandeisian ideas. In the 1950s and 1960s, members of Congress struggled to make sense of how banking was similar to or different from other areas of the economy, with profound results for bank supervision. Ultimately, Congress wanted good big banks and good small banks, and it wanted to terminate bad big banks and bad small ones—yet it lacked the capacity, on its own, to draw these divisions. Given the complexity of resolving those issues and given how poorly size fit as a proxy for desirability, Congress pushed these questions onto supervisors, making bank size and the discretion to manage it one of the key tools of bank supervisory discretion from that point forward. When conflict within the administrative state and between supervisors and the courts initially infringed on that discretion, Congress gave supervisors yet more power with still less clarity on how to use it.

Before those debates could take shape and find resolution, though, bank supervisors had to fight two wars: first, World War II and second, a rearguard war against bureaucracy that followed thereafter. Supervisors would win both, in a sign of the victories to come.

War Mobilization, 1941–1945

Before the antimonopoly debates took off in the postwar era, the conceptual and institutional battles of the second Roosevelt administration yielded to the demands of the wartime economy. As they had during World War I, supervisors played a proactive role in war finance, both by supporting bond sales and encouraging patriotic lending by the nation's banks. They also took on new responsibilities, as the administration sought to harness supervisors' expertise and turn it to new purposes. Despite perennial complaints that supervisors were both doing too much and doing too little to manage residual risk, bankers readily accepted the wartime partnership. Others, newly subject to supervisory oversight, were less enthusiastic.

Supervisory involvement in the war effort began through yet another process of institutional layering. With war on the horizon, the Roosevelt administration enlisted bank examiners to identify and manage foreign property held within the United States, which might be mobilized to aid the nation's enemies. Beginning in April 1940, Roosevelt issued a series of executive orders freezing the assets of nations occupied by the Axis powers, and in June 1941, the president froze all Axis-owned assets. The tasks of examining foreign-owned businesses and banks, cataloging their assets, and advising them on how to comply with the freeze policy proved beyond the capabilities of the Treasury Department's Office of Foreign Funds Control. In August, the administration assigned several hundred federal bank examiners to temporary duty.[4]

Within hours of the Japanese bombardment of the American Pacific Fleet at Pearl Harbor on December 7, 1941, supervisory monitoring turned into outright confiscation. The Treasury Department wired all national bank examiners, instructing those to the east of the Mississippi River to travel immediately to New York, and those to the west to San Francisco. Along with other Treasury officials, the examiners took possession of all Japanese-owned businesses. "Uncle Sam moved silently and swiftly to take over all Japanese-owned property," one news outlet reported. "Restaurants, banking agencies, apartment houses, vineyards, silk caches in storage warehouses, bakeries, importing firms, stores, many a lesser business—all were caught in the dragnet." On December 8, the order was expanded to German and Italian firms once those countries declared war on the United States.[5]

Over the remainder of the war, federal supervisors played key roles conserving, managing, and liquidating "alien" property, eventually including that of interned Japanese Americans. In the months before Pearl Harbor, Roosevelt recruited FDIC Chairman Leo T. Crowley (1934–1945) to head the office of Alien Property Custodian, a role Crowley would hold simultaneously with his FDIC post. By then, the questions about Crowley's past had largely subsided. His administrative prowess, demonstrated by the FDIC's maturation into a robust supervisory agency, convinced the president to hand Crowley this sensitive responsibility. Crowley, in turn, brought his top FDIC lieutenants into the Alien Property Custodian's office, where their expertise in investigation, supervision, and liquidation all proved valuable.[6]

As they shouldered new wartime roles, the supervisory agencies considered shrinking or outright pausing routine bank oversight. At the outbreak of the war, federal supervisors suspended bank examinations as they focused on confiscating alien property. In February 1942, the Federal Reserve Board began formulating a program to "reduce the number of complete examinations during the war period or eliminate them altogether." Fuel and tire rationing proved a particular impediment to supervisory work, reflecting the continued importance of examiner mobility with respect to government oversight of the nation's many banks. Agencies also experienced significant staff shortages, as personnel joined the armed forces. By June, the Board was ready to shift to biennial examinations for the soundest banks but ultimately elected to continue annual examinations "in full so far as possible," in part to undertake new supervisory functions required by the war effort.[7]

In some ways, the war economy made core risk management functions easier by providing banks a range of profitable, government-guaranteed investments. Bank examiners encouraged bankers to buy government bonds on their own account and to lend to individuals and firms that wished to purchase such bonds. Between 1941 and 1945, commercial banks purchased $70 billion in U.S. government obligations, which increased from 27.6 percent to 56.6 percent of all bank assets. In March 1942, the Roosevelt administration also created a program of loan guarantees for war contractors, called Regulation V loans. The program enabled defense agencies like the War Department to insure working capital loans related to war contracts against default. At their peak in 1943, Regulation V loans accounted for $3.5 billion, or 18.6 percent of commercial bank loans. Finally, supervisory officials recognized that wartime rationing and strategic procurement were disrupting preexisting lending arrangements in important industries. Examiners, understanding that the administration would not allow firms in such industries to fail, were actively and vocally "sympathetic" toward such problems.[8]

All told, during the war, federal officials pressed bankers to acquire large balances of government bonds and federally guaranteed loans, which made banks liquid and safe during the war years and—importantly—provided the foundation for bank safety well into the postwar era.

So long as the war went well, the nation's banks would remain safe, but wartime introduced novel supervisory challenges centered on inflation. Almost as quickly as Congress declared war on Japan, the Federal Reserve, as the nation's central bank, announced that it would accommodate a fixed interest-rate policy to keep rates for short-term U.S. debt at 3/8 percent. By fixing rates, the Fed sacrificed the power to control inflation through monetary policy. After a decade of battling the deflationary effects of the Depression, Fed Chairman Marriner Eccles worried that rising prices would be his next challenge. To meet it, Eccles revived his project, never truly dormant, of using bank supervision to manage the business cycle. In the policy that emerged, Roosevelt, through the War Powers Act, granted the Federal Reserve authority to control the price and terms of consumer credit. The aim, under Roosevelt's vision, was to reduce consumption and promote patriotic saving. "We must discourage credit and installment buying, and encourage the paying off of debts, mortgages, and other obligations" for the express purpose of making those savings "available to the creditors for the purchase of war bonds," the president explained.[9]

The Fed accomplished this through bank supervision, made applicable to a wide variety of nonbank lenders, including auto dealers and department stores. Through Federal Reserve Regulation W, the Fed fixed the price and terms of all consumer installment credit—later, of other forms as well—and required lenders to obtain a license from their local Federal Reserve Bank. When the regulation went into effect in September 1941, the Board urged a forbearing approach. Reserve Banks should treat violations as "the result of inadvertence or of misunderstanding," the Board instructed, and seek compliance through informal dialogue with lenders. By May 1942, the bank supervisory agencies had divided oversight responsibility and incorporated consumer credit supervision into their regular bank examination procedures (one key reason the Fed chose to continue annual examinations was to ensure its state member banks complied with Regulation W). The Reserve Banks also performed spot checks of licensed retail lenders, continuing to seek compliance through dialogue without resorting to criminal sanctions.[10]

Occasionally the Fed made examples out of offending firms. In November 1942, following an investigation by examiners from the Federal Reserve Bank of Atlanta, the Reserve Board suspended the license of eight furniture stores across Tennessee and Georgia. The stores agreed to close for a week as a condition of retaining their license once they reopened. The Board meted out similar punishments to clothing stores, appliance retailers, and consumer finance companies. Retailers chafed at the new rules and new federal oversight, contributing to a massive political backlash against consumer credit controls after the war.[11]

Two important themes emerged from the war experience. First, supervisors' collective reputation for competence, forged during the holiday and fortified during the 1930s, enabled the Roosevelt administration to layer on new responsibilities in adjacent policy areas where supervisory expertise appeared relevant. Some extensions of supervisory authority, like control of alien property, were temporary and shifted back to relevant agencies once personnel shortages and war exigency abated. Others, like consumer credit controls, met strong political opposition, even as some supervisors wished for the policies to continue. Although Eccles fought to retain credit control authority after the war in support of countercyclical economic policy, he was defeated by a Congress more sympathetic to industry calls to let credit and prosperity flow. Nevertheless, the supervisory agencies performed their wartime duties without scandal or crisis, leaving their reputations intact.[12]

The second important outcome was that during the war, banks built up balance sheets stocked with secure government obligations and profitable loans secured by government guarantees. The banking industry was profitable, and with supervisory encouragement, it used profits to strengthen balance sheets, for example, by increasing bank capital. During the prosperous postwar years, this strong position provided a foundation for bank safety, while federal loan guarantees spread into new policy areas, like small business lending, GI housing, and even shipbuilding. All this ensured a positive cycle of bank safety and supervisory reputation that further encouraged new policy responsibilities.[13]

Institutionalizing Supervisory Fragmentation: The (Rejection of the) Hoover Report

The war had also provided bank supervisory agencies with a unity of purpose—or at least some significant distraction—that prolonged the tense truce achieved under the 1938 Uniform Agreement on Bank Supervisory Procedures. With the war ended, debates about fragmented bank oversight and conflicting risk management approaches reemerged with a vengeance. Some of the players had changed: In 1938, Jefty O'Connor (1933–1938) resigned as head of the OCC to run for governor of California. To replace him, Treasury Secretary Henry Morgenthau put forward the eminently forgettable Preston Delano, governor of the Federal Home Loan Bank Board and a man Morgenthau was confident he could control. Delano served from 1938 to 1953, leaving almost no trace that he had done anything at all. Leo Crowley retired from government in 1945 and was replaced at the FDIC by Maple T. Harl (1946–1953). A former state banker and Colorado bank commissioner, Harl maintained the insurance agency's allegiance to small state banks and the dual banking system, as well as the agency's posture as staunch defender of bank depositors and, behind them, the insurance fund.[14]

And then there was Marriner Eccles, who remained ferociously at the center of every fight about bank supervision, first as Fed Chair under Truman until 1948 and then as a cantankerous member of the Reserve Board until his retirement from public life in 1951. Eccles continued to push for consolidated, countercyclical bank supervision under Federal Reserve authority, making his 1944 reappointment as Fed chair contingent on it. According to Eccles, Roosevelt had promised his support, which perhaps explains a curious 1943 press release in Eccles's files announcing that the Fed and OCC had been consolidated (they had not).[15]

Yet it was Herbert Hoover, the ex-president resurrected as administrative reorganizer, not Eccles, who did the most to place supervisory consolidation on the postwar political agenda. Hoover entered the picture under the guise of the eponymous Hoover Commission, created by Congress in 1947 to rationalize (and, the Republican-controlled Congress hoped, scale back) the institutional innovations of the New Deal and wartime government. Harry S. Truman, initially ambivalent about reorganization, embraced the effort and Hoover with it, an ironic outcome given the antipathy each had for the other on first meeting. "I had to talk to him in words of one syllable," Hoover recalled. Hoover, Truman felt, was "to the right of Louis the Fourteenth" and didn't "understand what's happened in the world since McKinley."[16]

In 1949, Hoover's commission published its report outlining plans to streamline the federal government (the 500-page document, to the apparent surprise of its publisher, became a bestseller). In the hunt for "efficiency and economy," Hoover and his colleagues saw what bankers and supervisors had been complaining about since the 1930s: inexplicable supervisory fragmentation. "At present, bank examinations are conducted by three agencies," the commissioners wrote. The Commission noted that "as a practical matter, a more or less satisfactory *modus vivendi* has been reached for the elimination of major duplication among the functions," referring to the 1938 decree reached by Crowley, Eccles, and O'Connor. Yet such divided authority was precisely what Hoover aimed to stamp out. The Commission wanted to move the FDIC inside the Treasury Department and make the Comptroller, then inside the Treasury but functionally independent, entirely under Treasury control. A newly created National Monetary and Credit Council, in turn, would consolidate bank supervision from the three federal supervisors, which would survive in name only. The hard-fought, informal *modus vivendi*—which encouraged complementary supervisory epistemologies of chartering, liquidity, and insurance to flourish—would be eliminated.[17]

Hoover saw the problem only through duplication, inefficiency, and opaque lines of authority; he wanted the prerogatives of an institutional designer starting afresh. This was not, however, how Congress had established bank supervisory institutions, and it was not how institutional change had worked in U.S. banking. The problem was not simply that agencies multiplied after major crises—the Civil War, 1907, or the Great Depression. The problem— and solution—was that Congress created agencies to address similar risk management challenges from different, sometimes conflicting and sometimes complementary, positions. By contrast, the Hoover Commission urged Congress to choose one governing risk management paradigm, and to subordinate all others.

The political fights which emerged from Hoover's proposals set the Federal Reserve against the FDIC (with the state supervisors and Comptroller, as chartering supervisors, closely aligned with the insurance corporation). The Fed, despite its constant enthusiasm for supervisory consolidation under its roof, was cool to the idea of a separate ur-supervisor to which it would report. Instead, Eccles—ever persistent—sought to capture Hoover's reform momentum. "Soundness of the individual bank and soundness of the economy must go hand in hand," Eccles proclaimed to Congress. Examination "should be integrated with and responsive to monetary and credit policy." Failure to do so could "nullify" the Fed's other operations.[18]

Harl, like Crowley before him, argued that macroeconomic management was fundamentally incompatible with insurance supervision. "Federal deposit insurance cannot function successfully as a mutual insurance fund while subjected and subordinated to the vagaries of the monetary or fiscal policies of the Federal Reserve Board or the Treasury Department," Harl wrote to the Senate in response to the Commission report. Rather, as Congress developed and debated reform proposals, Harl sought supervisory consolidation under the FDIC. "Fundamental to any system of insurance," Harl argued, "is the common-sense principle that the insurer should be able to examine and, to the extent possible, minimize his risk." The FDIC enjoyed this capacity through its partnerships with state bank supervisors and the Comptroller (still an ex officio member of the FDIC's board). What the agency needed was the unchecked authority to examine Fed member banks.[19]

Underlying these paradigmatic debates was a more pragmatic issue held over from the New Deal: Whether all federally insured banks should be required to meet the conditions of membership for the Federal Reserve System and abide by Federal Reserve policies, especially reserve requirements. When Congress considered the Hoover Commission's report, the Federal Reserve still maintained pegged interest rates to support federal borrowing, which in turn made reserve management one of the central bank's few functional monetary policy tools. Yet only Fed member banks were subject to the Fed's reserve requirements, while state nonmember banks enjoyed a layer of federal protection through the FDIC, without supporting Fed monetary policy. "I favored Federal deposit-insurance legislation at a time when most of my fellow bankers were denouncing it," Eccles told Congress. "But I never expected, and I am certain Congress never intended, that this protection for depositors would be used either to hamper effective national monetary policy or to give any class of banks special advantages over others." That the advantaged class was the small, weak, and unstable banks that Eccles most loathed was especially galling to the by then former Federal Reserve chairman.[20]

Although Eccles's proposals to consolidate supervision in the Fed and compel all insured banks to abide by Fed reserve requirements accorded with the

substance of the Hoover Commission's findings, Harl had the political lever-
age that came with a larger constituency of state bankers. State bankers liked
to participate in federal deposit insurance without also becoming subject to
either the Comptroller's chartering—and thus supervisory—authority, or to
the burdens of membership in the Federal Reserve System. Harl also had gifts
to offer. With few bank failures since the founding of the corporation, the
insurance fund was flush. After repaying the Treasury's initial capital investment, with interest, in 1948, Harl proposed trading a substantial cut in deposit
insurance premiums for greater independence and autonomy.[21]

In the end, the FDIC prevailed completely over the Hoover Commission's
efforts at efficiency and the Fed's efforts to secure countercyclical supervision. In 1950, after adopting about a third of the Commission's recommenda-
tions, Congress passed a special law that went in the other direction. The
Federal Deposit Insurance Act of 1950 was the first standalone statute to
address deposit insurance (prior legislation had attached the insurance corporation to the Federal Reserve Act). The FDIC had its own statute, its own
building, and its own mandate. Congress also empowered the agency to
examine any insured bank, expanding the scope of insurance supervision
and increasing, rather than decreasing, the overlapping lines of federal risk
management.[22]

The FDIC had arrived, no matter what anyone at the Fed had to say about
it. "I want to say that I do not think there is any agency of the Government that
is more entitled to the gratitude of the people than the Federal Deposit Insurance Corporation," fawned Brent Spence, a Democrat from Kentucky and
chairman of the House Committee on Banking and Currency. The other members of Congress were similarly enthusiastic.[23]

The Hoover Commission did not end calls for supervisory consolidation,
and throughout the postwar decades a stream of commissions considered various ways to unify the federal risk management agencies. Yet in bank supervision, the Commission's legacy is that it created political space for Harl to fortify
the already strong position of depositor safety and overall bank safety as the
era's primary risk management ethos. It was undoubtedly a major victory for
the dual banking system, and more than that, for an enduring vision of the
American political economy with small business and small banks at the center.
Although the postwar decades are often characterized as an era of big business,
big government, and big labor, strong countercurrents of antimonopoly sentiment pushed to retain smallness and competition as defining values in the
American economy and in American finance.[24]

The Postwar Problem of Bigness

The FDIC's success distinguishing its examination authority mattered for more than the full and final institutionalization of federal deposit insurance and the vast bank supervisory apparatus that it would require. This success was also a profound move toward the preservation of unit banking as a viable form of financial organization, despite the growing attacks on that American tradition from a variety of corners.

Since the turn of the century, bankers and bank reformers had promoted bank size, especially through branching, as a private risk management strategy that offered banks internal liquidity and geographic diversification. In the 1910s and 1920s, bankers pursued geographic expansion along different lines, shaped by the regulatory contexts in which they operated. In states that allowed branch banking, like California, state-chartered and—after the 1927 McFadden Act and more liberal 1933 Glass-Steagall Act—nationally chartered banks could grow in this way. Banking entrepreneurs also used chain banking (common ownership) and group banking (ownership under a holding corporation) to grow within states that restricted branching, and to grow across state lines.[25]

Throughout the New Deal and into the postwar years, the question of bank size remained a deeply contentious political issue, driven by unit bankers who sought to retain their independence in the face of competition with larger, more diversified, better capitalized rivals. Unit bankers positioned themselves as champions of an economic democracy for small proprietors, and by extension champions of a political democracy shielded from totalitarian and monopolistic control. This symbolic language, which bankers mobilized first in opposition to federal control of banking during the New Deal, proved flexible. During World War II, they decried banking concentration as "the Hitler–Mussolini control attitude"; in the early Cold War they characterized it as a step on the road to communism. In speeches, letters to public officials, and articles in the banking press, small bankers and their allies beat the drum against bigness in banking.[26]

Cornerstones of the business and financial elite in every part of the country, these unit bankers enjoyed robust congressional support. Paul H. Douglas, former University of Chicago economist and senator from Illinois, a unit banking state, made the small bankers' case succinctly in 1956: "Big banks commonly find it much easier and more to their liking to do business with big business rather than with little business," a refrain that would be repeated again and again as the debates over bigness trundled on.[27]

For all the hue and cry over the death of unit banking, the effects of concentration on the nation's banking structure appeared mixed. In the states that permitted branching, branch banking grew rapidly in the postwar years. While the total number of banks declined slightly between 1945 and 1960, from around 14,700 to 14,000, the number of branches expanded from 4,200 to 11,100. Meanwhile, large holding companies, especially California's Transamerica, continued national expansion projects that had begun before the war. There was much to worry small bankers; yet politicized fears of banking concentration did not reflect market conditions in most places. The booming postwar economy raised all boats, and suburbanization tended to channel household savings into banks and thrifts outside downtown commercial districts. Thus, while branching increased and the largest banks got larger, banking concentration fell from the end of the war until at least 1960. Congress, still stocked with antimonopolists deeply averse to financial bigness, nevertheless became focused on two related issues: how to supervise bank holding companies and how to manage bank mergers.[28]

The New Deal and the Problem of Banking Monopoly

The bank holding company problem had its origins in the unresolved institutional rivalries of the New Deal, simmering through the war before blowing up in the postwar years. Bank holding companies enabled entrepreneurs to overcome two limits in U.S. banking law: the division between commerce and banking, and branching restrictions that confined chartered banks in and among states. While holding companies could be justified as extralegal tools for geographic and industry diversification—for risk management under the corporate umbrella—holding companies also enabled bankers to accumulate risks that supervisors could not see or influence. Bank supervisors, of course, did not appreciate this avoidance and raised concerns repeatedly before and during the New Deal. Holding company executives, supervisors warned, could evade restrictions on branching by controlling nominally independent banks; they could hide risky assets from examiners by shuffling them between the holding company and the subsidiary banks; they could sell stock and buy banks at inflated prices; and they could weaken their subsidiary banks by siphoning profits to holding company shareholders rather than reinvesting in capital. The Detroit banking groups, which had crashed so spectacularly on the eve of Roosevelt's inauguration, embodied all these vices at once (so too, opponents believed, did Transamerica).[29]

The 1933 Glass-Steagall Act gave the Federal Reserve limited authority to check the growth of bank holding companies. When a holding company wished to exercise control over a bank in which it held a *majority* stake, it had to obtain a voting permit from the Federal Reserve Board, which the Board, "in its discretion, [could] grant or withhold . . . as the public interest may require." This authority proved inadequate, however, as holding companies found ways to exercise control through much smaller fragments of ownership.[30]

Deep internal division prevented the Roosevelt administration from crafting a functional bank holding company policy. In 1937, California Senator William G. McAdoo introduced legislation to enable interstate branch banking within Federal Reserve districts while forcing bank holding companies to dissolve (thus incentivizing their conversion into branch networks under a single charter). McAdoo, in effect, sought to enable risk management through bigness, subject to direct and consolidated supervisory oversight through chartering supervision. The thrust of reform quickly shifted as the Roosevelt administration, in the wake of the court packing fiasco and the deepening recession, pursued a new emphasis on antimonopoly. In April 1938, Roosevelt delivered a speech to congress on "curbing monopolies," in which he articulated specific plans for the "separation of banks from holding company control." Driven internally by Morgenthau and Crowley and aided in Congress by Senators McAdoo and Carter Glass, the administration set aside interstate branch banking and focused on preventing new bank holding companies, while freezing and dissolving those that existed.[31]

The administration's embrace of bank holding company dissolution accorded with its larger turn to antimonopoly, but it also targeted one holding company in particular: A. P. Giannini's Transamerica. Into the 1930s, Giannini remained America's most innovative and aggressive banker. He built his California-based Bank of America into a chain of nearly 500 branches to serve millions of households and small depositors. Through his holding company, Transamerica, Giannini also controlled branch banks in Oregon, Nevada, Washington, and Arizona, as well as major insurance, real estate, and industrial companies. "This company," James Bonbright and Gardiner Means wrote in their 1932 treatise on holding companies, "has an intercorporate structure so ramified as almost to pass beyond the bounds of comprehension." By the late 1930s, it was more ramified still.[32]

In the early years of the New Deal, Giannini had publicly supported Roosevelt and enjoyed cordial relations with O'Connor and Eccles. But concern about his empire's size—which had fueled Fed efforts to restrain its growth in the 1920s—and about the safety of Giannini's banking practices—which had led the San Francisco Fed to nearly deny Bank of America a license to reopen during the Bank Holiday of 1933—continued to plague Giannini's relationship with the federal government. By the late 1930s, the federal banking officials were determined to restrain Giannini, and Giannini was equally determined to thwart them. In a poignant episode, the Bank of America (a national bank) sought permission to open a branch in Del Monte, California, which O'Connor denied; then, one of the state banks owned by Transamerica sought a branch in the same city, which Crowley denied; finally, Giannini simply bought one of the town's two existing banks. His determination to grow into every community on the West Coast made Giannini a "well-loved and well-hated people's banker."[33]

Much of that hate emanated from the FDIC and the Treasury Department, where Crowley and Morgenthau saw Giannini's empire as a grave threat to the deposit insurance fund. In 1937, in a fiery memo denouncing Bank of America's weak capital position and dangerous policy of paying large dividends to Transamerica, Crowley steered the administration toward a confrontation. "If this one bank were to fail, the Federal Deposit Insurance Corporation would be required to pay out a greater amount than if the 4,000 smallest banks failed simultaneously," Crowley warned. "In fact, the one bank seems to be a greater problem . . . since it represents such a concentration of risk." Morgenthau joined the campaign to separate Bank of America from Transamerica and compel Giannini to clean up his too-big-to-fail California bank (ten full volumes of Morgenthau's famous diaries are dedicated to these fights).[34]

Marriner Eccles also opposed Giannini's rules-be-damned approach, but the Fed Chair sought to temper the administration's push to eliminate all bank holding companies. Before entering government service, Eccles had constructed his own multibank holding company from an inheritance bequeathed by David, his late father. David Eccles had emigrated from an impoverished Scotland to Mormon Utah in the 1860s and built an industrial empire from scratch. Marriner founded a holding company and skillfully used it to consolidate and control his father's interests in industries as varied as sugar beets, electricity production, coal, and banking—all at the expense of the bigamist David's other family. By 1928, Eccles had put together the Eccles-Browning Banking Group, owning and operating seventeen banks with consolidated back-office functions including "auditing, advertising, purchasing, [and] credit inspection." Once in government, Eccles disliked the holding company expedient, but he recognized that well managed holding companies offered managerial and diversification benefits to unit banks where branch banking remained legally prohibited.[35]

Internal conflict and a hostile Congress stymied the administration's legislative agenda, while Transamerica continued to grow. In January 1941, Roosevelt again instructed the banking agencies to "work together" to "make out a program." By then, positions had hardened. All continued to agree that Giannini and Transamerica posed a real and growing danger to the U.S. banking system. Officials disagreed about whether holding companies in general did the same, and if they did, what made such corporate agglomerations dangerous. Crowley and Morgenthau continued to object to bigness in general and the circumvention of branching restrictions in particular. They also claimed that the Fed, ostensibly responsible for supervising bank holding companies, had completely failed to restrain Giannini. With Roosevelt's support, Morgenthau introduced new legislation shifting bank holding company supervision, with the aim of dissolving them, from the Fed to the FDIC.[36]

Eccles and the Reserve Board saw the issue differently. In their experience, holding companies tended to work cooperatively with supervisory officials to strengthen their subsidiary banks. "In formulating a legislative program to deal generally with the bank-holding company situation," the Board advised, "it would be unjust and unwise to pattern it solely upon the experience in the Transamerica case." Still, Eccles was keen to demonstrate action. First, the Board sought to change the debate from one about size, to one about the dangers of comingling banking and "unrelated businesses" that could introduce risks into the holding company and its banks that supervisors could not manage. Here, too, Transamerica was the prime offender. In the early postwar years, the conglomerate doubled its sizeable insurance holdings and added war-related industries like aircraft manufacturing. It even owned a salmon cannery. Second, faced with Giannini's relentless push to build branches and buy banks, the Board forged an agreement with the FDIC and the Comptroller to prohibit any Transamerica-affiliated bank from securing any branch approvals.[37]

Met with a united supervisory front, Giannini raged. He insisted that his banks were safe. He howled that the federal supervisors had collectively used their discretion to refuse branches for any of his banks, while granting branches to his competitors. "Transamerica Corporation cannot submit to discrimination," he bellowed at Eccles in a November 1942 letter. And he did not submit; Transamerica acquired twenty-five more banks between 1942 and 1948, when the Fed finally found a way to try and stop him.[38]

Transamerica threatened to monopolize, as Eccles later recalled, "a good part of the banking business of the Western seaboard," and so, as World War II wound down, Eccles sought to challenge the Transamerica monopoly as a monopoly. First, Eccles asked the Justice Department to open an antitrust investigation in 1945. The results confirmed what Eccles believed: Transamerica banks "control[led] approximately 40% of the banking offices and approximately 36% of the commercial banking deposits in the five-state area" of California, Nevada, Arizona, Oregon and Washington. Yet, the Justice Department could not identify "any sustained policy of abuse of power," then a requirement to demonstrate unlawful monopolistic behavior. The antitrust effort stalled. Then, in 1946, the Supreme Court determined in an unrelated case that such a policy was not necessary to demonstrate monopolistic practices. Eccles ordered the Fed's lawyers to get to work.[39]

In light of the decades-long fight against Transamerica, it is remarkable that the Board took so long to exercise what appeared to be substantial antitrust authority. The 1914 Clayton Antitrust Act authorized the Federal Reserve Board to determine, via a hearing convened by the Board itself, whether a company's acquisitions of bank stocks substantially lessened competition and, if the Board so determined, to require divestment. The Board's legal staff recognized the strategy was risky, yet they were determined to move ahead. "When it is considered that the Board has repeatedly stressed . . . that the size of the Transamerica banking group has assumed dangerous if not monopolistic pro-portions," a Fed lawyer wrote, "the Board should exhaust the full reach of its powers for dealing with the problem."[40]

By employing its powers under the Clayton Act, the Board reached for a new tool (agency adjudication) and a new epistemology of risk (anticompetitive behavior). It proved, however, to be too much of a stretch, specifically with respect to the market definition the Fed adopted when ordering Transamerica to divest its interests. The Fed asserted, following the Justice Department's findings, that Transamerica had monopolized the western banking market. This focus, as opposed to one that was more fine-grained, proved too much and too little. By October 1948, when the hearing was held, Transamerica did control 40 percent of commercial bank deposits in the region the Fed identified, but among the states these figures diverged substantially from less than 5 percent in Washington to more than 75 percent in Nevada. When viewed locally, concentration figures diverged even further: "Banking, as the Board expressly finds, is essentially a local business; the monopoly by Transamerica banks and branches ranges from 100 percent in some towns to zero in other regions," Fed Governor Oliver S. Powell (1949–1952) argued as a dissent to the Board's eventual decision.[41]

Still, a majority of the Board found that Transamerica's acquisition of banks "tended to create a monopoly" and ordered Transamerica to divest itself from all bank holdings except Bank of America. Transamerica appealed the Fed's decision when it was issued in 1952, and the U.S. Court of Appeals for the Third Circuit eventually overturned the Fed's ruling in 1953. Echoing Powell's earlier arguments, the court found that "the Board's conclusion of a tendency to monopoly in the five-state area . . . flies in the face of its own finding that the local community is the true competitive banking area." In essence, the Fed was defeated in its effort to limit the concentration of financial power nationally by the then widespread belief that the proper geographic scope of banking was the community.[42]

Transamerica lived on. If the Fed and other supervisors wanted complexity and size to be added to the list of supervisory concerns, it would need a new theory of supervision.

Supervision and the Bank Holding Company Act

If existing antitrust law wasn't the right angle to pursue bank holding company supervision, Eccles reasoned, then banking law—or better, a revamped banking law—would be. Eccles had long avoided this path. He recognized from his professional and governmental experience that the definitional questions about what constituted a bank holding company and what it meant for such a company to control a bank were too technical and too difficult to be handled well by Congress. This concern was justified by the near perennial efforts by the Democratic Party's populist wing, led by Texas Congressman Wright Patman, to secure legislation liquidating all bank holding companies as quickly as possible. Indeed, in parallel with the Fed's efforts to control Transamerica through adjudication and then litigation, momentum built in Congress in the 1940s and 1950s to restrain—and perhaps eliminate—bank holding companies through legislation.[43]

Congressional momentum for bank holding company reform drew on a coalition of unit banking trade associations and liberal Congressmen— including Patman and Paul Douglas, the Senate's resident banking and monetary expert. This coalition united to protect community banking from firms like Transamerica by forcing bank holding companies to conform to the same regulations that governed the individual banks they owned, including, importantly, Glass-Steagall's division of insurance and commercial banking and the McFadden Act's restrictions on interstate branching.[44]

The coalition behind what would become the Bank Holding Company Act (BHCA) demonstrates an important reality about financial legislation in the U.S.: yesterday's enemies become tomorrow's allies. The bankers and liberals who had squabbled over so much during the New Deal recognized together that the aggregation of financial power through holding companies like Transamerica threatened both liberal and conservative ideals. The BHCA and the process behind its passage also illustrates an important reality about the evolution of bank supervision: While bank supervisors and bankers continued to press their negotiated risk management in secret, the purpose of that risk management had started to move beyond the safety and soundness of individual banks or even the financial system. The risks were instead political, understood through competing ideas about what made the American political economy democratic, and how that democracy could be preserved.

On the conservative side, the (small) bankers' trade groups argued that excessive market power, which gave larger firms competitive advantages over their independent rivals, was as dangerous to the free enterprise system as excessive government intervention. Bank holding company regulation, Independent Bankers Association President W. J. Bryan explained, "is necessary if we are to preserve our free enterprise banking system, the economic counterpart of our political system." Similarly, for Douglas, reining in Transamerica was emblematic of a lifelong quest to curtail the market power of large businesses and financial institutions. "Control over credit is moving into fewer and fewer hands," Douglas warned his congressional colleagues during the debates over the bank holding company legislation, sparking a cycle of concentration that linked industry to finance. "Industry has been moving out of competition into closer and closer concentration—monopoly and quasi-monopoly. This has been helped by the big banks." Douglas championed a vision of antimonopoly liberalism, where the free enterprise system preserved small competitors against the aggressive competition of larger rivals, and bank holding company legislation provided an essential pathway for that antimonopoly ethos.[45]

Neither of these thrusts connected squarely to the risk management concerns of bank supervision in its initial consolidation in the New Deal. Both would represent where bank supervision was destined to go in the postwar era (and beyond).

The final Bank Holding Company Act of 1956 represented a substantial expansion of the Fed's role as bank supervisor. The law's twin aims were, first, to prevent the growth of banks controlled by holding companies, and second, to limit the extent that nonbanking businesses were affiliated with insured banks—precisely the twin features (or defects, depending on one's perspective) of Giannini's empire. To fill these gaps, the bill defined "bank holding company" to mean "any company which directly or indirectly owns, controls, or holds with power to vote, 25 per centum or more of the voting shares of each of two or more banks." The law thus reduced the amount of stock needed to exert control from the 50 percent standard used in the 1933 legislation. The two-bank threshold, in turn, was part of a series of exceptions and firm-specific carveouts generated through congressional dealmaking that Eccles had anticipated, the Fed fought against, and Dwight Eisenhower complained about in his signing statement. Finally, any holding company that met the definition under the new legislation had to divest themselves of nonbanking voting interests.[46]

In its first supervisory action following the enactment of the law, the Federal Reserve ordered Transamerica to divest its shares of Occidental Life Insurance Company, the largest of Transamerica's nonbank holdings. To the surprise of most observers, Transamerica opted for another path, retaining its insurance and other nonbank holdings and spinning off its banking assets into a separate company, Firstamerica Corporation. A. P. Giannini had died in June 1949, followed shortly by his son, Mario, who had steered the banking empire alongside his father. Without Giannini's personal drive and with the prospect of consolidating the holding company's banks into an interstate branch network no closer in sight, Transamerica executives bowed finally to the relentless government pressure.[47]

The BHCA came at the end of a very long road toward reining in holding companies and placing them within the banking regulatory and supervisory system, yielding what one Fed official called "a sigh of relief—and exhaustion—almost without precedent in the annals of American banking." In some ways, it looked like the last gasp of the New Deal–era banking reforms, limiting as it did the prerogatives of big bankers. But in most ways, it was something different altogether. It expanded supervision into new and different forms of risk management in which the supervisors had never developed specific expertise. It also created an important—though unintended—semi-resolution to the federal battles for institutional supremacy in banking. Because the Act gave the Federal Reserve the prerogative of holding company supervision, any bank so owned would have the Fed as an active supervisor. In 1956, this was not a meaningful expansion of the Fed's responsibilities. By the end of the century, it made the Fed first among supervisory equals.[48]

As the dust settled on the legislation, it was the Fed that voiced the most concerns. Six months after the Act's passage, the Fed Governor (and eventual Vice Chairman) James L. Robertson (1952–1966, 1966–1973) strongly criticized the legislation in a speech before the Independent Bankers Association for essentially conflating the questions of supervisory risk management and anticompetition. "The express requirement of the Holding Company Act that [the Fed] consider the effect of a proposed transaction upon the preservation of competition presents problems that call for the wisdom of a Solomon—and there are not many of them around." By layering antitrust atop the Fed's discretionary evaluation of holding company applications, Congress had asked the Fed to significantly add to its supervisory burden but without the guidance the Fed itself wanted. The Fed didn't even know how to answer basic questions the statute presumed to be obvious. "What, for example, is a 'bank' within the meaning of the statute?" Robertson asked.[49]

The answer wasn't clear, but the implications of the answer would reverberate widely throughout the financial system. The result was that the "enactment of the statute, by itself, is by no means a solution of the 'holding company problem.'" Robertson concluded by quoting Thomas Brackett Reed's famous axiom: "One of the greatest delusions in the world is the hope that its evils can be cured by legislation." The BHCA represented a marked point of departure from the Fed's role as a supervisor. What it did not do was solve the related problem of how to supervise banks that threatened to monopolize a local market without recourse to a holding corporation, something that bank charters had essentially guaranteed for decades.[50]

The Merger Heard Round the World:
The Chase-Manhattan Merger of 1955

The Fed's attack on Giannini via antitrust didn't work, in large part because of the disarray that antitrust and banking had mutually encountered coming out of the Progressive Era and the New Deal. There was an antitrust regime, a banking regime, and rarely the two would meet. For a time, this lack of convergence posed little difficulty: The number of banks did not substantially decrease before the 1950s, meaning that banking competition remained relatively static. That would change. Between 1950 and 1955, 830 banks were absorbed through consolidation, a pace that only looked likely to increase. The acceleration of bank mergers set the stage for a major upheaval in the way that supervisors would encounter bank concentration through a new regime of bank antitrust. Although supervisors wanted more authority to evaluate the banking risks attendant to bank mergers, they, as Robertson suggested, sought to avoid the role of antitrust enforcers.[51]

The merger of two legendary financial institutions, the Manhattan Company and the Chase National Bank in the early months of 1955, initiated what would be a decade-long fight over bank antitrust. Between his stints as a U.S. senator and vice president of the United States, Aaron Burr secured a New York State charter for the Manhattan Company in 1799. Originally chartered to provide water services to New York City, Burr included a provision to use the corporation's "surplus capital" for "the purchase of public or other stock, or in any other monied transactions or operations, not inconsistent with the constitution and laws of this State or of the United States, for the sole benefit of the said company." So it was that the Manhattan Company became one of New York City's most important banks, with a specific focus in the early twentieth century on retail banking. By 1954, the bank operated fifty-eight branches, most of which were in the residential boroughs of Brooklyn, Queens, and the Bronx, giving it the second largest branch network in New York City.[52]

The Chase National Bank came seventy years later, built by and for national banks. Not only was it named in honor of Lincoln's Treasury Secretary Salmon P. Chase, sponsor of the National Banking Acts, two of the bank's early presidents were former Comptrollers of the Currency (Henry W. Cannon and A. Barton Hepburn). In roughly its first century of operation, the Chase National Bank operated as a "banker's bank" and served as a correspondent bank in New York City, mostly dealing with large commercial interests and industry. In the early twentieth century, Chase became affiliated with the Rockefeller interests through its longtime chairman Winthrop Aldrich, who was John D. Rockefeller, Jr.'s brother-in-law. By the end of the 1940s, Aldrich approached retirement and looked forward to the prospect of a Republican Eisenhower administration that was sympathetic to his fiercely international, business-oriented politics. He resigned as chair to accept Eisenhower's offer to become the U.S. ambassador to the Court of St. James, a plum appointment for a banker who saw in Ike a great hope for the future of U.S. financial policy.[53]

First, however, Aldrich had two pieces of unfinished business. First, he needed to name a successor but felt that Chase lacked viable options internally. He turned to John J. McCloy, a former Wall Street lawyer-turned-Assistant Secretary of War, who managed most of the U.S. war effort behind the aged and ailing Henry L. Stimson. After the war, McCloy served as the second president of the newly created World Bank and then as the first civilian U.S. Com-

missioner for Occupied Germany. While McCloy had never been a commercial banker, he accepted the position.[54]

Aldrich's other piece of business was converting Chase from a wholesale
bank that served institutional and corporate clients to one with a viable retail
banking business. As American corporations expanded globally in the Bretton
Woods era, U.S. banks struggled to grow large enough to serve their growing
corporate clients. Big business needed big banks. Meanwhile, affluent
households were moving to the suburbs, causing downtown banks like Chase
to lose access to stable household deposits. Chase could either expand slowly
through branching or quickly through acquisition. Aldrich preferred the latter,
and he targeted the Manhattan Company, with its extensive retail network. In
1951, as one of his last acts, Aldrich sought a friendly purchase of the Manhattan Company's assets. For reasons that remain mysterious, the Manhattan
Company's leadership balked after nearly consummating the sale, citing perhaps the second quirkiest provision of the original 1799 charter: Every major
decision required unanimous consent by the bank's shareholders.[55]

By 1955, McCloy, now chairman, resurrected Aldrich's plans and devised a
legal solution by having the much smaller Manhattan Company "acquire" the
Chase National Bank under the former's state charter. Such an acquisition
would not, McCloy and Chase's lawyers argued, require anything other than
a favorable vote from the Manhattan board of directors.[56]

By structuring the deal so that the state-chartered, Fed-member Manhattan
Company acquired the Chase National Bank, McCloy also limited the scope
for supervisory intervention. Only the New York Banking Department had
the formal authority to decide on the merger, while the Federal Reserve Board
could rule later on the opening of the former Chase National Bank's branches
by the new Chase Manhattan Bank. Behind the scenes, the Reserve Board
weighed its options carefully. Having satisfied itself that "the merger appeared
to be on a sound basis and would not seem to result in any substantial lessening of competition on Manhattan Island," it instructed the Federal Reserve
Bank of New York to inform the New York Banking Department "in confidence" that the Board would sanction the merger. Two days later, on March 31,
1955, New York Banking Superintendent George A. Mooney (1954–1959)
granted his approval.[57]

News coverage proved mostly favorable. The Chase Manhattan merger was
the largest in a growing trend of banking consolidations aimed at combining
big downtown banks with smaller—but growing—suburban institutions. The
newly merged bank would be the second largest in the nation, behind only the

Bank of America. Its combination of the formerly distinct wholesale and retail banks, the *New York Times* reported, marked the "new banking era" that reflected the "post-war world of expanded production and diffused individual buying power." The *Times* cast the merger in a populist and democratic tone: "The merger is striking testimony of the need of banking capital in modern society to strive aggressively to discern and serve all the needs of all the people, instead of sitting back, as in 'the good old days,' recognizing only a fraction of the needs of the few."[58]

The populist enthusiasm for bank mergers was not universal. Emanuel Celler, the chair of the House Judiciary Committee and Democratic congressman representing parts of Brooklyn and Queens, opposed the merger for fear of monopolistic concentration of New York City's banking. Given the sheer size of the Manhattan Company, with its fifty-eight branches, and the Chase National Bank, with its massive balance sheet, "it is highly questionable whether the resulting banking corporation can avoid conflict with the laws and policies of our Federal Government involving monopolies."[59]

This concern only mattered to the extent that the Eisenhower administration's Department of Justice thought it should. After its failure in the Transamerica case, the Federal Reserve had no interest in challenging the Chase-Manhattan merger under the Clayton Act. The Justice Department took a similar position. Section 7 of the Clayton Act, amended by Congress in 1950, prohibited mergers by a "corporation engaged in commerce" if "the effect of such acquisition may be substantially to lessen competition, or to tend to create a monopoly." The Justice Department determined, in effect, that banking was not commerce, meaning it "would not have jurisdiction to proceed" with any Clayton Act challenge. If a challenge was to come, then it would need to come from Congress.[60]

Bank Merger Supervision Before 1960

As the heat around the megamerger increased, members of Congress could point to little existing law that would reliably maintain the integrity of unit banking in the face of the bank consolidation wave sweeping the country. Antitrust, at the time, was "of little significance as applied to banks." This was not because the antitrust pioneers were ignorant of special circumstances in banking: After all, Louis Brandeis rocketed to public attention on his antitrust critique of large investment banks. The reformers responsible for the Sherman and Clayton Acts largely assumed that state-level branching restrictions and the prohibition against interstate branching would necessarily keep banks small and numerous, allowing competition to take care of itself. There could be no Standard Oil for banks because any bank with such ambitions was already limited by state and federal law.[61]

Through the New Deal era, there was at once a strong and persistent current of antimonopoly banking politics and no strong system to include antitrust concerns within the banking perimeter. Consolidation also took a decidedly different turn during the bank holiday and its aftermath: Supervisors needed healthy banks to absorb the liabilities of failing banks, making consolidation an instrument of stabilization policy. Into the postwar era, most federal supervisors (outside of the FDIC) roughly shared Marriner Eccles's view: Size and diversification—within vaguely defined limits—were far preferable to smallness and fragility. It is little wonder, then, that the incoherence of banking merger policy led first to the Fed's delay in using antitrust law against Transamerica, and then to its defeat in that effort. Federal supervisors operated in a world of financial risk management, not antitrust.

Moreover, as the Chase Manhattan merger made clear, the federal banking agencies had awkward and incomplete merger review authority. The Comptroller was the best positioned, having relatively robust control in cases where the resulting bank held a national charter (unless, for example, there was no change in capital for the acquiring bank). The Fed and the FDIC enjoyed much less. From 1955 to 1960, more than a third of mergers between state insured and Fed member banks occurred without any formal federal approval. Federal supervisors could often only nod and nudge. "As part of their regular supervisory function," the assistant chief of the Fed's Division of Examinations wrote in 1941, "the agencies endeavor to keep informed as to all such developments [i.e. mergers]—encouraging those which are constructive and discouraging those which are not." That policy still held a decade and a half later, embodied in the Reserve Board's confidential note, routed through the Federal Reserve Bank of New York, informing the New York State Banking Superintendent of its informal approval of the Chase Manhattan union.[62]

Thus, much bank merger policy rested on the statutes and supervisory practices of the forty-eight states (Alaska and Hawaii joined the union in 1959), meaning that bank merger policy was wildly incoherent from a national perspective. Figure 7.1 summarizes the diversity of state experience. The highly discretionary standard, "public interest," was the most important category of state merger analysis, a broad delegation also captured in categories such as "conformity with state law" and "public convenience." Meanwhile, competition

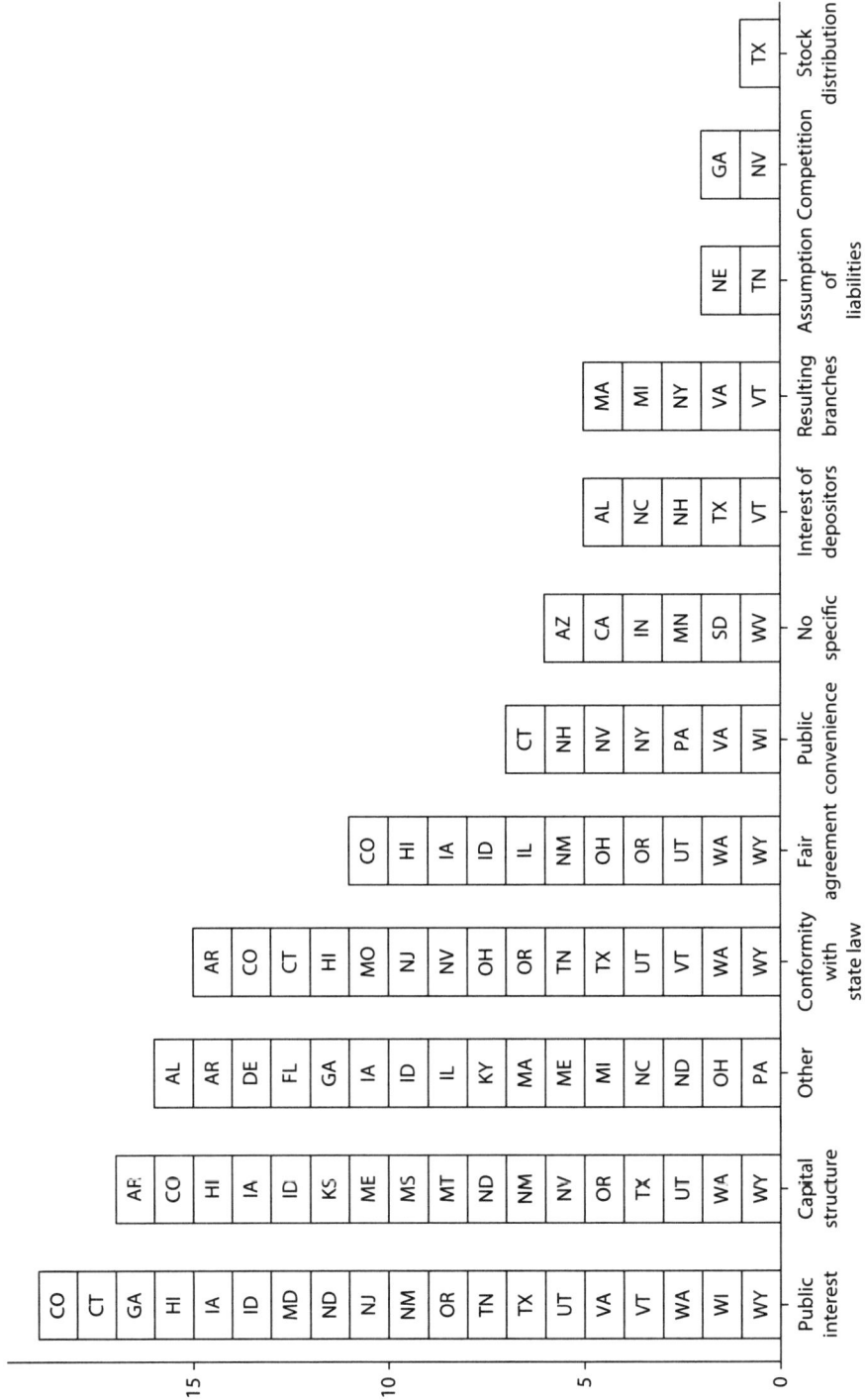

FIGURE 7.1. Merger approval standards by state, 1959

Public interest	Capital structure	Other	Conformity with state law	Fair agreement	Public convenience	No specific	Interest of depositors	Resulting branches	Assumption of liabilities	Competition	Stock distribution
CO	AR	AL	AR	CO	CT	AZ	AL	MA	NE	GA	TX
CT	CO	AR	CO	HI	NH	CA	NC	MI	TN	NV	
GA	HI	DE	CT	IA	NV	IN	NH	NY			
HI	IA	FL	HI	ID	NY	MN	TX	VA			
IA	ID	GA	MO	IL	PA	SD	VT	VT			
ID	KS	IA	NJ	NM	VA	WV					
MD	ME	ID	NV	OH	WI						
ND	MS	IL	OH	OR							
NJ	MT	KY	OR	UT							
NM	ND	MA	TN	WA							
OR	NM	ME	TX	WY							
TN	NV	MI	UT								
TX	OR	NC	VT								
UT	TX	ND	WA								
VA	UT	OH	WY								
VT	WA	PA									
WA	WY										
WI											
WY											

Source: U.S. Congress, Senate Committee on Banking and Currency, *Hearings on S. 1062, Regulation of Bank Mergers,* 86th Cong.,

as such was seldom an explicit category for supervisory consideration. Only two states, Georgia and Nevada, mentioned competition in state banking laws, despite the centrality of the concept to federal antitrust laws for decades. There was, in short, no coherent strategy on banking consolidation.[63]

Where states diverged and federal banking officials nodded and nudged, the federal government's primary antitrust enforcer, the Department of Justice, operated under the view that there was no such thing as "bank antitrust." Before the Chase Manhattan merger brought banking consolidation to public and political attention, the postwar DOJ had brought only one civil action under the Clayton Act and pursued some minor investigations. Banking simply did not occupy the DOJ's attention. Indeed, a major 1955 study, *The Report of the Attorney General's National Committee to Study the Antitrust Laws*—a 400-page effort to provide a "thoughtful and comprehensive study" of U.S. antitrust law—mentioned bank mergers not at all.[64]

Merger Mania in the U.S. Congress

It was not obvious what Congress wanted to do about bank mergers. Among opponents of banking consolidation—Emanual Celler, Paul Douglas, and Wright Patman—concern about such consolidation had been gaining momentum as bank mergers increased year by year. Until Chase Manhattan in 1955, and really until the great sigh of relief with the passage of the BHCA in 1956, bank holding companies held the spotlight. Only then did Congress turn to address the "Merger Fever" pulsing through the nation's banking markets, which raised two fundamental questions that lawmakers struggled to answer: Who, exactly, should supervise bank mergers? And how should they decide which mergers created banks that were bigger and better, and which created banks that were anticompetitive and monopolistic?[65]

On one side sat the staunch antimonopolists, led by Celler in the House and by Tennessee Democrat Estes Kefauver in the Senate. Both chaired their respective Judiciary Committees, and both wanted to answer these questions subject to their jurisdiction: The Department of Justice would be the "who," with limited advice from bank supervisors, and the DOJ would exercise its delegated authority largely through adversarial litigation proceedings under the Sherman and Clayton Acts. Under Celler's House proposal, the Justice Department would evaluate bank mergers solely on their effects on competition, blocking mergers that worked, in the words of Section 7 of the Clayton Act, "substantially to lessen competition, or to tend to create a monopoly." For the proponents of this approach, the foundational concern in banking consolidation was big banks getting bigger by eliminating competitors from the market.[66]

The Senate Banking Committee, aligned with the bank supervisory agencies, pursued a different path. Under the leadership of Democrats J. William Fulbright of Arkansas and then A. Willis Robertson of Virginia, the Senate Banking Committee sought to extend merger review to the interested federal banking agencies (granting the FDIC authority over state insured banks, and the Fed over Fed member banks) and to balance existing practices of banking oversight against the dominance of antitrust review. In this view, the federal bank supervisors—the Comptroller, the Fed, and the FDIC—would incorporate bank mergers into their usual supervisory process: bank risk management with a large dose of supervisory discretion, where competition would be part, but only part, of the overall equation. Supervisors strongly advocated for this approach, though they sought even more forcefully to rank what they called "banking factors" over "competitive factors." "We see no need for the application of the Clayton Act to banking transactions, since banking is an industry that is well regulated and supervised by both State and Federal Authorities," FDIC Chairman Henry E. Cook (1953–1957) wrote in 1956. "In the field of banking," Fed Vice Chairman C. Canby Balderston (1955–1966) concurred, "the test should be whether or not a merger would result in an 'undue' lessening of competition *that outweighs the banking factors.*" Bank risk management needed to remain primary.[67]

The debate between the congressional antimonopolists and the federal bank supervisors (via the sympathetic Senate Banking Committee) largely resolved in the supervisors' favor through the codification of merger review standards that weighed toward factors like capital adequacy and future earnings. Still, two key issues remained. First, where would the Department of Justice and its litigation ethos fit into the picture of supervising antitrust? And how much insight into the banking agencies' decisions, usually clouded in supervisory secrecy, would the public receive?

The banks and the supervisors thought that the answer to both questions should be "none." On the first question, the Attorney General thought the deprivation of mandatory Department of Justice review would run "afoul of basic—governmentwide—principles of comity between prosecuting and supervisory agencies." Such an exclusion would further "set up competitive tests for bank mergers different from those that apply to other sections of American businesses," which could, "even beyond the banking area, seriously dissipate enforcement efforts by decentralizing responsibility for decisions affecting" antitrust enforcement beyond the Department of Justice. The second question related to the first. Since 1890, DOJ antitrust policy had been a highly judicial affair. By contrast, from the 1860s, bank supervision made almost no space for judicial review. Whatever merger supervision outside of banking the Justice Department addressed was in the shadow of its ultimate authority: to file suit in federal court. Such suits were by their nature public and gave the public a variety of ways to orient themselves to merger decisions.[68]

Congressman Celler knew that bank supervision would play a primary role in bank merger review, but he did not want to foreclose bank merger decisions from public scrutiny. To that end, he preferred a "public hearing" associated with each merger application. A hearing, Celler insisted, "protects applicants against discriminatory denial of meritorious applications and safeguards the public interest against erosion of vital national principles." Celler essentially wanted to supervise the supervisors. "Without provision for hearings," he said, all kinds of problems would arise. The public would be "deprived of its only practical opportunity for appraising the quality" of, or the supervisory determination on, the merger; "uniformity of regulatory policy is most difficult to achieve," because each bank supervisor would go its own way; and "effective judicial supervision of agency action is greatly hampered." If Congress would give the supervisors formal merger supervision, Congress would need to have "assurance that the standards [the banking agencies] promulgate . . . would be administered in accordance with the congressional intent." This would only occur through a public hearing.[69]

Although this view had adherents in the Senate, it went nowhere. Subjecting each merger to a public hearing and judicial review would sow instability into the process. More than that, the DOJ would remain singularly focused on anticompetition as the reason for evaluating mergers, not on the variety of banking factors that might motivate the supervisory agencies to approve or prohibit a merger. Bank supervisors, Fulbright argued, had developed important expertise whose public airing would be detrimental to the supervisory apparatus. "The knowledge that the banking agencies possess concerning these factors is derived from constant examination and supervision of banks generally and of the particular banks to be involved in a proposed merger." If a public hearing forced disclosure of sensitive information, then the banks, their customers, and their depositors would all suffer. "Bank examination is an essential part of the protection of depositors and the public interest in banking generally. The Federal banking agencies cannot maintain the integrity of bank examination if bank examiners and the persons whom they interview in the process of examination know that the reports are liable to be disclosed to the public."[70]

The idea, too, that judicial review would strengthen the process did not compute: "The evaluation of such factors as the banking agencies must consider, such as character of the management, adequacy of the capital structure, and convenience and needs of the community, are not factors capable of court determination." This was a critique of both courts and the Department of Justice: "They necessarily involve evaluation based upon specialized experience and knowledge which neither the Attorney General nor the courts possess." Merger supervision remained fundamentally bound up in a larger risk management calculus, one which the federal banking agencies were uniquely situated to undertake because of their deep experience collecting and evaluating banking information and pursuing informed tradeoffs in partnership with bankers. The Celler view of bank merger review was squarely defeated shortly after Fulbright's statement, on a vote of 55–29.[71]

The final bill to emerge from these debates, the Bank Merger Act of 1960, was a major extension of the bank supervisory footprint. The law streamlined merger approval through the three federal banking supervisors, depending on the charter of the resulting bank: the Comptroller for national charters, the Fed for state member banks, the FDIC for state nonmembers. It did so without authorizing a public hearing. All that was required was a newspaper notice of the proposed merger, a move that favored supervisory control over bank disclosures.[72]

The law granted federal supervisors substantial leeway in reaching their decisions, guided by broad and potentially crosscutting factors. On the banking side, supervisors would consider financial history, capital structure, earnings prospects, management character, community needs, and the corporate powers of the resulting firm. Congress also instructed the agencies to "take into consideration the effect of the transaction on competition (including any tendency toward monopoly)," directing the agencies to balance the banking and competitive factors through the open category of "public interest." To meet Celler's call for uniformity of regulatory policy, the law also instructed the controlling supervisory agency to request a report from the Attorney General and the other two banking agencies, encouraging the evaluation of bank mergers from four relevant supervisory perspectives. What relative weights to assign the various factors when arriving at an evaluation of "the public interest," Congress provided no substantial clues.[73]

Finally, the Act mandated agencies to report annually to Congress on every merger. This last requirement may have been among the most important. While Congress granted supervisors substantial discretion in merger review, it did not want to be left out of the discussion. As a joint statement of four leading senators warned near the conclusion of the legislative debates, agencies' review decisions "will be closely scrutinized by Congress and the Country, and, if it should appear that" the agencies acted contrary to congressional priorities, "then at least some members of Congress will urge that stronger powers to be provided to the Department of Justice."[74]

The bottom line, from the perspective of the bill's sponsors, the banks, and the bank supervisors, was this: Bank merger review was now squarely an act of bank supervision. It would be left to the discretion of the supervisors to determine, even as the specific epistemology of supervision would be unlike anything the supervisors had done before.

The Failure of Resolution: The Bank Merger Act Amendments of 1966

As it happens, the idea that bank mergers would be exempted from antitrust enforcement and judicial review was welcome news to neither antitrust enforcers nor to judicial reviewers. Soon after the passage of the Bank Merger Act, the Comptroller of the Currency, Ray M. Gidney (1953–1961) reviewed an application by the Philadelphia National Bank to merge with the Girard Trust Corn Exchange. These were the second and third largest banks in Philadelphia, respectively. As required by the new bank merger law, the Comptroller received advisory opinions from the Fed, FDIC, and Department of Justice. All three agencies advised against the merger; Gidney approved it anyway. In his annual report to Congress, he argued that he did so because, "in the light of the statutory criteria" contained in the Bank Merger Act, "the merger would be in the public interest." That may have been the end of the story, but the new Attorney General, Robert F. Kennedy, decided to sue to block the merger the day after the Comptroller announced its decision.[75]

As litigation wound its way through the court system, the Federal District Court and the Comptroller both noted how strange it was that the American government was essentially suing itself. The DOJ did not conduct a "direct review of the Comptroller's decisions that the mergers would be in the public interest," that is, it did not evaluate whether the banking and competitive factors together weighed in favor of the combination. Rather, the DOJ focused only on the competitive effects, specifically whether the merger substantially lessened competition. The resulting case, which reached the Supreme Court in 1963, hinged on whether the Bank Merger Act had in fact given the Comptroller complete authority to decide federal bank merger policy and whether that policy could be resolved by giving attention to factors beyond competition.[76]

The first was easiest to resolve: The Act had not "immunize[d] approved mergers from challenge under the federal antitrust laws" because "no express immunity is conferred by the Act." Because Congress had not used the magic words—banks are hereby not subject to the antitrust laws—those laws could not be "repeal[ed] by implication." But what of the idea that Congress made clear that such mergers would be subject to a long list of relevant factors, all bound up in the amorphous category of "public interest"? Justice William J. Brennan Jr., writing for the majority, made equally quick, if somewhat dubious, work of this argument. The Comptroller and bankers' claims that "Philadelphia needs a bank larger than it now has in order to bring business to the area and stimulate its economic development" was irrelevant to the Court's conclusion, despite the explicit instruction from Congress in the Bank Merger Act to consider such public benefits. An anticompetitive merger, the majority concluded, "is not saved because, on some ultimate reckoning of social or economic debits and credits, it may be deemed beneficial. A value choice of such magnitude is beyond the ordinary limits of judicial competence." Congress "proscribed anticompetitive mergers, the benign and the malignant alike, fully aware, we must assume, that some price might have to be paid."[77]

Fulbright had anticipated this. The problem with the Court's analysis from the perspective of one of the bill's key proponents was that while the Department of Justice and the courts on which antitrust litigation relied did not have the competence to evaluate other factors beyond competition, the bank supervisors—by experimentation, legislative delegation, and hard-won expertise—did have that competence. And Congress in fact named "public interest" as the unit for reckoning the social or economic debits and credits of bank mergers. Justice John Marshall Harlan, in a related dissent from an opinion that reinforced the conclusions in *Philadelphia National Bank*, concluded archly that the Court had "preclude[d] any possibility that the will of the Congress with respect to bank mergers will be carried out."[78]

The Court, though, wasn't construing the congressional instructions from 1960 about bank mergers; it was focused on the viability and resilience of the antitrust laws passed in 1890 and 1914. On the back of the Supreme Court's decisions, the Department of Justice sued to block five additional major mergers, each approved by the Comptroller of the Currency, with each DOJ effort successful in the courts. To the Comptroller, this made no sense. "There is no serious dispute about the desirability of applying antitrust principles to the unregulated industries," Comptroller James J. Saxon (1961–1966) wrote in 1964. Such industries needed extra protection for freedom of entry so that "private initiative" and "free enterprise" could regulate these industries through competition. "In banking, however, entry and expansion are under public control." In that view, the only relevant determination necessary to assess the merits of bank mergers was that of the bank supervisor, the one holding the public end of the risk management bargain.[79]

This tussle between the Comptroller and the Department of Justice (and the Supreme Court) did not end the dispute over the allocation of supervisory authority for bank mergers. After these major reversals, Congress launched a legislative process that commentators would regard "as bizarre as that of any statute ever passed." It began in 1965 when Senator Robertson, a lead author of the Bank Merger Act of 1960, sought to "reinstate the original purpose and intent of Congress," a purpose and intention that the Supreme Court "erroneously" reversed in its interpretation of antitrust laws. In Robertson's view, when "the Bank Merger Act of 1960 was adopted it was generally agreed—in fact I think it was fair to say that it was universally agreed—that the restrictions of section 7 of the Clayton Act did not apply to bank mergers." He introduced new legislation to reflect that earlier view. "All my bill does," Robertson continued, "is seek to carry out the declared intention of Congress . . . in 1960— that these mergers should be under the exclusive control of the banking agencies."[80]

Liberal members of Robertson's committee, led by Wisconsin Senator William Proxmire, managed to exercise more influence than they had on the previous legislation. Proxmire sought a more formal role for the Department of Justice. He secured it in the form of a thirty-day window in which the DOJ could file suit—after the banking agencies had approved a merger, but before the merging banks began commingling assets. Federal Reserve Chair William McChesney Martin, Jr. (1951–1970) had suggested the time window as a kind of statute of limitations on DOJ action—a way to ensure that no more clouds of litigation would hang over approved bank mergers. With this compromise reached, the bill passed, in the words of one contemporaneous commentator, "almost casually by the Senate after a dull debate."[81]

The momentum stalled in the House of Representatives, especially at the hands of House Banking Committee Chair Wright Patman. Patman, perhaps the staunchest opponent of bigness in banking, considered all efforts to create a separate bank merger law as bad policy. "If you exempt banks from antitrust," he argued, "you might as well also shoot the policeman on the corner."[82]

In this era of committee chair power, Patman's opposition might have locked in divided federal authority over bank mergers, evaluated by banking agencies on primarily supervisory grounds and by the Department of Justice on competitive criteria. But Patman was not entirely in command. On October 19, 1965, in "one of the worst blow-ups in an important House committee in the memory of Capitol Hill old-timers," a group of House Democrats—Patman's own party—staged something of a coup. They entered the committee room under false pretense—one representative wanted to "get something" from his desk. That representative opened a side door and a small group of dissenting Democrats passed the Senate bill out of the House Banking Committee. Patman, as soon as he learned of the coup, called it a "sneak Pearl Harbor-type attack . . . on the nation's antitrust laws."[83]

Why the young Turks chose this moment to challenge their arthritic chairman is not clear. What is clear is that it worked. The result was essentially the compromise from the Senate. The mergers the bank supervisory agencies had already approved would remain approved, and the window for challenging approved mergers by the Department of Justice would be set at thirty days (a period that was ample for the DOJ's post–1960 lawsuits). The kicker was the question of competition: Would an anticompetitive merger ever be approved? The statutory language essentially punted: The responsible banking agency would not approve "any proposed merger transaction whose effect . . . may be to substantially lessen competition, or tend to create a monopoly . . . unless it finds that the anticompetitive effects of the proposed transaction are clearly outweighed by the public interest" in the community where the merger would occur.[84]

The statutory language, then, was hardly an improvement over what came before. Arguably, bank supervisory agencies had to prioritize the evaluation of anticompetitive effects when deciding on bank mergers—and in this sense, across the long fight over bank merger legislation, Congress gave the federal supervisory agencies antitrust responsibility that they had not sought and which could cut against more straightforward bank supervisory considerations. Yet as with the 1960 Bank Merger Act, Congress also rested the entire decision on "the public interest," in which banking risk management played an essential role. As it had following the enactment of the 1960 legislation, the Department of Justice retained a singular focus on competition policy and continued to aggressively challenge bank mergers for the next two decades.[85]

Conclusion

The New Deal banking reforms fundamentally settled the question of financial risk management. The federal government, not private shareholders, would hold and manage the risk. Marriner Eccles recognized, to his disgust, that this was especially a victory for the small banks and bankers whose cascading failures had contributed so much to the Depression's destructive forces. Ironically, the fostering hand of government secured small bankers' independence, at least with respect to holding company supervision (merger policy was more ambiguous). In the postwar years, this private-public partnership prospered within the New Deal's guardrails. In an important sense, though, Congress wanted bank supervisors to do more than manage financial risks of systemic crisis. It looked to bank supervisors to manage political risks in the form of antitrust policy. Bank holding company and bank merger legislation followed what would become a common pattern: Congress sought to shift divisive political questions with some financial risk content onto bank supervisors, who would use their information gathering prowess, their confidential engagement with banks, and their discretion to balance competing priorities of finance and politics alike. In many ways, this was an impossible task: There are irreconcilable conflicts in supervising bank risk for growth and managing the same risks for unit bank existence. Challenges to supervisors' performance, in turn, often resulted in Congress giving supervisory agencies yet more authority and discretion, expanding political risk management even further.

Interlude: Training Examiners (and Bankers) in the 1950s

IN 1954, the most closely supervised bank in the United States was the Inter-Agency Bank. It held solid assets, made reasonable loans, and had a pretty strong balance sheet. But its practices were riddled with errors—miscounted currency, poorly underwritten loans, and even a teller that perpetually "remove[d] the FDIC sign," a violation of banking regulations. It should have failed many times over, especially given that all of the bank's loans, depositors, and securities were fake. The only saving grace was that the Inter-Agency Bank was located in Room 2217 of the Federal Reserve Building on Constitution Avenue in Washington, DC. The bank was fake, too.[1]

The Inter-Agency Bank was "an interesting, easily dramatized gadget," observed a writer in *Banking*, the American Bankers Association's magazine, a gadget which the Federal Reserve, the FDIC, and the Comptroller of the Currency used to train bank examiners in two schools, the School for Examiners and the School for Assistant Examiners. Established in 1952, the schools offered students instruction in all subjects relevant to bank examinations in the 1950s. These included "analysis of financial statements, bank credit files, loan administration and supervision, function of reserves against deposits, Government securities and the money market, investments, bank tax problems, courses in credit, [and] examining techniques." In the senior school, seasoned examiners could expect to learn not only from bank supervisory personnel but also from "bankers from different parts of the United States, outstanding in various fields."[2]

The examiner schools were not, Federal Reserve Board Governor James L. Robertson (1952–1966) assured an audience of state bank examiners (who were also invited to participate), an effort "to impart our own opinions, but rather to furnish facts and kindle minds, with the view of contributing toward

the further development of broad-gauged examining forces, equal to their demanding tasks."[3]

As the industry's largest trade association, the American Bankers Association
(ABA) was keenly interested in banker—and bank examiner—education. And
to a considerable extent, they had always been one and the same thing. From the
beginning of federal banking supervision in the 1860s, the Comptroller had operated a revolving door from banking, into government service, and back into
banking. "Our best examiners are those in the prime of life, who work with
energy and fidelity, hoping to demonstrate their ability and worth, thereby securing for themselves a desirable and permanent position in some good bank,"
Comptroller Edward S. Lacy (1889–1892) wrote in 1892. This trend continued
into the twentieth century. "The best testimony to the high quality and character of the examining force is found in the fact that the bureau has constant difficulty in retaining the services of its skilled examiners because their special
qualifications constantly appeal to the best banks, which are continually draft-
ing them away from the bureau at greatly advanced compensation," Comptroller D. R. Crissinger (1921–1923) complained three decades later.[4]

In the nineteenth century, bank examiners learned their craft by examining banks, but in line with the larger professionalization of U.S. banking,
supervisory agencies gradually formalized and systematized examiner training. On the private side, the ABA led the way in banker education, following
the example set by British bankers in the 1880s. The ABA established the
American Institute of Bank Clerks (later the American Institute of Banking,
or AIB) in 1900, creating a series of credentialing courses for bankers of all
levels of experience. Formal bank examiner training followed closely behind.
Within a decade, Comptroller Lawrence O. Murray (1908–1913) reorganized
the examiner corps into regional districts and convened regular conferences
to standardize and improve examination methods. Training advanced somewhat haphazardly through the 1920s and the chaos of the Great Depression.
By the late 1930s, the FDIC, for example, required entry-level examiners to
have at least a year of banking experience, and was engaged in regular training programs, including mock examinations of its contrived "Bank A, Any-
town, Anystate."[5]

The intertwined professionalization of bankers and their examiners helps
explain the ABA's interest in the inner workings of the Inter-Agency Bank.
Indeed, by the 1950s, the collaboration between banks and bank supervisors
at the heart of supervision extended into joint training efforts. The ABA's
American Institute of Bankers invited examiners to participate in its banker

training courses, even providing the option to pursue this training via correspondence. Examiners are "'on the road' so much of the time that attendance at chapter or study group classes is impossible," the ABA reported. At the same time, supervisors provided periodic feedback on the content of the AIB's courses. Dr. Leroy Lewis, the AIB's national educational director, extolled the collaboration across the public-private divide: "Cooperation from the management of these agencies has been of an unusually high degree, even extending to the point where their representatives sit down with us once a year to consider how we can improve the quality of our educational materials."[6]

At the state level, formal training for state bank examiners worked in even closer collaboration with the industry than occurred between the federal agencies and the AIB. In states as diverse as Wisconsin, New York, and especially Pennsylvania, state bank superintendents formed close relationships not only with the banking trade groups while training examiners but with individual banks as well. In New York, bank examiners spent a full year "in one of several designated banks in the state learning the workings first hand." In Pennsylvania, recent college graduates "were placed in banks throughout the state for a 21-week course in the fundamentals of bank operations and procedures."[7]

For bankers and their examiners, the collaboration on training carried obvious benefits for improving skills and human capital, but there were also deeper motivations at work. The banking industry's interest in examiner training reflected the bankers' desire to structure their supervisory relationships in ways that permitted greater understanding of and control over the supervisory discretion that had expanded so dramatically following the Great Depression. By publicizing examiner training and the standardization of bank examination practices, the ABA in turn helped to render discretionary supervision legitimate in the eyes of those who would bear these costs.[8]

Collaboration on training also suggests shared anxiety around recruitment. By the mid-1950s, both banks and bank supervisory agencies faced what they perceived as an acute problem attracting qualified personnel. The banking industry's corporatist system of public and private risk management had perhaps succeeded too well in dampening excitement and entrepreneurial risk. The future was plastics, not banking. Seeking to hire recent college graduates, both bank supervisory agencies and banks placed increasing emphasis on early-career training as a means of competing with rival fields, such as engineering, accounting, sales, and general business. Persistent low salaries, exhausting work, and enormous responsibility weighed especially on examiner recruitment. "The position had ceased to be attractive," New York

State Bank Superintendent George Mooney (1954–1959) conceded in January 1957. Enticing new recruits was one of the key reasons New York and Pennsylvania sent their trainees into banks to learn the ropes. As the editors of *Mid-Continent Banker* declared in May 1957: "A Planned Training Program Can Attract Young Men!"[9]

In this sense, the public-private collaborations on training demonstrate the extent to which the pipeline into private employment remained a vital factor in recruiting capable employees into public service. Examiner training thus served a twofold purpose: the professionalization of examiners qua examiners, and then the training of examiners qua bankers, who, after leaving public service, would practice sound risk management within their banks.[10]

Pennsylvania Banking Superintendent Robert Myers (1955–1963) framed this explicitly through the problem—and implied risks—of successor management. The "lack of competent successor management personnel is a serious problem of many banks in Pennsylvania," Myers explained in a 1955 speech to his state's bankers. "Bank examination has been long recognized as an excellent training program for bank executives," and his program of training new examiners within banks was meant to "make available to the banking industry of the state men who have had sound training and experience as bank examiners." Myers noted that a poll commissioned by the American Bankers Association revealed "that 92% of banks polled indicated that failure to develop adequate successor leadership is the most glaring weakness of current bank management." Given that his own banking department was staffed by many examiners near or past retirement age, the new bank examiner program would give both the private sector and the examiners what they wanted.[11]

The Pennsylvania Bankers Association (PBA)—the industry lobbying group—responded enthusiastically to Myer's program, perhaps because it was tasked to design and implement it. The PBA started with a "one-week indoctrination period in the Department of Banking"—examiners had to learn, we suppose, that they were state employees first and foremost, and bankers only in their training. From there, the examiner trainees would spend sixteen weeks inside a bank to learn the affairs of the bank's major departments, including work on proof and transit (one week), demand ledgers (three weeks), the loan cage (three weeks), and a few days for review.[12]

This vision of bank examination as a pipeline for employment formalized a kind of corporatism that manifested itself in other parts of bank supervision at other points in history. It was also much more than this. The joint training of bankers and supervisors in the same skills and in the same locations reflects the view that the work of banking and bank supervision were inseparable: The skill set needed to perform well in both contexts looked very similar. Terminology that would become more common later—the revolving door, regulatory capture—was in this period not seen as something to mask or hide. Mutual reinforcement of the common enterprise of risk management was the point of the entire exercise.

8

The Saxon Invasion

THE SUPERVISORY BATTLE OVER RISK
AND FAILURE IN THE 1960S

WHATEVER ELSE the policy disputes over the supervision of bank concentration—whether through mergers or holding companies—accomplished, they unquestionably expanded the purview of bank supervision beyond the New Deal co-management of financial risk. What the New Deal apparently settled, however, did not remain settled. Old questions endured. For example, how much risk should bankers and their shareholders take in the name of growth and innovation? The immediate postwar era, scarred by the memory of the 1930s bank failures and swaddled in the FDIC's prudential oversight, erred on the side of little to none.

The election of John F. Kennedy in 1960 ushered in a new debate, though one the administration appears not to have anticipated. James J. Saxon (1961–1966), Kennedy's appointee as Comptroller of the Currency, turned out to be "a pugnacious political infighter" who, a friend observed, would "rather fight than be right." Saxon, who as a junior Treasury official orchestrated the removal of U.S. gold and greenbacks off the island of Corregidor as the Japanese were closing in during World War II, brought a renewed vigor to the Comptroller's office. "Congress didn't create the Comptroller's job for housekeeping," he told a reporter in one of his innumerable, on-the-record interviews.[1]

Behind Saxon's brash style was a substantial supervisory agenda. Since the New Deal, chartering supervision had been largely subsumed under the FDIC's insurance ethos, oriented not toward opening new banks and driving competition but toward managing competition to keep existing banks safe and sound. Saxon sought a new alignment. In the words of one sympathetic journalist, Saxon wanted to wake "the venerable office of the Comptroller from a

sleepy sinecure to a powerful instrument for infusing the staid banking industry with the spirit of competition and innovation." That meant reviving
chartering—creating more banks—as well as chartering competition—
encouraging differences in state and federal supervision that would enable
dynamic new business practices and industry growth. "Someone has to be the
leader of the banking industry," Saxon insisted—not the national banking industry but the entire banking industry. That someone would be him.[2]

In his campaign to revive chartering supervision, Saxon was not blazing a
trail back to the pre-New Deal world of predominantly private risk management. Rather, Saxon rested his self-nomination as leader of the banking industry on the New Deal infrastructure of private finance backed by public
power. He sought simply to emphasize the private finance in this relationship,
and to use the public power of chartering to invigorate more private risk-
taking. Saxon viewed the penchant for stability, and the outsized role of the
Fed and the FDIC in enforcing that stability, as a kind of hangover from the
Great Depression. He preferred instead a model of banking where national
banks were supervised exclusively by his office—and state banks similarly
under the purview of state authorities—with the result being a kind of charter competition that would benefit everyone. Supervision, in this sense, was
a recognition that private and public shared responsibility for managing financial risk, but it placed the supervisors in the position of pushing banks
toward risk-taking, not away from it. "We want a dynamic, thriving, risk-
taking business," he said in 1963. "If it becomes riskless, the government may
as well take it over."[3]

To the limited extent that he is remembered at all, Saxon has been characterized in almost universal disdain, as being illustrative of the "dangers in zeal
outstripping tact" and indicative of a Comptroller beholden to banks' efforts
to undermine important divisions between banking and the rest of the economy. This lack of historical reputation reflects, as well, Saxon's failure to achieve
his policy goals. By the end of his five-year tenure, he had changed little except
that, as recounted at the time of his retirement in 1966, he had "irritated two
U.S. Presidents and obstreperously tangled with such Washington Pooh-Bahs
as Robert Kennedy, William McChesney Martin, Nicholas Katzenbach, Senator John McClellan and Congressman Wright Patman—as well as leaders of
the Securities and Exchange Commission, the Federal Deposit Insurance Corporation and the Independent Bankers Association."[4] Indeed, Saxon's effort
to turn the dials in favor of more private risk-taking, coupled with the high-
profile failure of a handful of state and national banks in the mid-1960s, led

Congress to grant public officials yet more forceful powers to shape the decisions and direction of private bank management.

Although contemporaries focused on the personality conflicts and the turf wars that were Saxon's stock and trade, the fights Saxon initiated were part of an important shift in the balance between public and private in the question of financial risk management. In this critical period, including in his near-term, near-total losses, we see the institutionalization not of a specific resolution of the competing interests in bank supervision but of a very specific process for resolving those disputes prospectively. The public management of residual risk remained, even as some public risk managers pushed harder for more private responsibility, sometimes even against the wishes of those private actors.[5]

The Context of Bank Supervision in 1961

The embrace of unit banking in holding company reform and the continued suspicion of bank mergers by small bankers and their political allies reflected a profound commitment to protect the interests of banking stability and, as a result, incumbent bankers, at the expense of other factors, including economic growth. This protection was in part a function of the still resonant memories of the Depression years and of the consequent dominance of the FDIC's insurance ethos over other supervisory approaches. Politicians and bankers shared the fear that the postwar return to normalcy would trigger the same pathologies that created the Depression in the first place. "With the experience of thousands of bank failures between 1920 and 1934," the FDIC observed in 1960, "bank chartering authorities were alert to prevent a repetition ... and were determined that this should not happen again."[6]

This defensive conservatism meant that the Comptroller maintained a high perimeter around national bank charters. From 1934 to 1961, the number of national banks declined in every year but two (1935 and 1947). To a significant extent, this was the result of the mergers described in the previous chapter and the growth, where authorized by state law, of existing banks through branching. To take a typical year, in 1952 the Comptroller chartered 15 new national banks and authorized 177 national bank branches, while 46 national banks exited through merger. For 1959, the figures were 33 new banks, 456 branches, and 75 exits. Despite the steady decline of all banks during this period, national banks declined at a faster pace than state banks.[7]

Importantly, the absolute decline in the numbers of banks was the result of consolidations and not of bank failures, the latter of which had become mostly a thing of the past. From 1945 to 1961, there had been a total of fourteen national bank failures, out of roughly 4,500 national banks, and 34 state bank failures, out of 8,500 state banks. This was a time of unprecedented stability on both sides of the dual banking divide. The safety of the banking system rested in part on the massive buildup of government securities on bank balance sheets during World War II, which bankers gradually sold off to meet growing lending opportunities in the booming postwar economy. At the same time, the variety of federal credit programs and loan guarantees provided banks with publicly backed, profitable investments. In 1958, Bank of America told shareholders that a quarter of its loans were "guaranteed or insured by the United States Government or its agencies." And behind all of this stood the federal supervisors, who gave specific attention to monitoring and managing the composition of bank assets, aiming to minimize risk and improve diversification. As the American Bankers Association (ABA) observed in 1962, "the combined effect of these . . . supervisory operations has been a maintenance of a much higher quality of bank assets in bank portfolios and, as a consequence, has helped minimize the problem of bank failure."[8]

Commercial banks may not have been failing, but they were not growing either—or at least not growing apace with the American economy and competing financial institutions. From 1945 to 1958, commercial bank assets increased from $159 billion to $238 billion, while the total assets for all financial firms grew from $280 billion to $614 billion. Thus, while commercial bank assets grew by 50 percent, they declined relative to the financial sector, from 56.5 percent of total financial assets to 39.5 percent. Over the same period, the U.S. Gross Domestic Product grew by 100 percent, and the population—spurred by the postwar baby boom—increased from 140 million to 175 million. Home ownership jumped as well, from 44 percent to 62 percent, a change that benefited banks but even more so benefited savings and loans, as well as other thrifts that specialized in consumer lending and mortgage finance. "It is undoubtedly true . . . that the conservatism of some bank managements has been responsible" for the decline of commercial banks relative to nonbank competitors, the ABA conceded. But because of regulatory differences among different financial firms, "competing institutions have been able to operate more freely and profitably than commercial banks."[9]

The point is not that bank innovation had totally stalled in the postwar era. In the 1950s, much bank energy went into improving back-office processes, through the adoption of accounting and data storage technologies (like microfiche machines). The largest banks, led by Bank of America, developed bespoke computer systems that laid the groundwork for the digital transformation of banking in later decades. Spurred by the New Deal credit programs, bankers also continued to move into consumer lending, with the most ambitious experimenting with charge account programs—the forerunner of credit cards that were widely adopted in the mid 1960s.[10]

During the postwar transformation of the U.S. economy and its financial system, the Comptroller of the Currency remained essentially a background figure. Neither Preston Delano (1938–1953) nor his successor Ray M. Gidney (1953–1961) played significant roles in the legislative conflicts over bank holding companies or bank mergers. Before he was appointed by Dwight D. Eisenhower to head the Comptroller's office, Gidney had spent most of his career within the Federal Reserve System, most recently as president of the Federal Reserve Bank of Cleveland from 1944 to 1953. Gidney actively pursued cooperation with the Fed and the FDIC, and he used his public statements mostly to caution bankers toward safe lending. In 1956, during a period of economic expansion, Gidney urged bankers and supervisors to revisit the experience of the Great Depression, to "insure against possible untoward development in the future."[11]

Arguably, Gidney did not extend this caution to bank mergers. Soon after his appointment, Gidney disclaimed any preference for or against mergers and consolidations. "It is our duty under the law," Gidney wrote, "not to have a fixed policy, either in favor or in opposition [of mergers], since we believe that the law requires us to weight the merits of each individual case." Throughout the merger boom of the 1950s, Gidney found a lot of merit, frequently approving large national bank mergers despite pressure from congressional antimonopolists like Emanuel Celler. In support of these decisions, Gidney consistently argued that larger banks, by "add[ing] vitality to competitive banking," could better serve the public interest than smaller banks.[12]

Once the 1960 Bank Merger Act became official, Gidney continued to approve mergers on this logic, authorizing sixty-seven bank unions in 1961. By then, however, Eisenhower no longer headed the administration. John. F. Kennedy was president, and the Justice Department under Attorney General Robert F. Kennedy took a much more restrictive view of the effects of mergers on competition. In its advisory opinions, the DOJ only supported twenty-five of the mergers Gidney approved. The most controversial of these was the Philadelphia National Bank's merger with Girard Trust Corn Exchange in February 1961, which the DOJ immediately sued to stop. The administration also wanted Gidney's resignation but worried about the optics of removing him in relation to one specific case. For months the White House dithered, while Gidney continued approving mergers. In September, the administration botched the job further, announcing Gidney's resignation before they had secured it. In a public press conference, Gidney insisted that he had no plans to leave. After correcting the brushup, Saxon was appointed and duly confirmed a few months later.[13]

The New Sheriff in Town: The Saxon Appointment

Saxon upset the Kennedy administration's expectations almost immediately. Saxon initially expressed views about mergers that appeared in sync with those of the White House. But there was a careful distinction. Saxon did not share small bankers' insistence that any merger represented an "immoral application" that "might result in competition so destructive as to render it difficult for the smaller . . . banks to operate with reasonable chances for success." Instead, Saxon saw the problem of mergers as a problem of both competition *and* risk management, one unavoidably bound up with distinct processes of charter review and branch approvals. "As Saxon sees it," a profiler in *Newsweek* wrote, "the present system is a hodge-podge of antiquated, conflicting federal and state law" that "inhibits, rather than encourages, economic growth by unnaturally preventing adequate bank expansion." Saxon planned to make bank expansion much more efficient, not to protect monopolists but to resolve "delays of nine months or more in handling applications for new branches, mergers, and charters" in the spirit of injecting more entrepreneurial energy into the banking industry. Saxon wanted to turn the dials of risk tolerance toward private-sector dynamism, which the Depression had all but removed from the system.[14]

Bank mergers offered Saxon a central channel for promoting competition as he understood it, but one which placed him in continuous conflict with the Department of Justice. Saxon, like Gidney, believed that banks needed the size and scope to manage the increasingly demanding needs of America's massive economy. Bank mergers, Saxon argued, often resulted in stronger management for the consolidated banks, the ability of consolidated small banks to compete with already large rivals, and the extension of more banking services into new areas—all in the public interest. The problem was that, even after the Bank Merger Act of 1960 nominally placed merger approvals into supervisors' hands, the Department of Justice was staking a claim to independent merger authority in the courts. Here the DOJ's effort to maintain competition by maintaining the number of competitors, and thus limiting concentration in local banking markets, operated at cross-purposes with Saxon's ambitions.[15]

Although Saxon's appointment may have been triggered by a desire to co-ordinate bank merger policy more tightly with antitrust, Saxon and Robert Kennedy could not find common ground. In January 1962, Saxon sought a meeting with Kennedy to work out their differences. Kennedy refused to meet. Six months later, Saxon tried again, calling Kennedy twice. Receiving no response, he went public, calling the antitrust lawyers who contested national bank mergers "zealots" and, later, people for whom "the antitrust laws come first and the Ten Commandments come second."[16]

As the Philadelphia National Bank case wound through the court system, it was clear that the federal judiciary was on the DOJ's side, not Saxon's. His failure to push national banks into competitive markets with state banks through mergers did, however, have one lasting effect: Saxon resolved to more aggressively use the powers he had to encourage banks to grow and compete. Saxon found that path in the creation of new national bank charters at a pace not seen since at least the 1920s. During the entire postwar era until his confirmation in January 1962, Saxon's predecessors had chartered 562 national banks. During his five-year tenure, Saxon chartered 586. This process started slowly but gradually accelerated. Saxon chartered 65 new banks in 1962, 164 in 1963, and 205 in 1964. In that same period, 96 state-chartered banks—many being among the largest state banks—exercised the option to convert from their state charter to a national charter. Saxon also expanded the national bank branching system during the same period by 2,693 branches, compared to the 1,673 new state bank branches. The national banking business was booming, even if mergers were not the primary mechanism for accomplishing that growth. From Saxon's perspective, this was perhaps even better: Only the Comptroller could review charter and branching requests. Unlike bank mergers, there was no obvious cause of action for their denial.[17]

The ethos of risk tolerance Saxon sought to promote, and the growth of the national banking system he achieved, went hand in hand. Saxon wanted the government to trust private bankers more but not only that. He wanted more national bankers, period. "Each new generation produces a new group of men and women of skill and ability seeking outlets for the use of their talents," he wrote in 1964 to defend his expansive view of chartering. He wanted a banking system where decisional authority was not for the supervisors alone to exercise but for an ever-larger group of bankers. "It can never be in the public interest to protect banks against competitors who are either more efficient or more responsive to public demands." To accomplish these tasks of providing outlets in banking for the best and brightest of a rising generation, and of ensuring that the old guard had to earn their customers through open competition, Saxon pushed for as many bankers as possible to open as many banks and branches as possible and to try as many new banking products as possible.[18]

State bankers tracked Saxon's moves closely. They did not like what they saw. A Texas banker accused Saxon of "handing out charters like they were free hot dogs," while a North Carolina banker accused Saxon of being "dictatorial," "high-handed," and in need of being "throttled at once." They viewed the national bank expansion under Saxon as an affront to the dual banking system, fearing that if he "can accomplish his ends" of dramatic expansion, he would "completely wreck the dual banking system."[19]

Saxon relished the conflict and made no effort to change course. The critics were right that Saxon's vision of supervision would spare state banks—indeed, all banks—much less the rigors of competition. And while national bankers (mostly) cheered Saxon, it would be a mistake to cast Saxon's changes to the principles of supervision as simply doing the bidding of national bankers. To start, we can find no evidence that the Saxon invasion started with national bankers. Saxon's preference for banking growth was consistent with a long line of thinking among certain bank policymakers, and his emphasis on adding further competition through chartering was novel, at least in the post–New Deal context. Saxon did actively seek national bankers' advice on advantageous policy changes, surveying national bankers in 1962 and publishing a report, *National Banks and the Future*, authored by an advisory committee composed primarily of national bankers. This, too, was consistent with Saxon's intention to lead the banking industry toward more entrepreneurialism, innovation, and competition. He commissioned the survey, convened the group, published the study under the Comptroller's name, and then pursued policy change through every channel available to him.[20]

What's more, Saxon wanted to use national bank growth not only to correct problems of local concentration but also to address other social ills. For example, during the debates around the Civil Rights Act of 1964, Saxon wrote an op-ed in the *Afro-American*, a leading journal of the Black community, to describe his efforts to expand the banking franchise to bankers of all races: "In chartering National Banks, we do not inquire as to the racial origin of any organizing group, nor is racial origin a factor in the approval or denial of a National Bank application . . . Every citizen is treated exactly alike." He further touted that "some eleven National Banks have been chartered during my term of office in which colored citizens were members of the organizing group." After Lyndon Johnson launched the Great Society legislative program in 1965, Saxon expressed hope that a more innovative and less constrained banking system would be a partner in accomplishing these policies. And it was somewhat emphatic that he included "men and women" in his descriptions of the ideal banker, not merely men alone. In 1964, such locutions were not the norm.[21]

Whatever other benefits were obtained from charter liberalization, Saxon's primary effort was to reinvigorate competition in banking. Saxon credited an earlier generation of politicians and bankers for stabilizing a system in crisis in the 1930s. By the 1960s, however, the mania for safety—the public and private determination to defend against bank failure at all costs—had stunted the nation's banking system. "Much of today's banking legislation, borne in the aftermath of financial panics, is crisis-orientated. Thus, some state bankers, 'long accustomed to government shelters, are unwilling to release these crutches.'" Saxon did not want to provide shelter to "some businessmen's fear of competition," nor give credit to "some government officials' fear" of private initiative. He insisted on this view regularly. "The presumption," he said, "is against governmental restriction of this free discretion unless there is a clear public need which the Government can satisfy better than the individual." The tilting of the supervisory ethos away from government control and toward private initiative and private risk-taking is the throughline in all of Saxon's policy changes.[22]

Saxon's Conflicts: Imposing the Risk-Forward Vision of Supervision

By shifting the post-New Deal supervisory ethos back toward private initiative through, for example, chartering policy, Saxon did not want to eliminate public management of residual risk. He meant to give bankers and supervisors a close relationship, while preserving for each a separate domain. Banks were to take risks to promote economic growth; supervisors were to let them do so, while guaranteeing deposits, examining for compliance, and facilitating institutional expansion within (and sometimes beyond) the law. Saxon wanted the vision of supervision to be the exercise of light-touch supervisory discretion, where the residual risk for bank activity was still in the hands of the public, but the frontline risk was not.

Had Saxon operated in a world of consolidated supervision under the Comptroller's authority, his vision may have become national policy. Given the disharmony of federal banking supervision—that is, the spread of responsibilities among and across various institutions, not least the states, the Fed, the FDIC, the OCC, as well as the DOJ and the Securities and Exchange Commission—it is no surprise that Saxon's expansive view turned to conflict with other supervisors less keenly interested in reducing their own responsibilities. Indeed, it is no exaggeration to characterize the 1960s as a period of extended institutional disharmony in bank supervision unlike anything that had come before or that would follow after, including the sometimes bitter feuds of the 1930s covered in previous chapters. Three examples discussed further in this chapter—one each for the Fed, the FDIC, and the SEC—illustrate what the 1960s meant for changes in the supervisory ethos that Saxon tried but mostly failed to initiate.

To be clear, Saxon fought constantly, with everyone. It may have been his nature. This was more than a prima donna in a somewhat obscure office seeking to maximize his relevance, however. The common thread to these fights was to reassert the primacy of the nineteenth-century information regime of supervision, with the entrenched backstops of the Fed discount window and FDIC insurance firmly in place. Because he did not control those guarantees, Saxon viewed his job as pushing front-end risk management deeper into the private sector. In other words, the supervisory system as Saxon envisioned it was to focus less on the residual ownership of financial risk to which bank supervisors were mostly attentive and more on the private frontline risk management that included taking more adventurous risks in the name of supporting a better, stronger economy.

The Supervisory Approach of the SEC

By the 1960s, the consumer revolution had not quite landed in New Deal bank supervision, but it was a defining ethos in the New Deal securities laws. In the first hundred days of the Roosevelt administration, Congress not only fundamentally altered supervision by creating the FDIC through the 1933 Glass-Steagall Act, it also radically overhauled the way that capital markets were governed—away from the mostly private sector approach that had grown up around the New York Stock Exchange, and away from the state efforts at regulating securities prior to the Depression. In their place emerged the Securities Act of 1933, which required businesses to register every stock or bond with the

Federal Trade Commission (FTC), followed by the Securities Exchange Act of 1934, which removed that authority from the FTC and placed it into the newly created Securities and Exchange Commission (SEC). Thereafter the SEC would regulate the entire field, including the secondary markets where securities trades occurred.[23]

The new SEC also received supervisory authority of a kind. It performed audits and inspections of its registered broker-dealers. This examination authority was only loosely modeled on commercial bank supervision. The ethic of broker-dealer supervision was not about a shared commitment to managing financial risk; rather, the SEC was a compliance entity that issued fines and enforcement actions. The institutional framework for information sharing between brokers and the SEC was also very different than that which prevailed in commercial banking (though it had some resonance with the call-reporting regime of the nineteenth and early twentieth centuries). The SEC did not use examination to yield information useful to monitoring the activities of the brokers. It relied instead on informational disclosures and registrations required by law to be made to the investing public.[24]

This difference in orientations toward markets, information, and the class of stakeholders worthy of supervisory attention came to a head in the 1960s. The supervisory ethos that Saxon sought to accomplish was to push banks to the frontier of innovation (and away from reliance on examiners to address when and where bankers could undertake new products and services in the pursuit of profitable business opportunities). He wanted commercial banks—meaning, for him, national banks—to broaden their horizons such that, with "a vision of the future," they could "do a job that's needed for economic expansion." One place he wanted this expansion was in pushing banks to provide bank-adjacent financial services to their investing clients, including some that the Glass-Steagall Act had sought to limit or even eliminate. If that meant tripping over the SEC to get that expansion done, Saxon was more than happy to do it.[25]

The conflict began innocently enough. In early 1962, following advice laid out by his advisory committee in *National Banks and the Future*, Saxon lobbied Congress to transfer authority over commercial bank trust departments from the Federal Reserve—where, "by a historically inadvertent legislative action," it had been placed in 1913—to the Comptroller. Saxon urged the change as a simple streamlining of institutional responsibility. "We believe that it is essential that the national banking system be regulated as a whole entity and not subject to divided authority such as exists today." The Federal Reserve had no objection, and Congress enacted the change later that year.[26]

Once possessed of regulatory authority over bank trust departments, Saxon introduced significant changes aimed at pushing commercial banks into competition with investment firms. Saxon's vehicle for this transformation was the collective investment fund, a type of trust account which commercial banks traditionally used to pool the resources of small trusts to reduce administrative costs and increase trust returns. When regulated by the Federal Reserve, such funds were limited to "bona fide fiduciary purposes," meaning that banks could pool trust assets placed in their care but could not market their collective funds to investors as investments. Saxon scrapped the rule. "It has never made sense to me why a trust set up for the purpose of supporting one's children or aged parents has a more 'bona fide fiduciary' aspect than a trust set up to support one's self in one's old age," Saxon explained. The 1940 Investment Company Act explicitly exempted common trust funds from SEC regulation, and with the rule change, commercial banks could effectively offer mutual funds, supervised by the Comptroller rather than the SEC.[27]

SEC Chairman William L. Cary (1961–1964) did not welcome Saxon's efforts to encourage commercial banks to enter what the securities agency saw as plainly capital market activity. In April 1963, the fight burst into the open after the First National City Bank of New York (Citibank) announced plans to establish a "pooled investment agency" without registering with the SEC. In response, the SEC promised an injunction the moment First National City began operating the fund, unless it registered under the Investment Company Act and submitted to SEC oversight. "All investors in mutual funds, by whomever sponsored, should enjoy the same protections," Cary proclaimed in May 1963. That meant SEC registration, regulation, and oversight of national banks.[28]

Saxon struck back, claiming his own trust regulations were both "meticulous and thorough," reflecting "the product of years of thought and discussion by members of the banking community and their associations." He wanted to remove the monopolies that he claimed the investment banks enjoyed to the detriment of both national bankers and their customers. Cary responded, nonplussed by Saxon's legal and policy certainties. He did not want to ban banks from participating in a business they regarded as necessary to their work. He just wanted to ensure that securities were regulated as securities, which meant that the SEC must have a say. Commercial banks could enter the space occupied by investment banks; they would just have to be regulated by him in the process.[29]

The political economy of this dispute, and the tenor of Saxon's response, have to do with what Saxon regarded as the Depression-era mindset of financial supervision. In effect, the Glass-Steagall Act siloed financial firms by institution and market function. To oversimplify, commercial banks (institutions) took deposits and made loans (market functions). Investment banks (institutions) underwrote securities (market functions), work that included brokering deals, underwriting bond and equity issuances, and advising corporations. Congress had mostly placed underwriting activities within the regulatory purview of the SEC to be governed on a theory of registration and disclosure. This was not the work of thorough bank examination. Saxon, in a sense, sought to maintain the boundaries of oversight along institutional lines—anything that national banks did would be regulated and supervised by the Comptroller. "Our exercise of our responsibilities goes far beyond— through examination and other procedures—mere disclosure," Saxon argued. "We deal with the regulated industry of banking. There is no more intensively regulated business in this country."[30]

Cary and the SEC saw it differently. To them, the supervisory relationship was by product and market, not by institution. Any security management belonged to the SEC. This model reflected, at its core, a vastly different conception of risk management: activity, not institution. This epistemic difference set the two agencies up for a clear conflict.

Saxon would lose this fight. The interagency skirmish quickly became the concern of members of Congress who sought to resolve the conflict in favor of the activity-based, cautious risk management system of the New Deal. In testimony, the two agency heads sniped at one another. Cary "sprinkled his testimony with barbs directed at what he said were the Comptroller's past 'shortcomings' in guarding the interests of bank investors," reflecting a supervisory ethos that favored caution and investor protection rather than the private-sector innovation Saxon preferred. Cary further claimed that bank examiners are not sufficiently "trained to protect the interests of investors in bank securities or investment funds." Saxon dismissed these attacks, accusing Cary and the SEC of "posing as a St. George slaying the dragon of regulation" in an attempt to extend "the reach of the bureaucratic hand" to the banking industry. He contended that "the constant surveillance of state and federal bank examiners provides more than ample protection." What he did not say was that bank supervision answered to a conflicting supervisory ethos. Retail investors were not high on Saxon's list of stakeholders requiring his attention.[31]

In the final resolution, Saxon conceded by requiring more disclosures from the banks, necessitating, in part, that insiders (including officers, directors, and owners of over 10 percent) report their own stock trades. Saxon ultimately admitted: "maybe we've pushed too hard too rapidly . . . But it wouldn't be worth my time to be a nice, pleasant caretaker." His term as Comptroller was marked by this willingness to push for a banking industry "that is a competitive, viable force in the national economy" in the face of the recognition that "change is not the most welcome animal in the commercial banking industry."[32]

The Federal Reserve's Supervisory Ethos in the 1960s

The Federal Reserve's attitude toward supervision in the postwar era had continued the trajectory begun under Chairman Marriner Eccles (1934–1948), a trajectory that put supervision as the instrumentality of broader macroeconomic and monetary goals. After a temporary emphasis on bank holding companies as a mechanism for closing loopholes in bank supervision, the focus returned to the Fed's core priorities. William McChesney Martin Jr. (1951–1970), the Fed Chair appointed by Truman as part of the Fed-Treasury Accord of 1951, wanted the Fed to move away from dramatic interventions, including in bank supervision. In Martin's view, the Fed was designed to "minimize [the] convulsions" of the financial panics of the Gilded Age so as to "make possible the smooth functioning of monetary machinery so necessary to promote the growth of the country and to improve standards of living." To do this, the Fed must be "the main bulwark of our private banking system" that will preserve a banking system "of a free people with a minimum of Government interference." These kinds of light-touch approaches under Martin meant that the Fed would change much of how it approached its business. Supervision would not be the key to managing the appropriate level of government interference. The entire apparatus of Fed policy—monetary, supervisory, and otherwise—would be used to seek a smooth and even keel. The Fed would "lean against the wind, whichever way the wind is blowing."[33]

In some superficial respects, Saxon was simply joining Martin's view of a private-leaning, forward-looking bank supervisory system. The two approaches in practice were quite different. Saxon did not simply want to let the winds of private risk-taking blow of their own accord. He wanted to shape and direct them. He did not, therefore, want "a minimum of Government interference," but a government willing and interested in pointing the way toward bank risk management that would promote competition and economic vitality. Saxon wanted less cautious bankers, whereas Martin wanted more caution. "Unless banks are to pursue a policy of seeking only riskless loans," Saxon said, "it may be expected that the quality of their loan portfolios will be diverse and will vary with business conditions and monetary policies. This is as it should be, since, indeed, banking is a risk-taking business, as are all other forms of private enterprise."[34]

Despite Martin's enthusiasms for the private sector, he did not want banks to increase their risk exposure beyond a narrow band. Such differences in sensibilities meant that the Comptroller and the Fed, rarely the closest of allies, were headed for a collision. The main dispute came again in an area adjacent to the capital markets: municipal bond underwriting. When Saxon took office, commercial banks could underwrite general obligation bonds, those secured by the full faith and credit (and thus taxing power) of a borrowing entity, but they lacked similar power relative to revenue bonds, paid out of non-tax income like water charges or highway tolls. Saxon wanted commercial banks to participate in revenue bond underwriting, something that the Fed forbid for its member banks (which included, by law, all national banks) after the passage of Glass-Steagall.[35]

Claiming that the investment banking industry had a "full-fledged monopoly" on the underwriting of municipal bonds, Saxon authorized national banks to underwrite municipal revenue bonds in September 1963. He did so by expanding the definition of permitted investments under the Glass-Steagall Act, to include a category of "public securities," the eligibility of which the Comptroller would determine on a case-by-case basis. Saxon knew this was a provocative change and sought legislation that would authorize his maneuver. But he did not wait, either, permitting banks to immediately engage while he waited on Congress.[36]

Under the Glass-Steagall Act, Saxon's ruling nominally extended to Fed member banks as well, and the Fed immediately contradicted Saxon's ruling, which Martin denounced as "unwarranted." The Board wrote in November: "Since the Comptroller is not authorized by law to expand the category of exempt securities . . . the current Regulation does not have the force of law." The Fed flatly prohibited state member banks from joining the revenue bond business. In doing so, the Board played directly into Saxon's hands, since his goal above all else was to distinguish a national charter through its advantages vis-à-vis the states.[37]

These legal conflicts spilled quickly into the public, bringing Congress once again as mediator on what bank supervision and public-private risk management should be. The dispute reflected the difference between Saxon's vision for risk management and the contradictory supervisory priorities that the Fed (and the FDIC) wanted for the banking system. The Fed was clear that, given its macroeconomic stability mandate, it saw no need to cheer on banks that were rapidly expanding the indebtedness of cities at a time when the Fed wanted to lean against increased public borrowing and, in a larger sense, debt-fueled inflationary activity. Martin also worried that this entire enterprise was pro-cyclical. Referencing the bond underwriting bubble that burst during the Great Depression, Martin argued that the Glass-Steagall Act's division of commercial and investment banks was designed to restrain "undesirable conflicts of interest" inherent to too many commercial banks engaging too much in speculative finance. Martin wanted monetary policy to be the primary lever for managing municipal borrowing cycles, not supervisory policy (which would point in the other direction).[38]

Saxon saw it differently. It was not simply that Saxon wanted commercial banks doing more municipal bond offerings (though he was quite thorough in his defense of those prerogatives), it was that he wanted the national banks to reach beyond their traditional strictures. He wanted them to lean with the wind, not against it—taking risk was a healthy part of banking, something that supervisors should not only permit but encourage. Having battled the Fed on specific issues, he now challenged the basic premise that the central bank should undertake supervision at all. "In a democratic society," he said, "there are particular dangers in lodging broad regulatory powers with the central bank," namely, that "many a destructive policy may long escape notice or criticism" under the "guise of benevolent conservatism."[39]

For a time, Saxon prevailed. He promised Congress that commercial bank underwriting would increase competition and drive down the price of municipal bond issues, a promise that carried considerable weight as local governments competed for funds in an economy perpetually at war with inflation. Although Congress was skeptical about the legality of Saxon's maneuver, it did not follow Martin's call to equalize investment powers across national and Fed member banks, nor his call to ban revenue bond underwriting. Rather, Congress stalled. With no movement in sight, the Fed backed off its public outcry. Yet, as with collective investment funds, the meaningful challenge to Saxon's rule changes came through the courts. After a run of successful bids by commercial bank syndicates for revenue bond issues, ninety-seven investment banks sued to block a First National City Bank-headed syndicate from bidding on Port of New York Authority bonds in January 1966. In December, a federal judge ruled that Saxon had overstepped his authority, a decision upheld on appeal two years later. Here, again, Saxon lost. Banks stayed out of the business of revenue bond underwriting for almost forty years. Saxon's failure here wasn't unusual. He lost most of his battles in the short run, even as his reallocation of risk tolerance in bank supervision reverberated for many years to come.[40]

The State Supervisory Ethos: The Preservation of the Dual Banking System

The postwar addition of Alaska and Hawaii rounded the number of united states out to fifty. That also meant, with the District of Columbia and Puerto Rico (and other territories besides), that there were more than fifty alternative supervisory regimes adjacent to those being litigated at the federal level. It would be too much to say that each one varied from the others in their supervisory ethics, although each state's unique history meant that the experimentation and motivation of chartering and examination created remarkable variety. There was one common thread among these states and territories: They fiercely defended the dual banking system against the Comptroller and did all they could to protect it from Saxon's meddling.

This protective effort pitted Saxon against perhaps his most formidable foes, beginning a process of "preemption" of federal law over state efforts to limit the ability of national banks to participate in local economies. This idea comes from the Supremacy Clause of the U.S. Constitution: "The Constitution, and the Laws of the United States which shall be made in Pursuance thereof . . . shall be the supreme Law of the Land," even if state laws conflict. This supremacy meant that the Comptroller's interpretations of the national banking laws would override, or "preempt" in the legal term, any conflicting state laws so long as courts accepted that interpretation. Taking on the "highly controversial subject of whether federal law should take precedence over state law," state banking officials interpreted Saxon's goals "as a resumption of an old federal drive to break down the dual banking system that has been traditional in the U.S." State bank supervisors regarded this effort as "usurping their powers by trying to shift all regulatory authority to Washington."[41]

The story begins almost at the beginning of Saxon's tenure as Comptroller, through the chartering process discussed above. Saxon diagnosed bank supervision as a tool for establishing a "dynamic, thriving, risk-taking business," which meant that, through supervision, national banks would be urged to compete more fiercely with state-chartered banks. The OCC would not only support this competition but would facilitate national bank success through the exercise of federal preemption to protect national banks from state laws that applied to the state banks, creating distinct advantages for a national bank charter. Saxon defended his aggressive regime as necessary to revitalize the banking industry for which "the regulatory philosophy was formulated during the worst depression in modern times." The impacts of the Great Depression were part of the story, but only part. At its core, American banking history is a history of a peculiar form of political economy that placed states and the federal government in a kind of wrestling contest. In the twenty-first century, this contest is mostly over—the Feds have won, with entire domains of stability, liquidation, money laundering, consumer protection, foreign banking, and more all folded into the federal perimeter. In the middle of the twentieth century, however, the dominance was still hotly contested, although the writing was on the wall.[42]

Saxon sought to assert federal prerogatives in favor of the larger national banks. In Saxon's view—one shared by the bankers advising him—American banking in the 1960s was trending toward economies of scale and scope. "The thrust which now prevails for bank expansion is based to an important degree on the cost advantages of larger-scale operations," Saxon's advisory committee wrote in 1962. "The increased mechanization of banking operations involving heavy capital costs, and the broadening range of banking services entailing the use of highly specialized personnel, have produced both opportunities and incentives to expand operations in order to reduce unit costs." Mergers offered one means of growth but one subject to intense antitrust scrutiny by Robert Kennedy's Department of Justice. That left expansion through branching.[43]

Here, as in other places, Saxon was fairly limited in what he could do: Federal law left only a little room for preemption because, under the McFadden Act and 1933 Glass-Steagall Act, national banks were bound by state branching laws. Supervision and liberal supervisory interpretation were key, then, to Saxon's strategy of favoring national banks in the competition for charters and growth. The McFadden truce, Saxon believed, needed to be reworked. National banks needed to expand, they needed to meet the evermore sophisticated banking needs of the American economy, and they needed to do it with less direction from bank supervisors, including the Comptroller of the Currency—these were private risks to take, not public decisions of government. "We do not have, nor do we seek, the authority to initiate [chartering, branching, and merger] applications," Saxon explained to Congress. "The flow of such applications . . . reflects decisions on the part of private bankers."[44]

To give national banks an edge in branching, Saxon pursued two paths simultaneously. On the one hand, Saxon sought to change the law itself. From the beginning of his tenure, Saxon promoted legislative changes that would enable national banks to branch even in states which forbid branch banking. His initial proposal was cautious, aimed at enabling national banks to branch within a fixed geographic radius from their primary office (a weaker proposal than that advanced by Marriner Eccles in the 1940s, and before him, Carter Glass in the 1930s). The legislative path was a dead end. Unit bankers organized furiously against Saxon's plans, and they had a well-placed ally to defend their interests. "I wonder how Mr. Saxon plans to get this recommended change past Wright Patman's committee," Senate Banking Chairman A. Willis Robertson wryly observed when Saxon introduced the plan. As Patman explained to Saxon during hearings in 1963, the Texas Congressman had been in the House when they rejected Glass's branching proposals in 1933, and his committee would not revisit that decision.[45]

Blocked in Congress, Saxon focused on approving national bank branch applications that stretched—and as courts often determined, exceeded—the limits of state law. In Louisiana, which did not permit branching across parish lines, Saxon advised a national bank to create a holding company and to branch, in effect, through affiliate banks. North Dakota allowed state-chartered banks to operate limited-service branches. Saxon argued that state rules could govern national bank branch locations but not their functions. Because North Dakota allowed limited-service state branches, Saxon could allow full-service national branches. In Florida, Saxon authorized the First National Bank of Plant City to operate a full-service branch in the form of an armored car ("mobile drive-in") that could deliver banking services outside city limits. In Utah, the state effectively prohibited de novo branching but allowed banks to branch via merger. Saxon decided this was tantamount to authorizing branching, full stop, and he authorized two national banks to open de novo branches in 1964. When a federal judge decided a challenge to this last decision in Saxon's favor, the reaction was volcanic. "If national banks have this advantage," Jeff Burnett, head of the Arkansas Bankers Association, argued, "state banks all over the country will start to nationalize and it will be the end of the dual banking system."[46]

Over his term as Comptroller, Saxon fought many battles to reformulate the risk management divide between public and private in American banking. No battle was as fierce as the opposition from state bankers—not from other regulators, not from politicians. At the annual convention of the

American Bankers Association in 1963, an association that included both state and national bankers, the usually mild-mannered David Rockefeller, president of the largest state bank, the Chase Manhattan, urged "Mr. Saxon to review and revise his policy of non-coordination" with anyone who opposed him "and to substitute patience and persuasion for the use of outright power." Rockefeller attacked Saxon on all fronts. He attacked the Comptroller's proposals to liberalize national banks' lending powers. He attacked Saxon's rulings on municipal revenue bonds. And he especially attacked Saxon's proposals to enable national bank branching in contravention of state law. Rockefeller was sympathetic to Saxon's ambition "to provide flexibility," but he insisted that pursuing that flexibility by giving national banks specific and distinct advantages over state banks would "inevitably sound the death knell for dual banking."[47]

Saxon, undeterred, wanted not simply to start a debate about how government might push for greater innovation in banking. He wanted to see that greater innovation. For that reason, he largely agreed with the critique of state bankers like Rockefeller. He wanted the states—and through them, politically, the influential state bankers—completely out of the business of regulating national banks. If state banks could not compete, so be it.

For all his failures, Saxon's most important success came through Rockefeller and Chase Manhattan. Just eighteen months after Rockefeller's blistering defense of the dual banking system, Chase Manhattan switched back to a national charter, apparently able to overcome earlier legal concerns about the intricate provisions of the 1799 Manhattan Company charter. Within Chase, executives, with Rockefeller as a major participant, had debated the charter shift nearly as soon as Saxon began infusing flexibility into the New Deal bank regulatory system. Eventually, Chase executives could not shake the sense that Saxon had permanently altered the calculus of banking. The "basic advantage," Chase's former chairman and still board member George Champion wrote in 1965, "of a national charter is that it will permit the Bank greater flexibility in its operations, including the establishment of new services which cannot be carried out effectively under a state bank." This was, in summary, Saxon's entire purpose, one publicly acknowledged by Chase bankers, though without attribution. "It was embarrassing," one Chase official told *Businessweek*, "not to be able to offer the same [services] as leading national banks." Despite Rockefeller's recent and bitter critique, Saxon did not hold a grudge: "It's an old friend coming home." No other change during his tenure functioned as a stronger endorsement of his vision.[48]

Disputes between the states and the national banking system would get fiercer in the years ahead, including as future Comptrollers aggressively supported litigation to preempt state laws that sought to regulate national banks. Saxon was doing something subtly different: He was not only a proud partisan of the national banks, but he wanted to adopt a more aggressive risk tolerance through much more permissive supervisory decision-making. State banks would complain that his successes made them irrelevant. They would also, first quietly then quickly, follow suit.

The Failure of San Francisco National Bank and the Rise of Preventative Supervision

Saxon's supervisory ethos—to push risk-taking into private hands and away from rigid public control—always implied that there would be failure, as he anticipated in his fights with the Fed over "speculative" financial risk-taking. What Saxon did not anticipate was the near total public intolerance for bank failure. He would learn it in 1964, when the collapse of the San Francisco National Bank made it the largest bank failure since the Great Depression. That collapse was an axiomatic bank failure: It failed in the way that all banks fail—its liabilities outstripped its assets—while also failing in ways that were colorfully specific to its unique cast of characters. Unlike other major bank failures, however, this one also helped trigger a major overhaul in the legislative architecture of bank supervision.[49]

The story begins with Donald C. Silverthorne, the "portly" bank president who "cut an extraordinarily affluent figure in San Francisco financial circles," riding in a Rolls-Royce, collecting an estimated $800,000 in jewelry, and frequenting the Las Vegas gambling tables where he would lose extraordinary sums. Silverthorne had spent decades at the Bank of America, enough time to learn the arts and sciences of customer recruitment from A. P. Giannini himself. But Silverthorne was not content to stay in the great California banker's shadow. As Saxon opened the gates for new charters, Silverthorne stormed them and opened the San Francisco National Bank in June of 1962.[50]

Silverthorne would ultimately stand accused of a wide variety of malfeasance after his bank failed in January 1965, but it was a relatively garden-variety bank fraud that made Silverthorne's career such a critical juncture for the history of bank supervision. The basics of the fraud, laid out in the criminal prosecution that followed, were as follows: Silverthorne would grant loans to uncreditworthy borrowers from the San Francisco National Bank, with the requirement that the borrowed funds remain in the bank. Silver-thorne would separately require borrowers to write checks to him and an associate, which Silverthorne deemed bank fees, for the privilege of these accounts. He and his associate would then cash these "fee" checks at another bank. Silverthorne's borrowers tended to be friends whose business prospects were poor and who could not otherwise secure necessary loans. For a price—an exorbitant rate and a willingness to engage in bank fraud—Silverthorne would be their banker.[51]

One transaction illustrates the scheme. In March 1964, a customer—who we'll leave unnamed—applied to the bank for two loans in the amounts of $275,000 each. Silverthorne advised the customer that the loans would only be granted after "a fee or point charge of $100,000." The customer delivered a check payable to Silverthorne's associate, who then paid $70,000 to Silver-thorne. Silverthorne deposited the money into an account at a separate bank, causing San Francisco National "to lose custody and control" of the funds the government argued should never have been loaned in the first place. While somewhat convoluted, there was nothing particularly exotic about this fraud. These were just kickbacks that Silverthorne had engineered and attempted to obscure.[52]

Silverthorne's frauds became a major concern for bank supervisors in early 1964. In May, Victor Del Tredici, a seasoned bank examiner at the OCC, wrote a scathing examination report outlining the clear flaws of risk management that Silverthorne's risky and fraudulent approach introduced, with a special focus on Silverthorne' self-dealing and his efforts to obscure the transactions. Tredici wrote a letter to the U.S. Attorney's office and included it in the exami-nation report he shipped to the Comptroller's DC headquarters. Tredici then waited for something to happen. As Tredici later told Congress, Saxon shelved the report, failing to share it with other agencies or to act on it himself. Saxon never explained why.[53]

The examination report sat in the proverbial—maybe literal—drawer for seven months. In the days before the Comptroller finally triggered the bank's liquidation, Silverthorne sought and received a $1.5 million lifeline from the Federal Reserve Bank of San Francisco's discount window. It appears that the Reserve Bank never received word of the Comptroller's major supervisory concerns when determining whether the loan was an appropriate credit risk. This may have resulted, in part, because Saxon, ever the institutional pugilist, had dramatically raised the fees he charged other supervisory agencies for copies of national bank examiners' reports.[54]

The congressional hearings that followed created a public frenzy. Silverthorne appeared personally, giving testimony that was confessional, confrontational, accusatory, and incriminating. He claimed his bank was "run out of business" because other banks objected to his competition, denying any personal wrongdoing. He all but confessed to bribing bank examiners in one breath—"I don't give liquor by the bottle," he bragged, "I give it by the case"—and then in another accused them of stealing his liquor and cuff links (he had in fact given Saxon $125 cuff links that the latter returned with chagrin).[55]

Shortly after the congressional hearings that put Silverthorne on the front pages of the nation's newspapers, the U.S. Attorney in San Francisco indicted him for bank fraud. After two appeals, he was sentenced to eight years in prison. By that time, the premises of the bank's downtown San Francisco branch had been converted into a bar offering drinks such as the Preferred Issue ("a champagne cocktail priced at 50 cents plus 100% interest") or the Depositor's Downfall (brandy + vermouth + crème-de-menthe)."[56]

If Silverthorne had been less of a cartoon villain, the headlines for the ensuing congressional hearings might well have focused on the sustained congressional interrogation of Saxon's policies, and behind them, his entire banking philosophy. Saxon, as ever, stood ready to defend his record. He had never promised a system without bank failure; indeed, he had promised the opposite. Members of Congress showed little patience for this view. The San Francisco National Bank failure made visible, in ways Saxon's previous clashes had not, the extent to which the FDIC's insurance ethos still infused—and perhaps suffused—political understandings of what bank supervision was meant to accomplish. Saxon's push for liberalization and vitality could only proceed with a credible insurance backstop. When failure reemerged as a live concern, tolerance for Saxon's efforts to push more risk into the private sector crumbled. Wasn't it the case, asked John L. McClellan, the powerful Arkansas Senator and chairman of the subcommittee on investigations, that banks were so closely supervised as "to eliminate many of the risks that other free enterprise businesses are free to take?"[57]

With all the humility he could muster, Saxon explained that pushing risk into the private sector was always going to invite the potential for failure. "So far," he insisted, only "one bank that we have approved has failed." More could follow. "I don't know whether through misjudgment, embezzlement, dishonesty, that we might not have one or more in the future." For Saxon, the costs of these failures—Silverthorne's antics included—were the lesser potential cost. "The question in my mind," he said to his congressional critics, "is what price the Government, the country, is willing to pay to exclude new entry into the banking business. We can close the business forever, as I would see it, to bar entry, and thereby lose the driving force, initiative, and innovation that comes from a good new entry." Put another way, a banking system can be either over- or under-inclusive of risk. Should the supervisory system promote risk-taking that would, on the upside, support a vibrant and growing economy and, on the downside, lead to some bank failures? This was what Saxon had favored and tried to create. The alternative was a system with little banking innovation because such innovation would be blocked by skeptical supervisors, politicians, regulators, and even consumers. Saxon argued against the safe alternative. During his tenure, he lost. The San Francisco National failure, and with it the public and political repudiation of bank risk-taking, ended the discussion.[58]

In 1966, Congress enacted legislation in direct response to the San Francisco National failure and several other high-profile national and state bank failures, which—in typical fashion—reacted to perceived supervisory failure by dramatically expanding the authority of federal bank supervisors. The law, the Financial Institutions Supervisory Act of 1966 (FISA), was in essence a repudiation of the Saxon revolution and a further solidification of the FDIC's insurance ethos in bank supervision. Saxon recognized this: His office did not sign on with the other federal agencies when they sent the bill to Congress, and he did not testify in its favor. FISA gave federal supervisors new tools for what they called "preventative supervision," enabling government officials to directly intervene to change banking practices that they deemed "unsafe and unsound." While federal examiners, led by the FDIC, had incorporated management evaluations into their examinations since the New Deal, FISA gave them the power to compel changes in business practices and bank personnel. Instead of Saxon's view that private bank managers should lead by taking on more risk, under the logic of FISA, public officials would set the course of private risk management, holding the wheel and pumping the breaks when necessary.[59]

The sweeping return of the FDIC to predominance in bank supervision in the mid-1960s was somewhat of a surprise. The insurance agency had largely avoided public fights with Saxon during his comptrollership, in part because the FDIC cycled through a string of ineffectual chairmen and in part because Saxon, including during a period when he served as acting chairman of the insurance agency, used his seat on the FDIC board to impede the agency from within. In 1964, Lyndon Johnson appointed Kenneth A. Randall (1964–1965, 1965–1970), a Utah banker, to the board as its Republican member (Randall recalled that it was his support for the McFadden Act that won Johnson over). In 1965, Johnson elevated Randall to the chairmanship. "He wanted me to pick up the ball and run with it," Randall recalled. "He expected sound banks, he didn't want bank failure. We'd had some. He knew there were problems. He indicated again that he knew that there were problems of personality [with Saxon], but that I was to do a job, and he wanted sound banks."[60]

To give the president what he wanted, Randall led a coordinated campaign to secure FISA among the non-Saxon supervisors, including the Federal Home Loan Bank Board (FHLBB) and the Federal Savings and Loan Insurance Corporation (FSLIC), agencies which had gained new prominence with the postwar expansion of the savings and loan industry. Randall specifically sought the power "to order banks under [the FDIC's] supervision to cease and desist from unsafe and unsound practices and violations of law or regulations, and to suspend or remove officers and directors who are found to be engaged in such practices or violations." Encapsulated in the statement were two new tools that congress granted the five (including the FHLBB and FSLIC) supervisory agencies in FISA: supervisory cease and desist orders, which enabled agencies to correct any "unsafe or unsound practice" by ordering banks to change their behavior; and the "removal power," which could be invoked when the supervisor determined that a banker had committed "any violation of law," "engaged or participated in any unsafe or unsound practice," or "engaged in any act, omission, or practice which constitutes a breach of his fiduciary duty." As further evidence of Congress's embrace of the insurance ethos, FISA also included an increase in deposit insurance coverage from $10,000 to $15,000.[61]

In this way, Congress officially weighed in on an important part of the Saxon debates. Saxon wanted to break the vision of public supervision as the outcome of residual risk management. He wanted the private sector to bear those risks and the public sector to guide private enthusiasms. Congress saw it differently. By expanding the supervisors' police power, so to speak, it emphasized the point that had been introduced tentatively in the 1860s and more resoundingly in the New Deal: Bank supervisors, and the public they represented, stopped the buck. They were responsible for the final analysis, when all else had failed. The liquidation of banks like San Francisco National and the imprisonment of bankers like Silverthorne absorbed some of that risk, but only some. The supervisors were in charge of the rest.

Conclusion

On November 15, 1966, the James J. Saxon era of the Comptroller of the Currency ended. Saxon suggested he would have preferred to stay the course, to finish his revolution in bank supervision—forward looking, progressive, non-discriminatory, and an impetus to private enterprise. In making his case, he even offered supervision and the national banking system as the appropriate adjutant to the Great Society and its War on Poverty. In one of his parting shots, he condemned the static approach to supervision that preceded his rise and seemed to outflank him at every turn. "Enclaves of monopoly, and stagnant, unprogressive banks should not . . . be safeguarded," he said after Johnson became president. But Johnson had other plans, and his financial advisers had grown weary of Saxon's warring spirit. As one New York banker summarized: "I think the President realizes that we all need some time to digest what Mr. Saxon has done to us."[62]

Not everyone agreed. In Saxon's papers at the Kennedy Library, there are scores of letters praising his time in office, heralding his efforts to issue new charters, revitalize bank competition, and improve the vitality of the banking system (of course, Saxon deposited these papers; we don't have the letters he might have received from state bankers or FDIC board members who viewed him quite differently). "While your term in office has of course provoked some controversy," wrote one admirer, "you have revitalized this important office with progressive ideas and a sound approach to the supervisory function" of national banking. "The Comptroller's office will never be the same again," wrote a national banker. "Through your efforts the focus of thinking about banking has been enormously enlarged." Another "found it difficult to contain his emotions" at the announcement of Saxon's resignation. A Texas banker, who had received a charter from Saxon, went on in great detail about the benefits to his community that Saxon's push for competition and liberalized banking brought: "Anyone who believes that good competition is not necessary or needed in banking, in a community, is badly mistaken, and it is only from people with a backward trend of thought and those who do not desire progress, in my opinion, who have made the greatest protests and have found dissatisfaction in the progressive manner in which you have handled the job of Comptroller of the Currency."[63]

After his resignation, Saxon returned to the Midwest to accept the presidency of a mid-tier Indiana bank, but he only lasted a few years in the role. His death in 1980 was noticed in the newspapers, but barely. Historians rarely mention him when they assess the era. Of those that do, he is often only granted a brief mention, such as a quick dismissal of his policies and rulings as "ultimately reversed by court decisions." Saxon did lose most of his court battles, but he also built a foundation for a vision of bank risk-taking that was completed by others decades later. By the 1990s, Congress finally accepted Saxon's invitation and dismantled the last vestiges of unit and branch banking restrictions. The lead-up to the 2008 financial crisis was an era of pushing private risk-taking that Saxon would likely have cheered. Even in the efforts thereafter, while public ownership of residual risk has become the spirit and letter of the law, the same debates about the appropriate balance between private-sector risk-taking and public-sector preferences for stability dominate bank policy decisions in nearly every corner where they are discussed and debated.[64]

Interlude: Bunco

IN THE GILDED AGE, bank supervisors did not quite know what to do with fraud. Initially, Comptroller of the Currency Hugh McCulloch (1863–1865) urged Congress to legislate "that the failure of a national bank be declared prima facie fraudulent." Afterall, how could a bank fail except through the fraudulence of its officers and directors? In time, however, bank supervision flew the white flag in protecting banks and their stakeholders from fraudulent behavior. "It is not to be supposed that the short time usually spent in the examination of a national bank will be sufficient in all cases, to detect bad management or defalcations," Comptroller John Jay Knox Jr. (1872–1884) admitted in 1873, declining to suppose what his predecessors had earlier heralded as a key benefit of bank supervision.[1]

By the 1960s, that ambivalence had mostly disappeared in a curious way. Bank supervisors had declared victory against those bankers who, through fraudulence, would threaten their stakeholders and the entire banking system. In the early postwar years, the FDIC gained a reputation for exactness and criminal referrals that populated the federal penitentiary in Terre Haute, Indiana with an entire cadre of convicted banker-embezzlers. Some of the FDIC's "more humorous-minded staff" called the group "the FDIC Club." The club included an Indiana banker who cashed $200,000 in fake checks for his friends "just to be a good fellow." Another, a banker from New York, stole $110,000 from his bank "to buy hats." Some bought alfalfa farms, some bought sewer pipes, some bought apple orchards, and some bought lakeside cottages in Wisconsin. But when the bank supervisors (at the FDIC and elsewhere) discovered these excesses, the fact that these funds were now backstopped by the federal government made an enormous difference. Where previous examiners bemoaned their inability to track fraud through supervision, the transformation of "defalcation" to the federal crime of bank fraud meant that these con artists were no longer a concern for the county sheriff. They were for the Feds.[2]

The pursuit of such banker-fraudsters remained a core commitment into the 1960s and 1970s. In one case from Cartersville, Georgia, a banker named Lamar Hill became a pillar of the community by helping "people get loans they could not get from others." Hill, a former bank examiner himself, became bank president in the 12,000-person town and quickly turned to a life of "high living and hard drinking," with "the posh outsized house, the big car, the gambling jaunts to Las Vegas and the Bahamas" that, in retrospect, might have flagged more concern. "The gambling may not have been illegal," said one banking expert, "but it goes with banking about like whoring goes with preaching. Sooner or later a bank president who is a heavy gambler is going to get into a snit and go where the money's easy to get—and that's the till." In time, Hill embezzled $4.7 million, a fact only discovered—despite his colorful and well-traveled reputation—when an examiner-in-training refused to go along with an account he could not reconcile. "It was just a fluke," the student's supervisor later said. "An old-time examiner might have just let it pass; he caught it because he was young and inexperienced."[3]

This focus on fraud, such as it was, had an important limitation: Bank examiners were focused on frauds that could threaten the solvency of banks, not the solvency of individual bank customers. Fraud against consumers by third parties was outside their responsibility. Bank supervisors knew this division of authority could pose problems. "Banks have always been plagued with external and internal crimes," the OCC noted in 1974. "In the days gone by, it seemed the classic crimes were bank robberies and embezzlements." But "in the 60s, confidence men were able to get into the banks through fraudulent loan schemes," for example, by creating banking fronts in the Caribbean and on the Isle of Guernsey, and by securing loans from U.S. banks against "worthless certificates of deposit." In response to these schemes, bank supervisors tried to warn bankers but had few other answers than to make referrals to other agencies.[4]

Such referrals make good sense: Bank examiners were, obviously, there to examine banks, not to enforce criminal laws against third parties (especially on Guernsey). One of the key schemes, however, profited from the sterling reputation that bank examiners enjoyed in the public imagination. The scheme—variously called the "bank examiner game," the "bank examiner swindle," or the examiner bunco scheme—worked like this: A victim—often an elderly woman, targeted through the phone book with "an old-fashioned name, such as Lizzie or Bessie"—receives a phone call from someone posing as a "bank examiner" who is "seeking assistance in catching a bank teller that is suspected of being dishonest." The fake examiner's lie triggered both a sense of duty to report such fraud and a promise of reward. The "examiner" accompanied the victim to the bank, directed the victim to "the so-called dishonest teller," and asked the victim to make a "sizeable withdrawal." The examiner received the money, thanked the victim for their service, and disappeared. The victims often did not report the crimes until hours or days later, if they reported them at all.[5]

The scheme was remarkably successful. A Baltimore woman lost $1,800 in 1968. Two women in the Los Angeles area lost $8,000 in 1969. And in what was likely the largest such fraud, a wealthy woman from the Pacific Heights neighborhood of San Francisco was robbed of almost $700,000 in bonds and securities from her safety deposit box.[6]

And these are just the examples that were documented. Police officials at the time estimated that only one in five such thefts were reported, because the usually elderly victims failed to call authorities. "Even if they discover they've been taken [they] are often too embarrassed to report it." The rare report that included an arrest corroborated these kinds of figures: Fifteen victims were taken in by a former police officer perpetrating the scam, but only three were identified.[7]

Law enforcement officers, not bank examiners, led the way to preempt these swindlers. One patrolman from Chicago, 29-year-old James Kujawa, started an education program that sought to engage senior citizens about the bank examiner game, among other crimes and inconveniences. A film he created called "The Bunco Boys" even dramatized the "examiners" in action. Police efforts also included tough talk directed at both con artists and the victims themselves. Pittsburgh detectives characterized some swindlers as "con men and gypsies" who "appear to be likeable and humorous" and prey on the "not too well educated" who are eager to make a quick buck. "It's [victims'] desire to get something for nothing that sets them up as targets," Pittsburgh police inspector John Nee told journalists. "An honest man who knows you can't get something for nothing isn't susceptible to con games."[8]

It is difficult to determine exactly where the bank examiner bunco originated. Some experts thought it was a Canadian import from the mid-1960s. We have found one example that appears to be more spontaneous than orchestrated in postwar Japan, when a 19-year-old private first class from West Virginia walked away with ¥580,000 ($38,000) while posing as an Army bank examiner. He instructed compliant but shocked bankers in Yokohama that the transfer was required as part of the examination (he was caught the next day). The popularity of—or at least public reporting on—such flimflam artists impersonating bank examiners did not begin in earnest until the late 1960s.[9]

The prominence of this swindle was large enough that it generated major news coverage, including a page one article in the *New York Times* in 1976 that described a successful run of the scam taking in $400,000. That coverage, in turn, spread to copycat swindlers, including one whose case was published in a medical journal seeking to better understand lithium carbonate as a treatment of what was then called manic depression, now bipolar disorder. In that case, a manic reader of the *Times* saw the article and immediately sought to undertake the scam himself. Unfortunately for him, his target was the spouse of an FBI agent: he was promptly arrested.[10]

What the fake bank examiners understood was just how much examiner reputations for probity and rectitude meant to the millions of bank customers who would never in the usual course have anything to do with bank examiners. Their willingness to accede to the fake government officials was not a function of their greed—or at least not always (occasionally, the fake examiner would hand over a small amount of the victim's own cash as a reward before absconding with the rest). The success of the bank examiner swindle is best explained as a function of the public trust in the edifice of public-private risk management. For the generation that had heard Franklin Roosevelt explain the finer points of bank examination in his first fireside chat in 1933, confidence in bank examiners came naturally. They had seen films that trumpeted—even in comedic exaggeration—the incorruptible rectitude of bank examiners. And as a simple point in fact, until the mid-1970s, bank failures, through fraud or otherwise, had effectively ceased. What the fake examiners understood, but the real examiners had gradually forgotten, was that one of the key constituencies for that rectitude was not simply the bank itself, not simply the safety and soundness of these institutions, but the customer-depositors who relied on that rectitude to ensure the safety and soundness of their own deposits—and more broadly their safety and protection in the financial marketplace. It was a hole in the examiner mentality that consumer advocates and Congress would attempt to fill.[11]

9

The Expansion of Residual Risk

BANK SUPERVISION FOR
ANTIDISCRIMINATION, CONSUMER
PROTECTION, AND COMMUNITY
REINVESTMENT

JAMES SAXON'S attempts to turn the page on the New Deal ideologies of bank supervision failed to persuade most of his contemporaries—besides the national bankers, that is. However, shortly after Saxon's retirement, Congress carried forth a different divergence from the New Deal Order in a direction that Saxon had suggested was the next frontier for bank supervision: social policy. That so enthusiastic a bank defender as Saxon would also be in favor of broadening bank responsibilities in other areas, thereby equipping supervisors with those responsibilities too, is in surprising tension with the New Deal vision of bank supervision. That vision was anchored in preserving the safety and soundness of the financial system, sometimes at the cost of vitality and venturesome lending in the economy. This was Saxon's primary critique of that ecosystem. That critique, however, was about pushing supervisors away from managing the frontline *financial* risk of bank lending in order to let banks handle those tasks themselves.

But as Congress navigated the rising currents of the 1960s social movements and the waves of political change they drove forth, new expectations rose for the role of supervisors in managing residual *political risk*. This subtle shift put bank supervisors in a position that differed markedly from what had come before. It manifested itself in three important changes. First, civil rights and consumer groups demanded that federal banking officials ensure that minority borrowers enjoyed fair and equal access to the financial services, especially home mortgages, that had enabled their White counterparts to build wealth in the postwar era. Second, consumer groups called for supervisors to police a safe and transparent marketplace in consumer financial services for all bank clients, no matter their place in the economy. And third, community leaders pushed Congress to use bank supervision to incentivize banks to reinvest in their communities, after years of highly racialized redlining that bank supervisors had defended in the name of safety and soundness.

Through waves of legislation, from the Fair Housing and Truth-in-Lending Acts in 1968 through to the Equal Credit Opportunity Act of 1974 and the Community Reinvestment Act in 1977, Congress layered new responsibilities for antidiscrimination, consumer protection, and community reinvestment onto the federal supervisory agencies. These new supervisory purposes came with, Congress expected, a new supervisory posture: If safety and soundness was about identifying past problems and correcting them for future risk management, bank supervision should also be about rooting out past injustices and penalizing them through present enforcement.

Federal supervisors recognized these postures as reflecting a tension that could, at times, function at cross-purposes. Given these tensions and perhaps for other reasons, in each case the bank regulators argued against the expansion of their authority into these domains and the division of their attention away from prudential supervision—that is, supervising banks in the name of defending their safety and soundness. They lobbied against them in Congress and, once they became law, incorporated them into supervisory practice with deliberate sluggishness. "Remember that the historical context in which we have to view this, is that these agencies have come kicking and screaming into this dark night," explained a lawyer, whom the Federal Reserve hired to evaluate its consumer protection and antidiscrimination programs in 1978, just as Congress had expanded those programs. "I have this mental image of a Disney character, a grizzly bear clinging to a tree, being pulled away paw by paw very reluctantly." In a familiar pattern, as long as civil rights and consumer groups enjoyed political momentum, Congress responded to supervisory resistance to racial and consumer enforcement by enacting more laws that gave supervisors more tools. How the supervisors would use those tools remained up to the supervisors to decide.[1]

Racial Risk Management

Black Americans and other minority groups have long been excluded from participation in U.S. banking markets. People of color were seldom welcome customers in most financial institutions, which were almost uniformly owned and managed by White elites. Although the available evidence is sparse, federal supervisors appear to have helped maintain the financial color line in the years before the 1960s civil rights victories. From a strictly risk management perspective, this outcome followed a supervisory logic that was widely embraced, its moral defects notwithstanding. The endemic racism in American society created racial income and wealth gaps that persisted long after emancipation. As a result, minority borrowers had lower and less stable incomes than Whites, more difficulty repaying loans, and were thus more likely to default. From that perspective, bank supervisors engaged in collaborative risk management that pushed for bank decisions that reinforced these tendencies, making them worse.[2]

This racialized imposition of risk management was not simply passive, with examiners as complicit bystanders to the risk assessments made by racist bankers. In seeking to minimize financial risk, some federal examiners discouraged lending to minority borrowers. "A large amount of loans are to negro farmers," an examiner wrote in April 1920, critiquing a small southern bank. "The negro as a rule is poor pay and does not try to accumulate money to get ahead." The examiner repeated these criticisms at the next examination. Lending to Blacks was bad for business and would endanger the safety and soundness of the bank.[3]

The examiner's views, in this case, appear to reflect the wider culture of the Comptroller's office, at least in the 1910s and 1920s. Progressive president Woodrow Wilson embraced pseudo-scientific ideas about the necessity of racial segregation, and his Comptroller of the Currency, Virginia railroad magnate John Skelton Williams (1914–1921), was, as we have seen, a passionate advocate of racial exclusion policies. Williams, who one historian called an "especially steadfast and exuberant discriminator," served as Assistant Secretary of the Treasury for a year before assuming the comptrollership. In the former capacity, he mandated the segregation of Black and White Treasury Department employees, who had formerly worked side by side. Williams also promoted white supremacy in his public statements. Speaking to a group of Maryland bankers in June 1913, Williams adopted the coded idiom of purity and decay common to segregation's promotors. He urged the bankers to "aid in . . . the work of keeping our standards high, our finance clean, our business methods honest; to make sure that we shall not permit internal decay and corruption to sap away the life of our Republic." Williams's overt racism placed him on the leading edge of the hardening of racial barriers in the so-called Progressive Era.[4]

The thrust of national economic policy carried a heavily racialized inflection into and through much of the New Deal. Building on existing patterns of exclusion, racial risk management became explicit federal policy through the New Deal's housing programs. Around the turn of the century, Black migration from the southern countryside into northern and southern cities increased. White homeowners, city planners, and real estate professionals collectively promoted segregation as the way preserve order and property values, deliberately isolating Black Americans to "marginalize them socially, economically, and politically." During the New Deal, Roosevelt's administration sought to channel bank credit into the housing market by insuring mortgages that met specific quality standards. The Federal Housing Administration, created by Congress in 1934, relied on the same local elites who had imposed Progressive Era segregation to manage FHA mortgage programs. "The watchwords" of these public-private efforts, wrote Marriner S. Eccles, who helped design the policy, were "profits [and] decentralization." These supervision-adjacent modalities of economic policy were not aimed at remedying wrongs or providing equal access to government services. They were to provide economic opportunities for community elites to manage as they saw fit.[5]

Federal standards for insuring mortgages, in turn, explicitly embraced racial exclusion. "If a neighborhood is to retain stability, it is necessary that properties shall continue to be occupied by the same social and racial classes," explained the FHA's 1938 underwriting manual. "A change in social or racial occupancy generally contributes to instability and a decline in values."[6]

In this way, federal policymakers, as insurers, embraced redlining and racially restrictive deed covenants to maintain segregation, and with segregation, higher property values in all-White neighborhoods. After World War II, FHA and Veterans Administration (VA) lending programs funneled bank credit toward safe, all-White suburbs.[7]

Bank examiners encouraged these investments, seeing in them the solution to several bank supervisory and bank risk management problems. Federally insured loans provided guaranteed bank profits, encouraging bankers to lend in support of homebuilding and related activities, thus driving development and economic growth. In their onsite examinations, supervisors closely monitored banks' participation in these programs. That examiners promoted FHA and VA lending should not be surprising; federally subsidized mortgages were a cornerstone of New Deal economic and social policy, which extended forward into the era of booming postwar growth. In doing so, however, supervisors reinforced the financial color line, encouraging federally subsidized lending to White suburban borrowers, who in turn benefited from home price appreciation. Meanwhile, communities of color—marked out as risky, "inharmonious," and uninsurable—lacked access to mortgage finance.[8]

The implicit racial policy baked into federally backed mortgage lending paired with consistent examiner criticism of Black-owned banks. After the Bank Holiday of 1933, for example, two struggling Black-owned Washington, DC, banks merged to become the Industrial Bank of Washington. From that point forward, FDIC examiner reports read today as condescending, dismissive, and racially motivated. Examiners persistently criticized bank management, which one examiner in 1947 described as "sincere, but inept." Officials likewise looked down on the bank's clientele. The "bank has a generally undesirable class of customers," an FDIC examiner observed in 1952, while another commented in 1958 that "many of the customers who gravitate here are those who perhaps would not be desirable elsewhere."[9]

Examiners evaluated other Black-owned banks in similar fashion, so much so that by the late 1950s, examiners could generalize: The "problems" plaguing the Citizen's Trust Company of Atlanta were "those found in other Negro banks," one examiner wrote. In the postwar years, the overwhelming majority of Black-owned banks were placed on the FDIC's special examination list, subjecting them to heightened federal scrutiny.[10]

Persistent negative evaluations of Black-owned banks may have reflected the racial biases of federal bank examiners, but there was more at work here than can be attributed to personal examiner animus. The risks associated with Black banks reflected deeper systems of segregation and racial exclusion that limited the ability of Black banks to recruit talented managers and to find profitable lending opportunities. As Federal Reserve Governor Andrew F. Brimmer (1966–1974)—the Fed's first Black governor and a champion of racial financial inclusion during his public life—noted in a 1970 evaluation of Black bank performance, these firms earned lower profits and suffered much higher loan loss rates than White-owned banks, "experience [that] is intimately related to the inherent risk of doing business in the urban ghetto."[11]

Whether the supervisory policies were explicitly racist, as many were, or merely implicitly so, the result was generally the same. Even in the absence of racial animus, the logic of safety and soundness, imposed on top of the structural racism of American society, meant that denying capital to struggling communities not only made sense but followed perforce. The public-private partnership of bank supervisory management of financial risk exacerbated preexisting racial and social divides. The logic of prudential supervision that focused on the safety and soundness of banks and their services made pushing banks to accept deposits from minority and low-income customers—thus expanding banks' funding bases—easy to justify; investing in those same communities, by this logic, was much harder.

Vectors of Civil Rights Enforcement

As liberal Democrats embraced the civil rights movement in the mid-1960s, especially through and after the Civil Rights and Voting Rights Acts of 1964 and 1965, bank supervisory agencies took only tentative steps to promote a more inclusive bank supervision. In 1963, the Comptroller of the Currency hired Howard Law School graduate Roland W. Burris, and assigned him as a trust examiner based out of the Chicago office. Burris was the first Black examiner in the Comptroller's one-hundred-year history, something that came as a surprise to him: "I did not know at the time that there were no black examiners in America." In his first examination, Burris discovered that his federal authority was no shield against racial prejudice. Having arrived early to the Livestock National Bank and Trust Company on Chicago's Southside, one of the bank's officers let Burris in. "There were some seats where they sat customers," Burris remembered, and the officer told him, "'listen boy, you sit down right here until the examiners come.'" When Burris left the Comptroller's office to take a job at Continental Illinois National Bank, he was replaced in Chicago by a Howard Law School classmate, ensuring continuity for the nation's sole Black bank examiner.[12]

Other supervisory agencies were likewise cautious in their advocacy for civil rights. Following the enactment of the Civil Rights Act of 1964, which prohibited racial discrimination in employment and in federal assistance programs, the Federal Reserve pursued tepid internal compliance in its capacity as an employer, while seeking to narrowly tailor its external responsibilities as a bank supervisor. The Federal Reserve System "faithfully complies with the letter and spirit" of the Civil Rights Act in its own operations, the Board insisted in June 1965. In a concurrent memo, the Board argued that the Reserve Banks' discount and other operations did not qualify as "financial assistance," as defined by the Civil Rights Act's rules prohibiting discrimination in federal programs, and the Reserve Banks were thus free to operate according to their former safety and soundness logics, as racially exclusionary as those logics were.[13]

Indeed, the Board went further in its efforts to narrowly construe its obligations to protect civil rights within the banking industry: Its Wilsonian, quasifederalized structure meant that the Federal Reserve Banks, formally private institutions, were precluded from statutory responsibilities for the law. In response to allegations that the Alabama Exchange Bank in Tuskegee, Alabama, was blatantly violating the Act's equal employment provisions, the Board asserted that the "Reserve Banks clearly have no legal authority or responsibility to enforce or police the provisions of Title VII of the law."[14]

Lyndon Johnson had no patience for such reluctance. On September 24, 1965, Johnson issued Executive Order 11246, which required federal contractors to develop and implement affirmative action policies. This executive order was the birth of the federal government's affirmative action programs. It meant that federal contractors could no longer simply refrain from outright racial discrimination; they needed to demonstrate positive, affirmative efforts to recruit and employ underrepresented groups.[15]

Johnson's order also charged federal agencies working with contractors to ensure that the affirmative action provisions were followed. Over the next few years, the Treasury Department increased the scope of the order as it applied to banks contracting with the federal government—first to banks that held federal deposits, then to banks that served as paying agents on U.S. savings bonds, and finally covering all banks with fifty or more employees. Speaking at the American Bankers Association conference in September 1967, Assistant Treasury Secretary Robert A. Wallace conveyed the administration's policy bluntly: Bankers needed to take "'positive action' to hire Negroes in order to keep deposits of federal money."[16]

These efforts to promote diversity through hiring operated via a highly compliance-oriented form of supervision that was unusual under the reigning collaborative prudential supervisory regime. It also did not initially go through the supervisory agencies themselves. From 1965 to early 1971, the small Office of Federal Contract Compliance worked with the Treasury to undertake examinations of the department's bank contractors. Resource limitations, however, meant they were "unable to visit the majority of . . . banks." To expand the program's reach, the Treasury Department eventually convinced the Comptroller and the FDIC to incorporate equal opportunity compliance into regular bank examinations. The supervisors were now in the position of examining not only the inchoate risks to banks and the U.S. financial system, but also specific bank compliance with federal civil rights laws.[17]

Bank employment offered an avenue for improving economic outcomes for minority employees, but civil rights advocates were more eager to secure bank lending in minority communities. While many White families had built housing wealth through low-cost, federally insured mortgage programs, the deep legacies of redlining and racial exclusion had left minority communities without access to similar advantages. The 1964 and 1965 civil rights legislation focused on equality of access and political participation through mechanisms of antidiscrimination, without addressing financial exclusion. Congress, for example, omitted FHA and VA insurance from coverage under the Civil Rights Act of 1964.[18]

Black Americans increasingly demanded economic equality as the necessary pair to civil equality, which included access to credit. The year 1967 marked a turning point, as that year's "long, hot summer" of inner-city protests grew fiercer by the day. The multiple failures of federal housing policy and private banks were major factors, leading to consensus that housing needed to be addressed. This tumult prompted two influential government reports—the Kerner Commission and the President's Committee on Urban Housing—about the state of housing and, relatedly, the state of housing finance in the United States. These reports, though independent, reached similar conclusions: The social ills that plagued inner-city America could be traced in substantial part to residential segregation. In the ringing words of the introduction to the Kerner Commission's report: "What white Americans have never fully understood—but what the Negro can never forget—is that white society is deeply implicated in the ghetto. White institutions created it, white institutions maintain it, and white society condones it."[19]

In congressional hearings, civil rights groups, like the National Committee Against Discrimination in Housing, focused specific attention on the complicity of bank supervisors in maintaining the financial color line. "Nearly everything the Government touches turns to segregation, and the Government touches nearly everything." These activists highlighted the Federal Housing Administration's *Underwriting Manual*, which recommended restrictive covenants to separate "inharmonious racial groups." Activists also singled out supervisory agencies for failing "to promote among their member lending and financing institutions affirmative programs to eliminate discriminatory policies and practices."[20]

Congress took action through the Civil Rights Act of 1968, which included within it the Fair Housing Act. Congress's ambitions were grand: "It is the policy of the United States to provide, within constitutional limitations, for fair housing throughout the United States." The enforcement mechanisms, however, had been weakened through political compromise designed to secure the votes of increasingly reluctant Republican lawmakers. The Department of Housing and Urban Development (HUD) had no tools to compel compliance with the Housing Act's provisions. The Department of Justice, meanwhile, could only bring suit if there was "a pattern or practice" of discrimination. In both cases, these were antidiscrimination statutes, not bank supervisory ones. That meant that they were focused on policing violations of law rather than shaping bank behavior prior to such violations.[21]

HUD, recognizing that it stood at a profound information disadvantage, tasked bank supervisory agencies with ensuring compliance with the Act's antidiscriminatory provisions. The supervisory agencies in turn made banks and examiners aware of the new rules and relied on examiners to monitor compliance, under their own discretion, through their usual examination processes. In April 1969, the FDIC mailed out more than 22,000 copies of the Civil Rights Act of 1968 to all insured banks and included a letter about FDIC compliance plans to 7,855 insured non-Fed member banks, 1,650 FDIC examiners, and 52 state supervisory officials. "It is expected," FDIC Chairman K. A. Randall (1965–1970) wrote, "that all State nonmember insured banks will comply with the letter and spirit of this Federal law. The Corporation's examiners have been instructed to include in their reports any apparent violations of this Act disclosed during the course of any examination." In May, the Federal Reserve Banks, in an apparently coordinated effort, sent letters with nearly identical language to state member banks in their districts.[22]

There is little evidence that bank examiners did anything other than circulate these letters, leaving compliance up to the individual banks to handle. This policy of non-engagement was also consistent with the Nixon administration's lukewarm support for civil rights enforcement. Instead, supervisory officials relied on the 1968 Act's flimsy enforcement mechanisms to shield them from responsibility. The law authorized HUD to act only in response to consumer complaints, and the supervisory agencies, which intentionally made themselves invisible to the public, received very few complaints.

Give the complaint-oriented approach, the agencies manufactured a catch-22: Only public complaints could trigger investigations verifying noncompliance; but the bank supervisors did not open themselves to have much contact, if any, with the public; then, having heard no complaints, they could state that they knew of no discriminatory practices within the banks they supervised. "The Board does not know of any specific cases of discrimination, nor does it know of any specific institutions whose practices indicate discriminatory loan practices," the Fed wrote in response to a 1971 House Judiciary Committee inquiry into the experience of Housing Act enforcement. The Comptroller provided a nearly identical response. FDIC Chairman Frank Willie (1970–1976) was at least willing to concede space to doubt: "The Corporation is not aware of any bank practicing racial discrimination in mortgage lending," he wrote, joining the chorus. "However, the Corporation does not conclude . . . that there is a complete absence of racial discrimination in mortgage lending." These were remarkable omissions from a risk management system that was built on a prodigious information-gathering operation meant to restrain downside risk before it was too late. The difference was that the supervisors had not been willing to collect the relevant kinds of information.[23]

This systematic de-emphasis of their antidiscrimination efforts continued into the early 1970s as the banking agencies refused to undertake data gathering programs that might reveal patterns of discrimination. For example, when asked whether they required banks to maintain information on the race of loan applicants, federal banking officials uniformly confirmed that they did not. They also unanimously asserted that such recordkeeping would not be useful, and that they could not conceive of "any system of bank recordkeeping which would produce reliable or useful data in this area." Bank supervisors had been at the vanguard of generating unique information within government since the advent of the call report in the mid-nineteenth century. They had used that unique information-gathering apparatus to respond to the crises of the Great Depression and to revitalize merger review and expanded banking practices in the 1960s. Information-gathering capacity was perhaps the single most useful and powerful trait that defined bank supervision.[24]

It is thus hard to know exactly what they meant by this strange denial. In the face of such obstruction, civil rights advocates called for Congress to "meet the problem of dealing with bureaucrats who have learned over a long period of time how not to provide information."[25]

Depositor and Borrower Protection

The civil rights movement was not the only force putting pressure on bank supervisory practices in the 1960s and 1970s. Coming a few years later, but with similarly deep roots in American politics, another insurgent political movement soon gained the spotlight: consumerism. Like civil rights, and sometimes in parallel to it, the consumer protection movement had a long history of organization before it broke into the mainstream in the 1960s. Consumer and labor groups campaigned around fair prices in the first half of the twentieth century. After World War II, the movement shifted to focus on consumer harms caused to individuals (through faulty or dangerous products) and to society (through externalities like environmental degradation). Given the postwar economy's deep reliance on consumer credit, and the attendant risks consumer borrowing posed to American households, organized consumers placed increasing emphasis on fairness and safety in consumer lending markets. Strong enforcement provisions compelled supervisors to take the new consumer protection regime more seriously.[26]

Although federal supervision likely reinforced racial exclusion, consumer protection—in a broad sense—was a foundational if latent paradigm of government oversight. The very ambition of the Civil War–era National Banking Acts—to provide a uniform, redeemable banknote currency—protected consumers as currency holders from loss in the case of bank failure, a protection which would, through consumer confidence, redound to the government's benefit in the form of a stable currency. Likewise, the gradual adoption of a supervisory ethos of depositor protection in the later nineteenth century, through to the ultimate establishment of federal deposit insurance in the 1930s, reflected a growing depositor protection orientation among bank supervisors, one aligned with public residual risk management. The idea that protecting bank customers would protect banks is an old one going back at least to the deposit revolution in banking beginning in the 1870s, if not to New York's Safety Fund a generation earlier.

Longstanding consumer protection in bank supervision was not exclusively focused on the liability side of the balance sheet. On the lending side, too, the Civil War Congress sought to shield borrowers from excessive interest. In his first annual report, Comptroller Hugh McCulloch (1863–1865) made an extended argument in favor of a uniform, nationwide usury law to "protect the borrower from oppression." Congress pursued a federalist compromise: National banks followed their home-state's interest rate rules or observed a 7 percent limit if no local rule existed.[27]

Despite these provisions, later Comptrollers shied away from rigorous enforcement, because, as in other areas, the only extant penalty was a supervisory death sentence: liquidate the bank in the face of violations of any laws. As John Jay Knox Jr. (1872–1884) observed in 1872, "the Comptroller will not feel himself called upon to institute proceedings for the forfeiture of the charter of a bank for usurious transactions, when it is evident that the business of the association is conducted legitimately and safely in other aspects." Instead, Comptrollers left banks and borrowers to sort out alleged usury violations in court.[28]

The Comptroller's policy on usury enforcement changed dramatically in the 1910s under John Skelton Williams, the populist-segregationist who served under Woodrow Wilson. In 1914, amid market upheavals from World War I, several New York national banks raised call loan rates sharply. Williams, incensed, sought to root out usury across the national banking system. He used publicity to shame banks charging exorbitant rates, requiring them to list loans exceeding 6 percent interest in their published call reports. Bankers reacted with fury, calling it a "vicious assault" and demanding Williams's removal. Undeterred, Williams pressed his case through the war, arguing in 1918 that high interest rates stoked political unrest up to and including revolutionary socialism.[29]

Williams, like many critics of excessive interest, drew on biblical prohibitions to justify debtor protection. From the turn of the century through the New Deal, however, momentum built toward price control regulations rooted in economics, not morality. Consumer activists secured state-level legislation that allowed regulated consumer lenders to charge high interest rates on small loans. New Dealers, in turn, incorporated credit price controls into larger systems of economic management, like the Federal Reserve's Regulation Q, aimed at channeling private lending toward social priorities. These efforts went further during World War II, when the Fed administered consumer credit controls aimed at curtailing consumer purchases of scarce durable goods, a practice that endured in part after the war but was eventually abandoned in the face of stark opposition from retailers and lenders.[30]

Modern Consumer Supervision

Consumer financial protection—that is, the idea that banks should not be left to themselves to decide the structure and price of credit or other financial services, and that the law should prohibit or require specific acts or practices—emerged from these debates to become a standalone political issue largely through the initiative of Illinois Senator Paul H. Douglas, who began advocating for uniform credit price disclosure in the late 1950s. Through what became known as the Truth-in-Lending Act, Douglas sought "to require that the American consumer be given the truth, the whole truth, and nothing but the truth about the interest rates and finance charges he is asked to pay when he borrows money."[31]

A former University of Chicago economist, Douglas initially framed truth-in-lending around macroeconomic stability, arguing that transparent credit prices would encourage consumers to respond to Federal Reserve interest rate adjustments. Recognizing the emergence of organized consumer politics as a major national movement, Douglas shifted the policy's emphasis toward protecting consumers from harmful and deceptive lending practices. Over years of legislative hearings, Douglas cultivated a grassroots consumer base, while successfully convincing Democratic Presidents John F. Kennedy and Lyndon Johnson to make credit disclosure a cornerstone of pro-consumer politics.[32]

Here, as in the antidiscrimination context, the supervisory ethos of credit disclosures varied markedly from the risk management approach of safety and soundness supervision. Truth-in-lending violations were failures of clear compliance more akin to the supervisory ethos in securities regulation, and not to the give-and-take in bank supervision and risk management. Perhaps for this reason, Douglas, and later his legislative successor Wisconsin Senator William Proxmire, faced opposition from the Federal Reserve: Banking was the Fed's turf, and bank supervision wasn't really done that way. Recognizing the Fed's legitimacy with bankers and business interests, Douglas and Proxmire drafted truth-in-lending to give the Fed both regulatory and supervisory authority in line with the powers the Fed had previously exercised when administering wartime credit controls.

But the Fed did not want this authority, arguing instead that it would distract, not complement, the Fed's core monetary and supervisory policy functions. In hearings in 1967, Utah Senator Wallace F. Bennett asked Fed Vice Chairman James L. Robertson (1966–1973) whether he was aware that the Home Loan Bank Board sought the authority to write truth-in-lending regulations. "Yes, I am, Senator," Robertson replied, "and I would be delighted if you would give the entire job to the Home Loan Bank Board." As enactment became increasingly likely, however, the Fed accepted rule-writing responsibility so long as Congress distributed compliance responsibility among the federal banking and consumer protection agencies. "All we are trying to do," Robertson insisted, "is to make it very clear that the Board does not want the job of enforcing this statute." Writing the rules, they could do; supervising the risks, they would prefer to avoid, at least the exclusive responsibility.[33]

Thus, the 1968 Truth-in-Lending Act tasked the Federal Reserve with regulating credit disclosure—with writing the rules that creditors would have to obey—and tasked the remaining bank supervisory agencies with ensuring "compliance" with these rules. This division of responsibility in a sense formalized the informal division of responsibility hashed out in the late 1930s.

Subsequent consumer legislation, including the Fair Credit Reporting Act (1970) and the Fair Credit Billing Act (1974) would all adopt the same language, placing consumer enforcement with the federal banking agencies, and explicitly tying that enforcement to the increasingly dominant frame for all non-prudential bank supervision: compliance.[34]

In one sense, the evolution toward mandated price disclosure and post-hoc compliance oversight had some precedent, echoing as it did the nineteenth-century reporting and public surveillance regime. Like that system of public call reporting, disclosure made market participants—in this case, consumers—more effective monitors of financial institutions' behavior. Transparent prices enabled consumers to make informed decisions, to take action by changing banks, and to thus encourage banks to improve performance and lower prices. Consumers, in Douglas's view, would shop for the lowest price, increasing competition in consumer credit markets. But unlike the nineteenth-century disclosure regime, which left supervisors to manage noncompliance through direct and private supervisory engagement with bankers, truth-in-lending and subsequent consumer protection legislation enabled consumers to file class action lawsuits against firms that failed to comply. As Proxmire observed, "the law should be largely—I would anticipate—self-enforcing."[35]

Self-enforcing laws did not need bank supervision's public–private negotiation of residual risk. That was not a defect from the perspective of consumer activists' goals of consumer empowerment, but it also created challenges for supervisory officials who still had to implement the Fed's truth-in-lending rules. At first, supervisors incorporated consumer oversight into their existing examination practices. In June 1969, the FDIC issued examiners a new, seven-page truth-in-lending compliance checklist. Examiners would determine bank managers' knowledge about the new regulations and randomly sample consumer credit files to see if banks were following the rules. Talking to management and inspecting a bank's books aligned with the risk management work examiners were already doing to evaluate the soundness of a bank's business practices and the quality of its asset portfolio.[36]

Although they adopted these compliance-oriented checklists, even the FDIC's leadership recognized there was a tension between the new compliance oversight and the Corporation's core safety and soundness mission. The Truth-in-Lending Act's civil penalties, combined with new class action lawsuits that the law encouraged, "could conceivably threaten the solvency of a bank," a 1971 FDIC memo warned, an outcome antithetical to the very function and purpose of bank supervision.[37]

These were not idle concerns. Beginning in 1969, consumers filed a flurry of such lawsuits, including a $1 billion suit against Bank of America for alleged violations related to its credit card accounts (at the time the bank's capital was $1.35 billion). The FDIC did not want to foment such lawsuits. So it was that the FDIC began requiring its examiners to separate compliance paperwork from other examination forms, even filing work papers in separate envelopes. "All reference to" truth-in-lending, examiners were instructed, "should be omitted from Reports of Examination." Truth-in-lending may have been important to Congress and to consumers, but for the FDIC, it and later consumer compliance functions had to be hived off from their more important core safety and soundness focus. This separation made sense, to the supervisors, for another reason: Given the enforcement ethics of these consumer laws and the nature of the risk management, principles like supervisory pressure toward innovation or forbearance in the face of challenges to capital or liquidity did not have clear analogues to the consumer context. They simply did not know how to supervise consumer risks using the informational architecture of bank supervision.[38]

Consumer oversight threatened to radically disrupt ingrained norms of supervisory practice in another important way, beyond the change of ethos. By the postwar era, bank supervision relied on a largely confidential enforcement regime, worked out in bank offices between bank supervisors and bank management, with the strictest of privacy and penalties against disclosure. When examiners found violations of the rules, they explained those violations to bank management and determined the course of correction. If management met these demands by the next examination, supervisors took no further action, without disclosure to consumers, customers, investors, or any other third party, even when other federal laws (like the Truth-in-Lending Act or the federal securities laws) relied on public disclosure. To resolve this tension, the bank regulators ignored it. "We ... have concluded," the Comptroller explained in 1976, "that it was the intention and expectation of Congress that the banking agencies would use the same private approach to consumer law enforcement as they do in regard to other banking laws."[39]

The split went even further. In the nineteenth century, bankers faced litigation threats from disgruntled depositors, shareholders, and other financial stakeholders. The New Deal supervisory ecosystem funneled almost all such litigation risk away from banks and toward bank supervision. Depositors were made whole by the FDIC, shareholders had little to litigate in the face of non-failure, and other stakeholders would simply move on to other institutions, each backed and supervised by the government in the same way. Now, in the consumer context, the threat of class action lawsuits left bankers exposed to risks that bank supervisors found themselves in a position to manage along-side the banks, not against them. Bankers finding themselves crosswise with these new risks in the early days of consumer supervision looked unironically to their co-risk managers—their government bank supervisors—for advice and even protection. Bankers wanted assurance that they were following the rules and guidance on how to comply in the future more effectively, something that supervisors were eager to give. This orientation, however, was starkly at odds with the framework of consumer protection imagined by truth-in-lending and subsequent consumerist financial legislation. Truth-in-lending was premised on publicity—providing consumers the information necessary to make decisions. And it was oriented, through its civil penalties, toward rectifying past wrongs. Congress wanted bank supervisors to work on behalf of consumers to make amends for past mistakes, not—as supervisors had imagined their role—on behalf of bankers to prevent errors in the future. Bank supervisors unequivocally disdained the former in preference for the latter. Managing risks to the banks was their primary target; if consumers demanding justice exacerbated those risks, then supervisors would manage them in the way they best understood.[40]

Reflecting the way that supervisors had managed risk tradeoffs, by the mid-1970s, observers argued that federal supervisors were neglecting their compliance responsibilities. Consumer advocates, like Connecticut Bank Commissioner Lawrence Connell Jr. (1975–1977), noted somewhat blandly that federal agencies were not adequately enforcing the new laws because bank supervision was ill suited to the effort. "Truth-in-lending and other consumer type compliance," Connell argued at congressional hearings in 1976, "has been an appendage to an examination report that was really designed and employed to determine safety and soundness." Federal supervisors essentially demurred, feeling that consumer protection was undermining their hard-won relationships with bankers. The sheer volume of conversations about these issues between supervisors and bankers "served to keep the name of the Federal Reserve in the forefront of the bankers' mind in relation to a very distasteful subject," a senior vice president of the Federal Reserve Bank of New York complained. "Not that the bankers are against consumerism . . . but they are confused. In their confusion they place the blame on the federal reserve system."[41]

To lessen the confusion, the bank supervisory agencies began to develop separate consumer offices and experiment with separate compliance examinations of the banks they oversaw. By creating consumer departments and compliance teams, the supervisory agencies strengthened the compliance ethic, giving compliance an institutional identity by divorcing it from future-oriented safety and soundness supervision. The Comptroller moved first, creating its Consumer Affairs Division in 1974 and experimenting with separate compliance examinations in 1975. By 1976, the Comptroller converted 10 percent of its examination staff to consumer examiners. Individual Federal Reserve Banks began their own compliance examination trials, which ultimately became policy for the entire Federal Reserve System. The Federal Reserve gave jurisdiction for equal credit opportunity and fair housing to the Office of Saver and Consumer Affairs. The FDIC was a latecomer. In 1976, the corporation promised Congress that it would revamp its examiner training programs, which then included just one hour of compliance material for new examiners.[42]

The professionalization of supervisory compliance staff led, in turn, to the like professionalization of compliance staff in banks. The cascade of new consumer regulations, carrying varied penalties for noncompliance, compelled banks to construct internal, private risk monitoring programs, which public officials could then monitor externally. Beginning in 1977, the *Magazine of Bank Administration* ran a seven-part series on "Implementing a Program for Consumer Regulation Compliance," a topic also taken up in other industry publications. "Loan officers' 'gut feelings' are often colored by factors now prohibited from consideration," one writer warned, urging bankers to establish well-documented, consistently applied, and non-discriminatory lending criteria that would minimize vulnerabilities to charges of discrimination. Writers in the trade press also urged bankers and bank board members to make compliance a priority by hiring staff to centralize and implement consumer compliance programs. "The success of a bank's consumer compliance program depends a great deal upon the adequacy as well as the authority of the bank's compliance officer," the "compliance and procedures administrator" for a large Chicago bank observed. The "compliance officer" was officially born. Hiring in compliance was part of a larger explosion of compliance costs, a subject of perennial bank complaint.[43]

Pressure for Antidiscrimination Oversight

As they carved out separate consumer compliance programs, the federal banking agencies rolled civil rights oversight into that same, newly subordinated apparatus as a subsidiary category of compliance. In that sense, supervising bank civil rights laws became subordinated twice over: once as a second to prudential supervision, and once again second to consumer protection more generally. And again, the choice had both an institutional and political logic. Within the supervisory agencies, consumer protection took priority over racial equity because heavy consumer enforcement penalties posed more significant risks to banks than, for example, the relatively weak enforcement provisions of 1968 Fair Housing Act. At the same time, the politics of credit discrimination fundamentally transformed into a field of consumer protection itself. While Congress enacted fair housing as a civil rights measure intended to help economically disadvantaged, minority homebuyers, in the early 1970s, middle-class White women led new antidiscrimination campaigns in which they sought equal credit access *as consumers*. These women's calls for credit opportunity embraced not only mortgages but also upper-class forms of credit, especially credit cards. The origins of antidiscrimination supervision in banking were not, therefore, built on a foundation of civil rights; they were built on the foundation of the consumer revolution.[44]

This change was not because the fight for racial equity was making much progress in banking. Civil rights advocates continued to face institutional and political barriers to achieving antidiscrimination in mortgage and consumer lending. With the 1968 Housing Act clearly not meeting activists' goals, organizers in the early 1970s focused increasing attention on redlining, the practice of denying credit to specific neighborhoods that were seen as risky investments—riskiness that often correlated to the demographic makeup of the area. Redlining drove disinvestment and urban decay; the practice was especially galling when undertaken by financial institutions that drew deposits from redlined neighborhoods but refused to repurpose said deposits as loans to these same neighborhoods. Recognizing the political salience of consumerist claims, urban activists seized the logic of disclosure as a way to identify financial institutions that were not investing in their communities, thus enabling urban residents, as informed consumers, to move their money to banks that would. Grassroots advocates gained traction at the state and local level, before securing the Home Mortgage Disclosure Act (HMDA, pronounced "humda") in 1975. The law required federally chartered or insured banks to disclose the dollar amounts and geographic distribution of their mortgage lending, the enforcement of which was divided among the various banking agencies.[45]

As they pursued federal disclosure regulation, advocates also focused on bank supervision as they lobbied banking agencies to take a more assertive role in civil rights enforcement, specifically calling on agencies to collect the data on the race and sex of mortgage applicants. Through the early 1970s, the agencies steadfastly refused. "To compel the banking agencies to take the basic steps required to detect and remedy discrimination," a coalition of eleven civil rights groups sued the Comptroller, Fed, FDIC, and Federal Home Loan Bank Board in April 1976. Three of the four agencies settled and agreed to collect the data. The Federal Reserve, however, held out and eventually the case was dismissed for lack of standing.[46]

As it had from the beginning of the truth-in-lending debates, the Federal Reserve strongly resisted Congress's efforts to push social policy into the realm of bank supervisory risk management. Instead, the Fed sought to maintain its preferred practice of risk management through private engagement with bankers, which enabled Fed supervisors to confidentially discuss bank lending practices without exposing member banks to enforcement risk. Even as they had built out, albeit reluctantly, the institutional supervisory apparatus for consumer financial protection, the Fed continued to push supervising racial discriminatory practices to a deeper margin.

The Home Mortgage Disclosure Act was the partial answer to this resistance. The HMDA data would, in the first instance, empower consumers to impose their own kind of supervision, but one untethered from bank risk management. The government could share decisional authority with banks' interests in profitability—and thus, as a crude approximation, their safety and soundness. HMDA would allow consumers and investors (and anyone else with the sophistication to access this data) to separate fair lending from discriminatory practices.

But Congress did not intend HMDA to create a rival supervisory force headed by activists or lawyers. It also expected federal supervisory agencies to use geographic lending data to establish the patterns of discrimination that supervision by complaint had failed to reveal. The Fed balked. Fed Governor Philip C. Jackson (1975–1978) described the HMDA data as "of very limited use." Instead, Jackson continued to emphasize that supervisors' role was not to root out past illegal behavior but to use confidential supervisory dialogue with bankers "to instruct banks or to request changes in certain practices in order to 'prevent' discrimination in the future." By this, Jackson did not mean preventing actual instances of discrimination but rather preventing bank actions that were demonstrably illegal and thus subject to criminal enforcement or civil penalties. The supervisory task was to ensure that banks complied with the law—that disclosure and mandated data gathering were performed properly—and to guide banks through private dialogue when they were not.

The Board's job, Jackson explained in 1978 hearings, was to privately seek voluntary compliance. That was, after all, what shared risk management behind the veil of confidential supervisory information was meant to be. Even at face value, Jackson's (and the Fed's) reliance on that secrecy meant that it would not contemplate revealing the identity of violators to the public. Ultimately, Jackson concluded, the threat of consumer lawsuits was what should motivate banks to change behavior (and, by implication, the Fed would not willingly provide evidence against its bank members in such lawsuits).[47]

Congress, encouraged by civil rights groups, continued to apply pressure through frequent hearings in the late 1970s that evaluated the supervisory agencies' performance and considered new legislation that would integrate non-prudential supervisory goals into the prudential bank supervisory apparatus. By 1978, with the other agencies largely accepting consumer protection and civil rights responsibilities, the Fed came in for sustained criticism. By then, even the Fed could no longer defend itself. It commissioned an internal investigation of its consumer programs, which shared the critical view of the Fed's efforts as a failure of reluctance and stubborn refusals. "Our negative conclusions with respect to the Board's antidiscrimination enforcement efforts derive principally from our observation relating to the Board's not having recognized civil rights compliance as a discreet and separate area of responsibility differing from other consumer protection measures and requiring specialized expertise and policy consideration." Others cast the report's conclusions even more damningly: "The examiner instruction and training methods are deficient in almost every respect," civil rights advocates declared. "Examiners evidence . . . a mild hostility toward civil rights matters based partly on a perception that the devotion of their time and effort to civil rights matters would not materially advance their progress within the system, as it was not an area to which the Federal Reserve attached great importance." The problems came from the very top. Governor Jackson, advocates asserted, "candidly, is simply not sympathetic to consumer or civil rights compliance problems."[48]

The failure of the Fed's approach—and of the previous regime of supervision by complaint—was demonstrated by the agencies that settled with the civil rights groups. As part of its settlement, the Federal Home Loan Bank Board agreed to apply an effects test for civil rights violations. It began actively looking for patterns of discrimination in the data, not just qualitative allegations of racial animus. This seemed to work. Agency examiners reported very few violations before 1977 (when they depended reactively on complaints).

After changing their approach, the agency found 2,800 actual or possible violations, sent 1,949 supervisory letters, conducted 52 special investigations, and took more serious supervisory action in eight cases. Likewise, the FDIC began using the 1966 Financial Institutions Supervisory Act to issue cease-and-desist letters to banks for noncompliance with the Equal Credit Opportunity Act. When supervisors used their discretion to finally look for discrimination, they easily found it.[49]

The Passive Resistance to Community Reinvestment

One plausible hypothesis to explain why the banking agencies slow-walked the supervision of antidiscrimination and consumer protection is that these pieces of legislation often implied supervisory priorities without stating them. That is, they created new legal mandates and expected the already-functioning supervisory processes to verify compliance with those mandates. Jumping the gap between legal prohibition to active supervision was not an action the agencies willingly took, or even necessarily understood.

That plausible hypothesis, though, is probably wrong. In the creation of a community reinvestment program whereby banks were given supervisory attention and added incentives to make loans where they were already accepting deposits, Congress did not simply mandate legal requirements or issue legal prohibitions. It explicitly created new supervisory processes and criteria. That approach similarly failed, and for similar reasons.

Senator William Proxmire, the chief sponsor of HMDA and what later became the Community Reinvestment Act (CRA), explained the problem that he hoped HMDA disclosures would solve. Banks, he said, were all too eager to "welcome business [from lower-income and minority customers] at the deposit window . . . but when it comes time for the dream of homeownership, when they try to get a mortgage loan, they find they live on the wrong side of the tracks." The disclosures that HMDA produced were aimed to provide community leaders with the information necessary to right this wrong.[50]

After a few years, activists and other observers were not satisfied that the disclosure ethos would be sufficient to redress past wrongs of community divestment. Proxmire, following the lead of these community leaders, opted for another tack. In this approach, community activists would work with banks, not against them—adjudicating antidiscrimination not through the courts or markets, but through bank supervision.[51]

Congress passed the CRA, under Senator Proxmire's leadership, in 1977. Proxmire was an intriguing leader for the consumer finance movement. The son of a well-heeled Illinois family, he earned his undergraduate degree at Yale, served in Army counterintelligence during World War II, and then took successive degrees in business and public administration from Harvard. Proxmire then moved to Wisconsin, working first as a journalist before moving into politics. He served as a state assemblyman and tried but failed to capture the governorship throughout the 1950s before finally becoming Wisconsin's longest-serving U.S. senator. He was a party maverick, most associated as a severe critic of government waste—he created the "Golden Fleece Award" for the government project or contract he regarded as most indicative of inexcusable profligacy. He was also a steadfast critic of the banking industry, especially in its exclusion of women, minorities, and creditworthy borrowers in the inner-city. These were the areas he identified as key to his legislative focus when he ascended to the chairmanship of the Senate Banking Committee in 1974. Banks did not look forward to his work: "He loves publicity," one source told a journalist at the time. "He'll stage plenty of inquiries, insist on investigation, make loads of statements to the press about what's wrong with banking, and every banking official will be made to look like the big bad wolf about to devour Red Riding Hood."[52]

What bankers who feared Proxmire did not understand was that he wanted them not only to stop contributing to the problem of financial exclusion but to start contributing to the solution. To that end, Proxmire wanted to expand opportunities for bank lending, not limit them, including through some small erosions of the New Deal structural restrictions. The legislation of the 1970s reflected that spirit—using banking legislation and bank supervision to push banks into the posture of fixing the problems that they had helped to create in the first place.

The Community Reinvestment Act of 1978 reflected Proxmire's priorities. The law offered a fundamentally different approach to racial exclusion and discrimination in the banking and housing sectors. The key innovation was in the architecture of lending that the CRA created. At the time of its passage, the primary approach to solving the problems of inner cities was called "urban renewal," or, as the leading historian of community reinvestment activism describes it, a "federal strategy to remove 'blight' by empowering city agencies to clear 'slums' and build modern structures in their place." Unlike other efforts, the CRA was not meant for "clearing" those parts of the cities that had been ignored by private banks and the federal regulators that supported them.

It would also not attempt to "name and shame" the banks that failed, as John Skelton Williams had tried in the 1910s and as HMDA seemed to invite. The CRA was an activist-led partnership *with* banks that would create incentives, positive and negative, for banks to deploy lending back into those neighborhoods.[53]

While banker support was mixed for this model of supervision toward reinvestment, regulators were more uniformly opposed, for predictable reasons. The three main federal supervisors who would be responsible for the implementation of the new system felt, yet again, that such efforts would be duplicative, distracting, or even unnecessary. Robert L. Bloom, Acting Comptroller of the Currency (1976–1977) and by then the unquestioned primary supervisor of the largest banks in the country, argued that "in general, a bank serves its depositors best when it invests prudently in its community." The entire concept of forced reinvestment on anything other than a prudential basis was antithetical to that approach. He also argued that the Comptroller's robust "special consumer examination" already covered what was necessary to resolve the concerns of "community revitalization." Implicit in this critique is that a redirection of bank assets for purposes other than generating a profitable return would not do the community any services.[54]

Fed Chair Arthur F. Burns (1970–1978) agreed with Bloom. Bank supervisors were already in the business of encouraging banks to meet "the credit needs of their communities to the extent this is consistent with safe and sound operations." Thus, no new legislation was required. Similarly, FDIC Chairman Robert E. Barnett (1976–1977) wrote that while the federal insurance agency "fully support[ed] the objectives" of the proposed legislation, the approach considered would be "piecemeal" and create an "unnecessary reporting burden on financial institutions which would largely be duplicative of requirements already in effect."[55]

The ultimate statutory text reflected these concerns and provided a relatively weak set of instructions. The law formalized a requirement for all federal bank examiners to take community needs into consideration in their examinations and then went further: If banks wanted to grow, bank regulators needed to assess community reinvestment as part of the approval process. The chief innovation of the CRA, then, was to tie the banks' interest in growth to examiners' assessments of whether they had, in fact, reinvested in their communities.[56]

Given its weighty objectives, it may seem remarkable that the CRA did not attempt to accomplish more. Passed as part of the larger housing and community development law, the structure of the original CRA was just two pages and consisted primarily of an open-ended charge to federal bank examiners, much of it hortatory. Congress concluded that "regulated financial institutions are required by law to demonstrate that their deposit facilities serve the convenience and needs of the communities in which they are chartered to do business."[57] In light of that requirement, the relevant examiners were instructed "to use [their] authority when examining financial institutions ... to encourage such institutions to help meet the credit needs of the local communities in which they are chartered, consistent with the safe and sound operation of such institutions."[58]

Following the pattern in antidiscrimination and consumer protection supervision, these caveats were an important delegation to supervisors to determine exactly how they would go about approving requests to acquire new branches, banks, or lines of business (new "deposit facilities," in legalistic banking jargon). What was new and remarkable was the creation of the specific examination regime. Supervisors could make a pretense of the exercise Congress required of them, but they would have to undertake it all the same. Every application for a new deposit facility—and in the years following the passage of the CRA, there was explosion of such applications—had to pass through this examination process. These examinations would include an assessment of each bank's "record of meeting the credit needs of its entire community, including low- and moderate-income neighborhoods" and to "take such record into account in its evaluation of an application for a deposit facility by such institution."[59]

In January 1978, just two months after the statute's passage, the banking agencies announced that they would hold public hearings in Washington, DC, and throughout the country (including Atlanta, Chicago, San Francisco, Boston, and Dallas) to "receive suggestions from the public on how to implement the new law." The notice asked for help in defining nearly every term in the statute, from "community," to "credit needs," to the "assessment" that the statute required examiners to undertake. Perhaps most importantly for the way that the examination process mandated by Congress would proceed was the fact that they actively anticipated the tradeoffs that the safety and soundness examinations would face against the community reinvestment efforts. Supervisors asked: "What weight should be given to the record of an institution in meeting community credit needs compared to the weight given other factors such as competition, safety and soundness, and other managerial and financial factors?" And more, "under what conditions, *if any*, should the Agencies deny an application?"[60]

The National Archives preserve the answers of hundreds of respondents. Some took the opportunity to air grievances about just how much they hated the concentration of banking in their communities and disbelieved even the pretense of the statute. A president of a Pittsburgh manufacturing company complained that the "sole emphasis" of large banks "appears to be to grab the deposits out in the boondocks and send it downtown for the big deal." Many others raised similar concerns to those expressed by the regulators themselves. The Maryland State Bank Commissioner did not believe that the statute was necessary because the state had "never had a complaint involving 'redlining'" and, although the deputy commissioner admitted that they had not "conducted any studies" to confirm that fact, "our community needs are being met" and there was no need for further engagement. Other states made similar claims that redlining was a problem for other places, not for them.[61]

The comments came strongest from banks and thrifts of all kinds and sizes. They were, with few exceptions, hostile to the very idea of new examinations. "Inasmuch as we are already overtaxed and overburdened with rules and regulations," one state banker in Wisconsin argued, the agencies would do best by going back to Congress and seeking the Act's wholesale repeal. Another Wisconsin banker viewed the CRA examinations as "a case of where the medicine is going to be worse than the disease." Similarly, an Indiana banker lumped all such efforts with the "socialism" that had plagued all bank decisions since the passage of consumer protection laws. The whole consequence of the law was that the agencies were "no longer allowing the consumer to pick and choose between institutions" out of their own interests because the CRA meant that the government would now direct those policies. These were some of the more measured responses. The very prospect of a robust CRA examination system inspired banker vitriol. The few bankers who had supported the effort during the legislative debates did not leave a record of their thoughts on the shape of the examinations.[62]

Almost immediately, though, banks and their cooperative supervisors found ways to navigate the CRA's requirements, such as they were, to their liking. When Citibank applied to expand into South Dakota to launch its consumer credit card business—and with it, fundamentally change the provision of consumer credit in America—it committed to the principles of community reinvestment, with an important caveat: "The Bank will serve a broader 'community' which is comprised of the United States."[63]

Citibank was not playing fast and loose with its supervisors: It was merely following the conclusions that bankers and supervisors reached together. One of the first proposed mergers to test the CRA ran into community pressure because of alleged failures of reinvestment, with the Association of Community Organizations for Reform Now (ACORN) intervening to ask for the Fed to deny the application on CRA grounds. The Fed refused, siding with the banks and insisting that the CRA did not impose any specific quantitative or qualitative requirements on banks. "Legislation that could halt banks' redlining practices is not going to be used that way if the Federal Reserve Board can help it," ACORN complained before filing litigation to block the merger. This critique wasn't quite right. The legislation was designed to make community reinvestment a part of the Fed's (and the other agencies') supervisory discretion. That these agencies adopted the approach favored by the banks was a fact telegraphed well before the legislation ever passed.[64]

The Community Reinvestment Act has gone on to have a long life of constant change and controversy. Congress reformulated the examination requirements in 1989 when Proxmire noted that "redlining hasn't disappeared" and that the neighborhoods the CRA was meant to help were still "starving for credit." Proxmire's solution, then, was to render the examination records public, in a combination of the secret supervisory regime and the name-and-shame approach of HMDA; nearly every bank still received a passing grade in the decades that followed. In 2023, the agencies reformulated the CRA yet again, were promptly sued by the industry, and it is still to be seen whether courts find more congressional intent and statutory limits than the first regulators encountered. As of this writing, the CRA remains one of the bitterest frontiers between banks and supervisors.[65]

Conclusion

What is remarkable about the congressional efforts to expand the supervisory bailiwick beyond the risk management ecosystem that had evolved prior to the 1970s isn't that the banks (and regulators, initially) resisted it. What is remarkable is that it happened at all. As Philip Jackson, the Fed Board governor who opposed most efforts to bring greater attention to consumer and racial policies to bank supervision, explained after his retirement, the Fed "got thrust into [consumer and racial] issues, which, in my judgment, both distracted and detracted from the Board's primary function in our system of government, because it put the Board in the position of solving some problems involving some issues that, really, the Board shouldn't have been involved in." Given the extraordinary influence that the banking agencies had on shaping their relationship with Congress in each expansion of their authority from the 1860s onward, Congress's choice to impose more and greater tools and tasks into the unwilling hands of bank supervisors suggests a deeper legislative interest in this semisecret form of public-private governance.[66]

Congressional choices here are not hard to understand. There were many other approaches to redressing financial exclusion of racial minorities and the exploitation of informational asymmetries in consumer financial relationships, including especially the enforcement regimes that Congress also created in other agencies and in private hands that still, to this day, sit alongside bank supervision. Congress, however, chose to add complexity to supervisory discretion. That addition created institutional layering that generated important interactions between supervisory impulses among the approaches that had come before and those that would follow.

Antidiscrimination, consumer protection, and community reinvestment would not remain in the supervisory hinterlands forever. They became part of the dial of risk tolerance that supervisors turn in response to the elections that provide the appropriate boundaries of that risk tolerance. In time—especially after the 2008 financial crisis, but even before—the supervisory ethic for consumers and minorities would join that of the risk management system. That inflection point occurred in the critical period of the 1970s. It would also open up the door for the many more expansions of the supervisory ethic that would follow.

Conclusion

TO WHAT END, THE PUBLIC CONTROL
OF PRIVATE FINANCE

IN THE fall of 2014, news erupted that a bank supervisor, Carmen Segarra, had secretly recorded almost fifty hours of confidential deliberations from within the Federal Reserve Bank of New York. A leak of this kind is rare in American history: Federal law criminalizes the disclosure of "confidential supervisory information," and Segarra's recordings grabbed headlines as she accused the Fed of acting at the beck and call of the banks it was meant to supervise.[1]

Congress seized on the headlines and convened hearings to hold Segarra's boss, New York Fed President William C. Dudley (2009–2018), to account. Elizabeth A. Warren, a Democratic senator from Massachusetts, felt that the Federal Reserve had failed the public as the nation's leading supervisor of financial institutions. Dudley testified before the Senate Banking Committee, facing off with Warren in a memorable exchange. "I often describe our federal regulators as the cop on the beat," Warren explained. "That is, they are out there to look for illegal and unsafe conduct, try[ing] to stop that conduct before it happens."[2]

Dudley disagreed. Although he asserted that the Fed would refer any illegal conduct for appropriate investigation and punishment from "the enforcement agencies"—meaning, presumably but incorrectly, agencies other than the Fed—the job of banking supervision was not to be a "cop on the beat" but rather a "fire warden." Dudley explained that supervisors must "make sure that the institution is run well so that it is not going to catch on fire and burn on" such that it becomes a "threat to the rest of the financial system."[3]

Warren, Dudley, and the press focused on the dispute conceptually and ideologically, tussling over whether the appropriate role of government in identifying and reacting to political and financial risk should be more hostile to the incumbent banks or more cooperative with them. What they may not have known as they engaged in this debate is that they represented an important dynamic with much bigger theoretical, intellectual, legal, and political stakes. They were putting on the table the existential question of what bank supervision is in the first place.

Private Finance, Public Power has told that story. It is an origin story, but one that follows an evolutionary logic. The book explained how a growing army of public officials developed and deployed the power of the federal and state governments with enormous discretion—sometimes in collaboration with private industry, sometimes beholden to it, and sometimes as its taskmaster. It's a story that began in earnest with the iconic and constitutional battles for central banking in the founding generations through the wildcats of Michigan and the hapless examiners who sought (unsuccessfully) to verify the specie backing of their paper. The book ends with congressional delegation to supervisors to ensure not only the safety and soundness of banks, but also the protection of consumers, the enforcement of antidiscrimination, and the supervision of reinvestment in abandoned communities. Banking supervisors have managed these transitions in the face of constant pressure to reform—efforts by Warren and her predecessors eager to see more punitive approaches to risk management, and efforts by Dudley and his predecessors eager to see better collaboration; efforts to eliminate the institutional layering that arose through the fitful evolutionary processes by consolidating supervisory functions into a single organization, and efforts to further specialize and regularize those processes; efforts to use more supervisory discretion to push banks to take bigger risks through innovation, and efforts to use more supervisory discretion to get banks to hold back on innovation.

Supervisors have navigated all of this by using a growing set of tools—chartering, examination, liquidation, central bank lending policies, forbearance, merger review, compliance, investigations, risk management, consultations, litigation, and more—and by standing behind the financial system that has become the anchor of the entire global economy. They managed the residual risk of the financial system—and sometimes of the political system—because Congress wanted them to do so. No one would set out to design a supervisory system identical to what has evolved in the United States, because it is not the product of institutional design. Even so, the creaky set of institutions that has emerged through contingency and stress manages that risk in remarkably effective ways.

Private Finance, Public Power has told that story, but it has also made an argument. It has argued that bank supervision today stands as a kind of risk management system wherein frontline risk is held and managed by the banks with supervisors looming over their shoulders, while residual risk is owned by the supervisors. The private side of risk management has evolved in remarkable ways—sometimes cheering on the advantages of incumbency protected by the government, sometimes eager for liberation against those governmental strictures. The public side of risk management is accomplished deep in the shadows of the public-private divide. Bank supervision is not the echo of legislation. Congress has delegated this task in the broadest possible terms with the least amount of accountability for bank supervisors. They are firmly shielded by fierce traditions (and some legal protections) against such accountability. Instead, supervisors use their discretion to choose what kinds of risks they like, what they don't like, and what the banks must do as a result.

At times—including as of the printing of this book—there are many who regard this semi-secret form of government power as antidemocratic and inconsistent with principles of due process and the rule of law, what one bank lobbyist called "the most oppressive . . . component of the federal regulatory state." With the fall of *Chevron* deference in 2024—that is, the end of the judicial doctrine of deference to agency interpretations of their own authority—some have even questioned whether bank supervision in its present state will preserve the rich tradition of untrammeled power to manage private and public responsibilities for financial risk.[4]

This book should educate that debate. Claims that bank supervision has "lost its way" against an old tradition—when the public knew its place and knew how to stay out of the way of banks—cannot be taken seriously. Federal bank supervisors have, for 160 years, exercised extraordinary discretion over the private affairs of banks. Congress, in turn, has moved consistently over this period regarding the authority of these supervisors: with very few exceptions, that authority has only grown. We believe that the infrastructure of supervision is so entrenched in the American traditions of finance that there is virtually no path to remove it.

One basic feature of that institutionalization is the theme of the second half of the book—the institutional layering that has occurred over and over again, in the face of crises or in the face of stability, after scandals or for no particular reason at all. The institutions of bank supervision have proliferated during the period covered in the book and have only become more entrenched thereafter.

We focused mostly on the Comptroller, the Federal Reserve, the FDIC, the RFC, and the state banking authorities. We also discussed in passing the SEC, Federal Home Loan Bank Board, the FTC, and a few others. There are scores more supervisory entities in the United States, including those focused on credit unions at the state and federal level; savings banks, thrifts, and other similar firms, at both the state and federal level; money transmitters at the state level; digital currency providers; and more.

Private Finance, Public Power is about the political economy of such institutionalization. These entities became a power unto themselves, rendering efforts to remove their authority or abolish them as fruitless as they are regular. This is not merely the exercise of bureaucratic power, however, nor is it evidence of the (contested) idea that Congress creates but never abolishes federal bureaucracy. This book provides some evidence of bureaucratic skirmishes to ensure survival against the prevailing sentiments of powerful politicians—for example, Jefty O'Connor's protection of the OCC when no one, including Franklin Roosevelt, had any interest in its continuation (and long after the purpose of the "Office of the Comptroller of the Currency" had expired). But much more important than bureaucratic will is bureaucratic purpose, including when that purpose evolved. At the close of our history (and extending well past that period), the different supervisory agencies stood for different conceptions of risk and different approaches to risk management. The Comptroller wanted to ensure national consistency as a chartering authority, the truest form of common-law supervision, against the chaos of federalist experimentations. The states, by reciprocal turn, sought to preserve precisely that experimentation. The FDIC is focused on protecting depositors and, in so doing, preserving the value of the deposit insurance fund. It approaches bank risk like an insurance underwriter but of a peculiar sort: Because the FDIC has primary responsibility for the supervision for state-chartered banks that are not members of the Federal Reserve, this approach gives the FDIC a peculiarly state-based orientation on bank risk. And the Fed, especially in the postwar era, saw bank risk as macroeconomic risk, with stability as the key determinant in conceiving and managing the risks in the system. For each of these, supervision was the infrastructure of implementation on vastly different views of what constituted frontline risks for the banks to manage and residual risk for the agencies to own.[5]

As a result, when we write that bank supervision is the use of institutional discretion in managing bank risk, including where that risk is socialized to the public, we are writing about different modalities and epistemologies of bank supervision that will shift not only through a dynamic history but also through contested institutional lenses like those described above. Little wonder, then, that introductions of new responsibilities covered in this book—antitrust review, antidiscrimination, consumer protection, and community reinvestment—do not come out of that process with one clear orientation or direction.

The contingency and uncertainty of this history is, in an important sense, the book's primary argument. Bank supervision is not a point in time, but a large space to negotiate these different points and different claims. It is a negotiation not only across the public-private divide, but also a negotiation across these contested and competing modalities of risk and risk management among these disparate public actors. We do not resolve those debates in this book because the debates are not resolvable. We expect we will see William Dudley and Elizabeth Warren—just as we saw Robert Kennedy and James Saxon, or William Proxmire and Arthur Burns, or Marriner Eccles and Leo Crowley, or Lawrence Murray and national bankers—continue their debate for a long time to come.

———

There are two questions that remain as we conclude our account. First, why end the account in 1980? Second, although we are historians primarily interested in understanding the past and its relevance to the future, many of our readers will ask the question: What should be done as a result of this new understanding of bank supervision? Perhaps more fundamentally, is bank supervision a good thing or a bad thing? Is it an example of regulatory capture—ahem, supervisory capture—or is it good government?

First, why we ended in 1980. When we first embarked on this project almost a decade ago, we intended to tell the story of bank supervision, all of it, through to the time of publication. However, what we came to see was that, to paraphrase Virginia Woolf, on or about October 1979, the world of bank supervision changed. While it is true that the building blocks of bank supervision forged in the furnaces of the Civil War and Great Depression are still with us, the entire ideology of bank supervision shifted profoundly after this point.

Historians like to think in terms of epochs and orders. We end in the 1970s in part because it marks the end of what historians have called the "New Deal Order" and the beginning of what has become increasingly characterized as the "Neoliberal Order." There is plenty in such demarcations and neologisms to dispute. If we stipulate that these conventional boundaries hold, we ended the book in 1980 because, whatever the nature of these changes, the approach to managing residual risk during the Reagan-Bush-Clinton-Bush eras departed dramatically from the pendulum swings that had characterized the century before.[6]

The project of assessing the essentially corporatist institutions of bank supervision through this neoliberal period will be an important undertaking. Our book provides some of the antecedents of the transformations in this era, reaching as far back as the nineteenth century but also, more starkly, in the efforts of James Saxon in the 1960s chronicled in chapter 8. Gary Gerstle, one of the leading historians of the Neoliberal Order, defines the motivation of those who installed it as being "grounded in the belief that market forces had to be liberated from government regulatory controls that were stymieing growth, innovation, and freedom." In bank supervision, we see the reification of that ethos, growing from the early seeds planted in the immediate postwar period. When Saxon and his congressional allies sought to liberate banking because "a delicate and continuously changing balance must be maintained between public control and private initiative," a balance that needed to be corrected in favor of greater private initiative, he created the backdrop for the launch of the Neoliberal Order in bank supervision.[7]

But of course, this is not the whole story, nor anywhere near it. The New Deal order of bank supervision, if we can call it such, survived robustly after the fall of that political coalition's policy goals. It was not the "liberation" of markets from government that occurred in the 1980s and 1990s (and beyond), but the repurposing and reorientation of that relationship.

That is the story of bank supervision and of banking writ large. The neoliberal capture of bank supervision did not dismantle government intervention in private markets but institutionalized it in a specific form: Instead of public ownership of residual financial risk combined with efforts to minimize private risk-taking during the New Deal supervisory order, the neoliberal supervisory order retained the public backstop and gained new public encouragement of private risk-taking for economic and social good.

This transformation coincided with a series of unmitigated crises in the global financial system, beginning in 1979 and continuing unabated well into the twenty-first century. It begins with a crisis in monetary policy, sparked by Federal Reserve Chairman Paul A. Volcker's (1979–1987) famous monetary shock, decidedly a kind of financial (in)stability mechanism launched by the government on top of a brittle financial system. These moves in turn led to fragility in the banking and savings and loan industries, causing the S&L crisis and significant banking distress throughout the 1980s, including the collapse of Continental Illinois, the largest bank failure since the Great Depression (to say nothing of the international consequences). In important ways, the bank supervisors owned and managed that residual risk because they had cocreated it through channels of monetary policy and bank supervision. The reconception of risk continued through a series of crises with broker dealers and banks to the tumult of massive stock corrections in 1987, when the Fed, through its new Chair Alan Greenspan (1987–2006), assured markets that the Fed, "consistent with its responsibilities as the Nation's central bank, [would] serve as a source of liquidity to support the economic and financial system." When the Fed again raised interest rates in 1994, it sparked upheaval in the financial system, felt in Latin America and especially Mexico—tumult that the government sought once again to resolve in creative ways. It continued through the East Asian crisis, the Russian financial crisis, the catastrophes following the dot-com crash and 9/11, the global financial crisis of 2007–2009, the Eurozone crisis in 2010–2011, the financial and economic crises associated with the COVID-19 pandemic, and even the "mini-crisis" of 2023 that opened our account. The neoliberal supervisory order has not been a stable one.[8]

All the while, the regulators at the top of the supervisory system continued to be among the most politically engaged actors in managing legislation that directly impacted the authority and responsibilities of supervisors—including the Monetary Control Act of 1980, the dramatic expansion of anti-money laundering supervisory tools in successive legislative efforts, post-S&L reforms in 1989 and 1991, the removal of interstate branching restrictions in 1994, the dismantling of New Deal protections in Gramm-Leach-Bliley in 1999, and the post-2008 reforms in 2010. Each of these (and many others) reformed bank supervision to lesser or greater extents, but almost all in the same direction: the expansion of supervisory tools, supervisory discretion, and supervisory power, almost always at the behest of supervisors.

Through it all, we do not see a system of market-oriented deregulation, the withdrawal of government support, or the retreat of bank supervisors from their shadowy posture acting and reacting to the management of residual risk, contra the theme of the Neoliberal Order. We see something else. We see the active, interventionist use of state capacity to prevent full-scale catastrophe, with, at the same time, a continuous supervisory push for more private risk-taking and private risk management. Future scholarship must account for those ends and make sense of those interventions. Doing so in a single volume proved unworkable and unwise, diluting as it would the story of the origins of the supervisory framework that has been repurposed for so different a time.

That leaves the second important question posed in most law school workshops—the normative implications of our study of bank supervision. We are in this sense proud to carry the card of "presentist historians" because we believe deeply that our work can and should have policy relevance to the way we make decisions in the present, with implications for the future.

We hope policymakers who read this book can see important connections between this history and the work that they do. One important connection is the tight link between democratic accountability and bank supervision. Some will balk at the assertion of a link at all, making the contrary argument that bank supervision is the ultimate expression of unaccountable government power. But the history of bank supervision has not been the story of the deep state imposing its will on an unsuspecting public, free of democratic accountability. Secret, behind-the-scenes supervisory discretion is the mechanism by which politically accountable actors adjust the dials of their risk tolerance. In crass partisan terms relevant to the twenty-first century, we should expect to see (and do indeed see) Democrats adjust those dials in favor of greater systemic resilience and less risk-taking by banks and Republicans adjust those dials in favor of greater reliance on private bank innovations with fewer governmental restrictions on risk management (the partisan salience on these issues, of course, has changed over time). Bank supervisors do not lack accountability. Much to the contrary. Because bank supervision *is* the institutionalized management of residual risk, we should see changes—and should want to see changes—in risk tolerance that follow electoral cycles, the highest form of accountability available in a democracy.

A broader, related question we expect—and which we have frequently received—is about our wholesale evaluative and normative assessment of bank supervision. Considering our modest ambitions to influence the course of policy, is our contention that supervision is good, bad, or something in between? Or, to invoke the debate between Elizabeth Warren or Bill Dudley, is supervision good or bad when it looks like policing, good or bad when it looks like fire prevention and response, or is there some other better approach?

We think the normative exploration of supervision is vital, but framing it in such absolute terms is incoherent. Supervision in its shifting and varied forms is neither good nor bad; rather, it is the process for finding temporary answers to perennial questions of how to manage both frontline and residual risk, and then for negotiating and renegotiating those answers as circumstances change. Taken as a process, we can imagine alternatives for the banking system that look more like the ways we regulate other kinds of private activity, with less of a tether between the public and private, less secrecy in risk management, fewer efforts to manage future risks, and more efforts to punish past legal violations. There are countless instances in U.S. history where the government makes surprise inspections, and where government actors engage in informal counseling with private actors in the shadow of their exercise of regulatory power, litigation power, or even criminal enforcement. There is indeed some evidence that in the period following 2008, bank supervision migrated in part exactly in this direction. Many of the post–2008 reform discussions also imagined much more severe (from the banks' perspective) regulatory and legislative initiatives that might have obviated the need for public actors to cooperate, coordinate, and contest the actions of private institutions—ranging from the elimination of short-term debt issuance by nonbanks to the dramatic increase in bank capital required by those within the banking perimeter.[9]

Despite these efforts, bank supervision has stayed put. The secrecy, despite some breaches and leaks, remains very much intact. The discretion to adjust risk tolerance following changes of political guard remains alive and well. While few, if any, are particularly happy about it—the only people who complain more about bank supervision than policymakers are the bankers themselves—we cannot imagine an alternative system that more fully reflects the irreducible fact of banking, finance, and political economy in America. American policy reflects a divided country with inconsistent risk preferences, attitudes toward public control, and ideas about what the private sector should be. Bank supervision is the buffer that stabilizes that polarization even while it makes itself available to partisans for use through the electoral process.

We do not, for these reasons, think debates about wholesale alternatives to the supervisory system are particularly useful any more than other forms of counterfactual history. We think banking functions will continue to be performed by a wide array of institutions inside and outside the formal banking system. We think systemic risk management will always vacillate following changes in political alignments and coalitions. And we think we have not seen the last of financial crises, major or minor. When those events occur, bank supervisors will be the ones who know the most about what has happened, will have acted or failed to act in ways that will draw public scrutiny and public criticism, and will lead to the expansion, not elimination, of supervisory discretion.

———

Private Finance, Public Power told a story of origins and evolution—a story with temporary moments of real movement toward a longer arc that points forward awkwardly while pointing backward relentlessly. As Stephen Jay Gould, the evolutionary biologist whose quote opens this book, put it, "the useless, the odd, the peculiar, the incongruous" parts of bank supervision "are the signs of history." This book is part of that history, an account of the imperfect ecosystem of bank supervision showing where history failed to "cover . . . its own tracks." In following those tracks, we have come to many conclusions, but none stronger than this: The scholarly literature and the public discussion of bank supervision, long dormant and conflated with so many other lesser lights in government and finance, will only grow stronger over time. We did not initiate a research program on bank supervision in this book, but if we have succeeded, this book will contribute to continuing the important process of placing supervision at the center of study of the many fields we have explored, including, most important of all, the unsteady but ever-deepening relationship between private finance and public power.[10]

ACKNOWLEDGMENTS

THIS BOOK gathered so many debts in the ten years we have worked on it that it feels both exhilarating and daunting to thank the many colleagues and friends who contributed to its completion. Exhilarating because we can finally conclude the book in the deep gratitude we feel for an incredible team of supporters; daunting because, in so long a period, there are so many who have contributed to it that we fear the following words won't do our gratitude and this team the justice they warrant.

We will try anyway. Our first thanks go to our incredible team of research assistants—the undergraduates, MBA students, law students, and PhD students who contributed to organizing the vast quantity of primary and secondary qualitative and quantitative material that constituted our source base. In alphabetical order, they are James Blume, Edwin Bogert, Mary Jane Dumankaya, Sean Egan, Ria Ellendula, Maria Felix-Padilla, Caroline Hackley, Molly Hessel, Ashka Jhaveri, Luke Johnson, Finn Kiely, Daniel Kim, Anna Li, Josephine Phillips, Mary Pat Roche, Sophia Rosser, Joshua Schilowitz, Mark Shtrakhman, Pallavi Sood, Corey Stern, Richard White, Jacob Williams, Ola Dozier-Williams, and Mary Zimmerman. Thanks to each for being part of "team bank supervision."

Two additional research assistants deserve added thanks. Victoria Liu served as Peter's head RA for 2024, the year we reached the final conclusion on the manuscript. Despite her busy time as an MBA student, she coordinated final tasks and responsibilities with virtuosity and insight.

Kaleb Nygaard, a master's degree student and subsequently a fellow at the Perelman Center for Political Science and Economics, was Victoria's predecessor as head RA but was also much more than this. Kaleb organized a colossal amount of information and read through one of the final drafts of the manuscript with precision, focus, and an almost electric sense of the possibilities. Now an executive at Visa, Kaleb continues to be a colleague and a friend with a far-ranging set of passions and interests extending through this history and beyond.

We presented versions of this book and related articles to colleagues and audiences across the globe, receiving vital feedback along the way. In alphabetical order, we thank our hosts at the Accountability & Monetary Policy Conference (Annual Conference of the Journal of Financial Regulation), the Board of Governors of the Federal Reserve System, the Brookings Institution, the Business History Conference, the BYU Deals Conference, Cornell Law School, the European Central Bank, the Federal Deposit Insurance Corporation, the Federal Reserve Bank of Cleveland, George Mason Law School's Gray Center, Goethe University House of Finance, the Harvard-Wharton Conference on Bank Supervision, the International Monetary Fund, the Law & Macro Conference, the Monetary Committee of the International Law Association (at several conferences), NYU Law School, the Office of the Comptroller of the Currency, the Organization of American Historians, the Peterson Institute for International Economics, the Policy History Conference, Rutgers Business School, Rutgers University Department of Economics, University of Wisconsin Law School, various configurations of the Wharton FinReg Conference, the World Economic History Congress, and Yale Law School.

We benefited from wonderful archivists at the National Archives in College Park, MD and Kansas City, MO; the Library of Congress in Washington, DC; the LBJ Presidential Archives in Austin, TX; University of South Dakota, Vermillion, SD; Bancroft Library at University of California, Berkley, CA; Seeley G. Mudd Manuscript Library, Princeton University, Princeton, NJ; University of Pittsburgh Library System, Pittsburgh, PA; Herbert Hoover Presidential Library, Ames, IA; Federal Reserve Bank of New York Archives, New York, NY; Columbia University Archives and Special Collections, New York, NY; Gerald R. Ford Presidential Library, Ann Arbor, MI; John F. Kennedy Presidential Library, Boston, MA; and Yale University Library and Special Collections, New Haven, CT.

Since 2022, we have had the privilege of serving together on the advisory board of the Federal Reserve Archival System for Economic Research (FRASER), a service of the Federal Reserve Bank of St. Louis. The influence of FRASER librarians and archivists is on nearly every page, and this book simply would not have taken its shape without these wonderful colleagues, especially Katrina Stierholz and Jona Whipple. In a similar vein, we relied extensively on databases, including ProQuest, Google Books, Google Scholar,

HathiTrust, Hein, and Archive.org. Each of these tools is backed by its own hardworking staff, without whom we could not have written this book.

We published sections of Chapter 5 as "The Logic and Legitimacy of Bank Supervision: The Case of the Bank Holiday of 1933," in volume 95 of *The Business History Review* and sections of the introduction and some of our conclusions throughout the book as "Risk, Discretion, and Bank Supervision" in the *Columbia Business Law Review*. We thank the editors of both journals for their guidance, insights, and permission to republish the material here.

The community of scholars associated with financial regulation is very special. We benefited enormously from engagement with this community on chapters, articles, drafts, debates, and discussions, including in alphabetical order Vince Buccola, Brian Feinstein, Anna Gelpern, Randy Guynn, Dick Herring, Eric Hilt, Howell Jackson, Kate Judge, Steven Kelly, Jeremy Kress, Yair Listokin, Jonathan Macey, Josh Macey, Lev Menand, Geoff Miller, John Morley, Michael Ohlrogge, Saule Omarova, Morgan Ricks, David Skeel, Christina Skinner, Meg Tahyar, Rory Van Loo, Kevin Werbach, Art Wilmarth, David Wishnick, David Zaring, and Jeff Zhang. Few if any agree with all of our arguments here, but all of them made our work better. We are grateful for these scholars and to be members of this community.

In addition to the colleagues who read various iterations of the chapters over the years, a cadre of incredibly kind and dedicated colleagues read most or all of the full final manuscript in early 2024. We thank Dan Awrey, Chris Hughes, Naomi Lamoreaux, Rosa Lastra, Kaleb Nygaard, Joe Sommer, Meg Tahyar, Dan Tarullo, David Zaring, and Julian Zelizer, along with two anonymous reviewers for their help in bringing us from the penultimate draft to a much more elegantly written, less erroneous, and more interesting final version. It's a cliché to say that they aren't responsible for what is bad that remains—and admittedly, we didn't take every piece of advice—but what is good in this book flows right through their thoughtful and thorough engagement.

This book traveled a bit to find the right publisher and editor. It was well worth the journey. We could not have imagined better partners than our colleagues at Princeton University Press. Joe Jackson has been the editor par excellence, patient when we needed patience, stern when our fastidiousness needed reining in. Joe is probably the finest economics editor in the business, something that benefited us enormously as we sought to make our legal and historical arguments legible to a wider readership. We thank, too, Melody Negron, Jamie Thompson, Emma Wagh, and Enid Zafran for their work on various aspects of the book's production.

We each received significant financial and institutional assistance, which in different ways provided invaluable support for this project. Peter would like to thank the Wharton Dean's Office, the Hewlett Foundation's Economy and Society Project, and Open Philanthropy. Sean would like to thank the National Endowment for the Humanities-Hagley Postdoctoral Fellow in Business, Culture, and Society, as well as the University of Glasgow. We both thank the Wharton Initiative on Financial Policy and Regulation, of which Sean was a senior fellow and Peter a co-director.

Finally, in the course of this decade-long project, we have been blessed to have the constant support of our families, and of our friendship (tried as it has occasionally been on this long journey). Our spouses, Nikki and Sara, have lived with this project as long as we have, though we've done our best to spare them the details of dusty examination forms or bank merger fights. Our children—the Conti-Browns, Gabriel, Caleb, Nico, Simon; the Vanattas, Elliot, Sawyer, Finaly, and Cole—have done more, bringing joyful excuses to set the manuscript aside, pause, and be thankful that there is so much more to life than bank supervision. It is to them that this book is dedicated.

LIST OF ABBREVIATIONS

THE FOLLOWING abbreviations are used in the notes to designate frequently cited newspaper, archival, and online-archival sources.

Periodicals

BDR	*Buffalo Daily Republic*
BG	*Boston Globe*
BM	*Bankers' Magazine (and Statistical Register)*
BS	*Baltimore Sun*
CSM	*Christian Science Monitor*
CT	*Chicago Tribune*
DFP	*Detroit Free Press*
LAT	*Los Angeles Times*
NYH	*New York Herald*
NYHT	*New York Herald Tribune*
NYT	*New York Times*
NYTrib	*New York Tribune*
SLPD	*St. Louis Post-Dispatch*
WP	*Washington Post*
WSJ	*Wall Street Journal*

Archives

FDR Library	Franklin D. Roosevelt Presidential Library, Hyde Park, NY
Ford Library	Gerald R. Ford Presidential Library, Ann Arbor, MI
FRBNY	Federal Reserve Bank of New York Archives, New York, NY
Hoover Library	Herbert Hoover Presidential Library, Ames, IA
Johnson Library	Lyndon B. Johnson Presidential Library, Austin, TX
Kennedy Library	John F. Kennedy Presidential Library, Boston, MA
NARA II	National Archives of the United States, College Park, MD

Archival Collections

Aldrich Papers	Nelson W. Aldrich Papers, Library of Congress, Manuscript Division (accessed through FRASER)
Atkins Papers	Paul Moody Atkins Papers, Yale University Archives
Awalt Papers	Francis Gloyd Awalt Papers, Hoover Library
Burns Papers	Arthur F. Burns Papers, Ford Library
Douglas Papers	Paul H. Douglas Papers, Chicago Historical Society, Chicago, IL
Eccles Papers	Marriner S. Eccles Papers, University of Utah Libraries, Salt Lake City, UT (accessed through FRASER)
Evans Speeches	Statements and Speeches of Rudolph M. Evans, Board of Governors of the Federal Reserve System (accessed through FRASER)
FDIC Comment CRA Letters	Implementation of the Community Reinvestment Act folder, box 9, Comment Letters Concerning Proposed Changes to Regulations, 1975–1980, Office of the Executive Secretary, Records of the Federal Deposit Insurance Corporation (RG 34), NARA II
FDIC Crowley Memos	Letters and Memorandums of Leo T. Crowley, Office of the Chairman of the Board of Directors, Records of the Federal Deposit Insurance Corporation (RG34), NARA II
FDIC Directors Memos	Memorandums to Regional Directors, 1967–1975, Records of the Federal Deposit Insurance Corporation (RG 34), NARA II
FDIC Exam Reports Analysis	Analysis of Examination Reports, Records of the Federal Deposit Insurance Corporation (RG 34), NARA II
FDIC Minutes	Official Minutes of Meetings of the Board of Directors, Records of the Federal Deposit Insurance Corporation (RG34), NARA II
FDIC Supervisor Memos	Memorandums to Supervising Examiners, 1934–1969, Records of the Federal Deposit Insurance Corporation (RG 34), NARA II
Fed Board Minutes	Minutes of the Board of Governors of the Federal Reserve System, 1914–1966, NARA II (accessed through FRASER)
Fed System Records	Records of the Federal Reserve System (RG 82), NARA II (accessed through FRASER)

Hamlin Papers	Charles S. Hamlin Papers, Library of Congress, Manuscript Division (accessed through FRASER)
Janklow Papers	William J. Janklow Papers, University of South Dakota, Vermillion, SD
Letters and Statements of the Board	Mimeographed Letters and Statements of the Board, Board of Governors of the Federal Reserve System (accessed through FRASER)
Martin Papers	William McChesney Martin, Jr., Papers, Missouri Historical Society (accessed through FRASER)
Meyer Papers	Eugene Meyer Papers, Library of Congress, Manuscript Division (accessed through FRASER)
Morgenthau Diaries	Diaries of Henry Morgenthau, Jr., FDR Library (Accessed through FRASER)
OCC Clearing-house Letters	Letters and Reports Concerning State Clearing-houses, box 1, Organization Division, Records of the Office of the Comptroller of the Currency (RG 101), National Archives II
OCC Correspondence	Correspondence, 1863–1901, Division of Reports, Records of the Office of the Comptroller of the Currency (RG 101), NARA II
OCC Examiners Reports	Examiners Reports, Division of Reports, Records of the Office of the Comptroller of the Currency (RG 101), NARA II
OCC Insolvent Correspondence	General Correspondence File, 1865–1944, Insolvent National Banks, Records of the Office of the Comptroller of the Currency (RG 101), NARA II
OCC 1933 Records	Records Relating to the Banking Emergency of 1933, Records of the Organization Division, Records of the Office of the Comptroller of the Currency (RG 101), NARA II
O'Connor Diary	James Francis Thaddeus O'Connor Diary, James Francis Thaddeus O'Connor Diaries and Correspondence, 1933–1947, Bancroft Library, University of California, Berkeley
Saxon Papers	James Saxon Personal Papers, Kennedy Library
Silverthorne Case File	Case 21221, *Don C. Silverthorne v. U.S.*, National Archives Identifier 296040, Appeals Case Files and Briefs, 1891–1994, U.S. Court of Appeals for the Ninth Circuit, Records of the U.S. Courts of Appeals (RG 276), National Archives at Kansas City

Special Liquidator Brokers	Correspondence of the Special Liquidator of Securities with Brokers, 1932–39, Special Liquidator of Securities, Records of the Division of Insolvent National Banks, Records of the Comptroller of the Currency (RG 101), NARA II.
Special Liquidator Correspondence	General Correspondence of the Special Liquidator of Securities, 1932–1939, Special Liquidator of Securities, Records of the Division of Insolvent National Banks, Records of the Comptroller of the Currency (RG 101), NARA II
Special Liquidator NY Office	New York Office—Special Liquidator of Securities folder, box 7, Records of the Division of Insolvent National Banks, Records of the Office of the Comptroller of the Currency (RG 101), NARA II
Special Liquidator Vault Vouchers	Vault Vouchers, Special Liquidator of Securities, Records of the Division of Insolvent National Banks, Records of the Office of the Comptroller of the Currency (RG 101), NARA II
Strong-Miller Correspondence	Correspondence with the Board of Governors of the Federal Reserve System: Member Adolph C. Miller, 1914–1924, Other Members, Federal Reserve Board, Federal Reserve System, Papers of Benjamin Strong, Jr., Federal Reserve Bank of New York (accessed through FRASER)
Viner Papers	Jacob Viner Papers (MC# 138), Public Policy Papers, Department of Special Collections, Princeton University Library

Online Archives

APP	The American Presidency Project, edited by Gerhard Peters and John T. Woolley, http://www.presidency.ucsb.edu
FRASER	Federal Reserve Archival System for Economic Research, Federal Reserve Bank of St. Louis, https://fraser.stlouisfed.org/
FRED	Federal Reserve Economic Data, Federal Reserve Bank of St. Louis, https://fred.stlouisfed.org/

NOTES

Introduction

1. For more on the aftermath of SVB, see Board of Governors of the Federal Reserve System, *Review of the Federal Reserve's Supervision and Regulation of Silicon Valley Bank*, April 28, 2023, https://www.federalreserve.gov/publications/review-of-the-federal-reserves-supervision-and -regulation-of-silicon-valley-bank.htm ("Barr report").

2. Janet Yellen on *CBS Face the Nation*, March 12, 2023; Barak Obama, "Remarks on Signing the Dodd-Frank Wall Street Reform and Consumer Protection Act," July 10, 2010, APP. There is some dispute over whether the government's actions constitute a bailout. See Jeanna Smialek and Alan Rappeport, "Was This a Bailout? Skeptics Descend on Silicon Valley Bank Response," *NYT*, March 13, 2023. We view this mostly as a semantic question. See Adam Levitin, "In Defense of Bailouts," *Georgetown Law Journal* 99, no. 2 (2011): 435–514. We use the term to mean only that the government provided relief to parties not legally entitled to that relief in order to spare them from the downside risk of their own actions. For data on SVB's balance sheet, see Barr report, 17–22.

3. Barr report, 1 See also Jeanna Smialek, "A Big Question for the Fed: What Went Wrong with Bank Oversight," *NYT*, March 21, 2023; *Examining the Failures of Silicon Valley Bank and Signature Bank* (Testimony of Gregory W. Becker), 118 Cong. (2023).

4. For an elucidation of this blurry line between public and private, see William J. Novak, *The People's Welfare: Law and Regulation in Nineteenth-Century America* (University of North Carolina Press, 1996), 26.

5. In this sense, we stand in starkest contrast to scholars such as Lev Menand and Morgan Ricks, who look at golden eras of legislative founding in the Civil War and New Deal for insights into the purpose that the financial system was to take for decades thereafter. See Lev Menand, "Why Supervise Banks? The Foundations of the American Monetary Settlement," *Vanderbilt Law Review* 74, no. 4 (2021): 951–1022; Lev Menand and Morgan Ricks, "Federal Corporate Law and the Business of Banking," *University of Chicago Law Review* 88, no. 6 (2021): 1361–1418; Lev Menand and Morgan Ricks, "Rebuilding Banking Law: Banks as Public Utilities," *Yale Journal on Regulation* 41, no. 2 (2024): 591–651.

6. For an overview, see Jerome Van der Heijden, "Institutional Layering: A Review of the Use of the Concept," *Politics* 31, no. 1 (2011): 9–18. The leading theorist of institutional layering is Kathleen Thelen, e.g., "Institutional Change in Advanced Political Economies," *British Journal of International Relations* 47, no. 3 (2009): 471–98.

7. Our emphasis on layering and evolution offers a counterargument to proponents of the "iron law of financial regulation," in which new—and flawed—financial rules invariably arise in response to financial crises. See Roberta Romano, "Regulating in the Dark and a Postscript Assessment of the Iron Law of Financial Regulation," *Hofstra Law Review* 43, no. 1 (2014): 25–70. Sweeping congressional expansion of the supervisory purview after World War II often occurred with no financial crisis in sight.

8. Douglass C. North, *Institutions, Institutional Change and Economic Performance* (Cambridge University Press, 1990); Roy Suddaby, William M. Foster, and Albert J. Mills, "Historical Institutionalism," in *Organizations in Time: History, Theory, Methods,* ed. Marcelo Bucheli and R. Daniel Wadhwani (Oxford University Press, 2013), 100–123. For more on the application of institutional history to economic and financial history, see Peter Conti-Brown, "Institutions: A Research Program for Law, Macroeconomics, and History," *Law and Contemporary Problems* 83, no. 1 (2020): 157–79; Peter Conti-Brown and Brian D. Feinstein, "The Contingent Origins of Financial Legislation," *Washington University Law Review* 99 (2021): 145–222. The key text for institutional economics in the tradition we mean here is Douglass C. North and Barry R. Weingast, "Constitutions and Commitment: The Evolution of Institutional Governing Public Choice in Seventeenth-Century England," *Journal of Economic History* 49, no. 4 (1989): 803–32.

9. Stevenay Jay Gould, *The Panda's Thumb: More Reflections in Natural History* (W. W. Norton, 1980), 20–21, 28–29.

10. See, e.g., Menand and Ricks, "Federal Corporate Law"; Menand, "Why Supervise Banks?"; Christina Parajon Skinner, "The Monetary Executive," *George Washington Law Review* 91, no. 1 (2023): 164–223; Saule T. Omarova and Graham S. Steele, "Banking and Antitrust," *Yale Law Journal* 133, no. 4 (2024): 1162–1253.

11. *Annual Report of the Comptroller of the Currency* (1884), l; Randal Quarles, "Dean's Lecture" (lecture, Yale Law School, New Haven, CT, February 26, 2020) (transcript used with permission and on file with authors).

12. Randal Quarles, "Spontaneity and Order: Transparency, Accountability, and Fairness in Bank Supervision" (transcript of speech delivered at the American Bar Association Banking Law Committee Meeting 2020, Washington, DC, 2020, available online at https://www .federalreserve.gov/newsevents/speech/quarles20200117a.htm); Christina Parajon Skinner, "The Independence of Central Bank Supervision" (paper, Hoover Institution, Monetary Policy Conference, May 3, 2024); Daniel K. Tarullo, "Bank Supervision and Administrative Law," *Columbia Business Law Review* 2022, no. 1 (2022): 279–401; Todd Phillips, "In Support of Supervisory Guidance," *Corporate and Business Law Journal* 3 (2022): 344–80.

13. Jerry L. Mashaw, *Bureaucratic Justice: Managing Social Security Disability Claims* (Yale University Press, 1985). The first argument on "street level bureaucracy" is Michael Lipsky, *Street-Level Bureaucracy: Dilemmas of the Individual in Public Service* (Russell Sage Foundation, 1980). For an overview of the empirical literature that the latter book has spawned, see Daniel Ho and Sam Sherman, "Managing Street-Level Arbitrariness: The Evidence Base for Public Sector Quality Improvement," *Annual Review of Law and Social Science* 13 (2017): 251–72.

14. For an argument identifying different institutional conditions that predict when bureaucratic discretion moves in one way or another, see Quintin H. Beazer, "Bureaucratic Discretion,

Business Investment, and Uncertainty," *Journal of Politics* 74, no. 3 (2012): 637–52. Some economists have succeeded in identifying natural experiments that permit them to evaluate the presence or absence of supervisory resources. See John Kandrac and Bernd Schlusche, "The Effect of Bank Supervision and Examination on Risk Taking: Evidence from a Natural Experiment," *Review of Financial Studies* 34, no. 6 (2021): 3181–3212; Beverly Hirtle, Anna Kovner, and Matthew Plosser, "The Impact of Supervision on Bank Performance," *Journal of Finance* 75, no. 5 (2020): 2765–2808.

15. For a historical treatment of moral hazard, see David Rowell and Luke B. Connelly, "A History of the Term "Moral Hazard,"" *Journal of Risk and Insurance* 79, no. 4 (December 2012): 1051–75.

16. We thank Scott Shapiro for this pithy sentence. A boomlet in financial regulation scholarship focuses on the public-private nature of banking. See Mehrsa Baradaran, *How the Other Half Banks: Exclusion, Exploitation, and the Threat to Democracy* (Harvard University Press, 2018); Robert C. Hockett and Saule T. Omarova, "'Private' Means to 'Public' Ends: Governments as Market Actors," *Cornell Law Faculty Publications* 15 (2014): 53–76; Menand and Ricks, "Rebuilding Banking Law."

17. Morgan Ricks, *The Money Problem: Rethinking Financial Regulation* (University of Chicago Press, 2016); Gary B. Gorton, *Slapped by the Invisible Hand: The Panic of 2007* (Oxford University Press, 2010).

18. Kathryn Judge, "Fragmentation Nodes: A Study in Financial Innovation, Complexity, and Systemic Risk," *Stanford Law Review* 64, no. 3 (2012): 657–725; Dan Awrey, "The Mechanisms of Derivatives Market Efficiency," *New York University Law Review* 91, no. 5 (2016): 1104–82.

19. Sarah E. Light and Christina Parajon Skinner, "Banks and Climate Governance," *Columbia Law Review* 121, no. 6 (2021): 1895–956; Graham Steele, "Confronting the 'Climate Lehman Moment': The Case for Macroprudential Climate Regulation," *Cornell Journal of Law and Public Policy* 30, no. 109 (2020): 109–57.

20. Jeffrey N. Gordon and Christopher Muller, "Confronting Financial Crisis: Dodd-Frank's Dangers and the Case for a Systemic Emergency Insurance Fund," *Yale Journal on Regulation* 28, no. 1 (2011): 151–211; Iman Anabtawi and Steven L. Schwarcz, "Regulating Systemic Risk: Towards an Analytical Framework," *Notre Dame Law Review* 86, no. 4 (2011): 1349–412; Daniel Schwarcz and David Zaring, "Regulation by Threat: Dodd-Frank and the Nonbank Problem," *University of Chicago Law Review* 84, no. 4 (2017): 1813–81.

21. Erik F. Gerding, *Law, Bubbles, and Financial Regulation* (Routledge, 2011); John C. Coffee Jr., "The Political Economy of Dodd-Frank: Why Financial Reform Tends to Be Frustrated and Systemic Risk Perpetuated," *Cornell Law Review* 97, no. 5 (2012): 1019–82.

22. Romano, "Regulating in the Dark"; Peter Conti-Brown and Michael Ohlrogge, "Financial Crises and Legislation," *Journal of Financial Crises* 4, no. 3 (2022): 1–59.

23. Chris Brummer and Yesha Yadhav, "Fintech and the Innovation Trilemma," *Georgetown Law Journal* 107, no. 2 (2019): 235–307; Saule T. Omarova, "License to Deal: Mandatory Approval of Complex Financial Products," *Washington University Law Review* 90, no. 1 (2012): 63–140.

24. Gary B. Gorton and Jeffery Y. Zhang, "Taming Wildcat Stablecoins," *University of Chicago Law Review* 90, no. 3 (July 2021): 909–71; Hilary J. Allen, *Driverless Finance: Fintech's Impact on*

Financial Stability (Oxford University Press, 2022); Shaanan Cohney, David A. Hoffman, Jeremy Sklaroff, and David A. Wishnick, "Coin-Operated Capitalism," *Columbia Law Review* 119, no. 3 (2019): 591–676.

25. Mehrsa Baradaran, *The Color of Money: Black Banks and the Racial Wealth Gap* (Belknap Press, 2017); Nakita Q. Cuttino, "The Rise of 'FringeTech': Regulatory Risks in Earned-Wage Access," *Northwestern Law Review* 105, no. 6 (2022): 1505–79.

26. Dan Awrey and Kristin van Zwieten, "The Shadow Payment System," *Journal of Corporation Law* 43, no. 4 (2018): 775–816; Dan Awrey and Joshua Macey, "The Promise and Perils of Open Finance" (*Research Paper no. 956, University of Chicago Coase-Sandor Institute for Law and Economics*, May 2022); Peter Conti-Brown and David Wishnick, "Private Markets, Public Options, and the Payment System," *Yale Journal on Regulation* 27, no. 2 (2021): 380–434; Paolo Saguato, "The Ownership of Clearinghouses: When 'Skin in the Game' Is Not Enough, the Remutualization of Clearinghouses," *Yale Journal on Regulation* 34, no. 2 (2017): 601–66.

27. David A. Skeel. *The New Financial Deal: Understanding the Dodd-Frank Act and Its (Unintended) Consequences* (Wiley, 2010).

28. Jeremy C. Kress, "Reviving Bank Antitrust," *Duke Law Journal* 72, no. 3 (2022): 519–98. Jeremy C. Kress, "Modernizing Bank Merger Review," *Yale Journal on Regulation* 37, no. 2 (2020): 435–98.

29. Yair Listokin, *Law and Macroeconomics: Legal Remedies to Recessions* (Harvard University Press, 2019).

30. David T. Zaring, "The Government's Economic Response to the COVID Crisis," *Review of Banking and Financial Law* 40, no. 2 (2021): 315–421; Lev Menand, "Unappropriated Dollars: The Fed's Ad Hoc Lending Facilities and the Rules that Govern Them" (*Working Paper no. 518, European Corporate Governance Institute, Brussels*, 2020).

31. The book also grows from many insights from scholars active in that first generation of scholarship. We owe special debts to the following authors and their works: Jonathan R. Macey and Geoffrey P. Miller, "Double Liability of Bank Shareholders: History and Implications," *Wake Forest Law Review* 27 (1992): 31–62; Howell E. Jackson, "The Expanding Obligations of Financial Holding Companies," *Harvard Law Review* 107, no. 3 (1994): 507–619; Arthur E. Wilmarth Jr., "The Case for the Validity of State Regional Banking Laws," *Loyola of Los Angeles Law Review* 18, no. 4 (1985): 1017–51; Rosa María Lastra, *Central Banking and Banking Regulation* (Financial Markets Group, London School of Economics, 1996); Rosa María Lastra, *Legal Foundations of International Monetary Stability* (Oxford University Press, 2006); Rosa María Lastra, "Defining Forward-Looking, Judgement-Based Supervision," *Journal of Banking Regulation* 14, no. 3 (2013): 221–27.

32. To be very clear, this book did not discover bank supervision, as noted above, and as evidenced by the review essays prepared for the conference, "Bank Supervision: Past, Present, and Future," co-hosted by the Board of Governors of the Federal Reserve System, Harvard Law School, and the Wharton School of the University of Pennsylvania on December 11, 2020 (Beverly Hirtle, "Banking Supervision: The Perspective from Economics;" Julie A. Hill, "Bank Supervision: A Legal Scholarship Review;" Sean H. Vanatta, "Histories of Bank Supervision;" Johnathan Fiechter and Aditya Narain, "Enhancing Supervisory Effectiveness—Findings from IMF Assessments"). The literature reviewed in those pieces highlights a growing dynamism in the study of supervision in history, law, and economics. There is a reason, though, that almost

all of these scholarly efforts occurred within the last few years: As they recognize, the attention paid to supervision as a separate category is new and, in a word, undertheorized. What they lack is a unitary theory of supervision and a history of how supervisory institutions, broadly construed, have evolved. *Private Finance, Public Power* provides both.

33. See Theodore J. Lowi, *The End of Liberalism: Ideology, Policy, and the Crisis of Public Authority* (W. W. Norton & Co., 1969) and Stephen Skowronek, *Building a New American State: The Expansion of National Administrative Capacities, 1877–1920* (Cambridge University Press, 1982) for the still influential but almost completely repudiated view. The key architects of the revision are Novak, *The People's Welfare*; William J. Novak, *New Democracy: The Creation of the Modern American State* (Harvard University Press, 2023); Brian Balogh. *A Government Out of Sight: The Mystery of National Authority in Nineteenth-Century America* (Cambridge University Press, 2007); and Jerry L. Mashaw, *Creating the Administrative Constitution: The Lost One Hundred Years of American Administrative Law* (Yale University Press, 2012). Of the three key revisionists, only Mashaw discusses, briefly, the Comptroller of the Currency and the "broad visitation and inspection powers and the ability to place banks violating the [National Bank Act] or the terms of their federal charters in receivership and wind up their affairs" (*Creating the Administrative Constitution*, 242). Novak also mentions the Comptroller in a list of other agencies created prior to the Progressive Era (*New Democracy*, 223).

34. Eric Rauchway, *Winter War: Hoover, Roosevelt, and the First Clash over the New Deal* (Basic Books, 2018); Steve Fraser and Gary Gerstle, *The Rise and Fall of the New Deal Order, 1930–1980* (Princeton University Press, 1990); Alan Brinkley, *The End of Reform: New Deal Liberalism in Recession* (Alfred A. Knopf, 1995); Ira Katznelson, *Fear Itself: The New Deal and the Origins of Our Time* (Liveright, 2013); Mehrsa Baradaran, "Regulation by Hypothetical." *Vanderbilt Law Review* 67, no. 5 (2014): 1247–326; Baradaran, *The Color of Money*; Rebecca Marchiel, *After Redlining: The Urban Reinvestment Movement in the Era of Financial Deregulation* (University of Chicago Press, 2020); Kim Phillips-Fein, *Fear City: New York's Fiscal Crisis and the Rise of Austerity Politics* (Metropolitan Books, 2017).

35. Lipsky, *Street-Level Bureaucracy*.

36. Gretta R. Krippner, *Capitalizing on Crisis: The Political Origins of the Rise of Finance* (Harvard University Press, 2011).

37. James C. Scott, *Seeing like a State: How Certain Schemes to Improve the Human Condition Have Failed* (Yale University Press, 1998).

Chapter One

1. Bray Hammond, *Banks and Politics in America* (Princeton University Press, 1957), 600–604; Hugh Rockoff, "The Free Banking Era: A Reexamination," *Journal of Money, Credit, and Banking* 6, no. 2 (1974): 141–67.

2. State of Michigan, "*Bank Commissioners Report*," in *Documents Accompanying the Journal of the House of Representatives of the State of Michigan at the Annual Session in 1839*, ed. E. J. Roberts (J. S. and S. A. Bragg, 1839), 226–41; H. M. Utley, "The Wild Cat Banking System of Michigan," in *Report of the Pioneer Society of the State of Michigan*, vol. 5 (W. S. George, 1884), 207–22; Hammond, *Banks and Politics*, 601.

3. Utley, "The Wild Cat Banking System," 207–22.

4. Andrew D. Edwards, "Grenville's Silver Hammer: The Problem of Money in the Stamp Act Crisis," *Journal of American History* 104, no. 2 (2017): 337–62; Sharon A. Murphy, *Other People's Money: How Banking Worked in the Early American Republic* (Johns Hopkins University Press, 2017), 65; Robert E. Wright, *The Origins of Commercial Banking in America, 1750–1800* (Rowman and Littlefield Publishers, 2001), 61; Adam Smith, *The Wealth of Nations*, ed. Edwin Cannan (Bantam Books, 2003), 363–419. The first bank in the United States with a federal charter was Robert Morris's Bank of North America. For Morris's influence on Hamilton, see Wright, *Origins of Commercial Banking*, 100–101; Murphy, *Other People's Money*, 64.

5. Albert S. Bolles, *A Financial History of the United States, from 1789 to 1860* (D. Appleton & Company, 1894), 32; Drew R. McCoy, *The Elusive Republic: Political Economy in Jeffersonian America* (University of North Carolina Press, 1980); *Articles of Confederation* (1777), Article IX. For example, South Carolina's notes were not legal tender but traded at a premium because redemption was well established. Rhode Island, on the other hand, suffered from substantial inflation. See Arthur J. Rolnick, Bruce D. Smith, and Warren E. Weber, "In Order to Form a More Perfect Monetary Union," *Federal Reserve Bank of Minneapolis Quarterly Review* No. 1741 (1993): 1; Mary M. Schweitzer, "State-Issued Currency and the Ratification of the U.S. Constitution," *Journal of Economic History* 49, no. 2 (1989): 311–22.

6. Hammond, *Banks and Politics*, 89–93; James Madison, *Debates on the Adoption of the Federal Constitution*, ed. Johnathan Elliot (Johnathan Elliot, 1845), 435 (statement of Oliver Ellsworth). Farley Grubb argues that the clauses that prohibited state-issued currency were specifically intended to encourage the use of private banknotes—and ensure rents for private bankers. See Grubb, "Creating the U.S. Dollar Currency Union, 1748–1811: A Quest for Monetary Stability or a Usurpation of State Sovereignty for Personal Gain?," *American Economic Review* 93, no. 5 (2003): 1778–98.

7. Alexander Hamilton, *Second Report on the Further Provision Necessary for Establishing Public Credit* (1790).

8. Hamilton, *Second Report on the Public Credit*; Hammond, *Banks and Politics*, 89–114; Bolles, *Financial History of the United States*, 100–102; Wright, *Origins of Commercial Banking*, 77–110.

9. Thomas Jefferson to James Madison, October 1, 1792, in Gordon Wood, *Empire of Liberty: A History of the Early Republic, 1789–1815* (Oxford University Press, 2009), 294.

10. Thomas Jefferson to Albert Gallatin, December 13, 1803, in Thomas K. McCraw, *The Founders and Finance: How Hamilton, Gallatin, and Other Immigrants Forged a New Economy* (Harvard University Press, 2012), 290–311 (quote from 290).

11. McCraw, *Founders and Finance*, 296; Daniel Walker Howe, *What Hath God Wrought: The Transformation of America, 1815–1848* (Oxford University Press, 2007), 378–82.

12. McCraw, *Founders and Finance*, 290; Hammond, *Banks and Politics*, 208, 228–35, 244; Arthur Fraas, "The Second Bank of the United States: An Instrument for an Interregional Monetary Union," *Journal of Economic History* 34, no. 2 (1974): 447–67.

13. Sharon A. Murphy, *Banking on Slavery: Financing Southern Expansion in the Antebellum United States* (University of Chicago Press, 2023), 109–130; Howard Bodenhorn, *A History of Banking in Antebellum America: Financial Markets and Economic Development in an Era of Nation-Building* (Cambridge University Press, 2000), 9–17; Hammond, *Banks and Politics*, 19–26, 66, 144, 167; Fraas, "The Second Bank"; Joshua R. Greenberg, *Bank Notes and Shinplasters: The Rage*

for Paper Money in the Early Republic (University of Pennsylvania Press, 2020). Fraas articulates the non-trivial challenges that the Second Bank navigated—initially with profound failure—in securing a uniform currency by the late 1820s.

14. Eugene N. White, "Lessons from American Bank Supervision from the Nineteenth Century to the Great Depression," in *Macroprudential Regulatory Policies: The New Road to Financial Stability?*, ed. Stijn Claessens, Douglas D. Evanoff, George G. Kaufan, and Laura E. Kodres (World Scientific, 2011), 41–62; John T. Holdsworth and Davis R. Dewey, *The First and Second Banks of the United States*, Publications of the United States National Monetary Commission, Sen. Doc. 571 (Government Printing Office, 1910), 188–94; Arthur J. Rolnick, Bruce D. Smith, and Warren E. Weber, "Establishing a Monetary Union in the United States," in *Evolution and Procedures in Central Banking*, ed. David E. Altig and Bruce D. Smith (Cambridge University Press, 2003), 227–55. For a useful summary of the Currency versus Banking School debates, see Charles Goodhart and Meinhard Jensen, "Currency School Versus Banking School: An Ongoing Confrontation," *Economic Thought* 4, no. 2 (2015): 20. As Goodhart and Jensen state, a frequently debated position of the Currency School is that the provision of currency is a sovereign, not a private, function. These debates continue to resonate today. See Morgan Ricks, *The Money Problem: Rethinking Financial Regulation* (University of Chicago Press, 2016). Lev Menand has recently written a historical treatment of bank supervision that we identify as a proponent of the "currency view" of supervision—see Lev Menand, "Why Supervise Banks?" *Vanderbilt Law Review* 74, no. 4 (2021): 951–1022.

15. Hammond, *Banks and Politics*, 127, 241–44, 256, 272–73, 306–10 (Biddle quote at 307); Fraas, "The Second Bank"; White, "Lessons from American Bank Supervision"; Jane E. Knodell, *The Second Bank of the United States* (Routledge, 2019).

16. M. St. Clair Clarke and David A. Hall, *Legislative and Documentary History of the Bank of the United States* (Gales and Seaton, 1832), 159; Judge Glock, "The Forgotten Visitorial Power: The Origins of Administrative Subpoenas and Modern Regulation," *Review of Banking & Financial Law* 37 (2017): 205–65.

17. Holdsworth and Dewey, *First and Second Banks*, 73; Charles F. Dunbar, "Accounts of the First Bank of the United States," *Quarterly Journal of Economics* 6, no. 4 (1892): 471–74.

18. Holdsworth and Dewey, *First and Second Banks*, 131, 172, 277, 281; Clarke and Hall, *Legislative and Documentary History*, 714–34.

19. Knodell, *Second Bank*, 6–13; Gouge, quoted in Hammond, *Banks and Politics*, 608; William Johnson, dissenting, *Osborn v. Bank of the United States*, 22 U.S. 873, quoted in James W. Hurst, *A Legal History of Money in the United States* (University of Nebraska Press, 1973), 274n155.

20. It is hard to overstate the profound impact that the Bank War had on the political fabric of the time: e.g., Howe, *What God Hath Wrought*, 373–94; Sean Wilentz, *Rise of American Democracy: Jefferson to Lincoln* (W. W. Norton, 2005), 204–10. Peter Temin famously disputed the economic importance of the Bank War, but his argument is about the inflationary consequences of the failure at rechartering. See Temin, "The Economic Consequences of the Bank War," *Journal of Political Economy* 76, no. 2 (1968): 257. Our argument is about the consequences of that failure for bank supervision.

21. Murphy, *Other People's Money*, 165–85; Jane E. Knodell, "Rethinking the Jacksonian Economy," *Journal of Economic History* 66, no. 3 (2006): 541–43; Peter L. Rousseau, "Jacksonian

Monetary Policy, Specie Flows, and the Panic of 1837," *Journal of Economic History* 62, no. 2 (2002): 460–62; Howe, *What God Hath Wrought*, 594.

22. Hammond, *Banks and Politics*, 145, 164–66, 171, 323; Ross M. Robertson, *The Comptroller and Bank Supervision* (Office of the Comptroller of the Currency, 1968), 19; Davis R. Dewey, *State Banking Before the Civil War*, Publications of the National Monetary Commission, Sen. Doc. 581 (Government Printing Office, 1910), 126–35; Murphy, *Banking on Slavery*, 277–80.

23. Nathan Appleton, *A Defence of Country Banks: Being a Reply to a Pamphlet Entitled an Examination of the Banking System of Massachusetts, in Reference to the Renewal of the Bank Charters* (Stimpson and Clapp, 1831), 21–22.

24. Rockoff, "Free Banking Era," 141–67. There is significant disagreement in the contemporary banking literature on what free banking meant: e.g., Ricks, *The Money Problem*, 10 (describing "free banking" as the idea that the state should leave banking activity "unhindered."); Mehrsa Baradaran, *How the Other Half Banks: Exclusion, Exploitation, and the Threat to Democracy* (Harvard University Press, 2015), 34 (equating "free banking" with "wildcat banking" and stating that the period "is considered a disaster by most scholars" and that the system operated "without government support").

25. Howard Bodenhorn, "Bank Chartering and Political Corruption in Antebellum New York," in *Corruption and Reform: Lessons from America's Economic History*, ed. Edward L. Glaeser and Claudia Goldin (University of Chicago Press, 2006), 231–57; Howard Bodenhorn, "Free Banking and Bank Entry in Nineteenth-Century New York," *Financial History Review* 15, no. 2 (2008): 175–201; Eric Hilt, "Early American Corporations and the State," in *Corporations and American Democracy*, ed. Naomi R. Lamoreaux and William J. Novak (Harvard University Press, 2017), 37–73; Naomi R. Lamoreaux and John J. Wallis, "Economic Crisis, General Laws, and the Mid-Nineteenth-Century Transformation of American Political Economy" (working paper no. w27400, National Bureau of Economic Research, 2020).

26. Rockoff, "Free Banking Era," 142. For more on the trend toward general incorporation, see Hilt, "Early American Corporations and the State."

27. Warren E. Weber, "Antebellum State Bank Balance Sheets Compiled," Federal Reserve Bank of Minneapolis (2018), available online at https://researchdatabase.minneapolisfed.org /concern/datasets/9c67wm86f.

28. Hugh McCulloch, *Men and Measures of a Half Century* (Charles Scribner's Sons, 1888), 125–26; Hugh Rockoff, "New Evidence on Free Banking in the United States," *American Economic Review* 75, no. 4 (1985): 886–89.

29. Howard Bodenhorn, "Small-Denomination Banknotes in Antebellum America," *Journal of Money, Credit and Banking* 25, no. 4 (1993): 812–827, 822–23; Stephen Mihm, *A Nation of Counterfeiters: Capitalists, Con Men, and the Making of the United States* (Harvard University of Press, 2009), 235–45; Robert T. Bicknell, *Bicknell's Counterfeit Detector and Bank Note List* (Lilly, Wait & Co., 1833); J. W. Clark & Co., *Clark's New England Bank Note List, and Counterfeit Bill Detector, for December 1846* (J. N. Bank, 1846); T. B. Peterson & Bros., *Peterson's Philadelphia Counterfeit Detector and Bank Note List* (T. B. Peterson & Bros., 1860).

30. Howard Bodenhorn, "Making the Little Guy Pay: Payments-System Networks, Cross-Subsidization, and the Collapse of the Suffolk System," *Journal of Economic History* 62, no. 1 (2002): 147–69; State of Connecticut, *Report of the Bank Commissioners to the General Assembly* (1848), 9; Charles Calomiris and Charles Kahn, "The Efficiency of Self-Regulated Payment

Systems," *Journal of Money, Credit and Banking* 28, no. 4 (1996): 766–97. Calomiris and Kahn draw from the nineteenth-century examples as lessons for the present, at least as of 1996, but, as we will see in the chapters ahead, the changing landscape makes those parallels much harder to draw.

31. State of Ohio, *First Annual Report of the Bank Commissioners of Ohio* (1839), 9.

32. Ohio's banks are the exception that proves the rule, in that the legislature, angry about suspension, required specie payments in 1839 when neighboring states did not, which led to massive redemptions and the failure of Ohio's banks. See State of Ohio, "Special Report of the Bank Commissioner's Office" (July 26, 1842), in *Journal of the Senate of the State of Ohio* (1842), 8–23.

33. "Purchase of a Maryland Bank Charter," *BS*, June 27, 1854; Dewey, *State Banking Before the Civil War*, 103; Mihm, *Nation of Counterfeiters*; Jeff Forrett, "'How Deeply They Weed into the Pockets': Slave Traders, Bank Speculators, and the Anatomy of a Chesapeake Wildcat, 1840–1843," *Journal of the Early Republic* 39, no. 4 (2019): 709–36.

34. Hammond, *Banks and Politics*, 569–70; Dewey, *State Banking Before the Civil War*, 78–79; Bodenhorn, *History of Banking*, 169–70.

35. Bank examination derives from medieval "visitorial powers," which persisted in the common law as the right of a chartering authority to ensure that charter provisions were being followed. Glock, "The Forgotten Visitorial Power"; Hammond, *Banks and Politics*, 187; Robertson, *The Comptroller and Bank Supervision*, 24–25; Dewey, *State Banking Before the Civil War*, 126–35. Apparently, Nicholas Biddle refused a congressional committee entrance, so New York Congressman Abijah Mann hired workers to tunnel into the Second Bank's Philadelphia offices, leading Biddle to relent and let the congressmen in (Hammond, *Banks and Politics*, 583).

36. Howard Bodenhorn, *State Banking in Early America: A New Economic History* (Oxford University Press, 2003), 155–82; Carter H. Golembe and Clark Warburton, "Insurance of Bank Obligations in Six States," Federal Deposit Insurance Corporation (1958), VI-5–VI-7 (FRASER); Warren E. Weber, "Bank Liability Insurance Schemes in the United States Before 1865" (working paper no. 679, *Federal Reserve Bank of Minneapolis*, 2010), 10–12.

37. Bodenhorn, *State Banking*, 159–62.

38. Golembe and Warburton, "Insurance of Bank Obligations"; Weber, "Bank Liability Insurance Schemes."

39. Commonwealth of Massachusetts, *Annual Report of the Bank Commissioners* (1854), 37–48; State of Connecticut, *Report of the Bank Commissioners to the General Assembly* (1848), 9–10.

40. Hurst, *A Legal History of Money*, 157; Robert E. Chaddock, *The Safety Fund Banking System in New York*, Publications of the National Monetary Commission, Sen. Doc. 581 (Government Printing Office, 1910), 315–20, 326; Howard Bodenhorn, "Zombie Banks and the Demise of New York's Safety Fund," *Eastern Economic Journal* 22, no. 1 (1996): 28; "Commercial Affairs–Money Market," *NYH*, July 14, 1848; "A Bank Trap," *BDR*, July 18, 1848; Hammond, *Banks and Politics*, 556–63, 593; Bodenhorn, *State Banking*, 155–82.

41. Jeremy Atack, Matthew Jaremski, and Peter L. Rousseau, "Did Railroads Make Antebellum U.S. Banks More Sound?" in *Enterprising America: Businesses, Banks, and Credit Markets in Historical Perspective*, ed. William J. Collins and Robert A. Margo (University of Chicago Press, 2015), 152–53.

42. Charles Edwards, *On Receivers in Equity; and Under the New York Code of Procedure; with Precedents*, 2nd ed. (John S. Voorhees, 1857), 162–307; New York, *Annual Report of the Superintendent of the Banking Department of the State of New York* (1859), 14–15.

43. Edwards, *On Receivers in Equity*, 162–307.

44. New York, "Acts Related to the Safety Fund," in *Laws of New York Passed at the Sixty-Fourth Session of the Legislature* (Thurlow Weed, 1841), 338–50 (quote at 348); Chaddock, *The Safety Fund Banking System*, 302–303; Bodenhorn, *State Banking*, 161–64, 176–78.

45. State of Ohio, *Annual Report of the Bank Commissioners* (1839), 13. With the exception of the five publicly-traded banks (Bank of England, Bank of Scotland, Royal Bank of Scotland, the British Linen Company Bank, and the Bank of Ireland), British banks were not permitted to adopt limited liability before 1857 (Graeme G, Acheson and John D. Turner, "Shareholder Liability, Risk Aversion, and Investment Returns in Nineteenth-Century British Banking," in *Men, Women, and Money: Perspectives on Gender, Wealth, and Investment, 1850–1930*, ed. David R. Green, Alastair Owens, Josephine Maltby, and Janette Rutterford [Oxford University Press, 2011], 209–10). The question of bank shareholder liability has become en vogue again for scholars since the late 1980s (Jonathan Macey and Geoffrey Miller, "Double Liability of Bank Shareholders," *Wake Forest L. Rev.* 32 [1992]: 37; Peter Conti-Brown, "Elective Shareholder Liability," *Stanford Law Review* 64 (2012): 409–68, 414–17; Charles Goodhart and Rosa Lastra, "Equity Finance: Matching Liability to Power," *Journal of Financial Regulation* 6, no. 1 [2020]: 8–10).

46. Howard Bodenhorn, "Double Liability at Early American Banks" (*working paper no. 21494*, National Bureau of Economic Research, 2015), 2–10; Dewey, *State Banking Before the Civil War*, 115–20; State of Michigan, *Governor's Message* (1849), 18.

47. State of Michigan, *Laws of Michigan* (1849), 122–27.

48. Bodenhorn, "Zombie Banks," 23; Bodenhorn, "Double Liability," 10.

49. Hammond, *Banks and Politics*, 730; Bray Hammond, *Sovereignty and an Empty Purse* (Princeton University Press, 1970), 60–62, 168–69; Margaret G. Myers, *A Financial History of the United States* (Columbia University Press, 1970), 149–53; Robert P. Sharkey, *Money, Class, and Party: An Economic Study of Civil War & Reconstruction* (Johns Hopkins Press, 1959), 22–28. See also John Sherman, *John Sherman's Recollections* (Werner, 1895), 269–300. Sherman notes that the greenback and national banking questions were so entwined that they had to be discussed together. He never discusses examiners. His faith is in the system itself, especially in note redemption.

50. Paul Studenski and Herman E. Krooss, *Financial History of the United States* (McGraw-Hill, 1952), 141–43; Sharkey, *Money, Class, and Party*, 255–69.

51. Hammond, *Banks and Politics*, 718–25; Bruce G. Carruthers and Sarah Babb, "The Color of Money and the Nature of Value," *American Journal of Sociology* 101, no. 6 (1996): 1565; Sharkey, *Money, Class, and Party*, 168; Hammond, *Sovereignty and an Empty Purse*, 94–105; David F. Weiman and John A. James, "The Political Economy of the US Monetary Union," *American Economic Review* 97, no. 2 (2007): 271.

52. Myers, *Financial History*, 154–57; Hammond, *Sovereignty and an Empty Purse*, 290, 339–40.

53. Patrick Newman, "The Origins of the National Banking System," *Independent Review* 22, no. 3 (2018): 383–401; John A. James and David F. Weiman, "The National Banking Acts and the Transformation of New York City Banking During the Civil War Era," *Journal of Economic History* 71, no. 2 (2011): 338–62; National Banking Act of 1864, c. 106, 13 Stat. 99, §21.

54. Hammond, *Banks and Politics*, 727–34; Robertson, *The Comptroller and Bank Supervision*, 41, 47–48. Hammond suggests this point but does not follow the story forward.

55. White, "Lessons from the History of Bank Examination and Supervision," 18–22; Daniel P. Carpenter, *The Forging of Bureaucratic Autonomy: Reputations, Networks, and Policy Innovation in Executive Agencies, 1862–1928* (Princeton University Press, 2001).

Interlude: Supervision on Suspicion

1. For a sympathetic biography of Fillmore, see Robert J. Rayback, *Millard Fillmore: Biography of a President* (Henry Stewart, 1959).

2. *Annual Report of the Comptroller*, New York (January 4, 1849), 36.

3. *Annual Report of the Comptroller*, 36.

4. Sean Wilentz, *The Rise of American Democracy: Jefferson to Lincoln* (W. W. Norton, 2005), 531; *Annual Report of the Comptroller*, 37; Reprint of "The Canal Bank," *Albany Atlas*, July 13, 1848 in "The Canal Bank—Disgraceful Failure," *The Evening Post*, July 14, 1848.

5. "Astounding Disclosures of the Canal Bank, Albany," *NYH*, August 14, 1848; "The Canal Bank—Legal Proceedings," *BDR*, July 19, 1848.

6. "Astounding Disclosures of the Canal Bank, Albany."

7. "Local Matters," *BDR*, July 17, 1848; "Pratt Bank of Buffalo," *Buffalo Commercial Journal*, August 2, 1848; "Pratt Bank of Buffalo," *BDR*, August 3, 1848; "Astounding Disclosures of the Canal Bank, Albany."

8. "Failure," *Brooklyn Daily Eagle*, July 12, 1848; *Annual Report of the Comptroller*, 36.

9. *Annual Report of the Comptroller*, 36.

10. "The Republicans," *NYT*, October 10, 1855; "The Latest News Received by Magnetic Telegraph," *New York Daily Tribune*, September 8, 1858; Thurlow Weed Barnes, *Memoir of Thurlow Weed* (Houghton, Mifflin, 1884), 251; State of New York, *Annual Report of the Superintendent of the Banking Department* (January 5, 1859), 14–15.

11. *Annual Report of the Superintendent of the Banking Department*, 14.

12. *Annual Report of the Superintendent of the Banking Department*, 15.

13. *Annual Report of the Superintendent of the Banking Department*, 16.

Chapter Two

1. Hugh McCulloch, quoted in Thomas P. Kane, *The Romance and Tragedy of Banking: Problems and Incidents of Governmental Supervision of National Banks*, 2nd ed. (Bankers Publishing Co., 1923), 24.

2. Jerry L. Mashaw, *Creating the Administrative Constitution: The Lost One Hundred Years of American Administrative Law* (Yale University Press, 2012), 187–208 (quote at 195); Act of July 7, 1838, c. 191, 5 Stat. 304; Ross M. Robertson, *The Comptroller and Bank Supervision: A Historical Appraisal*, 2nd ed. (Office of the Comptroller of the Currency, 1995), 48–49; *National Banking Act of 1863*, 12 Stat. 665 § 51; *National Banking Act of 1864*, 13 Stat. 99 § 54; Sean H. Vanatta, "Revolving Door Governance: Bank Supervisors in the United States, 1863–1933," *Management and Organizational History* 19 (2024): 153–81, 6–7.

3. National Banking Act of 1864, §§ 12, 34, 46, and 53–55.

4. Comptroller of the Currency, *Instructions and Suggestions of the Comptroller of the Currency in Regard to the Organization and Management of National Banks* (1864); Howard Bodenhorn, "Double Liability at Early American Banks" (working paper no. 21494, National Bureau of Economic Research, August 2015); Hugh McCulloch, *Men and Measures of Half a Century* (Charles Scribner's Sons, 1889), 113–14; Richard Franklin Bensel, *Yankee Leviathan: The Origins of Central State Authority in America, 1859–1877* (Cambridge University Press, 1990); Brian Balogh, *A Government Out of Sight: The Mystery of National Authority in Nineteenth-Century America* (Cambridge University Press, 2009); Mashaw, *Creating the Administrative Constitution*; Comptroller of the Currency, *Instructions* (July 7, 1863), reproduced in U.S. Senate, *Message from the President of the United States, transmitting a letter from the Secretary of the Treasury, in response to Senate resolution of December 6, 1881, concerning instructions to and reports of certain examiners of national banks, &c.* 47 Cong. 1, Sess. Ex. Doc. 31 (1881), 12.

5. Daniel P. Carpenter and George A. Krause, "Reputation and Public Administration," *Public Administration Review* 72, no. 1 (2012): 26–32.

6. National Banking Act of 1864 §§ 8 and 18.

7. Bruce Champ, "The National Banking System: A Brief History" (working paper no. 07-23R, Federal Reserve Bank of Cleveland, 2011); John Sherman, quoted in Bray Hammond, *Sovereignty and an Empty Purse: Banks and Politics in the Civil War* (Princeton University Press, 1970), 346–47; Comptroller, *Instructions and Suggestions*, 7; Comptroller, *Instructions* (July 7, 1863); S. T. Howard to S. M. Cutcheon, May 17, 1865, F. Clarke to Andrew B. Mygatt, June 22, 1865, reproduced in *Response to Senate Resolution of December 6, 1881*, 12–13; *Annual Report of the Comptroller of the Currency* (1863), 58.

8. Robertson, *Comptroller and Bank Supervision*, 59–61; F. Cyril James, *Growth of Chicago Banks: Volume I, The Formative Years, 1816-1896* (Harper & Brothers, 1938), 318; Robert P. Sharkey, *Money, Class, and Party: An Economic Study of Civil War & Reconstruction* (Johns Hopkins Press, 1959), 231–37; *Annual Report of the Comptroller of the Currency* (1864), 51–52.

9. National Banking Act of 1864 §§ 1 and 54; McCulloch, *Men and Measures*, 166 (emphasis added).

10. United States, *Register of Officers and Agents, Civil, Military, and Naval, in the Service of the United States on the Thirtieth September 1867* (Government Printing Office, 1868), 54–55; United States, *Register of Officers and Agents, Civil, Military, and Naval, in the Service of the United States on the Thirtieth September 1869* (Government Printing Office, 1870), 55; George W. Cowles, ed., *Landmarks of Wayne County, New York* (D. Mason, 1895), 188 (part I), 21 (part II).

11. Connecticut Office of the Bank Commissioner, *Report of the Bank Commissioners of the State of Connecticut* (J. R. Hawley, 1862); "The State Bank of Iowa," *Bankers Magazine and Statistical Register* 12 (June 1858): 945–61 (esp. 959); State of Vermont, *Annual Report of the Banking Commissioner* (1865), 1; "Banking in Massachusetts: Annual Report of the Bank Commissioners, December 31, 1864," *Bankers Magazine and Statistical Register* 19 (April 1864): 800–809; "Hon. Sullivan M. Cutcheon," in John Beresy, *Cyclopedia of Michigan* (Western Publishing, 1890), 87–88; "List of the Civil Government of the Commonwealth of Massachusetts," in Commonwealth of Massachusetts, *Acts and Resolves Passed by the General Court of Massachusetts* (William White, 1856), 380; R. W. Derrickson, "Examiner's Report, First National Bank of Meadville, Pennsylvania," September 2, 1867, charter no. 115, box 10, OCC Examiners Reports; Butler Ward, "Examiner's Report, First National Bank of LeRoy, New York," October 16, 1866, charter no. 937, box 124, OCC Examiners Reports; Vanatta, "Revolving Door Governance."

12. *Annual Report of the Comptroller of the Currency* (1866), iii.

13. *Annual Report of the Comptroller of the Currency* (1869), xiii–xiv; Milton Friedman and Anna J. Schwartz, *A Monetary History of the United States, 1867–1960* (Princeton University Press, 1963), 66.

14. *Merchants' National Bank of Washington*, 42 Cong., Mis. Doc. No. 108 (1866) (testimony of John Bull), 10, 19; F. Clarke to Andrew B. Mygatt, June 22, 1865, in *Response to Senate Resolution of December 6, 1881*, 12; Butler Ward to Hugh McCulloch, January 20, 1864, box 5, OCC Examiners Reports.

15. *Failures of National Banks*, 42 Cong., Mis. Doc. 153 (1872) (testimony of John Bull), 36.

16. Grace Ballor, Gabriela Recio, and Sean H. Vanatta, "Surveillance Archive: Using Reports in Business History," *Management & Organizational History* 18, no. 1 (2023): 43–53; *Merchants' National Bank of Washington* (testimony of John Bull), 16.

17. *Failures of National Banks* (testimony of Henry H. Smith), 22; *Merchants' National Bank of Washington* (testimony of John Bull), 16; *Failures of National Banks* (testimony of John Bull), 5; Chandler R. Ransom, "Examiner's Report of the North National Bank of Boston," December 18, 1868, charter no. 525, box 63, OCC Examiners Reports.

18. Comptroller, *Instructions and Suggestions*, 13; Butler Ward to Hugh McCulloch, February 25, 1864, box 5, OCC Examiners Reports.

19. Charles R. Ransom to John Jay Knox, March 24, 1873, charter no. 525, box 113, OCC Correspondence; *Failures of National Banks* (testimony of Henry H. Smith), 18–19, 29; Kane, *Romance and Tragedy*, 366.

20. Comptroller, *Instructions* (July 7, 1863); Comptroller, *Instructions and Suggestions*.

21. Hugh McCulloch to Charles Callender, September 15, 1864, in *Response to Senate Resolution of December 6, 1881*, 9–10; R. W. Derrickson, [Bank Examiners Book] (1868–1869), University of Pittsburgh Special Collections, 104; McCulloch in Kane, *Romance and Tragedy*, 31.

22. Derrickson, [Bank Examiners Book], 42, 46; Naomi R. Lamoreaux, *Insider Lending: Banks, Personal Connections, and Economic Development in Industrial New England* (Cambridge University Press, 1994).

23. Derrickson, [Bank Examiners Book], 60. For similar critiques, see *Merchants' National Bank of Washington* (testimony of James Buffinton), 129; James, *Growth of Chicago Banks*, vol. 1, 315.

24. *Annual Report of the Comptroller of the Currency* (1867–1876).

25. National Banking Act of 1864 §§ 15, 31, 32, 35, and 50; Thomas J. Fitzpatrick IV, Moira Kearney-Marks, and James B. Thomson, "The History and Rationale for a Separate Bank Resolution Process," *Economic Commentary* no. 2012–01 (February 2, 2012); *Annual Report of the Comptroller of the Currency* (1866), xii; Kane, *Romance and Tragedy*, 60–61; National Banking Act of 1864 § 50; "Our Banking System and Its Dangers," *BM* 10, no. 10 (April 1876): 753; *In re Mfr.'s Nat. Bank*, 16 F. Cas. 665, 669 (N.D. Ill. 1873).

26. *Kennedy v. Gibson*, 75 U.S. 505 (1869); Fitzpatrick, Kearney-Marks, and Thomson, "The History and Rationale for a Separate Bank Resolution Process"; *In re Mfr's Nat' Bank*; "Bankruptcy Law," in *Sloan's Legal Register*, ed. W. H. Sloan (Eagle Print, 1874), 11.

27. Kane, *Romance and Tragedy*, 60; *Annual Report of the Comptroller of the Currency* (1869), v; "The Power of the Comptroller over National Banks," *Financier* 4, no. 40 (October 4, 1873): 182–83; Chapter 156, 44 Cong. §§ 1, 63 (1876); *Washington Nat. Bank v. Eckels*, 57 F. 870, 872 (C.C.D. Wash. 1893).

28. *Failures of National Banks* (testimony of Henry H. Smith), 21; Kane, *Romance and Tragedy*, 156, 177–80; "Third National," *CT*, November 23, 1877, 5.

29. *Ocean National Bank*, 43 Cong. 21-22 (1874), 126–29, 197, 291–92; *Investigation of Ocean National Bank*, H.R. Rep. No. 46-1463, at 13 (1880); Kane, *Romance and Tragedy*, 103.

30. Balogh, *Government out of Sight*; *Annual Report of the Comptroller of the Currency* (1869), viii.

31. *Annual Report of the Comptroller of the Currency* (1867), vii; *Annual Report of the Comptroller of the Currency* (1868), xx; Amendments to the National Currency Act, 1869, An Act Regulating the Reports of National Banking Associations, c. 130 (March 3, 1869); *Annual Report of the Comptroller of the Currency* (1869), vii. Eugene White also discusses some of the implications of this transition. See Eugene N. White, "Lessons from American Bank Supervision from the Nineteenth Century to the Great Depression," in *Macroprudential Regulatory Policies: The New Road to Financial Stability?*, ed. Stijn Claessens, Douglas D. Evanoff, George G. Kaufman, and Laura E. Kodres (World Scientific, 2012), 41–62.

32. National Banking Act of 1864 § 54; Nicholas R. Parrillo, *Against the Profit Motive: The Salary Revolution in American Government, 1780–1940* (Yale University Press, 2013), 1, 125; *Failures of National Banks* (testimony of John Bull), 5.

33. Derrickson, [Bank Examiners Book], 112–26; *Annual Report of the Comptroller of the Currency* (1869), x–xi; Vanatta, "Revolving Door Governance."

34. Charles W. Calomiris and Mark A. Carlson, "National Bank Examinations and Operations in the Early 1890s," Board of Governors of the Federal Reserve System (U.S.), Finance and Economics Discussion Series: 2014-19 (2014), 2.

35. Derrickson, [Bank Examiners Book], 50.

36. *Correspondence between the Comptroller of the Currency and First National Bank of Marlboro', Massachusetts, Relating to Charges for Examinations* (Geo. C. Rand & Avery, 1867), 6; *Annual Report of the Comptroller of the Currency* (1869), x; Robertson, *The Comptroller and Bank Supervision*, 77–79.

37. *Correspondence between the Comptroller of the Currency and First National Bank of Marlboro'*, 10–11; Bodenhorn, "Double Liability."

38. *Annual Report of the Comptroller of the Currency* (1871), vii.

39. *Annual Report of the Comptroller of the Currency* (1873), xlix–l.

40. On the climate of corruption in the Grant administration, see Richard White, *The Republic for Which It Stands: The United States During Reconstruction and the Gilded Age, 1865–1896* (Oxford University Press, 2017), 205–212; Leonard D. White, *The Republican Era, 1869–1901: A Study in Administrative History* (Macmillan, 1958).

41. *Failures of National Banks* (testimony of George R. Rutter), 15, 39.

42. *Failures of National Banks*, 19, 24, 30, 50.

43. Commonwealth of Massachusetts, *Annual Report of the Adjutant General of the Commonwealth of Massachusetts* (Wright and Potter, 1863), 452; United States, *Register of Officers and Agents, Civil, Military, and Naval, in the Service of the United States on the Thirtieth September 1865* (Government Printing Office, 1865), 49; "Charles Callender's Loans," *NYT*, March 31, 1874; *Failures of National Banks* (testimony of John Bull), 5.

44. "The Case of Callender—Examination of the President of the Ocean Bank," *NYT*, December 28, 1871; Jeffrey D. Broxmeyer, "Political Capitalism in the Gilded Age: The Tammany Bank Run of 1871," *Journal of the Gilded Age and Progressive Era* 16 (2017): 44–64.

45. "The Case of Callender"; "Financial Troubles," *NYTrib*, December 13, 1871.

46. "The Bank Examination Fraud," *CT*, December 24, 1871; "Local Miscellany: The Callender Case," *NYT*, June 1, 1874; "Callender, the United States Examiner," *NYT*, November 10, 1871.

47. "Stability of the Monetary Situation," *Commercial and Financial Chronicle* 13, no. 338 (December 16, 1871): 794.

48. "Prospectus," *Financier* 1, no. 1 (January 6, 1872): 3; "The Examination of Banks," *Financier* 1, no. 3 (January 20, 1872): 39.

49. "The Examination of Banks"; John A. James and David F. Weinman, "The National Banking Acts and the Transformation of New York City Banking During the Civil War Era," *Journal of Economic History* 71, no. 2 (2011): 338–62; Patrick Newman, "The Origins of the National Banking System: The Chase-Cooke Connection and the New York City Banks," *Independent Review* 22, no. 3 (2018): 383–401; James G. Cannon, *Clearing-House Methods and Practices*, Publications of the National Monetary Commission, 61 Cong. Sen. Doc. 491 (Government Printing Office, 1910); Gary Gorton, "Clearinghouses and the Origin of Central Banking in the United States," *Journal of Economic History* 45, no. 2 (1985): 277–83; Jon R. Moen and Ellis W. Tallman, "Clearinghouse Membership and Deposit Contraction During the Panic of 1907," *Journal of Economic History* 60, no. 1 (2000): 145–63.

50. "The Examination of Banks," *Financier*, January 20, 1872, 1; for Boston, "A New Bank Examiner for Boston," *WP*, August 6, 1881.

51. Comptroller, *Instructions* (July 7, 1863), 12.

52. John Jay Knox, *A History of Banking in the United States* (B. Rhodes & Company, 1900).

53. Walter Bagehot, *Lombard Street: A Description of the Money Market* (Henry S. King, 1873).

54. National Banking Act of 1864 §§ 31 and 32.

55. John A. James, *Money and Capital Markets in Postbellum America* (Princeton University Press, 1978); Margaret G. Myers, *The New York Money Market* (Columbia University Press, 1931).

56. National Banking Act of 1864 § 31; Edward S. Meade, "The Deposit-Reserve System of the National-Bank Law," *Journal of Political Economy* 6, no. 2 (1898): 209–24.

57. *Annual Report of the Comptroller of the Currency* (1872), xix.

58. James, *Growth of Chicago Banks*, vol. 1, 402–9.

59. "The Comptroller and the Banks," *Financier* 1, no. 14 (April 6, 1872): 272; Elmus Wicker, *Banking Panics of the Gilded Age* (Cambridge University Press, 2000), 126.

60. *Annual Report of the Comptroller of the Currency* (1872), xix.

61. "The Breach of the United States Banking Law by the New York National Banks," *Economist*, December 7, 1872, 1487; "The Legal-Tender Reserves," *NYT*, December 27, 1872; "Our Monetary Evils," *Financier* 2, no. 51 (December 21, 1872): 534. Bagehot would formalize these writings in *Lombard Street*, published a year later.

62. O.M.W. Sprague, *History of Crises Under the National Banking System*, Publications of the National Monetary Commission, 61 Cong. Doc. No. 538 (Government Printing Office, 1910), 55, 89.

63. As discussed in chapter 1, there were two pieces of legislation that were sometimes called the "national banking acts." Even a generation later, these related statutes were referred to together as the "National Banking Act." We adopt this singular usage from here.

64. Clearinghouse Committee, quoted in Sprague, *History of Crises*, 95; *Annual Report of the Comptroller of the Currency* (1873), xvii–xxvi (quote at xxv).

65. Bagehot, *Lombard Street*, 15; Michael D. Bordo, "Lender of Last Resort: Alternative Views and Historical Experience," *Federal Reserve Bank of Richmond Economic Review* (January/February

1990): 18-29. The Treasury Secretary could and did pump money into the banking system by using its available cash to redeem federal bonds ahead of schedule (see Margaret Myers, *A Financial History of the United States* [Columbia University Press, 1970], 232–34).

66. "Broken Banks and Lax Directors," *Century Illustrated Magazine* 23, no. 5 (March 1882): 768–77; *Response to Senate Resolution of December 6, 1881*, 30, 32; "Song of the Fugitive Bank Cashier," *Life* 4, no. 98 (November 13, 1884): 276.

67. *Annual Report of the Comptroller of the Currency* (1881), xxxvi; *Annual Report of the Comptroller of the Currency* (1884), xliv

68. *Annual Report of the Comptroller of the Currency* (1881), xxxvii. The banking press largely adopted Knox's restrained view of examination. See "Bank Examinations and Bank Directors," *BM* 36, no. 6 (December 1881): 414; "Bank Examinations," *BM* 36, no. 7 (January 1882): 542; "Bank Examinations," *Independent*, January 12, 1882; "Broken Banks and Lax Directors"; "Bank Examinations and Bank Directors," *BM* 39, no. 4 (October 1884): 241; "Bank Examinations," *BM* 39, no. 7 (January 1885): 483; "Bank Examinations Once More," *BM* 39, no. 9 (March 1885): 651.

69. "Instructions to National Bank Examiners," in *Response to Senate Resolution of December 6, 1881*, 4.

70. *Annual Report of the Comptroller of the Currency* (1881), xxxv.

Interlude: The Freedman's Bank

1. Charles A. Meigs to John Jay Knox, February 5, 1873, in *Report of the Comptroller of the Currency on the Condition of the Savings Banks in the District of Columbia*, 42 Cong. 10, Mis. Doc. No. 88 (1873); Jonathan Levy, *Freaks of Fortune: The Emerging World of Capitalism and Risk in America* (Harvard University Press, 2012), 115.

2. Shennette Garrett-Scott, *Banking on Freedom: Black Women in U.S. Finance Before the New Deal* (Columbia University Press, 2019), 13–40; Meigs to Knox, February 5, 1873.

3. Freedman's Savings and Trust Company, *Freedman's Savings and Trust Company [Charter and By-Laws]* (Wm. C. Bryant & Co., Printers, 1865), 12; Library of Congress, https://lccn.loc.gov/06031793; John Thom Holdsworth and Davis R. Dewey, *The First and Second Banks of the United States*, Publications of the National Monetary Commission, 62 Cong. Sen. Doc. 571 (Government Printing Office, 1910), 131, 142–43, 154–55, 172, 277, 281; Ch. XCII, 38 Cong. Sess. II (1864), 510–13; Abby L. Gilbert, "The Comptroller of the Currency and the Freedman's Savings Bank," *Journal of Negro History* 57, no. 2 (1972): 125–43.

4. Freedman's Savings and Trust Company, *Freedman's Savings and Trust Company*, 9.

5. Levy, *Freaks of Fortune*, 126–29; Carl R. Osthaus, *Freedmen, Philanthropy, and Fraud: A History of the Freedman's Savings Bank* (University of Illinois Press, 1976), 140–44.

6. Henrietta M. Larsen, *Jay Cooke, Private Banker* (Harvard University Press, 1936), 186.

7. Act of May 6, 1870, 16 Stat. 119; Gilbert, "The Comptroller of the Currency and the Freedman's Savings Bank," 126–27; Levy, *Freaks of Fortune*, 143; Osthaus, *Freedmen, Philanthropy, and Fraud*, 144–66; *Report of the Comptroller of the Currency on the Condition of the Savings Banks in the District of Columbia*, 42 Cong. 3, Mis. Doc. No. 88 (1873).

8. Meigs to Knox, February 5, 1873; Act of May 6, 1870, 16 Stat. 119; Chapter XLIII, 24 Cong, 3 Sess. (January 20, 1873); *Report of the Comptroller of the Currency*, Senate Misc. Doc. No. 88, 42 Cong., 3 Sess. (1873), 3, 9.

9. *Report of the Commissioners of the Freedman's Savings and Trust Company* 43 Cong., Mis Doc. 16 (1874).

10. *Report of the Commissioners of the Freedman's Savings and Trust Company* (1874), 59–83; Gilbert, "The Comptroller of the Currency and the Freedman's Savings Bank," 130–31; Frederick Douglass, *The Life and Times of Frederick Douglass* (De Wolfe, Fiske & Co., 1892), 493.

11. *Annual Report of the Commissioner of the Freedman's Savings and Trust Company* 47 Cong., Mis. Doc. 10 (1882), 19. By the 1920s, the Comptroller's staff abandoned this view, arguing that the federal government "had no supervision whatever" over the Freedman's Bank, so that "the only ground upon which the government can be urged to assume [the bank's] remaining liabilities is purely one of sentiment," in Thomas P. Kane, *The Romance and Tragedy of Banking* (Bankers Publishing Company, 1923), 83–84.

12. Gilbert, "The Comptroller of the Currency and the Freedman's Savings Bank," 135–42; Justene Hill Edwards, *Savings and Trust: The Rise and Betrayal of the Freedman's Bank* (W. W. Norton, 2024); Mehrsa Baradaran, *Color of Money: Black Banks and the Racial Wealth Gap* (Harvard University Press, 2017).

Chapter Three

1. "The Breach of the United States' Law by the New York National Banks," *Economist*, December 7, 1872, 1486.

2. William F. G. Shanks, "The Romance of Finance," *WP*, May 25, 1884; "Miscellaneous Bank Items," *Rhodes Journal of Banking* 10, no. 1 (December 1883). For the Panic of 1884 generally, see Elmus Wicker, *Banking Panics of the Gilded Age* (Cambridge University Press, 2000), 34–51.

3. "Wall Street Startled," *NYT*, May 7, 1884; Shanks, "Romance of Finance"; "Suspending in a Hurry," *WP*, May 7, 1884; Ron Chernow, *Grant* (Penguin Press, 2017), 17; "Five Millions in Debts," *NYT*, May 11, 1884; "The Marine Bank Failure," *NYT*, May 14, 1884.

4. "Two Millions Absorbed," *NYT*, May 14, 1884; "On the Verge of Panic," *NYT*, May 15, 1884.

5. "The Metropolitan Bank," *NYT*, May 15, 1884; "The Money Market and Financial Situation," *Commercial and Financial Chronicle*, May 17, 1884, 589, quoted in O.M.W. Sprague, *History of Crises Under the National Banking System*, Publications of the National Monetary Commission, 61 Cong. Doc. No. 538 (Government Printing Office, 1910), 111.

6. Shanks, "Romance of Finance."

7. "The Bank Doors Besieged," *NYT*, May 15, 1884; "Wall Street Wrecks," *DFP*, May 15, 1884; "The Second National," *CT*, May 16, 1884. Scriba's was a common supervisory tactic. See "Suicide of W. F. Coolbaugh," *NYT*, November 15, 1887; "The Northampton Bank Robbery," *NYT*, January 29, 1876.

8. "A Succession of Failures," *BS*, May 15, 1884; "The Storm Not Yet Spent," *NYT*, May 16, 1884.

9. "Metropolitan Bank"; *Annual Report of the Comptroller of the Currency* (1884), xxxii–xxvi, xli–xliv; Sprague, *History of Crises*, 114.

10. "Fisk & Hatch Go Under," *WP*, May 16, 1884; "Wall-St. Again Agitated," *NYTrib*, May 16, 1884; Gary Gorton and Ellis W. Tallman, "Too Big to Fail Before the Fed," *American Economic Review: Papers & Proceedings* 106, no. 5 (2016): 528–32.

11. *Annual Report of the Comptroller of the Currency* (1884), xxxvi, xliv.

12. George C. Coe, "Banking Reform Proposals in New York in 1884," *BM* (July 1884): 44–51, reproduced in Sprague, *History of Crises*, 373; Fritz Redlich, *The Molding of American Banking: Men and Ideas [1781–1910]*, vol. 2 (Hafner, 1951), 424–38.

13. *Annual Report of the Comptroller of the Currency* (1869), viii.

14. Coe, "Banking Reform Proposals," in Sprague, *History of Crises*, 372.

15. Coe, "Banking Reform," 372; Shanks, "Romance of Finance."

16. Milton Friedman and Anna J. Schwartz, *A Monetary History of the United States, 1867–1960* (Princeton University Press, 1963), 144–45; John A. James, "The Conundrum of the Low Issue of National Bank Notes," *Journal of Political Economy* 84, no. 2 (1976): 362; John A. James, *Money and Capital Markets in Postbellum America* (Princeton University Press, 1978), 22–27; Charles W. Calomiris and Joseph R. Mason, "Resolving the Puzzle of the Underissuance of National Bank Notes," *Explorations in Economic History* 45, no. 4 (September 2008): 327–55; Matthew Jaremski and Peter L. Rousseau, "The Dawn of an 'Age of Deposits' in the United States," *Journal of Banking & Finance* 87 (February 1, 2018): 264–81.

17. H. G. Moulton, "Commercial Banking and Capital Formation: I," *Journal of Political Economy* 26, no. 5 (1918): 498; Milton Friedman and Anna J. Schwartz, *Monetary Statistics of the United States* (National Bureau of Economic Research, 1970), 4–13; Bruce G. Carruthers and Sarah Babb, "The Color of Money and the Nature of Value: Greenbacks and Gold in Postbellum America," *American Journal of Sociology* 101, no. 6 (1996): 1556–91; "Comptroller Knox on the Currency," *WP*, August 15, 1881.

18. Moulton, "Commercial Banking," 497–98.

19. Jaremski and Rousseau, "The Dawn of an 'Age of Deposits,'" 264–81; "The National Bank Act," *NYT*, December 22, 1884.

20. Jonathan Levy, *Ages of American Capitalism: A History of the United States* (Random House, 2021); James, *Money and Capital Markets*, 58–71.

21. *Annual Report of the Comptroller of the Currency* (1884), l. Hugh McCulloch had tried to formalize this conception of failure as fraud in the National Bank Act. "I would suggest that section 12 be so amended that the failure of a national bank be declared prima facie fraudulent, and that the officers, and directors, under whose administration each insolvency shall occur, be made personally liable for the debts of the bank, and be punished criminally, unless it shall appear, upon investigation, that its affairs were honestly administered." *Report of the Secretary of the Treasury* (1863), 51.

22. *Annual Report of the Comptroller of the Currency* (1884), xlix.

23. *Annual Report of the Comptroller of the Currency* (1884), l.

24. On the spread of clearinghouses, see Matthew Jaremski, "Clearinghouses as Credit Regulators Before the Fed?" *Journal of Financial Stability* 17 (2015): 10–21.

25. Matthew Jaremski, "State Banks and the National Banking Acts: Measuring the Response to Increased Financial Regulation, 1860–1870," *Journal of Money, Credit and Banking* 45, no. 2–3 (2013): 379–99; Eugene White, *The Regulation and Reform of the American Banking System, 1900–1929* (Princeton University Press, 1983), 12–23; Ross Robertson, *Comptroller and Bank Supervision* (Office of the Comptroller of the Currency, 1995), 64–69; George Barnett, *State Banks and Trust Companies Since the Passage of the National-Bank Act*, Publications of the National Monetary Commission, 61 Cong. Sen Doc. 659 (Government Printing Office, 1911), 39–50, 87–93, 207.

26. Richard Page, *Banks and Bankers* (Forgotten Books, 2019), 1; "Comptroller Knox on the Currency," 2.

27. *Annual Report of the Comptroller of the Currency* (1864), 49; *Annual Report of the Comptroller of the Currency* (1881), xi; Robertson, *The Comptroller and Bank Supervision*, 61–71.

28. Kris Mitchener and Matthew Jaremski, "The Evolution of Bank Supervisory Institutions," *Journal of Economic History* 75, no. 3 (September 2015): 819–59; *Annual Report of the Comptroller of the Currency* (1932), 4; Barnett, *State Banks and Trust Companies*, 174.

29. Barnett, *State Banks and Trust Companies*, 12, 52–53, 59, 162.

30. W. W. Flannagan, "Address of Mr. W. W. Flannagan of New York, on Security for National Bank Deposits"; Samuel Merrill, "Address of Hon. Sml. Merrill of Iowa, on Bank Deposits and Panics," *BM* 40 (1886): 123–24. Scholars have generally not pursued political arguments for deposit guarantees earlier than the Panic of 1893. See, e.g., Michael Kazin, *A Godly Hero: The Life of William Jennings Bryan* (Anchor, 2007). Most focus on the Panic of 1907, including C. W. Shaw, "'The Man in the Street Is for It': The Road to the FDIC," *Journal of Policy History* 27, no. 1 (January 2015): 36–60. Our emphasis on 1884 indicates the long gestation of deposit insurance as an alternative to (or compliment for) central banking.

31. "Guarantee Deposit Funds," *CT*, February 15, 1886.

32. "The Bank Doors Besieged."

33. *Annual Report of the Comptroller of the Currency*, vol. 1 (1893), 5; *Annual Report of the Comptroller of the Currency* (1898), xxii, xiv.

34. "A New Clearing-House," *WP*, May 12, 1887. On clearinghouses, see James G. Cannon, *Clearing-House Methods and Practices*, Publications of the National Monetary Commission, 61 Cong. Sen. Doc. 491 (Government Printing Office, 1910), 137–47; Richard J. Timberlake Jr., "The Central Banking Role of Clearinghouses," *Journal of Money, Credit and Banking* 16, no. 1 (1984): 1–15; Gary Gorton, "Clearinghouses and the Origin of Central Banking in the United States," *Journal of Economic History* 45, no. 2 (1985): 277–83; Charles Goodhart, *The Evolution of Central Banks* (MIT Press, 1988), 29–46.

35. Matthew Jaremski, "The (Dis)advantages of Clearinghouses before the Fed," *Journal of Financial Economics* 127, no. 3 (2018): 435–58; Dudley Bailey, *The Clearing House System* (Kessinger Publishing, 2010), 4; *Annual Report of the Comptroller of the Currency* (1905), 383–84; A. B. Hepburn, "National Banking and the Clearing-House," *North American Review* 156, no. 436 (1893): 375.

36. Jaremski, "The (Dis)advantages of Clearinghouses," 436–37, 450–51.

37. Hepburn, "*National Banking and the Clearing-House*," 375.

38. Jaremski, "The (Dis)advantages of Clearinghouses," 436; Cannon, *Clearing-House Methods*, 137–47; *Annual Report of the Comptroller of the Currency* (1907), 66.

39. Gorton and Tallman, "Too Big to Fail," 528–32; Jaremski, "The (Dis)advantages of Clearinghouses," 435–58.

40. *Annual Report of the Comptroller of the Currency*, vol. 1 (1891), 27; William B. Ridgely, "Bank Examination and Failures—Address of Hon. William Barret Ridgely," *BM* 69, no. 5 (1904): 821–22.

41. *Annual Report of the Comptroller of the Currency*, vol. 1 (1892), 94; Eugene N. White, "Lessons from American Bank Supervision from the Nineteenth Century to the Great Depression," in *Macroprudential Regulatory Policies: The New Road to Financial Stability?*, ed. Stijn

Claessens, Douglas D. Evanoff, George G. Kaufman, and Laura E. Kodres (World Scientific, 2012), 12; "Bank Examinations and Failures," *WSJ*, October 20, 1904; Thomas J. Fry, "Bank Examination Reform," *NYT*, December 9, 1900; *Annual Report of the Comptroller of the Currency* (1905), 60; *Annual Report of the Comptroller of the Currency* (1900), xxvii.

42. *Annual Report of the Comptroller of the Currency*, vol. 1 (1891), 26–27; Calomiris and Mason, "Resolving the Puzzle."

43. Cannon, *Clearing-House Methods*, 137–38.

44. Sprague, *History of Crises*, 141; "Firms Fail, Banks Shaken," *NYT*, November 12, 1890.

45. "Villard Stocks Attacked," *NYT*, November 14, 1890; "Three More Suspensions," *NYT*, November 13, 1890; Wicker, *Banking Panics*, 44–47; "Near Utter Ruin," *WP*, November 16, 1890; *Annual Report of the Comptroller of the Currency*, vol. 1 (1891), 13–15; "The National Banks All Right," *WP*, November 14, 1890.

46. Mark Carlson, "Causes of Bank Suspensions in the Panic of 1893," *Explorations in Economic History* 42, no. 1 (2005): 56–80; Brandon Dupont, "Panic in the Plains," *Journal of Historical Economics and Econometric History* 3, no. 1 (2009): 27–54; Sprague, *History of Crises*, 168.

47. Alexander Noyes, "The Banks and the Panic of 1893," *Political Science Quarterly* 9, no. 1 (1894): 18; Thomas P. Kane, *The Romance and Tragedy of Banking; Problems and Incidents of Governmental Supervision of National Banks*, 2nd ed. (Bankers Publishing Co., 1923), 190–91; *Annual Report of the Comptroller of the Currency*, vol. 1 (1893), 11, 13–14; Wicker, *Banking Panics*.

48. Noyes, "The Banks and the Panic of 1893," 21–22; "George S. Coe Suddenly Stricken," *NYTrib*, November 24, 1893; "Many Changes in National Banks," *NYT*, January 10, 1894. Noyes explicitly invokes Walter Bagehot, *Lombard Street: A Description of the Money Market* (Henry S. King & Co., 1873).

49. Kane, *Romance and Tragedy*, 209, 211.

50. Kane, *Romance and Tragedy*, 195.

51. *Annual Report of the Comptroller of the Currency*, vol. 1 (1893), 11; Wicker, *Banking Panics*.

52. Kane, *Romance and Tragedy*, 195; *Annual Report of the Comptroller of the Currency*, vol. 1 (1893), 10; Calomiris and Mason, "Resolving the Puzzle."

53. Noyes makes this point regarding New York City, but for longer term bank distrust in the interior, see Carlos D. Ramírez, "Bank Fragility, 'Money Under the Mattress,' and Long-Run Growth: US Evidence from the 'Perfect' Panic of 1893," *Journal of Banking & Finance* 33, no. 12 (2009): 2185–98.

54. Jon Moen and Ellis Tallman, "The Panic of 1907: The Role of Trust Companies," *Journal of Economic History* 52, no. 3 (1992): 611–30; Carola Frydman, Eric Hilt, and Lily Zhou, "Economic Effects of Runs on Early 'Shadow Banks,'" *Journal of Political Economy* 123, no. 4 (2015): 907–8.

55. Wicker, *Banking Panics*, 89; Robert F. Bruner and Sean D. Carr, *The Panic of 1907: Heralding a New Era of Finance, Capitalism, and Democracy* (John Wiley & Sons, 2023).

56. Sprague, *History of Crises*, 247; "Clears the Banking Air," *BS*, October 21, 1907; "Wall Street Storm Comes to an End," *LAT*, October 19, 1907; "Ridgely May Head Bank," *WP*, October 18, 1907; "Ridgely to Stay Here," *WP*, October 20, 1907.

57. Sprague, *History of Crises*, 258; Wicker, *Banking Panics*, 121; Frydman, Hilt, and Zhou, "Economic Effects of Runs."

58. Wicker, *Banking Panics*, 91, quoting New York Clearinghouse Executive Committee minutes, October 21, 1907; "Gotham Shaking on Panics' Brink," *CT*, October 23, 1907; Frydman, Hilt, and Zhou, "Economic Effects of Runs," 910.

59. F. Cyril James, *The Growth of the Chicago Banks, Volume 2—The Modern Age, 1897–1938* (Harper & Brothers, 1938), 766.

60. "Banks Call for Currency," *WP*, November 3, 1907; Wicker, *Banking Panics*, 99–100; James, *Growth of the Chicago Banks*, 760; "Calls Banks to Show," *WP*, December 5, 1907; "Secrecy as to Banks," *WP*, November 6, 1907.

61. Wicker, *Banking Panics*, addresses the real economic effects.

62. *Annual Report of the Comptroller of the Currency* (1907), 74.

63. *Annual Report of the Comptroller of the Currency* (1869), xiii–xiv; *Annual Report of the Comptroller of the Currency* (1907), 73.

64. *Annual Report of the Comptroller of the Currency* (1907), 71.

Interlude: O. Henry and J.F.C. Nettlewick

1. O. Henry, *Roads of Destiny* (Doubleday, Page, and Co., 1922). The story was originally published in 1901 in *Ainslee's Magazine* and appeared in 1902 in London as Oliver Henry, "The Frigid Bank Inspector," *The Idler: An Illustrated Monthly Magazine* (1902): 98–105.

2. Trueman O'Quinn, "O. Henry in Austin," *Southwestern Historical Quarterly* 43, no. 2 (1939): 143–57; Frederick Tabor Cooper, *Some American Story Tellers* (Henry Holt, 1911), 225.

3. Frederick Jackson Turner, "The Significance of the Frontier in American History," paper read to the American Historical Association in Chicago, July 12, 1893; Frederick Winslow Taylor, *The Principles of Scientific Management* (Harper & Bros, 1911); *Money Trust Investigation* 62 Cong., pt. 15, 1084 (1913) (Testimony of J. Pierpont Morgan).

4. O. Henry, "The Call Loan," in *The Heart of the West* (McClure, 1907).

Chapter Four

1. F. Cyril James, *The Growth of Chicago Banks: Volume 2, The Modern Age, 1897–1938* (Harper & Brothers, 1938), 727–95. On the politics of banking reform in this era, see James Livingston, *Origins of the Federal Reserve System: Money, Class, and Corporate Capitalism, 1890–1913* (Cornell University Press, 1986); M. Elizabeth Sanders, *Roots of Reform: Farmers, Workers, and the American State, 1877–1917* (University of Chicago Press, 1999), 232–60.

2. Carter Glass, *Adventures in Constructive Finance* (Page & Company, 1927), 82.

3. Federal Reserve Act of 1913, Pub. L. 63-43, 38 Stat. 251 (December 23, 1913), Introduction.

4. Lyman Gage et al., "The Financial Situation," *North American Review* 187 (1908): 161–92.

5. "Bryan's Relief Plan," *NYTrib*, November 22, 1907; 53 Cong. Rec. 1700 (statement of William Jennings Bryan); Paul W. Gard, *The Trumpet Soundeth: William Jennings Bryan and His Democracy, 1896–1912* (University of Nebraska Press, 1960), 92–93; J. Laurence Laughlin, "The Aldrich-Vreeland Act," *Journal of Political Economy* 16, no. 8 (1908): 491–92.

6. James, *Growth of Chicago Banks*, vol. 2, 746–47, 773, 776–77, 799; *Report of Charles N. Fowler*, 60 Cong. H.R. No. 1126 (1908), 26–27.

7. Aldrich-Vreeland Act of 1908, Pub. L. 60-169 § 18 (May 27, 1908).

8. E. W. Kemmerer, "Banking Reform in the United States," *American Economic Review* 3, no. 1 (1913): 52; Kris James Mitchener and Matthew Jaremski, "The Evolution of Bank Supervisory Institutions: Evidence from American States," *Journal of Economic History* 75, no. 3 (2015):

819–59; Lawrence O. Murray, "Co-Operation as a Factor in Effective Bank Supervision," *Banking Law Journal* 27, no. 10 (1910): 894–901; "State Bank Examiners," *DFP*, July 31, 1902.

9. Eugene Nelson White, "State-Sponsored Insurance of Bank Deposits in the United States, 1907–1929," *Journal of Economic History* 41, no. 3 (1981): 539; Michael Kazin, *A Godly Hero: The Life of William Jennings Bryan* (Knopf, 2007), 154; Michael J. Hightower, *Banking in Oklahoma: 1907–2000* (University of Oklahoma Press, 2014), 14–19; Christopher W. Shaw, "'The Man in the Street Is for It': The Road to the FDIC," *Journal of Policy History* 27, no. 1 (2015): 41–42; *Annual Report of the Comptroller of the Currency* (1908), 70–72.

10. White, "State-Sponsored Insurance of Bank Deposits," 552–54; Clark Warburton, *Deposit Guaranty in Eight States During the Period 1908–1930* (Federal Deposit Insurance Corporation, 1959), 18 (FRASER). Some states sought to strengthen their funds by allowing national banks to participate, but the U.S. Attorney General barred such participation in 1908 (*Annual Report of the Comptroller of the Currency* [1908], 70–72).

11. Hightower, *Banking in Oklahoma*, 21–25.

12. James, *Growth of Chicago Banks*, vol. 2, 714–23; Fritz Redlich, *The Molding of American Banking: Men and Ideas*, pt. 2 (Edwards Brothers, 1947), 285–87.

13. Lawrence O. Murray to William J. Gilpin, September 18, 1911, OCC Clearinghouse Letters; C. E. Woodside to Lawrence O. Murray, June 29, 1908, OCC Clearinghouse Letters; Charles W. Reihl, "Practical Banking: Clearing-House Bank Examinations," *BM* 78, no. 5 (1909): 781; "To Make California Bank-Failure Proof," *LAT*, October 15, 1908; "California Banks' New Safeguards," *LAT*, November 6, 1908; *Annual Report of the Comptroller of the Currency* (1907), 66.

14. James, *Growth of Chicago Banks*, vol. 2, 792; "Clearing House Examinations," *NYT*, January 7, 1912.

15. "Deputy Comptroller of the Currency," *NYT*, September 2, 1898; "Mr. Murray's Resignation," *WP*, June 7, 1899; "Plans Sweeping Reform," *NYTrib*, June 17, 1905; "Shake-Up of Inspectors," *WP*, September 25, 1905; "President Plays Tennis," *BG*, April 5, 1906; "Inspectors Shifted," *BS*, March 10, 1907; "President Plays Tennis," *WP*, May 26, 1907.

16. Lawrence O. Murray, "Statement of Lawrence O. Murray," in *Administrative Features of the National Banking Laws and European Fiscal and Postal Savings Systems*, Publications of the National Monetary Commission (Government Printing Office, 1911), 268; Thomas P. Kane, *The Romance and Tragedy of Banking; Problems and Incidents of Governmental Supervision of National Banks* (Bankers Publishing Company, 1922), 302.

17. "New Plan for Bank Examiners," *CT*, October 9, 1908; "National Bank Examiner at Large," *WSJ*, January 11, 1909; "Bank Examinations Rigid," *NYT*, January 3, 1912; "Bank Examining Systematized by Controller Murray," *NYT*, September 3, 1911; *Annual Report of the Comptroller of the Currency* (1911), 82; "Controller Warns Bank Examiners," *NYT*, September 22, 1908; Sean H. Vanatta, "Revolving Door Governance: Bank Supervisors in the United States, 1863–1933," *Management and Organizational History* 19, no. 3 (2024): 153–81.

18. Kane, *Romance and Tragedy*, 392–93; Lawrence O. Murray, "Co-Operation as a Factor in Effective Bank Supervision," *Banking Law Journal* 27, no. 10 (1910): 899.

19. "State Bank Examiners," *DFP*, July 31, 1902; Murray, "Co-Operation as a Factor in Effective Bank Supervision," 899.

20. *Correspondence Between Comptroller of Currency and First National Bank of Canton, Pa.*, Sen. Doc. 2505 (1919) (Proquest accession no. T12.2-16.1), 24–28, 35–38.

21. "Bank Examining Systematized by Controller Murray"; "To Inform Bank Examiners," *WSJ*, May 18, 1910; "Comptroller's Credit Bureau," *WSJ*, September 28, 1910; "Shakeup of Bank Examiners," *CT*, September 8, 1910; Murray, "Co-Operation as a Factor in Effective Bank Supervision," 894; "Tracing Big Bank Loans," *WP*, September 17, 1908; J. L. Rue to Lawrence O. Murray, March 24, 1910, OCC Clearinghouse Letters; J. L. Rue to Lawrence O. Murray, April 20, 1910, OCC Clearinghouse Letters; Francis B. Sears to Lawrence O. Murray, April 11, 1910, OCC Clearinghouse Letters; Charles C. Homer to Lawrence O. Murray, June 11, 1909, OCC Clearinghouse Letters; "Would Guard Banks," *WP*, July 14, 1911; "Clearing House Examinations Tend to Prevent Over-Extension," *WSJ*, February 10, 1912.

22. Alfred D. Chandler, *The Visible Hand: The Managerial Revolution in American Business* (Harvard University Press, 1977); "Bank Examining Systematized by Controller Murray."

23. Lawrence O. Murray, quoted in William Henry Smith, "The United States Treasury—VI," *BM* 80, no. 6 (1910): 885.

24. J. Lawrence Broz, *The International Origins of the Federal Reserve* (Cornell University Press, 1997), 34; Elmus Wicker, *The Great Debate on Banking Reform: Nelson Aldrich and the Origins of the Fed* (Ohio State University Press, 2005), 52–69. The addition of the Federal Reserve on top of the Comptroller of the Currency, while failing to resolve the obvious conflicts between them, is a strong example of what Kathleen Thelen has called "institutional layering" and is a key mechanism for understanding the institutional evolution of supervision. For an overview of this literature, see James Mahoney and Kathleen Thelen, eds., *Explaining Institutional Change: Ambiguity, Agency, and Power* (Cambridge University Press, 2010) and Jeroen van der Heijden, "Institutional Layering: A Review of the Use of the Concept," *Politics* 31, no. 1 (2011): 9–18.

25. See Roger Lowenstein, *America's Bank: The Epic Struggle to Create the Federal Reserve* (Penguin, 2015); Broz, *International Origins*; Allan H. Meltzer, *A History of the Federal Reserve*, vol. 1, *1913–1951* (University of Chicago Press, 2003). For accounts of the Fed's founding from those who actively participated in it, compare Glass, *Adventure in Constructive Finance*, Paul M. Warburg, *The Federal Reserve System: Its Origin and Growth* (Macmillan, 1930), and H. Parker Willis, *The Federal Reserve System* (Blackstone Institute, 1920).

26. Glass, *Adventure in Constructive Finance*, 112–32; Woodrow Wilson, quoted in Broz, *International Origins*, 196.

27. Eugene N. White, "To Establish a More Effective Supervision of Banking," in *A Return to Jekyll Island: The Origins, History, and Future of the Federal Reserve*, ed. Michael D. Bordo and William Roberds (Cambridge University Press: 2013), 7–54.

28. *The National-Bank Act as Amended and Other Laws Relating to National Banks* 63 Cong. Sen. Doc. 197 (1913), 79; Federal Reserve Act § 21; National Monetary Commission, *National Monetary Commission: Replies to Circular Letter of Inquiry of September 26, 1908 on Suggested Changes in Administrative Features of the National Banking Laws* (Government Printing Office, 1908); National Monetary Commission, *Hearings Before the National Monetary Commission on Changes in the Administrative Features of the National Banking Laws* (Government Printing Office, 1908); J. L. Mohundro et al., "Bank Examinations, State and National," December 15, 1911, folder 6, box 81, reel 56, National Monetary Commission Archives, Miscellany, Aldrich Papers (FRASER); Carter Glass, H.R. Rep. 6454, 63 Cong. 34-36 (June 26, 1913).

29. Federal Reserve Act §§ 2, 3, 4, and 9; Sarah Binder and Mark Spindel, *The Myth of Independence: How Congress Governs the Federal Reserve* (Princeton University Press, 2017); E. E. Agger, "The Federal Reserve System," *Political Science Quarterly* 29, no. 2 (1914): 265–81.

30. Federal Reserve Act § 21.

31. Meltzer, *History of the Federal Reserve*, 22, 31, 34–35, 70–71.

32. Nelson W. Aldrich, *The Work of the National Monetary Commission: An Address by Senator Nelson W. Aldrich Before the Economic Club of New York, November 29, 1909*, Publications of the National Monetary Commission, 61 Cong. Sen. Doc. 406 (Government Printing Office, 1909); Broz, *International Origins*, 47; S. E. Harris, *Twenty Years of Federal Reserve Policy, Including an Extended Discussion of the Monetary Crisis, 1929–1933* (Harvard University Press, 1933), 269–80; Federal Reserve Act §13.

33. Letter from Charles A. People to W.P.G. Harding, January 23, 1922, Eligibility of Paper: Financial Statements (1919–1921), pt. 2, folder 2, box 1348, Fed System Records (FRASER); Caroline Whitney, *Experiments in Credit Control* (Columbia University Press, 1934), 89–90; James, *Growth of Chicago Banks*, vol. 2, 969–71.

34. Federal Reserve Bank of New York, "Eligible Paper," Circular No. 25 (June 19, 1915), Federal Reserve Bank of New York Circulars (FRASER); Whitney, *Experiments in Credit Control*, 86–89; "Uniform Accounts," *Federal Reserve Bulletin* (April 1917), 270–84.

35. Harris, *Twenty Years*, 272–80; George L. Harrison to Charles A. People, December 8, 1921, Eligibility of Paper: Financial Statements (1919–1921), pt. 2, folder 2, box 1348, Fed System Records (FRASER).

36. Whitney, *Experiments in Credit Control*, 42–44; Harris, *Twenty Years*.

37. Complicating matters even further, some Reserve Banks also used acceptability, in addition to the discount rate, to make monetary policy decisions.

38. Harris, *Twenty Years*, 294–95; "The Examination and Audit of Federal Reserve and Member Banks Under the Direction of the Federal Reserve Board," December 3, 1914, Letters and Statements of the Board, vol. 1 (FRASER); Federal Reserve Board, Memo, "Department of Examination—Federal Reserve Banks," December 23, 1918, Letters and Statements of the Board, vol. 9 (FRASER).

39. Benjamin Strong to Adolph Miller, July 14, 1922, Strong-Miller Correspondence (FRASER); White, "To Establish a More Effective Supervision of Banking." Harris offers robust evidence that the Reserve Banks took most high-quality collateral for themselves and left the depositors with nothing (*Twenty Years*, 293).

40. Federal Reserve Board, Memo, "Excessive Rediscounts by Member Banks," November 19, 1918, Letters and Statements of the Board, vol. 9 (FRASER).

41. Adolph Miller to Benjamin Strong, July 6, 1922, Strong-Miller Correspondence (FRASER).

42. Arthur Blaser, *The Federal Reserve Bank of Cleveland* (Columbia University Press, 1942), 193.

43. Kane, *Romance and Tragedy*, 444; Eric Yellin, *Racism in the Nation's Service* (University of North Carolina Press, 2013), 3, 96–105; Committee on the History of the Federal Reserve System, "Interview with Mr. Charles J. Rhoads at Bryn Mawr," folder 6, box 2, Committee on the History of the Federal Reserve System (FRASER).

44. M. G. Tucker, "The Slow Column," July 1, 1936, folder 5, box 81, Viner Papers; *Correspondence Between Comptroller of Currency and First National Bank of Canton, Pa.*, 93–98. On 1890s

examination forms, the terms were "bad debts" and "suspended or overdue paper" (OCC Examiners Reports).

45. *Annual Report of the Comptroller of the Currency*, vol. 1 (1916), 27; *Annual Report of the Comptroller of the Currency* (1917), 28; *Annual Report of the Comptroller of the Currency* (1918), 7.

46. *Annual Report of the Comptroller of the Currency* (1918), 6; Kane, *Romance and Tragedy*, 469, 484–90.

47. *Amendment to Abolish the Office of the Comptroller of the Currency* 67 Cong. 39–43 (1921) (statement of W.P.G. Harding, Governor of the Federal Reserve).

48. *Annual Report of the Comptroller of the Currency*, vol. 2 (1916), 700; *Correspondence Between Comptroller of Currency and First National Bank of Canton, Pa.*, 57.

49. *Correspondence Between Comptroller of Currency and First National Bank of Canton, Pa.*, 64, 68.

50. *Correspondence Between Comptroller of Currency and First National Bank of Canton, Pa.*, 82; Thomas Kane, Affidavit, in *First National Bank of Canton v. John Skelton Williams*, May 12, 1919 (Proquest accession no. T12.2-16.8).

51. "Attacks J. S. Williams," *WP*, February 16, 1919; "Williams, McFadden Row Gets Personal," *LAT*, March 3, 1919.

52. Kane, *Romance and Tragedy*, 479–84.

53. Stoddard Jess to W. G. Harding, October 9, 1917, Letters and Statements of the Board, vol. 6; Memorandum, J. A. Broderick, n.d., ca. November 1917, Letters and Statements of the Board, vol 6; "Clearing House Examinations," Letters and Statements of the Board, vol. 6 (FRASER); "Defends Comptroller," *BS*, November 15, 1915; "Would Oust Williams," *BS*, November 18, 1915.

54. D. R. Crissinger Jr. to W.P.G. Harding, "Directors' Right of Access to Reports of Examination," January 30, 1922, Letters and Statements of the Board, vol. 16 (FRASER). The original provisions were in section 4 of the Federal Reserve Act. This provision is among the most amended of the Federal Reserve Act, but the bankers still retain much of their influence. See Peter Conti-Brown and Simon Johnson, *Governing the Federal Reserve System After Dodd-Frank* (Peterson Institute, 2013).

55. Charles Starek, Sherrill Smith, and James D. Brennan to the Comptroller of the Currency, July 16, 1915, Letters and Statements of the Board, vol. 2 (FRASER); Charles S. Hamlin, October 14, 1915, *Diary*, vol. 3, folder 17, Hamlin Papers; Hamlin, November 11, 1915, *Diary*, vol. 3, folder 18, box 356, Hamlin Papers (FRASER); Federal Reserve Board, Meeting Minutes, October 15, 1915 and October 20, 1915, vol. 2, pt. 2, Fed Board Minutes (FRASER); Ross M. Robertson, *The Comptroller and Bank Supervision: A Historical Appraisal* (Office of the Comptroller of the Currency, 1968), 108–9; Frederick A. Delano II to Comptroller of the Currency, December 22, 1914, quoted in D. R. Crissinger Jr. to W.P.G. Harding, "Directors' Right of Access to Reports of Examination."

56. Richard Grossman, *Unsettled Account: The Evolution of Banking in the Industrialized World Since 1800* (Princeton University Press, 2010), 162–67, esp. 164.

57. Charles S. Hamlin, October 21, 1914, *Diary*, vol. 2, folder 15, Hamlin Papers (FRASER); Memorandum, W.P.G. Harding, "Department of Examination, Federal Reserve Banks," December 23, 1918, Letters and Statements of the Board, vol. 9; Memorandum, W.P.G. Harding, March 29, 1918, Letters and Statements of the Board, vol. 7; Memorandum, W.P.G. Harding,

August 31, 1917, Letters and Statements of the Board, vol. 6 (FRASER); White "To Establish a More Effective Supervision of Banking," 42.

58. *Amendment to Abolish the Office of the Comptroller of the Currency* 67 Cong. 39-43 (1921) (statement of W.P.G. Harding, Governor of the Federal Reserve); W.P.G. Harding, *The Formative Period of the Federal Reserve System* (Constable, 1925), 6–7; Eugene N. White, *The Regulation and Reform of the American Banking System* (Princeton University Press, 1983), 131–55.

59. *Amendment to Abolish the Office of the Comptroller of the Currency*, 48 (statement of Harding).

60. White, "To Establish a More Effective Supervision of Banking," 29–30, 43–44.

61. White, *Regulation and Reform*, 156; Eugene Meyer Jr., "The War Finance Corporation and Agricultural Finance," *Bankers Magazine* 104, no. 6 (1922): 983–90.

62. Virgil Willit, *Selected Articles on Chain, Group and Branch Banking* (H. W. Wilson Company, 1930); White, *Regulation and Reform*, 156–65.

63. White, *Regulation and Reform*, 160; Shirley Southworth, *Branch Banking in the United States* (McGraw-Hill, 1928), 36–111; Howard Preston, "Branch Banking with Special Reference to California Conditions," *Journal of Political Economy* 30, no. 4 (1922): 494–517, esp. 500; Howard Preston, "Recent Developments in Branch Banking," *American Economic Review* 14, no. 3 (1924): 443–62; Marquis James and Bessie R. James, *Biography of a Bank: The Story of Bank of America* (Harper & Row, 1954), 40–43, 104.

64. *Annual Report of California Superintendent of Banking* (1921), 42 (quoted in Southworth, *Branch Banking*, 51); California Bank Act (1925) § 9 (quoted in Southworth, *Branch Banking*, 73); Southworth, *Branch Banking*, 74; James and James, *Biography of a Bank*, 136; John S. Drum, Charles F. Stern, and J. F. Sartori to the Federal Reserve Board, October 8, 1923, Letters and Statements of the Board, vol. 19 (FRASER).

65. J. F Johnson to Bank of America Los Angeles, March 5, 1926, quoted in James and James, *Biography of a Bank*, 178; Southworth, *Branch Banking*, 84.

66. *Annual Report of the Comptroller of the Currency* (1922), 4; Walter Wyatt to Federal Reserve Board, "Past Policy of Board in Acting Upon Applications of State Member Banks for Additional Branches," July 31, 1923, Letters and Statements of the Board, vol. 19 (FRASER).

67. *Annual Report of the Comptroller of the Currency* (1922), 4; James and James, *Biography of a Bank*, 156; *Annual Report of the Comptroller of the Currency* (1923), 7 (emphasis in original).

68. White, *Regulation and Reform*, 161–62; *Annual Report of the Comptroller of the Currency* (1922), 88; Preston, "Recent Developments in Branch Banking," 448; James and James, *Biography of a Bank*, 95; Wyatt, "Past Policy of Board in Acting Upon Applications of State Member Banks for Additional Branches."

69. James and James, *Biography of a Bank*, 95.

70. James and James, *Biography of a Bank*, 185–201.

71. H. H. Preston, "The McFadden Banking Act," *American Economic Review* 17, no. 2 (June 1927): 204.

72. Wright Patman, 112 Cong. Rec. 15,031 (1966).

73. *Annual Report of the Comptroller of the Currency* (1924), 18.

Interlude: Sioux Falls Falls

1. "Sioux Falls Bank Closed," *NYT*, January 12, 1924; "Bank at Sioux Falls Fails to Open Doors," *Atlanta Constitution*, January 12, 1924; Comptroller of the Currency, *Reports of Condition for Individual National Banks* (1923), 219.

2. Memo, To All Depositors from W. E. Stevens et al., February 16, 1924, box 563, OCC Insolvent Correspondence; *Annual Report of the Comptroller of the Currency* (1923), 507; "Sioux Falls Bank Clearings," *The Northwestern Banker* 29, no. 437 (January 1924): 62; "State Takes Over South Dakota Bank," *Atlanta Constitution*, January 15, 1924; "U.S. Bank Aid in Wheat Area Gets Approval," *Minneapolis Morning Tribune*, January 19, 1924; Eugene Meyer Jr., "The War Finance Corporation and Agricultural Finance," *Bankers Magazine* 104, no. 6 (1922): 983–90; "Farmers Blamed for Bank Crashes," *NYT*, February 3, 1924.

3. "Bankers Held in $5,000,000 Failure," *Louisville Courier-Journal*, June 28, 1924; Charles H. Wilcox to Comptroller of the Currency, May 13, 1924, box 563, OCC Insolvent Correspondence.

4. R. Alton Lee, *A New Deal of South Dakota: Drought, Depression, and Relief, 1920–1941* (South Dakota Historical Society Press, 2016), 3; David C. Wheelock and Subal C. Kumbhakar, "'The Slack Banker Dances:' Deposit Insurance and Risk-Taking in the Banking Collapse of the 1920s," *Explorations in Economic History* 31, no. 3 (July 1, 1994): 357–75.

5. Memo, To All Depositors from W. E. Stevens et al., February 16, 1924; Charles H. Wilcox to Henry Dawes, April 14, 1924, box 563, OCC Insolvent Correspondence. This procedure would later be called a "Spokane Sale," after the reorganization of a national bank in Spokane, Washington, in 1928 (J.F.T. O'Connor, *The Banking Crisis and Recovery Under the Roosevelt Administration* [Callaghan and Co., 1938], 46–47).

6. "Bank Loans in South Dakota," *WSJ*, March 10, 1924; John Oakwood, "A Federal Reserve Bank Hits Back," *Barron's*, April 7, 1924.

7. Wilcox to Comptroller of the Currency, May 13, 1924.

8. Cyril B. Upham and Edwin Lamke, *Closed and Distressed Banks: A Study in Public Administration* (Brookings Institution, 1934), 94–96, 117; J. W. McIntosh to Charles H. Wilcox, April 30, 1924, box 563, OCC Insolvent Correspondence; Wilcox to Comptroller of the Currency, May 13, 1924.

9. Charles H. Wilcox to Henry M. Dawes, May 8, 1924, box 563, OCC Insolvent Correspondence; Upham and Lamke, *Closed and Distressed Banks*, 79; Charles H. Wilcox to Comptroller of the Currency, November 4, 1925, box 563, OCC Insolvent Correspondence; *Annual Report of the Comptroller of the Currency* (1926), 228.

10. *Annual Report of the Comptroller of the Currency* (1924), 661; *Annual Report of the Comptroller of the Currency* (1925), 611; Herbert S. Schell, *History of South Dakota*, 3rd ed. rev. (University of Nebraska Press, 1975), 277.

11. *Annual Report of the Comptroller of the Currency* (1934), 337, 446.

Chapter Five

1. Franklin D. Roosevelt, "Fireside Chat on Banking," March 12, 1933, APP. A version of this chapter appeared as Peter Conti-Brown and Sean H. Vanatta, "The Logic and Legitimacy of Bank Supervision: The Case of the Bank Holiday of 1933," *Business History Review* 95, no. 1 (2021): 87–120.

2. Gary Richardson, "Categories and Causes of Bank Distress During the Great Depression, 1929–1933: The Illiquidity Versus Insolvency Debate Revisited," *Explorations in Economic History* 44, no. 4 (October 2007): 593; Hugh Rockoff, "The Meaning of Money in the Great Depression" (historical working paper no. 52, National Bureau of Economic Research, December 1993), 36–37; Roosevelt, "Fireside Chat on Banking."

3. Christina D. Romer, "The Nation in Depression," *Journal of Economic Perspectives* 7, no. 2 (1993): 19–39.

4. Eugene N. White, "'To Establish a More Effective Supervision of Banking': How the Birth of the Fed Altered Bank Supervision," in *A Return to Jekyll Island: The Origins, History, and Future of the Federal Reserve*, ed. Michael D. Bordo and William Roberds (Cambridge University Press, 2013), 46.

5. Roosevelt, "Fireside Chat on Banking."

6. Eric Rauchway argues that these actions were simultaneous and that devaluation took precedence (*The Money Makers: How Roosevelt and Keynes Ended the Depression, Defeated Fascism, and Secured a Prosperous Peace* [Basic Books, 2015], 19–72). Many economic historians disagree, arguing that the devaluation stands alone in its impact on recovery. See Peter Temin and Barrie A. Wigmore, "The End of One Big Deflation," *Explorations in Economic History* 27 (1990): 483–502; Scott Sumner, *The Midas Paradox: Financial Markets, Government Policy Shocks, and the Great Depression* (Independent Institute, 2015).

7. For those who credit charisma, see Charles A. Beard and George E. Smith, *The Old Deal and the New* (Macmillan, 1940), 78; Arthur M. Schlesinger Jr., *The Age of Roosevelt: The Coming of the New Deal* (Houghton Mifflin, 1959), 6; William L. Silber, "Why Did FDR's Bank Holiday Succeed?" *Federal Reserve Bank of New York Economic Policy Review* (July 2009): 19–30; Ben S. Bernanke, "Nonmonetary Effects of the Financial Crisis in the Propagation of the Great Depression," *American Economic Review* 73, no. 3 (1983): 272. But cf. Susan E. Kennedy, *The Banking Crisis of 1933* (University of Kentucky Press, 1973).

8. Matthew S. Jaremski, Gary Richardson, and Angela Vossmeyer, "Signals and Stigmas from Banking Interventions: Lessons from the Bank Holiday in 1933" (working paper no. 31088, National Bureau of Economic Research, March 2023).

9. Eugene N. White, *The Regulation and Reform of the American Banking System, 1900-1929* (Princeton University Press, 1983), 126–87, esp. 132; Elmus Wicker, *The Banking Panics of the Great Depression* (Cambridge University Press, 1996), 5; Kris James Mitchener, "Bank Supervision, Regulation, and Instability During the Great Depression," *Journal of Economic History* 65, no. 1 (March 2005): 152–85; *Branch, Chain, and Group Banking*, 71 Cong., vol. 1, pt. I, 28–32, 68–70 (statement of Comptroller John Pole). In theory, branching promotes bank stability. Scholars debate whether it did so in fact during the Depression; see Mark Carlson and Kris James Mitchener, "Branch Banking as a Device for Discipline: Competition and Bank Survivorship During the Great Depression," *Journal of Political Economy* 117, no. 2 (April 2009): 165–210.

10. *Annual Report of the Comptroller of the Currency* (1934), 3–4; Leo T. Crowley to Marriner S. Eccles, February 9, 1938, in Diaries of Henry Morgenthau Jr., vol. 120, 289 (FRASER); Walter A. Morton, "Liquidity and Solvency," *American Economic Review* 29, no. 2 (1939): 279.

11. Federal Reserve, Committee on Branch, Chain, and Group Banking, "225 Bank Suspensions: Case Histories from Examiners' Reports," May 1933, 15 (FRASER). The Federal Reserve lists this report as circa 1932, but the final version was completed in 1933.

12. *Correspondence Between Comptroller of Currency and First National Bank of Canton, Pa.*, Senate Doc. 2505 (1919) (Proquest accession no. T12.2-16.1); *Annual Report of the Comptroller of the Currency* (1931), 11–12; *Annual Report of the Comptroller of the Currency* (1915), 63.

13. Committee on Branch, Chain, and Group Banking, "225 Bank Suspensions," 17; *Stock Exchange Practices, Part 12*, 73 Cong. 5846 (1934) (statement of Francis G. Awalt, Deputy Comptroller of the Currency).

14. Ray B. Westerfield, "Marginal Collateral to Discounts at the Federal Reserve Banks," *American Economic Review* 22, no. 1 (March 1932): 42–43; Caroline Whitney, *Experiments in Credit Control: The Federal Reserve System* (New York, 1934), 41–42. For a good historical overview of the real bills doctrine and the Great Depression, see Judge Glock, "The 'Reifler-Keynes' Doctrine and Federal Reserve Policy in the Great Depression," *History of Political Economy* 51, no. 2 (2019): 297–327. For the influence of the doctrine, see Kathryn Judge, "The Federal Reserve: A Study in Soft Constraints," *Law and Contemporary Problems* 78 (2015): 64–96.

15. Mark Carlson, Kris James Mitchener, and Gary Richardson, "Arresting Banking Panics: Federal Reserve Liquidity Provision and the Forgotten Panic of 1929," *Journal of Political Economy* 119, no. 5 (2011): 893–906.

16. Carlson, Mitchener, and Richardson, "Arresting Banking Panics," 893–906.

17. Walter Bagehot, *Lombard Street: A Description of the Money Market* (Henry S. King, 1873), 51.

18. Warren Randolph Burgess, *The Reserve Banks and the Money Market* (Harper, 1927), 231–37; White, "To Establish a More Effective Supervision of Banking," 46; Memo, Mr. Smead to the Federal Reserve Board, June 10, 1929, folder 3, box 362, Charles S. Hamlin Scrap Book–Volume 192 (FRASER); Memo, Mr. Smead to Governor Meyer, April 27, 1931, Federal Reserve Board, Reports–Div. of Bank Ops., folder 5, box 120, Meyer Papers (FRASER); Benjamin Strong to Adolph Miller, July 14, 1922, Strong-Miller Correspondence (FRASER).

19. *Branch, Chain, and Group Banking*, 71 Cong. 27 (1930) (testimony of John Pole, Comptroller of the Currency); John Berry McFerrin, *Caldwell & Company* (Chapel Hill, 1939), 123; Board of Governors of the Federal Reserve System, Committee on Branch, Group, and Chain Banking, *Banking Groups and Chains*, ca. 1932, 171 (FRASER); Memo, Mr. Smead to Federal Reserve Board, April 21, 1931, folder 6, box 364, Charles S. Hamlin Scrap Book–Volume 214 (FRASER).

20. McFerrin, *Caldwell & Company*, 24–36, 127–29, 176; Wicker, *Banking Panics of the Great Depression*, 24–36; *Operation of the National and Federal Reserve Banking Systems, Part 5*, 71 Cong. 632 (1931) (statement of J. W. Pole, Comptroller of the Currency).

21. McFerrin, *Caldwell & Company*, 178, 184; Gary Richardson, "The Check Is in the Mail: Correspondent Clearing and the Banking Panics of the Great Depression," *Journal of Economic History* 67, no. 3 (September 2007): 659–61; Gary Richardson and William Troost, "Monetary Intervention Mitigated Banking Panics During the Great Depression: Quasi-Experimental Evidence from a Federal Reserve District Border, 1929–1933," *Journal of Political Economy* 117, no. 6 (December 2009): 1031–73.

22. "Reserve Cash Idle in Banks," *Knoxville News-Sentinel*, November 13, 1930; "Tennessee Upset by Bank Failures," *NYT*, November 16, 1930.

23. Richardson and Troost, "Monetary Intervention Mitigated Banking Panics"; Wicker, *Banking Panics of the Great Depression*, 52–55.

24. Milton Friedman and Anna J. Schwartz, *Monetary History of the United States, 1867–1960* (Princeton University Press, 1963), 408–12; Wicker, *Banking Panics of the Great Depression*, 37–38, 40, 49.

25. Throughout the 1920s, national bank security portfolios had also increased relative to loans, so that while loans comprised 56 percent of bank assets in 1920, compared to 19 percent for securities, by 1930, loans made up 50 percent and securities 25 percent. In December 1933, securities and loans made up a nearly identical 37.25 percent of national bank assets, though the securities values were likely inflated by forbearance. *Annual Report of the Comptroller of the Currency* (1921), 12; *Annual Report of the Comptroller of the Currency* (1931), 41; *Annual Report of the Comptroller of the Currency* (1934), 65.

26. Paul M. Atkins, "The First Pentad of the Office of the Special Liquidator of Securities for the Comptroller of the Currency," ca. 1963, Special Liquidator of Securities—First Pentad folder, box 10, Atkins Papers; *Stock Exchange Practices, Part 10*, 73 Cong. 4702, 4704 (1933) (statement of Alfred P. Leyburn, Chief National Bank Examiner, Fourth Federal Reserve District). The Comptroller used similar forbearance during the financial upheaval caused by World War I: *Annual Report of the Comptroller of Currency* (1917), 7.

27. Gary Richardson, "Quarterly Data on the Categories and Causes of Bank Distress During the Great Depression" (working paper no. 12715, National Bureau of Economic Research, December 2006), 44; Memo, J. W. Pole to National Bank Examiners, December 18, 1931, quoted in *Stock Exchange Practices, Part 10*, 4644 (statement of Alfred P. Leyburn); Douglas W. Diamond and Philip H. Dybvig, "Bank Runs, Deposit Insurance, and Liquidity," *Journal of Political Economy* 91, no. 3 (1983): 410; Eugene M. Lokey, "Along the Highways of Finance," *NYT*, September 20, 1931; Walter Ferguson to F. G. Awalt, November 9, 1931, folder 10, box 3, Awalt Papers; "Banking Situation in the Second District," December 8, 1931, folder 3, box 117, Meyer Papers (FRASER). Our emphasis on forbearance on banks' bond portfolios contrasts in particular with Friedman and Schwartz, who argue that "[b]y reducing the market value of the bond portfolios of banks, declines in bond prices in turn reduced the margin of capital as evaluated by bank examiners, and in this way contributed to subsequent bank failures" (*Monetary History*, 312). Moreover, the Comptroller's effort to save banks by declaring assets worth what examiners said they were worth contextualizes other policy (in)actions, especially the Fed's failure to counteract the shrinking money supply. See Friedman and Schwartz, *Monetary History*, 312–17; Allan H. Meltzer, *A History of the Federal Reserve, Volume 1, 1913–1951* (University of Chicago Press, 2003), 336–37, 412–13; Wicker, *Banking Panics of the Great Depression*, 85–86.

28. Herbert Hoover, *American Individualism* (Hoover Institution, 1922), 52–55; Ellis W. Hawley, "Herbert Hoover, the Commerce Secretariat, and the Vision of an 'Associative State,' 1921–1928," *Journal of American History* 61, no. 1 (June 1974): 116–40; Brian Balogh, *The Associational State: American Governance in the Twentieth Century* (University of Pennsylvania Press, 2015), 75.

29. Friedman and Schwartz, *Monetary History*, 315; Meltzer, *History of the Federal Reserve*, 392–93; Wicker, *Banking Panics of the Great Depression*, 62; Gerald D. Nash, "Herbert Hoover and the Origins of the Reconstruction Finance Corporation," *Mississippi Valley Historical Review* 46, no. 3 (1959), 455–68; Kennedy, *Banking Crisis of 1933*, 33–36; *Literary Digest*, October 17, 1931, 5–6, quoted in Kennedy, *Banking Crisis of 1933*, 35.

30. James S. Olson, "The End of Voluntarism: Herbert Hoover and the National Credit Corporation," *Annals of Iowa* 41, no. 6 (1972): 1104–13; Kennedy, *Banking Crisis of 1933*, 35–36;

James S. Olson, *Saving Capitalism: The Reconstruction Finance Corporation and the New Deal, 1933–1940* (Princeton University Press, 1988), 1–24.

31. Charles W. Calomiris, Joseph R. Mason, Marc Weidenmier, and Katherine Bobroff, "The Effects of Reconstruction Finance Corporation Assistance on Michigan's Banks' Survival in the 1930s," *Explorations in Economic History* 50 (2013): 528; Joseph R. Mason, "The Political Economy of Reconstruction Finance Corporation Assistance During the Great Depression," *Explorations in Economic History* 40 (2003): 107–9.

32. Richardson, "Categories and Causes," 606; *Operation of the National and Federal Reserve Banking Systems, Part 2*, 72 Cong. 435 (1932) (statement of J. W. Pole, Comptroller of the Currency); Open Market Policy Conference for the Federal Reserve System, Meeting, April 12, 1932, Minutes of the Meetings of the Open Market Policy Conference (FRASER); J. W. Pole to All Chief National Bank Examiners, July 1, 1932, folder 8, box 1, Awalt Papers.

33. *Stock Exchange Practices, Part 10*, 4646 (statement of Alfred P. Leyburn).

34. "Pole to Leave Currency Post Due to Strain," *WP*, September 1, 1932; Francis G. Awalt to Ogden Mills, November 12, 1932, folder 1, box 4, Awalt Papers; Francis G. Awalt, Memorandum for Files, November 15, 1932, folder 10, box 3, Awalt Papers.

35. John T. Flynn, "Michigan Magic," *Harper's Magazine*, December 1932, 5; Darwyn H. Lumley, *Breaking the Banks in the Motor City: The Auto Industry, the 1933 Detroit Banking Crisis and the Start of the New Deal* (McFarland, 2009), 38; *Stock Exchange Practices, Part 12*, 5762 (statement of Alfred P. Leyburn); Alfred Leyburn to the Comptroller of the Currency, June 14, 1932, quoted in *Stock Exchange Practices, Part 10*, 4638 (statement of Alfred P. Leyburn); Francis Gloyd Awalt, "Recollections of the Banking Crisis," *Business History Review* 43, no. 3 (1969): 349–55; Kennedy, *Banking Crisis of 1933*, 77–93.

36. Awalt, "Recollections of the Banking Crisis," 355–56, 359–60; Kennedy, *Banking Crisis of 1933*, 93–96, 134; Rockoff, "The Meaning of Money in the Great Depression," 37; Charles W. Calomiris and Joseph R. Mason, "Fundamentals, Panics, and Bank Distress During the Great Depression," *American Economic Review* 93, no. 5 (December 2003): 1615–47; Wigmore, "Was the Bank Holiday of 1933 a Run on the Dollar," 739–56.

37. Kennedy, *Banking Crisis of 1933*, 103–35; Wicker, *Banking Panics of the Great Depression*, 71, 131–32; Robert Lynn Fuller, *"Phantom of Fear": The Banking Panic of 1933* (McFarland, 2012), 158–61; Arthur A. Ballantine, "When All the Banks Closed," *Harvard Business Review* 26, no. 2 (March 1948): 133-38; Schlesinger, *Coming of the New Deal*, 3; George W. Norris, *Ended Episodes* (Philadelphia, 1937), 220–30.

38. Eric Rauchway, *Winter War: Hoover, Roosevelt, and the First Clash over the New Deal* (New York, 2018), 205–9, 222; Emanuel A. Goldenweiser, Contemporaneous Notes, March 3, 1933, folder 11, box 1, Awalt Papers.

39. Kenneth Whyte, *Hoover: An Extraordinary Life in Extraordinary Times* (Knopf, 2017), 521–23; Schlesinger, *Coming of the New Deal*, 4; Goldenweiser, Contemporaneous Notes, March 3, 1933.

40. Franklin D. Roosevelt, "Inaugural Address," March 4, 1933, APP.

41. Will Rogers, "Will Rogers Remarks," *LAT*, March 6, 1933; Franklyn Waltman Jr., "Roosevelt Proclaims National Bank Holiday to Last Until Friday," *BS*, March 6, 1933.

42. Franklin D. Roosevelt, "Proclamation 2039—Declaring Bank Holiday," March 6, 1933, APP.

43. Ogden Mills to William Woodin, March 4, 1933, folder 7, box 1, Awalt Papers.

44. Francis G. Awalt, ["Personal Account of F. G. Awalt"], March 1933, folder 11, box 1, Awalt Papers.

45. Awalt, ["Personal Account of F. G. Awalt"]; Goldenweiser, Contemporaneous Notes, March 3, 1933; Ogden Mills to William Woodin, March 4, 1933, folder 7, box 1, Awalt Papers; Kennedy, *Banking Crisis of 1933*, 168–74; Marcus Nadler and Jules I. Bogen, *The Banking Crisis: The End of an Epoch* (Dodd, Mead & Co., 1933), 162–65.

46. Kennedy, *Banking Crisis of 1933*, 168–74; Nadler and Bogen, *The Banking Crisis*, 176; Federal Reserve Board, Meeting Minutes, March 8, 1933, vol. 20, pt. 1, Fed Board Minutes (FRASER); Awalt, "Recollections of the Banking Crisis," 366; Awalt, ["Personal Account of F. G. Awalt"].

47. Federal Reserve Board, Meeting Minutes, March 9, 1933, vol. 20, pt. 1, Fed Board Minutes (FRASER); Awalt, "Recollections of the Banking Crisis," 368n5; Kennedy, *Banking Crisis of 1933*, 183–84; Federal Reserve Board, Meeting Minutes, March 11, 1933, vol. 20, pt. 1, Fed Board Minutes (FRASER).

48. Kennedy, *Banking Crisis of 1933*, 175; Awalt, ["Personal Account of F. G. Awalt"].

49. Awalt, ["Personal Account of F. G. Awalt"]; 77 *Cong. Rec.* 58 (1933) (statement of Senator Glass).

50. 77 *Cong. Rec.* 62 (1933) (statement of Senator Vandenberg); Kennedy, *Banking Crisis of 1933*, 176-77.

51. Franklin D. Roosevelt, "Executive Order 6073—Reopening Banks," APP; J.F.T. O'Connor, *The Banking Crisis and Recovery Under the Roosevelt Administration* (Callaghan and Co., 1938), 19; Federal Reserve Board, Meeting Minutes, March 11, 1933.

52. Frederick L. Allen, *Only Yesterday: An Informal History of the Nineteen-Twenties* (Harper & Bros., 1939), 110; Barry Eichengreen, *Hall of Mirrors: The Great Depression, and the Uses—and Misuses—of History* (Oxford University Press, 2015), 296.

53. Committee on the History of the Federal Reserve System, "Interviews with Mr. J. Herbert Case," February 26, 1954, folder 1, box 2, Committee on the History of the Federal Reserve System (FRASER); George Seay to David R. Coker, quoted in Fuller, *Phantom of Fear*, 198.

54. Awalt, "Recollections of the Banking Crisis," 369n6; Ernest K. Lindsey, quoted in Kennedy, *Banking Crisis of 1933*, 237; Norris, *Ended Episodes*, 232–33.

55. L. R. Rounds to Governor Harrison, May 15, 1931, Federal Reserve Board: Transamerica Corporation, 1931–32, Subject File, folder 9, box 121, Meyer Papers (FRASER); Bessie R. James and Marquis James, *Biography of a Bank: The Story of Bank of America* (Harper & Row, 1954), 362–74; Kennedy, *Banking Crisis of 1933*, 186–87; Awalt, "Recollections of the Banking Crisis," 369; Woodin, quoted in Kenneth Davis, *FDR: The New Deal Years, 1933–1937* (Random House, 1986), 62.

56. Grace Tully, *FDR: My Boss* (Charles Scribner's Sons, 1949), 88, quoted in Geoffrey Storm, "FDR and WGY: The Origins of the Fireside Chats," *New York History* 88, no. 2 (2007): 178; Amos Kiewe, *FDR's First Fireside Chat: Public Confidence and the Banking Crisis* (Texas A&M University Press, 2007), 76–82; Awalt, "Recollections of the Banking Crisis," 370.

57. Eugene M. Stephens to Eugene R. Black, June 2, 1933, Policy and Procedure in Connection with Banking Holiday Proclamations, April 1933–1940, folder 2, box 2165, Fed System Records (FRASER).

58. Roosevelt, "Fireside Chat on Banking."

59. "White House Hails Bank Reopenings," *NYT*, March 14, 1933; "City Recovers Confidence as 34 banks reopen," *CT*, March 14, 1933; S. A. Hayes, "Local Bank Rides Financial Storm," *Philadelphia Tribune*, March 16, 1933; Kennedy, *Banking Crisis of 1933*, 187; "Bank Openings by States," *NYT*, March 17, 1933; Federal Reserve Bank of Boston, *Nineteenth Annual Report of the Federal Reserve Bank of Boston* (1933), 7.

60. "Hoarders of Gold Will Be Identified," *WP*, March 9, 1933; "Hoarders in Fright Turn in $30,000,000," *NYT*, March 1, 1933; "Gold Inflow Brings in $20,000,000 in Day," *NYT*, March 11, 1933; "Confidence Increasing as More Banks Reopen," *WSJ*, March 15, 1933; *Annual Report of the Federal Reserve System* (1933), 14.

61. Raymond Moley, *After Seven Years* (Harper and Brothers, 1939), 155; *Annual Report of the Federal Reserve System* (1933), 22; *Annual Report of the Federal Reserve System* (1935), 176.

62. Roosevelt, "Fireside Chat on Banking"; Kennedy, *Banking Crisis of 1933*, 188–89 (Awalt quote at 189).

63. *Annual Report of the Comptroller of the Currency* (1923) 20; Thomas J. Sargent, *Rational Expectations and Inflation* (Harper and Row, 1986).

Interlude: Banking on Bonds, for Better and Worse

1. *Annual Report of the Comptroller of the Currency* (1932), 3.

2. "Memorandum Re Sales of General Market Securities Owned by Insolvent National Banks," March 3, 1932, Organization & Procedures of the Office of Special Liquidator of Securities folder, box 14, Special Liquidator Correspondence.

3. Paul M. Atkins, "The First Pentad of the Office of the Special Liquidator of Securities for the Comptroller of the Currency," ca. 1963, Special Liquidator of Securities—First Pentad folder, box 10, Atkins Papers.

4. Paul W. Drake, *The Money Doctor in the Andes: The Kemmerer Missions, 1923–1933* (Duke University Press, 1989), 212–48.

5. Paul M. Atkins, "The Scientific Organization of a Secondary Reserve," *BM* 121, no. 2 (1930): 217; P. M. Atkins, "Difference Between Bank Secondary Reserve and Investment Accounts," *BM* 121, no. 3 (1930): 343; Paul M. Atkins, "Business and Bonds," *BM* 121, no. 5 (1930): 633; Paul M. Atkins, "Distortions in the Composition of Bank Secondary Reserves," *BM* 122, no. 1 (1931): 53; Paul M. Atkins, *Bank Secondary Reserve & Investment Policies* (Bankers Publishing Company, 1930).

6. George W. Norris to Paul M. Atkins, April 16, 1929, Ames, Emerich and Co.—Corresp. 1929–31 folder, box 3, Atkins Papers.

7. Paul M. Atkins to Victor S. Buchanan, March 19, 1930, Ames, Emerich and Co.—Reports 1928 Sep. folder, box 3, Atkins Papers.

8. Atkins to Buchanan, March 19, 1930.

9. "Memorandum Re Sales of General Market Securities Owned by Insolvent National Banks," March 3, 1932.

10. Allan H. Meltzer, *A History of the Federal Reserve, Volume 1, 1931–1951* (University of Chicago Press, 2003), 348n84; Atkins, "The First Pentad of the Office of the Special Liquidator of Securities."

11. L. F. Sailer to F. G. Awalt, January 29, 1932, Special Liquidator NY Office; Memo, J. W. Pole to the Secretary of the Treasury, n.d., ca. January 1932, Special Liquidator NY Office; C. B. Upham to Ralph D. Williams, February 21, 1932, Special Liquidator NY Office; Paul M. Atkins to J. E. Fouts, n.d., ca. February 1932, Special Liquidator NY Office; Paul M. Atkins to J. E. Fouts, March 25, 1932, Special Liquidator NY Office.

12. Atkins, "The First Pentad of the Office of the Special Liquidator of Securities."

13. Atkins, "The First Pentad of the Office of the Special Liquidator of Securities."

14. Paul M. Atkins, "A Bit of Financial History," ca. 1938, Special Liquidator of Securities— First Pentad folder, box 10, Atkins Papers.

15. Bond Receipt, no. 22048, Trust of Noble County National Bank, May 28, 1934, box 60, Foreign Bonds, Special Liquidator Vault Vouchers; Bond Receipt, no. 22049, Trust of Noble County National Bank, May 28, 1934, box 60, Foreign Bonds, Special Liquidator Vault Vouchers; Bond Receipt, no. 9328, First National Bank of Waterloo, December 17, 1932, box 60, Foreign Bonds, Special Liquidator Vault Vouchers; Bond Receipt, no. 9348, First National Bank of Waterloo, December 17, 1932, box 60, Foreign Bonds, Special Liquidator Vault Vouchers; Bond Receipt, no. 9289, First National Bank of Waterloo, December 17, 1932, box 60, Foreign Bonds, Special Liquidator Vault Vouchers; Edward I. Bradley, "$10 Third Prize Essay: 'Proper Diversification of a Bank's Secondary Reserve,'" *Northwestern Banker* 32, no. 478 (1927): 57; J. C. Lutweiler, "Future Opportunity in Foreign Bonds Based on Past Developments," *Mid-Continent Banker* (1927): 73; Clyde W. Phelps, "Turn Your Eyes to Latin America," *Mid-Continent Banker* (January 1929): 49.

16. Paul M. Atkins to J. E. Fouts, April 8, 1932, Special Liquidator NY Office.

17. Paul M. Atkins to J. E. Fouts, July 21, 1932, Special Liquidator NY Office; Atkins, "The First Pentad of the Office of the Special Liquidator of Securities."

18. Paul M. Atkins to J. A. Anderson, May 9, 1933, A—Brokers Letters folder, box 1; Paul M. Atkins to B. F. Madden, May 31, 1933, A—Brokers Letters folder, box 1; Paul M. Atkins to S. T. Pernell, January 19, 1934, D—1934 folder, box 10, Special Liquidator Brokers.

19. E. G. Olwell to Paul M. Atkins, December 29, 1933, Memorandums folder, box 12, Special Liquidator Correspondence; Paul M. Atkins to J. E. Fouts, June 15, 1932, Special Liquidator NY Office; Atkins to Office Staff, March 1, 1934, Memorandums folder, box 12, Special Liquidator Correspondence.

20. J. E. Fouts to Paul M. Atkins, November 9, 1933, Special Liquidator NY Office.

21. E. G. Olwell to Paul M. Atkins, August 30, 1933, Memorandums folder, box 12, Special Liquidator Correspondence; E. G. Olwell to Paul M. Atkins, November 8, 1934, Memorandums folder, box 12, Special Liquidator Correspondence; Memo re: 38855–38861 incl., ca. November 1936, Special Liquidator of Securities—Analysis of Sales, Section II (3) folder, box 7, Atkins Papers.

22. Atkins, "The First Pentad of the Office of the Special Liquidator of Securities"; Atkins, "A Bit of Financial History," cf. *Annual Report of the Comptroller of the Currency* (1939), 46.

Chapter Six

1. Franklin D. Roosevelt, "Message to Congress on Stimulating Recovery," April 14, 1938, APP.

2. Samuel Merrill, "Address of Hon. Sml. Merrill of Iowa, on Bank Deposits and Panics," *BM* 40 (1886): 123–24; Federal Deposit Insurance Corporation, *Federal Deposit Insurance Corpora-*

tion: The First Fifty Years: A History of the FDIC, 1933–1983 (Federal Deposit Insurance Corporation, 1984), 24–31; Eugene N. White, "State-Sponsored Insurance of Bank Deposits in the United States, 1907–1929," *Journal of Economic History* 41, no. 3 (1981): 537–57.

3. Susan Estabrook Kennedy, *The Banking Crisis of 1933* (University Press of Kentucky, 1973), 214–20; Raymond Moley, *The First New Deal* (Harcourt, Brace & World, 1966), 318–19; Henry Steagall, quoted in Jacob H. Gutwillig, "Glass Versus Steagall: The Fight over Federalism and American Banking," *Virginia Law Review* 100, no. 4 (2014): 805.

4. Kennedy, *Banking Crisis of 1933*, 214–16; Richard H. K. Vietor, *Contrived Competition: Regulation and Deregulation in America* (Harvard University Press, 1994), 246–52; Carter Glass, *Operation of the National and Federal Reserve Banking Systems*, S. Rep. 70-584, April 22, 1932, 10.

5. White, "State-Sponsored Insurance," 543; Christopher W. Shaw, "'The Man in the Street Is for It': The Road to the FDIC," *Journal of Policy History* 27, no. 1 (2015): 44–50; James F. T. O'Connor, Diary entry, June 1, 1933, reel 1, O'Connor Diary.

6. Glass, "Regulation of Banking," 3729; Banking Act of 1933, Pub. L. 73-66 § 8 (amendments to the Federal Reserve Act § 12B(e)) (1933).

7. Banking Act of 1933, Pub. L. 73-66 § 8 (amendments to the Federal Reserve Act § 12B(b-d)) (1933); *Annual Report of the Federal Deposit Insurance Corporation* (1934), 8. The initial provisions of the law required capital subscriptions from participating banks and made the Treasury's obligation callable (implying it would only be called in an emergency), but because the fund was temporary, the Board called the Treasury capital and held off on requiring participant banks to make their capital subscriptions.

8. Herbert Hoover, *The Memoirs of Herbert Hoover Volume 3: The Great Depression 1920–1941* (Macmillan Company, 1951), 161–62; Alan Brinkley, *Voices of Protest: Huey Long, Father Coughlin, & the Great Depression* (Knopf, 1982), 129–31; Gerald D. Nash, "Herbert Hoover and the Origins of the Reconstruction Finance Corporation," *Mississippi Valley Historical Review* 46, no. 3 (1959): 455; Eugene Meyer and Sydney Hyman, Unpublished Autobiography of Eugene Meyer, 216–19, box 81, Eugene Meyer Papers, Library of Congress, Manuscript Division; James S. Olson, *Saving Capitalism: The Reconstruction Finance Corporation and the New Deal, 1933–1940* (Princeton University Press, 1988), 18; Charles W. Calomiris, Joseph R. Mason, Marc Weidenmier, Katherine Bobroff, et al., "The Effects of Reconstruction Finance Corporation Assistance on Michigan's Banks' Survival in the 1930s," *Explorations in Economic History* 50, no. 4 (2013): 526–47; Joseph R. Mason, "Do Lender of Last Resort Policies Matter? The Effects of Reconstruction Finance Corporation Assistance to Banks During the Great Depression," *Journal of Financial Services Research* 20, no. 1 (2001): 77–95.

9. Francis G. Awalt, ["Personal Account of F. G. Awalt"], March 1933, folder 11, box 1, Awalt Papers; Kennedy, *Banking Crisis of 1933*, 170–71, 177; Emergency Banking Act of 1933, Pub. L. 73-1, 48 Stat. 1, Title II.

10. Olson, *Saving Capitalism*, 66, 69–71; Helen M. Burns, *The American Banking Community and the New Deal Reforms, 1933–1935* (Praeger, 1974), 120–23; Cyrus B. Upham and Edwin Lampke, *Closed and Distressed Banks: A Study in Public Administration* (Brookings Institution, 1934), 15–16.

11. Olson, *Saving Capitalism*, 73; Jesse Jones, *Fifty Billion Dollars: My Thirteen Years at the RFC (1932–1945)* (Macmillan Company, 1951), 45–50 (quote at 49); Memorandum, "re: Mechanics Bank, Richmond, California," December 4, 1933, box 3, OCC 1933 Records.

12. Jones, *Fifty Billion Dollars*, 49.

13. Jones, *Fifty Billion Dollars*, 26; Matthew Jaremski, Gary Richardson, and Angela Voss-meyer, "Signals and Stigmas from Banking Interventions: Lessons from the Bank Holiday in 1933" (working paper no. 31088, National Bureau of Economic Research, March 2023); Olson, *Saving Capitalism*, 71.

14. Banking Act of 1933, Pub. L. 73-66, 48 Stat. 162 § 12A(y).

15. "Takes Woodin's Posts," *NYT*, March 4, 1933; "Moves to Reopen More State Banks," *NYT*, April 9, 1933; "Bankers' Help for Reopening Here Is Asked," *WP*, April 9, 1933; "Accepts O'Connor for Controller," *NYT*, May 9, 1933; "Gibson Is Named Envoy to Brazil," *NYT*, May 2, 1933; "O'Connor Enters Race," *LAT*, February 19, 1938.

16. "Insurance Unit," *WSJ*, August 24, 1933; Meeting of the Directors of the Federal Deposit Insurance Corporation, September 11, 1933, vol. 1, box 1, FDIC Minutes.

17. Howard Wood, "O'Connor Tells Bank Deposit Guarantee Plan," *CT*, September 8, 1933; "State Bank Supervisors Act to Forestall Possible Crisis," *CSM*, September 14, 1933.

18. Diary entry, September 19, 1934, O'Connor Diary; "Bank Tests Ready in Guarantee Plan," *NYT*, September 19, 1933; State of New York, *Annual Report of the Superintendent of the Banks for the Year Ending December 31, 1933* (J. B. Lyon Company, 1934), 8; "Seek Credit Men to Aid Deposit Insurance Corp," *CT*, September 26, 1933; *Annual Report of the Federal Deposit Insurance Corporation* (1934), 14; *Annual Report of the Comptroller of the Currency* (1933), 145–47; *Annual Report of the Comptroller of the Currency* (1931), 80–85 (the Comptroller did not publish exam-iner lists after 1931); Meeting of the Directors of the Federal Deposit Insurance Corporation, September 20, 1933–November 9, 1933, vol. 1, box 1, FDIC Minutes.

19. Arthur M. Schlesinger Jr., *The Age of Roosevelt: The Coming of the New Deal* (Houghton Mifflin, 1959), 428; "Full Clearance by New Year Is Seen for Banks," *WP*, Septem-ber 14, 1933.

20. "Defines Deposit Guaranty Banks," *WSJ*, September 8, 1933.

21. "Roosevelt Urges Banks to Ease Credit," *NYT*, September 6, 1933; "Bankers Gather in Critical Mood," *NYT*, September 4, 1933; "Bankers of Nation Bow to 'New Deal,'" *NYT*, Sep-tember 10, 1933; Jones, *Fifty Billion Dollars*, 27. Jones misremembered that Black had already left the Board for Atlanta, but that did not occur until the following summer.

22. Jones, *Fifty Billion Dollars*, 27; Schlesinger, *Coming of the New Deal*, 429–30.

23. Olson, *Saving Capitalism*, 80–81; *Report of the Reconstruction Finance Corporation* (Fourth Quarter of 1933), 73 Cong. H. Doc. 297 (1934), 33 (FRASER).

24. *Annual Report of the Federal Deposit Insurance Corporation* (1934), 15–16; Schlesinger, *Coming of the New Deal*, 430; Jesse H. Jones to Walter J. Cummings, January 1, 1934, vol. 2, box 1, FDIC Minutes; *Banking Act of 1935*, 74 Cong. 41 (1935) (statement of Leo Crowley, Chairman of the Board, Federal Deposit Insurance Corporation).

25. Memorandum, "re: Citizens Bank, Pekin, Indiana," December 1, 1933, box 3, OCC 1933 Records. The bank remained in operation until at least the early 1950s ("Indiana News," *Mid-Continent Banker* 49, no. 9 [1953], 62 [FRASER]).

26. *Annual Report of the Federal Deposit Insurance Corporation* (1934), 15; Diary entry, De-cember 30, 1933, O'Connor Diary; Meeting of the Directors of the Federal Deposit Insurance Corporation, September 11, 1933, vol. 1, box 1, FDIC Minutes; New York, *Annual Report of the Superintendent of the Banks for the Year Ending December 31, 1933*, 5.

27. National Association of Supervisors of State Banks, *Proceedings of the Thirty-Second Annual Convention of the National Association of Supervisors of State Banks* (Brando Printing, 1933), 25, 27, 36.

28. Jones to Moley, April 1934, in Steven Fenberg, *Unprecedented Power: Jesse Jones, Capitalism, and the Common Good* (Texas A&M University Press, 2013), 221.

29. Diary entries, May 9 and 10, 1934, O'Connor Diary; Marriner S. Eccles, "Reconstructing Economic Thinking," October 27, 1933, folder 5, box 74, Eccles Papers (FRASER); Mark Wayne Nelson, *Jumping the Abyss: Marriner S. Eccles and the New Deal, 1933–1940* (University of Utah Press, 2017), 145–56; Jones, *Fifty Billion Dollars*, 48–49.

30. *Extension of Temporary Plan for Deposit Insurance*, 73 Cong. 131-150 (statement of J.F.T. O'Connor, Comptroller of the Currency) (1934); Roland I. Robinson, "The Capital-Deposit Ratio in Banking Supervision," *Journal of Political Economy* 49, no. 1 (1941): 41; *Extension of Temporary Plan for Deposit Insurance* 73 Cong. 16 (statement of Leo T. Crowley, Chairman of the Board, Federal Deposit Insurance Corporation); *Report of the Reconstruction Finance Corporation* (Fourth Quarter of 1934), 74 Cong. H. Doc. 139 (1935), 75 (FRASER); *Report of the Reconstruction Finance Corporation* (Fourth Quarter of 1933), 33.

31. *Federal Reserve Bulletin* (December 1933), 746; *Federal Reserve Bulletin* (December 1935), 803; Fenberg, *Unprecedented Power*, 217, 221–23 (Jones quote at 217); Allan H. Meltzer, *A History of the Federal Reserve, Volume 1, 1913–1951* (University of Chicago Press, 2003), 435.

32. Roosevelt, quoted in Fenberg, *Unprecedented Power*, 222 (emphasis in original).

33. Meeting summary, August 1, 1934, p. 7, vol. 2, pt. 1, Morgenthau Diaries (FRASER); Memorandum on Meeting in Office of the Secretary of the Treasury, August 1, 1934, folder 3, box 9, Eccles Papers (FRASER); Report of the Meeting Held August 2, 1934, in the Board Room of the Federal Reserve Board, folder 3, box 9, Eccles Papers (FRASER).

34. Report of the Meeting Held August 2, 1934.

35. Report of the Meeting Held August 2, 1934.

36. Report of the Meeting Held August 2, 1934.

37. Meeting summary, August 1, 1934.

38. Meeting summary, August 1, 1934; "Expansionists at Hyde Park," *WSJ*, September 10, 1934; Schlesinger, *The Coming of the New Deal*, 496–503.

39. Roderick P. Stewart and Thomas Phelps, "Roosevelt Backs Charges Examiners Balk Good Loans," *WSJ*, September 13, 1934; Stuart L. Weiss, *The President's Man: Leo Crowley and Franklin Roosevelt in Peace and War* (Southern Illinois University Press, 1996), 42; "Drop in Loans Laid to Federal Rules," *NYT*, September 12, 1934; Proposed Speech to Bankers, October 22, 1934, folder 4, box 9, Eccles Papers (FRASER).

40. Charles O. Hardy and Jacob Viner, *Report on Bank Credit Availability in the Seventh Federal Reserve District* (Government Printing Office, 1935), 22; Weiss, *President's Man*, 43.

41. Memo, J. Eigelberner to Crowley, November 21, 1935, Examining Division: Eigelberner, J. folder, box 1, FDIC Crowley Memos; Memo, "Classification of Loans," n.d., ca. September 1934, FDIC Crowley Memos; Report of the Meeting, September 10, 1934, Examining Division: Hopkins, R. L. folder, box 2, FDIC Crowley Memos; Memo, R. L. Hopkins to Leo T. Crowley, "Necessity for Continued Examination of Banks in the Manner Now Adopted," April 27, 1935, Examining Division: Hopkins, R. L. folder, box 2, FDIC Crowley Memos.

42. Meeting summary, August 1, 1934.

43. Weiss, *President's Man*, 17–21, 36–38, 61 (citing Morgenthau's diaries, May 22, 1936).

44. Weiss, *President's Man*, xii, 44.

45. Memo to FDR, November 2, 1934, p. 158, vol. 2, pt. 1, Morgenthau Diaries (FRASER); Jacob Viner, "Preliminary Report to Secretary Morgenthau on Bank Examinations," October 1, 1934, folder 7, box 50, Viner Papers; "Plan to End Duplicate Bank Examinations by Merging Controller's Office and FDIC," *NYT*, November 28, 1934; Diary entries, November 15–16, 1934, O'Connor Diary.

46. Telephone transcript, Henry Morgenthau Jr. and Marriner S. Eccles, December 19, 1934, pp. 328–29, vol. 2, pt. 2, Morgenthau Diaries (FRASER).

47. Ali Anari, James Kolari, and Joseph Mason, "Bank Asset Liquidation and the Propagation of the U.S. Great Depression," *Journal of Money, Credit and Banking* 37, no. 4 (2005): 758; Upham and Lampke, *Closed and Distressed Banks*, 40.

48. *Banking Act of 1935*, 74 Cong. 38 (statement of Leo T. Crowley) (1935); *Annual Report of the Federal Deposit Insurance Corporation* (1934), 26–27; *Annual Report of the Federal Deposit Insurance Corporation* (1936), 9.

49. Federal Deposit Insurance Corporation, *Federal Deposit Insurance Corporation: The First Fifty*, 85.

50. "U.S. Begins Paying Depositors of First 'Insured' Bank to Fail," *NYHT*, July 4, 1934; "Reopening Closed Banks for Business and Lifting of Restrictions: Illinois," *Commercial and Financial Chronicle*, July 7, 1934, 63 (FRASER); *Annual Report of the Federal Deposit Insurance Corporation* (1934), 249.

51. Report of the Meeting, September 12, 1934, p. 42, Examining Division: Hopkins, R. L. folder, box 2, FDIC Crowley Memos; Meeting Minutes, June 27, 1934, 3:00 P.M., vol. 21, pt. 3, Fed Board Minutes (FRASER).

52. *Annual Report of the Federal Deposit Insurance Corporation* (1934), 26; Banking Act of 1933 § 12B(1), available in Federal Reserve Bulletin, June 1933, codified at 12 U.S.C. § 1821; "Business: Pay Off," *Time*, July 16, 1934, 53; "Bank Insurance Brings Joy to Humble Hoarder," *Los Angeles Evening Post-Record*, July 4, 1934; "Payments Begun Under Bank Insurance; First Go to Depositors at East Peoria, Ill.," *NYT*, July 4, 1934; "Deposits: First Insured Bank to Fail Refunds 99 Percent," *Newsweek*, July 14, 1934, 29.

53. "Deposits: First Insured Bank to Fail"; Richard L. Strout, "New Deal Is Ready to Jump into Second Chapter in Fall Under Title 'Social Security,'" *CSM*, July 5, 1934; David M. Kennedy, "What the New Deal Did," *Political Science Quarterly* 124, no. 2 (July 2009): 251–68.

54. Report of the Meeting, September 12, 1934, p. 42, Examining Division: Hopkins, R. L. folder, box 2, FDIC Crowley Memos; *Annual Report of the Federal Deposit Insurance Corporation* (1936), 9, 16.

55. *People ex rel. Barrett v. Fon Du Lac State Bank*, 295 Ill. App. 71, 14 N.E.2d 686 (Ill. App. Ct. 1938); *People ex rel. Barrett v. Fon Du Lac State Bank*, 309 Ill. App. 139, 33 N.E.2d 144 (Ill. App. Ct. 1941); *People ex rel. Barrett v. Fon Du Lac State Bank*, 310 Ill. App. 28, 33 N.E.2d 714 (Ill. App. Ct. 1941).

56. *Annual Report of the Federal Deposit Insurance Corporation* (1934), 67.

57. Jacob Viner, Report on Meeting Held August 7, 1934, folder 3, box 9, Eccles Papers (FRASER); "Credit Aid Survey Pushed in Chicago," *NYT*, September 29, 1934; Viner, "Preliminary Report to Secretary Morganthau on Bank Examination."

58. Roderick P. Stewart, "Chicago Opinion," *WSJ*, September 13, 1934; Hardy and Viner, *Report on Bank Credit Availability*, 14.

59. Hardy and Viner, *Report on Bank Credit Availability*, 19–21 (quote at 21); Henry Edmiston, Digest of Report on Bank Examinations and Bank Reports Prepared by H. W. Riley Under the Supervision of Dr. Viner, January 3, 1935, folder 1, box 9, Eccles Papers (FRASER).

60. Hardy and Viner, *Report on Bank Credit Availability*, 22.

61. Hardy and Viner, *Report on Bank Credit Availability*, vii–viii, 14–23; Jacob Viner, "Recent Legislation and the Banking Situation," *American Economic Review* 26, no. 1 (1936): 106–19.

62. Telephone transcript, Henry Morgenthau Jr. and Marriner Eccles, December 19, 1934, p. 329, vol. 2, pt. 2, Morgenthau Diaries (FRASER). The explicit plan was to eliminate the office, which Carter Glass opposed (Diary entry, November 26, 1934, O'Connor Diary; Glass quoted: "I'll go to the Sec. and tell him he must not destroy the Comptroller's office").

63. Memorandum Re Leo T. Crowley, January 2, 1934, p. 13, vol. 3, pt. 1, Morgenthau Diaries (FRASER); Diary entries, December 14–15, 1934, O'Connor Diary.

64. Meeting Minutes, Interdepartmental Loan Committee, January 17, 1935, pp. 171, 183, vol. 3, pt. 1; "March 15th [1935]," p. 109, vol. 4, pt. 2; Meeting Minutes, Sub-Committee on Banking of the Interdepartmental Loan Committee, April 29, 1935, p. 47, vol. 5, pt. 1, Morgenthau Diaries (FRASER).

65. *Banking Act of 1935*, 74 Cong. 39 (statement of Leo Crowley).

66. *Banking Act of 1935*, 74 Cong. 31-32, 45 (statement of Leo Crowley).

67. Banking Act of 1935, Pub. L. 74-305, Title I, §§ 12B(g), 12B(i)(1–2), 12B(k)(2), 12B(n)(4–5), 12B(v)(4), 12B(y)(1); *Annual Report of the Federal Deposit Insurance Corporation* (1935), 17, 82.

68. Nelson, *Jumping the Abyss*, 200–201, 212–13; Carter Glass to Prof. Frederick E. Lee, December 6, 1935, folder 5, box 47, Viner Papers.

69. Franklin D. Roosevelt, "Address at Madison Square Garden, New York City," October 31, 1936, APP.

70. Meeting Minutes, April 29, 1935, pp. 46–47, vol. 5, pt. I, Morgenthau Diaries (FRASER); Marriner S. Eccles, *Beckoning Frontiers: Public and Personal Recollections* (Knopf, 1951), 266; Memo, Marriner S. Eccles to the President, November 12, 1936, folder 6, box 5, Eccles Papers (FRASER); Nelson, *Jumping the Abyss*, 227, 324.

71. Eccles, *Beckoning Frontiers*, 267.

72. Memo, Eccles to the President, November 12, 1936, folder 6, box 5, item 22, Eccles Papers (FRASER); Meeting Transcript, November 17, 1936, p. 137, vol. 45, Morgenthau Diaries (FRASER); Telephone Transcript, December 11, 1936, p. 60, vol. 48, Morgenthau Diaries (FRASER); Meeting Transcript, December 17, 1936, p. 237, vol. 48, Morgenthau Diaries (FRASER).

73. Meeting Transcript, December 18, 1936, p. 140, vol. 48, Morgenthau Diaries (FRASER); Meeting Transcript, January 12, 1937, p. 250, vol. 51, pt. 2, Morgenthau Diaries (FRASER).

74. Nelson W. Cheney to President Franklin D. Roosevelt, March 25, 1938, Correspondence Regarding Nelson W. Cheney, folder 4, box 7, Eccles Papers (FRASER); Memo, Marriner Eccles to the President, April 6, 1938, Correspondence Regarding Nelson W. Cheney, folder 4, box 7, Eccles Papers (FRASER); Nelson, *Jumping the Abyss*, 329–31; Franklin D. Roosevelt, "Message to Congress on Stimulating Recovery," April 14, 1938, APP.

75. Leo Crowley to Marriner Eccles, April 30, 1937, Examining Division, Chief of, Nichols, John folder, box 1, FDIC Crowley Memos; Marriner Eccles to Leo Crowley, August 18, 1937, Examining Division, Chief of, Nichols, John folder, box 1, FDIC Crowley Memos; Marriner Eccles to Leo T. Crowley, August 18, 1937, folder 5, box 51, Eccles Papers (FRASER); Crowley to Marshall Diggs (and Mr. Eccles), February 9, 1938, folder 5, box 81, Viner Papers.

76. Meeting Minutes, April 21, 1938, p. 128, vol. 120; Meeting Minutes, June 20, 1938, p. 57, vol. 130, Morgenthau Diaries (FRASER).

77. Meeting Minutes, April 21, 1938, p. 120, vol. 120, Morgenthau Diaries (FRASER).

78. Donald G. Simonson and George H. Hempel, "Banking Lessons from the Past: The 1938 Regulatory Agreement Interpreted," *Journal of Financial Services Research* 7, no. 3 (September 1, 1993): 249–67; Paul M. Atkins, *Bank Secondary Reserve & Investment Policies* (Bankers Publishing Company, 1930); Meeting Minutes, April 25, 1938, p. 284, vol. 120, Morgenthau Diaries (FRASER).

79. *Annual Report of the Federal Deposit Insurance Corporation* (1938), 62; Meeting Minutes, May 4, 1938, pp. 6, 47, vol. 123, pt. 1, Morgenthau Diaries (FRASER).

80. Sarah L. Quinn, *American Bonds: How Credit Markets Shaped a Nation* (Princeton University Press, 2019), 124–49.

81. Meeting Minutes, June 21, 1938, p. 198, vol. 130, Morgenthau Diaries (FRASER). In a preliminary report to Morgenthau in October 1934, Jacob Viner expressed the problem succinctly: "We have as many banking systems as there are examiners." Viner, "Preliminary Report to Secretary Morgenthau on Bank Examination."

82. Simonson and Hempel, "Banking Lessons from the Past," 249–67; Nelson, *Jumping the Abyss*, 333; "Revision of Procedure in Bank Examinations as Agreed to by the Secretary of the Treasury, the Board of Governors of the Federal Reserve System, the Directors of the Federal Deposit Insurance Corporation, and the Comptroller of the Currency, June 25, 1938," folder 9, box 9, Eccles Papers (FRASER); "Revised Bank Examinations Urged by Eccles," *WP*, May 14, 1938; G. L. Bach, "Bank Supervision, Monetary Policy, and Governmental Reorganization," *Journal of Finance* 4, no. 4 (December 1949); Meeting Minutes, June 14, 1938, p. 351, vol. 128, Morgenthau Diaries (FRASER); Marriner Eccles to Arthur Vandenberg, June 14, 1938, folder 1, box 64, Eccles Papers (FRASER); "Morgenthau Opposes Chairman Eccles' View on Bank Examinations," *WSJ*, June 21, 1938; Harold Fleming, "U.S. Agencies Battle Over Uniform Bank Examinations," *CSM*, May 25, 1938.

83. Stephen Jay Gould, *The Panda's Thumb: More Reflections in Natural History* (W. W. Norton & Company, 1980).

84. Francois Velde, "The Recession of 1937: A Cautionary Tale," *Economic Perspectives* 33, no. 4 (2009): 16–37.

Interlude: Supervising Japanese Banking

1. Sen Matsuda to Paul M. Atkins, October 19, 1949, Japan—General Correspondence, June 1948–May 1950, box 21, Atkins Papers; Paul M. Atkins to Chu Okazaki, September 29, 1948, Japan—General Correspondence, June 1948–May 1950, box 21, Atkins Papers; Sen Matsuda to Paul M. Atkins, December 5, 1948, Japan—General Correspondence, June 1948–May 1950, box 21, Atkins Papers; Sen Matsuda to Paul M. Atkins, October 19, 1949, Japan—General Correspondence, June 1948–May 1950, box 21, Atkins Papers.

2. Arthur W. Hodges to Paul M. Atkins, July 16, 1948, Japan—General Correspondence, June 1948–May 1950, box 21, Atkins Papers; Press release, Department of the Army, "American Expert to Study Japanese Banking Statistics," August 5, 1948, Japan—General Correspondence, June 1948–May 1950, box 21, Atkins Papers; Norio Tamaki, *Japanese Banking: A History, 1859–1959* (Cambridge University Press, 2010), 191.

3. Paul M. Atkins to Major General W. F. Marquat, September 8, 1948, Japan—General Correspondence, June 1948–May 1950, box 21, Atkins Papers; Mark D. Metzler, *Capital as Will and Imagination: Schumpeter's Guide to the Postwar Japanese Miracle* (Cornell University Press, 2013), 139–44.

4. Tamaki, *Japanese Banking*, 30–33; William M. Tsutsui, *Banking Policy in Japan: American Efforts at Reform During the Occupation* (Routledge, 2010), 16–18; Metzler, *Capital as Will and Imagination*, 86–87.

5. Tsutsui, *Banking Policy in Japan*, 19–21; Metzler, *Capital as Will and Imagination*, 80; Tamaki, *Japanese Banking*, 188.

6. Tsutsui, *Banking Policy in Japan*, 22.

7. Tsutsui, *Banking Policy in Japan*, 22; Tamaki, *Japanese Banking*, 189; Metzler, *Capital as Will and Imagination*, 88–92.

8. Tsutsui, *Banking Policy in Japan*, 28–29, 35; Tamaki, *Japanese Banking*, 190.

9. Sean H. Vanatta, *Plastic Capitalism: Banks, Credit Cards, and the End of Financial Control* (Yale University Press, 2024), 18–26; Welsh, quoted in Tsutsui, *Banking Policy in Japan*, 36.

10. Tsutsui, *Banking Policy in Japan*, 38–39.

11. J. Robert Brown Jr., *Opening Japan's Financial Markets* (Taylor Francis, 2018), 15; LeCount, quoted in Tsutsui, *Banking Policy in Japan*, 38, 40.

12. Paul M. Atkins, "Report on Banking Statistics in Japan," November 1, 1948, 16, Japan—Reports folder, box 21, Atkins Papers; Tsutsui, *Banking Policy in Japan*, 49–50.

13. G. W. Blattner, Caroline E. Cagle, and B. Magruder Wingfield, to Messrs. Morrill, Wyatt, Paulger, Goldenweiser, and Smead, folder 1, box 17, Eccles Papers (FRASER).

14. Tsutsui, *Banking Policy in Japan*, 42.

15. Economic and Scientific Section, Finance Division to Chief, Economic and Scientific Section, May 28, 1948, Japan—Banking Laws and Regulations May–October 1945 folder, box 21, Atkins Papers; Tamaki, *Japanese Banking*, 51–52.

16. Metzler, *Capital as Will and Imagination*, 137–57; Bank of Japan, "Tentative Program of Future Activities of the Financial Statistics Sub-committee in the Field of Banking Statistics," ca. October 1948, Japan—Banking: Miscellaneous c. August–November 1948 folder; Memo, Research Division of the Ministry of Finance, October 11, 1948, Japan—Banking: Miscellaneous c. August–November 1948 folder; Paul M. Atkins, "Report on Banking Statistics in Japan," November 1, 1948, 2, Japan—Reports folder, box 21, Atkins Papers.

17. Atkins, "Report on Banking Statistics in Japan."

18. Paul M. Atkins to Major General W. F. Marquat, October 25, 1948, Japan—Banking Laws and Regulations folder, box 21, Atkins Papers.

19. Eiji Hotori, "Sengo Fukkoki niokeru Okurasho Kensa Nihon Ginko Kosa no Kaikaku" [Reform of Bank Examination by the MOF and the BOJ During Postwar Years of Recovery in Japan], *Journal of Economic Studies (University of Tokyo)* 47 (2005): 25–36 (authors' translation using Google Translate).

20. Metzler, *Capital as Will and Imagination*, 157.

Chapter Seven

1. Chase National Bank, *The Report of the Chairman to the Governing Board of Shareholders* (1942), 4, as quoted in John Donald Wilson, *The Chase: The Chase Manhattan Bank, N.A., 1945–1985* (Harvard Business School Press, 1986), 17.

2. *Annual Report of the Comptroller of the Currency* (1929), 15, 89; *Annual Report of the Federal Deposit Insurance Corporation* (1945), 37; Donald Bailey Marsh, "Canada," in *Banking Systems*, ed. Benjamin Haggott Beckhart (Columbia University Press, 1956), 127; *Annual Report of the Federal Deposit Insurance Corporation* (1953), 80–81.

3. National Monetary Commission, *Report of the National Monetary Commission on Branch, Group, and Chain Banking* (Government Printing Office, 1910); Memo, Marriner S. Eccles to the President, November 12, 1936, folder 6, box 5, Eccles Papers (FRASER); Marriner Eccles, "The Dual Banking System: Address Before the National Association of Supervisors of State Banks," September 17, 1943, folder 7, box 8, Eccles Papers (FRASER).

4. Carl F. Goodman, "United States Government Foreign Property Controls," *Georgetown Law Journal* 52, no. 4 (1964): 767–69; Stuart L. Weiss, *The President's Man: Leo Crowley and Franklin Roosevelt in Peace and War* (Southern Illinois University Press, 1996), 115; E. H. Foley Jr. to Secretary Morgenthau, May 9, 1942, p. 23, vol. 527, pt. 1, Morgenthau Diaries (FRASER); "U.S. Agents Check Japan Firms Here," *San Francisco Examiner*, August 5, 1941.

5. Henry Morgenthau Jr., Telegram, to the Presidents of All Federal Reserve Banks, December 7, 1941, p. 34, vol. 470, Morgenthau Diaries (FRASER); "Roundup of Alien Property," *The National Week* (January 30, 1942), p. 396, vol. 489, pt. 2, Morgenthau Diaries (FRASER); "In 1942, Business Owners Forced into Concentration Camps," *U.S. News*, December 5, 2016.

6. Weiss, *President's Man*, 114–47; Federal Reserve Bank of San Francisco, *Evacuation Operations Pacific Coast Military Areas 1942* (1943) (FRASER); Office of Alien Property Custodian, *Annual Report* (1943), 1–32, 53–86. For a comprehensive view of the Fed's work preserving the property of interned Japanese Americans, see Records of the War Relocation Authority (RG 210) (FRASER).

7. Meeting Minutes, December 9, 1941, 9:30 A.M., p. 205, vol. 470, Morgenthau Diaries (FRASER); Meeting Minutes, February 10, 1942, vol. 29, pt. 1, Fed Board Minutes (FRASER); Memorandum to Supervising Examiners, March 18, 1943, Memoranda to Supervising Examiners folder, box 1, FDIC Supervisor Memos; Meeting Minutes, June 26, 1942, vol. 29, pt. 3, Fed Board Minutes (FRASER); *Annual Report of the Board of Governors of the Federal Reserve System* (1943), 43.

8. *Annual Report of the Federal Deposit Insurance Corporation* (1943), 15; *Annual Report of the Comptroller of the Currency* (1943), 2; *Annual Report of the Federal Deposit Insurance Corporation* (1945), 43; William P. Dunn Jr., "Regulation V Loans," *Journal of Accountancy* 77, no. 1 (1944): 43–47; Gerald M. Conkling, "Loans for War Purposes," *Federal Reserve Bulletin* 31, no. 11 (1945): 1109–5; C. B. Upham to Secretary Morgenthau, May 12, 1942, p. 226, vol. 527, pt. 2, Morgenthau Diaries (FRASER).

9. Jonathan Rose, "Yield Curve Control in the United States, 1942 to 1951," *Economic Perspectives* No. 2 (October 2021), available online at https://www.chicagofed.org/publications/economic-perspectives/2021/2. Franklin D. Roosevelt, "Message to Congress on an Economic Stabilization Program," April 7, 1942, *APP*. For the credit control policy generally, see Louis Hyman, *Debtor Nation: A History of America in Red Ink* (Princeton University Press, 2011),

98–131; Sean H. Vanatta, *Plastic Capitalism: Banks, Credit Cards, and the End of Financial Control* (Yale University Press, 2024), 27–33.

10. Vanatta, *Plastic Capitalism*, 26–27; Letter from Secretary Morrill re Procedure to Be Followed in Case of Apparent Violations of Regulation W, October 10, 1941, p. 336, vol. 55, no. S-368, Letters and Statements of the Board (FRASER); Allan H. Meltzer, *A History of the Federal Reserve, Volume 1: 1913–1951* (University of Chicago Press, 2003), 557–58, 602–3.

11. "Fail to Observe Credit Rulings, Close Stores," *Daily News Journal (Murfreesboro, TN)*, November 13, 1942; Meeting Minutes, November 9, 1942, vol. 29, pt. 6, Fed Board Minutes (FRASER); Meeting Minutes, June 24, 1943, vol. 30, pt. 2, Fed Board Minutes (FRASER); Meeting Minutes, December 29, 1943, vol. 30, pt. 4, Fed Board Minutes (FRASER); Meeting Minutes, March 14, 1945, vol. 32, pt. 1, Fed Board Minutes (FRASER); *Consumer Credit Control*, 80 Cong. (1947).

12. Vanatta, *Plastic Capitalism*, 29–30.

13. Sarah L. Quinn, *American Bonds: How Credit Markets Shaped a Nation* (Princeton University Press, 2019), 124–49; The Commission on Money and Credit, *Money and Credit: Their Influence on Jobs, Prices, and Growth* (Prentice-Hall, 1961), 181–211.

14. "O'Connor Enters Race," *LAT*, February 19, 1938; "Judge J.F.T. O'Connor Dies, Ex-Comptroller of Currency," *NYHT*, September 29, 1949; Meeting minutes, "Re: the Bank of America Situation," September 19, 1938, pp. 408–10, vol. 357, Morgenthau Diaries (FRASER); Marriner Eccles to William Benton, April 24, 1950, folder 15, box 57, Eccles Papers (FRASER); "M. T. Harl Sees Truman, May Get F.D.I.C. Post," *NYHT*, November 24, 1945.

15. Marriner Eccles, *Beckoning Frontiers: Public and Personal Recollections* (Alfred A. Knopf: 1951), 384–86; "Draft of Press Statement," n.d., ca. 1943, folder 7, box 4, Eccles Papers (FRASER); Franklin D. Roosevelt to Marriner Eccles, February 9, 1944, folder 7, box 4, Eccles Papers (FRASER); Marriner Eccles to Franklin D. Roosevelt, February 17, 1944, folder 7, box 4, Eccles Papers (FRASER).

16. *Reorganization Act of 1945*, Pub. L. 79-250, 59 Stat. 613; *Administrative Procedure Act of 1946*, Pub. L. 79-404, 60 Stat. 237; Roger A. Pemberton, "Struggle for the New Deal: Truman and the Hoover Commission," *Presidential Studies Quarterly* 16, no. 3 (1986): 511–27 (Hoover quote at 520); Harry Truman, quoted in David E. Lilienthal, *The Journals of David E. Lilienthal, Volume 2: The Atomic Energy Years* (Harper & Row, 1964), 564.

17. Commission on Organization of the Executive Branch of the Government, *The Hoover Commission Report on Organization of the Executive Branch of the Government* (Greenwood Press, 1970 [1949]), i, 3, 207; "Reorganization Snag," *WP*, April 14, 1950.

18. *Monetary, Credit, and Fiscal Policies*, 81 Cong. 219-220 (statement of Marriner Eccles, Board of Governors, Federal Reserve System) (1949).

19. "Harl Fights the Charge," *NYT*, July 8, 1949; *Monetary, Credit, and Fiscal Policies*, 81 Cong. 136-137 (statement of Maple T. Harl, Chairman, Federal Deposit Insurance Corporation) (1949); "F.D.I.C. Out to Spur Maybank Measure," *NYT*, May 11, 1950; Clark Warburton, "Co-Ordination of Monetary, Bank Supervisory, and Loan Agencies of the Federal Government," *Journal of Finance* 5, no. 2 (1950): 148–69.

20. Meltzer, *History of the Federal Reserve*, 658–67; E. A. Goldenweiser, "Douglas Committee Report," *American Economic Review* 40, no. 3 (1950): 389–96; *Monetary, Credit, and Fiscal Policies*, 81 Cong. 217, 222–25 (statement of Eccles) (1949).

21. George A. Mooney, "Hoover Study Held a Threat to Banks," *NYT*, March 27, 1949; *Monetary, Credit, and Fiscal Policies*, 81 Cong. 122-142 (statement of Maple T. Harl, Chairman, Federal Deposit Insurance Corporation) (1949); *Amendments to Federal Deposit Insurance Act*, 81 Cong. 86-88 (statement of Ben Dubois, Secretary, Independent Bankers Association) (1950); "FDIC Wipes Out Debt to Treasury," *NYT*, August 31, 1948; Charles W. Calomiris and Eugene N. White, "The Origins of Federal Deposit Insurance," in *The Regulated Economy: A Historical Approach to Political Economy*, ed. Claudia Goldin and Gary D. Libecap (University of Chicago Press, 1994), 178.

22. Lester B. Orfield, "The Hoover Commission and Federal Executive Reorganization," *Temple Law Quarterly* 24, no. 2 (1950): 214; *Federal Deposit Insurance Act: Conference Report*, H.R. Rep. No. 81-3049 (1950).

23. *Amendments to Federal Deposit Insurance Act*, 81 Cong. 21 (statement of Maple T. Harl, Chairman, Federal Deposit Insurance Corporation) (1950).

24. Commission on Money and Credit, *Money and Credit*; U.S. President's Commission on Financial Structure and Regulation, *The Report of U.S. President's Commission on Financial Structure & Regulation (Hunt Commission Report)* (Government Printing Office, 1971); Johnathan Levy, *Ages of American Capitalism: A History of the United States* (Random House, 2021), 524–27.

25. Virgil Willit, *Selected Articles on Chain, Group and Branch Banking* (H. W. Wilson Company, 1930); Eugene N. White, *The Regulation and Reform of the American Banking System* (Princeton University Press, 1983), 156–65.

26. Ben DuBois to Marriner S. Eccles, September 22, 1943, folder 8, box 80, Eccles Papers (FRASER); E. D. McCook to Marriner S. Eccles, October 8, 1943, folder 8, box 80, Eccles Papers (FRASER); Rudolph M. Evans, "America's Stake in the Independent Bank: Remarks at the Annual Independent Bankers Breakfast, Mayflower Hotel, Washington, D.C.," September 21, 1953, Evans Speeches (FRASER).

27. 102 Cong. Rec. 6857 (1956) (statement of Sen. Paul H. Douglas).

28. *Annual Report of the Federal Deposit Insurance Corporation* (1960), 30; *Annual Report of the Federal Deposit Insurance Corporation* (1961), 49; The American Banking Association, *The Commercial Banking Industry: A Monograph Prepared for the Commission on Money and Credit* (Prentice-Hall, 1962), 58.

29. John W. Hester, "The Blight on Holding Companies," *Current History* 39, no. 6 (1934): 680–81.

30. *Annual Report of the Board of Governors of the Federal Reserve System* (1941), 14–15.

31. "McAdoo Would Abolish Bank Holding Units," *WSJ*, May 7, 1937; Alan Brinkley, *The End of Reform: New Deal Liberalism in Recession and War* (Alfred A. Knopf, 1995), 48–64; Telegram, Ronald Ransom to Marriner Eccles, March 16, 1938, folder 3, box 17, Eccles Papers (FRASER); Meeting Minutes Re: Bank Holding Company Legislation, March 17, 1938, p. 261, vol. 115, pt. 1, Morgenthau Diaries (FRASER); Franklin D. Roosevelt, "Message to Congress on Curbing Monopolies," April 29, 1938, *APP*; George E. Anderson, "Move Against Monopolies to Hit Banks," *NYHT*, January 16, 1938.

32. "Foes Hit Bank of America in Expansion Plan," *NYHT*, May 16, 1937; "The March of Finance," *LAT*, May 18, 1937; Transamerica Corporation, *Annual Report* (1937) (Proquest ID: 88186518); Matthew Josephson, *The Money Lords* (Weybright and Talley, 1972), 77–79, 95, 98–99,

137–51; James C. Bonbright and Gardiner C. Means, *The Holding Company: Its Public Significance and Its Regulation* (McGraw-Hill, 1932), 333.

33. Meeting Minutes, "Bank Holding Companies," January 28, 1938, vol. 355, Morgenthau Diaries (FRASER); Matthew Josephson, "Big Bull of the West," *Saturday Evening Post*, September 13, 1947.

34. Leo Crowley, "Notes Concerning the Bank of America National Trust and Savings Association," October 22, 1937, vol. 354, Morgenthau Diaries; Eccles, *Beckoning Frontiers*, 36. O'Connor objected to Crowley's invasion of the Comptroller's turf. J.F.T. O'Connor to Henry Morgenthau Jr., January 28, 1938, vol. 354, Morgenthau Diaries (FRASER).

35. Eccles, *Beckoning Frontiers*, 36; George Eccles, *The First Security Corporation: The First Fifty Years, 1928–1978* (Newcomen Society in North America, 1978), 8–10; "Bank Holding Companies," January 25, 1938, folder 2, Eccles Papers (FRASER); Marriner Eccles to Franklin D. Roosevelt, January 23, 1941, folder 5, box 17, Eccles Papers (FRASER).

36. "Senate Shelves Bank Holding Company Bill," *WP*, May 4, 1938; "Bank Holding Company Legislation Now Likely Will Be Sidetracked," *WSJ*, February 15, 1939; Board of Governors of the Federal Reserve System, "United States of America Before the Board of Governors of the Federal Reserve System, in the Matter of Transamerica Corporation [Complaint]," June 24, 1948, folder 5, box 19, Eccles Papers (FRASER); F.D.R. to the Secretary of the Treasury, Chairman Crowley, Comptroller of the Currency, and Chairman Eccles, January 16, 1941, folder 5, box 19, Eccles Papers (FRASER); "Excerpt of Stenographic Transcript of Meeting at Treasury Department, January 21, 1941 at 3:00 P.M. in the Office of the Secretary," folder 5, box 17, Eccles Papers (FRASER); Jesse H. Jones to Henry Morgenthau Jr., March 17, 1938, folder 3, box 17, Eccles Papers (FRASER); Henry Morgenthau Jr. to Franklin D. Roosevelt, March 17, 1938, folder 4, box 17, Eccles Papers (FRASER); J.F.T. O'Connor to Marriner S. Eccles, March 30, 1938, folder 4, box 17, Eccles Papers (FRASER); Marriner S. Eccles to Franklin D. Roosevelt, January 23, 1941, folder 5, box 17, Eccles Papers (FRASER).

37. Marriner S. Eccles to Franklin D. Roosevelt, January 23, 1941, folder 5, box 17, Eccles Papers (FRASER); "Statement of the Reserve Board Relating to Certain Views Expressed at the Conference in the Office of the Secretary of the Treasury on January 21, 1941," March 14, 1941, folder 5, box 17, Eccles Papers (FRASER); "Arguments in Support of Board of Governors Policy in Matter of Bank of America and Transamerica Corporation," n.d., ca. March 1943, folder 7, box 20, Eccles Papers (FRASER); Chester Morrill to Members of the Board, January 18, 1944, folder 7, box 17, Eccles Papers (FRASER); Marriner Eccles to Tom C. Clark, October 16, 1945, folder 8, box 17, Eccles Papers (FRASER); "Letter to the Board of Governors," July 9, 1943, folder 8, box 20, Eccles Papers (FRASER); Chester Morrill to Transamerica Corporation, February 12, 1942, folder 4, box 19, Eccles Papers (FRASER).

38. A. P. Giannini to Marriner S. Eccles, November 25, 1942, in Group No. 1 [Transamerica Correspondence], folder 1, box 23, Eccles Papers (FRASER); Board of Governors of the Federal Reserve System, "United States of America Before the Board of Governors of the Federal Reserve System, in the Matter of Transamerica Corporation [Complaint]," June 24, 1948, folder 5, box 19, Eccles Papers (FRASER).

39. Eccles, *Beckoning Frontiers*, 443; Tom C. Clark to Marriner S. Eccles, October 31, 1945, folder 5, box 19, Eccles Papers (FRASER); Marriner Eccles to Tom C. Clark, February 26, 1947, folder 5, box 19, Eccles Papers (FRASER); M. S. Eccles to John W. Snyder, April 15, 1947, in

376 NOTES TO CHAPTER 7

"Group No. 2 [Transamerica Documents]," folder 5, box 19, Eccles Papers (FRASER); Memo, Leonard J. Townsend to Board of Governors, October 31, 1947, folder 4, box 19, Eccles Papers (FRASER); *American Tobacco Co. v. United States*, 328 U.S. 781 (1946).

40. Pub. L. 63-212, 38 Stat. 730; Townsend to Board of Governors, October 31, 1947, folder 4, box 19, Eccles Papers (FRASER).

41. "Clayton Act Proceeding: Transamerica Corporation," *Federal Reserve Bulletin* 38, no. 4 (April 1952): 387, 396.

42. "Clayton Act Proceeding: Transamerica Corporation," 391; James and James, *Biography of a Bank*, 512–15; Oliver S. Powell, quoted in "Control and Regulation of Bank Holding Companies," 75 (Appendix); *Transamerica Corp. v. Bd. of Governors of Fed. Reserve Sys.*, 206 F.2d 163, 169 (3d Cir. 1953).

43. "Drafts Bill to Liquidate All Bank Holding Companies," *NYT*, January 25, 1938; "Bill Proposes Curb on Bank Holding Units," *LAT*, June 2, 1943; *Providing for Control and Regulation of Bank Holding Companies*, 80 Cong. (1947); *Bank Holding Bill*, 81 Cong. (1950); *Control and Regulation of Bank Holding Companies*, 82 Cong. (1952); *Bank Holding Legislation*, 83 Cong. (1953). For an overview of some the challenges in defining a bank holding company, see Margaret Tahyar and Saule Omarova, "That Which We Call a Bank: Revisiting the History of Bank Hold Company Regulations in the United States," *Review of Banking & Financial Law* 31 (2011–2012): 113–98; Gerald C. Fischer, *Bank Holding Companies* (Columbia University Press, 1961).

44. Benjamin J. Klebaner, "The Bank Holding Company Act of 1956," *Southern Economic Journal* 24, no. 3 (1958): 314.

45. "Control and Regulation of Bank Holding Companies," 119 (statement of W. J. Bryan, President, Independent Bankers Assn. of Amer.); 102 Cong. Rec. 6857 (1956) (statement of Sen. Paul H. Douglas).

46. Benjamin J. Klebaner, "The Bank Holding Company Act of 1956," *Southern Economic Journal* 24, no. 3 (January 1958): 313–26; Dwight D. Eisenhower, "Statement by the President Upon Signing the Bank Holding Company Act of 1956," May 9, 1956, *APP*.

47. "Application of Transamerica Corporation Relating to Occidental Life Insurance Company of California," *Federal Reserve Bulletin* (September 1957): 1014–35; "Transamerica Ordered to Get Rid of Its Stock in Occidental Life," *WSJ*, August 21, 1957; "Transamerica's Plan for Reorganization Is Ruled Tax-Free," *WSJ*, February 7, 1958.

48. J. L. Robertson, "A Long View of the Bank Holding Company Act: Remarks Before the Independent Bankers Association at the American Bankers Convention, Los Angeles, California," October 22, 1956 (FRASER).

49. Robertson, "A Long View."

50. Robertson, "A Long View."

51. *Regulation of Bank Mergers*, 84 Cong. 25 (statement of L. A. Jennings, Deputy Comptroller, Office of the Comptroller of the Currency) (1956).

52. *New York State Law*, Ch. 84 (1799); Gregory Hunter, *The Manhattan Company: Managing a Multi-Unit Corporation in New York, 1799–1842* (Routledge, 1989); Beatrice G. Reubens, "Burr, Hamilton, and the Manhattan Company, Part I," *Political Science Quarterly* 72, no. 4 (1957): 578–607; Beatrice G. Reubens, "Burr, Hamilton, and the Manhattan Company, Part II," *Political Science Quarterly* 73, no. 1 (1958): 100–125; Bank of the Manhattan Company, *Annual Report* (1954), 13–16.

53. Thomas P. Kane, *The Romance and Tragedy of Banking: Problems and Incidents in the Governmental Supervision of National Banks* (Bankers Pub., 1922), 115; Wilson, *The Chase*, 9–19, 50–53; "Plan Sweeping Banking Reform," *BG*, March 9, 1933.

54. Kai Bird, *The Chairman: John J. McCloy & The Making of the American Establishment* (Simon & Schuster, 2017); Wilson, *The Chase*, 52.

55. Wilson, *The Chase*, 43–45, 56–73; Commission on Money and Credit, *Money and Credit*, 165; "Bank of Manhattan Board Faces Showdown in Move to Sell Stock," *NYT*, August 17, 1951.

56. "Two Large Banks in Merger Talks: Proposal Is for Chase to Give Up National Charter to Join the Manhattan Company: Assets Top $7 Billion: Planned Institution Would Be City's Largest," *NYT*, January 1, 1955.

57. Meeting Minutes, March 29, 1955, vol. 42, pt. 2, Fed Board Minutes (FRASER); "Chase, Manhattan Banks 'Wed' with State's Blessing," *NYT*, April 1, 1955.

58. "The Week in Business: Merger Fever Keeps Rising," *NYHT*, January 16, 1955; Lief H. Olsen, "U.S. Growth Spur to Bank Mergers," *NYT*, February 24, 1955; "Merger Confirms New Banking Era," *NYT*, January 16, 1955.

59. 101 Cong. Rec. 648 (1955) (statement of Hon. Emanuel Celler).

60. Meeting Minutes, February 9, 1955, vol. 42, pt. 1, Fed Board Minutes (FRASER); Celler-Kefauver Act of 1950, Pub. L. 81-899, 64 Stat. 1125; Richard B. Blackwell, "Section 7 of the Clayton Act: Its Application to the Conglomerate Merger," *William & Mary Law Review* 13, no. 3 (1972): 624; Stanley N. Barnes to Lawrence Bennett, Esq., March 23, 1955, in *Recent Antitrust Problems, Part 3*, 84 Cong. 2141 (1955) (quoted in turn in J. Harlan, dissent, *United States v. Philadelphia Nat'l Bank*, 374 U.S. 321 (1963), at 377).

61. *A Study of the Antitrust Laws*, 84 Cong. 681 (statement of William McChesney Martin, Chairman, Board of Governors, Federal Reserve System) (1955); Louis D. Brandeis, *Other People's Money, and How the Bankers Use It* (Frederick A. Stokes, 1914). Martin's point was that the Act on its own terms essentially only applied to bank holding companies, but he also expressed the view that the single effort to use the Act to limit the power of such companies—the Transamerica case—failed as a legal strategy.

62. *Regulation of Bank Mergers*, 86 Cong. 6 (statement of Ray M. Gidney, Comptroller of the Currency) (1960); R. F. Leonard, "Supervision of the Commercial Banking System," in *Banking Studies by Members of the Staff of the Board of Governors of the Federal Reserve System*, ed. E. A Goldenweiser, Elliott Thurston, and Bray Hammond (Waverly Press, 1941), 205.

63. "Compilation of State Laws Relating to Delegation of Authority in Bank Mergers and Consolidations," in *Regulation of Bank Mergers*, 86 Cong. 182-183 (1959).

64. *United States v. Firstamerica Corp.*, Civil No. 38139 (N.D. Cal. 1959); *Bank Mergers*, 84 Cong. 7 (statement of Stanley N. Barnes, Assistant Attorney General, Antitrust Division, Department of Justice) (1955); Attorney General's National Committee to Study the Antitrust Laws, *Report of the Attorney General's National Committee to Study the Antitrust Laws* (Government Printing Office, 1955). A major part of the DOJ's reluctance to proceed under the Clayton Act had to do with the Department's perception that the Clayton Act only applied to the purchase of bank stock, not bank assets, and as such it was also a dead letter for the DOJ, just as it was for the Fed. This was not a conclusion reached in court, to be clear, but a determination made unilaterally by the Department (*Regulation of Bank Mergers*, 86 Cong. 162 [statement of Robert A. Bicks, Acting Assistant Attorney General, Antitrust Division, Department of Justice]

[1960]). The decision, in turn, by the Attorney General's National Committee to Study the Antitrust Laws, to ignore bank mergers did not escape congressional ire. Congressman Emanuel Celler expressed bafflement that "a committee composed of 61 members expert in antitrust matters" would ignore banks altogether (*Current Antitrust Problems*, 84 Cong. 1859 [statement of Hon. Abraham J. Multer] [1955]). The Committee's Chairman, S. Chesterfield Oppenheim, confessed ignorance: "Maybe it is a reflection on us, but we weren't conscious of the problem at the time" (*Current Antitrust Problems*, 84 Cong. 1967 [statement of S. Chesterfield Oppenheim, Cochairman, Attorney General's National Committee to Study Antitrust Laws] [1955]).

65. *Bank Mergers and Concentration of Banking Facilities*, 82 Cong. (Staff Report to Subcommittee No. 5 of the Committee on the Judiciary House of Representatives) (1952); "The Week in Business: Merger Fever Keeps Rising."

66. Martin A. Traber, "A Legislative History of the 1960 Bank Merger Act and Its 1966 Amendment: Judicial Misuse and a Suggested Approach," *Indiana Law Journal* 44, no. 4 (Summer 1969): 596–623; H.R. 5948, 84 Cong. (1955); "Celler Tells Meeting Currency Comptroller Favors Giant Banks," *WSJ*, April 29, 1957.

67. H. E. Cook to Percival F. Brundage, in *Regulation of Bank Mergers*, 84 Cong. 8 (1956); *Regulation of Bank Mergers*, 84 Cong. 36 (statement of C. Canby Balderston, Vice Chairman, Federal Reserve System) (1956).

68. *Study of Banking Laws: Financial Institutions Act of 1957*, 85 Cong. 1012, 1030 (statement of Herbert Brownell Jr., Attorney General).

69. *Regulation of Bank Mergers*, 86 Cong. 130 (statement of Hon. Emanuel Celler) (1960).

70. 105 Cong. Rec. 8113 (1959) (statement of Joseph O'Mahoney); Subcommittee No. 2 of the Committee on Banking and Currency House of Representatives, *Regulation of Bank Mergers* (Government Printing Office, 1960), 92.

71. 105 *Cong. Rec.* 8144 (1959) (statement of J. William Fulbright).

72. Bank Merger Act of 1960, Pub. L. 86-463, 72 Stat. 129; Traber, "Legislative History of the 1960 Bank Merger Act."

73. *Bank Merger Act of 1960*; Traber, "Legislative History of the 1960 Bank Merger Act," 608.

74. *Bank Merger Act of 1960; Regulation of Bank Mergers*, 86 Cong. 28, S. Rep. No. 196 (supplemental views of Mr. Douglas, Mr. Clark, Mr. Proxmire, and Mr. Muskie) (1959).

75. *Annual Report of the Comptroller of the Currency* (1961), 18-19. The antitrust and banking context of the decade is analyzed well in William Lifland, "The Supreme Court, Congress, and Bank Mergers," *Law & Contemporary Problems* 32, no. 1 (Winter 1967): 15–39. *See also* Douglas V. Austin, "The Evolution of Commercial Bank Merger Antitrust Law," *Business Lawyer* 36, no. 2 (1981): 297–396.

76. *Annual Report of the Comptroller of the Currency* (1961), 18; *United States v. Philadelphia National Bank*, 374 U.S. 321 (1963).

77. *United States v. Philadelphia National Bank*, 374 U.S. 321, 350, 371 (1963); Traber, "Legislative History of the 1960 Bank Merger Act," 608-10.

78. *United States v. First National Bank & Trust Co. of Lexington*, 376 U.S. 665, 679 (1964).

79. Austin, "The Evolution of Commercial Bank Merger Antitrust Law"; *Annual Report of the Comptroller of the Currency* (1964), 5. The Supreme Court reached a similar conclusion in a case around the same time that merely reinforced the availability of antitrust application to banking mergers. See *United States v. First National Bank & Trust Co. of Lexington*, 376 U.S. 665 (1964). The difference in the cases had to do with which statute—the Clayton Act in *Philadel-*

phia National Bank, the Sherman Act in *Lexington*. Both involved a merger approved by the Comptroller of the Currency that was then challenged through litigation by the Department of Justice, with the mergers reversed by the Supreme Court.

80. David T. Searls and Harry M. Reasoner, "The Bank Merger Act of 1966: Its Strange and Fruitless Odyssey," *Business Lawyer* 25, no. 1 (November 1966): 139; 111 Cong. Rec. 6919 (1965) (statement of Sen. A. Willis Robertson).

81. Traber, "Legislative History of the 1960 Bank Merger Act," 610-13; *Amend the Bank Merger Act of 1960*, 89 Cong. 13 (statement of William McC. Martin, Chairman, Board of Governors, Federal Reserve Board) (1965); Arlen Large, "The Bank Merger Bill's Zany Journey," *WSJ*, February 8, 1966.

82. Wright Patman, quoted in Searls and Reasoner, "The Bank Merger Act of 1966," 139.

83. "House Banking Panel Approves Merger Bill in Chairman's Absence," *WSJ*, October 20, 1965; Large, "The Bank Merger Bill's Zany Journey"; "Trust Bills Termed 'Pearl Harbor Attack,'" *LAT*, November 9, 1965.

84. 12 U.S.C. § 1842(c)(3).

85. Austin, "The Evolution of Commercial Bank Merger Antitrust Law."

Interlude: Training Examiners (and Bankers) in the 1950s

1. John L. Cooley, "A School for Bank Examiners," *Banking*, June 1954, 51–53.

2. Cooley, "A School for Bank Examiners," 51; "Inter-Agency Bank Examination School," *Federal Reserve Bulletin* 40, no. 1 (1954): 23–25.

3. J. L. Robertson, "Men Who Count," October 14, 1954, Statements and Speeches of James Louis Robertson, 1952–1972 (FRASER).

4. *Annual Report of the Comptroller of the Currency*, vol. 1 (1892), 43; *Annual Report of the Comptroller of the Currency* (1922), 5.

5. C. W. Haskins, "The Scope of Banking Education," *BM* 63, no. 6 (1901): 955; Wilbert M. Schneider, *The American Bankers Association: Its Past and Present* (Public Affairs Press, 1956), 53–66; "New Plan for Bank Examiners," *Chicago Daily Tribune*, October 9, 1908; "Bank Examining Systematized by Controller Murray," *NYT*, September 3, 1911; *Annual Report of the Comptroller of the Currency* (1911), 82; "Controller Warns Bank Examiners," *NYT*, September 22, 1908; Peter G. Cameron, "Securing Competency in Bank Examiners," *Annals of the American Academy of Political and Social Science* 113, no. 1 (1924): 357–61; Leo T. Crowley to the Chief Executive Officer of the Insured Bank Addressed, September 2, 1941, Examining Division—Miscellaneous folder, box 2, Letters and Memorandums of Leo T. Crowley; John G. Nichols to All Supervising Examiners, February 26, 1941, Memoranda to Supervising Examiners, 1940–1945 folder, box 1, FDIC Supervisor Memos.

6. "How A.I.B. Aids Bank Examiners," *Banking* 47, no. 5 (1954): 102.

7. Albert L. Kraus, "Experts Wanted, but Pay's Small," *New York Times*, January 20, 1957; "College Men as Bank Examiners," *Banking* 49, no. 3 (1956); Robert C. Forrey, "How One State Trains Its Examiners," *Banking* 50, no. 4 (1957): 48.

8. For more on the standardization, legitimacy, and institutionalization, see Rakesh Khurana, *From Higher Aims to Hired Hands: The Social Transformation of American Business Schools and the Unfulfilled Promise of Management as a Profession* (Princeton University Press, 2007).

9. "'Here's Why I Like Banking as a Career,'" *Northwestern Banker* 61, no. 820 (1956): 18–20; "What Are the Salary Trends for College Graduates?" *Mid-Continent Banker* 53, no. 5 (1957): 31; "What Are Some Answers to the Personnel Problem?" *Mid-Continent Banker* 53, no. 5 (1957): 21–22; Harry E. Mertz, "Bank Recruitment Techniques Need Some Improvement!" *Mid-Continent Banker* 53, no. 5 (1957): 32, 34; Kraus, "Experts Wanted"; "A Planned Training Program Can Attract Young Men" *Mid-Continent Banker* 53, no. 6 (1957): 25.

10. Sean H. Vanatta, "Revolving Door Governance: Bank Supervisors in the United States, 1863–1933," *Management and Organizational History* 19 (2024); David Lucca, Amit Seru, and Francesco Trebbi, "The Revolving Door and Worker Flows in Banking Regulation," *Journal of Monetary Economics* 65 (2014): 17–32.

11. "College Men as Bank Examiners," 152–54.

12. Forrey, "How One State Trains," 48.

Chapter Eight

1. Edward T. O'Toole, "Views of New U.S. Comptroller on Bank Mergers Are Awaited," *NYT*, September 22, 1961; "New Frontiersman," *Newsweek*, October 4, 1962; "Controversial Ex-Chief of Currency James Saxon Dies," *LAT*, February 4, 1980; Irwin Ross, "Scrappy, Happy James J. Saxon," *Fortune*, April 1966; Mr. Foley to Secretary Morgenthau, July 23, 1941, p. 30, vol. 424, Morgenthau Diaries (FRASER); Secretary of State to American Embassy, Madrid, March 16, 1944, p. 262, vol. 710, Morgenthau Diaries (FRASER).

2. "Mr. Saxon's Shocker," *WP*, December 11, 1964; Thomas B. Storrs "'This Will Drive Them Wild . . . Wild': Comptroller James Saxon's Transformation of American Banking, 1961–1966," *Management & Organizational History* 14, no. 4 (2019): 411; "New Frontiersman."

3. "Saxon: Let States Run State Banks," *LAT*, October 27, 1964; "Feud Climax Due on Bank Control," *CSM*, September 18, 1963.

4. "Banking: Cool Camp," *Time*, November 18, 1966. For critics of Saxon, see Mark H. Rose, *Market Rules: Bankers, Presidents, and the Origins of the Great Recession* (University of Pennsylvania Press, 2019); Storrs, "This Will Drive Them Wild . . . Wild"; Arthur E. Wilmarth, *Taming the Megabanks: Why We Need a New Glass-Steagall Act* (Oxford University Press, 2020). For an interpretation in line with the one developed here, see Charles T. Brumfield, "James J. Saxon's Influence on Commercial Banking in the United States" (doctoral diss., University of South Carolina, 1978).

5. "War or Peace, Slump Isn't Likely—Fowler," *LAT*, October 25, 1966.

6. *Annual Report of the Federal Deposit Insurance Corporation* (1960), 36; Sam Peltzman, "Entry in Commercial Banking," *Journal of Law and Economics* 8 (1965): 11–60.

7. *Annual Report of the Comptroller of the Currency* (1952), 19; *Annual Report of the Comptroller of the Currency* (1959), 33.

8. *Annual Report of the Comptroller of the Currency* (1945), 1; *Annual Report of the Comptroller of the Currency* (1961), 1; Bank of America, *Bank of America National Trust and Savings Association Annual Report* (1958), 9 (ProQuest ID: 88192321); Richard K. Vedder, "The Impact of the Federal Deposit Insurance Corporation on Banking Stability," *Papers of the Annual Meeting of the Business History Conference* 15 (1968): 86–93; Hyman P. Minsky, *Stabilizing an Unstable*

Economy: A Realistic Approach to Economic Theory (Yale University Press, 1986), 71–77; American Bankers Association, *The Commercial Banking Industry: A Monograph Prepared for the Commission on Money and Credit* (Prentice-Hall, 1962), 3–8, 32–43. Bank figures are for 1961. In 1945, there were 5,023 national banks and 8,279 state banks.

9. The Commission on Money and Credit, *Money and Credit: Their Influence on Jobs, Prices, and Growth* (Prentice-Hall, 1961), 2, 167, 177–78; Raymond W. Goldsmith, Robert E. Lipsey, and Morris Mendelson, *Studies in the National Balance Sheet of the United States*, vol. 2 (Princeton University Press, 1963), 88–89, 114–15, 162–63; U.S. Bureau of Economic Analysis, *Gross Domestic Product*, FRED; U.S. Census Bureau, *Historical National Population Estimates: July 1, 1900 to July 1, 1999*, available online at https://www.census.gov/data/tables/time-series/demo/popest/pre-1980-national.html; U.S. Census Bureau, *Homeownership Rates: 1900 to 2000*, available online at https://www.census.gov/data/tables/time-series/dec/coh-owner.html; American Bankers Association, *Commercial Banking Industry*, 11.

10. Sean H. Vanatta, *Plastic Capitalism: Banks, Credit Cards, and the End of Financial Control* (Yale University Press, 2024), 34–78.

11. "Currency Comptroller Views Big Job Ahead," *LAT*, November 17, 1953; "Accuses Some Banks of Lax Credit Terms," *CT*, August 19, 1953; "Gidney Calls on Banks for Tougher Attitude When Granting Loans," *WSJ*, January 24, 1956; "U.S. Depression Study Is Urged," *NYHT*, May 26, 1956.

12. *Annual Report of the Comptroller of the Currency* (1954), 6; "Comptroller Asks Tighter Laws on Bank Mergers," *CSM*, September 23, 1955; "Gidney for Merger of Banks Here," *NYT*, March 22, 1955.

13. *Annual Report of the Comptroller of the Currency* (1961), 34–94; Bernard D. Nossiter, "Comptroller Exits to Echo of Old Issues," *WP*, September 22, 1961; "Currency Chief Irked by Forced Resignation," *LAT*, September 22, 1961; "Kennedy Picks Chicago Lawyer J. J. Saxon as Comptroller After Announcement Snarl," *WSJ*, September 21, 1961; "Saxon Airs Accord with Justice Dept," *WP*, November 18, 1961.

14. "Comptroller Promises New York Bank Merger Decision This Month," *WSJ*, December 5, 1961; "New Frontiersman"; Oliver S. Goodman, "Broad Reforms in Banking Promised by Comptroller," *WP*, June 8, 1962.

15. James J. Saxon, "Meeting the Shortage of Capable Personnel," *Banking*, October 1965, 33; *To Amend the Bank Merger Act of 1960*, vol. 2, 89 Cong. 730-733 (statement of James J. Saxon, Comptroller of the Currency) (1965).

16. "Angriest Man in Washington," *Newsweek*, January 5, 1962; "New Frontiersman"; "Scrappy, Happy James J. Saxon."

17. "Fast Approval of New Charters Raises National Bank Number; California Active," *NYT*, January 17, 1963; *Annual Report of the Comptroller of the Currency* (1961–65); Brumfield, "Saxon's Influence," 198; "Scrappy, Happy James J. Saxon."

18. *Annual Report of the Comptroller of the Currency* (1964), 2–3.

19. "Pinstripe War," *Newsweek*, May 6, 1963; Richard F. Jassen, "Battling Bankers: State Banks Push New Tactics in Fight with U.S. Comptroller Saxon," *WSJ*, October 9, 1963. For extensive criticism of Saxon's chartering and branching policies, see *Conflict of Federal and State Banking Laws*, 88 Cong. (1963).

20. Office of the Comptroller of the Currency, *National Banks and the Future: Report of the Advisory Committee on Banking to the Comptroller of the Currency* (Government Printing Office, 1962); *Nomination of James J. Saxon*, 87 Cong. 9-13 (1962) (statement of James J. Saxon).

21. James J. Saxon, "The National Banking System," *Afro-American*, October 2, 1965; "Saxon Ruling Enables National Banks to Join in the 'War on Poverty,'" *WSJ*, June 9, 1964.

22. "Saxon Assails Critics for 'Narrow Views,'" *WP*, May 4, 1963; James Saxon, "Speech: Commercial Bankers Forum," May 6, 1964, box 6, Series 1: Comptroller of the Currency, 1961–1966, Saxon Papers.

23. Joel Seligman, *The Transformation of Wall Street: A History of the Securities and Exchange Commission and Modern Corporate Finance* (Houghton Mifflin, 1982); see Michael Perino, *The Hellhound of Wall Street: How Ferdinand Pecora's Investigation of the Great Crash Forever Changed American Finance* (Penguin Publishing, 2011) for the antecedent.

24. Andrew Downey Orrick, "Organization Procedures and Practices of the Securities and Exchange Commission," *George Washington Law Review* 28, no. 1 (1959): 50–85; Seligman, *Transformation of Wall Street*, 267–68, 280-81.

25. David R. Francis, "Debate on Banking Warms," *CSM*, January 21, 1963; "Banking: Fighting Words," *Newsweek*, October 1, 1962.

26. *Authority Over the Trust Powers of National Banks and National Bank Branches*, 87 Cong. 4-5 (statement of James J. Saxon, Comptroller of the Currency) (1962); Advisory Committee, *National Banks and the Future*, 31–37; Brumfield, "Saxon's Influence," 78–80.

27. James J. Saxon, "Remarks at the Midwinter Trust Conference of the American Bankers Association," February 4, 1963, in *Annual Report of the Comptroller of the Currency* (1963), 331; "Regulation of Bank-Operated Collective Investment Funds—Judicial or Legislative Resolution of an Administrative Controversy?" *Yale Law Journal* 73, no. 7 (1964): 1249–64.

28. "Big New York Bank Is Not Filing with SEC Plan to Pool Investment Funds It Manages," *WSJ*, April 9, 1963; "ABA Seeks a Meeting with SEC in Dispute on Investment Funds," *WSJ*, April 12, 1963; "Banks' Joint Investment Funds Would Be Subject to SEC Regulation, Agency Says," *WSJ*, May 11, 1963; "House Unit Hears SEC, Comptroller in Dispute on 'Pooled' Bank Funds," *WSJ*, May 21, 1963; *Common Trust Funds—Overlapping Responsibility and Conflict in Regulation*, 88 Cong. 3-15 (statement of William L. Cary, Charman, Securities and Exchange Commission) (1963).

29. "House Unit Hears SEC, Comptroller in Dispute"; *Common Trust Funds—Overlapping Responsibility and Conflict in Regulation*, 32–33 (statement of James J. Saxon, Comptroller of the Currency); "Saxon Claims Monopoly by Investment Bankers in Municipals Dealings," *WSJ*, September 24, 1963.

30. *Common Trust Funds—Overlapping Responsibility and Conflict in Regulation*, 44 (statement of Saxon).

31. "House Unit Hears SEC, Comptroller in Dispute"; *Common Trust Funds—Overlapping Responsibility and Conflict in Regulation*, 26 (statement of Cary); "The Saxon-Cary Bout," *NYT*, June 10, 1963.

32. "National Banks' Disclosure Rules Stiffened by Saxon," *WSJ*, June 25, 1963; "Comptroller of the Currency: He's Rocking Financial Boats," *LAT*, July 7, 1963. In 1971, the Supreme Court finally ruled that Saxon had exceeded his authority by allowing pooled investment accounts

(*Investment Co. Inst. v. Camp*, 401 U.S. 617 [1971]). By that point, Congress had authorized national banks to offer mutual funds (Pub. L. 91-547, 84 Stat. 1413 [1970]).

33. Sarah Binder and Mark Spindel, *The Myth of Independence: How Congress Governs the Federal Reserve* (Princeton University Press, 2018), 124–64; Robert L. Hetzel and Ralph F. Leach, "The Treasury-Fed Accord: A New Narrative Account," *Federal Reserve Bank of Richmond Economic Quarterly* 87, no. 1 (2001): 33–55; William M. Martin, "Our Federal Reserve System," October 2, 1951, Statements and Speeches of William McChesney Martin (FRASER); *Hearings Before the Committee on Finance*, 85 Cong. 1929 (1957) (testimony of Senator Martin); Robert Bremner, *Chairman of the Fed: William McChesney Martin Jr.* (Yale University Press, 2004); Allan H. Meltzer, *A History of the Federal Reserve*, vol. 1, *1913–1951* (University of Chicago Press, 2009); Robert L. Hetzel, *The Federal Reserve: A New History* (University of Chicago Press, 2022).

34. J. A. Livingston, "Business Outlook: Saxon, Martin at Odds on Lender Prudence," *WP*, September 29, 1963.

35. Advisory Committee, *National Banks and the Future*, 26–30.

36. "Saxon Claims Monopoly"; "Banks and Bonds," *WP*, August 28, 1963; "Law Department," *Federal Reserve Bulletin* 49, no. 11 (1963): 1505; "Feud Climax Due on Bank Control."

37. "Application of Investment Securities Regulation to Member State Banks," *Federal Reserve Bulletin* 49, no. 11 (1963): 1509; "FRB Head Opposes Saxon's Effort to Let Banks Underwrite Local Revenue Bonds," *WSJ*, September 25, 1963; "Fed Issues Bond Ruling Contradicting Saxon's," *WP*, September 6, 1963.

38. "Martin Cautions Banking Committee," *CSM*, September 26, 1963; Joseph R. Slevin, "Banks Making 'Risky Loans,' Martin Claims," *LAT*, August 13, 1963; *To Permit National Banks to Underwrite and Deal in "Revenue Bonds,"* 89 Cong. 6–10 (statement of C. Canby Balderston, Vice Chairman, Board of Governors of the Federal Reserve System) (1965).

39. "Saxon Speaks Out: Federal Reserve Called Autocratic," *The Sun* (Baltimore), June 16, 1967.

40. *To Permit National Banks to Underwrite and Deal in "Revenue Bonds,"* 10–13, 19–34 (statement of James J. Saxon, Comptroller of the Currency); "2 Issues Approved for National Banks," *NYT*, August 20, 1963; "Wisconsin Building Issue of $35,335,000 Is Sold at 3.2062% Annual Cost," *WSJ*, February 18, 1965; "Bonds Marketed by Pennsylvania," *NYT*, March 2, 1966; "Securities Firms Sue Comptroller on Bond Rulings," *WSJ*, January 17, 1966; "National Banks Can't Underwrite or Deal in Tax-Exempt Revenue Bonds, Court Decides," *WSJ*, December 16, 1966; *Baker, Watts & Co. v. Saxon*, 261 F. Supp. 247 (D.D.C. 1966); *The Port of New York Authority, Appellant, v. Baker, Watts & Co. et al., Appellees*, 392 F.2d 497 (D.C. Cir. 1968).

41. "New Frontiersman." For an overview of federal preemption, see Caleb Nelson, "Preemption," *Virginia Law Review* 86, no. 2 (2000): 225–305; for a specific critique of the OCC's efforts in this space, see Arthur E. Wilmarth Jr., "The OCC's Preemption Rules Exceed the Agency's Authority and Present a Serious Threat to the Dual Banking System and Consumer Protection," *Annual Review of Banking & Financial Law* 23 (2004): 225–364.

42. "Feud Climax Due on Bank Control"; Paul G. Edwards, "Saxon Endorses Public Airing of Federal Agency Differences," *WP*, April 19, 1967; "Banking Law: An Overview of Federal Preemption in the Dual Banking System," Congressional Research Service, January 23, 2018; Kenneth E. Scott, "The Dual Banking System: A Model of Competition in Regulation," *Stanford Law Review* 30, no. 1 (1977): 1–50.

43. Advisory Committee, *National Banks and the Future*, 45.

44. J. A. Livingston, "Saxon Stirs Bankers' Blood," *WP*, October 6, 1963; *Conflict of Federal and State Banking Laws*, 275 (statement of James J. Saxon, Comptroller of the Currency).

45. Advisory Committee, *National Banks and the Future*, 51; Edward T. O'Toole, "Bankers Assail Saxon's Report," *NYT*, September 25, 1962; *Conflict of Federal and State Banking Laws*, 368 (statement of Saxon).

46. Brumfield, "Saxon's Influence," 236–58; Erin Cully, "Turf War: Interstate Banking and Industry Consolidation, 1965–1998" (PhD diss., City University of New York, 2024); *First Nat'l Bank in Plant City v. Dickinson*, 396 U.S. 122 (1969); *Walker Bank Trust Company v. Saxon*, 234 F. Supp. 74 (N.D. Utah 1964); Jeff Burnett, quoted in Storrs, "This Will Drive Them," 416.

47. "Chase Bank President Scores Saxon Policies on National Banks," *WSJ*, October 8, 1963; Edward Cowan, "Controller Is Urged to Show Restraint," *NYT*, October 8, 1963.

48. Memorandum from George Champion to Chase Board, July 2, 1965, as quoted in John Dover Wilson, *The Chase: The Chase Manhattan Bank, N.A., 1945–1985* (Harvard Business School Press, 1986), 145; "Chase Manhattan Says U.S.-Chartered Banks Have Edge in Suburbs," *WSJ*, January 21, 1964; "Saxon Charm Draws Chase Bank," *Business Week*, July 24, 1965; Robert Frost, "Chase Bank Seeks a National Charter," *NYT*, July 15, 1965.

49. "California Bank Ruled Insolvent; Failure in San Francisco Is First Since Depression," *NYT*, January 24, 1965. The idea that such a legislative response to bank failure is unusual is somewhat contested. See Roberta Romano, "Regulating in the Dark and a Postscript Assessment of the Iron Law of Financial Regulation," *Hofstra Law Review* 43, no. 1 (2014): 25–94. The empirical support for the idea that Congress only enacts major legislation in response to financial panic is also contested. See Peter Conti-Brown and Michael Ohlrogge, "Financial Crises and Legislation," *Journal of Financial Crises* 4, no. 3 (2022): 1–59.

50. "Investigations: Banky Panky," *Newsweek*, March 29, 1965; Comptroller of the Currency, "Quiet Hero: Victor Del Tredici and the Fall of the San Francisco National Bank," n.d., available online at https://www.occ.treas.gov/about/who-we-are/history/1936-1966/1936-1966-quiet-hero-victor-del-tredici.html.

51. Appellant's Opening Brief, June 1, 1967, *Silverthorne* Case File.

52. Appellant's Opening Brief, 13, *Silverthorne* Case File.

53. Comptroller of the Currency, "Quiet Hero: Victor Del Tredici"; "Saxon's Subordinates Blame Him for Lag," *WSJ*, March 18, 1965; *Investigation into Federally Insured Banks*, 89 Cong. 313-316, 320-321 (statement of Victor Del Tredici) (1965).

54. Robert S. Boyd, "Senate Hearings Bare Bank Control Flaws," *WP*, March 21, 1965; *Consolidation of Bank Examining and Supervisory Functions* 89 Cong. 345-353, 455-485 (1965).

55. "Run Out of Business, Banker Says," *Atlanta Constitution*, March 19, 1965; "Banking: Trouble Among the Regulators," *Time*, March 26, 1965; *Hearings Before the Permanent Subcommittee on Investigations of the Committee on Government Operations, Part 2*, 89 Cong. 297 (testimony of Arnold Larsen) (1965).

56. "Don C. Silverthorne, Former Bank President, Loses U.S. Court Appeal," *WSJ*, September 2, 1970; "Former Bank President In San Francisco Gets Eight-Year Sentence," *WSJ*, August 11, 1969; "Frenzied Finance: The Fantastic Story of the San Francisco National Bank," *Barron's National Business and Financial Weekly*, April 11, 1966.

57. *Investigation into Federally Insured Banks*, 89 Cong. 18 (1965) (statement of James J. Saxon).

58. *Investigation into Federally Insured Bank*, 89 Cong. 18, 70 (statement of Saxon).

59. *Financial Institutions Supervisory Act of 1966*, 89 Cong. 113-114, 212 (1966); Pub. L. 95-630, 92 Stat. 3657 (1978); Kenneth A. Randall oral history, March 14, 1969, 47–50, Lyndon B. Johnson Presidential Library (ProQuest ID: 2986470763); Kenneth G. Heisler, "A New Approach to Supervisory Legislation," *Business Lawyer (ABA)* 22, no. 1 (November 1966): 257–64.

60. Randall oral history, 16–21, 42–43, 46–47. Randall also suggested the creation of an informal supervisory coordinating committee among the federal supervisors (after Saxon's retirement made such coordination possible), formalized as the Federal Financial Institutions Examination Council as part of the Financial Institutions Regulatory and Interest Rate Control Act of 1978 (Pub. L. 95-630, 92 Stat. 3641).

61. Randall oral history, 47–50; *Investigation into Crown Savings Bank Failure*, 89 Cong. 456 (1965) (statement of K. A. Randall, Chairman, Federal Deposit Insurance Corporation); Da Lin and Lev Menand, "The Banker Removal Power," *Virginia Law Review* 108, no. 1 (2022): 1–79; Joseph M. Korff, "Banking: The Financial Institutions Supervisory Act of 1966," *Boston College Commercial Law Review* 8, no. 3 (1967): 599–625; Lyndon B. Johnson, "Statement by the President upon Signing Bill Increasing Insurance of Accounts in Banks and Savings and Loan Associations," October 17, 1966, APP.

62. Thomas J. Foley, "Outgoing Comptroller Claims U.S. Needs More Giant Banks," *LAT*, November 15, 1966; "Saxon Ruling Enables National Banks to Join in the 'War on Poverty'"; "Scrappy, Happy James J. Saxon"; "Saxon Cites Reforms in Bank Regulations," *WP*, October 18, 1964; Philip W. McKinsey, "U.S. Bank Official 'Cleaned House,'" *CSM*, November 9, 1966.

63. Fred Korth, Letter to James Saxon, October 27, 1966, box 3, Saxon Papers; J. Harvie Wilkinson Jr. to James Saxon, October 22, 1966, box 3, Saxon Papers; Jacob Shermano to James Saxon, October 24, 1966, box 3, Saxon Papers; A. B. Hammett to Saxon, October 25, 1966, box 3, Saxon Papers.

64. Arthur E. Wilmarth Jr., "The Expansion of State Bank Powers, the Federal Response, and the Case for Preserving the Dual Banking System," *Fordham Law Review* 58, no. 6 (1990): 1133–256. See, for example, the 2023–24 debates on bank capital. Michael S. Barr, "Holistic Capital Review," Washington, DC, July 10, 2022, available online at https://www.federalreserve.gov /newsevents/speech/barr20230710a.htm; "Basel III Endgame and the Cost of Credit for American Business," *Bank Policy Institute* (Basel), January 10, 2022.

Interlude: Bunco

1. *Report of the Secretary of the Treasury* (1863), 51; *Annual Report of the Comptroller of the Currency* (1873), xlix–l.

2. "Bank Losses Stopped by Federal Surety," *NYT*, July 22, 1951; Greer Williams, "Bank Failures Take a Holiday," *Nation's Business* 38, no. 10 (1950): 33–35, 68–69.

3. Niel Maxwell, "Passing Judgment," *WSJ*, August 9, 1972; Rex Granum, "Banker Admits Guilt in $4.7 Million Fraud," *Atlanta Journal Constitution*, January 10, 1973; "The Tired Embezzler," *Time*, February 12, 1973.

4. *Annual Report of the Comptroller of the Currency* (1974), 15, 288.

5. Fred E. Waddell et al., *Consumer Frauds and Deceptions: A Learning Module*, Consumer Education for Older Persons Project, U.S. Department of Health, Education & Welfare (1976), 11–12; Victoria H. Jaycox, Lawrence J. Center, and Edward F. Ansello, *Effective Responses to the*

Crime Problem of Older Americans: A Handbook, The National Council of Senior Citizens, Legal Research and Services for the Elderly Criminal Justice and the Elderly Program (January 1982), 155, 163; Kenneth Hansen, "Old Con Game Nets $8,000 in Valley," *LAT,* February 28, 1969; Ken Lubas, "Woman Duped of $8,000," *LAT,* June 18, 1972.

6. "Bank 'Officer' Robs Woman," *BS,* January 17, 1968; Hansen, "Old Con"; "Aged Widow Bilked of Bonds Worth $700,000," *Atlanta Constitution,* September 17, 1972.

7. Jaycox, Center, and Ansello, *Effective Responses to the Crime Problem of Older Americans,* 163; Lubas, "Woman Duped"; Robert D. McFadden, "2 Held Here as Confidence Men," *NYT,* January 13, 1976.

8. "Cop's Aid to Elderly Stings Thieves," *CT,* October 24, 1974; "Slippery Swindlers Prey on Elderly," *Pittsburgh Press,* March 4, 1973.

9. Joan Prevete, "The Con Game—How to Prevent It from Reaching a Sad Ending for Your Depositor," *Bank Systems & Equipment* 14, no. 6 (1977): 38; "Flimflams Seen on Rise Here," *Atlanta Constitution,* April 25, 1974; "Marine Admits Stealing $38,800 in Japan Bank," *NYHT,* March 30, 1946.

10. R. A. Ratner, "Mania, Crime and the Insanity Defense: A Case Report," *Bulletin of the American Academy of Psychiatry and the Law* 9, no. 1 (1981): 23–33.

11. Federal Deposit Insurance Corporation, *1980 Annual Report of the Federal Deposit Insurance Corporation* (Government Printing Office, 1980), 290. *It's A Wonderful Life* starring Donna Reed and Jimmy Stewart and *The Bank Dick* starring W. C. Fields, for example, were two films of the 1940s that prominently featured bank examiners in roles of sober probity and rigid adherence to safe and sound banking practices. *The Bank Dick,* directed by Edward F. Cline, Universal Pictures, 1940; *It's A Wonderful Life,* directed by Frank Capra, RKO Studios, 1946.

Chapter Nine

1. *Banking Regulatory Agencies' Enforcement of the Equal Credit Opportunity Act and the Fair Housing Act,* 95 Cong. 102 (statement of Warren L. Dennis, attorney, Troy, Malin & Pottinger) (1978).

2. Mehrsa Baradaran, *The Color of Money: Black Banks and the Racial Wealth Gap* (Harvard University Press, 2017); Shennette Garrett-Scott, *Banking on Freedom: Black Women in U.S. Finance Before the New Deal* (Columbia University Press, 2019); Ellora Derenoncourt, Chi Hyun Kim, Moritz Kuhn, and Moritz Schularick, "Wealth of Two Nations: The US Racial Wealth Gap, 1860–2020," *Quarterly Journal of Economics* 139, no. 2 (2024): 693–750.

3. Federal Reserve, Committee on Branch, Chain, and Group Banking, "225 Bank Suspensions: Case Histories from Examiners' Reports," (May 1933), 254–55 (FRASER). The Federal Reserve lists this report as circa 1932, but the final version was completed in 1933.

4. Thomas P. Kane, *The Romance and Tragedy of Banking: Problems and Incidents of Governmental Supervision of National Banks,* 2nd ed. (Bankers Publishing Co., 1923), 80; Eric Steven Yellin, *Racism in the Nation's Service: Government Workers and the Color Line* (UNC Press, 2013), 4, 97–98, 104, 117–19, 123–24. For an account of aggressive state supervision of Black-owned banks in Virginia, see Garrett-Scott, *Banking on Freedom,* 101–5.

5. Ira Katznelson, *When Affirmative Action Was White: An Untold History of Racial Inequality in Twentieth-Century America* (Norton, 2006); Douglas S. Massey, "The Legacy of the 1968 Fair

Housing Act," *Sociological Forum* 30, no. S1 (2015): 572; Marriner Eccles, "Comments on Public Works," November 11, 1934, folder 5, box 9, Eccles Papers (FRASER).

6. Federal Housing Administration (FHA), *Underwriting Manual* (Government Printing Office, 1938), 937 (FRASER).

7. Kenneth T. Jackson, *Crabgrass Frontier: The Suburbanization of the United States* (Oxford University Press, 1985); Richard Rothstein, *The Color of Law: A Forgotten History of How Our Government Segregated America* (Liveright, 2017); Jacob W. Faber, "We Built This: Consequences of New Deal Era Intervention in America's Racial Geography," *American Sociological Review* 85, no. 5 (October 1, 2020): 739–75; Price Fishback, Jonathan Rose, Kenneth A. Snowden, and Thomas Storrs, "New Evidence on Redlining by Federal Housing Programs in the 1930s," *Journal of Urban Economics* 141 (2024), 103462.

8. FHA, *Underwriting Manual*, 982, 1360, 1412(c). Monitoring of FHA and VA lending participation is visible throughout the examination reports from the era. See, for example, Federal Deposit Insurance Corporation (FDIC), Bank of America, April 30, 1957 and November 30, 1962, box 11, FDIC Exam Reports Analysis; Acosta National Bank, December 6, 1948 and April 24, 1950, box 18, FDIC Exam Reports Analysis.

9. Garrett-Scott, *Banking on Freedom*, 101–5; FDIC, Industrial Bank of Washington, May 15, 1947, January 3, 1952, and January 9, 1958, box 18, FDIC Exam Reports Analysis.

10. FDIC, Citizens Trust Company of Atlanta, August 17, 1959, box 23, FDIC Exam Reports Analysis; FDIC, Industrial Bank of Washington, November 25, 1947 and February 13, 1951, box 18, FDIC Exam Reports Analysis; FDIC, Citizens Trust Company, Atlanta, Georgia, February 10, 1964 and March 14, 1968, box 23, FDIC Exam Reports Analysis; FDIC, Carver State Bank, Savannah Georgia, June 26, 1956 and August 24, 1961, box 27, FDIC Exam Reports Analysis; FDIC, Freedom National Bank, New York, New York, February 1, 1968, box 165, FDIC Exam Reports Analysis; FDIC, Mechanics & Farmers Bank, Durham, North Carolina, May 18, 1939, box 172, FDIC Exam Reports Analysis; FDIC, Tri-State Bank, Memphis, Tennessee, September 1, 1948, box 229, FDIC Exam Reports Analysis; FDIC, Citizens Savings Bank and Trust Company, Nashville, Tennessee, June 9, 1967, box 230, FDIC Exam Reports Analysis; FDIC, Riverside National Bank of Houston, Texas, September 22, 1967, box 240, FDIC Exam Reports Analysis; FDIC, First State Bank, Danville, Virginia, February 7, 1949, box 254, FDIC Exam Reports Analysis; FDIC, Consolidated Bank and Trust Company, Richmond, Virginia, April 14, 1948, box 256, FDIC Exam Reports Analysis. The Douglas State Bank in Kansas City, Missouri, and the Victory Savings Bank in Columbia, South Carolina, were the only two Black-owned banks not added to the special problems list between 1937–1969.

11. Andrew F. Brimmer, "The Black Banks: An Assessment of Performance and Prospects," December 28, 1970, Statements and Speeches of Andrew F. Brimmer, 1966–1974 (FRASER).

12. Roland W. Burris, Oral History Interview, February 2, 2021, author's possession; Roland Burris, *The Man Who Stood Up to Be Seated* (Hunter Heart, 2015).

13. Merritt Sherman to Bureau of the Budget, June 7, 1965, Meeting Minutes, June 7, 1965, vol. 52, pt. 6, Fed Board Minutes (FRASER).

14. Merritt Sherman to the Presidents of All Federal Reserve Banks, June 7, 1965, vol. 52, pt. 6, Fed Board Minutes (FRASER); Merritt Sherman to Malcolm Bryan, June 7, 1965, Meeting Minutes, June 7, 1965, vol. 52, pt. 6, Fed Board Minutes (FRASER).

15. Memo, Lyndon Johnson to Hubert Humphrey, September 24, 1965, APP; Lyndon B. Johnson, Executive Order 11246—Equal Employment Opportunity, September 24, 1965, APP; Bernard E. Anderson, "The Ebb and Flow of Enforcing Executive Order 11246," *AEA Papers and Proceedings* 86, no. 2 (1996): 298–301; James E. Remmert, "Executive Order 11,246: Executive Encroachment," *American Bar Association Journal* 55, no. 11 (1969): 1037–40.

16. Federal Reserve Bank of Dallas, "Executive Order 11246, Which Requires That Contractors with the Government Not Discriminate Against Employees or Applicants for Employment Because of Race, Color, Creed or National Origin," August 31, 1966, District Notices (Federal Reserve Bank of Dallas) (FRASER); Federal Reserve Bank of Chicago, "Information to Meet the Equal Employment Opportunity Requirement," November 16, 1967, Federal Reserve Bank of Chicago Bulletins and Circular Letters (FRASER); Federal Reserve Bank of Dallas, "Treasury Regulations on Equal Opportunity Executive Order 112146, as Amended," March 7, 1969, District Notices (Federal Reserve Bank of Dallas) (FRASER); Department of the Treasury, Press Release, "Treasury Official Calls for Positive Action from Banks on Hiring Negroes, September 22, 1967," Press Releases of the United States Department of the Treasury, vol. 159, pp. 198–200 (FRASER).

17. Charles E. Walker to Frank Wille, February 25, 1971, box 1, FDIC Directors Memos; Edward J. Roddy to Regional Directors, March 31, 1971, box 1, FDIC Directors Memos.

18. Massey, "Legacy of the 1968 Fair Housing Act," 574.

19. Andrew F. Brimmer, "Equal Opportunity in Banking: An Urban Perspective," July 11, 1968, Statements and Speeches of Andrew Brimmer (FRASER); Keeanga-Yamahtta Taylor, *Race For Profit: How Banks and the Real Estate Industry Undermined Black Ownership* (University of North Carolina Press, 2019); President's Committee on Urban Housing, *A Decent Home: The Report of the President's Committee on Urban Housing* (Government Printing Office, 1968); National Advisory Board on Civil Disorders, *Report of the National Advisory Commission on Civil Disorders* (1968), 1.

20. National Committee Against Discrimination in Housing, "How the Federal Government Builds Ghettos," in *Fair Housing Act of 1967*, 90 Cong. 284, 294, 299; FHA, *Underwriting Manual*, 301.

21. Civil Rights Act of 1968, Pub. L. 90-284, 82 Stat. 73, Title VIII (Fair Housing) §§ 801, 805; Fair Housing Act, 42 U.S.C. §§ 3612–3614 (enforcement provisions of the Fair Housing Act as applicable, respectively, to the Secretary of Housing and Urban Development, private litigants, and the Department of Justice); Taylor, *Race for Profit*. Racial discrimination in housing had been illegal for over a century prior to 1968, but in the absence of a federal enforcement mechanism, that prohibition was a dead letter (Civil Rights Act of 1866, 14 Stat. 27-30).

22. Publication Distribution Sheet #13, April 1969, box 21, FDIC Supervisor Memos; K. A. Randall to Chief Executive Officer of the Bank Addressed, April 25, 1969, box 21, FDIC Supervisor Memos; "Circular No. 69-113," May 2, 1969, *District Notices (Federal Reserve Bank of Dallas)* (FRASER); "Civil Rights Act of 1968," May 2, 1969, *Federal Reserve Bank of New York Circulars* (FRASER).

23. Robert C. Holland to Theodore M. Hesburgh, March 12, 1971, *Federal Government's Role in the Achievement of Equal Opportunity in Housing*, 92 Cong. 841-842 (1971); Frank Willie to Theodore M. Hesburgh, April 19, 1971, *Federal Government's Role in the Achievement of Equal Opportunity in Housing*, 92 Cong. 849-850 (1971).

24. William B. Camp to Theodore M. Hesburgh, April 13, 1971, *Federal Government's Role in the Achievement of Equal Opportunity in Housing*, 92 Cong. 852.

25. *Federal Government's Role in the Achievement of Equal Opportunity in Housing*, 92 Cong. 109 (statement of Aileen C. Hernandez, National Organization for Women).

26. Matthew F. Delmont, *Why Busing Failed: Race, Media, and the National Resistance to School Desegregation* (University of California Press, 2016); Lizabeth Cohen, *A Consumers' Republic: The Politics of Mass Consumption in Postwar America* (Knopf, 2003); Meg Jacobs, *Pocketbook Politics: Economic Citizenship in Twentieth-Century America* (Princeton University Press, 2005).

27. Charles R. Geisst, *Beggar Thy Neighbor: A History of Usury and Debt* (University of Pennsylvania Press, 2018); Geisst, *Loan Sharks: The Birth of Predatory Lending* (Brookings Institution Press, 2017); *Annual Report of the Comptroller of the Currency* (1863), 54.

28. *Annual Report of the Comptroller of the Currency* (1872), xxvi; John A. James, *Money and Capital Markets in Postbellum America* (Princeton University Press, 1978), 82.

29. *Annual Report of the Comptroller of the Currency* (1915), 20–21; "Controller Urges Remedy for Usury," *NYT*, January 11, 1916, 4; *Annual Report of the Comptroller of the Currency* (1918), 209. "Asks Stronger Law to Stop Bank Usury," *NYT*, January 22, 1916, 16. "Seeks to Prevent Usury," *NYT*, January 7, 1916. "William's Fight on Usury to Go On," *NYT*, November 19, 1915; "Oklahoma Banks Resent Comptroller's Charges," *WSJ*, July 1, 1916; *Annual Reports of the Comptroller of the Currency* (1915, 1918).

30. Louis Hyman, *Debtor Nation: A History of America in Red Ink* (Princeton University Press, 2012), 304; Lendol Calder, *Financing the American Dream: A Cultural History of Consumer Credit* (Princeton University Press, 2001), 115; Anne Fleming, *City of Debtors: A Century of Fringe Finance* (Harvard University Press, 2018), 9; Federal Reserve Bank of Atlanta, "The Control of Instalment Credit," *Economic Review* 26, no. 8 (1941): 41, 46 (FRASER); Federal Reserve Bank of New York, "Regulation W, Consumer Instalment Credit Control," circular no. 3365, August 26, 1948, *Federal Reserve Bank of New York Circulars* (FRASER); William McChesney Martin Jr., Reports: 1949–1951, folder 4, box 15, Martin Papers (FRASER); *Standby Economic Controls*, 83 Cong. Sen. Rep. 138 (1953), esp. 20.

31. *Consumer Credit Labeling Bill*, 86 Cong. 1 (1960) (statement of Sen. Paul Douglas). For a history of the Act, see Edward L. Rubin, "Legislative Methodology: Some Lessons from the Truth-in-Lending Act," *Georgetown Law Journal* 80 (1991): 233 (quote from 242). Rubin argues that the Act demonstrates Congress's inability to craft regulatory legislation. See also Anne Fleming, "The Long History of 'Truth in Lending,'" *Journal of Policy History* 30 no. 2 (2018): 236–71; Christopher L. Peterson, "Truth, Understanding, and High-Cost Consumer Credit: The Historical Context of the Truth in Lending Act," *Florida Law Review* 55 (2003): 807.

32. Speech, "Douglas Before the National League of Insured Savings Associations," May 10, 1960, Douglas Statements 1960, box 1297, Douglas Papers; Douglas to Winnie Christmas, August 9, 1961, Douglas Correspondence 1961, box 1299, Douglas Papers; John F. Kennedy, "Special Message to the Congress on Protecting the Consumer Interest," March 15, 1962, APP; Lyndon Johnson, "Special Message to the Congress on Consumer Interests," February 5, 1964, APP; Sean H. Vanatta, *Plastic Capitalism: Banks, Credit Cards, and the End of Financial Control* (Yale University Press, 2024), 111–13.

33. *Truth in Lending—1967*, 90 Cong. 680-681 (1967) (statement of J. L. Robertson, Vice Chairman, Board of Governors).

34. Truth in Lending Act of 1968, Pub. L. 90-321, 82 Stat. 146 § 108; Fair Credit Reporting Act of 1970, Pub. L. 91-508 § 621; Fair Credit Billing Act of 1974, Pub. L. 93-495 § 704; Robert M. Fisher and James F. Smith to Board of Governors, "Growth of Credit Card Credit Outstanding, 1970–1975," February 23, 1976, box 20, Burns Papers. The Fed saw the explosion of bank credit cards in the late 1960s as the common denominator to all of this consumer legislation. Also, as a brief point of comparison, the Bank Security Act, Pub. L. 90-389, also enacted in 1968—which promulgated rules for "the installation, maintenance, and operation of security devices and procedures . . . to discourage robberies, burglaries, and larcenies," and which also distributed enforcement authority to the various agencies—does not use this structure or terminology. For discussion of FDIC compliance work under this Act, see Frank Wille to Theodore S. Hesburgh, October 19, 1971, box 1, FDIC Directors Memos.

35. Federal Reserve System, *Truth in Lending—1967*, 90 Cong. 681 (statement of J. L. Robertson).

36. Memo, Edward H. DeHority to Supervising Examiners, June 23, 1969, box 21, FDIC Supervisor Memos. The Federal Reserve Banks and the Comptroller also used a checklist. Memo, James H. Booth to John T. McClintock, June 4, 1973, 403.1A, Loans, Commercial Paper, Truth in Lending, FRBNY; Letter, Robert Bloom to Richard L. Wheatley Jr., April 15, 1971, in *Oversight on Consumer Protection Activities of Federal Banking Agencies*, 94 Cong. 57 (1976) (statement of James A. McCaffrey, Deputy Administrator, Oklahoma Department of Consumer Affairs).

37. Memo, Edward J. Roddy to Regional Directors, September 24, 1971, box 1, FDIC Directors Memos; Memo, Edward J. Roddy to Examiners and Assistant Examiners, June 30, 1971, box 1, FDIC Directors Memos. By 1976, at least 160 class action cases had been brought against financial and other credit-granting institutions. Congressional Research Service, "Class Actions Brought In Federal Courts Under Section 130 of the Truth in Lending Act," March 9, 1976, CRS-1976-AML-0049.

38. Richard Phalon, "Credit Suits May Result in Refunds for Millions," *NYT*, September 19, 1970; "Chemical Bank Illegally Omitted Data Truth-in-Lending Act Requires, Judge Rules," *WSJ*, June 21, 1971; Robert A. Wright, "Consumers Suing Bank of America," *NYT*, December 8, 1971; Memo, Edward J. Roddy to Examiners and Assistant Examiners, June 30, 1971, box 1, FDIC Directors Memos.

39. *Oversight on Consumer Protection Activities of Federal Banking Agencies*, 94 Cong. 461 (statement of Thomas W. Taylor, Associate Deputy Comptroller of the Currency for Consumer Affairs). For some discussion of the origins of "confidential supervisory information," see Margaret A. Tahyar, "Are Banking Regulators Special," *Banking Perspectives* (2018): 22–29.

40. *Oversight on Consumer Protection Activities of Federal Banking Agencies*, 94 Cong. 565 (FDIC sample enforcement letter). For a discussion of the role of information in U.S. consumer protection legislation, see Gunnar Trumbull, *Consumer Capitalism: Politics, Product Markets, and Firm Strategy in France and Germany* (Cornell University Press, 2006).

41. *Oversight on Consumer Protection Activities of Federal Banking Agencies*, 94 Cong. 2, 24 (statement of Lawrence Connell Jr., Connecticut Bank Commissioner); Fred W. Piderit Jr. to Frederick Solomon, June 23, 1976, 403.1 Loans—Truth in Lending—Reg Z, FRBNY.

42. *Oversight on Consumer Protection Activities of Federal Banking Agencies*, 94 Cong. 241-245, 447, 453, 457 (letter from Arthur F. Burns to Sen. William Proxmire and statement of Thomas W. Taylor); *Home Mortgage Disclosure and Equal Credit Opportunity*, 94 Cong. 3-4 (1976) (statement of Philip Jackson, Member, Board of Governors, Federal Reserve System); *Banking Regulatory Agencies' Enforcement of the Equal Credit Opportunity Act and the Fair Housing Act*, 95 Cong. 305 (statement of Carmen J. Sullivan, Acting Director, Office of Consumer Affairs and Civil Rights, Federal Deposit Insurance Corporation).

43. Joyce M. Saxon, "Implementing a Program for Consumer Regulation Compliance," *Magazine of Bank Administration* 53, no. 11 (1977): 21; Karen A. Oswald, "Developing and Maintaining an Ongoing Consumer Compliance Program," *Journal of Retail Banking* 1, no. 2 (1979): 34; William L. Hearn, "Why Have a Compliance Officer?" *Journal of Commercial Bank Lending* 60, no. 12 (1978): 29; Neil B. Murphy, "Economies of Scale in the Cost of Compliance with Consumer Credit Protection Laws: The Case of the Implementation of the Equal Credit Opportunity Act of 1974," *Journal of Bank Research* 10, no. 4 (1980): 248. On the later shift from supervisory discretion to the monitoring of internal bank processes in other realms of financial risk management, see Lev Menand, "Too Big to Supervise: The Rise of Financial Conglomerates and the Decline of Discretionary Oversight in Banking," *Cornall Law Review* 103, no. 6 (2018): 1527–88.

44. Hyman, *Debtor Nation*, 173–219; Cohen, *Consumers' Republic*, 370–86; Vanatta, *Plastic Capitalism*, 231–32.

45. Rebecca K. Marchiel, *After Redlining: The Urban Reinvestment Movement in the Era of Financial Deregulation* (University of Chicago Press, 2021), 119; Robert P. Voyles, "Red-Lining and the Home Mortgage Disclosure Act of 1975: A Decisive Step Toward Private Urban Redevelopment," *Emory Law Journal* 25, no. 3 (1976): 668; Pub. L. 94-200 § 305.

46. "Agencies Held Lax on Bias," *WP*, June 1, 1976; "Rights Groups Sue Banking Regulators Alleging Race, Sex Bias in Home Loans," *WSJ*, April 27, 1976; *Banking Regulatory Agencies' Enforcement of the Equal Credit Opportunity Act and the Fair Housing Act*, 95 Cong. 4 (statement of William L. Taylor, Director, Center for National Policy Review, School of Law, Catholic University).

47. *Home Mortgage Disclosure and Equal Credit Opportunity*, 94 Cong. 28, 32-34 (statement of Philip Jackson); *Banking Regulatory Agencies' Enforcement of the Equal Credit Opportunity Act and the Fair Housing Act*, 95 Cong. 305 (statement of Philip Jackson, Member, Board of Governors, Federal Reserve System).

48. *Banking Regulatory Agencies' Enforcement of the Equal Credit Opportunity Act and the Fair Housing Act*, 95 Cong. 8 (statement of William L. Taylor).

49. *Banking Regulatory Agencies' Enforcement of the Equal Credit Opportunity Act and the Fair Housing Act*, 95 Cong. 7, 306 (statements of William L. Taylor and Carmen J. Sullivan).

50. *Home Mortgage Disclosure Act of 1975*, 94 Cong. 1 (1975) (opening statement of Senator William Proxmire).

51. Some of the insights from this section are drawn from Peter Conti-Brown and Brian D. Feinstein, "Banking on a Curve: How to Restore the Community Reinvestment Act," *Harvard Business Law Review* 13 (2023): 335–91.

52. Dan Dorfman, "The Bottom Line: Proxmire vs. Banks," *New York Magazine*, July 15, 1974, 10. For biographical context for Proxmire, see Jonathan Kasparek, *Proxmire: Bulldog of the Senate*

(Wisconsin Historical Society Press, 2019); "William Proxmire, Maverick Democratic Senator from Wisconsin, Is Dead at 90," *NYT,* December 16, 2005.

53. Marchiel, *After Redlining,* 5. The CRA is codified in 12 U.S.C. § 2901. For overviews of the CRA's passage, see Marchiel, *After Redlining* and Michael Barr, "Credit Where It Counts: The Community Reinvestment Act and Its Critics," *New York University Law Review* 80, no. 514 (2005).

54. *Community Credit Needs,* 95 Cong. 12 (1977) (letter, Robert Bloom, Acting Comptroller of the Currency to William Proxmire, March 28, 1977). Compare statement of Ronald Grywiniski, Chairman of the Executive Committee, South Shore National Bank of Chicago, supporting the legislation (at page 296), to A. A. Milligan, President-elect, American Bankers Association, opposing it (at page 314).

55. *Community Credit Needs,* 95 Cong. 14, 16 (letter, Arthur Burns, Chairman of the Board of Governors of the Federal Reserve System, to William Proxmire, March 21, 1977).

56. Community Reinvestment Act of 1977, as codified, 12 U.S.C. § 2903; Barr, "Credit Where It Counts."

57. Housing and Community Development Act of 1977, Pub. L. 95-128, 91 Stat. 1111; 12 U.S.C. § 2901(a)(1). This was a fair statement of the chartering and quasi-chartering law as it existed at the time. By quasi-chartering, we refer to the legal requirements for otherwise chartered depository institutions to apply for (and receive) deposit insurance, administered by the FDIC, and access to master accounts, administered by the Federal Reserve. For a critical overview of this practice, see Peter Conti-Brown, *The Fed Wants to Veto State Banking Authorities. But Is That Legal?* Brookings Institution, November 14, 2018.

58. 12 U.S.C. § 2901(b)

59. 12 U.S.C. § 2903(a)(2).

60. FDIC News Release, January 19, 1978, FDIC CRA Comment Letters; FDIC News Release, January 19, 1978, FDIC CRA Comment Letters.

61. L. C. Schmitt to FDIC, February 1, 1978, FDIC CRA Comment Letters; Charles A. Knott Jr., Maryland Deputy State Bank Commissioner to FDIC, January 23, 1978, FDIC CRA Comment Letters; W. E. Wintrode, South Dakota Director of Banking and Finance, FDIC CRA Comment Letters.

62. Tom Ebenreiter to FDIC, February 3, 1978, FDIC CRA Comment Letters; L. L. Riley to FDIC, February 8, 1978, FDIC CRA Comment Letters; Lawrence A. Stevens to FDIC, February 3, 1978, FDIC CRA Comment Letters. One president of an inner-city bank in Louisville requested that any funds deployed under the Act be deposited in minority banks but was otherwise silent on the main questions (V. Joseph Shipman, February 17, 1978, FDIC CRA Comment Letters).

63. Citicorp, "Application to Organize a National Bank," March 12, 1980, Citibank 1979 folder, box 35, accession 94-4, Janklow Papers; Vanatta, *Plastic Capitalism,* 267–72, 278–84.

64. William H. Kester, "Fed Is Asked to Review Bank Merger," *SLPD,* July 27, 1978; Paul Wagman, "ACORN Assails Reserve Board Over Red-Lining," *SLPD,* August 10, 1978; Paul Wagman, "Federal Reserve Reaffirms Approval of Firm's Acquisition," *SLPD,* August 16, 1978; Paul Wagman, "Decision on Bank Merger Seen as Support for Red-Lining," *SLPD,* August 17, 1978.

65. *Community Reinvestment Act*, 100 Cong. 7 (1989) (statement of Sen. William Proxmire); Financial Institutions Reform, Recovery, and Enforcement Act of 1989, Pub. L. 101-73 § 1212, 103 Stat. 183, 526–27; "Community Reinvestment Act: Interagency Final Rulemaking to Implement the CRA," OCC Bulletin 2023-32 (October 24, 2023); Press Release, "Trade Associations Sue Regulators for Exceeding Statutory Authority in New Community Reinvestment Act Rules," American Bankers Association, February 5, 2024, available online at https://www.aba.com /about-us/press-room/press-releases/cra-joint-trades-lawsuit. See also Peter Conti-Brown and Brian Feinstein, "The Contingent Origins of Financial Legislation," *Washington University Law Review* 99 (2021): 145–219.

66. Federal Reserve Board, *Federal Reserve Board Oral History Project: Interview with Philip C. Jackson, Jr.* (March 11, 2010), 32.

Conclusion

1. Jake Bernanke, "Inside the New York Fed: Secret Recordings and a Culture Clash," *ProPublica*, September 26, 2014; Nathaniel Popper and Peter Eavis, "Secret Goldman Sachs Tapes Put Pressure on New York Fed," *NYT*, October 2, 2014.

2. Housing and Urban Affairs Subcommittee on Financial Institutions and Consumer Protection of the Senate Committee on Banking, "Improving Financial Institution Supervision: Examining and Addressing Regulatory Capture: Hearing," 113 Cong. 20 (2014).

3. "Improving Financial Institution Supervision," 21. The "fire" metaphor was a common one from 2008—the joint memoir of Ben Bernanke, Timothy Geithner, and Henry Paulson was called *Firefighting: The Financial Crisis and Its Lessons* (Penguin Random House, 2019).

4. "Are Bank Examiners Next on Industry Lawsuit List?" *Capitol Account* (blog), July 10, 2024, https://www.capitolaccountdc.com/p/are-bank-examiners-next-on-industry.

5. We have highlighted many efforts to remove or abolish supervisory authority between 1933 and 1980 in this book; others have documented even more. See the Volcker Alliance, *Reshaping the Financial Regulatory System: Long Delayed, Now Crucial*, April 19, 2015, available online at https://www.volckeralliance.org/sites/default/files/Reshaping%20the%20Financial%20Regulatory%20System%20-%20The%20Volcker%20Alliance.pdf. For the idea that Congress never abolishes administrative agencies, see Theodore J. Lowi, *The End of Liberalism: Ideology, Policy, and the Crisis of Public Authority* (W. W. Norton, 1969), 309. For the empirical repudiation of this idea, see David E. Lewis, "The Politics of Agency Termination: Confronting the Myth of Agency Immortality," *Journal of Politics* 64, no. 1 (2002): 89–107.

6. Daniel Rodgers, "The Uses and Abuses of 'Neoliberalism,'" *Dissent* 65, no. 1 (2018): 78–87; Gary Gerstle, *The Rise and Fall of the Neoliberal Order: America and the World Without the Free Market Era* (Oxford University Press, 2022); Quinn Slobodian, *Globalists: The End of Empire and the Birth of Neoliberalism* (Harvard University Press, 2018); Mehrsa Baradaran, *The Quiet Coup: Neoliberalism and the Looting of America* (W. W. Norton, 2024).

7. Gerstle, *Rise and Fall of the Neoliberal Order*, 2; *Annual Report of the Comptroller of the Currency* (1962), 32.

8. Ned Eichler, *The Thrift Debacle* (University of California Press, 1989); James R. Adams, *The Big Fix: Inside the S&L Scandal - How an Unholy Alliance of Politics and Money Destroyed*

America's Banking System (Wiley, 1990); James P. McCollum, *The Continental Affair: The Rise and Fall of the Continental Illinois Bank* (Dodd, Mead, & Co., 1987); Statement by Alan Greenspan on October 20, 1987, as quoted in Tom Redburn and Robert Rosenblatt, "Fed Injects Funds into Bank System," *LAT*, October 21, 1987.

9. Pierre-Hugues Verdier, *Global Banks on Trial: U.S. Prosecutions and the Remaking of International Finance* (Oxford University Press, 2020). For the the proposal to eliminate short-term debt, see Morgan Ricks, *The Money Problem: Rethinking Financial Regulation* (University of Chicago Press, 2016); for the proposal to dramatically increase bank capital, see Anat Admati and Martin Hellwig, *The Bankers' New Clothes: What's Wrong with Banking and What to Do About It* (Princeton University Press, 2013).

10. Steven Jay Gould, *The Panda's Thumb: More Reflections in Natural History* (W. W. Norton, 1980), 28–29.

INDEX

Figures are indicated by "f" following page numbers.

affirmative action programs, 291, 292

African Americans: bank chartering and, 260–61; bank ownership by, 163, 289, 386n4, 387n10; civil rights movement and, 17, 285–87, 290–94, 301–4; Freedman's Bank and, 75–78, 347n11; postwar migration of, 288. *See also* antidiscrimination provisions; race and racism

agricultural depression (1920s), 6, 133, 140, 145, 175

Aldrich, Nelson W., 111–13, 118–20

Aldrich, Winthrop, 234–35

Aldrich-Vreeland Act of 1908, 112, 117

Allen, Frederick Lewis, 160

Alvord, John W., 76

American Bankers Association (ABA), 136–37, 180, 182, 188, 248–51, 256, 272, 291

American Institute of Banking (AIB), 249–50

anti-bank movement, 27–28

antidiscrimination provisions: affirmative action programs, 291, 292; bank chartering and, 260–61; bank supervision and, 17, 286, 293–94, 302–5, 311, 314; Civil Rights Acts, 260, 290–93; consumer revolution and, 302; Fair Housing Act, 286, 292–93, 302; institutional layering and, 286; New Deal debates regarding, 6

antitrust law: attorney general's study of (1955), 239, 377–78n64; Clayton Act, 16, 229, 236, 239–40, 245, 377n64, 378–79n79;

competition and, 210, 223–24, 229–31, 236, 239–40; debates regarding, 6, 215; holding companies and, 229–31; institutional layering and, 233; Japanese banks and, 209–10; Justice Department enforcement of, 229, 239–46, 270; mergers and, 234, 236, 244–46, 270, 378–79n79; New Deal and, 209, 233, 237; politics of, 215, 237; risk management and, 233, 237; Sherman Antitrust Act, 236, 239, 379n79; special chartering in opposition to, 22

Articles of Confederation, 23

Association of Community Organizations for Reform Now (ACORN), 310

Atkins, Paul M., 167–71, 207–8, 211–12

Awalt, Francis G., 147, 154–55, 158–62, 164, 187

Bagehot, Walter, 70, 71, 79, 149, 345n61, 350n48

Bailey, T. M., 141

bailouts, 2, 12, 331n2

Baker, Elihu, 51–52

Balderston, C. Canby, 240

Baldwin, Oscar L., 72

bank chartering: antidiscrimination provisions and, 260–61; during Civil War, 5, 38; competition and, 6, 88–89, 145, 253–54, 259–61, 269–70; Comptroller and, 49–51, 89, 132, 145, 255, 259–60, 316; corruption related to, 64; discretion and,

Bank Merger Act Amendments of 1966, 245–46

bank mergers. *See* mergers

Bank of America (formerly Bank of Italy), 134–36, 161–62, 215, 226–27, 230, 256, 273, 299

Bank of England, 23, 84, 97, 100–101, 118, 149, 340n45

Bank of Italy. *See* Bank of America

Bank of North America, 336n4

bank reform: Aldrich Plan and, 119; branch banking and, 134, 224; central banking and, 110, 114, 118; Comptroller and, 115–18; deposit insurance and, 112–13; Federal Reserve System and, 15, 174, 190, 196; holding companies and, 230; Japanese banks and, 209–12; New Deal and, 137, 212, 232, 247; politics of, 109, 111, 351n1 (Ch. 4); risk management and, 109, 110, 247

bank regulation: bank supervision vs., 3–4, 10; branch banking and, 121, 224; of capital, 18, 36, 185; chartering and, 50; commercial banking and, 176; consumer protection and, 296–302; credit control policies, 218–19, 296, 372–73n9; discount eligibility and, 123–24; free banking and, 29, 30; Great Depression's impact on, 270; holding companies and, 215, 230–33; in Japanese banking system, 211; merger review standards, 240–46; New Deal system of, 272; preemption and, 269–70, 273; securities and, 262–65, 297; self-regulation, 74; system stability and, 128; of trusts, 263–64; violation of, 129, 150, 248, 277. *See also specific pieces of legislation*

banks and banking industry: anti-bank movement, 27–28; bigness in, 134–36, 214–16, 224–26, 228; Black-owned, 163, 289, 386n4, 387n10; by charter and assets (1890–1925), 146f; country banks, 31, 68, 70–71, 97, 104–5, 139; distrust of, 27, 350n53; diversification of, 111, 118, 134, 137,

224; free banking, 21–22, 29–30, 37–38, 41, 43, 49, 338n24; innovation within, 256–57, 260–61, 263, 272, 314; lenders of last resort, 67, 71, 88, 93, 103, 167; moral hazard within, 11–12; wildcat banks, 21, 32, 314, 338n24. *See also* branch banking; central banking; deposits; dual banking system; financial crises; liquidity; loans; reserve banks; unit banking; *specific banks*

Bank Security Act of 1968, 390n35

Banks of the United States: First Bank of the United States, 23–26, 76; note redemption under, 25, 30–31; supervision models used by, 25–27. *See also* Second Bank of the United States

bank supervision: administrative, 28–30, 35, 36, 77, 78; in antebellum era, 22, 28–37; antidiscrimination provisions and, 17, 286, 293–94, 302–5, 311, 314; Bank Holiday and, 15, 16, 144–45, 158–65; bank regulation vs., 3–4, 10; chartering as, 15, 28–30, 49–51, 89, 253–55, 316; community reinvestment and, 286, 305–11, 314; competition and, 6, 15, 128; consolidation of, 175, 187, 190, 195–205, 220–23; consumer protection and, 17, 286, 295–305, 311, 314; corporate governance and, 73, 76, 83, 84, 94; currency model of, 25–31, 39, 337n14; defined, 3–5, 332n7; democratic accountability and, 320; as economic management, 194–95, 198–201; failures of, 6, 17, 72, 80; as field of study, 13, 322, 334–35n32; forbearance and, 15, 16, 152, 165; formalist vision of, 67, 94; free banking and, 29, 30; in Gilded Age, 83–87, 94–95; Great Depression and, 143–44, 153–54, 157, 294, 317; holding companies and, 135, 228, 232, 247; informational approach to, 16, 80, 111, 143, 178, 294; institutional fragmentation and, 130–33, 195–200, 220–23; institutional history and evolution of, 7–9, 231, 353n24; institutional layering and, 5–7,

institutional history and evolution, 7–9, 88, 212, 332n8, 353n24

institutionalized discretion, 4–6, 10–11, 15, 18, 32, 51

institutional layering: antidiscrimination provisions and, 286; antitrust law and, 233; bank supervision and, 5–7, 110, 130, 311, 314–16, 332n7, 353n24; community reinvestment and, 286; consumer protection and, 286; deposit insurance and, 175–77; risk management and, 5–7, 37, 174–75, 205, 316; Thelen on, 331n6, 353n24; during World War II, 216–19

Inter-Agency Bank, 248, 249

Interest Rate Control Act of 1978, 385n60

interest rates, 1, 68, 100–101, 128, 218, 222, 295–97, 319

Interstate Commerce Commission, 14, 120

Investment Company Act of 1940, 264

investment funds, 264, 265, 268

iron law of financial regulation, 332n7

Jackson, Andrew, 27, 37, 41

Jackson, Philip C., 303–4, 310

James, F. Cyril, 102

Japan: banking system in, 207–12; Pearl Harbor bombings (1941), 216–17

Japanese Americans, internment during World War II, 217, 372n6

Jefferson, Thomas, 23, 24, 27, 75

Jensen, Meinhard, 337n14

Johnson, J. Franklin, 135

Johnson, Lyndon B., 261, 277, 278, 291, 297

Jones, Jesse H., 173, 177–79, 182–86, 200, 204, 366n21

Justice Department (DOJ), 229, 236, 239–46, 257–59, 270, 293

Kahn, Charles, 339n30

Kane, Thomas P., 97, 98, 129–30

Katzenbach, Nicholas, 254

Kefauver, Estes, 239

Kemmerer, Edwin, 167

Kennedy, John F., 17, 253, 257, 258, 297

Kennedy, Robert F., 243, 254, 259, 270

Kerner Commission, 292

Knox, John Jay, Jr.: on chartering discretion, 89; on consumer protection, 295; experience prior to Comptroller appointment, 52, 67; forbearance extended by, 98; on Freedman's Bank failure, 78; on limitations of bank examination, 63, 72–73, 280, 346n68; on reserve banks, 69–70, 71

Kujawa, James, 282

Lacy, Edward S., 94, 95, 127, 249

Law, Francis M., 188

LeCount, Walter, 210

Lee, Robert E., 39

lenders of last resort, 67, 71, 88, 93, 103, 167

Lewis, Leroy, 250

Leyburn, Alfred, 155

liability insurance, 15, 33–34, 37, 175

limited liability, 36, 37, 340n45

Lincoln, Abraham, 37, 47, 74

Lindsey, Ernest K., 161

Lipsky, Michael, 332n13

liquidations: bank failures and, 35, 140, 191–93, 274; Comptroller and, 57–59, 147; discretion and, 57–58; FDIC and, 191–93, 196, 197; federal dominance over, 270; fire sales, 168, 192; Freedman's Bank and, 77; holding companies and, 230; National Banking Acts on, 58; receiverships and, 35, 57, 140–42; reserve deficiencies and, 70; of securities, 168–71

liquidity: bank supervision and, 16, 144, 145, 188, 191; bond markets and, 137, 167, 168, 202; central banking and, 110, 122, 319; clearinghouses and, 5, 80, 83, 92, 93, 99, 113; consumer risks and, 299; discounting practices and, 15, 124, 148, 191; discretion and, 151, 159; evaluation of, 127; Great Depression and, 151, 156, 177; injections of, 149; internal, 134, 224; private, 67, 83, 131–33, 151; real bills doctrine and, 87, 187, 194; risk management and, 111, 138, 145,

A NOTE ON THE TYPE

This book has been composed in Arno, an Old-style serif typeface in the classic Venetian tradition, designed by Robert Slimbach at Adobe.